Marcu Nelson
118 Falconer St
Flensburg

Better Homes and Gardens.

COMPLETE
QUICK AND EASY COOK BOOK

CREDITS

On the cover:
Sausage Lasagna Rolls
Rye Rolls
Vanilla-Mocha Desserts
(See index for page numbers.)

Better Homes and Gardens® Books
Editor: Gerald M. Knox
Art Director: Ernest Shelton
Managing Editor: David A. Kirchner

Food and Nutrition Editor: Doris Eby
Department Head—Cook Books: Sharyl Heiken
Senior Food Editor: Elizabeth Woolever
Senior Associate Food Editors: Sandra Granseth, Rosemary C. Hutchinson
Associate Food Editors: Jill Burmeister, Julia Martinusen, Diana McMillen,
    Alethea Sparks, Marcia Stanley, Diane Yanney
Recipe Development Editor: Marion Viall
Test Kitchen Director: Sharon Stilwell
Test Kitchen Home Economists: Jean Brekke, Kay Cargill, Marilyn Cornelius,
    Maryellyn Krantz, Marge Steenson

Associate Art Directors (Creative): Linda Ford, Neoma Alt West
Associate Art Director (Managing): Randall Yontz
Copy and Production Editors: Nancy Nowiszewski,
    Lamont Olson, Mary Helen Schiltz, David A. Walsh
Assistant Art Directors: Faith Berven, Harijs Priekulis
Graphic Designers: Mike Burns, Alisann Dixon, Mike Eagleton, Lynda Haupert,
    Deb Miner, Lyne Neymeyer, Trish Podlasek, Bill Shaw, D. Greg Thompson

Editor in Chief: Neil Kuehnl
Group Editorial Services Director: Duane Gregg
Executive Art Director: William J. Yates

General Manager: Fred Stines
Director of Publishing: Robert B. Nelson
Director of Retail Marketing: Jamie Martin
Director of Direct Marketing: Arthur Heydendael

Complete Quick and Easy Cook Book Editors
Editors: Jill Burmeister, Rosemary C. Hutchinson,
    Marcia Stanley, Elizabeth Woolever
Copy and Production Editors: David A. Kirchner, Nancy Nowiszewski
Graphic Designer: Linda Ford

Our seal assures you that every recipe in the *Complete Quick and Easy Cook Book* is endorsed by the Better Homes and Gardens Test Kitchen. Each recipe is tested for family appeal, practicality, and deliciousness.

INTRODUCTION
QUICK AND EASY COOKING

If you find yourself having less and less time for cooking as your daily schedule gets busier and busier, the *Complete Quick and Easy Cook Book* can help you ease the strain. You'll find this book to be a complete guide to short-cutting meal preparation. It contains menus to fill almost any need from spur-of-the-moment suppers to planned parties. The recipes vary from fast (taking 45 minutes or less to prepare), to easy but longer-cooking, to make-ahead. This way, you can choose the type of recipe that fits the time you have. In addition, there are dozens of cooking tips designed to help you make the best use of your time and effort.

In collecting the recipes for this book, we began by looking for recipes that are not only wholesome and delicious but that are also quick or easy to prepare. We've included an assortment of recipes, so you have the option of making foods completely from scratch or starting with a convenience product. We've also chosen recipes with a minimum of ingredients and made sure that those ingredients are in an easy-to-use form. We've shortened and streamlined the recipes, numbering each preparation step to make everything easier to understand and to follow. We've also tried to use as few utensils as possible so you'll have fewer dishes, pots, and pans to wash.

To help you decide if a particular recipe fits into your schedule, we've included an estimate of the preparation and cooking times for each recipe. Since these figures are only approximations, the actual time it takes you may differ. But our timings should give you a guideline for organizing your schedule. Where there is a choice of ingredients, the timings are based on the first option listed; they also include the minutes it takes to do such chores as chop celery or onion, hard-cook eggs, or thaw frozen fish, vegetables, or fruit.

We hope that after you've tried a few recipes, the *Complete Quick and Easy Cook Book* will become one of your favorites and you'll refer to it often—whenever you have a culinary time problem to solve.

CONTENTS

SHORTCUT COOKING TIPS

This easy-to-read mini-encyclopedia is packed full of helpful information to save you time while cooking.

TIMESAVING MENUS

Choose from over three dozen tasty meals that are designed not only to cut short your time in the kitchen but also to accommodate a variety of dining situations.

OFF-THE-SHELF COOKING

The recipes in this chapter go together in a flash with common ingredients you probably have on hand in your refrigerator, freezer, or cupboard.

FAST COOKING

The next time you're in a hurry to get a meal on the table, look to these tempting recipes. Each one can be made from start to finish in 45 minutes or less.

EASY COOKING

On those days when you're busy at home, you can put these recipes together in minutes and then let them cook, chill, or freeze on their own with just an occasional check.

MAKE-AHEAD COOKING

When you have time to spare, whip up several of these recipes and store them in your refrigerator or freezer. Then serve them on those days when you're pressed for time by adding just a few final touches.

CHAPTER 1

SHORTCUT COOKING TIPS

When time is at a premium and you have cooking questions, turn to this chapter to find lots of information to aid you in cooking quickly and easily. First, you can choose from the tips that will help you short-cut all types of cooking tasks as well as select a few items from the list of timesaving gadgets to add to your kitchen. Next, you can pick up a few pointers on how to use appliances such as the microwave oven, blender, food processor, crockery cooker, pressure saucepan, or toaster oven to your advantage. Then, you can try out some of the meal planning, nutrition, or entertaining hints. Finally, you'll find a grouping of charts and tables to assist you with everything from stocking your kitchen with the basics to freezing foods to substituting ingredients.

MEAL PREPARATION SHORTCUTS

With increased demands on your time, it's important to get the most out of every minute you spend in the kitchen. Here are some meal preparation shortcuts that will help you minimize your KP time—everything you'll need from make-ahead ideas to time-saving ingredients to short-cut and work-saving tips.

MAKE-AHEAD IDEAS

• Skip last-minute food preparation by making casseroles ahead of time. Most can be made and refrigerated up to 24 hours before cooking. Just add 15 to 20 minutes to the normal cooking time.

• Or, freeze casseroles after baking. Be sure to cool the food quickly before wrapping for freezing. Then cover the casserole with moisture-vaporproof material, such as freezer paper, heavy foil, or a tight-fitting lid. Use frozen casseroles within three months for best quality. Allow 1¾ hours baking time for a 1-quart casserole in a 400° oven. Or defrost the casserole completely in the refrigerator overnight and heat.

• A handy way to freeze a casserole is to line the baking dish with heavy foil three times the length of the dish. Add the prepared food and cool. Seal foil over food and freeze. When the wrapped food is frozen, lift it from the dish and store it in the freezer. To serve, unwrap the frozen casserole and return it to the same dish for reheating.

• Take advantage of the time controls on your oven. Put a frozen casserole or a pot roast with seasonings into the oven before leaving home in the morning. Then, preset the oven to turn on automatically. Plan on a cooking time of ½ to 1 hour longer than the specified cooking time in your recipe. The food should be ready to eat when you arrive home. You can safely leave the *frozen* food for five hours in the unheated oven, but don't try this with freshly made or chilled casseroles or meat that's not frozen because harmful bacteria may grow during the waiting time.

• Slightly undercook vegetables that you plan to use in make-ahead casseroles. They will finish cooking when the casserole is baked.

• When preparing spaghetti sauce, make more than you need. Freeze the extra sauce for quick dinners at a later date. Or use it in other recipes such as lasagna or pizza.

• Make a double batch of meat loaf. Then bake one half and freeze the other. Or, form the meat mixture into small individual loaves (⅓ to ⅔ cups meat mixture for each) and freeze. Later, remove the exact number of mini-loaves you need. The small loaves will thaw and cook faster than one large loaf.

• For quick burgers, package ground meat into individual patties and freeze. To ensure easy separation of the frozen patties, stack them with two layers of waxed paper between. Cover with moisture-vaporproof wrap; seal, label, and freeze. Before serving, simply remove the desired number of patties without having to pry them apart.

- For faster thawing, freeze homemade soup, stew, and chili in serving-size portions. Then, at mealtime, take out just the number of servings you need. Remember that when you cook the frozen meat mixtures, you can shorten the thawing time even more by stirring frequently. Stir gently, however, to avoid breaking up food.
- Short - cut the last - minute preparation of stuffed meats or poultry by preparing the stuffing mixture ahead. Cover and refrigerate the stuffing *separately* from the meat. Then, before cooking, stuff the meat or bird.
- To avoid the hassle of making lunches each morning, keep a supply of frozen sandwiches on hand. Make the sandwiches all at once and store them in the freezer for up to two weeks. Sandwich fillings that freeze well include cream cheese, hard-cooked egg yolks, sliced or ground cooked meat and poultry, tuna, salmon, and peanut butter. *Do not freeze* sandwiches containing celery, tomatoes, lettuce, cucumbers, egg whites, or mayonnaise.
- For a ready-when-you-are meal accompaniment, slice a loaf of French bread to, but not through, the bottom crust. Spread the cut edges with softened butter or garlic butter. Wrap the loaf in foil; label and freeze. Then, simply heat the loaf in the oven in the foil.
- Make quick breads in small loaf pans. Not only do you save baking time, but you can freeze extra loaves and take out only as many loaves as you need for a meal. In addition, fruit and nut breads generally improve in flavor when baked a day or two before serving.

- To speed last-minute tossed salad preparation, clean salad ingredients and chop firm vegetables such as carrots, celery, and green peppers early in the day. Wrap and chill vegetables till serving time. Make and chill the salad dressing separately. Lightly toss dressing with salad just before serving.

TIMESAVING INGREDIENTS

- Prepare ingredients for several days' recipes at one time. For example, shred cheese and chop vegetables and nuts. Seal food in plastic bags; label and store as needed.
- Save time by making soft bread crumbs in batches and storing them in the freezer till needed. Freeze in a tightly covered freezer container. To measure the frozen crumbs, stir them with a spoon and press lightly into a measuring cup.
- When available, purchase ingredients in the form needed for a recipe. For example, buy shredded cheese, cut-up chicken, chopped nuts, cracker crumbs, and bread crumbs.
- Other speed-up-preparation foods are minced dried onion, minced dried garlic, and diced dried bell pepper. Additional foods available include frozen fruit juice concentrates; canned and dried soups; frozen chopped onion; canned meat, fish, and poultry; quick-cooking rice and potatoes; and sliced cheeses.
- When you need a quick sauce, heat a can of undiluted condensed cream of mushroom, cream of celery, cream of chicken, cream of shrimp, cream of onion, cheddar cheese, or tomato soup.

(continued)

Keep a supply of toasted nuts and coconut on hand to use for quick trims and in recipes. Place *nuts* in a pie plate in a 350° oven for 5 to 10 minutes, stirring once or twice. Spread *coconut* in a thin layer in a shallow baking pan; bake in a 350° oven for 6 to 8 minutes, stirring once or twice.

To quick-set gelatin for folding into other ingredients, chill the mixture over ice cubes. Make gelatin salads in just 20 to 25 minutes by placing them in individual molds or custard cups and chilling them in the freezer.

There are several ways to speedily shape meatballs. Shape the meat mixture into a log and cut off slices; roll the slices into balls. Or, use a small ice cream scoop to portion out the meat. Or, pat ground meat into a square and cut it into cubes. The small cubes will then roll easily into evenly sized meatballs.

To unmold a gelatin salad, loosen edge of gelatin with tip of a small metal spatula or table knife. Dip mold just to rim in warm water for a *few seconds*. Tilt slightly to let air in. Rotate mold so air can loosen gelatin all the way around. Center plate over mold. Invert plate and mold together. Shake mold gently and lift mold off.

• Hard-cook eggs several at a time so they'll be ready to use in salads and casseroles. Store hard-cooked eggs in the refrigerator for as long as one week.

• Measure stick butter or margarine the easy way by using the markings on the wrapper. If your brand doesn't have markings, just remember that one stick is ½ cup, one-half stick is ¼ cup, and one-quarter stick equals 2 tablespoons.

WORKSAVING SHORTCUTS

• To finely chop hard-cooked eggs, use a hand potato masher in a flat-bottomed bowl, or use a pastry blender in a bowl of any shape. Use the eggs for a simple garnish.

• To drain canned vegetables, make a hole on each of two opposite sides of can lid. Then invert the can in a bowl and drain.

• When preparing biscuits, roll out all the dough at once and cut into squares. There will be no rerolling and less waste. Or, make drop biscuits rather than regular biscuits.

• Grease and flour baking pans in one step. Thoroughly mix ½ cup *shortening* and ¼ cup all-purpose *flour*, then use a pastry brush to apply the coating to the pans. Store coating, covered, at room temperature.

• Except for cakes, breads, cookies, and delicate puffs and soufflés, omit the step of preheating the oven.

• Use as few utensils as possible to cut dishwashing time. Choose cookware that you can use for more than one job, such as freezer-to-oven-to-table baking dishes and casseroles.

• To reduce thawing time of fish, place wrapped one-pound blocks of frozen fish under cold running water. Or, better still, cook the fish without thawing. (See tip on page 260.)

Sift flour only when using cake flour because it has a tendency to pack down. For general baking, however, sifting all-purpose flour is an extra step. Instead, just stir all-purpose flour, spoon it lightly into a measuring cup, and level it off with a straight-edged knife. Never pack the flour into the measuring cup.

• To roast frozen meat, add ⅓ to ½ more time as needed to roast fresh meat. To broil frozen steaks, chops, or patties, place the meat 4 to 5 inches from heat to allow even cooking without burning. Broil until done.

• Freeze leftovers in the divided foil trays. Then the individual frozen dinners can be reheated for a no-fuss meal. Check information on pages 26 and 27 when selecting foods to freeze.

• To speed up the rising process for yeast breads and rolls, proof them in a warm oven. Turn the oven on to 200° for 1 minute; turn the oven off. Then place the dough in the oven and let rise. Keep the oven door closed to retain heat.

• To shorten time for baking potatoes, cut the potatoes in half lengthwise and place them, cut side down, on a lightly greased baking sheet. Bake in a 425° oven for 35 minutes. Or, boil the whole potatoes for 5 minutes in salted water. Cool slightly. Dry with paper toweling and bake in a 425° oven for about 35 minutes or till they are tender.

A kitchen shears has many uses. To simplify snipping fresh herbs and parsley, place uncut herb in a measuring cup and snip finely, using the kitchen shears. To cut up canned tomatoes quickly, use the shears to snip the tomatoes right in the can.

To separate frozen fruits and vegetables easily, put the food in a colander and rinse under hot tap water. Pieces should separate easily without your having to pry them apart.

Freeze chicken pieces individually on cookie sheets, then package in moisture-vaporproof wrap and freeze. When ready to cook, you can remove the exact number of pieces you need. The pieces will thaw more quickly than a whole chicken, or you can use them frozen (see the tip on page 252).

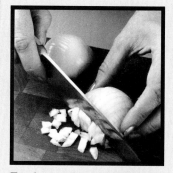

To chop onions quickly, cut them in half with a sharp knife. Using the cut side as a base, slice the onion half in one direction. Now holding the slices together with one hand, slice in the other direction.

SHORTCUT COOKING TIPS
TIMESAVING GADGETS

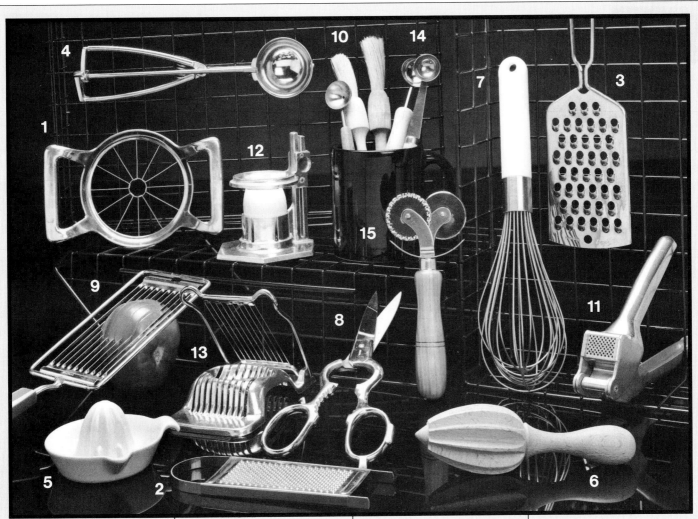

There are a number of kitchen gadgets that can short-cut your cooking and save you time in the kitchen. Buy them at cookware specialty shops and department store kitchen sections.

1. Core and wedge apples or pears all in one motion with this metal wedger.
2–3. Freshly grated citrus peel or finely shredded cheese is a snap with these mini-stainless steel graters.
4. Ice cream scoops of various sizes can be used for scooping other foods, too.
5–6. Citrus reamers are handy for extracting juice.

7. Use a wire whisk for whipping eggs and blending sauces.
8. Use kitchen shears to snip fresh herbs, parsley, and dried fruit.
9. A tomato slicer makes *beautiful*, even slices.
10. Pastry brushes make easy work out of basting poultry, glazing meat, or buttering bread loaf tops.

11. A garlic press quickly produces crushed garlic.
12–13. An egg wedger and slicer make perfect garnishes every time.
14. Melon balls are fun and easy to make with these wood-handled ball scoops.
15. This double-headed pastry wheel gives you the option of cutting both pizza and pastry.

SHORTCUT COOKING TIPS
MICROWAVE OVEN

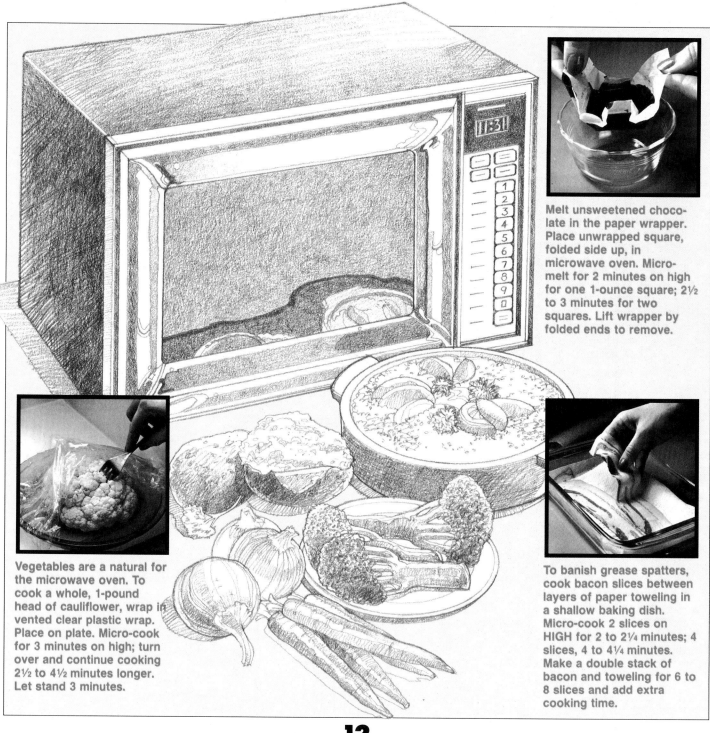

Melt unsweetened chocolate in the paper wrapper. Place unwrapped square, folded side up, in microwave oven. Micro-melt for 2 minutes on high for one 1-ounce square; 2½ to 3 minutes for two squares. Lift wrapper by folded ends to remove.

Vegetables are a natural for the microwave oven. To cook a whole, 1-pound head of cauliflower, wrap in vented clear plastic wrap. Place on plate. Micro-cook for 3 minutes on high; turn over and continue cooking 2½ to 4½ minutes longer. Let stand 3 minutes.

To banish grease spatters, cook bacon slices between layers of paper toweling in a shallow baking dish. Micro-cook 2 slices on HIGH for 2 to 2¼ minutes; 4 slices, 4 to 4¼ minutes. Make a double stack of bacon and toweling for 6 to 8 slices and add extra cooking time.

Rely on your microwave oven to speed up recipe preparations. Even if recipe directions call for conventional cooking, you can use your microwave oven to shorten preliminary chores such as melting butter or chocolate, softening cream cheese, thawing frozen foods, or cooking bacon.

For starters, try the following shortcuts. (The timings specified are at HIGH power unless noted otherwise. Timings are approximate, since oven speeds vary by manufacturer.)

RECIPE SHORTCUTS

- Save time by micro-cooking and serving in the same dish. Be sure to use oven-proof glass or ceramic dishes without metal trim. Or use cookware designed for microwave ovens. If you're not sure whether a dish is suitable for the microwave oven, perform this test. Pour ½ cup *cold water* into a glass measure. Set it inside or beside the dish you wish to test. Micro-cook for 1 minute at HIGH. If the water is warm but the dish remains cool, the dish can be used for micro-cooking. If the water is warm and the dish feels lukewarm, the dish is suitable only for heating or reheating food. If the water stays cool while the dish becomes hot, do *not* use the dish at all in the microwave oven.

- Foods will cook more quickly and evenly if they are cut into uniform-size pieces and are stirred and rearranged often.
- Since many foods continue to cook after you remove them from the microwave oven, take advantage of the standing time when planning meals. Use the time to put the finishing touches on the rest of the meal. Or, plan to microwave another food during these last minutes.
- To cook onion and/or celery on the double, use the microwave oven. Combine the *chopped vegetables* with *unmelted butter or margarine* in a glass measure or casserole. Cook, uncovered, for 2 to 3 minutes, stirring once.
- If a recipe calls for cooked chicken, you can prepare it quickly. Place 12 ounces of *chicken breasts* in a 2-quart casserole. Add 1 tablespoon *water*. Micro-cook, covered for 6 to 8 minutes or till done, turning chicken after 4 minutes. Cool, then bone and cube, if desired. Makes 1 cup. For 1½ cups cooked chicken, use 16 ounces chicken breasts and cook 9 to 12 minutes.
- Warm fresh and frozen breads in a flash. To avoid tough, hard results, heat breads just till they are warm to the touch. Two fresh sweet rolls or hamburger buns take 20 seconds, while frozen sweet rolls should heat for 35 seconds. Two frozen hamburger buns take 30 seconds. Two fresh bread slices take 10 seconds; for frozen try 20 seconds.
- Be sure to stack bread slices or rolls during heating so they will stay moist. Also, slip a paper towel or napkin under fresh breads to prevent sogginess.

- To freshen day-old or stale breads, fill a custard cup ¾ full of water and set the container in the corner of your microwave oven when you heat the bread. The steam from the water moistens the bread.
- Save time when barbecuing by precooking meat in your microwave oven. Micro-cook the meat about three-fourths done, then grill it over charcoal.
- Prepare and bake a crumb crust in the same dish. For a 9-inch pie, micro-melt 5 tablespoons *butter or margarine* in a 9-inch glass pie plate for 45 seconds. Stir in 1¼ cups finely crushed *graham crackers* and ¼ cup *sugar*. Press over bottom and sides of the pie plate. Micro-cook, uncovered, for 2 minutes, turning dish once.

TEAM THE MICROWAVE OVEN WITH THE FREEZER

- Package leftovers for quick microwave defrosting. Cut up your leftover meat or poultry as directed in the recipe that you plan to use later. Freeze recipe-size amounts in shallow packages. Label packages with the current date and intended use.
- To freeze soups or single servings of leftover casseroles for quick microwave reheating, line a microwave-oven-proof soup bowl with a double thickness of foil or clear plastic wrap. Fill with one serving of soup or casserole. Freeze until solid. Remove from bowl, seal, label, and store in the freezer. To reheat, unwrap and return soup or casserole to original bowl. (Do not freeze soups containing flour or cornstarch, because these ingredients break down and the soups become grainy.)

- To defrost fish fillets, open the package. If fillets can be separated, place them in the dish that you will use to cook them in later. Fish also may be thawed in the paper or plastic package. Defrost on 50% (MEDIUM) for 3 to 5 minutes per pound. After half the time, separate, rearrange, or turn fish over. Defrost for remaining time, or until fish is pliable on the outside, yet icy in the center of thick areas. Let stand 5 minutes, then rinse.

MICRO-COOKING VEGETABLES

- Heat canned vegetables in a microwave-oven-proof serving bowl only a minute or so till vegetables are hot.
- You can cook vegetables in paper cartons and plastic pouches. Be sure to slit the packaging before cooking so steam can escape. Vegetables packaged in foil containers should be removed to a non-metal bowl before cooking.
- Save time by preparing baked potatoes in the microwave oven. It takes 3 to 5 minutes to cook one whole, medium baking potato; 10½ to 12½ minutes to cook four potatoes. Be sure to wash and prick the skins with a fork before cooking and place potatoes on paper toweling in the oven. When cooking two or more potatoes, rearrange them once. Let potatoes stand for 5 minutes before serving.
- Cook corn on the cob in the microwave oven. Place four 7- to 8-ounce ears of *husked corn* in a tightly covered 12x7½x2-inch baking dish with 2 tablespoons *water*. Cook for 12 to 16 minutes, rotating once. Let stand 3 to 5 minutes.

SHORTCUT COOKING TIPS
BLENDER

When chopping vegetables, cut them into ½- to 1-inch pieces before putting into blender. When chopping more than ½ cup, cover vegetables with cold water. Replace lid; turn blender on and off quickly to chop.

When preparing meat loaf, make bread crumbs and combine the liquid, eggs, and seasonings in one blending operation. Then mix the blended mixture with ground meat in a separate bowl.

At the flick of a switch, this versatile kitchen helper trims minutes from food preparation time while it blends, chops, crumbs, emulsifies, or purees foods to suit your recipe needs. Here are some blender tips to help you.

- For ease in regulating the size of ingredient pieces when chopping, turn the blender on and off quickly. Obtain more uniform pieces by breaking or cutting up the ingredients before blending.
- Place liquid ingredients into the blender container first unless the recipe instructions say to do otherwise. (Many blender containers are marked to cups and ounces for quick measuring right into the container.)
- Blend large quantities of foods such as cracker crumbs or raw vegetables in several small batches so you can control the fineness of the pieces.
- Use the blender to make short work of chopping parsley. (Parsley should be dry). One-half cup of stemmed parsley yields ¼ cup chopped parsley.
- Chill hard-cooked eggs before chopping in the blender. Three eggs yield 1 cup.
- Dips, spreads, sauces, soups, gravies, and salad dressings are smoother and take less time to prepare when blended.
- When making creamy dressings, pour oil in a slow stream into blender container with blender running slowly. (Use the opening in the lid of your blender if it has one.)

- Use your blender to make soft bread crumbs. Prepare the crumbs by tearing pieces of bread into quarters. Then blend two or three slices at a time. One slice of bread makes ¾ cup soft bread crumbs. Store crumbs in the refrigerator or freezer to use in recipes and as a quick casserole topper.
- Use the blender to turn dry bread into fine dry crumbs.
- Use the blender to puree foods till smooth for the baby or to use in cooking.

To wash blender, fill ⅓ full with lukewarm water and add a small amount of detergent. Replace lid and run motor a few seconds till blender container is clean. Rinse, dry, and return container to base.

- When making a vanilla wafer or graham cracker crust, the blender crushes the crackers or cookies in seconds. Fourteen square graham crackers or 22 vanilla wafers make about 1 cup fine crumbs.
- Make quick work out of preparing fruit juice concentrates or dissolving gelatin by whirling them in the blender.
- Grate hard cheeses, such as Parmesan, in the blender.

SHORTCUT COOKING TIPS
FOOD PROCESSOR

A food processor can not only perform many of the same chopping and mixing jobs as the blender, but it also can help you with such chores as making yeast breads, slicing fruits

and vegetables, and mixing ground meat mixtures. The interchangeable cutting tools provide a great deal of control in processing foods to the right shape and size. Here are some guidelines to help you make the most use of your food processor.

• Keep your food processor handy to help you short-cut every aspect of meal preparation. Think through your menus, looking for ways to consolidate preparations before starting to work. For example, if you need chopped onion for a meat loaf and for a vegetable casserole, process enough onion for both foods at the same time.

• If several foods in a recipe require chopping, it is often possible to process similar-textured foods together, such as apples and pears. But, don't process more than the recommended amount at one time.

Instead of using a knife and cutting board, use the food processor to chop, slice, or shred foods. By limiting the amount of food processed at once, you get a more uniformly chopped product.

The slicing disk (left) will slice soft foods as well as firm ones. The shredding disk (above) makes fast and easy work out of shredding food, yet eliminates finger nicks and cuts that you may get from hand shredders.

• To prepare cheeses, grate very hard cheeses, such as Parmesan and Romano, with the steel blade in the work bowl. Shred firm or processed cheese, such as cheddar and Swiss, with the shredding disk. Use the steel blade to puree cottage cheese for use in dips.

• There's no need to bring butter or cream cheese to room temperature before processing. Simply quarter or cube these ingredients before adding them to the work bowl.

To eliminate excess bowl washing, process dry foods before wet ones, even though the dry ingredients may not be needed till last.

• Chop up to 1 cup dried fruit with the steel blade in the work bowl. Add ¼ cup flour or sugar per cup of fruit to prevent blade from gumming up. Process with on/off turns. Remember to subtract the flour or sugar used in chopping from the amount needed in the recipe. You also can chop candied fruit in the same manner. Add ½ cup flour or sugar per cup of fruit.

• Use cooked vegetables to thicken gravies instead of cornstarch or flour. When making a pot roast or stew, take out some of the vegetables (include a few pieces of cooked potato) and process till smooth. Add enough of the meat juices through the feed tube to make the desired consistency gravy.

• The key to an easy cleanup of the food processor is to rinse parts immediately after using. There's no need to thoroughly dry the work bowl and its parts unless further processing requires a dry bowl.

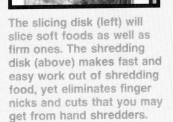

SHORTCUT COOKING TIPS
CROCKERY COOKER, PRESSURE SAUCEPAN, TOASTER OVEN

ELECTRIC SLOW CROCKERY COOKER

The electric crockery cooker gives you the option of fix-and-forget meals. With many recipes, you can cook foods for as long as 12 hours without tending. Here are some tips to help you use your crockery cooker to best advantage.

• Before using your electric slow crockery cooker, read the instruction booklet carefully so you are familiar with all its specific features. Depending on the model, you may need to adjust cooking times or occasionally stir the foods you cook.

To maintain the heat in your cooker, keep it covered. When you lift the cover to stir, be sure to replace it immediately, especially when cooking on the low-heat setting. If you leave the pot uncovered, it can lose as much as 20° of important cooking heat in only 2 minutes. A quick peek will cool the food only one or two degrees.

• Proper handling of foods before and after cooking is important. While you may want to do some advance preparation the night before, to ensure food safety you must store the ingredients in the refrigerator overnight and then transfer them to the cooker in the morning.

• Likewise, as soon as the meal is served, remove the extra food from the crockery cooker. Refrigerate the food while still warm, or cool it quickly over a bowl of ice water before refrigerating or wrapping and freezing the leftovers.

• To take advantage of the large quantities of food you can prepare in the crockery cooker, cook more food than you need for one meal and freeze the rest for another time.

• Use the cooker as a serving container. If you're serving buffet style, place the cooker right on the table and let guests help themselves.

• For parties, use your crockery cooker to keep a warm punch heated or in place of a fondue pot or chafing dish.

• For all-day cooking, plug your crockery cooker into an automatic timer to start cooking while you're away. Just before you leave, place the chilled food in the cooker, then cover. Set the timer to turn the cooker on at the appropriate time, making sure the uncooked food stands no more than two hours before the cooker comes on.

• Steam breads or puddings in the crockery cooker using a can (shortening or coffee cans work well), a heat-proof mold, or a special steamed pudding pan. But make certain that the container fits inside the crockery cooker before filling it with the batter or dough. Be sure to cover containers that have no lids with a piece of foil.

• For easy cleanup of the crockery cooker, add warm water to the cooker just after removing food rather than waiting till the cooker cools. This will help keep the food from sticking. Clean the liner with a soft cloth and soapy water, but avoid abrasive cleaners and cleansing pads. Never immerse the cord or cooker in water. If your crockery cooker has a removable liner, remove it for easy washing.

PRESSURE SAUCEPAN

Because heating steam under pressure raises the temperature of liquids higher than the boiling point of water, pressure saucepans cook foods faster than conventional saucepans. Not only do these handy appliances save you time, but because you can cook for a short time in a small amount of water, the foods you prepare will lose fewer nutrients. Here are some timesaving pressure cooking dos and don'ts to keep in mind.

• Before using a pressure saucepan, review the manufacturer's directions carefully. Pay particular attention to the instructions about the air vent and safety fuse. Also, follow the directions for the proper care of the saucepan.

• For safety's sake, never fill the pressure cooker more than two-thirds full.

• Make sure the vent pipe is always clean before you start. Particles of food can clog the vent and prevent steam from escaping.

If you're converting a favorite recipe that's ordinarily cooked in the oven or on the top of the range, cut cooking time by about one-third and be sure to include some form of liquid.

• After cooking, you can reduce the pressure two ways. One way is to place the cooker under cold running water to remove any steam buildup; if no steam comes out when the pressure control is moved, you can remove the top.

• The other way is to let the temperature and pressure in the saucepan drop on their own. Be sure to follow the recipe directions in the instruction book for this method of cooling. Also, do not remove the gauge or cover until pressure is down.

TOASTER OVEN

Toaster ovens are ideal for spur-of-the-moment cooking for small families. Depending on the brand of oven, you can bake, toast, and top-brown foods—all without turning on your regular oven. The next time you use your toaster oven, remember these tips:

• Toast oversize breads, such as bagels, French rolls, or English muffins in a toaster oven.

For quick sandwiches, freeze sandwich spreads in individual-size pats. Then place them on the bread and toast them in the toaster oven. Or, use the oven to melt cheese over open-face sandwiches.

• A toaster oven is great for baking one or two potatoes or broiling a steak or a few chops.

• Use your toaster oven to recrisp crackers or cookies, or to heat bread, rolls, pastries, or coffee cake portions. For breakfast, use your oven to keep the first batch of pancakes or waffles warm while you're working on the second batch.

• Toast coconut, seeds, and nuts in small amounts to use for garnishes and in recipes.

• Cut meal preparation time by using two ovens at once. Cook small items such as individual dessert servings in your toaster oven while you prepare large dishes such as roasts or casseroles in your conventional oven.

Toaster ovens are handy, portable appliances that are just the right size for small cooking tasks or when cooking for one or two people.

Electric slow crockery cookers short-cut cooking by shifting meal preparation time to earlier in the day. Dinner can cook practically all by itself.

A pressure saucepan helps you cook foods in about one-third the normal cooking time. It's great for speeding up slow-cooking foods such as stews or pot roasts.

SHORTCUT COOKING TIPS
PLANNING AND ORGANIZING MEALS

Planning and getting organized are important if you're going to short-cut your menu time in the kitchen. Use these hints to help you get the most out of your time.

● Plan meals for several days or a week in advance so you can compile one master grocery list and avoid last-minute confusion over what to serve.

● Shop only once a week. This way, you'll save the time spent on unnecessary trips to the supermarket.

● When planning meals, count on leftovers—they can be a real asset. Use cooked leftovers to prepare recipes such as sandwiches and casseroles. Or, if you have some uncooked leftovers, stir-frying is one quick way to use small amounts of vegetables and meats.

Streamline meals by planning two- or three-course menus. For example, serve a meat and vegetable main dish with a salad. Or, skip the salad and opt for dessert.

● Use a prepared food for one of the courses. Keep frozen yogurt or ice cream on hand for dessert. And for easy last-minute salads, try avocado or tomato halves filled with cottage cheese and bottled dressing.

● Serve cold meals more often. Make-ahead main-dish salads, sandwiches, and soups can be just as appetizing as hot meals.

● To save time, serve foods in big pieces when possible. For example, try a melon wedge in-stead of a fruit cup for dessert or a lettuce wedge instead of torn greens for a salad.

● Serve one-dish meat-vegetable combinations often. They save cooking, serving, and clean-up time.

MENU TIPS

● Consider textures and colors of foods when menu planning. Serve a variety of textures and colors. If your main dish is a soft food, include a crisp salad as part of the meal.

● Balance flavors. Serve a tart food with a bland one. Watch seasonings and make sure that one flavor doesn't dominate the meal. Beware of spicy ingredients. Unless it's an ethnic meal, one highly seasoned food per menu is usually enough.

● Avoid serving foods that are all mixtures. For example, team a tossed vegetable salad with a piece of meat, fish, or poultry rather than with a casserole that's also a mixture of pieces.

● Make sure that foods are really hot or cold, not lukewarm. And, plan a balance of hot and cold foods in the meal.

● Fit the dessert to the rest of the meal. Plan to serve a light dessert with a hearty meal and vice versa.

● Read the recipes carefully before you begin cooking, then gather the ingredients and utensils you'll need. This way, you won't be surprised by hidden steps or ingredients in the method, and you'll be able to organize your time to do the longest or most involved cooking steps first.

● Interweave as many of the steps in a meal or recipe as you can. For example, you can cook pasta for the main dish at the same time you're fixing the salad and dessert.

Plan cook-it-together meals where most of the foods are combined at the table. Pizzas, fondue, hot pot, and main-dish salads are all good choices.

Have the whole family prepare a meal. Divide the meal into parts and let each member, from Dad down to the youngest child, prepare something for the meal.

SHORTCUT COOKING TIPS
BASIC FOOD GROUPS

While short-cutting time, you need not short-cut nutrition. When planning menus, select a variety of foods for each day's meals. Make sure your menus are well balanced by using the Basic Five Food Groups.

Vegetable-Fruit Group: Fruits and vegetables provide vitamins A and C. Good vitamin C sources include citrus fruits, while good vitamin A sources include dark-green or deep-yellow vegetables. One serving equals ½ cup or a portion ordinarily served, such as a lettuce wedge or half of a grapefruit.

Bread-Cereal Group: These foods supply thiamine, niacin, riboflavin, and iron. A serving equals 1 slice whole grain or enriched bread, 1 ounce ready-to-eat cereal, or ½ to ¾ cup cooked cereal, pasta, or rice.

Milk-Cheese Group: Foods in this group supply calcium, riboflavin, protein, vitamin A, and sometimes vitamin D. Children under 9 years should have 2 to 3 servings daily; children 9 to 12, 3 servings; teens, 4 servings; and adults, 2 servings. One serving is 1 cup milk or yogurt, 2 ounces process cheese food, 2 cups cottage cheese, 1⅓ ounces cheddar or Swiss cheese, or 1½ cups ice cream.

Meat - Poultry - Fish - Beans Group: These foods are the main sources of protein, phosphorus, and iron. A serving equals 2 to 3 ounces cooked lean meat, poultry, or fish without bone; 2 eggs; ½ to 1 cup nuts; ¼ cup peanut butter; or 1 cup cooked dried beans.

Fats-Sweets-Alcohol Group: Foods in this group supply mainly calories with few nutrients. These foods include butter, margarine, mayonnaise, salad dressings, candy, sugar, soft drinks, alcoholic beverages, and unenriched breads.

Vegetable-Fruit Group: Select four servings every day. Include one good vitamin C source. Every other day include one good source of vitamin A.

Bread-Cereal Group: Four servings should be eaten every day. Included in this group are products made with whole grains, enriched flour or meal, and cereals, pasta, and rice.

Milk-Cheese Group: The recommended daily servings vary in this group, depending primarily on age. See paragraph at left for recommended servings. Pregnant and nursing women need additional servings. Other foods in this group are yogurt, ice cream, and buttermilk.

Meat - Poultry - Fish - Beans Group: You should eat two servings from this group every day. Besides meat, poultry, fish, and beans, other foods in this group include eggs, dried peas, soybeans, lentils, seeds, and nuts.

Fats-Sweets-Alcohol Group: No serving numbers or sizes are suggested for this group since the amounts depend on calorie needs.

SHORTCUT COOKING TIPS
ENTERTAINING TIPS

Saving time is especially important when you're entertaining because you want to get out of the kitchen fast and spend maximum time with your guests. Whether it be a large party, an informal get-together for a few, or guests for the entire weekend, you can entertain without a hitch if you keep some of these hints at your fingertips:

• When planning a menu, stick to recipes that you know will work. If serving buffet-style, don't plan any food that will melt easily, collapse, or toughen if it must stand a few minutes before it is served.
• Choose a menu that includes some foods that can be prepared in advance. Last-minute foods should be easy to fix.
• Consider asking guests to bring part of the menu. Offer your recipes or ask them to make their own choices.
• Another way to get help with food preparation is to make it part of the entertainment. Plan a participation party where you ask guests to chop, fry, toss, or flambé the food.
• Get organized by writing out a master plan. Jot down the complete menu and make a list of the food, serving pieces and bowls, rental equipment (if any), and other supplies that you'll need. Also, make out a timetable of last-minute preparations so you don't forget a food item tucked away in a cupboard or the refrigerator.

• If you're cooking for a large group, you may want to borrow large mixing bowls and baking pans from a school or church. But first measure your refrigerator and oven to be sure the pans will fit. Also, get some help, if possible. The simplest preparations will take longer than you expect with the larger quantities of food.
• An informal approach that features self-service and combine-it-yourself recipes is an easy way to simplify a menu for a large group. Guests help themselves to everything from beverages to the dessert. All you do is prepare the raw materials ahead, then set up a separate area for each course of the meal, including the necessary food, equipment, and how-to guidelines.
• Assembling supplies to feed a crowd needn't be a headache. To seat larger groups, rent folding tables and chairs. Use pastel sheets as table cloths. Mix and match china, glassware, and flatware borrowed from friends.
• For a very large party, hire older neighborhood children to help you with serving, baby-sitting, and cleaning up.
• For a table decoration, a centerpiece made of food is easy to make. Arrange some cheese with strawberries, melon wedges, pineapple spears, or sliced apple.
• Save time and money by doubling up on your entertaining. Make decorations and house-cleaning count twice by planning two parties for the same weekend or week—for instance, a Saturday brunch followed by a Sunday open house. Be sure to plan for most

of the food to be made ahead of time, and allow time to recover between parties.
• If your refrigerator or freezer won't hold large platters of food, check with the neighbors for additional storage space. Or, have a large cooler on hand to keep foods and/or beverages chilled.
• Try to have the dishwasher and/or sink empty before the meal so that you have a place to stash dirty dishes.
• Keep a record of menus and shopping lists for your next party. It will make the next party easier to plan if you have something to refer to.
• Let the food itself be the star and don't overdo the garnishes. Keep the trims on the foods simple and easy to make. Here are some suggestions for food garnishes:

Besides parsley sprigs, pineapple slices, and lemon wedges, consider some of these main-dish garnishes. Add pieces of spiced apple or pear to a serving platter of roast beef. Use kumquats with roast lamb. Garnish pork with French-fried onion rings.

When garnishing fish and seafood, set off whole fish with fresh mint sprigs; top casseroles or skillet dishes with cherry tomatoes, hard-cooked egg slices, or radish roses; and spruce up broiled or baked fish portions with carrot curls or green onion fans.

Don't forget those easy-to-do extra touches. A sprinkling of paprika on a main dish or a dollop of whipped cream on a dessert can turn everyday dishes into company fare.

Use meat garnishes to decorate main dishes. Save a few slices of frankfurter or chunks of ham to dress up a meaty casserole. Or, form one half of a large thin slice of sausage into a cornucopia shape, fasten with a wooden pick, and place atop a baked dish.

Cheese makes an attractive and tasty garnish for many dishes. Shredded cheese is an easy trim. Or, cut square slices of cheese in half diagonally for triangles, or cut round slices in half for semicircles. Arrange cut pieces around the edge of the hot casserole to form a decorative border.

Other casserole toppers include prebaked pastry cutouts or small biscuits, buttered bread crumbs, crushed chow mein noodles, potato chips, corn chips, or crackers.

To garnish light or clear soups, make them look and taste rich by adding pats of butter. Or, float lemon slices, cucumber rounds, snipped chives, or sliced olives atop. Garnish a creamed soup with croutons, sieved hard-cooked egg yolk, dairy sour cream, or crumbled bacon.

Glamorize desserts by sprinkling cakes with toasted coconut and/or nuts or grated citrus peel. Spruce up puddings or ice cream with fresh fruit, crumbled cookies, or crushed peppermint or toffee.

FEEDING HOUSEGUESTS

- If possible, plan your menus and do your shopping in advance. Put the emphasis on make-ahead foods you can refrigerate or freeze. Before the out-of-towners arrive, have a cooking spree and stow away the dishes till they are needed for a particular meal.
- Keep breakfasts and lunches simple—juice and rolls or cereal for breakfast and soup and sandwiches for lunch. Then plan fancier menus for the evening meals.
- Let guests help by setting the table, tossing the salad, or assisting in cleanup. They'll feel more at home and you can probably use the help.
- If plans include a busy day of shopping, sight-seeing, and such, take advantage of your electric slow crockery cooker. Put dinner in the pot, then take off and let the crockery cooker do the cooking. When you return home, keep the rest of the menu simple and the dining casual so there's no last-minute fuss before you serve.
- Plan meals and snacks on a self-serve basis. Post lists explaining where breakfast and snack foods are located.
- Round out a special homemade entrée with store-bought foods. Select the salad, bread, and dessert from a local shop that prides itself on quality food.
- For a change of pace, treat your houseguests to a tour of the city followed by a relaxing dinner at a favorite ethnic restaurant or a neighborhood spot. You might even make the evening a "progressive dinner," and eat each course at a different restaurant.

SHORTCUT COOKING TIPS
FOOD BUYING AND SHOPPING HINTS

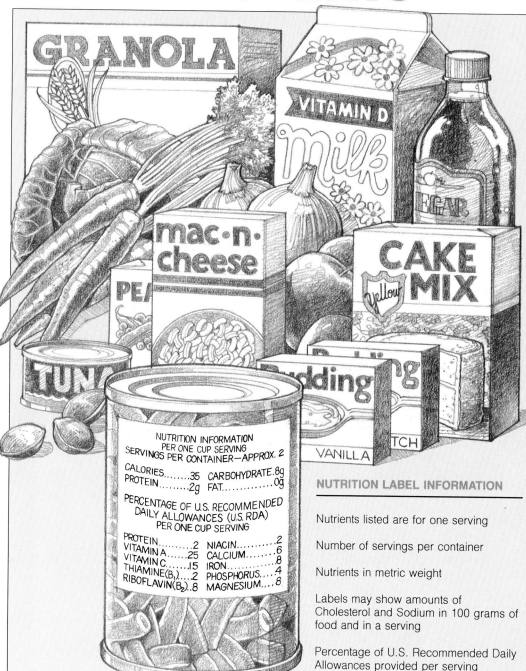

NUTRITION INFORMATION
PER ONE CUP SERVING
SERVINGS PER CONTAINER—APPROX. 2

CALORIES.........35 CARBOHYDRATE.8g
PROTEIN.........2g FAT.............0g

PERCENTAGE OF U.S. RECOMMENDED
DAILY ALLOWANCES (U.S. RDA)
PER ONE CUP SERVING

PROTEIN...........2   NIACIN...........2
VITAMIN A......25   CALCIUM.......6
VITAMIN C......15   IRON.............8
THIAMINE(B₁)....2   PHOSPHORUS....4
RIBOFLAVIN(B₂).8   MAGNESIUM....8

NUTRITION LABEL INFORMATION

Nutrients listed are for one serving

Number of servings per container

Nutrients in metric weight

Labels may show amounts of Cholesterol and Sodium in 100 grams of food and in a serving

Percentage of U.S. Recommended Daily Allowances provided per serving

Avoid extra trips to the store by making out a shopping list. While at the store, be a wise shopper. Consider the nutrition information on the label. Also, use the Availability of Fresh Produce chart to help when planning fresh produce for your menus.

One of the best times to make out your shopping list is when you are planning menus. By doing so, you know you won't forget any of the ingredients you need. Also, you can check your cupboard for ingredients you already have on hand.

To make assembling your list easier, keep a note pad handy to jot down ingredients as you use them up—especially staple items (see page 25). Divide the shopping list so that you group like items, perhaps even list them in the order in which you find them in your grocery store. Beside the food items and specified amounts needed, list any specially advertised prices and the brands of the specials. Also indicate on your shopping list whether you have coupons to use for the items.

Use newspaper food ads to help you make out your shopping list. Not only can the ads spark menu ideas but you may be able to plan several meals around a weekly special.

Choose a time of the week to grocery shop when the store isn't very crowded, yet the shelves are fully stocked. Also, it's best not to shop when you're hungry or you may find yourself purchasing unnecessary food items that you "just can't resist."

Select frozen foods that are frozen solid and are frost-free. Frost indicates the packages may have been thawed and re-frozen. To insure minimum thawing before you get home, make the frozen food section your last stop before you head for the check-out counter.

When selecting cans and packaged foods, avoid bulging and bent cans and leaky or opened packages.

Buy fresh produce that looks fresh and is in good condition. It's a waste of time and money if you have to cut away bad spots and discard poor quality produce. Plan to buy fruits and vegetables in season. Check the Availability of Fresh Produce chart at right for the best months for specific food items.

Become a comparison shopper. Consider cost per serving or per unit. Also, read the labels. Consider the grade and quality of the foods you buy, keeping in mind how you intend to use them. Take a look at the nutrition information on the label. As required by the Food and Drug Administration, the type of label shown on the page at left must be on all foods to which vitamins or minerals have been added and those that are advertised as having special nutritional qualities. The U.S. RDAs are based on the levels of protein, vitamins, and minerals needed by most adults to maintain good health.

Finally, take your grocery purchases straight home and store them properly as soon as possible. Be sure to overwrap meats you plan to freeze with moisture-vaporproof wrap.

AVAILABILITY OF FRESH PRODUCE

PERCENTAGE OF TOTAL ANNUAL SUPPLY

	JAN.	FEB.	MAR.	APR.	MAY	JUNE	JULY	AUG.	SEPT.	OCT.	NOV.	DEC.
Apples	9	9	10	9	8	6	3	4	9	12	10	11
Apricots					7	58	29	6				
Asparagus	*	7	25	34	20	9	*	*	1	2	1	
Beans, Snap	6	5	6	9	10	12	11	10	9	8	7	7
Beets	5	5	8	7	7	11	13	12	10	9	7	6
Blueberries					2	24	48	24	2			
Broccoli	9	8	12	8	8	8	7	5	7	8	9	11
Brussels Sprouts	13	12	11	8	4	*	*	2	6	14	16	13
Cabbage	9	8	10	9	9	9	7	7	8	8	8	8
Cantaloupes	*	*	3	4	9	19	24	23	12	4	1	*
Carrots	10	9	10	9	8	8	7	7	8	8	8	8
Cauliflower	8	7	9	8	8	7	6	6	8	12	11	9
Cherries, Sweet						6	42	46	6			
Corn, Sweet	3	2	4	7	16	18	17	14	7	5	4	3
Cranberries	*									10	25	45	20
Cucumbers	6	5	6	9	11	13	12	9	7	8	8	6
Grapefruit	12	12	13	11	9	6	3	3	4	7	10	10
Grapes, Table	3	2	4	3	2	6	10	19	19	15	10	7
Lemons	8	7	8	8	9	10	10	10	8	7	7	8
Lettuce	7	8	9	9	9	9	9	9	8	8	8	7
Mushrooms	9	8	9	8	9	8	7	8	8	8	9	9
Nectarines	*	1	*		*	19	32	30	16	1		
Oranges	12	11	12	11	10	7	5	4	4	5	8	11
Peaches	*	*	*	*	6	23	29	27	13	1		
Pears	7	6	7	6	5	4	4	13	16	14	10	8
Peas, Green	13	15	11	11	13	14	8	5	3	2	*	4
Peppers, Bell	8	7	7	8	9	10	10	9	9	8	8	7
Pineapples	7	7	11	10	12	13	10	7	4	5	6	8
Potatoes	9	8	9	8	8	8	8	8	9	9	8	8
Radishes	9	8	11	12	11	9	7	6	5	5	9	8
Rhubarb	8	15	17	22	21	10	2	1	1	1	1	1
Spinach	9	9	11	10	9	9	6	6	7	8	8	8
Squash	7	6	6	8	9	10	9	9	9	9	10	8
Strawberries	2	3	8	19	29	16	9	5	4	2	1	2
Sweet Potatoes	9	8	9	8	4	3	2	5	9	11	19	13
Tangerines	19	11	9	5	1	*	*		*	6	20	28
Tomatoes	7	6	8	9	11	10	11	9	7	8	7	7
Turnips and Rutabagas	12	10	10	8	5	4	4	5	8	11	13	10
Watermelons	*	*	1	3	12	28	29	18	6	1	*	*

*Supply is less than .5% of annual total
Chart provided courtesy of United Fresh Fruit Vegetable Association

SHORTCUT COOKING TIPS
STOCKING THE KITCHEN

BASIC KITCHEN EQUIPMENT

A well-equipped, organized kitchen can reduce the time and effort you spend preparing meals. When selecting equipment, make sure that each item you buy is durable and easy to clean. Choose pieces you can use for more than one job, such as freezer-to-oven-to-table baking dishes and oven-going skillets.

Preparation and Cooking Utensils:

set of mixing bowls
set of dry measuring cups
liquid measuring cup
set of standard measuring spoons
wooden spoons
rubber spatulas
flexible metal spatula
serrated knife for bread and tomatoes
paring knife with 3-inch blade
utility knife with 6-inch blade
French cook's or chef's knife
vegetable peeler
meat mallet
long-handled fork
long-handled spoon
ladle
slotted spoon
pancake turner
tongs
kitchen scissors
bottle opener; can opener
rotary beater and/or electric mixer
grater or shredder
small and large strainers
colander
kitchen timer
cutting board
rolling pin with cover
pastry cloth
pastry brush

Bakeware:

baking sheet or jelly roll pan
wire cooling racks
6-ounce custard cups
various sizes of round, oblong, and square baking dishes and pans
muffin pan
pie plate
loaf baking pan
various sizes of casserole dishes
roasting pan with rack
meat thermometer

Range-Top Cookware:

1-, 2-, and 3-quart covered saucepans
4- to 6-quart covered kettle or Dutch oven
6- to 8-inch covered skillet
10-inch covered skillet

Food Storage:

assorted refrigerator-freezer dishes
assorted canisters

STAPLES TO KEEP ON HAND

Nothing is more frustrating than starting to prepare a meal and discovering you don't have the ingredients you need. Avoid all the hassle and skip those last-minute trips to the store by keeping this list of ingredients on hand.

granulated sugar
brown sugar
all-purpose flour
salt
pepper
baking powder
baking soda
coffee and/or tea
shortening
cooking oil
butter and/or
 margarine
assorted herbs and
 spices
vanilla
unsweetened cocoa
 powder
mayonnaise and/or
 salad dressing
prepared mustard
catsup
Worcestershire sauce
bread

cereals
pasta
eggs
meat
salad greens
vegetables
fruits
cheese
juices
milk

Optional items to
keep on hand:

canned pie filling
canned pudding or
 pudding mixes
canned frosting and/or
 frosting mixes

soups to use in
 cooking—
 cream of mushroom,
 cream of chicken,
 and cream of celery
instant beef and
 chicken bouillon
 granules
evaporated milk
sweetened condensed
 milk
cold cuts, frankfurters,
 and/or canned
 meats
cooked bacon pieces
canned fish or seafood
bottled salad dressings
canned tomato
 products—
 sauce, paste, etc.
peanut butter
ice cream

Home-prepared pro-
ducts that are
helpful to keep on
hand in the refriger-
ator or freezer:

toasted chopped
 coconut
soft bread crumbs
chopped onion
shredded cheese

SHORTCUT COOKING TIPS
STORING FOOD

MAXIMUM STORAGE TIMES

FOOD	REFRIGERATOR (36°F. to 40°F.)	FREEZER (0°F. or lower)
MEAT		
Beef	2 to 4 days	6 to 12 months
Pork	2 to 4 days	3 to 6 months
Ground meats	1 to 2 days	3 months
Ham	7 days	2 months
Bacon	5 to 7 days	1 month
Frankfurters	4 to 5 days	1 month
Sausage, bulk	7 days	2 months
Sausage, dry	2 to 3 weeks	do not freeze
Sausage, smoked	3 to 7 days	do not freeze
Luncheon meats	7 days	do not freeze
Lamb	2 to 4 days	6 to 9 months
Veal	2 to 4 days	6 to 9 months
Variety meats	1 to 2 days	3 to 4 months
Cooked meats	4 to 5 days	2 to 3 months
POULTRY		
Chicken, whole	1 to 2 days	12 months
Chicken, pieces	1 to 2 days	9 months
Turkey, whole	1 to 2 days (thawed)	12 months
Poultry, cooked (without liquid)	1 to 2 days	1 month
FISH		
Fat fish	1 to 2 days	4 months
Lean fish	1 to 2 days	8 months
EGGS (see tip at right)		
Whole eggs	4 weeks	6 to 12 months
Egg whites	7 days	6 to 12 months
Egg yolks	2 to 3 days	6 to 12 months
DAIRY PRODUCTS		
Butter	7 days	3 to 6 months
Cheese, hard	several months	6 months
Cheese, soft	2 weeks	4 months
Cheese, cottage	5 days	do not freeze
Ice cream		1 to 3 months
Milk	5 to 7 days	do not freeze
Sour cream	3 to 4 days	do not freeze
Yogurt	2 weeks	do not freeze

Use the freezer for long-term storage and the refrigerator for storing perishable foods that are to be used within a few days. Nonperishable staples can be stored in a cool, dry, well-ventilated place.

When freezing foods, start with high-quality ingredients and observe strict sanitary procedures. Remember, freezer temperatures of 0°F. or below merely stop the multiplication of bacteria, but do not kill them. Avoid freezing certain foods because of the texture and flavor changes that occur. These foods include lettuce, celery, tomatoes, cucumbers, hard-cooked egg whites, mayonnaise, and sour cream.

For freezing, use moisture-vaporproof wrap such as foil, laminated freezer wrap, and polyethylene bags. Other freezer containers include freezer boxes with polyethylene bag liners, glass freezer jars, rigid plastic containers, and lightweight aluminum containers.

Be sure to date and label foods for the freezer. Keep a list on the freezer door and check items in and out when used.

The best place to thaw frozen foods is in the refrigerator or in a microwave oven. Or, thaw food in a sealed bag under cold running water.

Certain foods need special care when storing.

Canned foods—Store canned vegetables, fruits, and meats in a cool, dry place away from sunlight. Ideal storage temperature is between 50°F. and 70°F.

Cooked foods — Promptly cover and refrigerate or freeze cooked foods or leftovers.

Dairy products — Store cheese, milk, and butter or margarine tightly covered in the refrigerator. Refrigerate strong-flavored cheese such as blue cheese or feta in a tightly covered jar.

Dried fruits and nuts—Store dried fruit in a tightly closed container at room temperature. Nuts will keep longer if refrigerated or frozen in tightly covered containers.

Eggs—Keep eggs in the covered egg carton in the refrigerator. You can refrigerate leftover separated eggs in tightly covered containers (cover yolks with cold water). To freeze eggs, break into a bowl, stir to blend, and add 1½ teaspoons sugar or corn syrup or ⅛ teaspoon salt per 2 whole eggs or 4 egg yolks. Egg whites require no additions. Use freezer containers. Thaw in the refrigerator and use within 24 hours. Remember to allow for the added sugar, corn syrup, or salt when using them in recipes.

Fresh fish—Tightly wrap fish in moisture-vaporproof material before freezing or refrigerating.

Fresh fruits and vegetables—Store these in the refrigerator crisper. Keep items such as potatoes and dry onions in a cool, well-ventilated place.

Meat and poultry—Refrigerate fresh meat and poultry as purchased in clear packaging. To freeze, remove clear packaging. Divide meat into desired sized portions, then wrap tightly in moisture-vaporproof material. (Prepackaged meat and poultry can be frozen for one to two weeks without rewrapping.)

FREEZING PREPARED FOODS

FOOD AND PREPARATION FOR FREEZING	HOW TO SERVE	STORAGE TIME
BREADS		
Biscuits and muffins: Bake as usual; cool. Seal in a freezer container or wrap with moisture-vaporproof material; seal and label.	Thaw breads in the package at room temperature 1 hour or wrap in foil and reheat in a 300° oven for 20 minutes.	2 months
Yeast breads and rolls: Bake as usual; cool. Wrap with moisture-vaporproof material; seal and label. (Frost sweet rolls after thawing and heating, if desired.)	Thaw in package at room temperature or reheat yeast rolls in foil in a 300° oven about 15 minutes.	4 to 8 months
CAKES		
General: Bake cake or cupcakes as usual. Remove from pan; cool. (If cake is frosted, freeze it before wrapping.) Wrap in moisture-vaporproof material; seal and label. (Unfrosted cakes freeze better; frosted and filled cakes may become soggy.)	Thaw cakes at room temperature (allow 3 hours for a large cake, 1 hour for layers, and 40 minutes for cupcakes). Thaw frosted and filled cakes in the refrigerator.	6 months
Frostings and fillings recommended for freezing include cream cheese and butter cream frostings and fillings. Seal frostings in freezer containers. Those not recommended are soft frostings, frostings made with egg whites, and cream fillings.	Thaw frostings and fillings, covered, in the refrigerator.	6 months
CASSEROLES		
Poultry, fish, or meat with vegetables or pasta: Cool hot mixtures quickly. Turn into a freezer-to-oven casserole dish. Cover tightly with casserole lid or foil. Seal and label.	Bake, covered, in a 400° oven for half of baking time; uncover for second half of baking time. Allow 1¾ hours for one quart.	3 to 6 months
COOKIES		
Unbaked, general: Pack unbaked dough in freezer containers; seal and label. Don't freeze meringue-type cookies.	Thaw in container at room temperature till dough is soft. Bake as usual.	6 months
Refrigerator cookies: Shape unbaked dough into a roll. Wrap in moisture-vaporproof material.	Thaw slightly. Slice roll and bake.	6 months
Baked, general: Bake as usual; cool. Pack in containers with waxed paper between layers.	Thaw in package at room temperature.	6 to 12 months
PIES		
Fruit, general, two-crust, unbaked: Treat light-colored fruits with ascorbic acid color keeper to prevent fruit from darkening. Prepare pie as usual but do not slit top crust. Use a freezer-to-oven or metal pie plate. Cover top with an inverted paper plate to protect crust. Wrap with moisture-vaporproof material; seal and label. If desired, place in a sturdy container.	Unwrap; cut vent holes in top crust. Cover edge of crust with foil. Without thawing, bake in a 450° oven for 15 minutes, then in a 375° oven for 15 minutes. Uncover edge and bake about 30 to 35 minutes longer or till done.	3 months
Fruit, general, two-crust, baked: Bake as usual in a glass or metal pie plate. Cool and package as above.	Thaw in package at room temperature or covered with foil in a 300° oven.	2 to 3 months

SHORTCUT COOKING TIPS
INGREDIENT EQUIVALENTS

Use these charts for ingredient equivalents and emergency substitutions when you run short of an item. Check the high-altitude information if you live 1,000 feet or more above sea level.

INGREDIENT EQUIVALENTS

FOOD	AMOUNT BEFORE PREPARATION	APPROXIMATE MEASURE AFTER PREPARATION
CEREALS		
Macaroni	1 cup (3½ ounces)	2½ cups cooked
Noodles, medium	3 cups (4 ounces)	3 cups cooked
Spaghetti	8 ounces	4 cups cooked
Long grain rice	1 cup (7 ounces)	3 cups cooked
Quick-cooking rice	1 cup (3 ounces)	2 cups cooked
Popcorn	¼ cup	5 cups cooked
CRUMBS		
Bread	1 slice	¾ cup soft *or* ¼ cup fine dry cumbs
Saltine crackers	28 squares	1 cup finely crushed
Rich round crackers	24 crackers	1 cup finely crushed
Graham crackers	14 squares	1 cup finely crushed
Gingersnaps	15 cookies	1 cup finely crushed
Vanilla wafers	22 cookies	1 cup finely crushed
FRUITS		
Apples	1 medium	1 cup sliced
Apricots	1 medium	¼ cup sliced
Bananas	1 medium	⅓ cup mashed
Lemons	1 medium	3 Tbsp. juice; 2 tsp. shredded peel
Oranges	1 medium	¼ to ⅓ cup juice; 4 tsp. shredded peel
Peaches, pears	1 medium	½ cup sliced
Strawberries	4 cups whole	4 cups sliced
VEGETABLES		
Beans and peas, dried	1 pound (about 2½ cups)	6 cups cooked
Cabbage	1 pound (1 small)	5 cups shredded
Carrots, without tops	1 pound (6 to 8 medium)	3 cups shredded *or* 2½ cups diced
Celery	1 medium bunch	4½ cups chopped
Green beans	1 pound (3 cups)	2½ cups cooked, cut up
Green onions	1 bunch (7)	½ cup sliced
Green peppers	1 large	1 cup diced
Mushrooms	1 pound (6 cups)	6 cups sliced *or* 2 cups cooked
Onions	1 medium	½ cup chopped
Potatoes	1 medium	⅔ cup cubed *or* ½ cup mashed
Spinach	1 pound (12 cups)	1½ cups cooked
MISCELLANEOUS		
Cheese	4 ounces	1 cup shredded *or* cubed
Whipping cream	1 cup	2 cups whipped
Boneless meat	1 pound	2 cups cooked, cubed
Cooked meat	1 pound	3 cups diced

SUBSTITUTIONS AND HIGH-ALTITUDE HINTS

EMERGENCY SUBSTITUTIONS

IF YOU DON'T HAVE:	SUBSTITUTE:
1 cup cake flour	1 cup minus 2 tablespoons all purpose flour
1 tablespoon cornstarch	2 tablespoons all-purpose flour
1 teaspoon baking powder	1 teaspoon baking soda plus ½ cup buttermilk or sour milk (to replace ½ cup liquid called for)
1 cup granulated sugar	1 cup packed brown sugar or 2 cups sifted powdered sugar
1 cup honey	1¼ cups granulated sugar plus ¼ cup liquid
1 cup corn syrup	1 cup granulated sugar plus ¼ cup liquid
1 square (1 ounce) unsweetened chocolate	3 tablespoons unsweetened cocoa powder plus 1 tablespoon butter or margarine
1 cup buttermilk	1 tablespoon lemon juice or vinegar plus enough whole milk to make 1 cup (let stand 5 minutes)
1 cup whole milk	½ cup evaporated milk plus ½ cup water or 1 cup reconstituted nonfat dry milk
1 cup light cream	2 tablespoons butter plus 1 cup minus 2 tablespoons milk
2 cups tomato sauce	¾ cup tomato paste plus 1 cup water
1 cup tomato juice	½ cup tomato sauce plus ½ cup water
1 clove garlic	⅛ teaspoon garlic powder
1 small onion	1 teaspoon onion powder or 1 tablespoon minced dried onion
1 teaspoon dry mustard	1 tablespoon prepared mustard
1 tablespoon fresh snipped herbs	1 teaspoon dried herbs, crushed

COOKING AT HIGH ALTITUDES

If you live in the mountains, you probably wish there was a foolproof way to adapt recipes to high-altitude conditions. Unfortunately there is no magic formula. You'll need to become familiar with how altitude affects food, then experiment with your own recipes.

BAKING
When baking, many ingredients are affected by the lower air pressure found at high altitudes, especially leavenings, liquids, and sugar.

For leavenings, with less air pressure to control expansion, baked products rise too quickly and are coarse and crumbly.

For liquids, evaporation is accelerated at high elevations, causing foods to dry.

For sugar, as liquid evaporates, sugar becomes more concentrated. This weakens the cell structure of cakes and breads, causing them to fall.

Here are some tips on specific baked products:
● Cookies, biscuits, and muffins are more stable than cakes and need little adjustment. Experiment by reducing sugar and baking powder and increasing the liquid in the recipe.
● For cakes and cookies, increase the oven temperature about 20°F. and decrease the baking time. This allows cakes to set before leavening expands them too much, and it keeps cookies from drying out.
● Cakes leavened by air, such as angel cake, expand too much if egg whites are beaten at sea-level directions. Beat whites only to soft peaks.
● Cakes leavened with baking powder or baking soda need more adjustment depending on the altitude. When two amounts appear in the following recipe adjustment suggestions, try the smaller first, then adjust ingredients next time, if necessary.

At 3,000 feet, for each cup of liquid, add 1 to 2 tablespoons. For each teaspoon baking powder, decrease by ⅛ teaspoon. For each cup sugar, decrease up to 1 tablespoon.

At 5,000 feet, for each cup liquid, add 2 to 4 tablespoons. For each teaspoon baking powder, decrease by ⅛ to ¼ teaspoon. For each cup sugar, decrease up to 2 tablespoons.

At 7,000 feet, for each cup liquid, add 3 to 4 tablespoons. For each teaspoon baking powder, decrease by ¼ teaspoon. For each cup sugar, decrease by 1 to 3 tablespoons.
● Yeast doughs rise quickly at high altitudes, resulting in a weaker structure. Shorten rising time and add extra liquid.

RANGE-TOP COOKING
Since liquids boil at lower temperatures at high altitudes than at sea level, foods cooked in liquid take longer to cook. Be sure to increase the cooking time rather than the heat, since foods may scorch easily.

CHAPTER 2

TIMESAVING MENUS

Looking for tasty new meals to serve your family or friends? Take your pick from over three dozen menus in this chapter. There are meal plans to fit almost any size group and eating situation, from a company brunch to an informal family dinner. What's more, there's a complete weekend of meals in which you can transform foods leftover from one meal into entirely new recipes for the next meal. The menus feature a variety of cooking times. You can prepare an all make-ahead menu, a jiffy 30-minute meal, an easy but slow-cooking meal, or a combination of all three. Each of the menus also has its own timetable to show you the most efficient way to organize the KP duty.

Just one example of these easy-on-the-cook menus is Super Sandwich Supper (see recipes, page 50) headlining Pork and Olive Burgers, Oriental Salad, Glazed Sweet Potatoes, and lemonade.

Have you ever awakened on a Sunday morning and thought it would be fun to serve a special brunch—but you didn't know what to prepare, so you just made "the usual." With this delicious brunch menu, you'll never have that problem again! You can fix it anytime because the recipes call for ingredients you can easily keep on hand. And it only takes 50 minutes to prepare from start to finish.

RAID-THE-CUPBOARD BRUNCH

SALMON OMELET

SWEET BANANA-RAISIN MUFFINS

ELEGANT FRUIT COMPOTE

BEVERAGE

50 MINUTES BEFORE SERVING
■ Prepare Sweet Banana-Raisin Muffins.
■ Stir together mushroom soup, salmon, celery, sour cream, and paprika for the Salmon Omelet.
■ Beat the egg whites for the Salmon Omelet.

20 MINUTES BEFORE SERVING
■ Reduce oven temperature to 325°.
■ Finish preparing Salmon Omelet.
■ While omelet bakes, prepare Elegant Fruit Compote.
■ Prepare beverage.

SALMON OMELET

Total preparation time: 35 minutes

1 7¾-ounce can salmon, drained, flaked, and skin and bones removed
1 7½-ounce can semi-condensed savory cream of mushroom soup
½ cup dairy sour cream
¼ cup thinly sliced celery
½ teaspoon paprika
4 egg whites
2 tablespoons water
¼ teaspoon salt
4 egg yolks
2 tablespoons butter *or* margarine

1 In a saucepan stir together flaked salmon, mushroom soup, sour cream, sliced celery, and paprika. Heat through. *Do not boil.* Keep warm while preparing omelet.

2 For omelet, in a large mixer bowl beat egg whites till frothy. Add water and salt; continue beating about 1½ minutes or till stiff peaks form. Set aside.

3 In a small mixer bowl beat egg yolks at high speed of electric mixer about 5 minutes or till thick and lemon colored. Fold egg yolks into egg white mixture.

4 In a 10-inch oven-proof skillet heat the butter till a drop of water sizzles. Pour in egg mixture, mounding it slightly higher at the sides. Cook over low heat, uncovered, for 8 to 10 minutes or till eggs are puffed and set and the bottom is golden.

5 Place in a 325° oven; bake about 10 minutes or till a knife inserted near center comes out clean. Loosen the sides of the omelet with a metal spatula. Make a shallow cut across the omelet, slightly off center.

6 Fold the smaller portion of the omelet over the larger portion. Slip omelet onto a serving platter. Unfold the omelet and spoon in *½ cup* of the salmon mixture. Fold the smaller portion of the omelet over the salmon mixture. Top with *½ cup* of the salmon mixture; pass remaining. Serves 3.

SWEET BANANA-RAISIN MUFFINS

Assembling time: 10 minutes
Cooking time: 15 minutes

1 15-ounce package banana quick bread mix
¼ teaspoon ground nutmeg
1 8-ounce carton plain yogurt
½ cup raisins

1 Stir together dry bread mix and nutmeg. Prepare bread mix according to package instructions, *except* substitute yogurt for the liquid. Stir in raisins. Grease muffin cups or line with paper bake cups; fill ²/₃ full. Bake in a 350° oven about 15 minutes or till done. Makes 14 muffins.

ELEGANT FRUIT COMPOTE

Assembling time: 5 minutes

1 8¾-ounce can fruits for salad
¼ cup sliced almonds
2 tablespoons Amaretto
¼ cup dairy sour cream
1 tablespoon Amaretto

1 Cut any large pieces of fruit in half. In a mixing bowl stir together *undrained* fruit, almonds, and the 2 tablespoons Amaretto. Spoon into 3 individual dessert dishes.

2 In another bowl stir together dairy sour cream and the 1 tablespoon Amaretto. Dollop some of the sour cream mixture atop the fruit in the dessert dishes. Serves 3.

When you're entertaining, it can be hard to balance your time in the kitchen and the time you spend with your guests. This elegant brunch offers you a solution to that problem—make your meal ahead. Just prepare these delicate Individual Swiss Puffs beforehand and freeze them until the day of your brunch. Then simply pop them in the oven, and you're free to chat with your guests. Before you serve, take time for a few final touches and you'll end up with a mouth-watering meal that will win rave reviews.

MAKE-AHEAD BRUNCH

INDIVIDUAL SWISS PUFFS

ORANGE SLICES

APRICOT BREAD

DESSERT COFFEE

UP TO 1 WEEK BEFORE SERVING
- Prepare Apricot Bread.

UP TO 5 DAYS BEFORE SERVING
- Prepare and freeze Individual Swiss Puffs.

55 MINUTES BEFORE SERVING
- Bake Individual Swiss Puffs.

15 MINUTES BEFORE SERVING
- Peel oranges.
- Prepare Dessert Coffee.

INDIVIDUAL SWISS PUFFS

For a light, delicate texture and maximum volume, be sure to serve Individual Swiss Puffs within five days of preparation—

Advance preparation time: 40 minutes
Final preparation time: 1 hour and 5 minutes

- ½ **cup shredded carrot**
- 1 **small onion, finely chopped (¼ cup)**
- ⅓ **cup butter or margarine**
- ⅓ **cup all-purpose flour**
- 1 **teaspoon ground nutmeg**
  Dash pepper
- 2 **cups milk**
- 2½ **cups process shredded Swiss cheese**
- ¼ **cup grated Parmesan cheese**
- 6 **eggs**
- ½ **teaspoon cream of tartar**

1 In a saucepan cook carrot and onion in butter or margarine till tender but not brown. Stir in flour, nutmeg, and pepper. Add milk all at once. Cook and stir till mixture is thickened and bubbly. Cook and stir 1 minute more.

2 Add Swiss cheese and Parmesan cheese; stir till melted. Remove from heat. Separate eggs; beat yolks till thick and lemon colored. Gradually stir cheese mixture into yolks; cook about 5 minutes. Thoroughly wash beaters.

3 In a mixer bowl beat the egg whites and cream of tartar till stiff peaks form (tips stand straight). Fold yolk mixture into egg white-cheese mixture. Pour into 8 ungreased 1-cup soufflé dishes. Cover soufflé dishes with moisture-vaporproof wrap. Seal, label, and freeze.

Before serving: Set frozen soufflés in a shallow baking pan. Fill baking pan with boiling water to a depth of ½ inch. Bake in a 300° oven about 55 minutes or till a knife inserted near center comes out clean. Serve immediately. Makes 8 servings.

APRICOT BREAD

Advance preparation time: 1 hour and 5 minutes

- 2 **cups all-purpose flour**
- 1 **teaspoon baking soda**
- ½ **cup packed brown sugar**
- ½ **cup butter or margarine**
- 2 **eggs**
- 1 **teaspoon vanilla**
- 1 **6-ounce can apricot nectar**
- ¼ **cup apricot brandy or brandy**
- 1 **8¾-ounce can unpeeled apricot halves, drained and chopped**
- 1 **cup chopped pecans**

1 In a mixing bowl stir together flour, soda, and ½ teaspoon *salt*. Set aside. In a large mixer bowl beat together brown sugar, butter, eggs, and vanilla till fluffy.

2 Combine apricot nectar and the ¼ cup brandy. Add flour mixture and nectar mixture alternately to sugar mixture. Beat after each addition just till combined.

3 Fold in apricots and pecans. Divide batter between two lightly greased 7½x3½x2-inch loaf pans. Bake in a 350° oven about 40 minutes. Cool in pan 10 minutes. Remove from pan; cool on racks.

4 Wrap in *brandy*-moistened cheesecloth. Overwrap with foil. Store in the refrigerator overnight or up to 1 week. Remoisten cheesecloth as needed. Makes 2.

DESSERT COFFEE

Assembling time: 15 minutes

- 1 **cup ground coffee**
- ½ **cup coffee liqueur**
  Pressurized dessert topping

1 Brew coffee with 6 cups *water* in an 8-cup percolator for 6 to 8 minutes. Remove; discard grounds. Stir liqueur into brewed coffee. Pour into 8 cups. Top with pressurized dessert topping. Serves 8.

You can sleep-in this weekend and still put a nutritious midmorning meal on the table without hours of preparation. With a little early preparation, this tasty brunch can be made in less than 1 hour. Simply make part of the juice appetizer ahead of time and finish it while making the sausage patties and the puffed pancake on the morning of the brunch.

LATE-RISERS' BRUNCH

PUFFY GERMAN PANCAKE

MUSHROOM AND SAUSAGE PATTIES

SUNRISE COOLER

UP TO 2 WEEKS BEFORE SERVING
- Prepare cranberry-apple drink mixture for Sunrise Cooler.

50 MINUTES BEFORE SERVING
- Place oil in skillet and preheat oven for Puffy German Pancake. (*Do not* start preparing pancake until the oven is hot.)
- Thaw fruit for pancake.

40 MINUTES BEFORE SERVING
- Prepare Puffy German Pancake.
- Prepare Mushroom and Sausage Patties.

15 MINUTES BEFORE SERVING
- Make fruit sauce for pancake.
- Finish preparing Sunrise Cooler.

MUSHROOM AND SAUSAGE PATTIES

Assembling time: 5 minutes
Cooking time: 20 minutes

- 1 slightly beaten egg
- 2 tablespoons milk
- ½ cup quick-cooking rolled oats
- 1 2-ounce can chopped mushrooms, drained
- 1 pound bulk pork sausage
  Fresh mint leaves (optional)

1 In a mixing bowl combine egg and milk. Stir in rolled oats and mushrooms. Add sausage; mix well. Shape into 4 patties. Place patties on cold griddle or skillet.

2 Cook sausage patties over medium heat for 15 to 20 minutes, turning once. Transfer patties to a serving platter. Garnish with mint leaves, if desired. Serves 4.

SUNRISE COOLER

Advance preparation time: 35 minutes
Final preparation time: 5 minutes

- 3 cups cranberry-apple drink
- 1 tablespoon honey
- 3 inches stick cinnamon
- ¼ teaspoon whole cloves
- ⅛ teaspoon ground ginger
- 2 cups peach nectar, chilled

1 In a saucepan combine cranberry-apple drink, honey, cinnamon, cloves, and ginger. Cook over low heat for 30 minutes. Cover and refrigerate at least several hours or up to 2 weeks.

Before serving: Stir cranberry-apple drink mixture. Remove cloves and cinnamon stick. Pour cranberry-apple drink mixture into four tall glasses. Carefully pour chilled peach nectar down the sides of the glasses. *Do not mix.* Juices should form two layers. Makes 4 (10-ounce) servings.

PUFFY GERMAN PANCAKE

Assembling time: 21 minutes
Cooking time: 28 minutes

- 2 tablespoons cooking oil
- 3 eggs
- ½ cup all-purpose flour
- ½ cup milk
- 2 tablespoons cooking oil
- ½ teaspoon salt
- 1 10-ounce package frozen mixed fruit (in quick-thaw pouch)
- 2 teaspoons cornstarch

1 Place 2 tablespoons cooking oil in a 10-inch oven-going skillet. Place skillet in oven. Preheat oven to 450°. Meanwhile, in a small mixer bowl beat eggs at high speed of electric mixer till combined.

2 Add the flour, milk, 2 tablespoons cooking oil, and salt. Beat till mixture is smooth. Immediately pour into the hot skillet. Bake in a 450° oven for 18 minutes.

3 Prick bottom of pancake with the tines of a fork. Reduce the oven temperature to 350°. Bake 8 to 10 minutes longer. Serve immediately with fruit sauce.

4 For fruit sauce, thaw fruit according to package directions. Drain mixed fruit, reserving syrup. Measure syrup. Add enough water, if necessary, to make ⅔ cup liquid. In a saucepan stir together fruit syrup mixture and cornstarch.

5 Cook and stir till fruit syrup mixture is thickened and bubbly. Cook and stir 2 minutes more. Stir in drained fruit; cook till the fruit is heated through. Spoon over pancake. Makes 4 servings.

**Mushroom and Sausage Patties
Puffy German Pancake
Sunrise Cooler**

Need to get lunch in a hurry? Then this appealing menu is for you! It takes just 40 minutes from the time you step into the kitchen until lunch is on the table. And the menu is designed so you can make use of every minute. For example, while the salad is chilling, you can prepare and bake the rolls. And while the rolls are baking, you can make the dessert. Finally, chill the dessert while you eat the main course.

LAST-MINUTE LUNCH

BEEF 'N' CHEESE SALAD

QUICK SAVORY ROLLS

RUM-CHERRY TOSS

BEVERAGE

40 MINUTES BEFORE SERVING
- Set pea pods and dessert topping out to thaw.
- Cook rice for Beef 'n' Cheese Salad.
- Start chopping vegetables for salad.

20 MINUTES BEFORE SERVING
- Finish preparing Beef 'n' Cheese Salad.
- Prepare Quick Savory Rolls.
- Prepare Rum-Cherry Toss.
- Prepare beverage.

AT SERVING TIME
- Chill Rum-Cherry Toss while eating lunch.

BEEF 'N' CHEESE SALAD

If you have leftover cooked rice, you can save even more time by substituting 2 cups cooked rice for the 1 cup quick-cooking rice in the recipe—

Assembling time: 25 minutes

- 1 cup quick-cooking rice
- 1 12-ounce can corned beef, drained
- ½ cup shredded cheddar cheese
- 1 medium carrot, thinly sliced
- ½ of a 6-ounce package frozen pea pods, partially thawed
- ¼ cup chopped green pepper
- 1 cup mayonnaise or salad dressing
- 2 tablespoons prepared mustard
- ½ teaspoon Worcestershire sauce
  Lettuce leaves
- 2 tablespoons pumpkin seed (optional)

1 Cook rice according to package directions, *except* omit the salt. Chop the corned beef into bite-size pieces. In a mixing bowl combine rice, corned beef, cheddar cheese, sliced carrot, pea pods, and chopped green pepper.

2 To make the dressing, in a mixing bowl stir together the mayonnaise or salad dressing, prepared mustard, and Worcestershire sauce. Toss the dressing with the rice mixture.

3 Spoon the rice mixture into a lettuce-lined salad bowl. Top with pumpkin seed, if desired. Chill till serving time. Makes 4 servings.

QUICK SAVORY ROLLS

Assembling time: 5 minutes
Cooking time: 13 minutes

- 1 package (4) refrigerated crescent rolls
- ½ teaspoon Italian seasoning

1 Unroll crescent roll dough. Separate into 4 triangles. Sprinkle Italian seasoning atop roll dough. Starting at the widest end, roll the dough up. Place point side down on baking sheet. Bake in a 375° oven for 10 to 13 minutes or till golden brown. Makes 4 servings.

RUM-CHERRY TOSS

Assembling time: 8 minutes

- 1 8½-ounce can pear halves
- 2 tablespoons rum
- 1 16-ounce can pitted dark sweet cherries, drained
  Frozen whipped dessert topping, thawed
  Ground nutmeg

1 Drain pears, reserving ¼ cup syrup. Halve pears lengthwise. In a mixing bowl combine the reserved pear syrup and the rum. Stir in pears and cherries.

2 Spoon fruit and syrup mixture into individual dessert dishes. Chill till serving time. Dollop each with dessert topping and sprinkle with nutmeg. Makes 4 servings.

Tired of canned soup and bologna sandwiches for lunch? This easy-to-make soup-and-sandwich lunch could be just what you need! The mouth-watering flavor combination of pita sandwiches, savory tomato soup, and oatmeal bar cookies is truly unique. And, the menu goes together 1-2-3. Prepare the bar cookies the day before the lunch. Then combine the soup ingredients in a saucepan and let the soup simmer. Finally, make the sandwiches and you're ready to eat.

NO-FUSS LUNCH

TUNA- 'N' CHEESE-FILLED PITAS

HERBED TOMATO SOUP

CHEWY OATMEAL BARS

BEVERAGE

UP TO ONE DAY BEFORE SERVING
- Prepare Chewy Oatmeal Bars and store.

30 MINUTES BEFORE SERVING
- Prepare Herbed Tomato Soup.
- Prepare Tuna- 'n' Cheese-Filled Pitas while soup is simmering.
- Prepare beverage.

TUNA- 'N' CHEESE-FILLED PITAS

Try substituting slices of whole wheat bread for the pita bread for a more conventional sandwich—

Assembling time: 15 minutes

- 1 9¼-ounce can tuna, drained and flaked
- ½ cup shredded cheddar cheese (2 ounces)
- ¼ cup thinly sliced celery
- ¼ cup broken pecans (optional)
- ¼ cup dairy sour cream
- ¼ cup mayonnaise *or* salad dressing
- 2 pita bread rounds
     Lettuce leaves
     Alfalfa sprouts

1 In a mixing bowl stir together the tuna; shredded cheddar cheese; sliced celery; pecans, if desired; sour cream; and mayonnaise or salad dressing. Split pita bread in half crosswise to make "pockets."

2 Line the inside of each pita "pocket" with lettuce leaves. Spoon tuna-cheese mixture atop the lettuce leaves. Top tuna-cheese mixture with the alfalfa sprouts. Makes 4 servings.

HERBED TOMATO SOUP

Assembling time: 5 minutes
Cooking time: 26 minutes

- 3 cups tomato juice
- ¼ cup dry red wine
- 1 teaspoon instant beef bouillon granules
- 1 teaspoon dried basil, crushed
- ½ teaspoon sugar
- ½ teaspoon dried thyme, crushed
     Snipped chives

1 In a saucepan combine tomato juice, wine, bouillon granules, basil, sugar, thyme, 1 cup *water*, and ⅛ teaspoon *pepper*. Bring to boiling; reduce heat. Simmer, uncovered, about 20 minutes. If desired, garnish with snipped chives. Serves 4.

CHEWY OATMEAL BARS

- ⅔ cup packed brown sugar
- ½ cup butter *or* margarine
- 2 eggs
- 1 package (4-serving size) *instant vanilla pudding mix*
- ¾ cup all-purpose flour
- ¾ cup quick-cooking rolled oats
- ½ cup flaked coconut
- ½ cup chopped nuts
     Powdered sugar

1 In a mixer bowl combine brown sugar and butter or margarine. Beat on medium speed of electric mixer till light and fluffy. Add eggs; beat till well combined. By hand, stir in pudding mix, flour, oats, coconut, and nuts till well combined.

2 Turn into greased 9x9x2-inch baking pan. Bake in 350° oven for 20 to 25 minutes or till wooden pick inserted in center comes out clean. Cool 10 minutes; sprinkle with powdered sugar. Cut into bars. Serve warm or cool. Makes 24 bars.

When you find yourself in between a hectic morning and a busy afternoon, it can be hard to think about preparing lunch for friends. But relax—it's easy to dazzle them with this all-around speedy lunch that's ready in just 30 minutes. The pleasing no-cook salad is a great way to use leftover ham or cheese. It is complemented by your choice of a tangy blender drink/dessert or elegant tarts. And this fast lunch makes for a fast cleanup as well. There are just three preparation dishes to wash.

30-MINUTE LUNCH

SOUPER STRATA SALAD

RYE ROLLS

BUTTER OR MARGARINE

DESSERT-IN-A-GLASS OR CHOCO-BANANA TARTS

BEVERAGE

30 MINUTES BEFORE SERVING
- Prepare Dessert-in-a-Glass or Choco-Banana Tarts and chill till serving time.
- Prepare Souper Strata Salad.
- Prepare beverage.

Souper Strata Salad
Dessert-in-a-Glass

SOUPER STRATA SALAD

To give the salad a different flavor, substitute cans of chicken or turkey for the ham—

Assembling time: 20 minutes

- 1 11-ounce can condensed tomato bisque soup
- ½ cup vinegar
- ½ cup salad oil
- 1 tablespoon sugar
- 1 tablespoon Dijon-style mustard
- 1½ teaspoons Worcestershire sauce
- 1 medium head lettuce, torn (6 cups)
- 2 6¾-ounce cans chunk-style ham, drained and flaked
- 1 4-ounce package (1 cup) shredded mozzarella cheese
- 1 4½-ounce jar sliced mushrooms, drained
- 2 cups croutons

1 In a screw-top jar combine tomato bisque soup, vinegar, salad oil, sugar, Dijon-style mustard, and Worcestershire sauce. Cover jar and shake well. In a large salad bowl layer *half* of the lettuce, *half* of the chunk-style ham, *half* of the shredded mozzarella cheese, *half* of the sliced mushrooms, and *half* of the croutons.

2 Repeat layers using the remaining lettuce, chunk-style ham, shredded mozzarella cheese, sliced mushrooms, and croutons; drizzle some soup mixture atop salad and toss. Pass remaining soup mixture. Makes 6 servings.

DESSERT-IN-A-GLASS

Assembling time: 10 minutes

- 2 8-ounce cartons lemon yogurt
- 1 15½-ounce can crushed pineapple
- 1 cup milk
- 4 to 6 ice cubes (about 1 cup)
- 1 to 2 tablespoons sugar
- Mint sprigs

1 In a blender container combine yogurt, *undrained* crushed pineapple, and milk. Cover and blend till mixture is smooth. With blender running, add ice cubes, one at a time through hole in lid, till slushy.

2 Sweeten to taste with sugar. Chill till serving time. Pour into glasses. To serve, garnish with fresh mint, if desired. Makes 6 servings.

CHOCO-BANANA TARTS

Assembling time: 10 minutes

- ¼ cup chopped walnuts
- ¼ cup chocolate-flavored syrup
- 1 4½-ounce container frozen whipped dessert topping, thawed
- 1 tablespoon crème de cacao (optional)
- 1 medium banana
- 6 baked tart shells
- Lemon juice

1 In a mixing bowl fold nuts and chocolate syrup into whipped topping; fold in liqueur, if desired. Thinly slice *half* of the banana into the bottom of the tart shells. Spoon chocolate mixture into shells.

2 Thinly slice remaining banana. Brush with lemon juice. Place atop tarts. Drizzle with a little additional chocolate syrup, if desired. Makes 6 servings.

Here's a lunch that's easy to fix because it calls for ingredients you most likely have on hand. If you don't have a certain product, simply substitute a similar item. For example, if you don't have pepper cheese on hand, try substituting mozzarella cheese or cheddar cheese. Sour cream or yogurt can be substituted for the sour cream dip with French onion. In addition, a slice of bread or a frankfurter bun can take the place of a split pita round, and fully cooked sausage links can replace the frankfurters.

MIX-AND-MATCH LUNCH

CHEESE-FRANK WRAP-UPS

CARROT AND APPLE SALAD

SPICY CHOCOLATE SHAKE

45 MINUTES BEFORE SERVING
- Prepare Carrot and Apple Salad and chill till serving time.
- Prepare Cheese-Frank Wrap-Ups.
- While frankfurters bake, prepare Spicy Chocolate Shake.

CHEESE-FRANK WRAP-UPS

Assembling time: 15 minutes
Cooking time: 15 minutes

- 4 pita bread rounds
  Bottled barbecue sauce
- ¼ cup chopped pitted ripe olives
- 1 1-pound package (8) frankfurters
- 4 ounces pepper cheese, cut into 16 strips
  Sour cream dip with French onion
- 8 ripe olives

1 Split pita bread in half horizontally to make 8 rounds. Brush cut side of each pita half with some barbecue sauce. Sprinkle with chopped olives. Make a lengthwise cut in each frankfurter that is almost, but not all the way, through the frankfurter.

2 Place 2 strips of pepper cheese inside each frankfurter. Place a filled frankfurter on each pita round; roll pita around frankfurter. Secure with a wooden pick. Place on a baking sheet.

3 Cover baking sheet with foil. Bake in a 375° oven about 15 minutes or till cheese is melted and frankfurters are heated through. Remove wooden picks; dollop each with sour cream dip and top with a ripe olive. Makes 4 servings.

CARROT AND APPLE SALAD

Assembling time: 15 minutes

- 1 large apple
- 2 cups coarsely shredded carrot
- ½ cup raisins
- ½ of a 3-ounce package cream cheese
- ½ cup mayonnaise *or* salad dressing
- 1 tablespoon orange juice
  Ground nutmeg

1 Core and slice apple. In a mixing bowl combine apple, shredded carrot, and raisins. To make dressing, in a small bowl beat cream cheese till fluffy. Stir in mayonnaise or salad dressing and orange juice.

2 Spoon dressing over apple-carrot mixture. Toss mixture to coat with dressing. Sprinkle lightly with nutmeg. Cover and chill till serving time. Makes 4 servings.

SPICY CHOCOLATE SHAKE

Assembling time: 8 minutes

- 3 cups vanilla ice cream
- 1 cup milk
- ⅓ cup chocolate-flavored syrup
- ¾ teaspoon ground cinnamon
- ½ teaspoon vanilla

1 In a blender container combine ice cream, milk, chocolate-flavored syrup, cinnamon, and vanilla. Cover and blend till of desired consistency. Pour into tall glasses. Makes 4 (8-ounce) servings.

This lunch is ideal for sports fans. By combining make-ahead items with a no-watch soup, you can have lunch during or after the game and still not miss any of the action. Here's how it works: prepare the green pepper and cauliflower, biscuit snacks, and cookies well in advance of game time. Then right before the game starts, make the soup and put it on to simmer. Simply run to the kitchen and give the soup a quick stir during time-outs. You'll be ready to serve the feast at half time or whenever you're hungry.

GAME-TIME LUNCH

NO-WATCH SOUP

CHEESY BISCUIT SNACKS

GREEN PEPPER STRIPS AND CAULIFLOWER FLOWERETS

OATMEAL-CHOCOLATE CHIP BARS

BEVERAGE

UP TO 1 DAY BEFORE SERVING
- Prepare the Cheesy Biscuit Snacks and store.
- Cut the green pepper and cauliflower and refrigerate in water.
- Prepare the Oatmeal-Chocolate Chip Bars and store.

UP TO 4 HOURS BEFORE SERVING
- Prepare the No-Watch Soup and simmer till serving time.
- Prepare beverage.

NO-WATCH SOUP

Assembling time: 15 minutes
Cooking time: 1¼ hours to 3¼ hours

- 1 pound bulk pork sausage
- ½ pound ground beef
- 2 12-ounce cans vegetable juice cocktail
- 1 16-ounce can yellow hominy, drained
- 1 10½-ounce can condensed beef broth
- 1 cup beer
- 1 medium onion, thinly sliced into rings
- ¼ cup sliced pitted ripe olives
- 1 teaspoon sugar
- 1 teaspoon Worcestershire sauce
- ½ teaspoon ground sage
  Dash pepper

1 In Dutch oven cook sausage and beef till browned; drain. Stir in vegetable juice cocktail, hominy, broth, beer, onion, olives, sugar, Worcestershire sauce, sage, and pepper. Bring to boiling. Reduce heat. Cover; simmer for 1 to 3 hours, stirring occasionally. Skim off fat. Serves 4.

CHEESY BISCUIT SNACKS

Assembling time: 16 minutes
Cooking time: 18 minutes

- 1 cup all-purpose flour
- 1 teaspoon baking powder
  Dash salt
- ½ of a 5-ounce jar cheese spread with bacon (about ⅓ cup)
- ⅓ cup milk

1 In a mixing bowl stir together flour, baking powder, and salt. Cut in cheese spread till the mixture resembles coarse crumbs. Make a well in center; add milk all at once. Stir just till dough clings together.

2 Knead gently on a lightly floured surface for 8 to 10 strokes. Roll or pat to ¼-inch thickness. Cut with a 2½-inch biscuit cutter. Transfer to a greased baking sheet.

3 Bake in a 400° oven for 10 to 12 minutes. Use a sharp knife to horizontally split the hot rounds. Spread out, cut sides up, on the same baking sheet.

4 Return to the oven and bake 6 to 8 minutes longer or till golden brown. Cool to room temperature. Store in a tightly covered container till serving time. Makes 24.

OATMEAL-CHOCOLATE CHIP BARS

Assembling time: 12 minutes
Cooking time: 25 minutes

- ⅔ cup all-purpose flour
- ⅓ cup quick-cooking rolled oats
- 1 teaspoon baking powder
- ⅛ teaspoon salt
- ¼ cup butter *or* margarine
- ¾ cup packed brown sugar
- 1 egg
- ½ teaspoon vanilla
- ½ cup broken pecans
- ½ cup semisweet chocolate pieces

1 In a bowl stir together flour, rolled oats, baking powder, and salt; set aside. In a medium saucepan melt butter or margarine; remove from heat. Stir in brown sugar. Add egg and vanilla; beat till well combined.

2 Stir flour mixture, pecans, and chocolate pieces into sugar mixture. Spread in a greased 13x9x2-inch baking pan. Bake in a 350° oven for 20 to 25 minutes or till done. Cool. Cut into bars. Makes 24.

If sack lunches are getting boring, why not add some variety to yours with this innovative brown bag lunch! It's easy to put together in the morning because everything is made ahead of time. All you do is put it in the bag. To ensure that the sandwich will still be cool at lunch time, wrap and freeze it at least the night before. The carrot and celery sticks also can be prepared ahead of time and stored in water in the refrigerator.

BROWN BAGGIN' LUNCH

CHICKEN SALAD SANDWICHES

CELERY AND CARROT STICKS

SPICY APRICOT COMPOTE

YOGURT CUPCAKES

UP TO 1 WEEK BEFORE SERVING
■ Prepare Chicken Salad Sandwiches and freeze.

UP TO 2 DAYS BEFORE SERVING
■ Prepare Spicy Apricot Compote and refrigerate.
■ Prepare Yogurt Cupcakes and store.
■ Cut celery and carrot sticks and refrigerate in cold water.

CHICKEN SALAD SANDWICHES

Advance preparation time: 15 minutes
Final preparation time: 5 minutes

1 4-ounce container whipped cream cheese with chives
¼ cup thinly sliced celery
2 tablespoons sweet pickle relish
½ teaspoon Worcestershire sauce
1 5-ounce can chunk-style chicken, drained and chopped
6 slices whole wheat bread
Lettuce leaves

1 To make chicken filling, in a bowl stir together whipped cream cheese with chives, sliced celery, sweet pickle relish, and Worcestershire sauce; stir in chicken till well combined. Spread *three* of the bread slices with the chicken filling. Top with remaining bread slices.

2 Cut chicken salad sandwiches in half diagonally. Wrap the sandwiches in moisture-vaporproof wrap. Freeze at least 4 hours or up to 1 week.

Before serving: Wrap lettuce leaves in moisture-vaporproof wrap. Pack frozen sandwiches and lettuce leaves separately. Place a lettuce leaf in each sandwich immediately before eating. Makes 3 sandwiches.

SPICY APRICOT COMPOTE

Assembling time: 10 minutes

1 tablespoon sugar
1 teaspoon cornstarch
¼ teaspoon ground cinnamon
¼ teaspoon ground nutmeg
1 8-ounce can crushed pineapple (juice pack)
¼ cup snipped dried apricots
2 tablespoons raisins

1 In a small saucepan combine sugar, cornstarch, cinnamon, and nutmeg. Stir in *undrained* pineapple, snipped apricots, raisins, and ½ cup *water*.

2 Cook and stir till thickened and bubbly; cook and stir 2 minutes more. Spoon into 3 small containers; cover tightly. Chill till ready to pack lunch. Serves 3.

YOGURT CUPCAKES

Assembling time: 15 minutes
Cooking time: 20 minutes

1 package 1-layer-size yellow cake mix
½ cup plain yogurt
1 egg
½ cup regular rolled oats
¼ cup packed brown sugar
2 tablespoons chopped walnuts
2 tablespoons butter, melted

1 To make batter, in a mixing bowl combine cake mix, yogurt, and egg. Stir just till all is moistened. Line muffin pans with paper bake cups; fill ½ full with batter.

2 Stir together rolled oats, brown sugar, and walnuts. Stir in butter. Sprinkle some oat mixture atop each cupcake. Bake in a 350° oven about 20 minutes or till done. Cool. Store in a tightly covered container till ready to pack lunch. Makes 12.

What do you do when you want to serve an elegant luncheon, but you have the busiest morning schedule of the entire week? You plan a meal like this one that waits for you. This entire menu can be prepared ahead with the exception of the muffins. To make the meal even easier, serve it buffet style.

READY-AND-WAITING BUFFET

24-HOUR SALAD

FRUIT MUFFINS

ORANGE CHEESECAKE

BEVERAGE

UP TO 2 DAYS BEFORE SERVING
- Prepare muffin batter.
- Prepare Orange Cheesecake.

1 DAY BEFORE SERVING
- Prepare 24-Hour Salad.

40 MINUTES BEFORE SERVING
- Bake muffins.
- Prepare beverage.

FRUIT MUFFINS

Total preparation time: 40 minutes

- 2 cups all-purpose flour
- 1 teaspoon baking soda
- ½ teaspoon ground cinnamon
- ¼ teaspoon ground nutmeg
- ⅛ teaspoon ground cloves
- ⅔ cup shortening
- ½ cup packed brown sugar
- 2 eggs
- ½ cup dairy sour cream
- ½ cup milk
- 1 8¼-ounce can crushed pineapple, drained

1 Mix first five ingredients and ¼ teaspoon *salt*. In mixer bowl beat shortening and brown sugar till fluffy. Beat in eggs, sour cream, and milk. Stir in flour mixture.

2 Fold in pineapple. Store in airtight container in refrigerator up to 2 days.

Before serving: *Do not* stir batter. Fill greased muffin cups ⅔ full. Bake in a 350° oven for 25 to 30 minutes. Makes 12 to 14.

24-HOUR SALAD

Advance preparation time: 25 minutes

- ½ pound bacon, sliced
- 8 cups torn salad greens
- 1¼ cups shredded mozzarella cheese
- 1 10-ounce package frozen peas
- 1 cup cauliflower flowerets
- 1 cup chopped tomato
- ⅔ cup mayonnaise
- ⅓ cup green goddess salad dressing
- 2 tablespoons sunflower nuts

1 Cook bacon. Drain; crumble. Place *half* of greens in large bowl. Top with *1 cup* cheese, peas, cauliflower, remaining greens, tomato, and bacon. Mix mayonnaise and salad dressing. Spread atop. Cover; chill 3 to 24 hours. Top with remaining cheese and nuts. Serves 6.

ORANGE CHEESECAKE

Finely shredded lemon peel may be substituted for the orange peel—

Advance preparation time: 1 hour

- ½ cup crushed gingersnaps (8 cookies)
- ⅓ cup graham cracker crumbs
- 3 tablespoons butter *or* margarine, melted
- 1 tablespoon sugar
- 1 8-ounce package cream cheese, cut up
- ½ teaspoon finely shredded orange peel
- ¼ teaspoon vanilla
- ⅓ cup sugar
- 1 tablespoon all-purpose flour
  Dash salt
- 1 egg
- 2 tablespoons orange juice

1 In a bowl toss together gingersnaps, graham cracker crumbs, butter or margarine, and the 1 tablespoon sugar. Spread evenly in a 7-inch pie plate. Press onto bottom and up sides.

2 In mixer bowl beat cream cheese with electric mixer till fluffy. Beat in peel and vanilla. Stir together the ⅓ cup sugar, flour, and salt; beat into cream cheese mixture.

3 Add egg; beat till combined. Stir in orange juice. Turn into pie plate. Bake in a 350° oven for 30 to 35 minutes or till knife inserted near center comes out clean. Cool at room temperature. Chill at least 4 hours. Makes 6 servings.

When your time is short but your appetite is hearty, prepare this quick Italian dinner. You can put it all together in only 45 minutes. Double the recipes and have enough to serve company, or cut the recipes in half to serve two.

SPEEDY ITALIAN SUPPER

PIZZA PORK CHOPS

ITALIAN POTATO SALAD

TOASTY GARLIC BREAD

STRAWBERRY DAIQUIRIS

BEVERAGE

45 MINUTES BEFORE SERVING
- Set out butter for Toasty Garlic Bread.
- Cook vegetables for Italian Potato Salad; marinate potatoes.
- Prepare salad greens.
- Preheat broiler for Pizza Pork Chops.

20 MINUTES BEFORE SERVING
- Start broiling Pizza Pork Chops.
- Assemble topping ingredients for chops.
- Complete salad.
- Prepare Strawberry Daiquiris.
- Prepare Toasty Garlic Bread for broiling.
- Broil chops and bread at the same time.

AT SERVING TIME
- Arrange chops atop bread on plates.

Italian Potato Salad
Pizza Pork Chops
Strawberry Daiquiris

PIZZA PORK CHOPS

Assembling time: 3 minutes
Cooking time: 20 minutes

4 pork chops, cut ½ inch thick
4 slices mozzarella cheese
¼ cup chili sauce
4 thin green pepper rings
1 2-ounce can mushroom stems and pieces, drained
Toasty Garlic Bread

1 Place chops on a rack in an unheated broiler pan; sprinkle with salt and pepper. Broil chops, 3 to 4 inches from heat till well-done, turning once (allow about 20 minutes total time). Meanwhile, halve cheese slices diagonally.

2 Brush chops with chili sauce; top *each* with *two* cheese triangles. Place *one* green pepper ring and *one-fourth* of the mushrooms atop *each* chop. Broil for 1 to 1½ minutes more or till cheese melts. Serve atop hot slices of Toasty Garlic Bread. Makes 4 servings.

TOASTY GARLIC BREAD

Assembling time: 3 minutes
Cooking time: 1½ minutes

4 slices French *or* sourdough bread, cut 1 inch thick
Butter *or* margarine, softened
Garlic salt

1 Spread bread with butter or margarine. Sprinkle with garlic salt. Place bread slices, buttered-side up, on broiler pan with chops; broil 3 to 4 inches from heat for 1 to 1½ minutes. Makes 4 servings.

ITALIAN POTATO SALAD

Assembling time: 20 minutes

1½ cups frozen loose-pack cauliflower, broccoli, and carrots
¼ cup creamy Italian salad dressing
¼ cup plain yogurt
1 16-ounce can sliced potatoes, drained
2 cups torn greens

1 Cook frozen vegetables, covered, in a small amount of boiling salted water for 2 to 3 minutes. Drain. Cover vegetables in pan with *very cold* water. Chill in freezer.

2 Stir together dressing and yogurt; fold in drained potatoes. Chill in refrigerator. Place greens in a serving bowl; chill in refrigerator. Just before serving, thoroughly drain vegetables. Add to greens. Top with potato mixture; toss. Makes 4 servings.

STRAWBERRY DAIQUIRIS

Assembling time: 10 minutes

1 10-ounce package frozen sliced strawberries, broken up
¾ cup light rum
½ cup frozen lemonade concentrate
20 to 24 ice cubes
Mint leaves (optional)

1 In a blender container combine strawberries, rum, and lemonade concentrate. Cover and blend till smooth. With blender running, add ice cubes, one at a time through hole in lid, to make about 5 cups slushy mixture. (If mixture becomes too thick, add a little water.) Pour into glasses. Garnish with mint leaves, if desired. Makes 4 (10-ounce) servings.

You can serve elegant entrées without a lot of work. How? With this easy Gourmet Dinner. We've taken some favorite gourmet foods and streamlined the preparation. In addition, several of the dishes can be made ahead so you won't have much last-minute work.

GOURMET DINNER

VEGETABLE ANTIPASTO OR EASY CRAB APPETIZERS

INDIVIDUAL BEEF WELLINGTONS

DUCHESS POTATO MOUNDS

ORANGE TOSSED SALAD OR THREE-FRUIT SALAD

MOCHA CUSTARDS

BEVERAGE

1 DAY BEFORE SERVING
■ Marinate vegetables for antipasto.
■ Make Individual Beef Wellingtons; chill.
■ Make Duchess Potato Mounds; chill.
■ Prepare Mocha Custards.

50 MINUTES BEFORE SERVING
■ Prepare salad and dressing for Orange Tossed Salad or Three-Fruit Salad.
■ Prepare Easy Crab Appetizers or arrange Vegetable Antipasto.

20 MINUTES BEFORE SERVING
■ Bake Potato Mounds and Beef Wellingtons.
■ Prepare sauce for Beef Wellingtons.

10 MINUTES BEFORE SERVING
■ Prepare beverage.
■ Top salad with dressing.
■ Unmold Mocha Custards.

INDIVIDUAL BEEF WELLINGTONS

Advance preparation time: 30 minutes
Final preparation time: 20 minutes

    4 beef tenderloin steaks *or* beef eye
        round steaks, cut 1 inch thick
      Cooking oil
    4 frozen patty shells, thawed
  ¼ cup canned liver spread
    1 beaten egg
  ½ cup water
1½ teaspoons cornstarch
    1 teaspoon instant beef bouillon
        granules
  ¼ teaspoon dried basil, crushed
    2 tablespoons dry red wine

1 Brush steaks with cooking oil; sprinkle with a little salt and pepper. In a hot skillet quickly brown steaks 2 minutes on each side. Cool at least 15 minutes.

2 Roll each thawed patty shell into an 8-inch circle. Spread the liver over the pastry circles to within 1-inch of the edge. Center *one* steak atop *each* pastry circle. Wrap meat in pastry; brush edge of the pastry with a little beaten egg. Press edges of pastry to seal. Place seam side down in a greased shallow baking pan. Use a sharp knife to make a small slash in top of each. Cover and chill up to 24 hours. Cover and chill remaining beaten egg.

Before serving: Brush remaining egg over pastry. Bake in a 425° oven about 20 minutes for medium doneness. Meanwhile, combine water, cornstarch, bouillon granules, and basil. Cook and stir till thickened and bubbly. Cook and stir 2 minutes more. Stir in wine. Serve with beef wellingtons. Makes 4 servings.

MOCHA CUSTARDS

Advance preparation time: 50 minutes
Final preparation time: 5 minutes

    3 eggs
    1 tablespoon instant coffee crystals
    1 tablespoon hot water
  ⅓ cup sugar
    1 tablespoon unsweetened cocoa
        powder
  ⅛ teaspoon salt
1½ cups milk
    1 teaspoon vanilla
      Boiling water
      Whipped cream (optional)
      Shaved German chocolate
        (optional)

1 In a medium mixing bowl lightly beat the eggs. Dissolve the instant coffee crystals in the hot water. Stir together sugar, unsweetened cocoa powder, and salt. Stir the dissolved coffee, sugar-cocoa mixture, milk, and vanilla into the beaten eggs.

2 Place four 6-ounce custard cups in a 9x9x2-inch baking pan on an oven rack. Pour the coffee-egg mixture into the custard cups. Pour the boiling water into the baking pan around custard cups to a depth of 1 inch.

3 Bake in a 325° oven for 30 to 40 minutes or till a knife inserted near center comes out clean. Carefully remove custard cups from water in the baking pan. Cool the custards to room temperature, then cover and chill in refrigerator for several hours or overnight.

Before serving: Unmold by loosening edges of custard with a spatula or knife; slip the point of the knife down sides to let air in. Invert onto serving plates. If desired, garnish with whipped cream and shaved chocolate. Makes 4 servings.

THREE-FRUIT SALAD

Assembling time: 15 minutes

½ cup dairy sour cream
¼ cup apricot nectar
¼ cup salad oil
1 tablespoon sugar
¼ teaspoon ground cinnamon
¼ teaspoon paprika
   Lettuce leaves
1 11-ounce can mandarin orange
   sections, drained
1 cup sliced fresh strawberries
1 kiwi, peeled and sliced

1 To make dressing, combine sour cream, nectar, salad oil, sugar, cinnamon, paprika, and a dash *salt*. Beat with a rotary beater till smooth. Cover and chill.

2 On four lettuce-lined salad plates, arrange orange sections, strawberries, and kiwi. Dollop fruit with dressing. Chill any remaining dressing. Makes 4 servings.

VEGETABLE ANTIPASTO

Advance preparation time: 8 minutes
Final preparation time: 5 minutes

1 cup water
3 cups frozen loose-pack zucchini,
   carrots, cauliflower, lima beans,
   and Italian beans
1 cup Italian salad dressing
½ teaspoon dried thyme, crushed
½ cup cherry tomatoes

1 In saucepan bring water to boiling. Add vegetables. Return to boiling; drain (vegetables should be crisp-tender). Combine dressing and thyme. In mixing bowl pour mixture over vegetables; stir to coat. Cover; chill in refrigerator 3 to 24 hours.
   Before serving: Drain vegetables. Arrange on a platter with tomatoes. Serves 4.

DUCHESS POTATO MOUNDS

It's easier to fill a pastry bag with the mashed potato mixture if you first fold the top 1½ inches of the bag to the outside. Spoon the potato mixture into the bag, filling it only ⅔ full. Unfold the top, twist closed, and squeeze to release the contents—

Advance preparation time: 55 minutes
Final preparation time: 20 minutes

3 medium potatoes, peeled
   (1 pound)
1 tablespoon butter *or* margarine
⅛ teaspoon salt
   Dash pepper
   Milk (about 2 tablespoons)
1 beaten egg
1 tablespoon butter *or* margarine

1 In a saucepan cook potatoes, covered, in enough boiling salted water to cover for 25 to 40 minutes or till tender. Drain. Mash potatoes with a potato masher or on low speed of an electric mixer.

2 Add 1 tablespoon butter or margarine, salt, and pepper. Gradually beat in enough of the milk to make potatoes light and fluffy. Cool slightly. Beat in egg.

3 Use a pastry bag with a large star tip to pipe potatoes (or spoon potatoes) into 8 mounds onto a greased baking sheet. Cover with moisture-vaporproof wrap and chill for several hours or overnight.
   Before serving: Melt 1 tablespoon butter or margarine. Drizzle potato mounds with butter. Bake in a 425° oven for 15 to 20 minutes or till heated through and tops are light brown. Makes 4 servings.

EASY CRAB APPETIZERS

Assembling time: 15 minutes

1 6-ounce package frozen crab
   meat, thawed, *or* one 6-ounce
   can crab meat, drained, flaked,
   and cartilage removed
½ cup dairy sour cream
¼ cup slivered almonds
⅛ teaspoon ground turmeric *or*
   curry powder
1 large cucumber, bias-cut into
   ¼-inch-thick slices

1 Stir together crab meat, sour cream, almonds, and turmeric or curry powder. Generously dollop each cucumber slice with some crab mixture. Makes 30 to 36.

ORANGE TOSSED SALAD

Assembling time: 15 minutes

4 cups torn salad greens
¾ cup sliced fresh mushrooms
¼ cup sliced radishes
2 tablespoons sliced green onion
⅓ cup mayonnaise *or* salad dressing
2 teaspoons frozen orange juice
   concentrate
¾ teaspoon sugar
⅛ teaspoon dry mustard
   Few drops bottled hot pepper
   sauce

1 In a salad bowl toss together greens, mushrooms, radishes, and green onion. For dressing, stir together mayonnaise or salad dressing, orange juice concentrate, sugar, dry mustard, and hot pepper sauce. Before serving, pour dressing over salad; toss lightly to coat. Makes 4 servings.

DINNER

Whip up this jiffy meal in just 50 minutes. The dessert chills in the freezer while you assemble and chop the ingredients for the stir-fry. Then just add the chopped ingredients to the hot wok and stir. In addition to being quick, your dinner will have the intriguing flavor of the South Seas.

STIR-FRY DINNER

PINEAPPLE-SAUSAGE STIR-FRY

TORN SPINACH SALAD WITH CREAMY CUCUMBER DRESSING

INSTANT PEACH-ALMOND SHERBET

FORTUNE COOKIES

LEMON SPICE TEA

50 MINUTES BEFORE SERVING
- Prepare Instant Peach-Almond Sherbet.
- Tear spinach for salad.

35 MINUTES BEFORE SERVING
- Prepare Pineapple-Sausage Stir-Fry.
- Prepare Lemon Spice Tea.
- Add salad dressing to spinach.

LEMON SPICE TEA

Assembling time: 5 minutes
Cooking time: 7 minutes

- 3 **cups water**
- 2 **tablespoons honey**
- 1 **lemon slice**
- 2 **inches stick cinnamon, broken up**
- 3 **tea bags**
  Lemon slices (optional)

1 In a saucepan combine water, honey, 1 lemon slice, and stick cinnamon. Bring to boiling; reduce heat and simmer, covered, for 3 minutes. Remove from heat; add tea bags.

2 Cover and steep for 4 minutes. Remove tea bags, cinnamon, and lemon slice. Pour tea into 4 cups; serve hot. Garnish with additional lemon slices, if desired. Makes 4 servings.

INSTANT PEACH-ALMOND SHERBET

Assembling time: 8 minutes

- ½ **cup water**
- 2 **tablespoons orange-flavored instant breakfast drink powder**
- ¼ **teaspoon almond extract**
- 2 **10-ounce packages frozen peach slices**
  Shredded coconut (optional)

1 In blender container combine water, breakfast drink powder, and almond extract. Use a fork to break up frozen peaches; add peaches to blender container. Cover and blend on high speed till smooth and sherbetlike in texture. If necessary, stop blender and push ingredients toward blades with a rubber spatula.

2 Spoon the mixture into sherbet dishes; store in the freezer till serving time. Garnish with shredded coconut, if desired. Makes 4 servings.

PINEAPPLE-SAUSAGE STIR-FRY

You don't need a wok to stir-fry. Any recipe that can be cooked in a wok can also be done in a large heavy skillet with deep sides. Just be sure to keep the food constantly moving—

- 2 **medium carrots, cut into 1-inch-long julienne strips**
- 1 **8-ounce can pineapple chunks (juice pack)**
- ¾ **cup unsweetened pineapple juice**
- 1 **6-ounce package frozen pea pods**
- 3 **tablespoons teriyaki sauce**
- 4 **teaspoons cornstarch**
- 1 **tablespoon brown sugar**
- 1 **12-ounce package fully cooked smoked sausage links, cut crosswise into thirds**
  Chow mein noodles

1 Cook carrots in a small amount of boiling salted water for 7 to 10 minutes or till tender. Drain pineapple chunks, reserving juice; set pineapple aside. Combine the reserved pineapple juice and enough unsweetened pineapple juice to make 1¼ cups liquid. Run hot water over frozen pea pods in a colander till thawed. Set aside.

2 In small bowl stir together teriyaki sauce, cornstarch, and brown sugar. Stir in pineapple juice mixture.

3 In a wok or large skillet stir-fry sausage about 5 minutes or till brown. Stir the teriyaki mixture; stir into wok or skillet. Cook and stir till mixture is thickened and bubbly. Stir in carrots, pineapple chunks, and pea pods. Cover and cook 2 minutes more. Serve at once over chow mein noodles. Makes 4 servings.

Instant Peach-Almond Sherbet
Pineapple-Sausage Stir-Fry

Here's a sensational supper that's heavy on appeal, but light on work. It takes only 40 minutes—from the time you step into the kitchen until the food is on the table. Yet you can be sure there's no compromise on taste. The Oriental Salad gives a tangy Far East flavor. Pork adds a new dimension to the traditional burger. And those foods are all complemented by the home-style flavor found in Glazed Sweet Potatoes.

SUPER SANDWICH SUPPER

PORK AND OLIVE BURGERS

GLAZED SWEET POTATOES

ORIENTAL SALAD

POTATO CHIPS

CHOCOLATE PUDDING

BEVERAGE

40 MINUTES BEFORE SERVING
- Prepare instant chocolate pudding.
- Thaw pea pods for Oriental Salad.
- Prepare dressing for salad and chill.
- Prepare salad and chill.

25 MINUTES BEFORE SERVING
- Prepare Pork and Olive Burgers.
- While meat is broiling, prepare Glazed Sweet Potatoes.
- Prepare beverage.
- Toss salad.

PORK AND OLIVE BURGERS

Pictured on pages 30 and 31—

Assembling time: 10 minutes
Cooking time: 15 minutes

1 slightly beaten egg
2 tablespoons milk
¼ cup fine dry bread crumbs
2 tablespoons chopped pimiento-stuffed olives
½ teaspoon minced dried onion
½ teaspoon dried oregano, crushed
Dash pepper
1 pound ground pork
4 slices French bread, toasted* (optional)
4 slices Swiss cheese *or* mozzarella cheese (4 ounces)
½ cup alfalfa sprouts

1 In a bowl combine egg and milk. Stir in bread crumbs, olives, dried onion, oregano, and pepper. Add ground pork; mix well. Shape into four ½-inch-thick patties. Place patties on the rack of an unheated broiler pan. Broil 3 inches from heat till well-done, turning once (allow about 15 minutes total time).*

2 Cut cheese to fit atop burgers, if necessary. Top each patty with one slice of cheese; broil about 1 minute more or just till cheese is melted. Serve burgers alone or on toasted French bread. Top with alfalfa sprouts. Makes 4 servings.

*Toast bread with burgers for 1 minute on each side.

ORIENTAL SALAD

Pictured on pages 30 and 31—

Assembling time: 10 minutes

½ of a 6-ounce package frozen pea pods
1 8-ounce can pineapple chunks (juice pack)
2 tablespoons soy sauce
2 tablespoons salad oil
1 tablespoon sesame seed
3 cups torn romaine
½ of an 8-ounce can sliced water chestnuts, drained

1 Run hot water over frozen pea pods in colander till thawed. Drain pineapple, reserving 2 tablespoons juice. For dressing, in a screw-top jar combine reserved pineapple juice, soy sauce, oil, and sesame seed. Cover; shake well. Chill.

2 Combine romaine, water chestnuts, pea pods, and pineapple. Chill. To serve, toss dressing and salad. Serves 4.

GLAZED SWEET POTATOES

Pictured on pages 30 and 31—

Total preparation time: 12 minutes

2 tablespoons brown sugar
1 teaspoon cornstarch
¼ teaspoon ground ginger
½ cup apple juice
1 teaspoon prepared mustard
1 17-ounce can sweet potatoes
⅓ cup cashews

1 In a saucepan mix brown sugar, cornstarch, ginger, and ¼ teaspoon *salt*. Add apple juice and mustard; cook and stir till bubbly. Cook and stir 2 minutes more. Drain sweet potatoes; stir into sugar mixture. Heat through. Stir in cashews. Serves 4.

It doesn't take hours of work to serve a full-flavored lamb dinner. This tasty menu can be prepared in a mere 45 minutes. The luscious lamb chops are served with a dramatic asparagus and tomato sauce. You'll find this easy dinner irresistible.

45-MINUTE LAMB DINNER

ASPARAGUS-TOPPED LAMB CHOPS

TOSSED FRUIT SALAD

DINNER ROLLS

ALMOND-COCOA CAKE

DESSERT

BEVERAGE

45 MINUTES BEFORE SERVING
- Put fruit for the Tossed Fruit Salad in the refrigerator to chill.
- Make dressing for salad and chill.
- Prepare Almond-Cocoa Cake Dessert and chill.

30 MINUTES BEFORE SERVING
- Arrange fruit for Tossed Fruit Salad atop greens.
- Broil lamb chops.
- While chops are broiling, prepare sauce for chops.
- Prepare beverage.

AT SERVING TIME
- Top fruit salad with dressing.
- Spoon sauce over chops.

ASPARAGUS-TOPPED LAMB CHOPS

Assembling time: 12 minutes
Cooking time: 14 minutes

8 lamb loin chops *or* lamb leg sirloin chops, cut ¾-inch thick
1 stalk celery, bias-sliced into ½-inch pieces
1 tablespoon butter *or* margarine
1 8-ounce can stewed tomatoes, cut up
½ teaspoon dried rosemary, crushed
¼ teaspoon salt
  Dash pepper
½ of a 10-ounce package frozen cut asparagus
1 tablespoon water
2 teaspoons cornstarch
  Grated Parmesan cheese

1 Place chops on the rack of an unheated broiler pan; season with salt and pepper. Broil 3 to 4 inches from heat to desired doneness (allow 12 to 14 minutes total time for medium doneness).

2 Meanwhile, in a medium saucepan cook celery in butter or margarine till tender but not brown. Stir in *undrained* tomatoes, rosemary, salt, and pepper; bring mixture to boiling.

3 Stir in asparagus; return to boiling; cover and simmer for 5 minutes. Combine water and cornstarch; stir into tomato mixture. Cook and stir till thickened and bubbly. Cook and stir 2 minutes more. Spoon sauce atop broiled lamb chops; sprinkle with grated Parmesan cheese. Makes 4 servings.

TOSSED FRUIT SALAD

Assembling time: 8 minutes

2 tablespoons sugar
2 tablespoons lemon juice
1 tablespoon water
¼ teaspoon celery seed
¼ teaspoon paprika
¼ teaspoon dry mustard
  Dash salt
⅓ cup salad oil
3 cups torn salad greens
1 17-ounce can chunky mixed fruit, chilled and drained

1 To make dressing, in a small bowl combine sugar, lemon juice, water, celery seed, paprika, dry mustard, and salt. Stir till sugar dissolves. Gradually add salad oil, beating till mixture is thick. Cover and chill.

2 Place greens in a salad bowl. Arrange fruit atop greens. Just before serving, pour desired amount of dressing over fruit. Toss to coat. Makes 4 servings.

ALMOND-COCOA CAKE DESSERT

Assembling time: 5 minutes

½ cup whipping cream
¼ cup presweetened cocoa powder
4 ½-inch-thick slices frozen pound cake, thawed, *or* four ½-inch thick slices angel food cake
  Sliced almonds

1 In a small mixer bowl whip together cream and cocoa powder till soft peaks form. Spoon atop cake slices; sprinkle with sliced almonds. Makes 4 servings.

DINNER

When it's late and the family is really hungry, rely on hearty, quick Meat Loaf Supper to ease your time bind. This filling menu can be prepared in just 50 minutes. It features Mini Surprise Meat Loaves—individual loaves of ground beef with a zesty cheese filling. Accompaniments include Walnut Rice and Cheese and Pea Salad. This dinner is sure to be a people-pleaser!

MEAT LOAF SUPPER

MINI SURPRISE MEAT LOAVES

CHEESE AND PEA SALAD

WALNUT RICE

COOKIES

BEVERAGE

50 MINUTES BEFORE SERVING
- Prepare Mini Surprise Meat Loaves.

30 MINUTES BEFORE SERVING
- Cook meat loaves.
- Begin cooking rice for Walnut Rice.
- Prepare Cheese and Pea Salad.

15 MINUTES BEFORE SERVING
- Prepare fruit mixture for rice.
- Prepare beverage.
- Make topping for meat loaves and spread on meat loaves.

MINI-SURPRISE MEAT LOAVES

Assembling time: 13 minutes
Cooking time: 30 minutes

- 1 beaten egg
- 1/3 cup catsup-style hamburger relish
- 1/4 cup milk
- 1 teaspoon minced dried onion
- 1/3 cup fine dry bread crumbs
- 3/4 teaspoon salt
- 1/8 teaspoon pepper
- 1 pound ground beef
- 2 ounces Swiss cheese, cut into 12 cubes
- 1/4 cup catsup-style hamburger relish
- 1 teaspoon prepared mustard

1 In a mixing bowl combine the beaten egg, the 1/3 cup catsup-style hamburger relish, milk, and minced dried onion. Let stand for 5 minutes. Stir in bread crumbs, salt, and pepper. Add ground beef; mix well.

2 Evenly spoon *half* of the meat mixture into 12 muffin cups till 1/2 full. Press a cheese cube into the center of each. Spoon remaining meat mixture atop cheese cubes. Slightly press the meat mixture down around cheese to seal, pulling meat slightly away from the sides of the muffin cups.

3 Bake in a 350° oven for 20 minutes. Meanwhile stir together the 1/4 cup catsup-style hamburger relish and mustard. Spoon relish mixture atop meat loaves. Bake about 10 minutes more or till done. Makes 6 servings.

CHEESE AND PEA SALAD

Assembling time: 13 minutes

- 1 10-ounce package frozen peas
- 1 cup cherry tomato halves
- 2 stalks celery, bias-sliced into 1/2-inch pieces
- 3 ounces Swiss cheese, cut into 1/2-inch cubes
- 1/2 cup mayonnaise *or* salad dressing
- 2 tablespoons milk
- 1/2 teaspoon dried dillweed
- Lettuce leaves

1 Run hot water over frozen peas in a colander till separated. In a bowl toss together peas, cherry tomato halves, celery, and cheese. Stir together mayonnaise, milk, dillweed, 1/4 teaspoon *salt*, and a dash *pepper*. Spoon mayonnaise mixture atop pea mixture. Toss and chill. Serve on lettuce-lined plates. Serves 6.

WALNUT RICE

Total preparation time: 30 minutes

- 1 10 3/4-ounce can condensed chicken broth
- 1 cup long grain rice
- 2 tablespoons butter *or* margarine
- 2 tablespoons honey
- 1 medium cooking apple, cored and chopped
- 1/2 cup chopped walnuts
- 1/2 cup raisins

1 In 2-quart saucepan mix chicken broth, rice, and 3/4 cup *water*. Bring to boiling. Reduce heat; cover; simmer 14 minutes (*do not* lift cover). Remove from heat. Let stand, covered, for 10 minutes.

2 Meanwhile, in a skillet melt butter. Stir in honey. Stir in apple, walnuts, and raisins. Cover and simmer for 3 to 4 minutes. Stir into the hot rice. Makes 6 servings.

Here's a nourishing dinner that you can fix and forget while your appliances do most of the work. First, prepare and chill the Black Cherry Pie. Do this the night before or at least 3½ hours prior to serving time. Next, fix the chicken. While it cooks, stir together the Cheese and Vegetable Bake. Put it in the oven with the chicken—it bakes at the same temperature. Your dinner will be ready in 40 minutes.

FIX-AND-FORGET DINNER

CRISPY HERB CHICKEN

CHEESE AND VEGETABLE BAKE

CELERY AND CARROT STICKS

DINNER ROLLS

BLACK CHERRY PIE

BEVERAGE

UP TO 1 DAY BEFORE SERVING
- Prepare Black Cherry Pie and chill.
- Prepare celery and carrot sticks and chill.

1¼ HOURS BEFORE SERVING
- Prepare Crispy Herb Chicken and bake.

55 MINUTES BEFORE SERVING
- Prepare Cheese and Vegetable Bake and bake.

5 MINUTES BEFORE SERVING
- Prepare beverage.

CRISPY HERB CHICKEN

Assembling time: 20 minutes
Cooking time: 60 minutes

1¼ cups crisp rice cereal, crushed
1 .6-ounce envelope Italian salad dressing mix
1 teaspoon dried parsley flakes
1 2½- to 3-pound broiler-fryer chicken, cut up
¼ cup butter *or* margarine, melted

1 In a mixing bowl combine crushed rice cereal, salad dressing mix, and parsley flakes. Brush chicken with melted butter or margarine; roll in cereal mixture.

2 Place chicken, skin side up, on a rack in an ungreased, large shallow baking pan. Sprinkle with any remaining crumbs. Bake in a 375° oven for 50 to 60 minutes or till tender. *Do not turn*. Makes 6 servings.

CHEESE AND VEGETABLE BAKE

Assembling time: 15 minutes
Cooking time: 40 minutes

1 10-ounce package frozen mixed vegetables *or* 2 cups frozen loose-pack mixed vegetables
1 5½-ounce package dry scalloped potato mix
1½ cups boiling water
⅔ cup milk
1 cup shredded Swiss cheese

1 Run hot water over frozen vegetables in a colander till separated. Place potatoes from scalloped potato mix in a 2-quart casserole. Set aside.

2 Meanwhile, combine boiling water, milk, and sauce mix from scalloped potato mix. Pour over potatoes. Stir in vegetables and cheese. Bake in a 375° oven for 40 minutes. Serves 6.

BLACK CHERRY PIE

Assembling time: 35 minutes
Chilling time: 3 hours

2 3-ounce packages cream cheese, cut up
1 3-ounce package black cherry-flavored gelatin
½ cup water
2 slightly beaten egg yolks
1 8-ounce carton plain yogurt
¼ teaspoon ground nutmeg
2 egg whites
2 tablespoons sugar
1 16-ounce can pitted dark sweet cherries, drained and halved
1 graham cracker pie shell
Unsweetened whipped cream

1 In a saucepan combine cream cheese, cherry gelatin, water, and beaten egg yolks. Cook and stir about 6 minutes or till the gelatin is dissolved and the mixture is slightly thickened. Remove from heat.

2 Beat the yogurt and nutmeg into the gelatin mixture till the mixture is smooth. Chill the mixture to the consistency of corn syrup, stirring occasionally.

3 Meanwhile, wash beaters thoroughly. Beat the egg whites till soft peaks form. Gradually add the sugar, beating till stiff peaks form. When the gelatin is the consistency of unbeaten egg whites (partially set), fold the egg whites into the gelatin mixture.

4 Fold the drained cherries into the gelatin mixture. Chill till the mixture mounds when spooned. Turn into the graham cracker pie shell. Chill at least 3 hours or till set. If desired, garnish with whipped cream. Makes 8 servings.

With a little creativity, you can transform ordinary deli food into an elegant dinner that's perfect to serve when you entertain. Deli fried chicken becomes Festive Peachy Chicken. Deli Bean and Potato Salad is based on purchased three-bean salad. And ready-to-eat pudding is layered with crumbled cookies and nuts to make Party Parfaits.

PARTY FROM THE DELI

FESTIVE PEACHY CHICKEN

DELI BEAN AND POTATO SALAD

FRENCH BREAD

PARTY PARFAITS

BEVERAGE

45 MINUTES BEFORE SERVING
- Make Deli Bean and Potato Salad; chill.
- Prepare Party Parfaits and chill.

20 MINUTES BEFORE SERVING
- Heat chicken and prepare sauce for Festive Peachy Chicken.

5 MINUTES BEFORE SERVING
- Slice French bread.
- Add chicken to sauce.
- Prepare beverage.

Festive Peachy Chicken
(see recipe, page 56)
Party Parfaits (see recipe, page 56)
Deli Bean and Potato Salad
(see recipe, page 56)

FESTIVE PEACHY CHICKEN

Pictured on pages 54 and 55—

Total preparation time: 25 minutes

12 pieces purchased fried chicken
1 small onion, chopped
1 tablespoon butter *or* margarine
1 4½-ounce jar strained peaches (baby food)
½ cup chili sauce
⅓ cup water
¼ cup light raisins
2 tablespoons brown sugar
1½ teaspoons Worcestershire sauce
4 fresh peaches *or* nectarines, peeled and sliced, *or* one 16-ounce can peach slices, drained

1 Place chicken pieces in a shallow baking pan and heat in a 350° oven for 15 minutes or till heated through. Meanwhile, in a 12-inch skillet cook the chopped onion in butter or margarine till the onion is tender but not brown.

2 Stir strained peaches, chili sauce, water, light raisins, brown sugar, and Worcestershire sauce into skillet. Bring mixture to boiling; reduce heat. Simmer, uncovered, for 3 to 5 minutes or till ingredients are combined and heated through.

3 Stir in fresh peach or nectarine slices or canned peach slices. Just before serving, add the hot chicken pieces, spooning sauce atop; heat mixture 1 to 2 minutes more. Makes 6 servings.

DELI BEAN AND POTATO SALAD

Pictured on pages 54 and 55—

Assembling time: 10 minutes

1 16-ounce can sliced potatoes
½ pint purchased marinated three-bean salad (1 cup)
4 cups torn romaine
1 small red onion, sliced and separated into rings
1 teaspoon dried dillweed
1 teaspoon paprika
½ teaspoon dry mustard

1 Drain potatoes; cut up any large slices. Drain three-bean salad, reserving marinade. In a bowl combine potatoes, salad, the torn romaine, and onion. Combine dillweed, paprika, mustard, and reserved marinade. Toss with salad. If desired, serve in a romaine-lined salad bowl. Serves 6.

PARTY PARFAITS

Pictured on pages 54 and 55—

Assembling time: 10 minutes

1 pint purchased lemon pudding
1 cup dairy sour cream
2 tablespoons sifted powdered sugar
2 tablespoons orange liqueur
8 crisp oatmeal cookies
¼ cup pecan halves

1 Stir together pudding, sour cream, powdered sugar, and liqueur. Crumble the cookies; stir in pecans. Spoon *half* of the pudding mixture into six parfait glasses.

2 Set aside *one-fourth* of the crumb mixture; divide remaining crumbs among parfait glasses. Top with remaining pudding and reserved crumb mixture. If desired, garnish each with a lemon slice. Serves 6.

Why try elaborate recipes when you entertain? Instead, make our Carefree Company Dinner. All the recipes are so easy you don't have to worry about a thing. Yet they're so elegant and flavorful, they'll dazzle your guests.

CAREFREE COMPANY DINNER

EASY SALMON APPETIZERS OR POCKET BREAD APPETIZERS

ORANGE AND SOY CHICKEN

LETTUCE WEDGES WITH VINEGAR AND OIL

BRANDIED PEAR SAUCE OR STRAWBERRY SAUCE

ICE CREAM

UP TO 3 DAYS BEFORE SERVING
■ Prepare spread for Easy Salmon Appetizers and chill.
■ Prepare Brandied Pear Sauce or Strawberry Sauce and chill.

1½ HOURS BEFORE SERVING
■ Prepare marinade and begin marinating chicken for Orange and Soy Chicken.
■ Prepare Pocket Bread Appetizers if you do not make Easy Salmon Appetizers.
■ Scoop ice cream for dessert and freeze.

30 MINUTES BEFORE SERVING
■ Finish Orange and Soy Chicken.
■ Prepare lettuce wedges and dressing.

EASY SALMON APPETIZERS

Let your guests spread their own—

Assembling time: 12 minutes

- 2 3-ounce packages cream cheese with chives, cut up
- 1 tablespoon vinegar
- ¼ teaspoon dried thyme, crushed
  Dash pepper
- 1 7¾-ounce can salmon, drained, flaked and skin and bones removed
- ¼ cup finely chopped celery
  Assorted crackers
  Pimiento-stuffed olives (optional)

1 In a mixer bowl beat together cream cheese with chives, vinegar, thyme, and pepper till fluffy. Stir in salmon and celery. Chill till just before serving time. Spread on crackers. If desired, garnish each with an olive. Makes about 1½ cups spread.

POCKET BREAD APPETIZERS

Assembling time: 5 minutes
Cooking time: 8 minutes

- 2 pita bread rounds
- ¾ cup shredded caraway cheese *or* hickory smoke-flavor cheese

1 Cut pita bread rounds in half horizontally. Cut each pita half into 8 wedges. Place on greased baking sheet. Sprinkle with shredded cheese. Bake in a 375° oven for 8 minutes or till cheese melts. Serve warm. Makes 32.

ORANGE AND SOY CHICKEN

Total preparation time: 1¼ hours

- 2 teaspoons sesame seed
- ⅓ cup orange juice
- 3 tablespoons soy sauce
- 2 whole large chicken breasts, skinned, halved lengthwise, and boned
- ⅓ cup water
- 1 tablespoon cornstarch
- 1 6-ounce package frozen pea pods
- ½ cup cashews
  Chow mein noodles, rice noodles, *or* hot cooked rice

1 Toast sesame seed, if desired. For marinade, in a bowl stir together orange juice, soy sauce, and sesame seed. Marinate chicken breasts at room temperature in orange juice mixture for 30 minutes.

2 Place chicken and marinade in a 10-inch skillet. Cover and simmer about 30 minutes or till done. Remove chicken and keep warm.

3 Combine water and cornstarch; add to marinade in skillet. Cook and stir till mixture is thickened and bubbly. Cook and stir 2 minutes more. Stir frozen pea pods and cashews into the thickened marinade. Cook and stir for 1 minute. Serve chicken and pea pod mixture over chow mein noodles, rice noodles, or hot cooked rice. Makes 4 servings.

BRANDIED PEAR SAUCE

Assembling time: 5 minutes
Cooking time: 8 minutes

- 1 8½-ounce can pear halves *or* slices
- 1½ teaspoons cornstarch
- ⅛ teaspoon ground cinnamon
- 1 tablespoon brandy
- 1½ teaspoons lemon juice
  Vanilla ice cream *or* orange sherbet
- 2 tablespoons slivered almonds

1 Drain pears, reserving ½ cup liquid. Coarsely chop pears; set aside. In a small saucepan combine reserved pear syrup, cornstarch, and cinnamon. Cook and stir till thickened and bubbly. Cook and stir for 2 minutes more. Remove from heat.

2 Stir in brandy and lemon juice; fold in pears. Cover and chill till serving time. Serve over ice cream or sherbet. Top with slivered almonds. Makes 4 servings.

STRAWBERRY SAUCE

Assembling time: 10 minutes
Cooking time: 8 minutes

- 1 10-ounce package frozen sliced strawberries (in quick-thaw pouch)
- 2 tablespoons sugar
- 2 teaspoons cornstarch
- ¼ cup strawberry jelly
  Vanilla ice cream

1 Thaw strawberries according to package directions; crush. In a medium saucepan combine sugar and cornstarch; stir in strawberries and jelly. Bring to boiling. Cook and stir till slightly thickened. Strain; cool. Serve over ice cream. Cover; chill any remaining sauce. Serves 4 to 6.

When it's 95° in the shade, the last thing you want to do is heat up your kitchen by turning on the range. And with Supper on Ice you can prepare a refreshing meal without ever touching the range. All of the ingredients come out of a package or can and need no cooking. Just put them together and chill the meal till serving time.

SUPPER ON ICE

PAELLA SALAD SUPPER

CRISPY RYE CRACKERS

FRUIT TORTE

APRICOT COOLER

45 MINUTES BEFORE SERVING
- Take cake for Fruit Torte from freezer and thaw.
- Prepare dressing for Paella Salad Supper and chill.
- Prepare Paella Salad Supper.

20 MINUTES BEFORE SERVING
- Prepare filling for Fruit Torte.
- Assemble Fruit Torte.
- Prepare Apricot Cooler.

AT SERVING TIME
- Toss Paella Salad Supper with dressing.

FRUIT TORTE

Assembling time: 15 minutes

1 frozen loaf pound cake, thawed
1 cup ricotta cheese
¼ cup sifted powdered sugar
1 teaspoon vanilla
1 large banana, thinly sliced
   Lemon juice
1½ cups fresh raspberries, blueberries, *or* sliced strawberries

1 Cut pound cake horizontally into three layers. Set aside. In a small mixer bowl beat together ricotta cheese, powdered sugar, and vanilla. Dip banana slices in lemon juice. Set aside several slices for garnish.

2 Arrange remaining slices over bottom layer of cake. Spread *one-third* of ricotta mixture atop banana slices. Set aside several berries for garnish. Top cheese layer with *half* the remaining berries.

3 Add middle cake layer. Spread with *half* the remaining cheese mixture and remaining berries. Top with last cake layer. Frost top of cake with remaining cheese mixture. Garnish with reserved banana slices and reserved berries. Serves 6 to 8.

APRICOT COOLER

Assembling time: 5 minutes

2 cups dry white wine *or* unsweetened white grape juice, chilled
1 12-ounce can (1½ cups) apricot nectar, chilled
1 10-ounce bottle lemon-lime carbonated beverage, chilled
   Ice

1 In a large pitcher combine wine and apricot nectar. Gradually pour in the carbonated beverage. Stir gently. Serve over ice. Makes 6 (6-ounce) servings.

PAELLA SALAD SUPPER

If you don't have cheddar cheese or ham on hand, try substituting another cheese such as Swiss or mozzarella or another meat such as canned turkey or chicken—

Assembling time: 20 minutes

½ cup catsup
2 tablespoons red wine vinegar
2 tablespoons cooking oil
1 teaspoon Worcestershire sauce
½ teaspoon dried oregano, crushed
¼ teaspoon onion powder
4 cups torn lettuce
2 cups shredded cabbage
1 15-ounce can Spanish rice
1½ cups cubed fully cooked ham *or* one 6¾-ounce can chunk-style ham, drained and flaked
1 6-ounce package frozen cooked shrimp, thawed, *or* one 4½-ounce can shrimp, rinsed and drained
1 cup sliced pitted ripe olives
½ cup shredded cheddar cheese
½ small cucumber, sliced
1 small tomato, cut into wedges

1 In a screw-top jar combine the catsup, vinegar, cooking oil, Worcestershire sauce, oregano, and onion powder. Cover; shake till well combined. Chill thoroughly.

2 In a large salad bowl layer or combine lettuce, cabbage, Spanish rice, ham, shrimp, olives, cheese, cucumber slices, and tomato wedges, as desired. To serve, pour dressing over salad; toss to coat. Makes 6 to 8 servings.

Paella Salad Supper
Fresh Fruit Torte
Apricot Cooler

Here's an all-around fuss-free meal that's energy efficient. It's easy because both preparation and cleanup are at a minimum. It's energy efficient because the main dish, bread, and dessert can all be baked in a 350° oven at the same time.

EASY OVEN MEAL

MEXICAN-STYLE PORK CHOPS

LETTUCE WEDGES

HORSERADISH BREAD

CHEESE-APPLE SQUARES

BEVERAGE

1¼ HOURS BEFORE SERVING
- Prepare Horseradish Bread and bake.
- Prepare Mexican-Style Pork Chops and bake.

30 MINUTES BEFORE SERVING
- Prepare Cheese-Apple Squares and bake.

5 MINUTES BEFORE SERVING
- Cut lettuce wedges.
- Prepare beverage.

MEXICAN-STYLE PORK CHOPS

Assembling time: 12 minutes
Cooking time: 40 minutes
Standing time: 10 minutes

6 pork chops, cut ½ inch thick
2 tablespoons cooking oil
½ cup chopped onion
1 17-ounce can whole kernel corn
1 15½-ounce can red kidney beans, drained
1 10¾-ounce can condensed tomato soup
1 cup quick-cooking rice
1 cup water
½ cup sliced pitted ripe olives
2 to 3 teaspoons chili powder
½ teaspoon salt
½ teaspoon dried oregano, crushed
Dash pepper
Snipped parsley (optional)

1 In a 12-inch oven-proof skillet brown pork chops on both sides in cooking oil; remove from skillet. Season chops with salt and pepper; set aside.

2 In the same skillet cook onion till tender but not brown. Add the *undrained* corn, drained beans, tomato soup, *uncooked* rice, water, olives, chili powder, salt, oregano, and pepper. Bring to boiling.

3 Arrange chops atop. Bake, uncovered, in a 350° oven about 40 minutes. Let stand 10 minutes before serving. Garnish with parsley, if desired. Makes 6 servings.

HORSERADISH BREAD

Assembling time: 10 minutes
Cooking time: 50 minutes
Cooling time: 10 minutes

1 beaten egg
½ cup sour cream dip with bacon and horseradish
½ cup milk
2 cups packaged biscuit mix
2 tablespoons sliced green onion

1 In a bowl combine the egg, sour cream dip, and ¼ teaspoon *salt*. Set aside ⅓ *cup* of the sour cream mixture. Stir milk into remaining sour cream mixture. Add biscuit mix and onion, stirring just till combined.

2 Turn into a greased 8x4x2-inch loaf pan. Spread reserved sour cream mixture atop. Bake in a 350° oven for 45 to 50 minutes. Cool 10 minutes before removing from pan. Serve warm. Makes 1 loaf.

CHEESE-APPLE SQUARES

Total preparation time: 40 minutes

¾ cup graham cracker crumbs
½ cup all-purpose flour
½ cup packed brown sugar
⅓ cup butter *or* margarine, softened
1 20-ounce can sliced apples
1 cup shredded cheddar cheese
¼ cup chopped walnuts

1 In a mixing bowl combine graham cracker crumbs, flour, and brown sugar. Cut in butter till crumbly. Set aside ¾ *cup* of the mixture. Pat remaining crumb mixture in the bottom of an 8x8x2-inch baking pan. Bake in a 350° oven for 10 minutes.

2 Drain apples. Stir together apples, cheese, and nuts; spoon atop crust. Sprinkle reserved crumb mixture over all. Bake 20 minutes. Serve warm. Serves 9.

You just need some shelf staples, a blender, a skillet, and 30 minutes to whip up this mouth-watering menu. Start by preparing either the luscious Easy Cherry Yogurt Pudding or the rich and creamy Chocolate-Mint Parfaits for dessert. Then while dessert is chilling, prepare the easy-to-make Skillet Hawaiian. It will all go together in a flash, and your family's sure to think it tastes great.

HURRY-UP HAWAIIAN DINNER

SKILLET HAWAIIAN

TOSSED SALAD WITH CREAMY FRENCH DRESSING

EASY CHERRY YOGURT PUDDING OR CHOCOLATE-MINT PARFAITS

BEVERAGE

30 MINUTES BEFORE SERVING
- Prepare Easy Cherry Yogurt Pudding or Chocolate-Mint Parfaits and chill.
- Prepare greens for tossed salad.
- Cut up the vegetables and meat for Skillet Hawaiian.

15 MINUTES BEFORE SERVING
- Prepare Skillet Hawaiian.
- Toss salad dressing with salad.
- Prepare beverage.

SKILLET HAWAIIAN

If you have a food processor, use it to slice the celery and green pepper—

Total preparation time: 12 minutes

- 1 12-ounce can luncheon meat *or* 1½ cups fully cooked ham cut into strips
- ¾ cup sliced green pepper
- 2 stalks celery, thinly sliced (1 cup)
- 2 tablespoons cooking oil
- 1 8-ounce can pineapple chunks (juice pack)
- ⅓ cup orange marmalade
- 1 tablespoon cornstarch
- 1 tablespoon soy sauce
- ¼ teaspoon ground ginger
  Chow mein noodles, rice noodles, *or* hot cooked rice

1 In a 10-inch skillet cook meat strips, green pepper, and celery in hot cooking oil till vegetables are crisp-tender. Meanwhile, drain the pineapple, reserving ⅓ *cup* of the juice.

2 In a small bowl combine the reserved pineapple juice, the orange marmalade, cornstarch, soy sauce, and ground ginger. Stir into meat mixture in skillet.

3 Cook and stir till the mixture is thickened and bubbly. Stir in the pineapple chunks; cook and stir about 2 minutes more or till the pineapple is heated through. Serve over chow mein noodles, rice noodles, or hot cooked rice. Makes 4 servings.

EASY CHERRY YOGURT PUDDING

Assembling time: 10 minutes

- ¼ cup sugar
- 1 envelope unflavored gelatin
- ½ cup milk
- ¾ cup drained crushed ice *or* six 1-inch ice cubes
- 1 8-ounce carton cherry yogurt
- 2 tablespoons sliced almonds

1 Stir together the sugar and unflavored gelatin. In a small saucepan heat milk just till boiling. Pour milk into a blender container. Add the sugar-gelatin mixture. Cover and blend for 2 minutes to dissolve gelatin and sugar.

2 With blender running, add ice a little at a time through hole in lid, till mixture is smooth. Add the cherry yogurt and blend just till combined. Pour mixture into sherbet dishes. Sprinkle with sliced almonds. Chill till serving time. Serves 4.

CHOCOLATE-MINT PARFAITS

Assembling time: 15 minutes

- 1 17½-ounce can chocolate pudding
- ½ cup dairy sour cream
- ½ of a 4-ounce container frozen whipped dessert topping, thawed
- 1 tablespoon crème de menthe liqueur

1 In a mixing bowl fold together chocolate pudding and dairy sour cream. In another bowl fold together dessert topping and crème de menthe. Spoon alternate layers of the pudding mixture and the topping mixture into 4 parfait glasses. Chill till serving time. Makes 4 servings.

At the end of a hurry-here, scurry-there day, take an imaginary vacation to Mexico for dinner. You won't need to do lots of hard work or spend hours in the kitchen to conjure up the flavors of Mexico. Just start by making our easy version of zesty sangria and a Mexican-Style Quiche. Then while the quiche starts to bake, prepare the Easy Fruit Cobbler—it bakes at the same temperature, so it can go into the oven with the quiche.

MEXICAN QUICHE SUPPER

MEXICAN-STYLE QUICHE

MIXED BEAN SALAD

EASY FRUIT COBBLER

EASY SANGRIA

55 MINUTES BEFORE SERVING
- Prepare Easy Sangria and chill.
- Prepare Mexican-Style Quiche and bake.

35 MINUTES BEFORE SERVING
- Prepare Easy Fruit Cobbler and bake.
- Open two 16-ounce cans three-bean salad; turn into a bowl. Top with red or green pepper rings and chill.

MEXICAN-STYLE QUICHE

Assembling time: 10 minutes
Cooking time: 25 minutes
Standing time: 5 minutes

- 4 6-inch flour tortillas
- 4 ounces Monterey Jack cheese with jalapeño peppers, sliced
- 1 3-ounce can French-fried onions
- 2 cups milk
- 4 beaten eggs
- ½ teaspoon salt
- ½ teaspoon chili powder
- ¼ teaspoon dry mustard
  Parsley sprigs (optional)

1 Gently press one flour tortilla in each of four individual au gratin dishes; top with cheese slices and about *three-fourths* of the French-fried onions (reserve remaining onions for garnish).

2 In a saucepan heat the milk almost to boiling. Gradually add the milk to beaten eggs, mixing well. Stir in the salt, chili powder, and dry mustard.

3 Place individual casseroles in a shallow baking pan; place on oven rack. Divide egg mixture evenly among the casseroles. Bake in a 350° oven for 20 to 25 minutes.

4 Sprinkle reserved onions atop. Bake 5 minutes more or till a knife inserted near center comes out clean. Let stand 5 minutes before serving. Garnish with parsley sprigs, if desired. Makes 4 servings.

EASY FRUIT COBBLER

Assembling time: 5 minutes
Cooking time: 25 minutes

- 1 21-ounce can fruit pie filling (any flavor)
- 1 11-ounce can mandarin orange sections, drained
- 2 tablespoons sugar
- ¼ teaspoon ground cinnamon
- ½ package (6) pre-baked heat-and-serve biscuits
- 2 tablespoons butter, melted

1 In a medium saucepan heat pie filling till bubbly; stir in orange sections. Turn mixture into 8x8x2-inch baking dish. Stir together sugar and cinnamon.

2 Dip tops of biscuits in melted butter, then in sugar-cinnamon mixture. Arrange atop fruit, sugar side up. Bake in a 350° oven for 20 to 25 minutes or till heated through. Makes 4 to 6 servings.

EASY SANGRIA

Assembling time: 5 minutes

- 1 750-milliliter bottle rosé, burgundy, *or* other red wine
- ¼ cup orange juice
- 2 tablespoons sugar
- 2 tablespoons lemon juice
- 2 tablespoons brandy (optional)
- 1 16-ounce bottle carbonated water, chilled (2 cups)
  Ice cubes

1 In a large pitcher combine wine, orange juice, sugar, lemon juice, and brandy. Stir to dissolve sugar. Chill, if desired. Just before serving, slowly add carbonated water. Pour over ice cubes in glasses. If desired, garnish with orange slices. Makes 6 (8-ounce) servings.

When you know you're going to have time on your hands one day and "no time at all" the next, take advantage of Next Night's Dinner. With this menu you can make everything at least one day ahead. Then, add a few last-minute touches and you'll have a hearty dinner pronto.

NEXT NIGHT'S DINNER

ZESTY MEAT ROLLS

SPINACH AND MUSHROOM SALAD

FRENCH BREAD

DESSERT COMPOTE

BEVERAGE

UP TO 7 DAYS BEFORE SERVING
- Prepare Zesty Meat Rolls and freeze.

1 DAY BEFORE SERVING
- Prepare Spinach and Mushroom Salad and chill.
- Prepare Dessert Compote; chill.

1½ HOURS BEFORE SERVING
- Bake Zesty Meat Rolls.

20 MINUTES BEFORE SERVING
- Cook spaghetti.
- Slice French bread.
- Prepare beverage.
- Toss Spinach and Mushroom Salad.

ZESTY MEAT ROLLS

Advance preparation time: 30 minutes
Final preparation time: 1¾ hours

- 2 **beaten eggs**
- 1 **8-ounce can pizza sauce**
- ½ **cup fine dry seasoned bread crumbs**
- ½ **teaspoon salt**
  Dash pepper
- 1½ **pounds lean ground beef**
- 6 **ounces mozzarella cheese**
- 1 **10½-ounce can tomato puree**
- ½ **cup sliced pimiento-stuffed olives**
  or sliced pitted ripe olives
- 2 **tablespoons dry red wine**
- 2 **teaspoons Worcestershire sauce**
- ½ **teaspoon sugar**
- ½ **teaspoon dried marjoram, crushed**
- ½ **teaspoon instant beef bouillon granules**
  Hot cooked spaghetti
  Grated Parmesan cheese

1 In a mixing bowl combine eggs and *half* of the pizza sauce. Stir in seasoned bread crumbs, salt, and pepper. Add ground beef; mix well. Divide the meat mixture into 6 equal portions.

2 Cut mozzarella cheese into 6 sticks measuring about 3½x1x½-inch. Using one stick of cheese for each, shape each meat portion into an individual meat loaf around the cheese. Make sure meat mixture is completely sealed around cheese.

3 Place meat loaves in an 8x8x2-inch freezer-to-oven baking dish. Stir together remaining pizza sauce, tomato puree, olives, wine, Worcestershire sauce, sugar, marjoram, and beef bouillon granules. Pour over meat loaves. Cover baking dish with moisture-vaporproof wrap. Seal, label, and freeze.

Before serving: Bake, covered, in a 375° oven for 1½ to 1¾ hours. Serve over hot cooked spaghetti. Pass Parmesan cheese. Makes 6 servings.

SPINACH AND MUSHROOM SALAD

Advance preparation time: 25 minutes

- 4 **cups torn fresh spinach**
- 1 **cup sliced fresh mushrooms**
- 1 **cup cherry tomatoes**
- 1 **medium carrot, bias-sliced**
- ½ **cup fresh *or* canned bean sprouts**
- ½ **cup mayonnaise *or* salad dressing**
- 2 **tablespoons milk**
- 2 **tablespoons grated Parmesan cheese**
- ⅛ **teaspoon dried marjoram, crushed**
  Dash garlic powder

1 Toss together spinach, mushrooms, tomatoes, carrot, and sprouts. Stir together mayonnaise, milk, cheese, marjoram, and garlic powder. Spoon atop vegetables, sealing to edge. Cover; chill in refrigerator 3 to 24 hours.

Before serving: Toss to coat vegetables. Makes 6 servings.

DESSERT COMPOTE

Advance preparation time: 10 minutes

- 1 **8¾-ounce can unpeeled apricot halves**
- 1 **8-ounce can pineapple chunks (juice pack)**
- ½ **cup whole walnuts**
- ¼ **cup raisins**
- 2 **tablespoons orange liqueur**
- ⅛ **teaspoon ground nutmeg**
- ⅛ **teaspoon ground cinnamon**
- 1 **cup sliced apples, halved cherries, halved strawberries, *or* seeded grapes**

1 Combine *undrained* apricots, *undrained* pineapple, walnuts, raisins, liqueur, nutmeg, and cinnamon. Add desired fresh fruit. Cover and chill overnight. Makes 6 servings.

This savory menu is ready in a snap with just a few pans and several common ingredients that you probably have on hand. The whole meal is conveniently prepared on top of the range in only 35 minutes.

QUICK PASTA DINNER

AD-LIB ANTIPASTO

PROSCIUTTO AND PASTA

BREADSTICKS

POACHED PEARS WITH ORANGE SAUCE

BEVERAGE

35 MINUTES BEFORE SERVING
- Start boiling water for pasta.
- Poach pears for Poached Pears with Orange Sauce.
- Arrange Ad-Lib Antipasto on a platter.

20 MINUTES BEFORE SERVING
- Cook pasta and asparagus, make sour cream sauce, and cut prosciutto for Prosciutto and Pasta.
- Prepare beverage.

AT SERVING TIME
- Top poached pears with whipped cream cheese and cinnamon.
- Toss together ingredients for Prosciutto and Pasta.

Prosciutto and Pasta
Ad-Lib Antipasto
Poached Pears with Orange Sauce

PROSCIUTTO AND PASTA

For the best texture and flavor, pasta should be cooked "al dente." That's when the pasta is still firm but no longer starchy. The best way to test pasta for doneness is to taste it. When done, pasta should be drained immediately to avoid further cooking by the hot water. Do not rinse the pasta—

Total preparation time: 35 minutes

- 1 10-ounce package frozen asparagus spears
- ¾ cup grated Parmesan cheese
- ½ cup dairy sour cream
- ¼ cup dry white wine
- ¼ cup butter *or* margarine, melted
- 4 ounces thinly sliced prosciutto *or* very thinly sliced smoked ham, cut into 1-inch-wide strips
- 8 ounces linguine *or* fettuccine Grated Parmesan cheese (optional)

1 Cook asparagus according to package directions till crisp-tender; drain well. Meanwhile, combine the ¾ cup Parmesan cheese, sour cream, white wine, and butter or margarine. Stir in cooked asparagus and prosciutto or ham.

2 Cook pasta in a large amount of boiling salted water for 10 to 12 minutes or till tender. Drain pasta well (*do not rinse*). Transfer to a warm serving platter; toss with sour cream mixture. Garnish with additional Parmesan cheese, if desired. Serve immediately. Makes 4 servings.

AD-LIB ANTIPASTO

Assembling time: 5 minutes

- 1 6½-ounce can tuna, drained and broken into large chunks
  Ripe olives
  Pickled sliced beets
  Cherry tomatoes
  Marinated artichoke hearts
  Leaf lettuce

1 Arrange tuna with *some or all* of the vegetable ingredients on a large lettuce-lined serving platter. Makes 4 servings.

POACHED PEARS WITH ORANGE SAUCE

Total preparation time: 10 minutes

- 1 16-ounce can pear halves
- ¼ cup frozen orange juice concentrate
- 1 inch stick cinnamon
  Dash salt
- ½ of a 4-ounce container whipped cream cheese
  Ground cinnamon

1 Drain pears, reserving liquid. In a medium saucepan stir together orange juice concentrate and pear liquid. Stir in stick cinnamon and salt.

2 Bring mixture to boiling. Add pear halves. Cook, uncovered, 1 to 2 minutes or till pears are heated through. Let stand till serving time; remove cinnamon.

3 To serve, spoon pear halves and spiced syrup into dessert dishes. Dollop each serving with whipped cream cheese. Sprinkle lightly with ground cinnamon. Makes 4 servings.

When you're hungry for pizza, you need look no farther than your cupboard and refrigerator shelves. There you'll most likely find all the ingredients necessary to put together this delicious 60-minute pizza dinner. To short-cut the last-minute preparation, just prepare the fruit topper and vegetable dip ahead.

OFF-THE-SHELF PIZZA

YOUR-CHOICE PIZZA

VEGETABLES AND DIP

CRUNCH-TOPPED FRUIT

BEVERAGE

1 HOUR BEFORE SERVING
- Prepare and bake topping for Crunch-Topped Fruit.
- Prepare pizza crust dough.
- While the dough rests, cut up vegetable dippers.
- Roll out pizza crust dough.

25 MINUTES BEFORE SERVING
- Bake pizza crusts.
- Assemble pizza toppers for Your-Choice Pizza.
- Add the toppers to the partially baked pizza crust.
- Prepare dip.
- Prepare beverage.

YOUR-CHOICE PIZZA

Assembling time: 35 minutes
Cooking time: 10 minutes

- 1 package active dry yeast
- ½ cup warm water (110° to 115°)
- 2½ cups packaged biscuit mix
  Cornmeal (optional)
- 2 8-ounce cans pizza sauce
  Pepperoni Pizza Topper, Ham Pizza Topper, or Salami Pizza Topper
  Grated Parmesan cheese (optional)

1 Soften yeast in warm water; add biscuit mix. Mix well. Turn out onto a lightly floured surface; knead 25 strokes. Cover; let rest for 10 minutes.

2 Grease a 15x10x1-inch baking pan; lightly sprinkle with cornmeal, if desired. Pat or roll dough out onto bottom and halfway up sides of prepared pan.

3 Bake crust in a 425° oven for 8 to 10 minutes. Spread pizza sauce over baked pizza crust. Spread desired pizza topper over sauce. Bake in a 425° oven about 10 minutes more or till cheese is melted and pizza is heated through. Pass grated Parmesan cheese, if desired. Serves 6.

Pepperoni Pizza Topper: Arrange two 4-ounce packages sliced *pepperoni*; ½ cup sliced pitted *ripe olives or pimiento-stuffed olives*, drained; and 2 cups shredded *mozzarella cheese* over the pizza sauce.

Ham Pizza Topper: Arrange one 8-ounce package sliced chopped *ham*; one 8¼-ounce can *crushed pineapple*, well drained; and 2 cups shredded *mozzarella cheese* over the pizza sauce.

Salami Pizza Topper: Arrange one 8-ounce package sliced *salami*; one 4-ounce can *mushroom stems and pieces*, drained; and 2 cups shredded *Swiss cheese* over the pizza sauce.

VEGETABLES AND DIP

Assembling time: 15 minutes

- ½ cup cream-style cottage cheese
- ½ cup dairy sour cream
- 1 teaspoon Italian salad dressing mix
  Paprika
  Assorted vegetable dippers

1 Stir together cottage cheese, sour cream, and Italian salad dressing mix. Sprinkle with paprika. Serve with assorted vegetable dippers. Makes 1 cup dip.

CRUNCH-TOPPED FRUIT

Assembling time: 10 minutes
Cooking time: 25 minutes

- ⅓ cup peach preserves
- 2 tablespoons butter or margarine
- ½ teaspoon ground cinnamon
- 2 cups regular rolled oats
- ½ cup broken pecans
  Canned fruit

1 In a saucepan combine peach preserves, butter or margarine, and cinnamon. Cook and stir till butter and preserves are melted. Stir in rolled oats and pecans till well coated.

2 Turn into a 13x9x2-inch baking pan. Bake in a 350° oven for 20 to 25 minutes, stirring every 5 minutes. Cool, stirring occasionally to break into pieces. Store in a tightly covered container. Serve over fruit. Makes 2⅔ cups topping.

When the weather's nice, everyone wants to enjoy the outdoors rather than be stuck in the kitchen cooking. Yet, it seems that outdoor activity drums up some very hearty appetites that simply have to be satisfied. That's when this no-watch dinner can save the day. Just purchase coleslaw at the deli and prepare the cream cheese-coffee mold for the Strawberry-Topped Coffee Creme ahead of time. Then about 2½ hours before serving, whip up the sweet-sour meat sauce and put the rump roast on the grill. Now all you have to do is to enjoy yourself till nearly dinner time!

NO-WATCH DINNER

PINEAPPLE-ORANGE RUMP ROAST

COLESLAW

DINNER ROLLS

STRAWBERRY-TOPPED COFFEE CREME

BEVERAGE

UP TO 1 DAY BEFORE SERVING
- Prepare coffee creme mold for Strawberry-Topped Coffee Creme.

2¾ HOURS BEFORE SERVING
- Prepare Pineapple-Orange Rump Roast.

10 MINUTES BEFORE SERVING
- Place coleslaw and rolls in serving containers.
- Halve and sweeten strawberries.
- Prepare beverage.

PINEAPPLE-ORANGE RUMP ROAST

Determine the temperature of hot coals by holding your hand just above the coals at the height where the roast will be cooking. Count the seconds you can hold your hand in that position. If you need to withdraw your hand after 4 seconds, coals are medium—

Assembling time: 20 minutes
Cooking time: 2½ hours

1 **small onion, finely chopped**
1 **tablespoon cooking oil**
2 **tablespoons brown sugar**
2 **teaspoons cornstarch**
½ **cup catsup**
½ **of a 6-ounce can (⅓ cup) frozen pineapple-orange juice concentrate**
2 **tablespoons steak sauce**
1 **4-pound boneless beef round rump roast**

1 For sauce, in saucepan cook onion in oil till tender. Stir in brown sugar, cornstarch, and ½ teaspoon *salt*. Stir in catsup, pineapple-orange juice concentrate, steak sauce, and ½ cup *water*. Cook and stir till mixture is thickened and concentrate is melted. Cook and stir 2 minutes more.

2 If desired, treat roast with meat tenderizer according to package directions. Insert a spit rod through center of roast. Insert a meat thermometer near the center of the roast (*do not* allow the thermometer to touch metal rod or fat). Arrange *medium coals* around the drip pan. Attach spit to grill; position drip pan directly under meat.

3 Roast meat over coals for 2 to 2½ hours or till meat thermometer registers 160° for medium. (Or roast in a 325° oven for 2 to 2½ hours.)

4 Brush frequently with sauce during the last 20 minutes of roasting. Let stand 15 minutes before slicing. Heat remaining sauce to pass with meat. Serves 8 to 10.

STRAWBERRY-TOPPED COFFEE CREME

Advance preparation time: 1¾ hours
Final preparation time: 10 minutes

1 **envelope unflavored gelatin**
1 **teaspoon instant coffee crystals**
¾ **cup cold water**
1 **8-ounce package cream cheese, cut up**
½ **cup sugar**
¼ **cup coffee liqueur**
1 **cup whipping cream**
1 **pint strawberries, halved**
¼ **cup sugar**

1 In a small saucepan soften gelatin in cold water. Add coffee crystals. Cook and stir over low heat till gelatin and coffee are dissolved. Cool to room temperature.

2 In a small mixer bowl beat together the cream cheese and the ½ cup sugar. Beat in gelatin mixture and coffee liqueur. Chill till the consistency of unbeaten egg whites (partially set).

3 Whip cream to soft peaks. Fold into gelatin mixture. Spoon into a 4-cup mold. Cover and chill several hours or overnight.

Before serving: Combine strawberries and the ¼ cup sugar. Unmold coffee creme onto a serving platter by dipping mold quickly into a basin of warm water and inverting over platter. Serve strawberries over coffee creme. Makes 8 servings.

If you enjoy picnics but don't want to be bothered with the hassle, try this zesty picnic menu. There's no fire to light and no last-minute food to prepare. Just make the Deviled Drumsticks, Picnic Coleslaw, and Chocolate Cupcakes ahead. Then the only thing you'll have to do before digging-in is toss the salad.

NO-HASSLE PICNIC

DEVILED DRUMSTICKS

PICNIC COLESLAW

POTATO CHIPS

CHOCOLATE CUPCAKES

BEVERAGES

UP TO 1 DAY BEFORE SERVING
- Prepare Deviled Drumsticks and chill.
- Prepare Chocolate Cupcakes and store.
- Prepare vegetables and dressing for Picnic Coleslaw and store.

AT SERVING TIME
- Toss dressing with vegetables for Picnic Coleslaw.

Deviled Drumsticks
(see recipe, page 70)
Chocolate Cupcakes
(see recipe, page 70)
Picnic Coleslaw
(see recipe, page 70)

DEVILED DRUMSTICKS

Pictured on pages 68 and 69—
Add a little variety to the drumsticks by crushing 1 teaspoon dried marjoram, basil, rosemary, or sage, and substituting it for the curry powder—

Assembling time: 10 minutes
Cooking time: 1 hour

½ cup fine dry bread crumbs
2 teaspoons onion powder
2 teaspoons curry powder
¾ teaspoon salt
½ teaspoon dry mustard
¼ teaspoon garlic powder
¼ teaspoon paprika
Dash ground red pepper
12 chicken drumsticks (about 2¼ pounds) *or* one 2½- to 3-pound broiler-fryer chicken, cut up
¼ cup milk

1 In a mixing bowl combine fine dry bread crumbs, onion powder, curry powder, salt, dry mustard, garlic powder, paprika, and ground red pepper. Dip chicken pieces in milk and then in crumb mixture.
2 Place chicken, skin side up, in a greased shallow baking pan. Bake in a 375° oven about 1 hour or till chicken is tender. Chill chicken till picnic time. Pack in a covered container. Makes 6 servings.

PICNIC COLESLAW

Pictured on pages 68 and 69—

Assembling time: 15 minutes

2½ cups shredded cabbage
1 cup shredded carrot
½ small red onion, thinly sliced and separated into rings
½ cup dairy sour cream
2 tablespoons tarragon vinegar
1 tablespoon sugar

1 Layer cabbage, carrot, and onion in a salad bowl. Cover surface with plastic wrap. Chill. To make dressing, stir together sour cream, vinegar, sugar, and ½ teaspoon *salt*. Pour into a container with a tight lid. Cover and chill. At picnic time, pour dressing over vegetables in the bowl. Toss to mix well. Makes 6 servings.

CHOCOLATE CUPCAKES

Pictured on pages 68 and 69—

Total preparation time: 35 minutes

1 package 2-layer-size chocolate cake mix
1 6-ounce package semisweet chocolate pieces
1 teaspoon finely shredded orange peel
½ teaspoon ground cinnamon
1 can sour cream white frosting

1 Prepare cake batter according to package directions. Stir in chocolate pieces, orange peel, and cinnamon. Divide chocolate mixture among 24 to 26 paper-bake-cup-lined muffin cups, filling each ⅔ full.
2 Bake in a 350° oven for 20 to 25 minutes or till done. Cool. Frost with sour cream white frosting. Makes 24 to 26.

It doesn't take hard work, just a little careful planning, to assemble a picnic outdoors. Start by deciding what essentials you'll need for your picnic and pack those first.

If there are no tables at your picnic site, you'll want to pack a blanket or plastic ground cover to sit on. Then you'll also need a tablecloth, napkins, paper plates, plastic or paper cups, plastic or regular silverware, moist towelettes, serving utensils, and paper or plastic garbage bags.

Pack for convenience and safety. For example, wrap each setting of silverware in a napkin to keep it from rattling in your picnic basket and to speed up "table" setting. Or, use the ground cover or tablecloth as a wrapper to protect any glass food or beverage containers.

When it comes to food, remember to keep cold foods cold and warm foods warm. Avoid taking creamed foods such as custards, puddings, and cream pies, since they are susceptible to bacterial growth at warm temperatures.

Pack refrigerated food last before leaving home. Have meats tightly wrapped and well chilled in advance. To ensure that they will stay cold, place them in the bottom of the cooler. If you're taking an oil-based or mayonnaise-based salad dressing, pack it separately from the salad and keep it chilled in the cooler.

Spaghetti, toasty bread, and brownies are surefire family favorites. And they're sure to be your favorites too, when you use these simple, fast, and delicious recipes. They start with ingredients you're likely to keep on hand. For example, Spicy Cream Cheese Brownies start with a walnut brownie mix and add a novel twist to the flavor with cinnamon and cream cheese. And Cheese-Topped Buns are an herb-and-cheese-flavored toasty bread that's super simple to make because you start with hamburger buns.

FAVORITE FAMILY DINNER

QUICK AND EASY SPAGHETTI

PEACH SLICES

CHEESE-TOPPED BUNS

SPICY CREAM CHEESE BROWNIES

BEVERAGE

UP TO 1 DAY BEFORE SERVING
■ Prepare Spicy Cream Cheese Brownies.
35 MINUTES BEFORE SERVING
■ Prepare Quick and Easy Spaghetti.
15 MINUTES BEFORE SERVING
■ Spoon peach slices into serving bowls.
■ Prepare Cheese-Topped Buns.
■ Prepare beverage.

QUICK AND EASY SPAGHETTI

This one-saucepan spaghetti sauce is so easy that it's ideal for the kids' night in the kitchen—

Assembling time: 15 minutes
Cooking time: 15 minutes

1 **pound ground pork** *or* **ground beef**
1 **large carrot, chopped**
1 **teaspoon cornstarch**
2 **15-ounce cans tomato sauce**
1 **4-ounce can sliced mushrooms, drained**
1 **teaspoon dried oregano, crushed**
1 **teaspoon Worcestershire sauce**
½ **teasoon sugar**
½ **teaspoon dried basil, crushed**
¼ **teaspoon garlic powder**
¼ **teaspoon salt**
  Hot cooked spaghetti
  Grated Parmesan cheese

1 In a 3-quart saucepan cook the ground pork or ground beef and carrot till the meat is browned. Drain off fat. Stir in cornstarch. Add tomato sauce, mushrooms, oregano, Worcestershire, sugar, basil, garlic powder, and salt.

2 Bring mixture to boiling; reduce heat. Simmer, uncovered, about 15 minutes, stirring occasionally. Serve over hot cooked spaghetti. Pass grated Parmesan cheese. Makes 6 servings.

CHEESE-TOPPED BUNS

Assembling time: 5 minutes
Cooking time: 3 minutes

¼ **cup butter** *or* **margarine, softened**
2 **tablespoons grated Parmesan cheese**
½ **teaspoon dried basil, crushed**
3 **hamburger buns, split**

1 In a small bowl stir together butter or margarine, cheese, and basil. Spread on split buns. Place on the rack of an unheated broiler pan. Broil 4 inches from heat for 2 to 3 minutes or till toasted. Serves 6.

SPICY CREAM CHEESE BROWNIES

Assembling time: 12 minutes
Cooking time: 35 minutes

1 **23¾-ounce package walnut brownie mix**
¾ **teaspoon cinnamon**
1 **3-ounce package cream cheese, cut up**
¼ **cup sugar**
1 **egg**
½ **teaspoon vanilla**

1 Grease a 13x9x2-inch pan. Stir together brownie mix and cinnamon; prepare according to package directions. In a small mixer bowl beat cream cheese for 30 seconds. Add sugar; beat till fluffy. Beat in egg and vanilla.

2 Spread *half* of the brownie mixture in the prepared pan. Top with the cream cheese mixture and the remaining brownie mixture. Swirl layers to marble. Bake in a 350° oven about 35 minutes or till done. Cool completely before cutting into bars. Makes 32 bars.

It's often difficult to get everyone together at a "regular" dinner hour. That's when you need a menu like Anytime Dinner. The real value of this taste-tantalizing meal is that it can be served hot or cold. Thus, the early birds can have an appetizing hot dinner, while those who come home later can enjoy it cold. If your time is on the short side, make and bake Summer Meat Loaf in advance.

ANYTIME DINNER

SUMMER MEAT LOAF

CREAMY BEAN AND BROCCOLI TOSS

COCONUT-GRANOLA BARS

BEVERAGE

UP TO 1 DAY BEFORE SERVING
- Prepare Coconut Granola Bars and store.
- Prepare vegetables and dressing for Creamy Bean and Broccoli Toss and chill.
- Prepare Summer Meat Loaf and chill, if serving it cold.

1¼ HOURS BEFORE SERVING
- Prepare Summer Meat Loaf, if serving it warm.

10 MINUTES BEFORE SERVING
- Fold together vegetables and dressing for Creamy Bean and Broccoli Toss.
- Slice meat loaf.
- Prepare beverage.

SUMMER MEAT LOAF

Assembling time: 15 minutes
Cooking time: 1½ hours

½ cup chopped onion
½ cup shredded carrot
¼ cup chopped green pepper
2 slightly beaten eggs
1½ cups soft bread crumbs
1 cup cottage cheese, drained
1 teaspoon salt
1 teaspoon poultry seasoning
2 pounds ground beef
¾ cup catsup

1 Cook onion, carrot, and pepper, covered, in a small amount of boiling water, for 5 minutes; drain. Mix eggs, crumbs, cheese, salt, and poultry seasoning. Stir in vegetables. Add beef; mix well. Pat into a 9x5x3-inch loaf pan.
2 Bake, uncovered, in a 350° oven about 1½ hours. Drain meat loaf. Serve either warm or chilled with catsup. Serves 8.

COCONUT-GRANOLA BARS

Assembling time: 5 minutes
Cooking time: 40 minutes

1 17-ounce package date quick bread mix
½ cup quick-cooking rolled oats
½ cup flaked coconut
½ teaspoon ground cinnamon
1 egg
1 cup orange juice

1 Grease and flour an 11x7x1½-inch baking pan. Combine bread mix, oats, coconut, and cinnamon. Beat together egg and orange juice. Stir into oat mixture just till moistened. Spoon into prepared pan. Bake in a 350° oven for 35 to 40 minutes. Cool on rack. Cut into bars. Makes 20 to 24.

CREAMY BEAN AND BROCCOLI TOSS

Total preparation time: 28 minutes

½ cup mayonnaise or salad dressing
⅓ cup buttermilk
1 .4-ounce envelope buttermilk salad dressing mix or .7-ounce onion salad dressing mix
2 teaspoons anchovy paste
¼ teaspoon onion powder
1½ cups green beans, cut into 1-inch pieces, or one 9-ounce package frozen cut green beans
1½ cups chopped broccoli or one 10-ounce package frozen chopped broccoli
1 16-ounce can whole small carrots, drained

1 In a mixing bowl stir together mayonnaise or salad dressing, buttermilk, salad dressing mix, anchovy paste, and onion powder. Cover and chill till serving time.
2 Meanwhile, in a large saucepan cook fresh green beans, covered, in boiling salted water for 10 minutes. Add chopped fresh broccoli; cook, covered, for 5 to 10 minutes more or till tender. (Or prepare frozen vegetables according to package directions.) Drain vegetables well.
3 Stir together green beans, broccoli, and carrots. Cover and chill. Just before serving, fold desired amount of salad dressing mixture into vegetables. Spoon into a lettuce-lined bowl, if desired. Cover and chill any remaining salad or dressing. Makes 8 servings.

Summer Meat Loaf
Coconut-Granola Bars
Creamy Bean and Broccoli Toss

After downhill sledding, there's no better way to warm people up than to involve them in preparing a quick hot snack. This delicious menu is tailored for such an occasion. Here's how it works. Divide the participants into three groups. Have the first group make and bake the simple Ham-Pineapple Nibbles. At the same time have the second group cut up the fruit and mix together the flavorful dip. Finally, have the third group heat and serve the Quick Warm-Up Cocoa—sure to warm everyone up in a jiffy!

AFTER-SLEDDING PARTY

HAM-PINEAPPLE NIBBLES

FRUIT AND ORANGE DIP

QUICK WARM-UP COCOA

30 MINUTES BEFORE SERVING

- Assemble the ingredients in three separate work areas.
- Start group 1 making the Ham-Pineapple Nibbles.
- Start group 2 preparing the Fruit and Orange Dip.
- Start group 3 preparing the Quick Warm-Up Cocoa.

HAM-PINEAPPLE NIBBLES

These meat-filled pastries are easy to make because you start with crescent rolls and ground fully cooked ham—

Assembling time: 15 minutes
Cooking time: 13 minutes

- 2 packages (8 rolls each) refrigerated crescent rolls
- 1 slightly beaten egg
- 1 8¼-ounce can crushed pineapple, drained
- ¼ cup soft bread crumbs
- 2 tablespoons sliced green onion
- ¼ teaspoon ground sage
- 1½ cups ground fully cooked ham
- ½ cup shredded mozzarella cheese *or* shredded cheddar cheese (2 ounces)

1 Separate crescent rolls into eight rectangles. Pinch diagonal seams together. Pat or roll each rectangle to about 8x4 inches. Cut each rectangle of dough crosswise into thirds.

2 In a mixing bowl stir together the egg, drained pineapple, bread crumbs, green onion, and sage. Stir in the ground ham and shredded cheese. Place *one rounded tablespoon* ham mixture on one end of each dough rectangle.

3 Fold other end of dough over filling. Seal with the tines of a fork. Place on a baking sheet and bake in a 375° oven for 10 to 13 minutes or till golden brown. Makes 24 appetizers.

FRUIT AND ORANGE DIP

Assembling time: 20 minutes

- 1 8-ounce package cream cheese, cut up
- 1 7-ounce jar marshmallow creme
- 2 teaspoons finely shredded orange peel
- 2 tablespoons orange juice
- ½ cup broken walnuts
- 3 medium apples, cut into wedges Lemon juice
- 1 11-ounce can mandarin orange sections, drained

1 In a mixer bowl beat together cream cheese, marshmallow creme, orange peel, and juice. Fold in broken walnuts. Brush apple wedges with lemon juice. Alternately thread orange sections and apple wedges on wooden picks. Serve with cream cheese mixture. Makes 2 cups.

QUICK WARM-UP COCOA

Assembling time: 13 minutes

- 2½ cups water
- 2 cups milk
- 6 envelopes instant cocoa mix
- 6 tablespoons rum *or* brandy (optional) Pressurized dessert topping
- 6 cinnamon sticks *or* peppermint sticks (optional)

1 In a large saucepan combine water and milk. Heat to almost boiling. In a large pitcher, empty the cocoa mix; add hot milk mixture. Stir till cocoa is dissolved.

2 Pour cocoa mixture into 6 mugs. Stir *1 tablespoon* rum or brandy into each mug, if desired. Top with dessert topping; add a cinnamon stick or peppermint stick, if desired. Makes 6 (6-ounce) servings.

Preparing a spectacular dinner party for a crowd doesn't have to mean spending all day in the kitchen. With this menu, you'll be able to make most of the dinner the day before the party.

DAZZLING DO-AHEAD DINNER

CHAMPAGNE

SNAP PEA HORS D'OEUVRES

PÂTÉ-STUFFED ROAST WITH WINE MAYONNAISE

WALNUT AND WILD RICE PILAF

ASPARAGUS SPEARS

ASSORTED GLACÉED FRUIT

CHOCOLATE CANDIES

1 DAY BEFORE SERVING
- Prepare and bake roast.
- Prepare and chill wine mayonnaise.
- Prepare and chill Snap Pea Hors d'Oeuvres.
- Prepare and chill the pilaf.
- Chill champagne.

30 MINUTES BEFORE SERVING
- Remove pilaf from refrigerator.
- Arrange fruit and candies on a platter.
- Thinly slice the roast.
- Prepare asparagus spears.
- Toss pilaf mixture with oil.

PÂTÉ-STUFFED ROAST WITH WINE MAYONNAISE

Advance preparation time: 3¼ hours
Final preparation time: 15 minutes

1 6-pound boneless beef rib roast
2 4¾-ounce cans liver pâté *or* liver spread
⅓ cup chopped pistachio nuts *or* pine nuts
2 teaspoons snipped parsley
1½ cups mayonnaise *or* salad dressing
¼ cup dry white wine
1 tablespoon snipped parsley

1 Untie and unroll beef rib roast. Stir together liver pâté or liver spread, chopped pistachio or pine nuts, and the 2 teaspoons snipped parsley. Spread pâté mixture over unrolled beef rib roast. Reroll and re-tie beef roast.

2 Place roast, fat side up, on a rack in a shallow roasting pan. Sprinkle with salt and pepper. Roast in a 325° oven to desired doneness. (Allow 2½ to 3 hours for rare or till thermometer registers 140°).

3 Cool to room temperature; cover and chill roast. For wine mayonnaise, in a small mixing bowl stir together mayonnaise or salad dressing, white wine, and the 1 tablespoon parsley. Cover and chill mayonnaise mixture till serving time.

Before serving: Thinly slice the chilled meat. Serve with the wine mayonnaise. Makes 12 to 15 servings.

SNAP PEA HORS D'OEUVRES

Advance preparation time: 15 minutes

½ pound sugar snap peas
1 cup cream-style cottage cheese with chives
1 3-ounce package cream cheese, cut up
2 tablespoons cocktail sauce
1 teaspoon dry mustard
Several dashes bottled hot pepper sauce
1 4½-ounce can tiny shrimp

1 Shell peas, reserving peas and pods. In a blender container or food processor bowl combine peas, cottage cheese, cream cheese, cocktail sauce, mustard, and pepper sauce. Cover and blend or process till smooth. Rinse and drain shrimp. Stir shrimp into cheese mixture. Chill till serving time. Serve pea pods as dippers for cheese-shrimp mixture. Makes about 2 cups dip.

WALNUT AND WILD RICE PILAF

Advance preparation time: 15 minutes
Final preparation time: 35 minutes

2 6¼-ounce packages quick-cooking long grain and wild rice mix
1 cup coarsely chopped walnuts
½ cup sliced pitted ripe olives
¼ cup walnut oil *or* salad oil
Lettuce leaves

1 Prepare long grain and wild rice mix according to package directions; cool. Toss cooked rice with chopped nuts and sliced olives. Cover and chill.

Before serving: Let rice mixture stand at room temperature for 30 minutes. Drizzle walnut oil or salad oil over rice mixture; toss. Turn into a lettuce-lined bowl or platter. Makes 12 to 15 servings.

A cocktail party is an easy way to entertain a large group of people—especially when you use this easy make-ahead menu. What's more, we've included a recipe for a champagne punch so you won't need to tend bar.

COCKTAIL PARTY

SHRIMP TURNOVERS

PORK MEATBALLS IN PINEAPPLE SAUCE

GAZPACHO VEGETABLE DIP

CHOCOLATE-DIPPED FRUIT

PEACH-PINEAPPLE CHAMPAGNE PUNCH

(Also see recipes on page 78)

UP TO 1 WEEK BEFORE SERVING
- Prepare and freeze meatballs.

UP TO 1 DAY BEFORE SERVING
- Prepare Gazpacho Vegetable Dip.
- Stir together and chill the pineapple preserve mixture for the meatballs.
- Chill the ingredients for the punch.
- Prepare and chill Chocolate-Dipped Fruit.

UP TO 6 HOURS BEFORE SERVING
- Prepare and chill Shrimp Turnovers.

30 MINUTES BEFORE SERVING
- Finish preparing meatballs.
- Bake the Shrimp Turnovers.
- Prepare the punch.

Peach-Pineapple Champagne Punch (see recipe, page 78)
Gazpacho Vegetable Dip
Shrimp Turnovers (see recipe, page 78)
Pork Meatballs in Pineapple Sauce
Chocolate-Dipped Fruit

PORK MEATBALLS IN PINEAPPLE SAUCE

Advance preparation time: 40 minutes
Final preparation time: 20 minutes

- 1 beaten egg
- 1/3 cup milk
- 1/2 cup corn bread stuffing mix
- 3/4 teaspoon salt
- 1/2 teaspoon ground sage
- 1/8 teaspoon ground pepper
- 1 pound ground pork
- 1/2 cup pineapple preserves
- 1/4 cup water
- 2 tablespoons vinegar
- 1/4 teaspoon ground ginger

1 In a mixing bowl combine egg and milk. Stir in stuffing mix, salt, sage, and pepper. Add ground pork; mix well. Shape meat mixture into 48 meatballs. Place on a rack in a shallow baking pan.

2 Bake in a 375° oven for 20 to 25 minutes or till done. Remove from pan. Drain on paper toweling. When cool, spread meatballs out on a shallow baking pan. Cover with moisture vaporproof wrap; freeze. When frozen, place meatballs in freezer containers; freeze.

3 Stir together the pineapple preserves, water, vinegar, and ground ginger. Cover and chill till just before serving time.

Before serving: Place pineapple mixture in a large saucepan. Cook and stir over low heat till heated through. Add frozen meatballs. Cover and cook over medium heat about 10 minutes or till meatballs are heated through, stirring occasionally. To serve, spear with cocktail picks. Makes 48 meatballs.

CHOCOLATE-DIPPED FRUIT

Advance preparation time: 35 minutes

- 3 squares (3 ounces) semisweet chocolate
- 1½ teaspoons shortening
  Assorted fresh fruit (fresh pineapple, peeled and cut into 2-inch chunks; fresh strawberries; oranges, peeled and sectioned)

1 In a small saucepan melt chocolate and shortening over low heat. Use paper toweling to pat the fruit dry. Dip the fruit pieces into melted chocolate (chocolate does not need to completely cover fruit).

2 Place the fruit on waxed-paper-lined baking sheets. Chill till chocolate is set. Cover with plastic wrap; chill till serving time. Makes about 40.

GAZPACHO VEGETABLE DIP

Cut up the vegetable dippers a day before the party. Then refrigerate in water—

Advance preparation time: 20 minutes

- 1 8-ounce package cream cheese, cut up
- 1/4 cup hot chili salsa
- 1 to 2 tablespoons jalapeño pepper relish
- 1 tablespoon lemon juice
- 1 teaspoon Worcestershire sauce
- 1 green pepper, chopped (1/2 cup)
  Assorted vegetables for dipping

1 Beat cream cheese till fluffy. Beat in salsa, relish, lemon juice, Worcestershire sauce, 1/4 teaspoon *salt*, and a dash *pepper*. Stir in green pepper. Cover and chill till serving time. Serve with vegetable dippers. Makes 1 3/4 cups.

SHRIMP TURNOVERS

Pictured on page 76—

Advance preparation time: 15 minutes
Final preparation time: 20 minutes

1 3-ounce package cream cheese
   with chives, cut up
½ of a 5-ounce jar neufchâtel cheese
   spread with pimiento (⅓ cup)
1 4½-ounce can tiny shrimp, rinsed
3 packages (6 rolls each)
   refrigerated flaky dinner rolls
1 egg white

1 Beat together cheeses. Drain shrimp; fold into cheese mixture. Separate *each* roll into 2 pieces. Form a "pocket" in each by separating the layers. Fill each with ½ *tablespoon* shrimp mixture. Brush edges with water; seal. Place on baking sheets. Cover; chill up to 6 hours.
   Before serving: Mix egg white and 1 tablespoon *water.* Brush rolls with mixture. If desired, top with sesame seed. Bake in 375° oven 15 to 18 minutes. Makes 36.

PEACH-PINEAPPLE CHAMPAGNE PUNCH

Pictured on page 76—

Total preparation time: 5 minutes

1 46-ounce can unsweetened
   pineapple juice, chilled
1 46-ounce can peach nectar, chilled
3 750-milliliter bottles champagne,
   chilled

1 Stir together juice, nectar, and 2 cups *water.* Add champagne; stir gently. If desired, garnish with orange and lemon slices. Makes 50 (4-ounce) servings.

A casual patio party is a great way to spend a warm summer evening with close friends. And this enticing selection of food is sure to make it a success. Enjoy the wholesome goodness of Orange-Maple Fruit Dip, Savory Ham Crescents, and Rosé Punch. The real plus in this menu is that it's easy on you—almost everything can be prepared ahead of time so there's not a lot of last-minute fuss.

PLAN-AHEAD PATIO PARTY

HAM CRESCENTS

ORANGE-MAPLE FRUIT DIP

MARINATED CAULIFLOWER

ROSÉ PUNCH

1 DAY BEFORE SERVING
■ Prepare Marinated Cauliflower.
■ Prepare the Orange-Maple Fruit Dip.
2 HOURS BEFORE SERVING
■ Prepare and chill the Ham Crescents.
45 MINUTES BEFORE SERVING
■ Bake the Ham Crescents.
■ Cut up the fruit to go with the fruit dip.
■ Prepare the Rosé Punch.
■ Drain the Marinated Cauliflower.

HAM CRESCENTS

Advance preparation time: 20 minutes
Final preparation time: 42 minutes

¾ pound ground fully cooked ham
½ cup meatless spaghetti sauce
¼ cup chopped green pepper
2 packages (8 rolls each)
   refrigerated crescent rolls

1 Stir together ham, spaghetti sauce, and green pepper. Separate rolls into 16 triangles. At wide end of each, place about *3 tablespoons* of the ham mixture.
2 Roll up, starting at wide end. Arrange on a greased baking sheet. Cover and chill for up to 2 hours.
   Before serving: Bake in a 375° oven 25 to 30 minutes. Let cool 10 minutes. Dollop with plain yogurt, if desired. Makes 16.

ORANGE-MAPLE FRUIT DIP

Advance preparation time: 18 minutes
Final preparation time: 10 minutes

2 3-ounce packages cream cheese,
   cut up
½ cup maple-flavored syrup
1 teaspoon shredded orange peel
¼ cup orange juice
1 cup whipping cream
⅔ cup broken pecans
   Assorted fresh fruit*
   Lemon juice

1 Beat cream cheese till fluffy. Beat in syrup, peel, and orange juice. Whip cream till soft peaks form; fold into cheese mixture. Fold in nuts. Cover; chill for up to 12 hours.
   Before serving: Brush fruit with lemon juice. Serve with dip. Makes 1⅔ cups.
   *Choose from any of the following: fresh berries; melon balls; sliced peaches; sliced nectarines; sliced plums; orange sections; sliced apples; *or* sliced bananas.

MARINATED CAULIFLOWER

Advance preparation time: 20 minutes

- 1 small head cauliflower, cut into flowerets
- 1 10-ounce package frozen cut broccoli
- 1½ cups frozen crinkle-cut carrots
- 1 small zucchini, sliced
- 1 green pepper, cut into strips
- ¾ cup cooking oil
- ½ cup wine vinegar
- 2 tablespoons brown sugar
- 2 tablespoons lemon juice
- 2 teaspoons celery seed
- 1 teaspoon ground ginger
- 1 teaspoon ground nutmeg

1 Cook cauliflower, covered, in a small amount of boiling salted water about 5 minutes or just till tender. Drain and cool slightly. Meanwhile, cook broccoli and carrots according to package directions; drain and cool slightly. Place cauliflower, broccoli, carrots, zucchini, and green pepper in a plastic bag set in a shallow pan.

2 For marinade, combine oil, vinegar, brown sugar, lemon juice, celery seed, ginger, nutmeg, and ¾ teaspoon *salt*. Pour over vegetables. Close bag. Chill several hours or overnight, turning occasionally.

Before serving: Drain vegetables; discard marinade. Makes about 7 cups.

ROSÉ PUNCH

Assembling time: 5 minutes

- 1 32-ounce bottle carbonated water
- 2 750-milliliter bottles rosé wine
- 1 orange, thinly sliced

1 In a pitcher slowly pour the carbonated water into the wine. Add orange slices. Pour into ice-filled glasses. Makes 16 (5-ounce) servings.

Your poolside party will be a "splashing" success when you serve these easy, zesty refreshments. You can prepare ahead for thirsty guests by doubling the recipe for Tropical Slush and freezing it in two containers. Take the slush out of the freezer when you start to swim. By the time everyone's ready for a break, the slush will be just right to mix with the carbonated beverage.

SPLASHING POOL PARTY

SALMON SPREAD

TROPICAL SLUSH

UP TO 8 WEEKS BEFORE SERVING
- Prepare and freeze Tropical Slush.

UP TO 2 DAYS BEFORE SERVING
- Prepare and chill Salmon Spread.
- Chill carbonated beverage for Tropical Slush.

2 HOURS BEFORE SERVING
- Remove Tropical Slush from the freezer.

AT SERVING TIME
- Spread Salmon Spread on melba toast or toasted bagels.
- Add carbonated beverage to slush.

TROPICAL SLUSH

Advance preparation time: 5 minutes
Final preparation time: 2 hours

- 1½ cups unsweetened pineapple juice
- 1 6-ounce can frozen lemonade concentrate
- 2 medium ripe bananas, cut up
  Lemon-lime carbonated beverage *or* club soda, chilled

1 In a blender container combine pineapple juice, lemonade concentrate, and bananas. Cover; blend till smooth. Pour into a freezer container. Seal, label, and freeze.

Before serving: Thaw slush for 1½ to 2 hours. Spoon *3 to 4 tablespoons* of slush into each glass. Pour about ⅓ cup carbonated beverage or club soda over slush in each glass. Makes 3¼ cups slush.

SALMON SPREAD

Advance preparation time: 10 minutes
Final preparation time: 5 minutes

- 1 8-ounce package cream cheese, cut up
- 1 tablespoon milk
- ⅛ teaspoon onion powder
  Several drops bottled hot pepper sauce
- 1 7¾-ounce can salmon, drained, finely flaked, and skin and bones removed
- ¼ cup finely chopped celery
- ¼ cup sliced pimiento-stuffed olives
  Melba toast rounds *or* toasted bagels

1 In a bowl beat cream cheese till fluffy. Beat in milk, onion powder, and hot pepper sauce. Stir in salmon, celery, and olives. Cover and chill till serving time.

Before serving: Spread on toast or bagels. Top bagels with lettuce and a tomato slice, if desired. Makes 2¼ cups spread.

WEEKEND OF GREAT MEALS

When you're having company for the weekend, don't think you have to be a "prisoner" of your kitchen. Let this weekend of great meals set you free!

This meal plan is designed to give you a head start on each meal through the use of carry-over foods. For example, the star of Friday's feast becomes the basis for a delicious spin-off featured in Saturday's breakfast. And this pattern continues throughout the whole weekend. Each meal adequately serves six people with enough surplus food to create new dishes for later in the weekend. Even though the meals are designed to go together, they'll each stand equally well on their own. For each recipe that calls for a carry-over food, we've suggested an alternate ingredient. This way you can prepare only those meals that fit into your weekend plans.

Mediterranean Stroganoff
Turmeric Rice (see recipe, page 84)
Rum 'n' Coffee Cream (see recipe, page 84)
Spice Diamonds (see recipe, page 84)
Bok Choy Salad (see recipe, page 84)
Marinated Shrimp and Artichoke Hearts

Start the weekend off right with a delicious Friday night dinner. Marinated Shrimp and Artichoke Hearts make a sophisticated appetizer for dinner. Mediterranean Stroganoff is a meatless version of the classic stroganoff that's complemented by Oriental-style Bok Choy Salad.

FRIDAY DINNER

MARINATED SHRIMP AND ARTICHOKE HEARTS

MEDITERRANEAN STROGANOFF

TURMERIC RICE

BOK CHOY SALAD

RUM 'N' COFFEE CREAM

SPICE DIAMONDS

(Also see recipes on page 84)

ONE DAY BEFORE SERVING
- Prepare Marinated Shrimp and Artichoke Hearts.
- Prepare the Spice Diamonds.

45 MINUTES BEFORE SERVING
- Cook vegetables for Mediterranean Stroganoff.
- Prepare Turmeric Rice.
- Finish preparing stroganoff.
- Drain and arrange appetizer.
- Prepare Bok Choy Salad.

5 MINUTES BEFORE SERVING
- Prepare Rum 'n' Coffee Cream.

MARINATED SHRIMP AND ARTICHOKE HEARTS

Pictured left and on pages 83 and 89—

Advance preparation time: 20 minutes

1 cup salad oil
½ cup vinegar
⅓ cup dry white wine
1 tablespoon snipped parsley
1 teaspoon sugar
1 teaspoon dried coriander, crushed (optional)
½ teaspoon salt
½ teaspoon paprika
¼ teaspoon whole black peppercorns
1 clove garlic, minced
2 pounds medium shrimp, cooked, drained, peeled, and deveined
2 9-ounce packages frozen artichoke hearts, thawed and halved, *or* two 14-ounce cans artichoke hearts, drained and halved
1 small onion, sliced into half-rings
1 8-ounce can sliced water chestnuts, drained

1 In a screw-top jar combine salad oil; vinegar; wine; parsley; sugar; coriander, if desired; salt; paprika; peppercorns; and garlic; cover and shake well to mix.

2 In a 4-quart container place shrimp, and remaining ingredients. Pour oil mixture over shrimp mixture. Cover and chill overnight; stir occasionally. Makes 12 cups.

Before serving: *For Friday dinner,* drain 4 cups mixture. Spoon into shrimp icers or goblets partially filled with crushed ice. If desired, serve with *bottled cocktail sauce.*

For Saturday breakfast, drain 4 cups of the mixture. Place in a lettuce-lined salad bowl; garnish with *caviar,* if desired.

For Sunday brunch, serve remaining mixture, drained, in 4 to 6 *lettuce cups.*

MEDITERRANEAN STROGANOFF

Total preparation time: 35 minutes

3 cups fresh broccoli cut into bite-size pieces *or* two 10-ounce packages frozen cut broccoli
4 carrots, thinly bias-sliced
1 pound fresh mushrooms, sliced
1 medium leek, sliced
1 clove garlic, minced
¼ cup butter *or* margarine
3 tablespoons all-purpose flour
1 teaspoon instant chicken bouillon granules
2 cups light cream *or* milk
2 tablespoons soy sauce
½ cup dry white wine
½ cup sliced pitted ripe olives
1 cup dairy sour cream
1 cup ricotta cheese
½ cup grated Parmesan cheese
Turmeric Rice (see recipe, page 84)
Grated Parmesan cheese

1 Cook broccoli and carrots together, covered, in boiling salted water about 5 minutes or till crisp-tender; drain. In skillet cook mushrooms, leek, and garlic in butter or margarine till mushrooms are tender.

2 Stir flour and bouillon granules into mushroom mixture. Stir in cream and soy sauce all at once. Cook and stir till thick and bubbly. Cook and stir 1 minute more. Stir in broccoli, carrots, wine, and olives.

3 Combine sour cream, ricotta cheese, and the ½ cup Parmesan. Gradually stir about *1 cup* of the hot mixture into sour cream mixture; return all to skillet. Cook over medium heat for 3 to 4 minutes or till heated through. *Do not boil.*

4 Reserve *1½ cups* of the mixture for Garden Frittata Parmesan (see recipe, page 82). Spoon remaining mixture over Turmeric Rice. If desired, garnish with carrot curls, whole olives, and parsley sprigs. Pass additional Parmesan. Makes 6 servings.

WEEKEND OF GREAT MEALS

You won't have to rise with the sun on Saturday to serve your guests this mouth-watering breakfast. Just use foods from Friday night's feast to create the basis for some of your dishes. Garden Frittata Parmesan calls for the stroganoff served Friday. And Friday's Marinated Shrimp and Artichoke Hearts creates a pleasant side dish. The Rum 'n' Coffee Cream dessert reappears as Rum Café au Lait. Add Honey Fruit Compote and Coconut Drop Biscuits and you're ready to serve a taste-tantalizing breakfast!

SATURDAY BREAKFAST

GARDEN FRITTATA PARMESAN

MARINATED SHRIMP AND ARTICHOKE HEARTS

COCONUT DROP BISCUITS

HONEY FRUIT COMPOTE

RUM CAFÉ AU LAIT

(Also see recipes on pages 81 and 84)

50 MINUTES BEFORE SERVING
- Prepare and chill Honey Fruit Compote.
- Brew coffee for Rum Café au Lait.
- Prepare Coconut Drop Biscuits.
- Drain the Marinated Shrimp and Artichoke Hearts; place in lettuce-lined bowl and garnish, if desired.

20 MINUTES BEFORE SERVING
- While biscuits are baking, prepare Garden Frittata Parmesan.
- Broil the frittata.
- Finish preparing Rum Café au Lait.

GARDEN FRITTATA PARMESAN

Assembling time: 5 minutes
Cooking time: 7 minutes

8 eggs
¼ cup grated Parmesan cheese
¼ teaspoon salt
⅛ teaspoon pepper
1½ cups reserved Mediterranean Stroganoff (see recipe, page 81) *or* cooked creamed vegetables
2 tablespoons butter *or* margarine
6 thin tomato slices
Cooking oil
1 tablespoon grated Parmesan cheese

1 In a medium mixing bowl beat together eggs and the ¼ cup Parmesan cheese, the salt, and pepper till frothy. Stir in reserved Mediterranean Stroganoff or creamed vegetables.

2 In a 10-inch oven-going skillet or omelet pan melt the butter or margarine. Pour egg mixture into the hot skillet. Cook over medium heat, lifting edges occasionally to allow uncooked portion to flow underneath. Cook about 4 minutes or till top is almost set and bottom is light brown.

3 Broil 4 to 5 inches from heat for 1 to 2 minutes or till set. Top with tomato slices; brush lightly with oil. Sprinkle tomato with the 1 tablespoon Parmesan cheese; broil about 1 minute more or till tomatoes are heated through. Cut into wedges to serve. Makes 6 servings.

HONEY FRUIT COMPOTE

This delightful combination of winter fruit is mildly sweetened with honey—

Assembling time: 15 minutes

1 20-ounce can pineapple chunks (juice pack)
2 11-ounce cans mandarin orange sections, drained
1½ cups seedless green *or* red grapes, seeded and halved
3 kiwi, peeled, halved lengthwise, and sliced
3 tablespoons pomegranate seeds (optional)
½ cup orange juice
¼ cup honey
1 tablespoon lemon juice

1 Drain pineapple, reserving juice. In a large bowl combine drained pineapple chunks, mandarin orange sections, green or red grapes, kiwi slices, and pomegranate seeds, if desired.

2 Add water, if necessary, to reserved pineapple juice to make 1 cup liquid. Combine pineapple juice mixture, orange juice, honey, and lemon juice; pour over fruit. Cover and chill till serving time.

3 Reserve *1 cup* of fruit mixture for Bacon-Stuffed Pork (see recipe, page 87). Serve remaining fruit mixture in dessert dishes. Makes 6 servings.

Garden Frittata Parmesan
Marinated Shrimp and Artichoke Hearts (see recipe, page 81)
Coconut Drop Biscuits (see recipe, page 84)
Honey Fruit Compote
Rum Café au Lait (see recipe, page 84)

TURMERIC RICE

Pictured on page 80—
It's important to use the short grain rice if you're planning to make the Sizzling Rice Soup (see recipe, page 85). If you're not making the soup, you can substitute quick-cooking rice. Just add the turmeric to the rice along with the butter and salt. Then cook according to package directions.

Assembling time: 5 minutes
Cooking time: 20 minutes

    2 cups short grain rice
    2 tablespoons butter *or* margarine
    ¼ teaspoon ground turmeric

1 Bring rice, butter, turmeric, 4 cups *water*, and 2 teaspoons *salt* to boiling. Reduce heat. Cover and simmer about 20 minutes or till rice is tender and water is absorbed. Reserve *1 cup* of the rice for Sizzling Rice Soup. Serve the remaining rice with Mediterranean Stroganoff (see recipe, page 81). Serves 6.

RUM 'N' COFFEE CREAM

Pictured on page 80—

Assembling time: 5 minutes

    1 quart coffee ice cream
    ½ cup rum *or* brandy
      Whipped cream
    2 1⅛-ounce bars chocolate-coated
      English toffee, coarsely chopped

1 Place ice cream and rum or brandy in a blender container; cover and blend till smooth. Freeze *½ cup* of the mixture for Rum Café au Lait (see recipe on this page). Pour remaining mixture into dessert goblets or wineglasses; top with whipped cream and sprinkle with chopped candy bars. Serve at once. Makes 6 servings.

BOK CHOY SALAD

Pictured on page 80—

Advance preparation time: 5 minutes
Final preparation time: 10 minutes

    ¼ cup salad oil
    3 tablespoons lemon *or* lime juice
    1 tablespoon honey
    1½ teaspoons soy sauce
    1 teaspoon sesame seed, toasted
    ½ teaspoon paprika
    6 cups torn bok choy
    ⅓ cup walnut halves
    ¼ cup raisins

1 Mix first six ingredients and ½ teaspoon *salt*. Cover; shake well. Toss with bok choy, nuts, and raisins. Serves 6.

SPICE DIAMONDS

Pictured on page 80—
Save half of this recipe for Eggnog Custard Pie (see recipe, page 85)—

Total preparation time: 30 minutes

    ½ cup shortening
    ¼ cup sugar
    ¼ cup packed brown sugar
    2 tablespoons milk
    1 egg yolk
    1 teaspoon vanilla
    1¼ cups all-purpose flour
    1 teaspoon cream of tartar
    ½ teaspoon baking soda
    ½ teaspoon ground cinnamon

1 Cream shortening and sugars; beat in milk, egg yolk, and vanilla. Combine flour, cream of tartar, soda, cinnamon, and ¼ teaspoon *salt*; add to sugar mixture. Mix well. Spread in greased 13x9x2-inch baking pan. Bake in 350° oven for 12 to 15 minutes. Cool; if desired, sprinkle powdered sugar atop. Cut into diamonds. Makes 24.

COCONUT DROP BISCUITS

Pictured on page 83—

Assembling time: 10 minutes
Cooking time: 12 minutes

    2 cups all-purpose flour
    ¾ cup coconut, toasted
    2 tablespoons sugar
    1 tablespoon baking powder
    ⅓ cup shortening
    1 cup milk
    ½ teaspoon vanilla

1 Stir together the flour, coconut, sugar, baking powder, and ½ teaspoon *salt*. Cut in shortening till mixture resembles coarse crumbs. Combine milk and vanilla.
2 Make a well in the center of the dry ingredients; add milk mixture all at once. Stir just till dough clings together. Drop dough from a tablespoon onto a greased baking sheet. Bake in a 450° oven for 10 to 12 minutes. Makes 12 to 15.

RUM CAFÉ AU LAIT

Pictured on page 83—
If you didn't make the Rum 'n' Coffee Cream dessert, substitute ½ cup softened vanilla ice cream mixed with 1 tablespoon rum or brandy for the dessert mixture—

Assembling time: 20 minutes

    6 cups hot strong coffee
    ½ cup reserved frozen Rum 'n'
      Coffee Cream mixture (see
      recipe on this page)

1 Pour coffee into mugs; top each with a scoop of the reserved cream mixture. If desired, garnish with cinnamon sticks. Serves 6.

Saturday dinner takes advantage of three carry-over dishes from the two previous meals. The fruit compote served for breakfast is transformed into a fruit sauce, which is poured over the Bacon-Stuffed Pork. Sizzling Rice Soup is Turmeric Rice from Friday night, formed into fried patties and slipped into bubbling chicken broth. And for a luscious dessert, Friday night's cookies return disguised as crumb crust in the Eggnog Custard Pie.

SATURDAY DINNER

SIZZLING RICE SOUP

BACON-STUFFED PORK

BASIL SCALLOPED POTATOES

STEAMED CABBAGE WITH MUSTARD BUTTER OR MUSHROOMS WITH CUCUMBERS

EGGNOG CUSTARD PIE

(Also see recipes and picture on pages 86 and 87)

UP TO 1 DAY BEFORE SERVING
- Prepare and chill Eggnog Custard Pie.

2¾ HOURS BEFORE SERVING
- Prepare Bacon-Stuffed Pork.
- Prepare Basil Scalloped Potatoes.
- Prepare rice patties for soup.

45 MINUTES BEFORE SERVING
- Prepare Fruit Sauce for the pork roast.
- Make Steamed Cabbage with Mustard Butter or Mushrooms with Cucumbers.
- Prepare the Sizzling Rice Soup.

SIZZLING RICE SOUP

Pictured on page 86—
If you're not making the Turmeric Rice (see recipe, page 84), you can substitute 1 cup cooked short grain rice—

Total preparation time: 20 minutes

- **4 cups chicken broth**
- **1 medium leek, thinly sliced (½ cup)**
- **½ cup water chestnuts, drained and thinly sliced**
- **1 cup reserved Turmeric Rice mixture (see recipe, page 84)**
- **Cooking oil**

1 To prepare rice patties, moisten hands and, using about *2 tablespoons* Turmeric Rice mixture for each, make 8 thin patties 2 inches in diameter. Cover and chill till serving time.

2 In a 10-inch skillet heat ½ inch cooking oil to 375°. Fry rice patties, all at once, about 5 minutes or till crispy and golden. Meanwhile, in a saucepan bring broth to boiling. Add leek and water chestnuts; reduce heat and simmer about 2 minutes. Keep warm over low heat.

3 Working quickly, use a slotted spoon to transfer the fried rice patties to a large heated serving bowl; pour the hot chicken broth mixture over rice patties (speed is important to obtain the desired sizzling). Serve immediately. Makes 6 servings.

EGGNOG CUSTARD PIE

Pictured on page 86—
If you didn't prepare the Spice Diamonds (see recipe, page 84) for Friday's Dinner, you can substitute a prepared 9-inch pastry shell that's been prebaked in a 450° oven for 5 minutes—

Assembling time: 15 minutes
Cooking time: 45 minutes
Cooling time: 2 hours

- **½ recipe reserved Spice Diamonds (see recipe, page 84), crushed**
- **3 tablespoons butter, melted**
- **1 8-ounce package cream cheese, cut up**
- **⅓ cup packed brown sugar**
- **2 eggs**
- **1½ cups canned *or* dairy eggnog**
- **1 teaspoon vanilla**
- **¼ teaspoon ground nutmeg**
- **1 cup whipping cream**
- **2 tablespoons powdered sugar**

1 To prepare crust, combine crushed Spice Diamonds and melted butter or margarine; toss thoroughly to combine. Press on the bottom and up the sides of a 9-inch pie plate, forming a high edge. Bake in a 350° oven for 5 to 8 minutes; cool while preparing filling.

2 For filling, in bowl beat cream cheese and brown sugar on medium speed of electric mixer till fluffy. Add eggs, beating on low speed just till combined.

3 Gradually stir in eggnog, vanilla, and nutmeg. Turn into the prebaked crust. Cover edges of crust with foil to prevent overbrowning. Bake in a 350° oven for 40 to 45 minutes or till knife inserted near center comes out clean. Cool; chill at least 2 hours.

4 In a mixer bowl beat cream and powdered sugar just till soft peaks form (tips curl over). Using a pastry tube fitted with a star tip, pipe whipped cream in a lattice design atop pie. Chill till serving time. Serves 8.

BASIL SCALLOPED POTATOES

Assembling time: 15 minutes
Cooking time: 1¾ hours
Cooling time: 15 minutes

¼ **cup butter** *or* **margarine**
1 **tablespoon all-purpose flour**
1 **teaspoon salt**
1 **teaspoon dried basil, crushed**
⅛ **teaspoon pepper**
2 **cups milk**
½ **cup snipped parsley**
6 **to 8 medium potatoes, peeled and**
   thinly sliced (6 cups)
½ **cup soft bread crumbs**
1 **tablespoon butter** *or* **margarine,**
   melted
¼ **cup snipped parsley**

1 To make sauce, in a small saucepan melt the ¼ cup butter or margarine; stir in flour, salt, basil, and pepper. Stir in milk all at once. Cook and stir over medium heat till mixture is thickened and bubbly. Cook and stir 1 minute more. Stir in the ½ cup parsley.

2 Grease an 8x8x2-inch baking dish. Combine the sliced potatoes and the hot sauce; pour into baking dish. Cover; bake in a 325° oven for 1 hour. Stir together bread crumbs and the 1 tablespoon melted butter or margarine.

3 Uncover baking dish; sprinkle the center with the bread crumb mixture. Bake 30 to 45 minutes longer or till potatoes are fork-tender.

4 Let stand 15 minutes before serving. Sprinkle with the ¼ cup snipped parsley; garnish with a parsley sprig, if desired. Makes 6 servings.

Basil Scalloped Potatoes
Steamed Cabbage with Mustard Butter
Bacon-Stuffed Pork
Eggnog Custard Pie
(see recipe, page 85)
Sizzling Rice Soup
(see recipe, page 85)

BACON-STUFFED PORK

Substitute ¾ cup chopped fresh fruit and ¼ cup orange juice for the Honey Fruit Compote, if desired—

Assembling time: 30 minutes
Cooking time: 2½ hours

8 **slices bacon**
1 **5-pound boneless pork loin roast**
2 **tablespoons brown sugar**
1 **tablespoon candied ginger,**
   finely chopped
1 **cup reserved Honey Fruit**
   Compote (see recipe, page 82)
¼ **cup dry white wine**
1½ **teaspoons thinly sliced orange**
   peel
¼ **cup orange juice**
½ **teaspoon instant beef bouillon**
   granules
1 **tablespoon cornstarch**

1 Cook bacon till crisp. Remove and drain; crumble and set aside. Cut and discard string of tied roast. Unroll roast; sprinkle with salt and pepper. Sprinkle surface of roast with bacon, brown sugar, and ginger. Reroll meat and tie securely. Place on a rack in a shallow roasting pan.

2 Insert a meat thermometer in center of meat so bulb reaches thickest part. Roast, uncovered, in 325° oven 2 to 2½ hours or till thermometer registers 170°. Transfer to platter; let stand 15 minutes.

3 Meanwhile, prepare fruit sauce. Drain Honey Fruit Compote mixture, reserving juice. Combine reserved juice, wine, orange peel, orange juice, and bouillon.

4 Combine cornstarch and ¼ cup *cold water*; add to juice mixture. Cook and stir till thickened. Cook and stir 2 minutes more. Stir in reserved fruit; heat through. Pour some of the sauce over the roast; pass the remaining sauce. Remove strings as meat is carved. Makes 8 servings. Reserve 2 servings meat for Pork-Filled Gougère (see recipe, page 88).

STEAMED CABBAGE WITH MUSTARD BUTTER

Total preparation time: 10 minutes

1 **medium head cabbage, cut into**
   bite-size pieces
¼ **cup butter** *or* **margarine, softened**
2 **tablespoons prepared mustard**
   Hard-cooked egg, cut into wedges

1 Place cabbage in a steamer basket or metal colander over boiling water in a 4-quart Dutch oven (water should not touch basket). Cover; steam about 5 minutes or till cabbage is tender. Drain well.

2 Combine softened butter or margarine and mustard; toss with cabbage. Season with salt and pepper to taste. Place in serving bowl; garnish with hard-cooked egg wedges. Makes 6 servings.

MUSHROOMS WITH CUCUMBERS

Total preparation time: 15 minutes

4½ **cups sliced fresh mushrooms**
2 **small cucumbers, seeded and cut**
   into julienne strips
1 **medium onion, thinly sliced**
¼ **cup butter** *or* **margarine**
1 **teaspoon all-purpose flour**
¼ **cup dairy sour cream**
⅓ **cup condensed chicken broth**
1 **tablespoon snipped parsley**

1 In a skillet cook mushrooms, cucumber, and onion in butter or margarine for 5 to 6 minutes or just till tender, stirring occasionally. Remove from heat.

2 In a bowl stir flour into the sour cream. Gradually stir chicken broth and parsley into sour cream mixture. Pour over vegetables. Heat through over low heat, stirring constantly. Serve immediately. Serves 6.

WEEKEND OF GREAT MEALS

Here's an elegant way to end a fabulous weekend—with a brunch. Start off with Spinach-Potato Soup, a tasty combination of Saturday night's scalloped potatoes, spinach, and a white sauce. Next move to the salad where the Marinated Shrimp and Artichoke Hearts makes its final appearance. Pork-Filled Gougère is a hearty main dish that calls for Saturday's pork. And end up with Cranberry-Apple Crisp, crowned with crunchy granola and coconut. A superb finalé to a weekend of great meals!

SUNDAY BRUNCH

SPINACH-POTATO SOUP

PORK-FILLED GOUGÈRE

MARINATED SHRIMP AND ARTICHOKE HEARTS

CRANBERRY-APPLE CRISP

BEVERAGE

(Also see recipe, page 81)

1¼ HOURS BEFORE SERVING
- Prepare and bake the gougère dough.
- Prepare and bake the Cranberry-Apple Crisp.
- Drain the Marinated Shrimp and Artichoke Hearts; place in lettuce cups.

30 MINUTES BEFORE SERVING
- Prepare the pork filling for the Pork-Filled Gougère.
- Finish baking the Pork-Filled Gougère.
- Prepare the Spinach-Potato Soup.
- Prepare beverage.

PORK-FILLED GOUGÈRE

Total preparation time: 50 minutes

⅓ cup butter *or* margarine
1 cup all-purpose flour
4 eggs
2 cups shredded Swiss cheese
1 large green pepper, cut into ½-inch squares (1 cup)
1 medium onion, sliced (½ cup)
2 tablespoons snipped parsley
1 clove garlic, minced
1 tablespoon butter *or* margarine
1 tablespoon cornstarch
1 8-ounce can tomato sauce
½ cup dry red *or* white wine
1 tablespoon Worcestershire sauce
1 teaspoon sugar
2 cups reserved Bacon-Stuffed Pork (see recipe, page 87), *or* cooked beef, ham, chicken, *or* turkey cut into bite-size julienne strips

1 Generously grease a 12x7½x2-inch baking dish with butter or margarine. Set aside. In a saucepan combine the ⅓ cup butter, 1 cup *water*, ½ teaspoon *salt*, and a dash *pepper*; bring to boiling. Add flour all at once; cook and stir vigorously till mixture forms a ball that doesn't separate. Remove from heat. Cool 5 minutes.

2 Add eggs one at a time, beating vigorously after each till smooth. Stir in 1¾ cups of the cheese. Spread over bottom and up sides of greased baking dish. Bake in a 400° oven about 20 minutes.

3 Meanwhile, in a saucepan cook green pepper, onion, parsley, and garlic in the 1 tablespoon butter. Cover and cook till vegetables are tender; stir in cornstarch.

4 Add tomato sauce, wine, Worcestershire, and sugar. Cook and stir till thickened and bubbly. Cook and stir 2 minutes more. Stir in meat strips. Pour into hot crust; sprinkle with the remaining ¼ cup cheese. Return to oven; bake 15 to 20 minutes longer or till puffed and golden brown. Serve immediately. Makes 6 servings.

SPINACH-POTATO SOUP

If you don't have any leftover Basil Scalloped Potatoes (see recipe, page 87), 1 cup of cooked sliced potatoes or mashed potatoes will work equally well in this hearty appetizer soup—

Total preparation time: 20 minutes

1 10-ounce package frozen chopped spinach, thawed
3 cups light cream *or* milk
1 cup reserved Basil Scalloped Potatoes (see recipe, page 87)
½ teaspoon dried dillweed
Dairy sour cream (optional)
Fresh dill sprigs *or* dried dillweed (optional)

1 Use paper toweling to squeeze out excess liquid from spinach. In a 2-quart saucepan combine chopped spinach, light cream or milk, reserved Basil Scalloped Potatoes, and the ½ teaspoon dillweed. Season with salt and pepper to taste.

2 Cook, uncovered, over medium heat about 15 minutes or till heated through. Transfer *half* of the hot mixture to a blender container or a food processor bowl. Blend or process till smooth. Repeat with the remaining hot mixture.

3 Pour into serving bowls or soup tureen; dollop with sour cream, and garnish with a sprig of fresh dill or some dried dillweed, if desired. Serve immediately. Makes 6 servings.

CRANBERRY-APPLE CRISP

You can also substitute a granola that has fruit or nuts added—

Assembling time: 5 minutes
Cooking time: 30 minutes

3 cups unpeeled, thinly sliced
   cooking apples
   (4 medium)
1 16-ounce can whole cranberry
   sauce
2 cups granola
½ cup coconut
⅓ cup butter *or* margarine,
   melted
   Whipped cream *or* vanilla ice
   cream (optional)

1 In a mixing bowl stir together the apples and cranberry sauce; turn apple mixture into a 10x6x2-inch baking dish. In another bowl stir together the granola, coconut, and melted butter or margarine till well combined; sprinkle evenly over fruit mixture in baking dish.

2 Bake, covered, in a 400° oven for 15 minutes; uncover and bake 10 to 15 minutes more or till topping is crisp and golden brown. Spoon the crisp into serving dishes. Serve warm topped with whipped cream or vanilla ice cream, if desired. Makes 6 to 8 servings.

Pork-Filled Gougère
Marinated Shrimp and Artichoke Hearts
(see recipe, page 81)
Cranberry-Apple Crisp
Spinach-Potato Soup

CHAPTER 3

OFF-THE-SHELF COOKING

The next time you forget to plan something for dinner, let the recipes in this chapter help you out of the jam. Each is based on ingredients most cooks have in their kitchens—products such as canned meat or fish, packaged meats, frozen fish, dinner mixes, canned soups, canned or frozen vegetables, gelatin, bread mixes, cake mixes, or cookie mixes. Here's how the recipes work. When you need a new idea, make a quick check of the ingredients in your cupboards and refrigerator. Then flip to the section of this chapter that fits one of the ingredients you have on hand. There you'll find both fast (under 45 minutes) and easy recipes. Or, better still, choose several dishes from this chapter and keep the ingredients on hand for cooking emergencies.

Put these raid-the-cupboard recipes together on the spur of the moment: Dilled Corned Beef (see recipe, page 92), Tossed Fish Salad (see recipe, page 108), and Granola Swirl Coffee Cake (see recipe, page 125).

OFF-THE-SHELF COOKING
START WITH CANNED MEAT AND FISH

CHEESY POTATO OMELET

Assembling time: 10 minutes
Cooking time: 18 minutes

1 12-ounce can luncheon meat
1 16-ounce can sliced potatoes, drained
3 green onions, sliced (3 tablespoons)
1/4 teaspoon dried thyme, crushed
2 tablespoons cooking oil
6 eggs
1/3 cup milk
1 teaspoon dried parsley flakes
   Dash pepper
1/4 cup shredded cheddar cheese (1 ounce)

1 Cut luncheon meat into bite-size pieces. In a 10-inch skillet toss luncheon meat, sliced potatoes, sliced green onions, and thyme in cooking oil.

2 Evenly spread meat mixture over bottom of skillet. Cook meat mixture over low heat about 10 minutes or till heated through. Meanwhile, beat together eggs, milk, parsley flakes, and pepper. Pour over hot potato mixture in skillet.

3 Cover; cook over medium heat for 6 to 8 minutes or till surface is set but still glossy and moist. Sprinkle cheddar cheese atop egg mixture. To serve, loosen edges of egg mixture and cut into wedges. Makes 6 servings.

BARBECUE-STYLE BEEF AND RICE

Total preparation time: 32 minutes

2 stalks celery, finely chopped
1 cup quick-cooking rice
2 tablespoons chopped canned green chili peppers
1 tablespoon minced dried onion
1 teaspoon dried oregano, crushed
1/2 teaspoon garlic salt
1 15-ounce can barbecue sauce and beef
4 ounces American cheese

1 Combine the first 6 ingredients and 1 cup *water*. Bring to boiling; reduce heat. Cover and simmer for 2 minutes. Stir in barbecue sauce and beef.

2 Cover; simmer 10 to 15 minutes. Remove from heat. Meanwhile, cut cheese into 1/2-inch cubes; stir into rice. Cover; let stand for 5 minutes. Serves 4.

REUBEN CHOWDER

Total preparation time: 35 minutes

3 cups milk
1 10¾-ounce can condensed cream of celery soup
1/2 cup shredded *process* Swiss cheese
1 16-ounce can sauerkraut, rinsed, drained, and snipped
1 12-ounce can corned beef
3 tablespoons butter, softened
4 slices rye bread
1 teaspoon caraway seed

1 Combine milk, soup, and cheese. Stir in sauerkraut. Cover; simmer 15 minutes. Chop beef; stir into soup. Heat 10 minutes. Meanwhile, butter both sides of bread; sprinkle with caraway. Cut into triangles; place on baking sheet. Toast in 300° oven 20 minutes. Serve with soup. Serves 4.

SOUTH-OF-THE-BORDER SUPPER

Total preparation time : 22 minutes

1 16-ounce can tomatoes, cut up
1½ cups quick-cooking rice
1/2 cup raisins
1 tablespoon minced dried onion
1 tablespoon vinegar
1 teaspoon sugar
1 teaspoon dried marjoram, crushed
1/4 teaspoon ground cinnamon
1 12-ounce can chopped beef, cut into 1/2-inch cubes
1 large cooking apple, peeled, cored, and chopped

1 Combine the first 8 ingredients, 1/3 cup *water*, and 1/2 teaspoon *salt*. Bring to boiling; stir frequently. Stir in beef and apple. Cover; simmer 5 to 7 minutes. Serves 3.

DILLED CORNED BEEF

Pictured on page 91—

Total preparation time: 25 minutes

1 30-ounce can corned beef brisket
2 16-ounce cans whole new potatoes, drained
1 10-ounce package frozen peas with pearl onions
1/2 teaspoon dried dillweed
2 medium tomatoes

1 Remove beef from can, reserving 1/4 cup liquid. Cut meat into 1-inch slices; arrange in a 10-inch skillet with potatoes. Break up peas and onions; sprinkle atop.

2 Combine reserved liquid, dillweed, and 1/4 cup *water*. Pour over all. Cook, covered, 8 to 10 minutes. Cut tomatoes into wedges; arrange atop. Spoon liquid over mixture. Cover; cook 5 minutes. Serves 6.

CREAMY CORNED BEEF SAUCE

Total preparation time: 32 minutes

¼ cup butter *or* margarine
2 tablespoons all-purpose flour
½ teaspoon dried basil, crushed
1½ cups milk
1 16-ounce can peas and carrots
1 cup shredded provolone cheese
1 12-ounce can corned beef, broken
   into small pieces
   Hot cooked fettucine *or* spaghetti

1 Melt butter. Stir in flour, basil, ⅛ teaspoon *salt*, and ⅛ teaspoon *pepper*. Add milk all at once. Cook and stir till bubbly. Cook and stir 1 minute more. Drain peas and carrots; stir into sauce along with cheese, stirring till cheese melts. Stir in beef; heat through. Serve over pasta. Serves 5.

INSTANT REUBEN CASSEROLE

Assembling time: 15 minutes
Cooking time: 30 minutes

4 slices rye bread
1 tablespoon prepared mustard
1 12-ounce can corned beef
1 16-ounce can sauerkraut, rinsed,
   drained, and snipped
1 10¾-ounce can condensed tomato
   soup
3 tablespoons sweet pickle relish
5 slices Swiss cheese, halved

1 Spread rye bread with mustard. Cut into cubes; place in bottom of a buttered 9x9x2-inch baking pan. Crumble corned beef evenly over bread.

2 Stir together sauerkraut, tomato soup, relish, and ¼ cup *water*; spoon atop corned beef. Bake, uncovered, in a 375° oven about 25 minutes. Arrange cheese atop; bake 5 minutes more. Serves 5.

HOT CORNED BEEF SANDWICHES

Assembling time: 15 minutes
Cooking time: 20 minutes

2 cups finely shredded cabbage
1 12-ounce can corned beef, broken
   into small pieces
¼ cup Russian *or* thousand island
   salad dressing
1 teaspoon minced dried onion
1 teaspoon prepared horseradish
   Butter *or* margarine
8 kaiser rolls *or* hamburger buns,
   split
   Dill pickle slices (optional)

1 For sandwich filling, in a mixing bowl stir together finely shredded cabbage, corned beef pieces, Russian or thousand island salad dressing, minced dried onion, and prepared horseradish.

2 Spread butter or margarine on both halves of rolls or buns. Spread about *one-third* of the filling on the bottom half of *each* roll or bun. Cover corned beef filling with tops of buns or rolls.

3 Wrap each sandwich in a 12x12-inch square of foil. Place foil-wrapped sandwiches on a baking sheet. Bake in a 375° oven about 20 minutes or till heated through. To serve, unwrap sandwiches. Serve with dill pickle slices, if desired. Makes 8.

DENVER SPECIAL

Total preparation time: 25 minutes

1 12-ounce can chopped ham
1 4-ounce can sliced mushrooms,
   drained
1 small onion, chopped
2 tablespoons butter *or* margarine
6 eggs
¾ cup cream-style cottage cheese
1 tablespoon dried parsley flakes
1 teaspoon Dijon-style mustard *or*
   prepared mustard
¼ teaspoon garlic powder
6 English muffins, split
   Butter *or* margarine
6 slices mozzarella cheese, cut into
   fourths

1 Slice ham into bite-size strips. In a 10-inch skillet cook ham strips, mushrooms, and onion in butter or margarine till onion is tender but not brown.

2 In a blender container combine eggs, cottage cheese, parsley flakes, Dijon-style mustard or prepared mustard, and garlic powder. Cover; blend till combined. Add egg mixture to hot skillet.

3 Cook, without stirring, till mixture starts to set on bottom and around edges. Lift and fold the partially cooked egg mixture so the uncooked portion flows underneath. Continue cooking about 4 minutes or till eggs are cooked throughout but still glossy and moist. Immediately remove from heat.

4 Meanwhile, broil the English muffin halves 3 to 4 inches from heat till toasted. Spread with butter or margarine. Spoon egg mixture atop English muffin halves. Cross 2 strips of cheese atop and broil till cheese is melted. Makes 6 servings.

OFF-THE-SHELF COOKING

HAM PATTIES STROGANOFF-STYLE

Total cooking time: 30 minutes

- 1 16-ounce can ham patties (8)
- 1 tablespoon cooking oil
- 1 cup water
- 1 large onion, sliced and separated into rings
- 1 4-ounce can sliced mushrooms, drained
- ¼ cup catsup
- 2 teaspoons dried parsley flakes
- 1 teaspoon instant beef bouillon granules
- ½ teaspoon dried dillweed
- ¾ cup dairy sour cream
- 1 tablespoon all-purpose flour
  Hot cooked noodles

1 In a large skillet cook the ham patties, half at a time, in the hot cooking oil about 3 minutes or till patties are heated through, turning once. Remove from skillet. Drain fat from skillet.

2 In the same skillet combine water, onion, sliced mushrooms, catsup, parsley flakes, bouillon granules, and dillweed. Bring to boiling; reduce heat. Cover; simmer about 10 minutes or till onion is tender.

3 Stir together sour cream and flour; stir a small amount of the hot onion mixture into the sour cream mixture. Return all to skillet. Cook and stir till thickened; heat just to boiling. Return ham patties to skillet; heat through. Serve over hot cooked noodles. Makes 4 servings.

Ham Patties Stroganoff-Style

GRILLED HAM AND CHEESE SANDWICHES

This easy version of the traditional ham and cheese sandwich can be put together on the spur of the moment—

Assembling time: 8 minutes
Cooking time: 10 minutes

- 8 slices rye, whole wheat, *or* pumpernickel bread
- 1 3-ounce can deviled ham
- 2 green onions, sliced, *or* 2 tablespoons chopped onion
- 4 slices Swiss *or* American cheese
  Mustard *or* Dijon-style mustard
  Butter *or* margarine

1 Spread *4 slices* of the bread with the deviled ham. Sprinkle each with the sliced green onion or chopped onion. Then place *1 slice* of Swiss or American cheese atop *each*.

2 Lightly spread the remaining 4 bread slices with mustard or Dijon-style mustard. Top cheese slice with bread, mustard side down. Spread butter or margarine on *outside* of each sandwich.

3 In a large skillet or on griddle cook sandwiches over medium heat about 8 minutes or till toasted and golden. Turn sandwich and cook about 2 minutes more or till toasted and golden. To serve, cut each toasted sandwich diagonally in half. Makes 4 sandwiches.

SAUSAGE AND MUSHROOM PIZZA

For an easy meal, serve this off-the-shelf pizza with a tossed salad—

Total assembling time: 30 minutes

- 1 13¾-ounce package hot roll mix
- 2 tablespoons yellow cornmeal
- 1 cup warm water (110°)
- 2 teaspoons dried oregano, crushed
- 1 15-ounce can tomato sauce
- 1 9-ounce can Vienna sausage, drained and halved lengthwise *or* cut into slices
- 1 8-ounce can mushroom stems and pieces, drained
- 2 cups shredded mozzarella, American, *or* Monterey Jack cheese

1 In a mixing bowl combine hot roll mix and cornmeal. Prepare hot roll mix according to package directions, *except* use warm water and omit the egg. *Do not let rise.* Divide dough in half.

2 On a lightly floured surface roll each half into a circle 13 inches in diameter. Transfer circles of dough to greased 12-inch pizza pans or baking sheets. Build up edges slightly. Bake in a 425° oven for 6 to 7 minutes or till light brown.

3 Stir oregano into tomato sauce. Spread *half* of the tomato sauce over *each* partially baked pizza crust. Top *each* pizza with *half* of the sausage and mushrooms.

4 Sprinkle *half* of the cheese atop *each*. Return to the 425° oven; bake for 10 to 15 minutes more or till bubbly. Makes two 12-inch pizzas.

SPICY SAUSAGE CHILI

Be prepared to curb any sudden hunger pangs by keeping the ingredients for this savory chili on the shelf—

Assembling time: 15 minutes
Cooking time: 30 minutes

1　16-ounce can tomatoes, cut up
1　15½-ounce can red kidney beans
1　15½-ounce can chili beans
1　15-ounce can tomato sauce
2　5-ounce cans Vienna sausage, sliced
2　celery stalks, chopped (½ cup)
1　medium onion, chopped (½ cup)
1　4-ounce can green chili peppers, rinsed, seeded, and chopped
2　teaspoons Worcestershire sauce
1½　teaspoons chili powder
1　teaspoon ground cumin
1　teaspoon celery salt
1　teaspoon dry mustard

1 In a large saucepan or Dutch oven combine *undrained* tomatoes, *undrained* kidney beans, *undrained* chili beans, tomato sauce, *undrained* Vienna sausage, celery, onion, chili peppers, Worcestershire sauce, chili powder, ground cumin, celery salt, and dry mustard.

2 Bring mixture to boiling; reduce heat. Cover and simmer for 30 minutes, stirring occasionally. Serve in soup bowls. Makes 4 servings.

POTATO-SHELL CHICKEN PIE

Total preparation time: 1 hour

1　12-ounce package frozen shredded hash brown potatoes
3　tablespoons butter *or* margarine, melted
¾　teaspoon salt
　Dash pepper
1　cup milk
1½　teaspoons minced dried onion
2　tablespoons butter *or* margarine
2　tablespoons all-purpose flour
1　teaspoon instant chicken bouillon granules
½　teaspoon Worcestershire sauce
¼　teaspoon dried basil, crushed
2　ounces American cheese, cubed (½ cup)
1　10-ounce package frozen peas and carrots
1　5-ounce can chunk-style chicken, drained and chopped
½　of a 3-ounce can French-fried onions

1 Run hot water over frozen potatoes in a colander about 5 minutes to thaw. Drain well; pat dry with paper toweling. In a mixing bowl combine potatoes, the 3 tablespoons melted butter, salt, and pepper.

2 Press mixture into the bottom and up sides of a 10-inch pie plate. Bake in a 425° oven for 20 minutes. Meanwhile, stir together milk and dried onion; set aside.

3 In a saucepan melt the 2 tablespoons butter or margarine. Stir in flour, bouillon granules, Worcestershire sauce, and basil. Add milk mixture all at once; cook and stir till thickened and bubbly. Cook and stir 1 minute more.

4 Add cheese. Cook and stir 1 to 2 minutes more or till cheese is melted. Stir in peas and carrots. Return to boiling. Layer chicken atop baked crust. Spread vegetable mixture atop chicken. Bake in a 375° oven about 30 minutes. Top with French-fried onions. Bake 5 minutes more. Serves 4.

CHICKEN ENCHILADAS

Assembling time: 35 minutes
Cooking time: 33 minutes

1　10¾-ounce can condensed cream of chicken soup
1　8¾-ounce can whole kernel corn, drained
8　green onions, sliced (½ cup)
1　tablespoon chili powder
2　5-ounce cans chunk-style chicken *or* turkey, drained and chopped
½　cup dairy sour cream
¼　cup milk
8　flour tortillas
1½　cups shredded cheddar cheese (6 ounces)
　Green pepper rings (optional)
　Pitted ripe olives (optional)

1 In a saucepan combine cream of chicken soup, corn, green onions, and chili powder; cook till onion is tender. Stir in chicken or turkey, sour cream, and milk; heat through but *do not boil.*

2 Place about ¼ cup of the chicken mixture on *each* tortilla; roll up. Spread remaining chicken mixture in the bottom of a 12x7½x2-inch baking dish.

3 Place filled tortillas, seam side down, on the chicken mixture in the baking dish. Cover with foil. Bake in a 350° oven about 30 minutes or till heated through.

4 Remove foil; sprinkle with cheese. Return to oven about 3 minutes more or till cheese is melted. Garnish with green pepper rings and olives, if desired. Makes 6 servings.

CHICKEN AND WILD RICE DINNER

Total preparation time: 20 minutes

1 10-ounce package frozen onions in cream sauce
1 6¾-ounce package quick-cooking long grain and wild rice mix
2 5-ounce cans chunk-style chicken *or* turkey, drained and chopped
1 4-ounce can mushroom stems and pieces, drained

1 Prepare onions and the rice mix according to package directions. In a saucepan combine onions, chicken or turkey, mushrooms, ½ teaspoon *salt*, and ⅛ teaspoon *pepper*. Cover; simmer 5 minutes. Stir in rice; heat through. Serves 3 or 4.

CHICKEN, VEGETABLE, AND NOODLE SOUP

Assembling time: 5 minutes
Cooking time: 20 minutes

1 10-ounce package frozen peas
2 5-ounce cans chunk-style chicken *or* turkey, drained and chopped
1 8½-ounce can cream-style corn
1 7½-ounce can tomatoes, cut up
1 tablespoon instant chicken bouillon granules
1 tablespoon minced dried onion
½ teaspoon dried rosemary, crushed
1 cup fine noodles

1 In a large saucepan combine peas, chicken, corn, *undrained* tomatoes, chicken bouillon granules, dried onion, rosemary, 2½ cups *water*, and ⅛ teaspoon *pepper*. Stir in *uncooked* noodles. Bring to boiling. Reduce heat; simmer, covered, about 10 minutes or till vegetables and noodles are tender. Makes 4 servings.

BROILED TUNA SANDWICHES

Assembling time: 10 minutes
Cooking time: 8 minutes

1 beaten egg
¼ cup milk
½ cup finely crushed saltine crackers (14 crackers)
2 teaspoons dried parsley flakes
½ teaspoon dried dillweed
¼ teaspoon salt
¼ teaspoon paprika
1 6½-ounce can tuna, drained and finely flaked, *or* one 7¾-ounce can salmon, drained, finely flaked, and skin and bones removed
4 slices Monterey Jack cheese
4 whole wheat hamburger buns, split, toasted, and buttered
4 lettuce leaves
4 tomato slices

1 In a mixing bowl combine egg and milk. Stir in crushed crackers, parsley flakes, dillweed, salt, and paprika. Stir in tuna or salmon. Shape mixture into patties, using about ⅓ cup mixture for *each*.

2 Place patties on a greased rack of an unheated broiler pan. Broil patties 4 inches from heat for 3 to 4 minutes per side or till golden brown.

3 During the last minute of cooking time, place a slice of cheese atop each patty. Serve patties on toasted hamburger buns with lettuce leaves and tomato slices. Makes 4 sandwiches.

DILL-TUNA CASSEROLE

Assembling time: 30 minutes
Cooking time: 45 minutes

2 eggs
1 cup tiny shell macaroni *or* elbow macaroni
1 10¾-ounce can condensed cream of mushroom soup
⅓ cup milk
¼ cup mayonnaise *or* salad dressing
1 tablespoon dried parsley flakes
½ teaspoon dried dillweed
1 6½-ounce can tuna, drained and flaked
1 cup shredded American cheese (4 ounces)
½ of a 3-ounce can French-fried onions (optional)

1 To hard-cook eggs, place eggs in a saucepan; cover with cold water. Bring to boiling; reduce heat to just below simmering. Cover and cook for 15 minutes. Run cold water over eggs till cool. Remove shells; chop eggs. Cook macaroni according to package directions; drain.

2 Meanwhile, in a mixing bowl combine cream of mushroom soup, milk, mayonnaise or salad dressing, parsley flakes, and dillweed. Stir in tuna and cheese. Gently fold the chopped eggs and cooked macaroni into the tuna mixture.

3 Turn into a 1½-quart casserole. Bake in a 350° oven for 40 minutes or till heated through. Remove from oven; sprinkle French-fried onions around edge of casserole, if desired. Bake 5 minutes more. Makes 4 or 5 servings.

ORIENTAL-STYLE TUNA TOSSED SALAD

Assembling time: 20 minutes
Chilling time: 20 minutes

⅓ cup vinegar
¼ cup salad oil
2 tablespoons sugar
1 tablespoon soy sauce
¼ teaspoon ground ginger
1 11-ounce can mandarin orange sections, drained
1 9¼-ounce can tuna, drained and broken into large pieces
1 8-ounce can bamboo shoots, drained
1 8-ounce can sliced water chestnuts, drained
1 medium green pepper, cut into strips
6 cups torn fresh spinach

1 To make salad dressing, in a screw-top jar combine vinegar, salad oil, sugar, soy sauce, and ground ginger. Cover and shake well to mix. In a large salad bowl combine the mandarin orange sections, tuna, drained bamboo shoots, sliced water chestnuts, and green pepper strips.

2 Pour salad dressing over mixture in salad bowl; toss to coat. Place in freezer for 20 minutes to chill. Add spinach and toss lightly. Makes 4 main-dish servings.

EASY SCALLOPED SALMON

Assembling time: 15 minutes
Cooking time: 40 minutes

½ cup hot water
1 teaspoon instant chicken bouillon granules
2 slightly beaten eggs
½ cup milk
2 tablespoons dried parsley flakes
1 tablespoon instant minced onion
½ teaspoon dry mustard
⅛ teaspoon salt
⅛ teaspoon pepper
2 cups herb-seasoned stuffing croutons
1 15½-ounce can salmon, drained, flaked, and skin and bones removed
1 cup shredded cheddar cheese (4 ounces)
Vegetable Sauce

1 In a bowl stir together water and bouillon granules till bouillon is dissolved. Combine the bouillon mixture, eggs, milk, dried parsley flakes, minced dried onion, dry mustard, salt, and pepper.

2 Stir in the herb-seasoned croutons, salmon, and cheddar cheese. Turn mixture into a 9-inch pie plate; bake, uncovered, in a 350° oven for 35 to 40 minutes. Cut into wedges and serve with Vegetable Sauce. Makes 4 servings.

Vegetable Sauce: In a saucepan stir together 2 tablespoons melted *butter* or *margarine*, 2 tablespoons *all-purpose flour*, ¼ teaspoon *salt*, and a dash *pepper*. Add 1 cup *milk* all at once; cook and stir till thickened and bubbly. Cook and stir 1 minute more. Stir in 1 drained 8½-ounce can *peas*; heat through.

TUNA CHOWDER

Assembling time: 15 minutes
Cooking time: 35 minutes

6 slices bacon
1 medium onion, chopped (½ cup)
2 cups water
1 10¾-ounce can condensed chicken broth
1 5½-ounce package dry au gratin potatoes
2 stalks celery, chopped (½ cup)
½ teaspoon salt
¼ teaspoon white pepper
3 cups milk
1 17-ounce can whole kernel corn
2 6½-ounce cans tuna, drained and flaked

1 In a Dutch oven cook bacon till crisp. Drain on paper toweling, reserving 1 tablespoon drippings in Dutch oven. Crumble bacon; set aside. Add chopped onion to the drippings in pan; cook till onion is tender but not brown.

2 Stir in water, chicken broth, the potatoes from the mix, the celery, salt, and pepper. Bring to boiling; reduce heat. Cover and simmer for 25 minutes, stirring often.

3 Stir *1 cup* of the milk into the packet of seasoning from the au gratin potato mix. Stir the milk mixture into the broth mixture along with the remaining 2 cups of milk, *undrained* corn, and flaked tuna.

4 Cook and stir till mixture thickens slightly and bubbles. To serve, ladle into soup bowls; sprinkle crumbled bacon atop each serving. Makes 8 servings.

RIGATONI WITH SHRIMP

Assembling time: 30 minutes
Cooking time: 30 minutes

4 ounces rigatoni *or* mostaccioli
  (2 cups)
6 green onions, sliced into ½-inch
  pieces
3 tablespoons butter *or* margarine
2 tablespoons all-purpose flour
1 tablespoon instant chicken
  bouillon granules
1 teaspoon dried basil, crushed
2 cups milk
2 4½-ounce cans shrimp, rinsed and
  drained
¼ cup grated Parmesan cheese

1 Cook rigatoni or mostaccioli according to package directions. Drain well. *Do not rinse.* Set aside. Meanwhile, in a saucepan cook green onion pieces in butter or margarine till tender but not brown.

2 Stir flour, chicken bouillon granules, and dried basil into green onion mixture. Add milk all at once. Cook and stir till mixture is thickened and bubbly. Cook and stir 1 minute more. Gently stir in cooked rigatoni or mostaccioli and drained shrimp.

3 Turn shrimp mixture into a 10x6x2-inch baking dish. Sprinkle grated Parmesan cheese atop. Bake, uncovered, in a 350° oven for 25 to 30 minutes or till heated through. Makes 6 servings.

LINGUINE WITH SHRIMP-WINE SAUCE

Crusty bread and a tossed salad are good accompaniments to this elegant sauce with pasta—
  Total preparation time: 20 minutes

¾ cup dry white wine
1 4-ounce can sliced mushrooms,
  drained
¼ cup water
1 tablespoon butter *or* margarine
1 tablespoon dried parsley flakes
2 teaspoons minced dried onion
1 teaspoon instant chicken bouillon
  granules
½ teaspoon garlic powder
¼ cup water
1 tablespoon cornstarch
2 4½-ounce cans shrimp, rinsed and
  drained
  Hot cooked linguine *or* spaghetti

1 In a large saucepan combine wine, the drained mushrooms, the ¼ cup water, butter or margarine, dried parsley flakes, minced dried onion, chicken bouillon granules, and garlic powder. Bring to boiling; reduce heat. Cover mixture and simmer for 5 minutes.

2 Stir together the ¼ cup water and cornstarch; add to wine mixture. Cook and stir till mixture is thickened and bubbly. Cook and stir 2 minutes more. Stir in shrimp; heat through. Serve over hot cooked linguine or spaghetti. Makes 4 servings.

SHRIMP AND CHICKEN SALAD

Assembling time: 20 minutes
Chilling time: 45 minutes

1½ cups elbow macaroni
2 5-ounce cans chunk-style chicken,
  drained and chopped
2 4½-ounce cans shrimp, rinsed and
  drained
1 8¾-ounce can peach slices,
  drained and chopped
1 8¼-ounce can pineapple chunks,
  drained
4 stalks celery, chopped (1 cup)
4 green onions, sliced (¼ cup)
½ of a 14-ounce can Eagle Brand
  sweetened condensed milk
½ cup lemon juice
2 tablespoons salad oil
2 tablespoons prepared mustard
¼ teaspoon salt
  Lettuce cups

1 In a saucepan cook macaroni in large amount boiling salted water according to package directions. Drain. Meanwhile, in a large mixing bowl combine chicken, shrimp, peaches, pineapple, celery, and sliced green onion. Stir in drained macaroni.

2 In another mixing bowl stir together sweetened condensed milk, lemon juice, salad oil, prepared mustard, and salt. Stir into macaroni-chicken mixture. Cover and chill in freezer for 30 to 45 minutes. To serve, spoon into lettuce cups. Makes 6 to 8 servings.

SEAFOOD SOUFFLÉ SANDWICHES

Assembling time: 25 minutes
Cooking time: 35 minutes

- 1 10¾-ounce can condensed cream of shrimp soup
- 1 cup shredded cheddar cheese (4 ounces)
- 1 teaspoon Dijon-style mustard *or* prepared mustard
- 4 egg yolks
- 4 egg whites
- 4 English muffins, split, toasted, and buttered
- 8 ounces sliced fully cooked ham
- 1 5-ounce can lobster, drained, broken into large pieces, and cartilage removed, *or* one 7-ounce can crab meat, drained, flaked, and cartilage removed, *or* one 6½-ounce can tuna (water pack), drained and flaked

1 In a saucepan combine cream of shrimp soup, cheddar cheese, and mustard; cook and stir over low heat till cheese is melted. Remove from heat. In a small mixer bowl beat yolks on high speed of electric mixer about 5 minutes or till thick and lemon colored. Slowly stir the beaten yolks into soup mixture.

2 Using *clean* beaters, beat egg whites on medium speed of electric mixer about 1½ minutes or till stiff peaks form. Fold soup mixture into beaten egg whites. On a baking sheet or an oven-going platter place muffin halves in 2 rows with sides touching.

3 Top each muffin with a slice of ham and some lobster, crab meat, or tuna. Spoon the egg mixture atop. Bake in a 350° oven for 30 to 35 minutes or till puffed and golden. Serve immediately. Makes 8 open-face sandwiches.

MARINER'S SPAGHETTI RING

Total preparation time: 30 minutes

- 8 ounces spaghetti
- 1 cup shredded Swiss cheese (4 ounces)
- 1 0.6-ounce package garlic *or* Italian salad dressing mix
- 2 tablespoons butter *or* margarine, melted
- 1 teaspoon dried parsley flakes
- ½ cup finely chopped onion
- 1 4-ounce can sliced mushrooms, drained
- 2 tablespoons butter *or* margarine
- 1 15-ounce can tomato sauce
- 1 6½-ounce can minced clams, drained
- 1 6½-ounce can tuna, drained and broken into chunks

1 Cook spaghetti according to package directions; drain. In a mixing bowl combine cooked spaghetti, shredded Swiss cheese, garlic or Italian salad dressing mix, 2 tablespoons melted butter or margarine, and parsley flakes.

2 Turn spaghetti mixture into a greased 4½-cup ring mold. Let stand 5 minutes. Meanwhile, in a saucepan cook onion and mushrooms in 2 tablespoons butter or margarine about 5 minutes or till the onion is tender but not brown.

3 Stir the tomato sauce and clams into the onion mixture; simmer for 5 minutes. Gently stir in tuna and heat through. Unmold spaghetti onto a serving plate; serve with sauce. Makes 6 servings.

SHRIMP-CASHEW STIR-FRY

This stir-fry is especially easy to prepare because it doesn't require any chopping of ingredients. All of the items are already small enough to cook quickly—

Total preparation time: 15 minutes

- 1 8¼-ounce can pineapple chunks
- 2 teaspoons cornstarch
- 2 tablespoons soy sauce
- ½ teaspoon dry mustard
- 1 tablespoon cooking oil
- 1 8-ounce can bamboo shoots, drained
- 1 4½-ounce can whole mushrooms, drained
- 1 6-ounce package frozen pea pods, thawed
- 2 4½-ounce cans shrimp, rinsed and drained
- 1 cup cashews
  Hot cooked rice *or* chow mein noodles
  Soy sauce (optional)

1 Drain pineapple, reserving liquid. Stir reserved pineapple liquid into cornstarch; stir in soy sauce and dry mustard. Preheat a large skillet or wok over high heat; add cooking oil.

2 Stir-fry bamboo shoots and whole mushrooms for 2 minutes. Stir pineapple liquid mixture and add to vegetable mixture in large skillet or wok. Cook and stir till mixture is thickened and bubbly.

3 Stir in drained pineapple chunks, pea pods, drained shrimp, and cashews. Cover and cook 2 minutes more. Serve shrimp mixture at once over hot cooked rice or chow mein noodles. Pass soy sauce, if desired. Makes 4 servings.

PANTRY-SHELF POTAGE

Total preparation time: 25 minutes

3½ **cups milk**
 1 **10¾-ounce can condensed cream of celery, chicken, mushroom, onion, potato, *or* shrimp soup**
 ¼ **teaspoon dried thyme, crushed**
 ⅛ **teaspoon pepper**
 1 **14½-ounce can cut asparagus *or* one 16-ounce can cut green beans *or* 2 cups frozen loose-pack cut broccoli *or* 2 cups frozen loose-pack peas**
 ½ **cup instant mashed potatoes**
 1 **12½-ounce can tuna *or* one 15½-ounce can salmon *or* two 6-ounce cans crab meat *or* two 5-ounce cans lobster, drained**

1 In a large saucepan combine milk, soup, thyme, and pepper. Bring mixture to boiling. Drain canned vegetables and stir into soup mixture; remove from heat. (If you're using frozen vegetables, add them to soup mixture; cover and cook till vegetables are just tender.)

2 Stir instant potatoes into soup mixture. Transfer *half* of the soup mixture to a blender container or food processor bowl. Cover and blend or process till smooth. Repeat with remaining mixture.

3 Return all of the mixture to the saucepan. Break the canned seafood into chunks. If necessary, remove cartilage or skin and bones. If desired, reserve a small amount of the fish or seafood for garnish.

4 Stir the remaining seafood into the vegetable mixture. Heat through. Sprinkle reserved seafood atop, if desired. Makes 6 servings.

Seafood Soufflé Sandwiches

101

TURKEY IN WALNUT SAUCE

Assembling time: 10 minutes
Cooking time: 12 minutes

1 cup coarsely chopped walnuts
1 medium onion, chopped (½ cup)
2 tablespoons butter *or* margarine
2 tablespoons all-purpose flour
1 tablespoon instant beef bouillon granules
½ teaspoon celery seed
¼ teaspoon ground allspice
¼ teaspoon salt
¼ teaspoon pepper
1½ cups water
2 4-ounce packages turkey breast luncheon meat, cut into bite-size strips
2 tablespoons chopped pimiento
1 to 2 tablespoons vinegar
1 tablespoon honey
Hot cooked rice

1 In a large saucepan cook chopped walnuts and chopped onion in butter or margarine till onion is tender but not brown. Stir in flour, beef bouillon granules, celery seed, allspice, salt, and pepper.

2 Stir in water, turkey strips, chopped pimiento, vinegar, and honey. Bring turkey mixture to boiling; reduce heat. Cook and stir till mixture is thickened and bubbly. Cook and stir 1 minute more. Serve over hot cooked rice. Makes 4 servings.

TURKEY CHOWDER

Total preparation time: 25 minutes

1 medium potato, peeled and cubed (1 cup)
1 stalk celery, chopped (½ cup)
3 cups milk
1 17-ounce can cream-style corn
2 4-ounce packages turkey breast luncheon meat, cut into ½-inch squares
1 teaspoon salt
⅛ teaspoon pepper
⅛ teaspoon ground nutmeg

1 In a large saucepan cook potato and celery in milk about 10 minutes or just till tender; mash slightly. Stir in corn, turkey, salt, pepper, and nutmeg. Simmer, uncovered, for 5 minutes more. Serves 4 to 6.

TORTILLA STACKS

Assembling time: 7 minutes
Cooking time: 8 minutes

4 6- or 7-inch tortillas
4 slices Swiss cheese, halved
4 slices boiled ham, halved
2 slices turkey breast luncheon meat, halved
⅓ cup cooking oil
1 8-ounce can whole cranberry sauce

1 Halve tortillas. For each stack, layer in order, a piece of cheese, ham, turkey, ham, and cheese *between* tortilla halves. In a 10-inch skillet heat oil.

2 Cook half of the stacks at a time in hot oil over medium-high heat about 4 minutes or till tortillas are crisp and cheese just begins to melt, carefully turning once. Drain on paper toweling. Keep warm in oven while cooking remaining stacks. Serve with cranberry sauce. Makes 4 servings.

TURKEY, SAUSAGE, AND BEAN CASSEROLE

The sausage lends a smoky flavor to this barbecue-style dish—

Assembling time: 25 minutes
Cooking time: 30 minutes

½ of a 12-ounce package fully cooked smoked sausage links, sliced
1 small onion, chopped (¼ cup)
1 tablespoon cooking oil
1 15½-ounce can red kidney beans, drained
⅔ cup water
1 4-ounce package turkey breast luncheon meat, cut into ½-inch squares
½ of a 6-ounce can tomato paste
¼ cup cranberry-orange relish
1 clove garlic, minced
2 teaspoons instant chicken bouillon granules
½ teaspoon dried thyme, crushed

1 In a large saucepan cook the sliced sausage and chopped onion in hot cooking oil till sausage is brown and onion is tender. Drain off fat.

2 Stir in drained kidney beans, water, turkey, tomato paste, cranberry-orange relish, minced garlic, instant chicken bouillon granules, and dried thyme.

3 Turn mixture into a 1½-quart casserole. Cover and bake in a 350° oven about 30 minutes or till heated through. Makes 4 servings.

SAUCY ORIENTAL-STYLE BEEF DINNER

Total preparation time: 25 minutes

  1 small onion, cut into thin wedges
  2 tablespoons butter *or* margarine
  1 15½-ounce can pineapple chunks
  ¼ cup packed brown sugar
  2 tablespoons cornstarch
  ⅛ teaspoon ground ginger
  ⅓ cup vinegar
  2 3-ounce packages sliced dried beef, cut into bite-size strips
  1 8¼-ounce can sliced carrots, drained
    Chow mein noodles *or* hot cooked rice

1 In a large saucepan cook onion wedges in butter or margarine till tender but not brown. Drain pineapple, reserving syrup. Add enough water to the reserved syrup to make 1¼ cups total liquid.

2 Combine brown sugar, cornstarch, and ground ginger; stir in pineapple liquid mixture and vinegar. Stir into the onion mixture in the saucepan. Cook and stir till the mixture is thickened and bubbly. Cook and stir 2 minutes more.

3 Stir in beef strips, sliced carrots, and pineapple chunks; heat through. Serve over chow mein noodles or hot cooked rice. Makes 3 servings.

BEEF-NOODLE SKILLET

Total preparation time: 22 minutes

  1½ cups medium noodles
  2 3-ounce packages sliced dried beef, cut into strips
  1 medium onion, chopped (½ cup)
  1 stalk celery, thinly sliced
  1 tablespoon butter *or* margarine
  1 8¾-ounce can whole kernel corn, drained
  ½ teaspoon dried oregano, crushed
  1 8-ounce package cream cheese, cut up
  ⅔ cup milk

1 Cook noodles according to package directions; drain. Meanwhile, in a 10-inch skillet cook beef, onion, and celery in butter or margarine till celery is tender.

2 To skillet add corn, oregano, ⅛ teaspoon *salt*, and ⅛ teaspoon *pepper*. Stir in cream cheese and milk, stirring till smooth. Stir in noodles; heat through. Serves 4.

SPICY GLAZED CANADIAN BACON

Assembling time: 5 minutes
Cooking time: 5 minutes

  8 ounces Canadian-style bacon, cut into ¼-inch-thick slices
  2 teaspoons butter *or* margarine
  ¼ cup orange marmalade
  2 tablespoons dry red wine *or* water
  1 to 2 teaspoons lemon juice
  ⅛ teaspoon ground ginger
    Dash ground cloves

1 Cook bacon in butter till brown. Combine marmalade, wine, lemon juice, ginger, and cloves; pour over bacon. Bring just to boiling; reduce heat slightly. Cook, uncovered, for 5 minutes. Serves 2 or 3.

HAM AND SPINACH ROLLS

Assembling time: 22 minutes
Cooking time: 30 minutes

  1 10-ounce package frozen chopped spinach
  1 10¾-ounce can condensed cream of chicken soup
  ½ cup mayonnaise *or* salad dressing
  ⅓ cup milk
  1 tablespoon lemon juice
  1 to 2 teaspoons curry powder
  ½ teaspoon Worcestershire sauce
  1 6-ounce package sliced fully cooked ham (8 slices)
  3 cups herb-seasoned stuffing mix

1 Cook spinach according to package directions; drain. Meanwhile, for sauce, in a mixing bowl combine cream of chicken soup, mayonnaise or salad dressing, milk, lemon juice, and curry powder. Remove ½ *cup* of the sauce; set remaining sauce aside.

2 Mix the ½ cup sauce with the cooked spinach and Worcestershire sauce. Spread some of the spinach mixture on each ham slice. Roll up; set aside.

3 Prepare the stuffing mix according to package directions; spoon into a 12x7½x2-inch baking dish. Place ham rolls, seam side down, atop stuffing. Spoon remaining sauce over all. Cover and bake in a 350° oven about 20 minutes. Uncover; bake 10 minutes more. Makes 3 servings.

START WITH PACKAGED MEAT

STUFFED FRANKS

Assembling time: 15 minutes
Cooking time: 6 minutes

- ½ cup herb-seasoned croutons
- 2 tablespoons sweet pickle relish
- 3 tablespoons water
- 1 8-ounce package (4) large frankfurters
- 4 slices bacon
- ½ of a 5-ounce jar American cheese spread
- 1 teaspoon prepared mustard
- 4 frankfurter buns, split

1 Stir together the herb-seasoned croutons and sweet pickle relish; toss with water. Cut frankfurters lengthwise almost to, but not through, other side. Mound crouton mixture inside the cut frankfurters.

2 Place bacon slices on a rack of an unheated broiler pan. Broil about 4 inches from heat for 2 minutes. Drain on paper toweling. Wrap each stuffed frankfurter with a partially cooked bacon slice; secure with wooden picks.

3 Place bacon-wrapped frankfurters, cut side up, on rack in the broiler pan. Broil about 4 minutes or just till bacon is crisp. Meanwhile, combine the American cheese spread and prepared mustard.

4 Carefully turn frankfurters. Place buns, cut side up, on broiler rack. Continue broiling about 2 minutes or till buns are toasted. Spread toasted buns with cheese-mustard mixture. Serve stuffed frankfurters in buns. Makes 4 sandwiches.

SWEET 'N' SOUR FRANKWICHES

Assembling time: 17 minutes
Cooking time: 6 minutes

- 1 16-ounce package frankfurters (8)
- 1 16-ounce can sauerkraut, drained
- ¼ cup chili sauce
- 1 tablespoon brown sugar
- 4 hamburger buns, split and toasted, or 8 slices bread, toasted
- ¾ cup dairy sour cream
- 2 tablespoons chopped pimiento-stuffed olives
- 1 tablespoon milk
  Sliced pimiento-stuffed olives (optional)

1 Use a sharp knife to slit each frankfurter crosswise into 7 sections, cutting almost to, but not through, other side. Shape each cut frankfurter into a circle; set aside.

2 In a small saucepan heat together drained sauerkraut, chili sauce, and brown sugar till bubbly; spoon some of sauerkraut mixture atop each toasted bun half or bread slice.

3 Place a frankfurter circle atop the sauerkraut mixture on each bun half. Stir together the sour cream, chopped pimiento-stuffed olives, and milk.

4 Fill centers of frankfurter rings with sour cream mixture. Place frankfurter-topped buns on a baking sheet; broil 3 to 4 inches from heat about 6 minutes. If desired, garnish with sliced pimiento-stuffed olives. Makes 8 open-face sandwiches.

BARBECUE-STYLE SANDWICHES

Total preparation time: 23 minutes

- ½ cup catsup
- 1 teaspoon minced dried onion
- ½ teaspoon steak sauce
- ¼ teaspoon dry mustard
- ⅛ teaspoon celery seed
  Dash bottled hot pepper sauce
- 1 cup cooked ham, chicken, or beef cut into thin, bite-size strips
- 4 individual French rolls, split and toasted

1 In a saucepan combine catsup, onion, steak sauce, dry mustard, celery seed, and hot pepper sauce. Bring to boiling; reduce heat. Simmer, covered, 10 minutes. Stir in meat. Cover and heat about 5 minutes. Spoon onto rolls. Makes 4.

SALAMI-BEAN SOUP

Assembling time: 10 minutes
Cooking time: 25 minutes

- 1 4-ounce package summer sausage or salami, chopped
- 2 medium carrots, chopped (1 cup)
- 1 medium potato, peeled and chopped
- 1 teaspoon minced dried onion
- 1 teaspoon Worcestershire sauce
- ½ teaspoon dried thyme, crushed
- 1 16-ounce can pork and beans in tomato sauce

1 Coarsely chop meat. In a saucepan cook meat till lightly browned. Stir in carrots, potato, onion, Worcestershire sauce, thyme, 2 cups *water*, ¼ teaspoon *salt*, and a dash *pepper*.

2 Bring to boiling; reduce heat. Cover and simmer for 15 to 20 minutes. Stir in pork and beans; heat through. Serves 4.

PEPPERONI-STUFFED PEPPERS

Assembling time: 25 minutes
Cooking time: 25 minutes

- 4 **large green peppers**
- ¾ **cup quick-cooking rice**
- ¾ **cup water**
- ¼ **teaspoon salt**
- 1 **4-ounce package sliced pepperoni**
- 1 **beaten egg**
- 1 **8¾-ounce can whole kernel corn, drained**
- 1 **cup shredded Monterey Jack *or* cheddar cheese (4 ounces)**
- ½ **cup chopped walnuts**
- ¼ **cup chili sauce**

1 Cut off tops of green peppers; set peppers aside. Chop tops. In a small saucepan combine chopped green pepper, rice, water, and salt. Bring to boiling; reduce heat. Cover and simmer for 5 minutes.

2 Meanwhile, remove seeds and membranes from peppers. If desired, precook peppers in boiling salted water for 3 minutes; drain. Halve pepperoni slices. In a mixing bowl stir together beaten egg, pepperoni, corn, cheese, nuts, and chili sauce. Stir in cooked rice mixture.

3 Stuff peppers with pepperoni-rice mixture. Place upright in an 8x8x2-inch baking dish. Bake in a 350° oven about 25 minutes or till heated through. Serves 4.

MUSHROOM-SAUSAGE KABOBS

Total preparation time: 22 minutes

- 1 **pound fully cooked Polish sausage**
- 1 **8-ounce can stewed onions, drained**
- 1 **green pepper, cut into 1½-inch pieces**
- 1 **2½-ounce jar whole mushrooms, drained**
- ½ **cup chili sauce**
- 1 **tablespoon soy sauce**
- ¼ **teaspoon lemon pepper**

1 Cut sausage into 1½-inch pieces. Alternately thread sausage, onions, green pepper, and mushrooms onto 4 skewers. Mix chili sauce, soy, and lemon pepper.

2 Place kabobs on a rack of an unheated broiler pan. Broil 4 to 5 inches from heat for 10 to 12 minutes, turning once. Brush occasionally with sauce mixture. Serve on hot cooked rice, if desired. Serves 4.

SALAMI TOSSED SALAD

Assembling time: 15 minutes

- 1 **4-ounce package sliced salami**
- 1 **head lettuce, torn (6 cups)**
- 1 **4-ounce package (1 cup) shredded cheddar cheese**
- 1 **small green pepper, cut into thin strips**
- ¼ **cup sliced pitted ripe olives**
- ⅓ **cup Italian salad dressing**
- 1 **teaspoon prepared horseradish Dash Worcestershire sauce**

1 Cut salami slices into 8 wedges. In bowl mix salami, lettuce, cheese, pepper, and olives. Combine salad dressing, horseradish, and Worcestershire. Pour over lettuce mixture; toss. Makes 4 servings.

HEARTY BRATWURST SUPPER

Fully cooked smoked knackwurst will make a tasty substitute for the bratwurst in this recipe—

Assembling time: 10 minutes
Cooking time: 15 minutes

- 1 **12-ounce package fully cooked smoked bratwurst**
- ⅓ **cup water**
- 3 **tablespoons vinegar**
- 2 **tablespoons brown sugar**
- 1 **teaspoon prepared mustard**
- 1 **16-ounce can whole new potatoes, drained**
- 1 **16-ounce can sauerkraut, drained and snipped**
- 1 **large apple, cored and cut into wedges**
  Snipped parsley (optional)

1 Cut bratwurst diagonally into thirds. In a large skillet stir together water, vinegar, brown sugar, and prepared mustard. Stir in drained potatoes, drained and snipped sauerkraut, apple wedges, and bratwurst.

2 Bring the bratwurst mixture to boiling; reduce heat. Cover and simmer for 10 to 15 minutes or till the apple is tender and the bratwurst is heated through. If desired, sprinkle with snipped parsley. Serves 4.

START WITH FROZEN FISH

SPAGHETTI WITH FISH SAUCE

Total preparation time: 40 minutes

- **1 pound frozen fish fillets**
- **¼ cup sliced green onion**
- **1 tablespoon cooking oil**
- **1 8-ounce can tomato sauce**
- **1 7½-ounce can tomatoes, cut up**
- **⅓ cup dry white wine**
- **1 teaspoon dried parsley flakes**
- **1 teaspoon instant chicken bouillon granules**
- **½ teaspoon dried basil, crushed**
- **⅛ teaspoon minced dried garlic**
- **2 tablespoons water**
- **4 teaspoons cornstarch**
- **Hot cooked spaghetti**
- **Grated Parmesan cheese**

1 Let frozen block of fish stand at room temperature for 15 minutes. Use a sharp knife to cut the block of fish into 1-inch cubes. Meanwhile, in a saucepan cook green onion in cooking oil till tender.

2 Stir tomato sauce, *undrained* tomatoes, white wine, dried parsley flakes, chicken bouillon granules, dried basil, and minced dried garlic into green onion mixture. Add fish; bring to boiling. Reduce heat; cover and simmer about 10 minutes or till fish flakes easily when tested with a fork.

3 Stir together water and cornstarch. Stir into fish mixture in saucepan. Cook and stir till mixture is thickened and bubbly. Cook and stir 2 minutes more. Serve sauce with hot cooked spaghetti. Pass Parmesan cheese. Makes 4 servings.

SWEET-SOUR FISH AND PEPPERS

Total preparation time: 37 minutes

- **1 pound frozen fish fillets**
- **3 tablespoons cornstarch**
- **1 medium red *or* green pepper**
- **1 15¼-ounce can pineapple chunks (juice pack)**
- **1 tablespoon cornstarch**
- **Dash pepper**
- **¼ cup soy sauce**
- **¼ cup honey**
- **¼ cup catsup**
- **3 tablespoons vinegar**
- **3 tablespoons dry sherry**
- **3 tablespoons peanut oil *or* cooking oil**
- **Hot cooked rice**

1 Let the block of fish stand at room temperature for 15 minutes. Use a sharp knife to cut the fillets into 1-inch cubes; coat the fish cubes with the 3 tablespoons cornstarch and set aside. Cut pepper into ¾-inch squares; set aside. Drain pineapple, reserving juice; set pineapple aside.

2 In a small mixing bowl combine the reserved pineapple juice, the 1 tablespoon cornstarch, and pepper. Stir in soy sauce, honey, catsup, vinegar, and dry sherry; set mixture aside.

3 In an electric skillet or wok cook fish pieces in hot oil for 2 to 4 minutes or till fish flakes easily when tested with a fork; remove from skillet. Add red or green pepper squares; stir-fry for 2 minutes. Remove peppers from skillet.

4 Stir pineapple juice mixture. Add to skillet; cook and stir till mixture is thickened and bubbly. Cook and stir 2 minutes more. Add pineapple chunks to pan; stir in fish and pepper squares. Heat about 1 minute more or till heated through. Serve over hot cooked rice. Makes 4 servings.

WINE-BAKED FILLETS

For a different flavor, substitute shredded mozzarella or fontina cheese for the Swiss cheese—

Assembling time: 5 minutes
Cooking time: 45 minutes

- **1 pound frozen fish fillets**
- **¼ cup dry white wine**
- **½ teaspoon dried oregano, crushed**
- **½ cup shredded Swiss cheese (2 ounces)**
- **2 medium carrots, cut into julienne strips**
- **2 stalks celery, cut into julienne strips**

1 Place frozen block of fish in a greased 10x6x2-inch baking dish. Season with salt and pepper. Pour wine over fish; sprinkle with oregano. Bake, covered, in a 350° oven for 35 minutes.

2 Sprinkle fish with shredded Swiss cheese. Bake, uncovered, 5 to 10 minutes more or till fish flakes easily when tested with a fork. Meanwhile, in a medium saucepan cook carrot and celery strips in a small amount of boiling salted water about 10 minutes or just till tender. Drain.

3 Cut fish into 4 equal portions. Transfer fish to a serving platter, spooning some of the fish juices atop. Arrange carrot and celery strips around fish on platter. Makes 4 servings.

Wine-Baked Fillets

START WITH FROZEN FISH

CURRIED COD

Assembling time: 20 minutes
Cooking time: 12 minutes

¼ **cup honey**
¼ **cup Dijon-style mustard**
2 **tablespoons lemon juice**
2 **teaspoons curry powder**
1 **teaspoon salt**
1½ **pounds frozen cod fillets, cut**
   ¾ inch thick
   Snipped chives *or* parsley

1 Stir together honey, mustard, lemon juice, curry powder, and salt. Place fish in a shallow dish. Spread honey mixture on both sides. Let stand 15 minutes.

2 Place fish on rack of unheated broiler pan, reserving honey mixture. Broil 4 inches from heat for 10 to 12 minutes; brush occasionally with honey mixture. Heat and pass remaining honey mixture. Garnish with chives or parsley. Serves 6.

TOSSED FISH SALAD

Assembling time: 26 minutes

1 **8-ounce package frozen fish sticks**
1 **6-ounce package sliced mozzarella**
   cheese
5 **cups torn lettuce**
1 **11-ounce can mandarin orange**
   sections, drained
1 **cup sliced celery**
⅓ **cup creamy cucumber salad**
   dressing

1 Prepare fish sticks according to package directions. Let cool for 5 to 10 minutes. Bias-slice into 1-inch pieces. Slice cheese into ¾ x ¼-inch strips, cutting through all slices of cheese at once.

2 In a large salad bowl combine lettuce, orange sections, celery, cheese, and fish. Pour dressing atop; toss. Serves 4.

OVEN-FRIED FISH

Assembling time: 20 minutes
Cooking time: 30 minutes

1 **pound frozen fish fillets**
⅓ **cup herb-seasoned stuffing mix**
¼ **cup grated Parmesan cheese**
1 **tablespoon butter *or* margarine,**
   melted
   Dash pepper

1 Let block of frozen fish stand at room temperature for 15 minutes. Use a sharp knife to cut the fish into 8 equal portions; pat dry. Meanwhile, combine stuffing mix, Parmesan, butter, and pepper.

2 Place fish in an ungreased shallow baking pan. Sprinkle with stuffing mixture. Bake in a 450° oven for 25 to 30 minutes or till fish flakes easily. Makes 4 servings.

WALNUT-TOPPED FISH FILLETS

Total preparation time: 37 minutes

1 **pound frozen fish fillets**
4 **tablespoons butter *or* margarine**
½ **cup broken walnuts**
1 **tablespoon lemon juice**
½ **teaspoon dried basil, crushed**

1 Let frozen fish stand at room temperature for 15 minutes. Cut crosswise into 1-inch slices. Season with salt and pepper. Melt *half* of the butter. Add fish slices; cook, covered, over medium heat for 4 minutes. Turn fish; cook, uncovered, 4 minutes more or till fish flakes easily when tested with fork.

2 Remove fish to a warm platter; keep warm. In the same skillet melt remaining 2 tablespoons butter. Add walnuts; cook and stir about 3 minutes or just till golden. Stir in lemon juice and basil; pour over fish slices. Makes 4 servings.

FISH STEW

Assembling time: 22 minutes
Cooking time: 10 minutes

1 **pound frozen fish fillets**
1 **medium onion, cut into wedges**
1 **tablespoon cooking oil**
1 **16-ounce can stewed tomatoes,**
   cut up
1 **16-ounce can sliced potatoes,**
   drained and cut up
1 **10¾-ounce can condensed**
   tomato soup
1 **8¾-ounce can whole kernel**
   corn, drained

1 Let frozen fish stand at room temperature for 20 minutes. Cut into 1-inch cubes; set aside. Meanwhile, in saucepan cook onion in hot oil till tender.

2 Stir fish, *undrained* tomatoes, potatoes, soup, corn, and a dash *pepper* into saucepan. Bring to boiling; reduce heat. Cover; simmer for 10 minutes. Serves 4 to 6.

GINGERED FISH STEAKS

Assembling time: 6 minutes
Cooking time: 15 minutes

3 **tablespoons butter, melted**
2 **tablespoons lemon juice**
1 **tablespoon honey**
⅛ **teaspoon ground ginger**
   Dash paprika
4 **frozen fish steaks *or* fillets**

1 Mix butter, lemon juice, honey, ginger, and paprika. Set aside. Place frozen fish on rack of unheated broiler pan.

2 Broil 4 inches from heat for 7 minutes; brush with honey mixture. Turn; broil 5 to 8 minutes more or till fish flakes easily. Sprinkle with salt. Brush with remaining honey mixture. If desired, serve with lemon wedges. Makes 4 servings.

SHRIMP WITH CREAMY ONION SAUCE

By keeping these ingredients on hand, you can have an elegant main dish ready for surprise guests in no time at all—

Total preparation time: 35 minutes

- 1 10-ounce package (6) frozen patty shells
- 1 16-ounce package frozen peeled and deveined shrimp
- 1 10¾-ounce can condensed cream of onion soup
- ¼ cup dry white wine
- 1 4-ounce can sliced mushrooms, drained
  Dash pepper
- 1 cup dairy sour cream

1 Bake patty shells according to package directions. Meanwhile, place frozen shrimp in a colander in the sink; run cold water over shrimp about 3 minutes or till partially thawed. Drain shrimp; set aside.

2 In a large saucepan combine condensed cream of onion soup, dry white wine, drained sliced mushrooms, and pepper. Stir in the drained shrimp. Bring the shrimp mixture to boiling; reduce heat. Cover and simmer for 3 to 5 minutes or till the shrimp turn pink.

3 Stir some sauce from the shrimp mixture into the sour cream. Return all to the saucepan. Heat through; *do not boil.* Serve shrimp mixture in baked patty shells. Makes 6 servings.

SHERRIED SEAFOOD DINNER

Total preparation time: 35 minutes

- 1 6-ounce package frozen crab meat and shrimp
- 1 7½-ounce can semi-condensed savory cream of mushroom soup
- ¼ cup milk
- 3 tablespoons dry sherry
- 2 teaspoons lemon juice
- ½ cup shredded Swiss cheese (2 ounces)
- ⅓ cup dairy sour cream
- 1 tablespoon all-purpose flour
- 3 English muffins, split and toasted
  Snipped parsley

1 Place the wrapped frozen crab meat and shrimp in cold water for 15 to 20 minutes to thaw. Remove the partially thawed crab meat and shrimp from the package; separate and spread the seafood out on paper toweling to continue to thaw.

2 Meanwhile, in a large saucepan stir together the semi-condensed cream of mushroom soup, milk, dry sherry, and lemon juice. Stir in the crab meat and shrimp; heat just to boiling.

3 In a mixing bowl stir together the shredded Swiss cheese, dairy sour cream, and flour. Stir the cheese mixture into the seafood mixture. Cook and stir till mixture is thickened and bubbly. Cook and stir 1 minute more. Serve the seafood mixture atop toasted English muffin halves. Garnish with snipped parsley. Makes 3 servings.

BROILED PINEAPPLE-SCALLOP KABOBS

Assembling time: 15 minutes
Cooking time: 12 minutes

- 1 12-ounce package frozen loose-pack scallops
- 1 tablespoon lemon juice
- 1 15½-ounce can pineapple chunks, drained
- 1 medium green pepper, cut into ¾-inch squares
- ⅓ cup chili sauce
- 2 tablespoons orange marmalade

1 Place frozen scallops in a colander in the sink; run cold water over scallops about 5 minutes or till partially thawed. Cut any large scallops in half. Sprinkle scallops with lemon juice.

2 On four skewers, alternate scallops with pineapple chunks and green pepper squares. Place kabobs on a rack of an unheated broiler pan. Stir together chili sauce and orange marmalade.

3 Broil kabobs 3 to 4 inches from heat for 6 minutes. Carefully turn kabobs; brush with chili sauce mixture. Broil 5 to 6 minutes more or till scallops are done. Brush with any additional sauce before serving. Makes 4 servings.

OFF-THE-SHELF COOKING
START WITH DINNER MIX

CHILI-TACO CASSEROLE

You can substitute shredded Monterey Jack cheese for the cheddar cheese—

Assembling time: 25 minutes
Cooking time: 15 minutes

- 1 16-ounce can stewed tomatoes
- 1 15½-ounce can red kidney beans, drained
- 1 8¾-ounce can whole kernel corn
- 1 8-ounce package frankfurters (5), cut into ¼-inch slices
- 1 7-ounce package taco dinner mix
- 1½ cups shredded cheddar cheese (6 ounces)

1 In a large saucepan combine *undrained* tomatoes, drained red kidney beans, *undrained* whole kernel corn, frankfurter slices, and taco seasoning mix from the dinner mix.

2 Bring the tomato-frankfurter mixture to boiling; reduce heat. Simmer, uncovered, for 10 minutes, stirring occasionally. Fill taco shells from the dinner mix with the hot tomato-frankfurter mixture.

3 Arrange filled taco shells lengthwise in three rows in a 13x9x2-inch baking dish. Sprinkle cheddar cheese over meat mixture in taco shells.

4 Bake in a 350° oven for 10 to 15 minutes or till all is heated through and shredded cheddar cheese is melted. Makes 6 servings.

TUNA-MACARONI BOWL

Assembling time: 25 minutes
Chilling time: 30 minutes

- 4 eggs
- 1 7¼-ounce package macaroni and cheese dinner mix
- ½ cup milk
- 1 9¼-ounce can tuna, drained and flaked
- ¾ cup mayonnaise *or* salad dressing
- ¼ cup cooked bacon pieces
- 2 tablespoons sweet pickle relish
- 1 tablespoon prepared mustard
  Lettuce leaves

1 To hard-cook eggs, place eggs in a small saucepan; cover with cold water. Bring to boiling; reduce heat to just below simmering. Cover and cook for 15 minutes. Run cold water over eggs till cool. Remove shells from eggs; chop eggs.

2 Prepare macaroni and cheese dinner mix according to package directions, *except* use ½ cup milk instead of the liquid called for in the directions.

3 Stir the drained and flaked tuna, mayonnaise or salad dressing, cooked bacon pieces, sweet pickle relish, and mustard into the cooked macaroni and cheese mixture. Fold the chopped hard-cooked eggs into the tuna-macaroni mixture. Turn the mixture into a mixing bowl.

4 Cover and place the tuna-macaroni mixture in the freezer for 30 minutes or till thoroughly chilled, stirring once. To serve, spoon the chilled mixture onto individual lettuce-lined salad plates. Makes 6 servings.

PEPPERONI SKILLET LASAGNA

Assembling time: 15 minutes
Cooking time: 35 minutes
Standing time: 4 minutes

- 1 medium onion, chopped (½ cup)
- 1 tablespoon butter *or* margarine
- 2½ cups water
- 1 7¾-ounce package lasagna dinner mix
- 1 7½-ounce can tomatoes, cut up
- 1 4-ounce package sliced pepperoni
- 1 2-ounce can mushroom stems and pieces, drained
- ⅛ teaspoon garlic powder
- 1½ cups cream-style cottage cheese
- 1 cup frozen loose-pack cut broccoli
- 1 4-ounce package (1 cup) shredded mozzarella cheese

1 In a 10-inch skillet cook onion in butter or margarine till tender. Stir in water, noodles from the dinner mix, sauce mix from the dinner mix, *undrained* tomatoes, sliced pepperoni, mushrooms, and garlic powder.

2 Bring mixture to boiling; reduce heat. Cover and simmer for 20 to 25 minutes or till noodles are tender, stirring occasionally. Stir in cottage cheese and broccoli.

3 Cover and cook over low heat for 7 to 10 minutes or till broccoli is tender. Sprinkle with mozzarella cheese. Cover and let stand for 3 to 4 minutes or till cheese melts. Makes 5 servings.

HAM-MAC BAKE

Assembling time: 30 minutes
Cooking time: 35 minutes

1 7¼-ounce package macaroni and cheese dinner mix
1 6¾-ounce can chunk-style ham, drained and broken into chunks, *or* one 5-ounce can chunk-style chicken, drained and broken into chunks
1 cup cream-style cottage cheese
½ cup dairy sour cream
2 green onions, sliced (2 tablespoons)
¼ teaspoon salt
¼ teaspoon dry mustard
¾ cup soft bread crumbs (1 slice bread)
2 tablespoons grated Parmesan cheese
1 tablespoon butter *or* margarine, melted
1 teaspoon dried parsley flakes (optional)

1 Prepare macaroni and cheese mix according to package directions. Stir in ham or chicken, cottage cheese, sour cream, green onion, salt, and dry mustard. Turn mixture into a 1½-quart casserole.

2 Combine bread crumbs, Parmesan cheese, melted butter or margarine, and dried parsley flakes, if desired. Sprinkle atop casserole. Bake the casserole in a 350° oven for 35 minutes or till heated through. Makes 4 servings.

SHRIMP FRIED RICE

Assembling time: 10 minutes
Cooking time: 11 minutes

1 7-ounce package quick-cooking Chinese-style rice mix
2 tablespoons dry white wine *or* water
½ teaspoon ground ginger
⅛ teaspoon garlic powder
2 tablespoons cooking oil
2 beaten eggs
3 stalks celery, bias-sliced (1½ cups)
1 6-ounce package frozen pea pods
1 6-ounce package frozen cooked shrimp

1 In a medium saucepan cook the rice from the Chinese-style rice mix according to package directions, *except* omit the seasoning mix. Meanwhile, combine wine or water, ginger, garlic powder, and the seasoning mix from the rice mix; set aside.

2 Preheat a large skillet or wok over high heat; add *1 tablespoon* of the cooking oil. Add beaten eggs; cook, without stirring, till eggs are set. Remove eggs from skillet or wok; cut up and set aside.

3 Add the remaining cooking oil to the skillet or wok. Add the sliced celery; stir-fry for 3 minutes. Add the frozen pea pods; cook, stirring frequently, 1 minute more or till the vegetables are crisp-tender. Remove vegetables from skillet or wok.

4 Add shrimp to skillet or wok; stir-fry for 3 minutes. Add cooked rice, celery, pea pods, and eggs. Add seasoning mixture; cook and stir just till mixture is heated through. Serve at once. Makes 4 servings.

SHRIMP, CHICKEN, AND NOODLE BAKE

Assembling time: 20 minutes
Cooking time: 25 minutes

1 7-ounce package noodles with chicken dinner mix
1 10-ounce package frozen chopped broccoli
2 cups milk
1 stalk celery, thinly sliced (½ cup)
1 3-ounce package cream cheese, cut up
½ teaspoon dried basil, crushed
1 4½-ounce can shrimp, rinsed and drained, *or* one 5-ounce can chunk-style chicken, chopped
1 teaspoon lemon juice
1 cup chow mein noodles

1 Prepare noodles from the noodles with chicken dinner mix according to package directions; drain. Meanwhile, run hot water over frozen broccoli in a colander in the sink till separated; drain.

2 In a saucepan combine chicken sauce mix from the dinner mix and milk. Cook and stir till heated through; add broccoli, celery, cream cheese, and dried basil. Bring mixture to boiling; stir in shrimp or chicken, lemon juice, and drained cooked noodles.

3 Turn mixture into a 10x6x2-inch baking dish. Sprinkle chow mein noodles atop. Bake in a 350° oven for 20 to 25 minutes or till heated through. Makes 3 servings.

OFF-THE-SHELF COOKING

START WITH
DINNER MIX

MACARONI AND CHEESE SAVORY SOUP

By starting this soup with the macaroni and cheese dinner mix, you'll have no cheese to shred or macaroni to measure—

Total preparation time: 35 minutes

- 1 7¼-ounce package macaroni and cheese dinner mix
- ¼ cup butter *or* margarine
- ¼ cup all-purpose flour
- 2 13¾-ounce cans (3¼ cups) chicken broth
- 1 12-ounce can (1½ cups) beer
- 1 10-ounce package frozen mixed vegetables, thawed
- 1 cup diced fully cooked ham (5½ ounces)

1 In a large saucepan cook macaroni from dinner mix in a large amount of boiling salted water about 7 to 10 minutes or till tender. Drain and set aside.

2 In the same pan melt butter or margarine. Stir in flour and cheese sauce mix from the dinner mix. Gradually stir in chicken broth and beer. Cook and stir till thickened and bubbly. Cook and stir 1 minute more.

3 Add vegetables and ham. Cook and stir about 5 minutes more or till vegetables are just tender. Stir in cooked macaroni; heat through. Makes 6 servings.

Macaroni and Cheese Savory Soup

DILLED SALMON CHOWDER

Total preparation time: 30 minutes

- 1 8¾-ounce package creamy noodles and tuna dinner mix
- 3 cups milk
- 2 teaspoons dried parsley flakes
- ½ teaspoon dried dillweed
- 1 15½-ounce can salmon, drained, flaked, and skin and bones removed
- 1½ cups shredded American cheese

1 In a saucepan combine noodles and sauce mix from dinner mix, milk, parsley, dillweed, and 4 cups *water*. Bring to boiling, stirring occasionally; reduce heat. Cover; simmer 10 minutes or till noodles are tender. Stir in salmon and cheese. Heat, stirring gently, till cheese melts. Serves 8.

CREAMY CHICKEN AND NOODLES

Total preparation time: 35 minutes

- 1 8¾-ounce package creamy noodles and tuna dinner mix
- 2 cups milk
- 1 10-ounce package frozen chopped spinach
- 1 teaspoon dried thyme, crushed
- ⅛ teaspoon ground nutmeg
- 2 5-ounce cans chunk-style chicken, chopped
- 1 cup cream-style cottage cheese
- ¼ cup grated Parmesan cheese

1 In a large skillet combine noodles from mix, sauce mix from dinner mix, milk, spinach, thyme, nutmeg, and 1 cup *water*. Bring to boiling; stirring occasionally. Reduce heat. Cover; simmer 20 minutes or till mixture is thickened. Stir chicken, cottage cheese, and Parmesan into spinach mixture; heat through. Makes 6 servings.

CHINATOWN OMELETS

Total preparation time: 25 minutes

- 1 29-ounce package sukiyaki dinner mix
- ¼ cup quick-cooking rice
- 2 tablespoons butter *or* margarine
- ¼ cup water
- 1 cup water
- 8 eggs
- ¼ cup water
- ¼ teaspoon salt
- ¼ teaspoon pepper
- 2 tablespoons butter *or* margarine

1 Drain the vegetables from the dinner mix. In a medium saucepan cook the drained vegetables and the quick-cooking rice in 2 tablespoons butter or margarine about 5 minutes or till the rice is golden brown and the vegetables are heated through, stirring occasionally.

2 Add ¼ cup water to the vegetable-rice mixture. Bring the mixture to boiling. Cover and remove from heat. Let stand at least 5 minutes. Meanwhile, in a small saucepan combine the sauce mix from the dinner mix and the 1 cup water; bring to boiling. Remove from heat; stir ¼ cup of the sauce into the vegetable-rice mixture. Cover and keep remaining sauce warm.

3 Beat together eggs, ¼ cup water, salt, and pepper. In a 10-inch oven-going skillet melt 2 tablespoons butter or margarine. Pour in egg mixture. Cook over medium heat. As eggs set, run a spatula around edge of skillet, lifting eggs to allow uncooked portion to flow underneath.

4 Continue cooking and lifting edges of eggs till mixture is almost set (surface will be moist and shiny). Place skillet under broiler, 5 inches from the heat. Broil 1 to 2 minutes or just till top is set.

5 Spoon the rice-vegetable mixture over the omelet. Cut into 4 wedges; loosen bottom and slide wedges out onto serving plates. Pass remaining sauce. Makes 4 servings.

POTATO-VEGETABLE SKILLET

Assembling time: 25 minutes
Cooking time: 5 minutes

2 eggs
1 10¾-ounce can condensed cream of celery soup *or* cream of chicken soup
¼ cup milk
½ teaspoon minced dried onion
¼ teaspoon dried dillweed
1 16-ounce can sliced potatoes, drained
1 16-ounce can mixed vegetables, drained
½ cup crushed potato chips

1 To hard-cook eggs, place eggs in a small saucepan; cover with cold water. Bring to boiling; reduce heat to just below simmering. Cover and cook for 15 minutes. Run cold water over eggs till cool. Remove shells from eggs; chop eggs.

2 In a large 10-inch skillet stir together soup, milk, dried onion, and dillweed. Stir in sliced potatoes, mixed vegetables, and chopped eggs.

3 Cook till mixture is heated through, stirring constantly. Just before serving, sprinkle with crushed potato chips. Makes 4 servings.

TUNA AND ZUCCHINI MACARONI

Total preparation time: 25 minutes

1¼ cups elbow macaroni
1 10¾-ounce can condensed cream of chicken soup
¾ cup milk
1 teaspoon dried basil, crushed
¼ teaspoon salt
Few drops bottled hot pepper sauce
2 medium zucchini, quartered lengthwise and sliced
1 cup frozen loose-pack peas
1 9¼-ounce can tuna, drained and flaked
1 cup shredded American cheese (4 ounces)

1 In a large covered saucepan cook the elbow macaroni in boiling salted water according to package directions; drain and set aside. Meanwhile, in a 3-quart saucepan stir together the condensed cream of chicken soup, milk, dried basil, salt, and bottled hot pepper sauce.

2 Stir the sliced zucchini and frozen peas into the chicken soup mixture. Cook over medium heat about 5 minutes or till the vegetables are heated through, stirring occasionally.

3 Stir the cooked macaroni, the drained and flaked tuna, and the shredded American cheese into the soup-vegetable mixture. Continue cooking and stirring till the mixture is heated through and the cheese is melted. Makes 6 servings.

ORIENTAL GARLIC TURKEY

Assembling time: 12 minutes
Cooking time: 12 minutes

½ cup water
1½ cups frozen loose-pack sliced carrots
1 10½-ounce can condensed beef broth
4 teaspoons cornstarch
1 tablespoon soy sauce
½ teaspoon garlic powder
1 tablespoon cooking oil
1 8-ounce can sliced water chestnuts, drained
½ cup peanuts
2 6-ounce packages turkey breast luncheon meat, cut into bite-size strips
1 6-ounce package frozen pea pods
Hot cooked rice

1 In a saucepan bring water to boiling; stir in carrots. Return to boil; cover and cook for 2 minutes. Drain. Meanwhile, stir together beef broth, cornstarch, soy sauce, and garlic powder; set aside.

2 Preheat a large skillet or wok over high heat. Add cooking oil. Stir-fry precooked carrots, sliced water chestnuts, and peanuts in hot cooking oil for 2 minutes.

3 Stir beef broth mixture; add to skillet or wok. Cook and stir till mixture is thickened and bubbly. Cook and stir 2 minutes more. Stir in turkey and pea pods. Cover and cook about 2 minutes or till heated through. Serve over hot cooked rice. Makes 6 servings.

SAUSAGE PUFF

Assembling time: 25 minutes
Cooking time: 20 minutes

1 8-ounce package brown-and-serve
   sausage links
6 egg yolks, slightly beaten
1 10¾-ounce can condensed cream
   of mushroom soup
1 teaspoon minced dried onion
½ teaspoon dry mustard
¼ teaspoon dried savory, crushed
6 egg whites
½ cup milk
¼ cup dairy sour cream
1 teaspoon dried parsley flakes

1 In a 10-inch oven-going skillet cook sausage links till brown; drain, reserving about 1 tablespoon drippings in skillet. Meanwhile, in a mixing bowl combine egg yolks, ⅔ *cup* of the cream of mushroom soup, the minced dried onion, dry mustard, and dried savory.

2 In a large mixing bowl beat egg whites on medium speed of electric mixer about 2½ minutes or till stiff peaks form. Fold yolk mixture into egg whites.

3 Arrange sausages spoke-fashion in skillet. Pour egg mixture over sausages. Bake, uncovered, in a 325° oven for 18 to 20 minutes or till golden.

4 Meanwhile, to make sauce, in a small saucepan combine remaining soup, milk, sour cream, and parsley flakes. Heat through but do not boil. Loosen puff from skillet; invert onto serving plate. Cut into wedges and serve with sauce. Makes 5 servings.

PORK-POTATO BAKE

Assembling time: 15 minutes
Cooking time: 35 minutes

4 pork chops, cut ½ inch thick
2 tablespoons cooking oil
2 16-ounce cans sliced potatoes,
   drained
1 cup frozen loose-pack peas
1 tablespoon lemon juice
1 10¾-ounce can condensed cream
   of mushroom soup
¼ cup milk
½ teaspoon dried dillweed

1 In skillet cook chops in hot oil about 10 minutes or till brown. Sprinkle with pepper. Combine potatoes, peas, and lemon juice in a 12x7½x2-inch baking dish.

2 Place chops atop vegetables. Combine soup, milk, and dillweed; pour over chops and vegetables. Cover with foil. Bake in a 350° oven for 35 minutes. Serves 4.

MUSHROOM-SAUCED POTATOES

Total preparation time: 20 minutes

1 10¾-ounce can condensed cream
   of mushroom soup
½ cup dairy sour cream
2 16-ounce cans sliced potatoes,
   drained
2 tablespoons sliced pitted ripe
   olives
1 teaspoon dried parsley flakes
1 teaspoon minced dried onion

1 In a saucepan combine soup and sour cream. Stir in sliced potatoes, olives, parsley flakes, and dried onion. Cook over medium heat about 10 minutes or till heated through, stirring occasionally. Turn into a serving bowl. Sprinkle with paprika, if desired. Makes 6 to 8 servings.

SAUCY SAUSAGE DINNER

Also serve this savory mixture as a stew—

Total preparation time: 38 minutes

1 small onion, chopped (¼ cup)
2 tablespoons butter *or* margarine
1 16-ounce can tomatoes, cut up
1 10¾-ounce can condensed tomato
   soup
1 4-ounce can sliced mushrooms
¼ teaspoon salt
½ teaspoon dried basil, crushed
½ teaspoon dried oregano, crushed
¼ teaspoon pepper
1 12-ounce package fully cooked
   smoked bratwurst, sliced, *or* one
   12-ounce can chopped beef,
   cubed
   Hot cooked rice *or* hot cooked
   noodles *or* toasted English
   muffin halves

1 In a large saucepan cook chopped onion in butter or margarine till tender but not brown. Stir in *undrained* tomatoes, condensed tomato soup, *undrained* sliced mushrooms, salt, dried basil, dried oregano, and pepper.

2 Bring tomato mixture to boiling. Reduce heat; simmer, uncovered, about 20 minutes. Stir in sliced bratwurst or chopped beef; continue cooking about 3 minutes or till mixture is heated through.

3 To serve, spoon meat mixture over hot cooked rice, hot cooked noodles, or toasted English muffin halves. Serves 4.

START WITH CANNED SOUP

SPICY TOMATO BOUILLON

Assembling time: 6 minutes
Cooking time: 8 minutes

1 10¾-ounce can condensed
  tomato soup
1 10½-ounce can condensed beef
  broth
⅔ cup water
1 tablespoon lemon juice
½ teaspoon ground cinnamon
  Lemon slices, halved (optional)

1 In a 2-quart saucepan combine tomato soup, beef broth, water, lemon juice, and cinnamon. Heat mixture to boiling, stirring occasionally. Serve in heat-proof mugs. Garnish each serving with a lemon slice, if desired. Makes 3 or 4 servings.

MEXICAN TOMATO SOUP

Total preparation time: 25 minutes

½ cup elbow macaroni
1 10¾-ounce can condensed
  tomato soup
1 8½-ounce can cream-style corn
¾ cup milk
2 tablespoons chopped canned
  green chili peppers
½ cup shredded American cheese
  (2 ounces)

1 In a medium saucepan cook macaroni according to package directions; drain and return to saucepan. Stir in tomato soup, corn, milk, and chili peppers. Bring just to boiling. Stir in cheese, stirring till melted. Makes 4 servings.

CORN CHOWDER

Total preparation time: 18 minutes

2 10¾-ounce cans condensed
  cream of potato soup
2½ cups milk
1 12-ounce can whole kernel corn
½ cup sliced green onion
¼ teaspoon celery seed
⅛ teaspoon pepper
3 tablespoons cooked bacon pieces
  Paprika (optional)

1 In a large saucepan combine cream of potato soup, milk, *undrained* corn, sliced green onion, celery seed, and pepper. Bring to boiling. Reduce heat; cook about 10 minutes, stirring frequently. Stir in bacon pieces. Sprinkle with paprika, if desired. Makes 6 servings.

TEXAS CHICKEN SOUP

Total preparation time: 20 minutes

1 10½-ounce can condensed
  vegetable soup
1 soup can (1⅓ cups) water
1 8¾-ounce can whole kernel corn
1 tablespoon minced dried onion
1 to 1½ teaspoons chili powder
  Dash bottled hot pepper sauce
2 5-ounce cans chunk-style chicken,
  chopped, *or* 1½ cups chopped
  cooked chicken

1 In a medium saucepan combine vegetable soup, water, *undrained* whole kernel corn, minced dried onion, chili powder, and hot pepper sauce. Bring to boiling; reduce heat. Cover and simmer about 15 minutes. Stir in chopped chicken; heat through. Makes 4 servings.

SPLIT PEA AND TOMATO SOUP

Assembling time: 18 minutes
Cooking time: 5 minutes

1 small onion, chopped (¼ cup)
1 clove garlic, minced
1 tablespoon butter *or* margarine
1 11½-ounce can condensed split
  pea with ham soup
1 soup can (1⅓ cups) water
1 8-ounce can stewed tomatoes
¼ cup dry white wine *or* water

1 In a medium saucepan cook onion and garlic in butter or margarine till tender but not brown. Stir in split pea with ham soup, the can of water, *undrained* tomatoes, and ¼ cup wine or water. Bring to boiling; reduce heat. Simmer, uncovered, about 5 minutes, stirring occasionally. Serves 4 to 6.

APPLE-VEGETABLE CHOWDER

Assembling time: 8 minutes
Cooking time: 15 minutes

1 19-ounce can chunky old-
  fashioned bean with ham soup
1 8-ounce can stewed tomatoes
1 small apple, peeled and chopped
2 tablespoons chopped canned
  green chili peppers

1 In a medium saucepan combine bean with ham soup, *undrained* tomatoes, apple, and green chili peppers. Bring to boiling; reduce heat. Cover and simmer about 15 minutes or till apple is crisp-tender. Makes 4 servings.

CHILLED CUCUMBER-YOGURT SOUP

Assembling time: 25 minutes
Chilling time: 6 hours

1 medium cucumber, seeded and chopped
2 green onions, sliced
1 tablespoon butter *or* margarine
2 cups milk
1 10¾-ounce can condensed cream of celery soup
¼ teaspoon dried basil, crushed
½ cup plain yogurt
Cucumber slices (optional)

1 In a saucepan cook chopped cucumber and sliced green onion in butter or margarine about 10 minutes or till tender. Stir in milk, soup, and basil. Cook and stir about 5 minutes or till heated through. Cool slightly; stir in yogurt. Cover and chill at least 6 hours. If desired, garnish with cucumber slices. Makes 6 to 8 servings.

CHEESE 'N' BEER SOUP WITH RICE

Total preparation time: 22 minutes

1 11-ounce can condensed cheddar cheese soup
1 cup beer
¾ cup quick-cooking rice
1 stalk celery, thinly sliced
½ teaspoon instant chicken bouillon granules
Dash bottled hot pepper sauce

1 In a medium saucepan stir together soup, beer, and 1 cup *water*. Stir in rice, celery, bouillon granules, and hot pepper sauce. Bring to boiling; reduce heat. Cover and simmer for 8 to 10 minutes or till rice is tender. Makes 4 to 6 servings.

BEER CHILI

Assembling time: 25 minutes
Cooking time: 35 minutes

1 pound ground beef
1 15½-ounce can red kidney beans
1 12-ounce can (1½ cups) beer
1 11¼-ounce can condensed chili beef soup
1 10¾-ounce can condensed tomato soup
1 cup water
2 stalks celery, cut into ½-inch slices
1 tablespoon diced dried bell pepper
1½ teaspoons chili powder
1 teaspoon minced dried onion
1 teaspoon Worcestershire sauce
½ teaspoon garlic powder
Shredded cheddar cheese
Dairy sour cream (optional)

1 In a large saucepan cook ground beef till browned; drain off fat. Stir in *undrained* kidney beans, beer, chili beef soup, tomato soup, water, celery, dried bell pepper, chili powder, dried onion, Worcestershire sauce, and garlic powder.

2 Bring ground beef mixture to boiling. Reduce heat; cover and simmer for 30 to 35 minutes. Top each serving with shredded cheddar cheese and dollop with sour cream, if desired. Makes 6 servings.

SPINACH-CLAM CHOWDER

Total preparation time: 20 minutes

⅓ cup water
1 10-ounce package frozen chopped spinach
1 small onion, chopped (¼ cup)
1½ cups milk
1 10¾-ounce can condensed cream of shrimp soup
1 7½-ounce can minced clams

1 In a medium saucepan bring water to boiling; add frozen spinach and chopped onion. Cover and cook about 7 minutes or till spinach is tender. *Do not drain.* Stir in milk, cream of shrimp soup, and *undrained* clams. Return just to boiling; reduce heat. Simmer, uncovered, about 5 minutes, stirring occasionally. Serves 6.

CREAMY BROCCOLI-SHRIMP SOUP

Total preparation time: 18 minutes

½ cup water
1 10-ounce package frozen chopped broccoli
1½ cups milk
1 10¾-ounce can condensed cream of shrimp soup
1 tablespoon lemon juice
⅛ teaspoon ground nutmeg
Lemon slices, halved

1 In a medium saucepan bring water to boiling; add frozen broccoli. Cover and simmer about 5 minutes or till broccoli is tender. *Do not drain.* Stir in milk, cream of shrimp soup, lemon juice, and nutmeg. Cook and stir about 5 minutes. Garnish with lemon slices. Makes 6 servings.

BROCCOLI-TOMATO SOUP

Assembling time: 9 minutes
Cooking time: 8 minutes

- 1 16-ounce can stewed tomatoes
- 1 cup water
- ¾ cup Italian cooking sauce
  Few dashes bottled hot pepper sauce
- 1 10-ounce package frozen chopped broccoli

1 In a medium saucepan combine *undrained* tomatoes, water, Italian cooking sauce, and hot pepper sauce. Add frozen broccoli. Bring mixture to boiling, stirring occasionally. Reduce heat. Cover and simmer for 7 to 8 minutes or till broccoli is tender. Makes 4 servings.

CREAMY BEAN SALAD

Assembling time: 10 minutes
Chilling time: 20 minutes

- 1 15½-ounce can red kidney beans, drained
- 1 8½-ounce can lima beans, drained
- 2 stalks celery, chopped
- 2 green onions, sliced
- ¼ cup mayonnaise *or* salad dressing
- 2 tablespoons Italian salad dressing
  Lettuce leaves

1 In a mixing bowl combine kidney beans, lima beans, celery, and green onion. Cover and place in the freezer for 20 minutes or till thoroughly chilled.

2 Stir together mayonnaise or salad dressing and Italian salad dressing; stir into bean mixture. Serve on individual lettuce-lined salad plates. Makes 6 servings.

ASPARAGUS-SPAGHETTI SALAD TOSS

Total preparation time: 45 minutes

- 6 ounces spaghetti
- 1 8-ounce package frozen cut asparagus
- ½ teaspoon dried basil, crushed
- ½ teaspoon dried thyme, crushed
- ½ teaspoon onion powder
- 1 7½-ounce can tomatoes, drained and cut up
- ½ cup Italian salad dressing
- 2 tablespoons lemon juice

1 Cook spaghetti and asparagus separately according to package directions; drain. Chill in ice water 5 minutes; drain.

2 Toss spaghetti with basil, thyme, and onion powder. Add asparagus, tomatoes, salad dressing, and lemon juice. Toss. Season with salt and pepper. Cover; chill in freezer for 10 to 15 minutes. Serves 6.

SAUCY SPICED TOMATOES

Total preparation time: 20 minutes

- 1 16-ounce can tomatoes, drained and cut up
- 1 stalk celery, sliced
- 1 2-ounce can chopped mushrooms, drained
- 1 teaspoon sugar
- ¼ teaspoon dried basil, crushed
- ⅛ teaspoon ground allspice
  Dash ground red pepper

1 In a saucepan combine tomatoes, celery, mushrooms, sugar, basil, allspice, red pepper, and ⅛ teaspoon *salt*. Bring to boiling; reduce heat. Cover and simmer about 10 minutes. Makes 4 servings.

DILLED POTATO SALAD

The dillweed adds a hint of summer freshness to the canned vegetables—

Assembling time: 8 minutes
Chilling time: 20 minutes

- 2 16-ounce cans sliced potatoes, drained
- 1 8½-ounce can peas and carrots, drained
- 1 2½-ounce jar sliced mushrooms, drained
- 1 2-ounce jar sliced pimiento, drained (optional)
- ⅓ cup mayonnaise *or* salad dressing
- 1 tablespoon vinegar
- 2 teaspoons prepared mustard
- ½ teaspoon salt
- ½ teaspoon dried dillweed
  Dash pepper
  Lettuce leaves (optional)

1 In a large mixing bowl combine the sliced potatoes, peas and carrots, sliced mushrooms, and sliced pimiento, if desired. In a small mixing bowl stir together the mayonnaise or salad dressing, vinegar, prepared mustard, salt, dried dillweed, and pepper.

2 Pour the mayonnaise mixture over the potato mixture and toss lightly to coat the vegetables. Cover and place in the freezer for 20 minutes or till thoroughly chilled. Spoon into a lettuce-lined salad bowl, if desired. Makes 6 servings.

Asparagus-Spaghetti Salad Toss

BUTTERED CORN MEDLEY

Total preparation time: 15 minutes

- 1 10-ounce package frozen whole kernel corn
- 1 small onion, sliced and separated into rings
- ½ cup water
- ⅛ teaspoon salt
- 1 6-ounce package frozen pea pods
- 2 tablespoons butter *or* margarine
- ¼ teaspoon dried dillweed

1 In a medium saucepan combine frozen corn, onion, water, and salt. Bring to boiling; reduce heat. Cover and cook according to the corn package directions.

2 Stir in pea pods; return to boiling. Cover and cook for 1 minute. Drain well. Turn into a serving bowl. In the same saucepan heat and stir butter or margarine about 2 minutes or till golden. Stir in dillweed. Toss with vegetables. Makes 6 servings.

CREAMY SPINACH AND CHEESE

Total preparation time: 15 minutes

- 2 10-ounce packages frozen chopped spinach
- 1½ cups cream-style cottage cheese
- 1 cup shredded American cheese (4 ounces)
  Dash nutmeg

1 Cook spinach according to package directions; drain well, pressing out excess liquid. Meanwhile, stir together the cottage cheese, American cheese, and nutmeg. Stir into spinach. Cook and stir about 3 minutes or till American cheese is melted. Makes 8 servings.

CHEDDAR-PECAN CAULIFLOWER

Total preparation time: 15 minutes

- 1 10-ounce package frozen cauliflower
- 1 tablespoon butter *or* margarine
- 1 3-ounce package cream cheese, cut up
- 2 tablespoons milk
- 2 tablespoons shredded cheddar *or* American cheese
- 2 tablespoons chopped pecans

1 Cook cauliflower according to package directions; drain well. Meanwhile, melt butter or margarine over low heat.

2 Add cream cheese and milk; heat and stir till cream cheese melts. Stir in cauliflower; heat through. Turn into serving bowl. Sprinkle with cheese and nuts. Serves 4.

SCALLOPED CORN

Assembling time: 10 minutes
Cooking time: 40 minutes
Standing time: 5 minutes

- 2 beaten eggs
- 1 17-ounce can cream-style corn
- 1 8¾-ounce can whole kernel corn
- 1 5⅓-ounce can (⅔ cup) evaporated milk
- ½ cup quick-cooking rolled oats
- 1 small green pepper, chopped
- ¼ cup grated Parmesan cheese
- 1 tablespoon minced dried onion

1 Combine eggs, cream-style corn, *undrained* whole kernel corn, and milk. Stir in rolled oats, green pepper, Parmesan cheese, and onion.

2 Turn corn mixture into an 8x1½-inch round or a 10x6x2-inch rectangular baking dish. Bake in a 350° oven for 30 to 40 minutes or till almost set. Let stand 5 minutes. Makes 6 to 8 servings.

LEMON-BUTTERED SWEET POTATOES

Assembling time: 5 minutes
Cooking time: 10 minutes

- 2 tablespoons butter *or* margarine
- ⅓ cup packed brown sugar
- ¼ cup water
- 2 tablespoons lemon juice
- 1 17-ounce can sweet potatoes, drained

1 In medium skillet melt butter or margarine. Stir in brown sugar, water, and lemon juice. Add sweet potatoes, cutting up any large ones; stir gently till coated. Cook over medium-low heat about 10 minutes or till heated through. Makes 4 to 6 servings.

PEANUT-TOPPED CREAMED ONIONS

Total preparation time: 15 minutes

- 1 tablespoon butter *or* margarine
- 2 teaspoons all-purpose flour
- ¼ teaspoon salt
- 1 cup milk
- 1 16-ounce can stewed onions, drained
- ¼ cup peanuts *or* cashews, coarsely chopped
- 2 tablespoons grated Parmesan cheese

1 In a medium saucepan melt butter or margarine; stir in flour and salt. Add milk all at once. Cook and stir till mixture is thickened and bubbly. Cook and stir 1 minute more. Stir in onions; heat through. Turn into a serving bowl. Sprinkle with chopped peanuts or cashews and Parmesan cheese. Makes 4 servings.

TANGY BEANS AND CELERY

Total preparation time: 15 minutes

1 9-ounce package frozen cut green beans
3 stalks celery, sliced
1 small onion, cut into thin wedges
3 tablespoons vinegar
1 teaspoon sugar
¼ teaspoon mustard seed

1 In a saucepan bring ⅓ cup *water* to boiling; add beans, celery, and onion. Reduce heat; cover and simmer for 6 to 8 minutes or just till vegetables are tender.

2 Meanwhile, combine vinegar, sugar, mustard seed, and ⅛ teaspoon *salt*. Spoon vegetables into serving bowl. Toss with vinegar mixture. Makes 6 servings.

MINESTRONE

Assembling time: 15 minutes
Cooking time: 15 minutes

4 slices bacon *or* ¼ cup cooked bacon pieces
1 15-ounce can great northern beans, drained
½ of a 20-ounce package (3 cups) frozen loose-pack mixed Italian green beans, chick-peas, red peppers, onion, and ripe olives
1 envelope *regular* vegetable soup mix
¾ teaspoon dried basil, crushed
Grated Parmesan cheese

1 If using sliced bacon, cook till crisp in a saucepan; drain and crumble. Set aside. In saucepan combine beans, vegetables, soup mix, basil, and 4 cups *water*.

2 Bring mixture to boiling. Reduce heat; cover. Simmer 10 to 15 minutes. Serve with bacon and cheese. Serves 6.

CURRIED VEGETABLE RAGOUT

Assembling time: 10 minutes
Cooking time: 10 minutes

1 small onion, chopped (¼ cup)
1 teaspoon curry powder
1 tablespoon butter *or* margarine
1 16-ounce can sliced potatoes, drained
1 8¼-ounce can sliced carrots, drained
1 8-ounce can stewed tomatoes
¼ cup raisins
Dash garlic powder
Chopped peanuts

1 In a medium skillet cook onion and curry powder in butter or margarine till onion is tender. Stir in potatoes, carrots, *undrained* tomatoes, raisins, garlic powder, and ¼ teaspoon *salt*. Bring to boiling; reduce heat. Simmer, uncovered, for 10 minutes. Sprinkle with peanuts. Serves 6.

OVEN VEGETABLES AND RICE

Assembling time: 10 minutes
Cooking time: 45 minutes

2 tablespoons butter or margarine
1 cup long grain rice
⅛ teaspoon dried basil, crushed
1 10-ounce package frozen mixed vegetables

1 In a 1½-quart casserole stir butter into 2 cups *boiling water*. Stir in rice, basil, 1 teaspoon *salt*, and ¼ teaspoon *pepper*. Place frozen vegetables atop.

2 Cover and bake in a 350° oven for 40 to 45 minutes or till rice is tender, stirring after 20 minutes. Stir before serving. Makes 8 servings.

BEETS POLYNESIAN

Assembling time: 5 minutes
Cooking time: 8 minutes

¼ cup packed brown sugar
2 tablespoons all-purpose flour
⅓ cup vinegar
1 8¼-ounce can crushed pineapple
½ cup raisins
2 tablespoons butter *or* margarine
2 16-ounce cans sliced *or* diced beets, drained

1 In a saucepan combine brown sugar, flour, and ¼ teaspoon *salt*; stir in vinegar and ¾ cup *water*. Add *undrained* pineapple, raisins, and butter or margarine.

2 Cook and stir till thickened and bubbly; cook and stir 1 minute more. Stir in beets; heat through. Serves 8 to 10.

DANISH LIMAS

Total preparation time: 20 minutes

1 10-ounce package frozen lima beans
¼ cup chopped celery
1 small onion, chopped (¼ cup)
½ cup dairy sour cream
¼ cup crumbled blue cheese
2 tablespoons chopped pimiento
1 tablespoon cooked bacon pieces

1 In a saucepan cook beans, celery, and onion in boiling salted water for 10 minutes or till tender; drain well. Stir in sour cream and blue cheese.

2 Cook and stir over low heat till mixture is heated through and cheese is melted. *Do not boil.* Stir in pimiento. Turn into a serving dish. Sprinkle bacon atop. Serves 4.

START WITH GELATIN

APPLE-RASPBERRY MOLD

Preparation time: 10 minutes
Chilling time: 30 minutes

- ¾ cup boiling water
- 1 3-ounce package raspberry-flavored gelatin
- 1½ cups ice cubes
- 2 tablespoons lemon juice
- 1 small apple, chopped
- ½ cup applesauce
- ¼ cup chopped walnuts
- 3 tablespoons raisins

1 In a bowl add boiling water to raspberry gelatin. Stir till gelatin is dissolved. Stir in ice cubes and lemon juice. Stir about 3 minutes or till gelatin thickens slightly; remove any remaining ice cubes.

2 Fold in chopped apple, applesauce, chopped walnuts, and raisins. Turn into a 3½-cup ring mold. Chill in freezer about 30 minutes or till firm. Unmold to serve. Makes 6 servings.

DOUBLE CHERRY RING

Preparation time: 6 minutes
Chilling time: 30 minutes

- 1 cup boiling water
- 1 3-ounce package cherry-flavored gelatin
- 1 3-ounce package cream cheese
- 1 cup frozen pitted tart red or dark sweet cherries

1 In blender container combine boiling water and gelatin. Cover; blend 15 to 30 seconds or till gelatin is dissolved. Cut up cream cheese. Add to blender along with frozen cherries. Cover; blend 30 to 45 seconds or till smooth. Turn into a 3½-cup ring mold. Chill in freezer about 30 minutes. Serves 6.

CRANBERRY-ORANGE SALAD

Preparation time: 12 minutes
Chilling time: 45 minutes

- 1 3-ounce package cherry-flavored gelatin
- ½ cup water
- 1 16-ounce can whole cranberry sauce
- 1 8-ounce carton dairy sour cream
- 1 11-ounce can mandarin orange sections, drained
- ¼ cup chopped walnuts
- ⅓ cup mayonnaise or salad dressing

1 In saucepan heat and stir gelatin and water till gelatin is dissolved. Remove from heat. Beat cranberry sauce and *half* of the sour cream into gelatin mixture with rotary beater. Stir in oranges and nuts.

2 Turn into an 8x8x2-inch pan. Chill in freezer about 45 minutes or till firm. To serve, combine remaining sour cream and the mayonnaise. Cut salad into squares; dollop with mayonnaise mixture. Serves 8.

THREE-BEAN-SALAD ASPIC

Preparation time: 15 minutes
Chilling time: 20 minutes

- 1 3-ounce package lemon-flavored gelatin
- ½ cup water
- 1 17-ounce can three-bean salad
- 1 8-ounce can pizza sauce
- ¼ cup finely chopped celery

1 In medium saucepan combine lemon gelatin and water. Heat and stir till gelatin is dissolved. Remove from heat. Stir in *undrained* bean salad, pizza sauce, and celery. Turn into 6 to 8 individual molds. Chill in freezer about 20 minutes or till firm. Unmold to serve. Makes 6 to 8 servings.

DILLY BEAN SALAD

Preparation time: 25 minutes
Chilling time: 20 minutes

- ¼ cup sugar
- 1 envelope unflavored gelatin
- 2 teaspoons minced dried onion
- 1 teaspoon instant chicken bouillon granules
- ¼ teaspoon salt
- ⅔ cup water
- ¼ cup lemon juice
- ½ teaspoon dried dillweed
- 1½ cups ice cubes
- 1 16-ounce can French-style green beans, drained
- 2 tablespoons chopped pimiento
  Lettuce
  Mayonnaise *or* salad dressing

1 In saucepan combine sugar, gelatin, dried onion, bouillon granules, and salt. Add water; heat and stir till ingredients are dissolved. Remove from heat.

2 Stir in lemon juice and dillweed. Add ice cubes; stir about 3 minutes or till gelatin starts to thicken. Remove any remaining ice cubes. Fold in green beans and chopped pimiento.

3 Pour mixture into six ½-cup molds. Chill in freezer about 20 minutes or till firm. Unmold salads onto lettuce-lined plates. Dollop with mayonnaise or salad dressing. Makes 6 servings.

GOLDEN CORN RELISH MOLD

Preparation time: 15 minutes
Chilling time: 30 minutes

½ **cup water**
1 **3-ounce package lemon-flavored gelatin**
¼ **cup Italian salad dressing**
2 **tablespoons vinegar**
2 **cups ice cubes**
1 **8-ounce can whole kernel corn, drained**
½ **cup chopped cabbage**
2 **tablespoons sweet pickle relish**

1 In medium saucepan combine water and gelatin. Heat and stir till gelatin is dissolved. Remove from heat. Stir in salad dressing and vinegar. Add ice cubes; stir about 3 minutes or till gelatin starts to thicken. Remove any remaining ice cubes.

2 Fold in corn, cabbage, and pickle relish. Turn mixture into a 3½-cup ring mold. Cover and chill in freezer about 30 minutes or till firm. Unmold to serve. Makes 6 servings.

ORANGE SHAKE

Total preparation time: 5 minutes

1 **cup cold milk**
1 **3-ounce package orange-flavored gelatin**
1 **pint vanilla ice cream**
1 **8-ounce carton orange yogurt**

1 In blender container combine the milk and orange gelatin. Cover; blend about 30 seconds or till gelatin is dissolved. Spoon in the ice cream and yogurt. Cover and blend about 1 minute more or just till mixed. Makes 3½ cups.

LEMON LIGHTNING CAKE

For a special treat, top this cake with scoops of vanilla ice cream—

Preparation time: 15 minutes
Cooking time: 30 minutes

3 **cups packaged biscuit mix**
½ **cup sugar**
1 **3-ounce package lemon-flavored gelatin**
4 **beaten eggs**
½ **cup milk**
⅓ **cup cooking oil**
1½ **cups sifted powdered sugar**
½ **cup orange juice**
Lemon slices, halved (optional)

1 Grease and flour a 13x9x2-inch baking pan. In a mixing bowl combine the biscuit mix, sugar, and dry gelatin. Combine eggs, milk, and oil; stir into dry ingredients till moistened. Beat vigorously by hand about 1 minute or till smooth. Pour batter into the prepared baking pan. Bake in a 350° oven for 25 to 30 minutes or till cake tests done. Cool in pan on a wire rack for 5 minutes.

2 Meanwhile, in a small bowl stir together the powdered sugar and orange juice till smooth. Using a long-tined fork, poke holes all over top of cake.

3 Pour sugar-orange juice mixture evenly over top of cake. Serve cake warm or cool thoroughly. Just before serving, garnish each portion with a half-slice of lemon, if desired. Makes 10 to 12 servings.

PEACH MELBA DESSERTS

Preparation time: 15 minutes
Chilling time: 20 minutes

1 **envelope unflavored gelatin**
½ **cup water**
1 **10-ounce package frozen peach slices**
½ **cup raspberry yogurt**
¼ **cup Amaretto**
2 **tablespoons grenadine syrup**

1 In medium saucepan combine gelatin and water. Let stand 5 minutes to soften. Heat and stir till gelatin dissolves. Remove from heat. Add frozen peach slices; stir for 3 to 5 minutes or till fruit thaws and gelatin starts to thicken.

2 Stir in yogurt, Amaretto, and grenadine. Spoon mixture into 5 or 6 sherbet or dessert dishes. Chill in refrigerator about 20 minutes. Makes 4 or 5 servings.

QUICK GELATIN IDEAS

For an easy ice cream topping, thaw a pouch of frozen mixed fruit, peaches, strawberries, or raspberries, and stir in a spoonful of your favorite fruit-flavored gelatin right from the package. This topper is especially good with sherbet.

For festive marbled cake, prepare a white cake mix and turn *half* the batter into the baking pan. Stir a spoonful of your favorite flavored gelatin right from the package into the remaining batter. Turn into baking pan. Then swirl with a spatula and bake.

OFF-THE-SHELF COOKING

START WITH BREAD MIX

HOMEMADE BISCUIT MIX

10 cups all-purpose flour
⅓ cup baking powder
¼ cup sugar
4 teaspoons salt
2 cups shortening that does not require refrigeration

1 In large mixing bowl stir together flour, baking powder, sugar, and salt. With pastry blender, cut in shortening till mixture resembles coarse crumbs. Store in covered airtight container up to six weeks at room temperature. (For longer storage, place in a sealed freezer container and store in the freezer for up to six months.) To use, allow mix to come to room temperature. Spoon mix lightly into measuring cup; level off with a straight-edged spatula. Makes 12½ cups.

CHILIES RELLENOS BREAD

Preparation time: 8 minutes
Cooking time: 35 minutes

1½ cups packaged biscuit mix or Homemade Biscuit Mix
1 4-ounce can chopped green chili peppers, drained
½ cup shredded cheddar cheese
2 tablespoons chopped pimiento
⅓ cup milk

1 In mixing bowl stir together biscuit mix, chili peppers, cheese, and chopped pimiento; stir in milk till combined. Spread into a greased 8x1½-inch round baking pan. Bake in a 350° oven for 30 to 35 minutes or till done. Cut into wedges to serve. Makes 6 to 8 servings.

TUNA SOUP WITH CHEESE DUMPLINGS

Another time, make this soup with salmon—

Preparation time: 20 minutes
Cooking time: 20 minutes

1 10-ounce package frozen mixed vegetables
1 14½-ounce can chicken broth
1 10¾-ounce can condensed cream of onion soup
1 cup water
1 9¼-ounce can tuna, drained and broken into chunks
1 cup packaged biscuit mix or Homemade Biscuit Mix
¼ cup grated Parmesan or Romano cheese
⅓ cup milk

1 In a 3-quart saucepan stir together the frozen mixed vegetables, the chicken broth, cream of onion soup, and water. Heat, stirring occasionally, till bubbly. Stir in tuna. Meanwhile, in mixing bowl combine biscuit mix and Parmesan or Romano cheese. Stir in milk just till moistened.

2 Drop dough from a tablespoon to make 8 mounds atop the bubbling soup. Simmer, uncovered, for 10 minutes. Cover and simmer 10 minutes longer (do not lift cover). Makes 4 servings.

CHICKEN-CORNMEAL CASSEROLE

For best results, be sure the chicken mixture is bubbling before you add the topper—

Preparation time: 15 minutes
Cooking time: 20 minutes

1 10¾-ounce can condensed cream of chicken soup
2 5-ounce cans boned chicken or turkey
½ of a 10-ounce package frozen peas
¼ cup sliced water chestnuts
2 teaspoons minced dried onion
⅔ cup packaged biscuit mix or Homemade Biscuit Mix
⅓ cup cornmeal
½ teaspoon dried basil, crushed
⅓ cup milk
1 beaten egg

1 In saucepan combine cream of chicken soup, *undrained* chicken, frozen peas, water chestnuts, and dried onion. Heat till bubbly, stirring occasionally.

2 In a bowl combine the packaged biscuit mix or Homemade Biscuit Mix, cornmeal, and basil. Stir in milk and egg just till moistened.

3 Turn chicken mixture into a 1½-quart casserole. Pour biscuit mixture over all, spreading evenly to edge of casserole. Bake in a 375° oven about 20 minutes or till biscuit topper is done. Makes 4 servings.

NUTMEG SCONES

Preparation time: 12 minutes
Cooking time: 12 minutes

2⅓ **cups packaged biscuit mix *or* Homemade Biscuit Mix**
¼ **cup sugar**
¼ **teaspoon ground nutmeg**
1 **egg**
¼ **cup milk**
2 **tablespoons butter, melted**
   Sugar

1 In bowl combine biscuit mix, the ¼ cup sugar, and nutmeg. Combine egg, milk, and melted butter or margarine; stir into flour mixture just till dough clings together. Knead gently on floured surface for 8 strokes.

2 Pat dough into a 6-inch circle. Cut into 10 wedges. Sprinkle with sugar. Place on ungreased baking sheet. Bake in a 425° oven for 10 to 12 minutes. Serve warm. Makes 10.

OLIVE BATTER BREAD

Preparation time: 10 minutes
Cooking time: 15 minutes

1½ **cups packaged biscuit mix *or* Homemade Biscuit Mix**
¼ **cup grated Parmesan cheese**
¼ **cup chopped pitted ripe olives**
2 **teaspoons minced dried onion**
½ **cup milk**
1 **beaten egg**
1 **tablespoon sesame seed**

1 In bowl combine biscuit mix, Parmesan cheese, chopped olives, and dried onion. Stir in milk and egg till moistened. Spread batter into a greased 8x1½-inch round baking pan. Sprinkle with sesame seed. Bake in a 450° oven about 15 minutes. Serve warm. Makes 6 to 8 servings.

GRANOLA SWIRL COFFEE CAKE

This cake will taste delicious with almost any flavor of fruit preserves—

Preparation time: 15 minutes
Cooking time: 30 minutes
Cooling time: 10 minutes

½ **cup granola**
¼ **cup packed brown sugar**
¼ **cup chopped walnuts**
2 **cups packaged biscuit mix *or* Homemade Biscuit Mix**
2 **tablespoons brown sugar**
⅔ **cup orange juice**
1 **beaten egg**
½ **cup strawberry preserves**
1 **cup sifted powdered sugar**
   Milk

1 In a bowl stir together the granola, the ¼ cup brown sugar, and walnuts; set aside. In a second bowl combine the biscuit mix and the 2 tablespoons brown sugar. Add the orange juice and egg; stir just till moistened.

2 Spread the batter into a greased 9x9x2-inch baking pan. Drop the strawberry preserves by spoonfuls over the batter. Sprinkle with *half* of the brown sugar mixture.

3 Using a narrow spatula, stir gently through the batter to marble. Sprinkle with the remaining brown sugar mixture. Bake in a 375° oven for 25 to 30 minutes or till the cake tests done.

4 Meanwhile, in a bowl stir together the powdered sugar and enough milk (about 1½ tablespoons) to make a glaze of pouring consistency. Cool the cake on a wire rack for 10 minutes. Drizzle glaze over warm cake. Serve slightly warm or cool thoroughly. Makes 9 servings.

PUMPKIN NUT BREAD

Preparation time: 10 minutes
Cooking time: 50 minutes

3 **cups packaged biscuit mix *or* Homemade Biscuit Mix**
½ **cup packed brown sugar**
1 **teaspoon pumpkin pie spice**
2 **beaten eggs**
1 **cup canned pumpkin**
½ **cup milk**
½ **cup sunflower nuts *or* chopped walnuts**

1 In bowl combine biscuit mix, brown sugar, and pumpkin pie spice. Combine the eggs, pumpkin, and milk; stir into biscuit mix mixture just till moistened. Fold in nuts. Turn batter into a greased 9x5x3-inch loaf pan. Bake in a 350° oven about 50 minutes. Cool. Makes 1 loaf.

PEANUT BUTTER COOKIES

Preparation time: 20 minutes
Cooking time: 10 minutes

¾ **cup peanut butter**
½ **cup sugar**
½ **cup packed brown sugar**
1 **egg**
¼ **cup orange juice**
2 **cups packaged biscuit mix *or* Homemade Biscuit Mix**

1 In a mixer bowl beat the peanut butter and sugars with electric mixer till well combined. Beat in egg and orange juice. Add biscuit mix and beat till well combined.

2 Drop dough from a teaspoon onto an ungreased cookie sheet. Flatten by crisscrossing with tines of a fork dipped in sugar, if desired. Bake in a 375° oven for 8 to 10 minutes. Cool 2 minutes on cookie sheet. Remove to rack; cool. Makes 48.

START WITH BREAD MIX

WHEAT GERM MUFFINS

These muffins are great accompaniments for main-dish salads—

Preparation time: 6 minutes
Cooking time: 25 minutes

2/3 **cup packaged biscuit mix** *or*
     Homemade Biscuit Mix
     (see recipe, page 124)
1/3 **cup toasted wheat germ**
1/4 **cup sugar**
  1 **egg**
1/3 **cup water**
  2 **tablespoons peanut butter**
1/2 **teaspoon vanilla**
     Butter curls (optional)
     Grape preserves (optional)

1 In a mixing bowl combine biscuit mix, wheat germ, and sugar. In another small bowl combine the egg, water, peanut butter, and vanilla; beat mixture with a rotary beater till smooth. Add egg mixture to dry ingredients, stirring just till dry ingredients are moistened (do not overmix).

2 Grease muffin cups or line with paper bake cups, fill 2/3 full. Bake in a 375° oven for 20 to 25 minutes or till muffins are golden brown. Serve with butter curls or preserves, if desired. Makes 6 muffins.

Wheat Germ Muffins

UPSIDE-DOWN PEACH CUPS

Preparation time: 17 minutes
Cooking time: 25 minutes

  1 **16-ounce can peach halves**
  1 **3-ounce package cream cheese**
  1 **cup packaged biscuit mix** *or*
     Homemade Biscuit Mix
     (see recipe, page 124)
1/4 **cup sugar**
  1 **beaten egg**

1 Grease five 6-ounce custard cups. Drain peach halves, reserving 1/3 cup syrup. Place each peach half, pitted side up, in a custard cup. Divide cream cheese into 5 equal portions; roll into balls. Place a cream cheese ball in each peach half.

2 In a bowl combine the biscuit mix, sugar, egg, and reserved peach syrup; mix well. Spoon batter over peaches, filling cups 3/4 full. Bake in a 350° oven about 25 minutes or till done. Cool for 5 minutes; invert onto serving plates. Drizzle with melted currant jelly, if desired. Makes 5 servings.

DATE-ORANGE BREAD

Preparation time: 22 minutes
Cooking time: 1 hour

  1 **beaten egg**
1/2 **cup frozen orange juice**
     concentrate, thawed
  1 **17-ounce package date quick**
     bread mix
3/4 **cup quick-cooking rolled oats**

1 In a bowl combine the egg, orange juice concentrate, and 2/3 cup *water*. Stir in the dry bread mix and rolled oats just till moistened. Turn into a greased 8x4x2-inch loaf pan. Bake in a 350° oven for 55 to 60 minutes or till done. Cool 10 minutes on wire rack; remove from pan. Cool. Makes 1.

MOCHA-YOGURT COFFEE CAKE

Preparation time: 30 minutes
Cooking time: 40 minutes

1/4 **cup packed brown sugar**
1/4 **cup chopped nuts**
  1 **tablespoon unsweetened cocoa**
     powder
1½ **teaspoons ground cinnamon**
  1 **teaspoon instant coffee crystals**
3/4 **cup sugar**
  6 **tablespoons butter** *or* **margarine**
  1 **teaspoon vanilla**
  2 **eggs**
1½ **cups packaged biscuit mix** *or*
     Homemade Biscuit Mix
     (see recipe, page 124)
3/4 **cup plain yogurt**
     Sifted powdered sugar

1 In a small bowl combine brown sugar, nuts, cocoa powder, cinnamon, and coffee crystals; set aside. In a mixer bowl beat sugar, butter or margarine, and vanilla on medium speed of electric mixer till fluffy. Add eggs, one at a time, beating well after each addition. Add biscuit mix and yogurt alternately to beaten mixture, stirring just till combined.

2 Spoon about *half* of the batter into a greased 8x8x2-inch baking pan. Sprinkle the nut mixture atop. Spoon the remaining batter over all. With a narrow spatula, swirl batter to marble. Bake in a 350° oven for 35 to 40 minutes or till the cake tests done. Cool slightly on rack. Sprinkle lightly with powdered sugar. Serves 8 or 9.

START WITH
BREAD MIX

GRANOLA NUT BREAD

Preparation time: 15 minutes
Cooking time: 50 minutes

- 1 16-ounce package nut quick bread mix
- ¾ cup milk
- 1 beaten egg
- 2 teaspoons finely shredded orange peel
- ¼ cup orange juice
- ½ cup granola
- ½ cup coconut

1 In a bowl stir together bread mix, milk, egg, orange peel, and orange juice just till moistened. Fold in granola and coconut. Turn into a greased and floured 9x5x3-inch loaf pan. Bake in a 350° oven for 45 to 50 minutes or till done. Cool for 10 minutes; remove from pan. Cool on rack. Makes 1.

APPLE-BANANA SQUARES

Preparation time: 15 minutes
Cooking time: 30 minutes

- 1 15-ounce package banana quick bread mix
- 1 8-ounce jar applesauce
- 1 teaspoon vanilla
- ½ cup snipped dried apples
- ½ cup chopped walnuts
- ¼ cup packed brown sugar
- ¼ cup all-purpose flour
- 2 tablespoons butter, softened

1 Prepare quick bread mix according to package directions, *except* substitute the applesauce for the water and stir in the vanilla. Fold in apples. Turn into a greased 9x9x2-inch baking pan. Mix nuts, brown sugar, flour, and butter; sprinkle over batter. Bake in a 375° oven about 30 minutes. Cool for 10 minutes; cut into squares. Serves 9.

CREAM CHEESE-FILLED DESSERT MUFFINS

Preparation time: 15 minutes
Cooking time: 25 minutes

- 2 3-ounce packages cream cheese, cut up
- 2 tablespoons sugar
- 1 egg
- 1 14½-ounce package gingerbread mix
- ¼ teaspoon ground nutmeg
- ¼ cup sugar (optional)
- ½ teaspoon finely shredded lemon peel (optional)

1 In a small mixer bowl beat the cream cheese and the 2 tablespoons sugar on medium speed of electric mixer till fluffy. Beat in the egg; set aside. Prepare the gingerbread mix according to package directions, *except* stir the nutmeg into the dry mix.

2 Grease muffin cups or line with paper bake cups; fill ½ full with batter. Drop about *1 tablespoon* of the cream cheese mixture atop each batter-filled cup. Dollop remaining batter atop cream cheese.

3 Bake muffins in a 350° oven about 25 minutes or till muffins test done. Remove from pan; cool slightly on wire rack. While muffins are still warm, dip the tops in a mixture of the ¼ cup sugar and the finely shredded lemon peel, if desired. Makes 14 or 15 muffins.

MEXICAN PIZZA

Preparation time: 10 minutes
Cooking time: 25 minutes

- **Cornmeal**
- 1 6½-ounce package pizza crust mix
- 1½ cups shredded cheddar cheese
- ½ teaspoon chili powder
- 1 15-ounce can chili with beans
- ¾ cup broken tortilla chips
- 1 16-ounce can tomato wedges, drained
- **Shredded lettuce**

1 Grease a 12-inch pizza pan; sprinkle with cornmeal. Prepare pizza crust mix according to package directions, *except* stir in *½ cup* of the cheese and the chili powder. Pat dough into pan; build up edges slightly. Bake in 425° oven 10 minutes or till golden.

2 Heat chili; spread over hot crust. Top with remaining cheese and tortilla chips. Bake 10 to 15 minutes or till bubbly. Top with tomatoes and lettuce. Makes 1.

OATMEAL BREAD

Preparation time: 52 minutes
Cooking time: 50 minutes

- 1¼ cups milk
- 1 13¾-ounce package hot roll mix
- 1 single-serving envelope instant oatmeal (any flavor)
- 1 slightly beaten egg

1 Grease an 8x4x2-inch loaf pan. Heat milk till warm (115° to 120°). Stir in the yeast from roll mix and the oatmeal; mix well. Stir milk mixture and egg into flour mixture from roll mix till blended. Turn into pan.

2 Cover; let rise till nearly double (about 40 minutes). Bake in a 350° oven for 45 to 50 minutes or till done. Cover with foil the last 10 minutes to prevent overbrowning. Remove from pan; cool on rack. Makes 1.

HOT ROLL SALLY LUNN

Preparation time: 1¾ hours
Cooking time: 40 minutes

1 cup milk
1 13¾-ounce package hot roll mix
6 tablespoons butter *or* margarine,
   softened
¼ cup sugar
2 eggs
   Butter *or* margarine (optional)
   Preserves (optional)

1 In saucepan heat milk just till warm (115° to 120°). Remove from heat. Add yeast from hot roll mix, stirring to dissolve yeast. Set yeast mixture aside.

2 In large mixer bowl beat the 6 tablespoons butter or margarine and sugar at medium speed of electric mixer till fluffy. Add eggs, one at a time, beating well after each addition.

3 By hand, stir the flour from the hot roll mix and the yeast-milk mixture alternately into butter-sugar mixture. Stir vigorously till dough is smooth; do not overbeat. Cover; let rise in a warm place till double (about 1 hour).

4 Stir batter down; pour into a greased 10-cup Turk's-head mold or fluted tube pan. Let rise till almost double (about 30 minutes).

5 Bake in a 350° oven for 35 to 40 minutes or till done. Remove bread from pan; cool completely on wire rack. Serve with butter or margarine and preserves, if desired. Makes 1.

CHILI PEPPER-CHEESE WEDGES

Preparation time: 15 minutes
Cooking time: 20 minutes

1 package (10) refrigerated biscuits
1 beaten egg
1½ cups shredded Monterey Jack
   cheese *or* cheddar cheese
   (6 ounces)
1 4-ounce can green chili peppers,
   rinsed, seeded, and chopped
1 teaspoon minced dried onion
   Milk
   Poppy seed

1 Separate refrigerated biscuits. On a lightly floured surface arrange *five* of the biscuits in a circle with edges touching. Pat or roll out biscuits into an 8-inch circle. Carefully transfer to a greased baking sheet.

2 In a bowl combine the egg, Monterey Jack or cheddar cheese, green chili peppers, and minced onion; spoon over biscuit circle to within ½ inch of edge. On a lightly floured surface roll remaining biscuits into an 8-inch circle as above. Place over cheese mixture. Moisten edges with water; seal. Flute edges.

3 Brush top of circle with milk; sprinkle with poppy seed. Prick circle with fork to let steam escape. Bake in a 350° oven about 20 minutes or till golden brown. To serve, cut into wedges. Serves 6 to 8.

BACON CORN MUFFINS

Preparation time: 5 minutes
Cooking time: 25 minutes

1 beaten egg
1 8½-ounce package corn muffin
   mix
1 8-ounce carton dairy sour cream
3 tablespoons cooked bacon pieces

1 In bowl combine egg, muffin mix, and sour cream, stirring just till moistened. Fold in bacon pieces. Grease muffin pans or line with paper bake cups; fill ⅔ full. Bake in a 400° oven for 20 to 25 minutes or till done. Makes 10 muffins.

CHIVE COTTAGE CHEESE CORN BREAD

Preparation time: 8 minutes
Cooking time: 30 minutes

1 10-ounce package corn bread mix
1 egg
1 8-ounce can cream-style corn
1 slightly beaten egg
1 cup cream-style cottage cheese
   with chives, drained

1 Prepare corn bread mix according to package directions, *except* add 1 egg and substitute the cream-style corn for the milk called for on package. Turn batter into a greased 9x9x2-inch baking pan.

2 In a bowl combine the slightly beaten egg and cottage cheese; pour over batter in pan. Swirl gently with spoon to marble mixtures. Bake in a 375° oven for 25 to 30 minutes or till done. Makes 9 servings.

START WITH CAKE MIX

COCONUT CAKE RING

Preparation time: 15 minutes
Cooking time: 30 minutes

- 3 **tablespoons butter** *or* **margarine**
- ¼ **cup packed brown sugar**
- 2 **tablespoons light corn syrup**
- ⅓ **cup flaked coconut**
- ⅓ **cup chopped pecans**
- 1 **package snack-type applesauce-raisin cake mix**

1 In saucepan melt butter; stir in brown sugar, corn syrup, and 1 tablespoon *water*. Pour into an ungreased 5½-cup oven-proof ring mold; sprinkle with coconut and pecans. Prepare cake mix according to package directions; pour into mold.

2 Bake in a 350° oven for 25 to 30 minutes or till cake tests done. Immediately loosen sides and invert cake onto a serving plate. Serve warm. Makes 8 servings.

PEANUT BUTTER STREUSEL CAKE

Preparation time: 12 minutes
Cooking time: 50 minutes

- ⅓ **cup all-purpose flour**
- ⅓ **cup sugar**
- ½ **cup peanut butter**
- 1 **16-ounce package pound cake mix**

1 Grease and lightly flour a 9x9x2-inch baking pan. In a mixing bowl combine flour and sugar. Cut in peanut butter just till mixture resembles coarse crumbs.

2 Prepare cake mix according to package directions. Turn *half* of the batter into prepared pan; sprinkle *half* of the peanut butter mixture over batter. Top with remaining batter; sprinkle with remaining peanut butter mixture. Bake in a 325° oven about 50 minutes or till done. Serve warm. Makes 9 servings.

CHERRY CUPCAKE TORTES

Preparation time: 50 minutes
Cooking time: 15 minutes

- 1 **package 1-layer-size chocolate cake mix**
- ½ **teaspoon ground cinnamon**
- ¼ **teaspoon ground nutmeg**
- 1 **can sour cream-chocolate** *or* **cream cheese frosting**
- 1 **21-ounce can cherry pie filling**

1 Line muffin pans with paper bake cups. Prepare and bake cake mix according to package directions for cupcakes, *except* add cinnamon and nutmeg. Cool on rack 30 minutes.

2 If desired, remove paper bake cups. Spread or pipe a border of frosting at edge of each cupcake. (Store remaining frosting for another use.) Carefully spoon a little cherry pie filling into the center of each cupcake. Chill. Makes 12 tortes.

CHOCOLATE-RAISIN CAKE

Preparation time: 8 minutes
Cooking time: 35 minutes

- 1 **2-layer-size German chocolate** *or* **Swiss chocolate cake mix**
- 1½ **teaspoons ground cinnamon**
- 1 **22-ounce can raisin pie filling**
- 3 **slightly beaten eggs**
  Sifted powdered sugar

1 Grease and flour a 13x9x2-inch baking pan. In a bowl combine cake mix and cinnamon. Add pie filling and eggs; stir just till combined. Turn into prepared pan. Bake in a 350° oven about 35 minutes or till done. Cool on wire rack. Sprinkle with powdered sugar. Serves 12.

APRICOT-ALMOND UPSIDE-DOWN CAKE

Preparation time: 20 minutes
Cooking time: 30 minutes

- 1 **8¾-ounce can unpeeled apricot halves**
- 2 **tablespoons butter** *or* **margarine**
- ⅓ **cup packed brown sugar**
- ¼ **cup slivered almonds**
- 1 **package 1-layer-size yellow cake mix**
- ¼ **teaspoon ground nutmeg**
  Frozen whipped dessert topping, thawed

1 Drain apricots, reserving 2 tablespoons syrup. Preheat oven to 350°. Place butter or margarine in a 9x1½-inch round baking pan. Melt butter in pan in oven while preheating. Remove pan.

2 Stir brown sugar and the reserved syrup into pan. Spread mixture evenly over bottom of pan; sprinkle almonds atop. Arrange apricot halves, cut side up, over brown sugar mixture.

3 Prepare cake mix according to package directions, *except* add nutmeg. Pour batter over apricots. Bake cake in a 350° oven about 30 minutes or till cake tests done. Cool on wire rack 5 minutes. Loosen sides; invert cake onto a serving plate. Serve warm topped with thawed whipped dessert topping. Makes 8 servings.

**Cherry Cupcake Tortes
Coconut Cake Ring**

START WITH CAKE MIX

MINCEMEAT CAKE RING

Preparation time: 20 minutes
Cooking time: 65 minutes

1 package 2-layer-size yellow
   cake mix
½ teaspoon pumpkin pie spice
1 cup prepared mincemeat
½ cup applesauce
¼ cup cooking oil
4 eggs
1 cup finely chopped walnuts

1 Grease and lightly flour a 10-inch fluted tube pan. In large mixer bowl combine cake mix and pumpkin pie spice. Add mincemeat, applesauce, cooking oil, and eggs. Beat at medium speed of electric mixer 3 minutes. Stir in nuts. Turn into pan.
2 Bake in a 350° oven for 60 to 65 minutes. Cool on rack 10 minutes. Remove from pan; cool. Sprinkle with sifted powdered sugar, if desired. Serves 8 to 10.

CRANBERRY-BANANA CAKE

Preparation time: 7 minutes
Cooking time: 30 minutes

1 package 1-layer-size yellow
   cake mix
1 ripe medium banana, mashed
1 8-ounce can whole cranberry
   sauce
½ cup flaked coconut

1 Grease and lightly flour an 8x8x2-inch baking pan. Prepare cake mix according to package directions, *except* add banana in place of liquid. Turn into pan. Bake according to package directions.
2 Combine cranberry sauce and coconut. Spread over warm cake in pan. Broil 4 to 5 inches from heat for 3 to 5 minutes or till bubbly. Serve warm. Serves 9.

EASY PECAN PIE BARS

For a special dessert, cut these bars larger and top them with vanilla ice cream—

Preparation time: 12 minutes
Cooking time: 40 minutes

1 package 2-layer-size white
   cake mix
¼ cup butter *or* margarine, softened
1 slightly beaten egg
3 eggs
¾ cup dark corn syrup
¾ cup packed brown sugar
1 teaspoon vanilla
¾ cup chopped pecans

1 Set aside ⅔ *cup* of the dry white cake mix. In medium mixing bowl combine the remaining cake mix, softened butter or margarine, and the egg. Stir by hand just till mixture is crumbly. With floured hands press mixture evenly over bottom and 1 inch up sides of an ungreased 13x9x2-inch baking pan. Bake in a 350° oven for 15 minutes.
2 Meanwhile, in a mixing bowl combine the 3 eggs, dark corn syrup, packed brown sugar, and vanilla. Add the ⅔ cup reserved cake mix; stir by hand just till mixture is blended (some specks of cake mix will remain).
3 Spread evenly over baked crust in pan; sprinkle pecans atop. Bake for 20 to 25 minutes or till filling is set. Cool completely in pan on wire rack; cut into bars. Makes 48.

PINEAPPLE PUDDING CAKE

Preparation time: 10 minutes
Cooking time: 45 minutes

1 package 1-layer-size yellow
   cake mix
2¼ cups unsweetened
   pineapple juice
1 package 4-serving-size *regular*
   lemon pudding mix

1 Grease and lightly flour a 9x9x2-inch baking pan. Prepare cake mix according to package directions. Turn batter into prepared pan. Gradually stir pineapple juice into pudding mix. Pour evenly over batter.
2 Bake cake in a 350° oven for 40 to 45 minutes or till cake tests done. Loosen sides; invert onto serving plate. Serve warm with whipped cream, if desired. Serves 9.

QUICK CHERRY COBBLER

Preparation time: 15 minutes
Cooking time: 25 minutes

1 16-ounce can pitted tart red
   cherries
⅓ cup sugar
2 tablespoons quick-cooking tapioca
   Few drops almond extract
1 package 1-layer-size yellow
   cake mix
½ cup plain yogurt
1 egg

1 In saucepan combine *undrained* cherries, sugar, tapioca, and almond extract. Let stand 5 minutes. In a bowl mix cake mix, yogurt, and egg till moistened.
2 Bring cherries to boiling. Turn into a 10x6x2-inch baking dish. Spoon cake batter atop hot cherry mixture in 6 mounds. Bake in a 350° oven about 25 minutes or till done. Serve warm. Makes 6 servings.

ORANGE-CARROT CAKE

Preparation time: 20 minutes
Cooking time: 40 minutes

- 1 package 2-layer-size spice *or* applesauce spice cake mix
- 1 1-inch-square piece orange peel
- 1 cup orange juice
- ¼ cup cooking oil
- 3 eggs
- 4 medium carrots, sliced (2 cups)
- ½ cup chopped walnuts
- ½ cup raisins
- 1 package creamy white frosting mix (for 1-layer cake)
- 1 3-ounce package cream cheese, cut up
- 1 to 2 teaspoons orange juice

1 Place dry cake mix in large mixer bowl. In blender container place orange peel, the 1 cup orange juice, cooking oil, and eggs. Add carrots. Cover and blend till carrots are finely chopped.

2 Pour carrot mixture over cake mix. Beat on low speed of electric mixer till blended, then on medium speed for 2 minutes. Stir in walnuts and raisins. Turn batter into a greased 13x9x2-inch baking pan. Bake in a 350° oven for 35 to 40 minutes or till cake tests done. Cool on wire rack.

3 In small mixer bowl beat frosting mix and cream cheese with electric mixer till blended. Beat in enough of the 1 to 2 teaspoons orange juice to make a frosting of spreading consistency. Spread over top of cake. Makes 12 servings.

PEANUT BUTTER-CHOCOLATE CHIP BARS

Preparation time: 10 minutes
Cooking time: 25 minutes

- 1 package 2-layer-size white cake mix
- ½ cup peanut butter
- 1 egg
- ¼ cup milk
- 2 tablespoons butter *or* margarine, softened
- 1 3-ounce package cream cheese, cut up
- 2 eggs
- 1 teaspoon vanilla
- 1 6-ounce package semisweet chocolate pieces
- ½ cup chopped peanuts

1 Set aside ¾ *cup* dry cake mix. In large mixer bowl combine remaining cake mix, peanut butter, the egg, milk, and butter or margarine. Beat on low speed of electric mixer for 1 minute. Press into bottom of a greased 13x9x2-inch baking pan. Bake in a 350° oven for 10 minutes.

2 Meanwhile, in small mixer bowl beat cream cheese, the 2 eggs, and vanilla till smooth. Beat in the reserved ¾ cup cake mix; stir in chocolate pieces and peanuts. Carefully spread over baked layer. Return to 350° oven; bake about 15 minutes more. Cool on wire rack. Cut into bars while warm. Makes 36 bars.

COCONUT-DATE CAKE

Preparation time: 20 minutes
Cooking time: 40 minutes

- Water
- 1 package 2-layer-size yellow cake mix
- 1 8-ounce package chopped pitted dates
- 1 egg
- 1 5⅓-ounce can (⅔ cup) evaporated milk
- ½ cup sugar
- ¼ cup butter *or* margarine
- 1 3½-ounce can (1⅓ cups) flaked coconut

1 Measure the amount of water called for on the cake mix package; bring to boiling. Set aside ½ *cup* of the dates. Add remaining dates to hot water; let stand about 15 minutes or till cooled slightly.

2 Grease and lightly flour a 13x9x2-inch baking pan. Prepare cake mix according to package directions, *except* use the date-water mixture in place of the water called for on the package. Turn batter into prepared pan. Bake in a 350° oven for 35 to 40 minutes or till cake tests done.

3 Meanwhile, in a saucepan beat egg slightly. Stir in the evaporated milk, sugar, and butter or margarine. Cook and stir over medium heat about 10 minutes or till mixture is thickened and bubbly. Stir in the flaked coconut and the reserved ½ cup dates; cool until cake has finished baking. Spread over warm cake. Serve warm or cool. Makes 12 servings.

START WITH COOKIE MIX

ORANGE-COCONUT DROPS

Preparation time: 8 minutes
Cooking time: 10 minutes

- 1 package 3-dozen-size sugar cookie mix
- 1/4 teaspoon ground cinnamon
  Dash ground cloves
- 1/2 cup coconut
- 1/4 cup orange marmalade

1 In a bowl combine cookie mix, cinnamon, and cloves; prepare according to package directions. Stir in the coconut and orange marmalade. Drop cookie batter from a teaspoon 2 inches apart onto an ungreased cookie sheet.

2 Bake cookies according to package directions. Cool cookies on a wire rack. If desired, spoon about 1/2 teaspoon additional orange marmalade onto *each* cookie and sprinkle with a little additional coconut. Makes about 36 cookies.

ALMOND SUGAR COOKIES

Preparation time: 16 minutes
Cooking time: 10 minutes

- 1 package 3-dozen-size sugar cookie mix
- 1/2 cup slivered almonds, chopped
- 1/2 teaspoon ground nutmeg, cardamom, *or* cinnamon

1 Prepare cookie mix according to package directions. Stir in chopped slivered almonds and nutmeg, cardamom, or cinnamon. Shape into 1-inch balls. Place on an ungreased cookie sheet.

2 Bake cookies according to package directions. Cool cookies on cookie sheet about 1 minute before removing to a wire rack; cool thoroughly. Makes 36 cookies.

ORANGE-OATMEAL COFFEE CAKE

Preparation time: 10 minutes
Cooking time: 25 minutes
Cooling time: 15 minutes

- 1 package 3-dozen-size oatmeal cookie mix
- 1/4 teaspoon ground cinnamon
- 2 beaten eggs
- 1/3 cup orange juice
- 1 11-ounce can mandarin orange sections, drained

1 For topping, measure *1/2 cup* of the cookie mix into a small bowl; stir in the cinnamon. Set aside. In a mixing bowl combine the eggs, remaining cookie mix, and orange juice. Stir till well combined.

2 Spread in a greased 8x8x2-inch baking pan. Arrange oranges atop batter; sprinkle with topping. Bake in a 375° oven for 20 to 25 minutes. Cool 15 minutes. Cut into squares; serve warm. Serves 9.

CHEESE-OATMEAL COOKIES

Preparation time: 11 minutes
Cooking time: 10 minutes

- 1 4-ounce package (1 cup) shredded sharp cheddar cheese
- 1/2 cup sunflower nuts
- 1 package 3-dozen-size oatmeal cookie mix
- 2 tablespoons honey

1 In a mixing bowl stir cheese and sunflower nuts into dry cookie mix. Prepare mix according to package directions; stir in honey. Drop from a teaspoon 2 inches apart on an ungreased cookie sheet.

2 Bake cookies according to package directions. Cool cookies on cookie sheet about 1 minute before removing to a wire rack; cool thoroughly. Makes about 48.

MOCHA-DATE DROPS

Preparation time: 10 minutes
Cooking time: 10 minutes

- 1 package 3-dozen-size chocolate cookie mix
- 2 tablespoons hot water
- 1 teaspoon instant coffee crystals
- 1 8-ounce package chopped pitted dates

1 Prepare cookie mix according to package directions. Combine hot water and coffee crystals; stir into cookie dough. Stir in dates. Drop from a teaspoon 2 inches apart onto an ungreased cookie sheet.

2 Bake cookies according to package directions. Cool cookies on cookie sheet about 1 minute before removing to a wire rack; cool thoroughly. Makes 48 cookies.

OATMEAL-CHIP COOKIES

For crisp cookies, omit the milk—

Preparation time: 15 minutes
Cooking time: 10 minutes

- 1 package 3-dozen-size chocolate chip cookie mix
- 1/3 cup milk (optional)
- 1 1/2 cups quick-cooking rolled oats
- 1/2 cup chopped peanuts

1 Prepare cookie mix according to package directions; stir in milk, if desired. Stir in rolled oats and peanuts. Drop from a teaspoon 2 inches apart onto an ungreased cookie sheet.

2 Bake cookies according to package directions. Cool cookies on cookie sheet about 1 minute before removing to a wire rack; cool thoroughly. Makes about 32.

PEANUT BUTTER-CHOCOLATE BARS

Preparation time: 15 minutes
Cooking time: 25 minutes

1 package 6-dozen-size peanut
   butter cookie mix
1 6-ounce package (1 cup)
   semisweet chocolate pieces
½ cup peanut butter
1 cup crisp rice cereal

1 Prepare cookie mix according to package directions. Press dough into an ungreased 15x10x1-inch baking pan. Bake in a 350° oven for 20 to 25 minutes or till done. Cool in pan on a rack for 5 minutes.

2 Meanwhile, melt chocolate over low heat; stir in peanut butter till melted. Spread over baked layer; sprinkle with rice cereal. Cool in pan on wire rack. Cut into bars. Makes about 48 bars.

GRANOLA-PEANUT BUTTER COOKIES

Preparation time: 11 minutes
Cooking time: 10 minutes

1 package 3-dozen-size peanut
   butter cookie mix
3 tablespoons orange juice *or* milk
1 cup granola
½ cup raisins

1 Prepare cookie mix according to package directions; stir in orange juice or milk. Stir in granola and raisins. Drop from a teaspoon 2 inches apart onto an ungreased cookie sheet.

2 Bake cookies according to package directions. Cool cookies on cookie sheet about 1 minute before removing to a rack; cool thoroughly. Makes 42 to 48 cookies.

PEANUT BUTTER-BROWNIE BARS

Preparation time: 15 minutes
Cooking time: 30 minutes

1 package 3-dozen-size peanut
   butter cookie mix
1 8-ounce package brownie mix
½ of a can chocolate frosting

1 Prepare peanut butter cookie mix according to package directions. Press cookie dough into bottom of an ungreased 9x9x2-inch baking pan. Bake in a 350° oven for 10 minutes.

2 Meanwhile, prepare brownie mix according to package directions. Spoon brownie mix in small spoonfuls evenly across top of cookie mix, spreading carefully. Return to oven; bake about 20 minutes more or till done. Cool thoroughly on a wire rack. Spread with chocolate frosting. Cut into bars. Makes 24 bars.

OATMEAL-CARROT DESSERT SQUARES

Preparation time: 10 minutes
Cooking time: 35 minutes

1 package 3-dozen-size oatmeal
   cookie mix
⅓ cup milk
1 egg
⅔ cup finely shredded carrot
⅓ cup raisins

1 Grease an 8x8x2-inch baking pan. Prepare cookie mix according to package directions, *except* stir in the milk and egg with the other ingredients called for on package. Stir in shredded carrot and raisins.

2 Spread mixture in prepared pan. Bake in a 350° oven for 30 to 35 minutes or till done. While warm, cut into squares. If desired, serve *each* topped with a scoop of ice cream or frozen yogurt. Serves 9.

CREAM CHEESE-MARBLED BROWNIES

Preparation time: 15 minutes
Cooking time: 45 minutes

1 15½-ounce package fudge
   brownie mix
1 8-ounce package cream cheese,
   cut up
½ cup sugar
1 egg
½ cup chopped nuts (optional)

1 Grease a 9x9x2-inch baking pan. Prepare the brownie mix according to package directions. Spread *half* of the brownie batter in the prepared pan. Bake in a 350° oven for 10 minutes.

2 Meanwhile, in a mixer bowl beat the cut-up cream cheese and sugar till fluffy. Add the egg; beat to combine. Stir in the chopped nuts, if desired. Pour the cream cheese mixture over partially baked layer.

3 Carefully spoon the remaining brownie batter over cream cheese mixture. To marble the brownies, use a narrow spatula to swirl through the light and dark layers, being careful not to touch the bottom layer. Return to the oven; bake 30 to 35 minutes more or till brownies test done. Cool in pan on a wire rack. Cut into bars. Makes 24 bars.

CHAPTER 4

FAST COOKING

If you're usually in a rush when it's time to make a meal, here's a helping hand. Since all of the foods in this chapter go together in 45 minutes or less, you can use them to ease your busy schedule. Just start with any of the shortcut meat, poultry, fish, seafood, or egg main dishes. Then add one or two of the quick-as-a-wink salads, vegetables, pasta, and rice side dishes, breads, or desserts. Presto—your meal is ready to bring to the table. Or

if you like, give an impromptu party with some of the appetizer, snack, or beverage ideas. To cut cooking time even further, refer to the time-saving tips and fix-ups.

This quartet of fast recipes is proof positive that foods can be both quick and delicious: Beef and Squash Dinner (see recipe, page 142), Parmesan Slices (see recipe, page 202), Oriental Sprout Salad (see recipe, page 187), and Cran-Orange Sipper (see recipe, page 221).

CURRIED HAMBURGER AND FRUIT

Assembling time: 15 minutes
Cooking time: 10 minutes

- 1 **pound ground beef**
- 1 **medium onion, chopped (½ cup)**
- 1 **tablespoon all-purpose flour**
- ½ **teaspoon salt**
- ¼ **teaspoon pepper**
- 1 **8¼-ounce can pineapple chunks**
- 2 to 3 **teaspoons curry powder**
- 1½ **teaspoons instant beef bouillon granules**
- 1 **medium apple, cored and chopped**
  Hot cooked rice
  Chopped nuts *or* **raisins (optional)**

1 In a 10-inch skillet cook ground beef and chopped onion till meat is browned and onion is tender. Drain off fat. Sprinkle the meat mixture with the flour, salt, and pepper. Stir to combine.

2 Drain pineapple, reserving the syrup. Add enough water to the reserved syrup to measure 1 cup liquid. Stir the pineapple liquid, curry powder, and bouillon granules into the meat mixture. Cook and stir till thickened and bubbly. Cook and stir 1 minute more.

3 Stir in pineapple chunks and chopped apple. Simmer, covered, about 5 minutes or till heated through. Serve over hot cooked rice. Top each serving with chopped nuts or raisins, if desired. Serves 4.

ZUCCHINI-SAUCED BEEF

Total preparation time: 25 minutes

- 1 **pound ground beef**
  Garlic salt
- 1 **medium zucchini, thinly sliced**
- 1 **8-ounce can pizza sauce**
- 1 **small onion, chopped (¼ cup)**
- 2 **slices mozzarella cheese**

1 Shape meat into one ½-inch-thick patty; sprinkle with garlic salt and pepper. Place on the rack of an unheated broiler pan. Broil 3 inches from heat to desired doneness, turning once (allow about 10 minutes total time for medium).

2 Meanwhile, combine zucchini, pizza sauce, and onion. Cover and cook 10 to 15 minutes. Top meat with cheese. Broil 1 minute or till cheese melts. Cut into wedges; serve with zucchini mixture. Serves 4.

PIZZA PATTIES

Assembling time: 8 minutes
Cooking time: 30 minutes

- 1 **8-ounce can tomato sauce**
- ¾ **teaspoon dried tarragon, crushed**
- ¾ **teaspoon dried basil, crushed**
- ⅛ **teaspoon garlic powder**
- 1 **beaten egg**
- ¼ **cup fine dry bread crumbs**
- 1 **pound ground beef** *or* **pork**
- ½ **cup shredded mozzarella cheese**

1 Combine first 4 ingredients and ⅛ teaspoon *pepper*. Combine ⅓ *cup* of tomato mixture, the egg, bread crumbs, and ¾ teaspoon *salt*. Add meat; mix well. Shape into five ½-inch-thick patties.

2 Place patties in a shallow baking pan. Bake, uncovered, in a 350° oven for 20 to 25 minutes. Drain off fat. Spoon remaining tomato mixture atop. Sprinkle with cheese. Bake 3 minutes more. Serves 5.

HEALTH BURGERS

Assembling time: 12 minutes
Cooking time: 10 minutes

- ½ **teaspoon instant beef bouillon granules**
- ⅓ **cup hot water**
- ¼ **cup toasted wheat germ**
- ½ **teaspoon minced dried onion**
- 1 **pound ground beef, pork, lamb,** *or* **veal**
- 1 **cup shredded zucchini**
- 1 **cup alfalfa sprouts** *or* **wheat sprouts**
- ¼ **cup chopped walnuts**
- ¼ **cup creamy cucumber salad dressing**
- 4 **whole wheat hamburger buns, split,** *or* **2 pita bread rounds, cut in half crosswise**

1 In a mixing bowl dissolve bouillon granules in hot water; stir in wheat germ and onion. Let stand a few minutes to rehydrate dried onion. Add ground meat; mix well. Shape into four ½-inch-thick patties.

2 If using lamb or veal options, melt 2 tablespoons *shortening* in a 10-inch skillet. In the skillet cook meat patties over medium-high heat to desired doneness, turning once. (Allow 8 to 10 minutes total time for medium doneness for beef or lamb; cook pork 12 to 15 minutes total time or till meat patties are well done.)

3 Meanwhile, combine shredded zucchini, sprouts, walnuts, and salad dressing. Place patties on bottoms of buns or in pita bread halves; top each patty with some of the zucchini mixture. If using buns, top with remaining bun halves. Serves 4.

TACO-CHEESE BURGERS

Assembling time: 18 minutes
Cooking time: 22 minutes

1 pound ground beef
1 medium onion, chopped (½ cup)
1 7½-ounce can tomatoes, cut up
¼ cup water
1½ to 2 teaspoons chili powder
1 teaspoon Worcestershire sauce
¾ teaspoon garlic salt
½ teaspoon sugar
½ teaspoon dry mustard
6 hamburger buns, split and toasted
1 cup shredded lettuce
1 cup shredded American cheese
   (4 ounces)
Taco sauce

1 In a 10-inch skillet cook ground beef and onion till beef is browned. Drain off fat. Stir in *undrained* tomatoes, water, chili powder, Worcestershire sauce, garlic salt, sugar, and dry mustard.

2 Bring to boiling; reduce heat. Boil gently, uncovered, for 15 to 20 minutes or till of desired consistency. Spoon onto bottoms of buns. Sprinkle with lettuce and American cheese. Add the bun tops. Pass the taco sauce. Makes 6 servings.

BROWNING GROUND MEATS

To evenly brown ground meats, use the back of a wooden spoon or a fork to break the meat into large chunks. Stir occasionally during cooking, but be sure to avoid breaking the meat into pieces that are too small.

FRANKFURTER LOGS

Assembling time: 12 minutes
Cooking time: 10 minutes

1 beaten egg
2 tablespoons grated Parmesan cheese
½ teaspoon salt
½ teaspoon dried oregano, crushed
⅛ teaspoon pepper
1 pound ground beef
3 frankfurters *or* smoked sausage links
½ cup pizza sauce *or* bottled barbecue sauce
6 frankfurter buns, split and toasted
   Grated Parmesan cheese (optional)

1 In a mixing bowl combine the beaten egg, 2 tablespoons grated Parmesan cheese, salt, oregano, and pepper. Add ground beef; mix well. Cut frankfurters or sausage links in half lengthwise. Shape *one-sixth* of the ground beef mixture around *each* frankfurter half.

2 Place on the rack of an unheated broiler pan. Broil 4 to 5 inches from heat till ground beef is of desired doneness, turning once. (Allow about 10 minutes total time for medium doneness.)

3 Meanwhile, in a small saucepan heat the pizza sauce or barbecue sauce. Serve ground-beef-coated frankfurters in toasted buns. Spoon warm sauce atop. Sprinkle with additional grated Parmesan cheese, if desired. Makes 6 servings.

OPEN-FACE PITAS

Total preparation time: 30 minutes

¼ cup cooking oil
3 tablespoons dry red wine
2 tablespoons lemon juice
1 tablespoon sugar
1 teaspoon dried basil, crushed
½ teaspoon salt
2 large pita bread rounds, halved horizontally
1 10-ounce package frozen chopped spinach
½ teaspoon ground nutmeg
1 pound ground beef, pork, lamb, veal, *or* ground raw turkey
1 clove garlic, minced
   Assorted toppers (crumbled feta cheese, chopped tomato, sliced pitted ripe olives, thinly sliced onion rings)

1 In a screw-top jar combine cooking oil, red wine, lemon juice, sugar, basil, and salt. Cover and shake well. Set aside. Place pita bread halves on a baking sheet; toast in a 350° oven for 8 to 10 minutes.

2 Meanwhile, cook spinach according to package directions; drain and press out excess liquid. Stir in nutmeg; cover and keep warm. In a 10-inch skillet cook ground meat and garlic till the meat is browned. Drain off fat. Season meat mixture to taste with salt and pepper.

3 To assemble, top each toasted pita bread half with *one-fourth* of the spinach mixture, then *one-fourth* of the meat mixture. Sprinkle with assorted toppers, as desired. Shake red wine mixture and pass with pitas. Serve immediately. Makes 4 servings.

ORIENTAL BEEF AND PEAS

Assembling time: 20 minutes
Cooking time: 20 minutes

- 1 **pound beef round steak**
- 2 **tablespoons cornstarch**
- 1 **tablespoon brown sugar**
- 1 **teaspoon instant beef bouillon granules**
- ¾ **cup water**
- ⅓ **cup dry white wine**
- ¼ **cup soy sauce**
- 1 **tablespoon cooking oil**
- 1 **medium onion, sliced**
- 1 **green pepper, cut into 1-inch pieces**
- 1 **cup frozen loose-pack peas**
- 1 **cup fresh bean sprouts**
  Chow mein noodles

1 Thinly slice round steak into bite-size strips. Set aside. Combine cornstarch, brown sugar, and bouillon granules; stir in water, wine, and soy sauce. Set aside.

2 Preheat a large skillet or wok over high heat; add oil. Stir-fry onion, green pepper, and peas in hot oil for 3 minutes. Remove from wok. Add more oil, if necessary.

3 Add *half* of the beef to hot skillet or wok; stir-fry 2 to 3 minutes or till done. Remove beef. Stir-fry remaining beef 2 to 3 minutes. Return all meat to skillet or wok.

4 Stir soy mixture; stir into meat. Cook and stir till thickened and bubbly. Cook and stir 2 minutes more. Return vegetables to skillet; stir in bean sprouts. Cover and cook 1 minute more. Serve over chow mein noodles. Makes 4 servings.

MEXICAN MEAT CUPS

Total preparation time: 28 minutes

- 1 **package (10) refrigerated biscuits**
- 1 **pound ground beef**
- 1 **15½-ounce can chili beans**
- 1 **15¼-ounce can Mexican-style sandwich sauce**
- 1 **cup shredded cheddar cheese**

1 Roll or pat each biscuit into a 3½- to 4-inch circle; fit over the backs of well-greased muffin pans. Bake in a 400° oven for 8 to 9 minutes or till golden brown.

2 Meanwhile, cook meat till brown. Drain off fat. Stir in beans, sandwich sauce, and ¼ cup *water*; bring to boiling. Remove biscuits from pans. Fill with meat mixture. Sprinkle with shredded lettuce and chopped tomato, if desired. Top with cheese. Makes 5 servings.

MEAT AND POTATO BURGERS

Assembling time: 10 minutes
Cooking time: 10 minutes

- 1 **pound ground beef**
- 2 **teaspoons minced dried onion**
- 1 **cup frozen loose-pack hash brown potatoes**
- ½ **cup dairy sour cream**
- ½ **teaspoon dried dillweed**
- 4 **hamburger buns, split and toasted**

1 Combine meat, onion, and ¼ teaspoon *salt*; mix well. Stir in potatoes. Shape into four ½-inch-thick patties. Place on the rack of an unheated broiler pan. Broil 3 inches from heat to desired doneness, turning once. (Allow 10 minutes total time for medium.)

2 Meanwhile, combine sour cream and dillweed. Serve patties in buns, spooning a dollop of the sour cream mixture atop each patty. Makes 4 servings.

BROILED STEAK AND VEGETABLES

Assembling time: 10 minutes
Cooking time: 22 minutes

- 2 **pounds boneless beef sirloin steak, cut 1½ inches thick**
- ½ **cup cooking oil**
- ½ **cup dry red wine**
- 2 **tablespoons minced dried onion**
- 2 **teaspoons sugar**
- 2 **teaspoons dried basil, crushed**
- 2 **teaspoons dried oregano, crushed**
- ½ **teaspoon garlic salt**
- ¼ **teaspoon pepper**
- 3 **or 4 medium tomatoes, halved**
- 12 **large whole fresh mushrooms**
- ¼ **cup grated Parmesan cheese**

1 With a knife, slash the fat edge of the sirloin steak at 1-inch intervals. Place steak on the rack of an unheated broiler pan. In a mixing bowl combine cooking oil, red wine, dried onion, sugar, basil, oregano, garlic salt, and pepper. Brush some of the wine mixture over steak.

2 Broil steak 3 to 4 inches from heat for 10 minutes, brushing occasionally with wine mixture. Turn steak with tongs. Arrange tomatoe halves and mushrooms on the rack around the steak.

3 Continue broiling for 6 to 8 minutes for medium or to desired doneness; brush steak occasionally with wine mixture. Sprinkle Parmesan cheese atop tomatoes. Broil 2 minutes more. Arrange steak on platter; cut across the grain into thin slices. Arrange vegetables around steak. Season to taste. Serve immediately. Makes 8 servings.

Mexican Meat Cups

BLUE CHEESE STROGANOFF

Total preparation time: 30 minutes

3 slices bacon
1 pound beef cubed steaks
½ cup hot water
1 teaspoon instant beef bouillon
  granules
1 10-ounce package frozen peas
  with pearl onions
1 8-ounce package cream cheese,
  cut up
⅔ cup milk
2 ounces blue cheese, crumbled,
  (½ cup)
3 tablespoons all-purpose flour
Hot cooked noodles

1 In a 10-inch skillet cook bacon till crisp; drain bacon, reserving drippings in skillet. Crumble bacon; set aside. Cut beef steaks into bite-size strips; cook meat in reserved drippings till brown.

2 Combine water and bouillon granules; pour over meat. Bring to boiling; add frozen peas with onions. Cover; cook 5 to 7 minutes or till vegetables are tender.

3 Meanwhile, in a small mixer bowl combine cream cheese, *half* of the milk, blue cheese, and flour; beat at low speed of an electric mixer till well mixed. Add remaining milk; beat till smooth.

4 Stir cream cheese mixture into meat mixture; cook and stir till thickened and bubbly. Cook and stir 1 minute more. Serve steak strips and sauce over hot cooked noodles; top with crumbled bacon. Serves 5.

BEEF AND SQUASH DINNER

Pictured on page 137—

Assembling time: 20 minutes
Cooking time: 26 minutes

1 pound beef round steak
2 tablespoons cooking oil
1½ cups water
1 ¾-ounce envelope mushroom
  gravy mix
1 teaspoon instant beef bouillon
  granules
½ teaspoon dried marjoram, crushed
¼ teaspoon garlic powder
¼ teaspoon minced dried onion
1 10-ounce package frozen summer
  squash
1 3-ounce can sliced mushrooms
2 tablespoons cold water
1 tablespoon cornstarch
1 cup cherry tomatoes, halved
Hot cooked noodles

1 Thinly slice round steak into bite-size strips. In a 10-inch skillet brown the meat, *half* at a time, in hot oil. Drain off fat. Return all meat to skillet. Stir in the 1½ cups water, mushroom gravy mix, beef bouillon granules, crushed marjoram, garlic powder, and minced dried onion.

2 Bring meat mixture to boiling, stirring constantly. Reduce heat. Cover and simmer about 15 minutes or till meat is tender. Add squash and *undrained* mushrooms to skillet. Bring to boiling, separating squash slices. Reduce heat; cover and simmer 3 minutes.

3 Stir together 2 tablespoons cold water and cornstarch; stir into meat mixture. Cook and stir till thickened and bubbly. Cook and stir 2 minutes more. Stir in tomatoes; cover and heat 1 minute. Serve over hot cooked noodles. Makes 4 servings.

FANCY BEEF AND RICE DINNER

Assembling time: 12 minutes
Cooking time: 20 minutes

1 pound beef top loin steak
6 green onions, sliced into ½-inch
  lengths
1 tablespoon butter *or* margarine
2 tablespoons butter *or* margarine
¼ cup dry red wine
¼ teaspoon salt
⅛ teaspoon pepper
½ cup dairy sour cream
2 teaspoons all-purpose flour
Hot cooked rice
Snipped parsley

1 Thinly slice beef into bite-size strips. Set aside. In a 10-inch skillet cook onions in 1 tablespoon butter or margarine till tender but not brown; remove and set aside.

2 Add 2 tablespoons butter or margarine to skillet. Add half of the beef; cook quickly over high heat, stirring frequently, for 2 to 3 minutes or till done. Remove beef from skillet. Repeat with remaining beef. Return all meat to skillet.

3 Stir wine, salt, pepper, and green onions into meat. Bring to boiling; reduce heat. Stir together sour cream and flour. Stir into meat mixture. Cook and stir till heated through; *do not boil.* Serve meat mixture over hot cooked rice. Garnish with snipped parsley. Makes 4 servings.

ONION-TOPPED STEAK

Assembling time: 15 minutes
Cooking time: 18 minutes

1 tablespoon butter *or* margarine
1 large onion, chopped (1 cup)
2 tablespoons dairy sour cream
¼ teaspoon dried tarragon, crushed
1 1½-pound beef sirloin steak, cut 1 inch thick

1 In a saucepan melt butter. Add onion; cook till tender. Remove from heat. Stir in sour cream and crushed tarragon.

2 Slash the fat edge of steak at 1-inch intervals. Place steak on the rack of an unheated broiler pan. Broil 3 inches from heat to desired doneness, turning once. (Allow 12 to 14 minutes total time for medium.) Season with salt and pepper. Top with onion mixture. Broil 2 minutes more. Serves 4.

SAUCY CUBED STEAKS

Assembling time: 10 minutes
Cooking time: 32 minutes

4 beef *or* pork cubed steaks
1 large onion, sliced and separated into rings
2 tablespoons cooking oil
1 7½-ounce can semicondensed cream of mushroom soup
1 2-ounce can sliced mushrooms, drained
¼ cup dry white wine

1 In a 10-inch skillet cook cubed steaks and onion in oil till meat is brown. Drain off fat. Stir together cream of mushroom soup, mushrooms, and wine. Add to steaks. Simmer, covered, for 20 to 25 minutes or till meat is tender. Uncover; simmer 5 minutes more or till sauce is of desired consistency. Transfer to serving platter. Serves 4.

BEEF AND ASPARAGUS

Assembling time: 15 minutes
Cooking time: 16 minutes

1 pound beef round steak
1 large onion, sliced and separated into rings
2 tablespoons butter *or* margarine
¾ cup water
1 5¾-ounce can steak sauce with mushrooms
2 teaspoons instant beef bouillon granules
½ teaspoon dried thyme, crushed
1 8-ounce package frozen cut asparagus
½ cup plain yogurt
1 tablespoon all-purpose flour
Hot cooked noodles

1 Thinly slice steak into bite-size strips. In 12-inch skillet cook steak and onion in butter till meat is browned.

2 Add the water, steak sauce, beef bouillon granules, and crushed thyme. Stir in the frozen cut asparagus. Bring to boiling; reduce heat. Cover and simmer for 5 to 6 minutes or till asparagus is just tender.

3 Stir together the yogurt and flour. Stir into the meat-asparagus mixture in the skillet. Cook and stir till thickened and bubbly. Cook and stir 1 minute more. Serve over hot cooked noodles. Makes 4 servings.

SLICING MEATS

To easily slice frozen meat into thin bite-size strips, allow it to partially thaw for 20 to 25 minutes at room temperature. Then cut the meat across the grain. If you're starting with fresh rather than frozen meat, freeze it for 15 to 20 minutes before you slice it.

MEXICAN BEEF SOUP

You can substitute shredded Monterey Jack cheese or mozzarella cheese for the cheddar that is sprinkled atop the soup—

Assembling time: 15 minutes
Cooking time: 25 minutes

½ pound beef round steak
1 large onion, chopped (1 cup)
1 stalk celery, sliced
1 tablespoon cooking oil
1 16-ounce can refried beans
1 10½-ounce can condensed beef broth
1 cup water
1 small green pepper, chopped
½ teaspoon chili powder
¼ teaspoon minced dried garlic
¼ teaspoon pepper
Several dashes bottled hot pepper sauce
Shredded cheddar cheese
Crushed tortilla chips

1 Cut the round steak into ½-inch pieces. In a 3-quart saucepan cook the meat, onion, and celery in hot oil till the meat is brown. Drain off fat.

2 Stir in refried beans, condensed beef broth, water, chopped green pepper, chili powder, dried garlic, pepper, and hot pepper sauce. Bring meat mixture to boiling. Reduce heat; cover and simmer for 15 minutes. Serve in soup bowls. Pass shredded cheddar cheese and crushed tortilla chips to sprinkle atop. Makes 4 servings.

SALAD-STYLE BEEF 'N' CHEESE TOSTADAS

Assembling time: 15 minutes
Chilling time: 15 minutes

1 12-ounce can chopped beef
⅓ cup salad oil
3 tablespoons vinegar
2 teaspoons chili powder
½ teaspoon onion powder
½ teaspoon sugar
1 8-ounce can red kidney beans, drained
1 cup shredded cheddar cheese (4 ounces)
1 small green pepper, cut into thin strips
½ cup sliced pitted ripe olives
5 cups shredded lettuce
6 tostada shells
  Taco sauce (optional)

1 Use a fork to break the chopped beef into bite-size chunks. In a mixing bowl combine salad oil, vinegar, chili powder, onion powder, and sugar; add beef chunks, drained red kidney beans, shredded cheddar cheese, green pepper strips, and sliced ripe olives. Toss to coat. Chill meat mixture in the freezer for 15 minutes.

2 Stir shredded lettuce into chilled beef mixture. Spoon about 1½ cups of beef-lettuce mixture atop *each* tostada shell. If desired, pass taco sauce. Serves 6.

BEEF AND NOODLE SOUP

Assembling time: 12 minutes
Cooking time: 20 minutes

1 pound ground beef *or* pork
2 10½-ounce cans condensed beef broth
1 10½-ounce can condensed onion soup
3 soup cans (3¾ cups) water
2 ounces medium noodles (1½ cups)
2 tablespoons dried parsley flakes

1 Cook meat till browned. Drain off fat. Stir in broth, soup, water, *uncooked* noodles, and parsley. Bring to boiling; reduce heat. Cover; simmer about 15 minutes or till noodles are tender, stirring occasionally. Sprinkle each serving with grated Parmesan cheese, if desired. Serves 6.

FIESTA BURGERS

Assembling time: 15 minutes
Cooking time: 10 minutes

1 beaten egg
¼ cup taco sauce
¾ cup soft bread crumbs (1 slice)
1 teaspoon chili powder
1 pound ground beef
  Taco sauce
4 lettuce leaves
4 hamburger buns, split and toasted
  Shredded cheddar cheese

1 Combine egg and ¼ cup taco sauce. Stir in bread crumbs, chili powder, and ½ teaspoon *salt*. Add ground beef; mix well. Shape mixture into four ½-inch-thick patties.

2 Place on rack of unheated broiler pan. Broil 3 inches from heat to desired doneness, turning once. (Allow 10 minutes for medium.) Brush with taco sauce. Place lettuce on bottoms of buns; top with patties, cheese, and bun tops. Serves 4.

VEAL CUTLETS IN SOUR CREAM SAUCE

Assembling time: 5 minutes
Cooking time: 10 minutes

1 pound veal leg round steak, cut ¼ inch thick
3 tablespoons butter *or* margarine
1 3-ounce can sliced mushrooms
2 tablespoons milk
⅛ teaspoon dried tarragon, crushed
⅓ cup dairy sour cream
1 teaspoon all-purpose flour

1 Cut veal leg round steak into 4 serving-size pieces; pound each piece with a meat mallet to about ⅛-inch thickness. Sprinkle with salt and pepper.

2 In a 12-inch skillet cook *half* of the veal in hot butter or margarine over medium-high heat about 1 minute on each side. Remove veal to a serving platter; keep warm. Add a little more butter or margarine to skillet, if necessary. Repeat cooking with remaining veal. Remove and keep warm.

3 To skillet drippings add *undrained* sliced mushrooms, milk, and crushed tarragon. Stir together the sour cream and flour. Stir the sour cream mixture into the milk mixture in the skillet. Cook and stir till heated through; *do not boil.* Serve over veal steak. Makes 4 servings.

SWEET-AND-SOUR LIVER KABOBS

Assembling time: 25 minutes
Cooking time: 10 minutes

12 to 16 small boiling onions
1 medium zucchini, cut into 1-inch
   slices
1 8¼-ounce can pineapple slices
⅓ cup cold water
¼ cup soy sauce
3 tablespoons dry sherry
2 tablespoons lemon juice
1 tablespoon cornstarch
1 clove garlic, minced
1 pound beef liver

1 In a medium saucepan cook small boiling onions and zucchini slices, covered, in boiling salted water for 3 minutes; drain. Set aside. Drain pineapple slices, reserving ¼ cup of the syrup; set aside. Quarter pineapple slices.

2 In a small saucepan combine the reserved pineapple syrup, cold water, soy sauce, dry sherry, lemon juice, cornstarch, and minced garlic clove. Cook and stir till thickened and bubbly. Cook and stir 2 minutes more.

3 Cut liver into 4x1x¼-inch strips. On six 10-inch skewers thread liver accordion-style alternately with partially cooked onions and zucchini slices and the quartered pineapple slices. Place skewers on the rack of an unheated broiler pan. Broil 3 inches from heat for 7 to 8 minutes or till meat is done, turning once. Brush kabobs often with soy mixture. Makes 6 servings.

PORK AND PEPPERS

Assembling time: 20 minutes
Cooking time: 20 minutes

1 pound lean boneless pork
3 tablespoons lime juice
3 tablespoons soy sauce
1 tablespoon sugar
1½ teaspoons cornstarch
¼ teaspoon ground ginger
2 tablespoons cooking oil
2 large onions, sliced and separated
   into rings
1 large carrot, coarsely shredded
1 4-ounce can chopped green chili
   peppers, drained
⅓ cup peanuts

1 Thinly slice the pork into bite-size strips. Set aside. In a small mixing bowl combine lime juice and soy sauce; stir in sugar, cornstarch, and ginger; set aside. Preheat a large skillet or wok over high heat; add cooking oil. Stir-fry onion and carrot in hot oil for 2 to 3 minutes. Remove from skillet.

2 Add more oil, if necessary. Add *half* of the pork; stir-fry 2 to 3 minutes. Remove. Stir-fry remaining pork 2 to 3 minutes. Return all pork to skillet or wok.

3 Stir soy mixture; add to pork in skillet or wok. Cook and stir till thickened and bubbly. Cook and stir 2 minutes more. Stir in onion, carrot, green chili peppers, and peanuts. Cover and cook 1 to 2 minutes or till heated through. Makes 4 servings.

PORK STIR-FRY WITH HOISIN SAUCE

Assembling time: 15 minutes
Cooking time: 18 minutes

1 pound boneless pork
⅓ cup water
2 tablespoons hoisin sauce
2 tablespoons soy sauce
1 teaspoon cornstarch
2 tablespoons cooking oil
1 large onion, sliced and separated
   into rings
1 large green pepper, cut into 1-inch
   pieces
1 8-ounce can bamboo shoots,
   drained
   Hot cooked rice

1 Thinly slice boneless pork into bite-size strips; set aside. In a small mixing bowl combine the water, hoisin sauce, soy sauce, and cornstarch; set hoisin sauce mixture aside. Preheat a large skillet or wok over high heat. Add cooking oil.

2 Stir-fry onion rings and green pepper pieces in hot cooking oil for 2 minutes. Remove from skillet or wok. Add more cooking oil, if necessary. Add *half* of the pork strips to the skillet or wok; stir-fry 2 to 3 minutes. Remove pork. Stir-fry remaining pork strips 2 to 3 minutes. Return all pork to skillet or wok.

3 Stir hoisin sauce mixture. Add to pork in skillet or wok. Cook and stir till thickened and bubbly. Cook and stir 2 minutes more. Stir in drained bamboo shoots and onion-green pepper mixture. Cover and cook 1 minute. Serve over hot cooked rice. Makes 4 servings.

PEPPERY FRIED RICE WITH PORK

Assembling time: 25 minutes
Cooking time: 15 minutes

- **1 pound boneless pork**
- **1½ cups quick-cooking rice**
- **2 beaten eggs**
- **1 tablespoon cooking oil**
- **1 6-ounce package frozen pea pods**
- **1 small sweet red *or* green pepper, cut into bite-size strips**
- **1 clove garlic, minced**
- **1 tablespoon cooking oil**
- **⅓ cup sliced water chestnuts**
- **3 tablespoons soy sauce**
- **¼ teaspoon ground ginger**
- **¼ teaspoon crushed red pepper**

1 Thinly slice the pork into bite-size strips. Prepare rice according to package directions *except* omit the salt. Meanwhile, in a 10-inch skillet cook the eggs in 1 tablespoon oil, without stirring, till set. Invert skillet over a baking sheet to remove cooked eggs; cut into short narrow strips.

2 In the same skillet cook frozen pea pods, red or green pepper strips, and minced garlic in 1 tablespoon cooking oil about 1 minute or till the pea pods are thawed. Remove from skillet.

3 Add more oil, if necessary. Add *half* of the pork to the skillet. Stir-fry pork 2 to 3 minutes or till done. Remove from skillet. Stir-fry remaining pork 2 to 3 minutes or till done. Return all of the pork to the skillet.

4 Stir in the cooked rice, egg strips, cooked vegetable mixture, water chestnuts, soy sauce, ginger, and crushed red pepper. Heat through. Pass additional soy sauce, if desired. Makes 6 servings.

Peppery Fried Rice with Pork

PORK CHOPS WITH CABBAGE

Total preparation time: 25 minutes

- **6 pork loin chops, cut 1 inch thick**
- **1 tablespoon butter *or* margarine**
- **1 small head cabbage, cored and chopped**
- **1 small onion, chopped (¼ cup)**
- **1 small clove garlic, minced**
- **1 tablespoon all-purpose flour**
- **1 teaspoon dried parsley flakes**
- **½ teaspoon salt**
- **¼ teaspoon dry mustard**
- **¼ teaspoon dried tarragon, crushed**
- **¼ teaspoon pepper**
- **¾ cup milk**

1 Place chops on the rack of an unheated broiler pan. Broil chops 3 to 4 inches from heat for 10 to 12 minutes. Season with salt and pepper. Turn chops; broil 10 to 12 minutes more or till done.

2 Meanwhile, in a small saucepan melt butter or margarine. Add chopped cabbage, chopped onion, and minced garlic. Cook cabbage mixture, covered, 3 to 4 minutes or till cabbage is tender.

3 In a small mixing bowl combine flour, dried parsley flakes, salt, dry mustard, crushed tarragon, and pepper. Stir into cabbage mixture. Add milk all at once. Cook and stir till thickened and bubbly. Cook and stir 1 minute more. To serve, spoon cabbage mixture over chops. Makes 6 servings.

PORK CHOPS WITH MUSTARD SAUCE

Total preparation time: 35 minutes

- **6 pork chops, cut ½ inch thick**
- **½ teaspoon salt**
- **¼ teaspoon pepper**
- **2 tablespoons cooking oil**
- **1 small onion, chopped (¼ cup)**
- **2 tablespoons all-purpose flour**
- **1 tablespoon dry mustard**
- **1 teaspoon instant beef bouillon granules**
- **¼ teaspoon dried oregano, crushed**
- **1 cup milk**
- **1 8-ounce can stewed tomatoes, cut up**
- **2 tablespoons vinegar**
- **Hot cooked rice**

1 Season pork chops with salt and pepper. In a 12-inch skillet cook pork chops, uncovered, in hot cooking oil over medium heat for 15 to 20 minutes, turning once. Remove pork chops from skillet; keep warm. Drain; reserve 1 tablespoon drippings.

2 In the same skillet cook chopped onion in reserved drippings till tender. Stir in flour, dry mustard, beef bouillon granules, and oregano. Add milk all at once; cook and stir till thickened and bubbly. Cook and stir 1 minute more. Stir in *undrained* stewed tomatoes and vinegar; heat through.

3 To serve, arrange the pork chops atop the hot cooked rice; spoon some of the mustard-tomato mixture over the pork chops. Pass remaining mixture. Serves 6.

PORK CHOPS WITH BRUSSELS SPROUTS

Smoked pork chops have an aromatic flavor similar to smoked ham—

Assembling time: 10 minutes
Cooking time: 20 minutes

- 1 tablespoon butter *or* margarine
- 3 smoked pork chops, cut ½ inch thick
- 1 10-ounce package frozen brussels sprouts
- 1 medium apple, sliced
- ¼ cup water
- 1 teaspoon lemon juice
- ½ teaspoon minced dried onion
- 1 tablespoon cold water
- 1 teaspoon cornstarch

1 In a 10-inch skillet melt the butter or margarine. Add the smoked pork chops, frozen brussels sprouts, and sliced apple to the skillet. Stir in the ¼ cup water, lemon juice, and onion. Bring to boiling; reduce heat. Cover and simmer about 15 minutes or till the pork chops are heated through and the vegetables are tender.

2 With a slotted spoon remove chops, sprouts, and apple to a serving platter. To make sauce, combine the 1 tablespoon cold water and the cornstarch; stir into the skillet drippings. Cook and stir till thickened and bubbly. Cook and stir 2 minutes more. Spoon sauce over pork chops, brussels sprouts, and apple. Makes 3 servings.

NEW ENGLAND-STYLE PLATTER

Assembling time: 10 minutes
Cooking time: 20 minutes

- 1 12-ounce can beer
- ¾ cup water
- 1 small onion, chopped (¼ cup)
- 1 tablespoon brown sugar
- 1 teaspoon dry mustard
- 1 bay leaf
- ½ teaspoon salt
- ¼ teaspoon pepper
- ⅛ teaspoon minced dried garlic
- 3 smoked pork chops, cut ¾ inch thick
- 1 16-ounce can whole new potatoes, drained
- 1 cup frozen crinkle-cut sliced carrots
- 1 small head cabbage, cored and cut into six wedges

1 In a Dutch oven combine beer, water, onion, brown sugar, dry mustard, bay leaf, salt, pepper, and garlic. Bring to boiling; reduce heat. Add the pork chops, potatoes, carrots, and cabbage to Dutch oven. Cover and simmer about 15 minutes or till cabbage and carrots are tender.

2 Remove pork chops and vegetables to a serving platter. Remove bay leaf from pan juices. Pass the pan juices with meat and vegetables. Makes 3 servings.

MEXICAN PORK CHOPS

Total preparation time: 25 minutes

- 4 pork chops, cut ½ inch thick
- ¼ cup taco sauce
- 1 canned green chili pepper, rinsed, seeded, and cut into four strips
- ¾ cup shredded Monterey Jack cheese

1 Place pork chops on the rack of an unheated broiler pan; season chops with salt and pepper. Broil 3 inches from heat for 8 to 10 minutes. Turn chops; broil 8 to 10 minutes more or till done.

2 Brush chops liberally with taco sauce; place chili pepper strips atop chops. Top evenly with shredded cheese. Broil just till cheese melts. Makes 4 servings.

PORK SUPPER IN A SKILLET

Assembling time: 10 minutes
Cooking time: 18 minutes

- 4 pork cubed steaks
- 2 tablespoons cooking oil
- 1 16-ounce can sliced potatoes
- 1 16-ounce can sauerkraut, drained
- 1 small green pepper, cut into strips
- ½ cup water
- 2 teaspoons minced dried onion
- 1½ teaspoons instant chicken bouillon granules
- 1 teaspoon caraway seed

1 In a skillet brown the meat on both sides in hot oil. Remove meat. Drain off fat. Drain the potatoes. Combine potatoes, sauerkraut, green pepper, water, onion, bouillon granules, and caraway in the skillet.

2 Bring the potato mixture to boiling. Place meat atop mixture. Reduce heat. Cover and simmer about 15 minutes or till green pepper is tender. Makes 4 servings.

BARBECUED PORK SANDWICHES

You can easily substitute ground beef for the ground pork in this recipe—

Assembling time: 20 minutes
Cooking time: 18 minutes

1 pound ground pork
1 small onion, chopped (¼ cup)
1 small green pepper, cut into bite-
   size strips
1 8-ounce can tomato sauce
¼ cup sliced pitted ripe olives
2 tablespoons vinegar
1 tablespoon brown sugar
2 teaspoons Worcestershire sauce
1 teaspoon chili powder
1 teaspoon prepared horseradish
½ teaspoon paprika
¼ teaspoon minced dried garlic
3 pita bread rounds, cut in half
   crosswise
1 cup shredded cheddar cheese
   (4 ounces)
   Alfalfa sprouts

1 In a 10-inch skillet cook ground pork, onion, and green pepper till meat is brown and onion is tender. Drain off fat. Stir in tomato sauce, olives, vinegar, brown sugar, Worcestershire sauce, chili powder, horseradish, paprika, and dried garlic.

2 Bring meat mixture to boiling. Reduce heat; cover and simmer for 15 minutes. To serve, spoon mixture into pita bread halves. Top with shredded cheddar cheese and alfalfa sprouts. Makes 6 servings.

PORK BEAN STEW

Assembling time: 15 minutes
Cooking time: 20 minutes

3 pork cubed steaks
1 large onion, chopped (1 cup)
2 tablespoons cooking oil
1 11½-ounce can condensed bean-
   with-bacon soup
2 medium carrots, sliced
1 teaspoon Worcestershire sauce
¼ teaspoon dry mustard

1 Cut steaks into bite-size pieces. Cook meat and onion in hot oil till meat is browned. Drain off fat. Stir in soup, carrots, Worcestershire sauce, dry mustard, and 2 cups *water*. Bring to boiling. Reduce heat; cover; simmer for 15 minutes. Serves 3.

CURRANT-GLAZED PORK PATTIES

Assembling time: 8 minutes
Cooking time: 15 minutes

2 tablespoons orange juice
1 green onion, sliced (1 tablespoon)
1 teaspoon Worcestershire sauce
1 pound ground pork
¼ cup currant jelly
1 tablespoon orange juice

1 In a bowl combine 2 tablespoons orange juice, green onion, Worcestershire sauce, ½ teaspoon *salt*, and dash *pepper*. Add ground pork; mix well. Shape into four ½-inch-thick patties. Place patties on the rack of an unheated broiler pan. Broil 3 inches from heat for 8 minutes.

2 Meanwhile, in a saucepan combine currant jelly and 1 tablespoon orange juice; heat to melt jelly. Brush patties with melted jelly mixture. Turn patties; broil 7 minutes more or till done. Drizzle with remaining jelly mixture. Makes 4 servings.

PORK STEW WITH CORNMEAL DUMPLINGS

Assembling time: 10 minutes
Cooking time: 23 minutes

¾ pound ground pork
½ of a 20-ounce package frozen
   loose-pack mixed zucchini,
   carrots, cauliflower, lima beans,
   and Italian beans
1 cup tomato juice
½ teaspoon ground cumin
¼ teaspoon salt
¼ teaspoon instant beef bouillon
   granules
⅛ teaspoon ground coriander
   Dash pepper
1 package (6) refrigerated biscuits
2 tablespoons butter *or* margarine,
   melted
   Yellow cornmeal

1 In an 8-inch skillet cook ground pork till browned; drain off fat. Stir in vegetables, tomato juice, ground cumin, salt, beef bouillon granules, coriander, and pepper. Bring to boiling. Reduce heat; cover and simmer for 5 minutes.

2 Meanwhile, for dumplings, dip biscuits in melted butter or margarine. Dip tops of biscuits in cornmeal. Break up the vegetables in ground pork mixture, if necessary. Place biscuits, cornmeal side up, atop bubbling meat mixture. Cover and simmer for 12 to 15 minutes more; *do not lift lid*. Serve immediately. Makes 3 servings.

STUFFED KNACKWURST AND POTATO SALAD

Assembling time: 15 minutes
Cooking time: 30 minutes

2 16-ounce cans German-style
    potato salad
1½ pounds fully cooked knackwurst
1 8-ounce can sauerkraut, drained
    and snipped
4 slices Swiss cheese, each cut into
    4 strips (4 ounces)
¼ cup dairy sour cream
¼ cup mayonnaise *or* salad dressing
¼ cup catsup
1 teaspoon dried dillweed
¼ teaspoon garlic salt
⅛ teaspoon pepper

1 Spread potato salad in a 12×7½×2-inch baking dish. Slice knackwurst lengthwise three-fourths of the way through; spread open. In *each* knackwurst spoon *2 tablespoons* sauerkraut; top with *2 strips* cheese. Press knackwurst, stuffed side up, into potato salad.

2 Bake, uncovered, in a 350° oven for 25 to 30 minutes. Meanwhile, combine sour cream, mayonnaise or salad dressing, catsup, dillweed, garlic salt, and pepper; mix well. If desired, heat over low heat just till warm. Pass the sour cream mixture to spoon over each serving. Makes 6 servings.

CHILI-SALAMI SALAD

Total preparation time: 20 minutes

1 medium onion, chopped (½ cup)
1 tablespoon butter *or* margarine
1 15½-ounce can chili beans
1 head lettuce, torn (6 cups)
8 slices salami, cut into eighths
    (6 ounces)
1 medium tomato, chopped
½ cup shredded cheddar cheese
1 cup slightly crushed corn chips *or*
    tortilla chips

1 In a small saucepan cook the onion in butter or margarine till tender; add chili beans and heat till bubbly. Meanwhile, in a large salad bowl combine lettuce, salami, tomato, and cheese. Pour the hot chili bean mixture atop salad. Top with chips. To serve, toss lightly to coat. Makes 4 servings.

CHILI-CHEESE FRANKS

Assembling time: 5 minutes
Cooking time: 8 minutes

1 15½-ounce can chili with beans
½ of an 11-ounce can condensed
    cheddar cheese soup
2 teaspoons minced dried onion
1 pound frankfurters (8 to 10)
8 to 10 frankfurter buns, split and
    toasted
1 to 1½ cups corn chips *or* tortilla
    chips, coarsely crushed

1 In a large saucepan combine chili, cheese soup, and onion. Add frankfurters; bring to boiling. Reduce heat; simmer, uncovered, about 5 minutes. To serve, place a frank in each bun; top with chili-cheese mixture and sprinkle with corn chips. Makes 4 or 5 servings.

SPICY FRANKFURTER SOUP

Assembling time: 20 minutes
Cooking time: 12 minutes

1 pound frankfurters (8 to 10)
1 large onion, chopped (1 cup)
2 stalks celery, sliced (1 cup)
1 small green pepper, chopped
    (½ cup)
2 tablespoons butter *or* margarine
1 16-ounce can refried beans
¼ teaspoon pepper
¼ teaspoon chili powder
⅛ teaspoon minced dried garlic
    Several dashes bottled hot pepper
    sauce (optional)
1 10¾-ounce can condensed
    chicken broth
1 8¾-ounce can whole kernel corn
½ cup water
    Shredded cheddar cheese
    Chopped tomato
    Tortilla chips

1 Thinly slice frankfurters; set aside. In a 3-quart saucepan cook onion, celery, and green pepper in butter or margarine till tender. Add refried beans, pepper, chili powder, minced dried garlic, and hot pepper sauce. Stir in chicken broth, *undrained* corn, water, and sliced frankfurters.

2 Bring frankfurter mixture to boiling. Reduce heat; cover and simmer for 10 minutes. Serve in soup bowls; pass shredded cheese, tomato, and tortilla chips to sprinkle atop each serving. Serves 5.

Chili-Salami Salad

SAUERKRAUT AND SAUSAGE SOUP

You can substitute fully cooked Polish sausage for the knackwurst—

Assembling time: 10 minutes
Cooking time: 15 minutes

½ **pound fully cooked knackwurst**
2 **cups water**
1 **16-ounce can sliced potatoes**
1 **8-ounce can sauerkraut, rinsed and drained**
1 **small onion, chopped (¼ cup)**
1 **tablespoon dried parsley flakes**
2 **teaspoons instant chicken bouillon granules**
¼ **teaspoon salt**
¼ **teaspoon caraway seed**
½ **cup dairy sour cream**
1 **tablespoon all-purpose flour**

1 Thinly slice knackwurst. In a large saucepan combine knackwurst slices, water, *undrained* potatoes, drained sauerkraut, chopped onion, dried parsley flakes, chicken bouillon granules, salt, and caraway seed. Bring to boiling. Reduce heat; cover and simmer for 5 minutes. Skim off any fat.

2 In a bowl combine sour cream and flour; stir in about ½ *cup* of the hot knackwurst mixture. Return all to the saucepan. Cook and stir till slightly thickened and bubbly. Cook and stir 1 minute more. Makes 3 servings.

ZIPPY SAUCED FRANKFURTERS

Assembling time: 8 minutes
Cooking time: 12 minutes

1 **pound frankfurters (8 to 10)**
⅓ **cup packed brown sugar**
1 **tablespoon cornstarch**
¼ **cup water**
¼ **cup red wine vinegar**
¼ **cup catsup**
1 **teaspoon Worcestershire sauce**
1 **4-ounce can green chili peppers, rinsed, seeded, and chopped**
6 **hamburger *or* frankfurter buns, split and toasted**

1 Thinly slice frankfurters. In a saucepan combine brown sugar and cornstarch; stir in water, red wine vinegar, catsup, and Worcestershire sauce. Stir in frankfurters and chili peppers. Bring to boiling. Reduce heat; simmer, uncovered, for 10 minutes. Serve in buns. Makes 6 servings.

SAUSAGE KABOBS

Assembling time: 10 minutes
Cooking time: 12 minutes

1 **pound fully cooked Polish sausage links**
1 **8¼-ounce can pineapple chunks**
1 **large green pepper, cut into 1-inch pieces**
⅓ **cup French salad dressing**

1 Cut sausage into 1-inch chunks. Drain pineapple, reserving 2 tablespoons syrup. On 4 skewers alternately thread sausage, pineapple, and green pepper. For sauce, combine syrup and salad dressing.

2 Broil kabobs 4 to 5 inches from heat for 10 to 12 minutes, turning occasionally and brushing with sauce. Brush with sauce before serving. Makes 4 servings.

BRATWURST SKILLET

For a different flavor, substitute knackwurst or Polish sausage for the bratwurst—

Assembling time: 15 minutes
Cooking time: 25 minutes

1 **pound fresh *or* fully cooked bratwurst**
1 **cup water**
1 **medium onion, chopped (½ cup)**
¼ **cup chopped green pepper**
2 **teaspoons instant beef bouillon granules**
1 **teaspoon dry mustard**
1 **small head cabbage, cored and cut into wedges**
4 **medium carrots, cut into 1-inch pieces**
½ **cup milk**
3 **tablespoons all-purpose flour**

1 Cut bratwurst crosswise into halves. Place bratwurst in an unheated, large skillet. Place over low heat and cook bratwurst about 10 minutes or till browned, turning occasionally.

2 Stir in water, chopped onion, chopped green pepper, beef bouillon granules, and dry mustard; mix well. Add cabbage wedges and carrot pieces to bratwurst mixture in skillet. Cook, covered, about 20 minutes or till vegetables are tender.

3 Remove bratwurst, cabbage, and carrots to a platter; keep warm. Stir together milk and flour; add to mixture in skillet. Cook and stir till thickened and bubbly. Cook and stir 1 minute more. Pour over meat and vegetables on platter. Makes 4 servings.

SAUSAGE PIZZA

Assembling time: 15 minutes
Cooking time: 24 minutes

1 package active dry yeast
¾ cup warm water (110° to 115°)
2¾ cups packaged biscuit mix
1½ cups shredded mozzarella cheese
   or Swiss cheese (6 ounces)
1 beaten egg
6 ounces sliced cooked sausage
   (choose a sausage such as
   bologna, salami, pepperoni, *or*
   summer sausage)
1 cup ricotta *or* cream-style cottage
   cheese, drained
½ cup grated Parmesan cheese
1 tablespoon dried parsley flakes

1 In a mixing bowl soften the yeast in warm water. Add biscuit mix; beat vigorously with a spoon till the dough forms a ball. Sprinkle a surface with a little additional biscuit mix. Turn dough out onto surface; knead 25 strokes. Cover; let rest 5 minutes.

2 Divide dough in half and roll each half into a circle 13 inches in diameter. Transfer each circle of dough to a greased 12-inch pizza pan. Build up edges slightly. Bake in a 425° oven for 6 to 8 minutes or till lightly browned.

3 Meanwhile, cut sausage into strips; set aside. In a mixing bowl combine egg, mozzarella or Swiss cheese, ricotta or cottage cheese, Parmesan cheese, and parsley flakes. Add sausage strips; mix well.

4 Spread *half* of the cheese-sausage mixture on *each* partially baked pizza crust. Return pizzas to the 425° oven; bake for 10 to 15 minutes longer or till mixture is bubbly. Makes two 12-inch pizzas.

SAUSAGE SUPPER

Assembling time: 15 minutes
Cooking time: 25 minutes

½ pound bulk Italian sausage
½ pound ground beef
4 ounces sliced pepperoni
1 medium onion, chopped (½ cup)
1 16-ounce jar Italian cooking sauce
2 medium potatoes, peeled and
   sliced
½ of a 20-ounce package frozen
   loose-pack mixed zucchini,
   carrots, cauliflower, lima beans,
   and Italian beans

1 Cook sausage, beef, pepperoni, and onion till sausage is browned. Drain. Stir in cooking sauce, potatoes, and ½ cup *water*. Cover; simmer for 10 minutes. Stir in vegetables. Cover; simmer 10 minutes more, stirring often. Serves 6.

ITALIAN SKILLET DINNER

Assembling time: 15 minutes
Cooking time: 30 minutes

1½ pounds bulk pork sausage
1 small onion, chopped (¼ cup)
¼ cup chopped green pepper
1 18-ounce can tomato juice
1 6-ounce can tomato paste
1 teaspoon dried basil, crushed
1½ cups macaroni

1 In a 12-inch skillet cook sausage, onion, and green pepper till the meat is browned and vegetables are tender. Drain off fat. Stir in tomato juice, tomato paste, basil, 3½ cups *water*, and ½ teaspoon *salt*.

2 Bring to boiling. Stir in *uncooked* macaroni. Reduce heat; cover and simmer about 20 minutes or till macaroni is tender, stirring frequently. Uncover and simmer 5 minutes more. Makes 6 servings.

ORANGE HAM AND SWEET POTATOES

Assembling time: 10 minutes
Cooking time: 25 minutes

2 tablespoons butter *or* margarine
1 1½-pound fully cooked center-cut
   ham slice, cut 1 inch thick
½ of a 10-ounce jar orange
   marmalade
2 tablespoons water
1 tablespoon lemon juice
½ teaspoon minced dried onion
⅛ teaspoon ground nutmeg
1 17-ounce can sweet potatoes,
   drained
1 tablespoon cold water
2 teaspoons cornstarch
¼ cup sliced almonds

1 In a 12-inch skillet melt the butter or margarine. Brown the ham quickly on both sides in butter. Combine marmalade, the 2 tablespoons water, lemon juice, onion, and nutmeg. Pour over ham. Cover and simmer for 10 minutes.

2 Arrange sweet potatoes atop the ham slice. Spoon the marmalade mixture over the potatoes. Cover and simmer 5 minutes longer or till the potatoes are heated through.

3 Transfer the ham slice and potatoes to a serving platter; keep warm. Skim fat from pan juices. Measure juices; add water, if necessary, to make ⅔ cup liquid. Return pan juices to the skillet.

4 Combine 1 tablespoon cold water and cornstarch; stir into juices. Cook and stir till thickened and bubbly. Cook and stir 2 minutes more. Spoon mixture over ham slice and potatoes. Sprinkle with almonds. Makes 6 servings.

HAM AND SWEET POTATO PIES

Assembling time: 15 minutes
Cooking time: 30 minutes

½ **of a 16-ounce package frozen loose-pack mixed broccoli, cauliflower, and carrots**
1 **beaten egg**
1 **tablespoon orange juice** *or* **milk**
3 **tablespoons fine dry bread crumbs**
¼ **teaspoon onion powder**
¼ **teaspoon dry mustard**
  Dash pepper
¾ **pound ground fully cooked ham**
1 **17-ounce can sweet potatoes, drained**
  Dash ground cloves
½ **of an 11-ounce can condensed cheddar cheese soup**
1 **tablespoon milk**

1 Cook frozen vegetables according to package directions; drain well. Set aside. Meanwhile, in a mixing bowl combine egg and 1 tablespoon orange juice or milk. Stir in bread crumbs, onion powder, mustard, and pepper. Add ham; mix well. Shape ham mixture into 12 meatballs, using about 1 rounded tablespoon for each.

2 Mash drained sweet potatoes; stir in cloves. Spread sweet potato mixture on the bottom and sides of four 10-ounce individual casseroles or au gratin dishes. Arrange 3 meatballs atop sweet potato mixture in each casserole; spoon vegetables atop meatballs and sweet potato mixture.

3 Stir together cheddar cheese soup and 1 tablespoon milk; spoon *one-fourth* of the soup mixture over *each* casserole. Bake, covered, in a 350° oven about 30 minutes or till meatballs are heated through. Makes 4 servings.

HAM CARBONARA

If you don't have linguine or fettucini, substitute spaghetti—

Total preparation time: 20 minutes

3 **eggs**
10 **ounces linguine** *or* **fettucini**
¼ **cup butter** *or* **margarine**
1 **6¾-ounce can chunk-style ham, drained and flaked**
1 **2½-ounce jar sliced mushrooms, drained**
2 **tablespoons snipped parsley** *or* **2 teaspoons dried parsley flakes**
2 **tablespoons light cream** *or* **milk**
½ **teaspoon dried marjoram, crushed**
¾ **cup grated Parmesan cheese**

1 Place whole eggs in a bowl of hot water to warm. Meanwhile, cook pasta in a large amount of boiling salted water about 10 minutes or till tender; drain.

2 While pasta cooks, in a large saucepan melt the butter or margarine; stir in ham and sliced mushrooms. Heat through. Remove eggs from water. Break into a mixing bowl and beat slightly; stir in parsley, cream or milk, and dried marjoram.

3 Toss hot cooked pasta with ham mixture. Pour egg mixture over ham-pasta mixture. Toss till pasta is well coated. Add Parmesan cheese; toss to mix. Serves 4.

GINGER-HAM MEDLEY

Fresh gingerroot may have a gnarled and knobby appearance, but it also has a sensational flavor and aroma. You'll find it in the produce section of your supermarket—

Total preparation time: 15 minutes

½ **of a 16-ounce package frozen loose-pack mixed green beans, broccoli, onions, and mushrooms**
1 **tablespoon cornstarch**
1½ **teaspoons grated gingerroot**
1½ **cups apricot nectar**
1 **teaspoon lemon juice**
1½ **cups cubed fully cooked ham**
1 **16-ounce can unpeeled apricot halves, drained and cut in half**
  Hot cooked rice
¼ **cup peanuts**

1 In a small saucepan cook the frozen mixed vegetables according to package directions; drain. Meanwhile, in a 2-quart saucepan combine the cornstarch and grated gingerroot. Stir in the apricot nectar and lemon juice. Cook and stir till mixture is thickened and bubbly. Cook and stir 2 minutes more.

2 Stir in cubed ham and cooked mixed vegetables. Fold apricot pieces into ham mixture. Cook and stir till heated through. Serve ham-apricot mixture over hot cooked rice. Top each serving with peanuts. Makes 4 servings.

Ham and Sweet Potato Pies

SAUCY BARBECUED HAM

Assembling time: 10 minutes
Cooking time: 20 minutes

1 medium onion, sliced
2 tablespoons butter *or* margarine
1 10-ounce package frozen succotash
1 8-ounce can stewed tomatoes
1 8-ounce can jellied cranberry sauce
¼ cup water
1 tablespoon vinegar
1½ teaspoons prepared mustard
½ teaspoon chili powder
¼ teaspoon ground cumin
1 pound fully cooked ham slice
1 tablespoon cornstarch
1 tablespoon cold water
Hot cooked rice

1 In a 10-inch skillet cook the sliced onion in the butter or margarine till tender but not brown. Stir in succotash, *undrained* tomatoes, cranberry sauce, ¼ cup water, vinegar, prepared mustard, chili powder, and cumin. Bring to boiling.

2 Meanwhile, cut ham into thin bite-size strips. Stir ham into tomato mixture. Reduce heat. Cover and simmer for 10 minutes. Stir together cornstarch and 1 tablespoon cold water; add to ham mixture in skillet. Cook and stir till thickened and bubbly. Cook and stir 2 minutes more. Serve ham mixture over hot cooked rice. Serves 4.

HAM-VEGETABLE SOUP

Assembling time: 5 minutes
Cooking time: 20 minutes

1 10¾-ounce can condensed cream of onion soup
1 teaspoon dry mustard
1 teaspoon lemon juice
½ teaspoon dried thyme, crushed
2½ cups cubed fully cooked ham
1 10-ounce package frozen peas with sliced mushrooms
1½ cups milk
⅔ cup quick-cooking rice

1 In a saucepan combine soup, dry mustard, lemon juice, thyme, and 1¼ cups *water*. Bring to boiling. Stir in ham and vegetables. Reduce heat. Cover and simmer 10 minutes. Stir in milk and rice. Return to boiling. Remove from heat; cover and let stand 5 minutes. Makes 6 servings.

SAUCY BROCCOLI-HAM SANDWICHES

Assembling time: 18 minutes
Cooking time: 3 minutes

1 10-ounce package frozen broccoli in cheese sauce
3 slices white *or* whole wheat bread Prepared mustard
6 slices boiled ham (6 ounces)
3 slices tomato
2 tablespoons sliced almonds

1 Prepare broccoli according to package directions. Meanwhile, toast bread; spread lightly with mustard. Top each toast slice with 2 slices ham and a tomato slice.

2 Place sandwiches on the rack of an unheated broiler pan. Broil 3 to 4 inches from heat for 2 to 3 minutes or till hot. Spoon broccoli and cheese sauce atop; sprinkle with almonds. Makes 3 servings.

HAM PATTIES WITH MUSTARD SAUCE

Assembling time: 20 minutes
Cooking time: 20 minutes

1 beaten egg
¼ cup milk
¾ cup soft bread crumbs (1 slice)
1 tablespoon brown sugar
2 teaspoons minced dried onion
Dash pepper
2 cups ground fully cooked ham
2 tablespoons butter *or* margarine
2 tablespoons mayonnaise *or* salad dressing
2 tablespoons prepared mustard
6 hamburger buns, split and toasted Lettuce leaves

1 In a mixing bowl combine the beaten egg and milk. Stir in the soft bread crumbs, brown sugar, minced dried onion, and pepper. Add the ground cooked ham; mix well. Shape the meat mixture into six ½-inch-thick patties.

2 In an 11×7½×1½-inch baking pan melt the butter or margarine. Place the ham patties in the butter or margarine; turn patties over to coat both sides with butter or margarine. Bake in a 450° oven about 20 minutes or till done.

3 Meanwhile, combine the mayonnaise or salad dressing and prepared mustard. Place ham patties on the bottoms of toasted buns. Top with mustard mixture, lettuce leaves, and top halves of buns. Makes 6 servings.

PASTA WITH HAM

Fettucini or spaghetti can be substituted for the linguine—

Assembling time: 15 minutes
Cooking time: 15 minutes

2 large carrots
3 green onions, sliced
    (3 tablespoons)
1 tablespoon butter *or* margarine
1 8-ounce package sliced chopped
    ham
1 8-ounce can stewed tomatoes
½ cup water
1 2-ounce can sliced mushrooms,
    drained
½ cup milk
2 tablespoons all-purpose flour
    Hot cooked linguine
    Grated Parmesan cheese

1 Halve carrots lengthwise and thinly slice. In a 2-quart saucepan cook carrots and green onion in butter about 5 minutes or till carrots are crisp-tender.
2 Cut ham slices into strips. Stir ham, *undrained* tomatoes, water, and drained mushrooms into carrot-onion mixture. Bring to boiling; reduce heat. Cover and simmer for 10 minutes.
3 Stir together the milk and flour. Stir the milk mixture into the tomato-ham mixture. Cook and stir till the mixture is thickened and bubbly. Cook and stir 1 minute more. Serve the ham-vegetable mixture over hot cooked linguine. Pass Parmesan cheese. Makes 4 servings.

DILLED LAMB-ZUCCHINI STEW

Assembling time: 8 minutes
Cooking time: 37 minutes

¾ **pound boneless lamb**
2 **tablespoons cooking oil**
1 **10¾-ounce can condensed cream**
    of potato soup
1 **7½-ounce can tomatoes, cut up**
1 **teaspoon dried dillweed**
½ **teaspoon minced dried onion**
1 **10-ounce package frozen zucchini**
2 **cups frozen sliced carrots**

1 Cut the lamb into bite-size pieces. Brown in hot cooking oil. Drain off fat. Stir in soup, *undrained* tomatoes, dillweed, onion, ¾ cup *water*, and ⅛ teaspoon *pepper*. Bring to boiling; reduce heat. Cover and simmer for 20 minutes. Stir in zucchini and carrots. Cover and simmer about 15 minutes more, stirring occasionally. Serves 4.

PLUM-SAUCED LAMB CHOPS

Total preparation time: 15 minutes

6 **lamb leg sirloin *or* shoulder chops,**
    cut ¾ inch thick
½ **of a 10-ounce jar plum jam**
¼ **cup chili sauce**
2 **tablespoons dry white wine**
1 **teaspoon lemon juice**
½ **teaspoon ground allspice**
¼ **teaspoon minced dried onion**

1 Slash fat edges of chops. Place on the rack of an unheated broiler pan. Broil 3 to 4 inches from heat 10 to 12 minutes for medium, turning once.
2 Meanwhile, combine jam, chili sauce, wine, lemon juice, allspice, and onion. Bring to boiling; reduce heat. Simmer, uncovered, 10 minutes. To serve, spoon atop chops. Serves 6.

MINTED LAMB KABOBS

To save even more time, ask your butcher for lean boneless lamb that has already been cut into 1-inch pieces—

Assembly time: 20 minutes
Cooking time: 16 minutes

⅓ **cup apple jelly**
1 **tablespoon vinegar**
1 **teaspoon cooking oil**
½ **teaspoon dried mint, crushed**
½ **teaspoon Worcestershire sauce**
¼ **teaspoon salt**
1 **pound lean boneless lamb**
1 **medium green pepper, cut into**
    1-inch squares
4 **small boiling onions**

1 In a small saucepan combine apple jelly, vinegar, cooking oil, mint, Worcestershire sauce, and salt. Cook and stir till jelly is melted and mixture is well blended.
2 Cut the boneless lamb into 1-inch pieces. Alternately thread lamb pieces and green pepper squares on 4 skewers; place an onion on the end of each skewer.
3 Place on the rack of an unheated broiler pan. Broil kabobs 5 inches from heat to desired doneness, turning frequently (allow 14 to 16 minutes total time for medium).
4 Baste kabobs with apple jelly mixture frequently during broiling. Baste with the remaining jelly mixture just before serving. Serve immediately. Makes 4 servings.

157

TURKEY AND CRANBERRY CLUB SANDWICHES

Try serving this delicious new flavor combination in the style of the familiar three-layer club sandwich—

Assembling time: 15 minutes

12 slices white *or* whole wheat bread, toasted
½ cup cranberry-orange relish
4 slices turkey breast luncheon meat *or* cooked turkey
4 slices American cheese
Mayonnaise *or* salad dressing
Leaf lettuce
4 slices honey loaf *or* chopped ham
1 medium cucumber, thinly sliced

1 To assemble sandwiches, spread 4 of the toasted bread slices with some of the cranberry-orange relish. Top with turkey slices and American cheese slices.

2 Spread one side of remaining slices of bread lightly with mayonnaise or salad dressing. Add 4 slices of bread, mayonnaise side up, to sandwiches. Top *each* sandwich with lettuce, 1 slice of honey loaf or ham, and some of the sliced cucumber.

3 Add remaining slices of bread, mayonnaise side down. Cut each sandwich diagonally into triangles and secure with wooden picks. Makes 4 sandwiches.

Barbecue-Style Fried Chicken

BARBECUE-STYLE FRIED CHICKEN

Assembling time: 3 minutes
Cooking time: 35 minutes

1 32-ounce package frozen fried chicken pieces
Garlic salt
1 cup apricot preserves
1 medium onion, chopped (½ cup)
½ cup bottled barbecue sauce
2 tablespoons soy sauce

1 Arrange frozen chicken pieces in a single layer in an ungreased 13×9×2-inch baking dish. Sprinkle lightly with garlic salt. Bake, uncovered, in a 375° oven for 15 minutes.

2 Meanwhile, in a small bowl combine the apricot preserves, onion, barbecue sauce, and soy sauce. Spoon over chicken. Bake, uncovered, 20 minutes more or till chicken is heated through. Serves 4 or 5.

CASUAL CACCIATORE

Assembling time: 3 minutes
Cooking time: 35 minutes

1 32-ounce package frozen fried chicken pieces
1 16-ounce jar Italian cooking sauce
1 2½-ounce jar sliced mushrooms, drained
¼ cup dry red *or* white wine
¼ teaspoon dried oregano, crushed

1 Arrange frozen chicken pieces in a 13×9×2-inch baking dish. Bake, uncovered, in a 375° oven for 15 minutes. Meanwhile, combine Italian cooking sauce, drained mushrooms, wine, and oregano. Pour over chicken.

2 Bake, uncovered, 15 to 20 minutes more or till chicken and sauce mixture is heated through. Makes 4 or 5 servings.

TURKEY TURNOVERS

These make a perfect spur-of-the-moment lunch or light supper entrée. While the turnovers bake, create a leafy green salad to round out the meal—

Assembling time: 15 minutes
Cooking time: 15 minutes

½ cup frozen peas and carrots
1 3-ounce package cream cheese, cut up
1 tablespoon milk
Dash pepper
2 5-ounce cans chunk-style turkey, drained and chopped
1 package (8) refrigerated crescent rolls
1 to 2 tablespoons butter *or* margarine, melted
2 teaspoons poppy seed

1 In a small saucepan cook frozen peas and carrots in a small amount of boiling salted water for 5 minutes; drain. Meanwhile, stir together cream cheese, milk, and pepper till smooth. Fold in turkey and cooked vegetables.

2 Unroll crescent roll dough; seal perforations to form 4 rectangles. Place ¼ of the turkey mixture in the center of each rectangle. Lift the four points of each rectangle to the center; pinch edges to seal.

3 Place turnovers on an *ungreased* baking sheet. Brush with melted butter or margarine; sprinkle with poppy seed. Bake in a 375° oven for 12 to 15 minutes or till golden brown. Serve warm. Serves 4.

CREAMY CHICKEN AND SPAGHETTI

Total preparation time: 18 minutes

1 7-ounce package spaghetti
1 8-ounce package cream cheese, cut up
3 tablespoons butter *or* margarine
2 teaspoons minced dried onion
1 teaspoon dried parsley flakes
½ teaspoon dried basil, crushed
 Dash garlic powder
2 tablespoons milk
2 5-ounce cans chunk-style chicken
⅓ cup grated Parmesan cheese

1 Cook spaghetti according to package directions; drain. Meanwhile, in a medium saucepan heat cream cheese, butter or margarine, onion, parsley flakes, basil, and garlic powder over low heat just till cream cheese is softened, stirring occasionally.

2 Stir in milk; fold in *undrained* chicken and Parmesan cheese. Heat through. Toss chicken mixture with spaghetti till coated. Serve immediately. Serves 4 to 6.

ORIENTAL CHICKEN SOUP

Total preparation time: 10 minutes

2 10½-ounce cans condensed chicken with rice soup
1 16-ounce can chop suey vegetables, drained
2 5-ounce cans chunk-style chicken *or* turkey chopped
1 tablespoon soy sauce

1 In a saucepan combine soup and 2 soup cans (2½ cups) *water*; bring to boiling. Reduce heat; stir in chop suey vegetables, *undrained* chicken or turkey, and soy sauce. Cook till heated through. Makes 4 or 5 servings.

ELEGANT CHICKEN WITH NOODLES

To make the best use of your time, put the noodles on to cook while preparing the chicken mixture—

Total preparation time: 15 minutes

½ of a 10-ounce package (1 cup) frozen peas
1 10¾-ounce can condensed cream of chicken soup
½ cup milk
1 2¼-ounce can (½ cup) sliced pitted ripe olives, drained
1 2-ounce can sliced pimiento, drained and chopped
¼ teaspoon dried marjoram, crushed
⅛ teaspoon pepper
2 5-ounce cans chunk-style chicken *or* turkey, chopped
¼ cup dry white wine
 Hot cooked noodles

1 Cook peas according to package directions; drain. Meanwhile, in a large saucepan combine condensed cream of chicken soup and milk. Stir in olives, pimiento, marjoram, and pepper; bring to boiling.

2 Stir in cooked peas, *undrained* chicken or turkey, and wine; cook till heated through. On a serving platter spoon chicken mixture over hot noodles. Makes 4 servings.

CHICKEN-MAC CASSEROLE

Assembling time: 18 minutes
Cooking time: 20 minutes

1 7¼-ounce package macaroni and cheese dinner mix
1 large zucchini, halved lengthwise and sliced (2 cups)
½ cup milk
¼ cup butter *or* margarine
½ teaspoon minced dried onion
¼ teaspoon dried oregano, crushed
2 5-ounce cans chunk-style chicken *or* turkey, large pieces broken up
½ cup bite-size shredded wheat squares, crushed

1 Cook macaroni from mix in a large amount of boiling salted water for 10 minutes, adding zucchini slices to the macaroni the last 5 minutes of cooking time. Drain.

2 Add cheese sauce from mix, milk, butter or margarine, dried onion, and oregano to macaroni mixture; stir till butter is melted and mixture is well blended. Stir in *undrained* chicken or turkey.

3 Turn mixture into a 1½-quart casserole. Bake, covered, in a 375° oven for 15 minutes. Top with crushed cereal; bake, uncovered, about 5 minutes more. Serves 4.

OFF-THE-SHELF POULTRY IS HANDY

Keep canned "chunk-style" chicken or turkey handy for recipes requiring chopped cooked poultry. It's perfect for casseroles, sandwiches, soups, or salads where the size of the poultry pieces isn't important. Just cut up the large chunks and gently stir in the poultry near the end of the recipe.

ARTICHOKE AND CHICKEN SALAD SANDWICHES

A classy way to serve an old favorite—

Assembling time: 15 minutes
Chilling time: 15 minutes

1   14-ounce can artichoke hearts
½   cup mayonnaise *or* salad dressing
¼   cup grated Parmesan cheese
1   teaspoon lemon juice
⅛   teaspoon garlic powder
2   5-ounce cans chuck-style chicken,
      drained
1   stalk celery, chopped (½ cup)
12   slices whole wheat, white, *or* rye
      bread
      Lettuce leaves
      Cherry tomatoes (optional)

1 Drain artichoke hearts thoroughly, pressing to remove excess liquid. Mash artichokes; stir in mayonnaise or salad dressing, Parmesan cheese, lemon juice, and garlic powder. Stir in chicken and celery. Cover and chill in the freezer for 10 to 15 minutes or in the refrigerator till serving time.

2 Spread the chilled artichoke-chicken mixture on 6 of the slices of bread; top each with lettuce. Place the remaining bread slices atop sandwiches. Garnish with cherry tomatoes, if desired. Makes 6 sandwiches.

TURKEY HASH

Assembling time: 5 minutes
Cooking time: 12 minutes

½   of a 24-ounce package (3 cups)
      frozen hash brown potatoes
      with onion and peppers
1   10½-ounce can chicken gravy
2   5-ounce cans chunk-style turkey,
      chopped, *or* 1½ cups chopped
      cooked turkey
1   stalk celery, thinly sliced

1 In a medium skillet combine frozen hash brown potatoes, chicken gravy, turkey, and celery. Bring to boiling; reduce heat. Cover and simmer 10 minutes. Makes 4 servings.

LAZY DAY CHICKEN A LA KING

Total preparation time: 20 minutes

2¼   cups light cream *or* milk
1   1¾-ounce envelope white sauce
      mix (makes 2¼ cups)
1   beaten egg yolk
2   5-ounce cans chunk-style chicken,
      large pieces broken up
2   tablespoons chopped pimiento
1   tablespoon dry sherry
      Toast points *or* rusks
      Paprika
      Sliced almonds

1 In a saucepan stir cream or milk into white sauce mix. Cook and stir till thickened and bubbly. Gradually stir about half of the hot sauce into the egg yolk; return all to the saucepan. Cook and stir just till bubbly.

2 Fold in *undrained* chicken, pimiento, and sherry; heat through. Serve over toast points or rusks. Sprinkle with paprika and sliced almonds. Makes 5 servings.

WHITE-BEAN CHILI

Great northern beans, chunks of turkey, green chili peppers, and beer unite in this out-of-the-ordinary chili—

Assembling time: 12 minutes
Cooking time: 12 minutes

1   small onion, chopped (¼ cup)
1   tablespoon butter *or* margarine
1   15-ounce can great northern
      beans
1   5-ounce can chunk-style turkey
½   cup beer
½   of a 4-ounce can (about
      3 tablespoons) chopped
      green chili peppers
1   teaspoon instant chicken bouillon
      granules
½   teaspoon chili powder
      Dash garlic powder
½   cup shredded Monterey Jack *or*
      mozzarella cheese (2 ounces)
      Parsley sprigs (optional)

1 In a medium saucepan cook onion in butter or margarine till tender but not brown. Stir in *undrained* beans, *undrained* turkey, beef, chili peppers, bouillon granules, chili powder, and garlic powder.

2 Bring to boiling; reduce heat. Cover and simmer 10 minutes. Ladle soup mixture into bowls. Sprinkle each serving with shredded cheese. Garnish with parsley sprigs, if desired. Makes 3 servings.

CHICKEN RAMEKINS

Assembling time: 10 minutes
Cooking time: 25 minutes

1 beaten egg
3 tablespoons plain yogurt
3 tablespoons fine dry bread
    crumbs
1 teaspoon dried parsley flakes
⅛ teaspoon onion salt
1 5-ounce can chunk-style chicken
    or turkey, chopped

1 In a bowl combine egg and yogurt. Stir in crumbs, parsley, and onion salt. Stir in *undrained* chicken. Pack mixture firmly into 2 buttered 6-ounce custard cups.

2 Bake in a 375° oven for 20 to 25 minutes. With a narrow spatula loosen edges; unmold onto a serving plate. Serve with additional yogurt, if desired. Serves 2.

CHICKEN SUB-GUMBO

Total preparation time: 18 minutes

1 10¾-ounce can condensed
    chicken gumbo soup
3 tablespoons cornstarch
1 soup can (1¼ cups) water
2 tablespoons soy sauce
2 5-ounce cans chunk-style chicken,
    large pieces broken up, *or* 1½
    cups chopped cooked chicken
½ cup sliced water chestnuts
2 green onions, sliced
    Chow mein noodles

1 In a medium saucepan combine soup and cornstarch. Stir in water and soy sauce. Cook and stir till thickened and bubbly. Cook and stir 2 minutes more.

2 Stir in *undrained* chicken, water chestnuts, and onions; heat through. Serve over chow mein noodles. Serves 4.

ORIENTAL EGG AND CHICKEN SALAD

Pea pods and water chestnuts give this salad crunch as well as an Oriental flair—

Total preparation time: 30 minutes

4 eggs
1 6-ounce package frozen pea pods
1 8-ounce can sliced water
    chestnuts, drained
1 5-ounce can chunk-style chicken,
    drained and chopped
⅓ cup sweet pickle relish
¼ cup mayonnaise *or* salad dressing
2 teaspoons prepared mustard
1 teaspoon minced dried onion
½ teaspoon salt
    Lettuce cups (optional)

1 To hard-cook eggs, place eggs in a saucepan; cover with cold water. Bring to boiling; reduce heat to just below simmering. Cover and cook for 15 minutes. Run cold water over eggs till cool. Remove shells; chop eggs.

2 Meanwhile, run hot water over frozen pea pods in a colander till separated; drain thoroughly. Combine pea pods, water chestnuts, and chicken.

3 Stir together sweet pickle relish, mayonnaise or salad dressing, prepared mustard, dried onion, and salt; add to pea pod-chicken mixture. Add chopped hard-cooked eggs. Toss lightly. Serve in lettuce cups, if desired. Makes 4 servings.

TURKEY PITA SANDWICHES

Assembling time: 15 minutes

2 pita bread rounds
1 5-ounce can chunk-style turkey,
    drained and chopped
¾ cup alfalfa sprouts
¾ cup shredded Swiss *or* Monterey
    Jack cheese (3 ounces)
⅓ cup creamy cucumber salad
    dressing
1 medium tomato, sliced and halved

1 Cut pita bread in half crosswise. Combine turkey, sprouts, cheese, and salad dressing. Fill each bread half with ¼ of the mixture. Add tomato slices. Makes 4.

CHICKEN RAREBIT STACK-UPS

Total preparation time: 20 minutes

1 10-ounce package frozen
    broccoli spears
1 10-ounce package frozen
    Welsh rarebit
1 5-ounce can chunk-style chicken,
    large pieces broken up
3 English muffins, split and toasted
1 tomato, sliced
1 tablespoon cooked bacon pieces

1 Cook broccoli according to package directions; drain. Keep warm. Meanwhile, in a saucepan heat frozen rarebit over medium heat for 7 to 8 minutes or till heated through, stirring occasionally. Stir in *undrained* chicken; heat through.

2 Arrange 2 muffin halves on each serving plate. Top with tomato slices and broccoli; spoon chicken mixture over all. Sprinkle with bacon pieces. Serve immediately. Makes 3 servings.

CHICKEN AND VEGETABLE SKILLET

Assembling time: 25 minutes
Cooking time: 15 minutes

- 2 slices bacon
- 1 10-ounce package frozen brussels sprouts
- 2 whole medium chicken breasts
- 1 small onion, chopped (¼ cup)
- 1 teaspoon lemon juice
- ½ teaspoon salt
- ½ teaspoon dried basil, crushed
- ⅛ teaspoon pepper
- 2 medium tomatoes, sliced and quartered

1 In a 10-inch skillet cook bacon till crisp; drain, reserving drippings in skillet. Crumble bacon and set aside. Meanwhile, run hot water over frozen brussels sprouts in a colander till separated; drain and halve brussels sprouts. Set aside.

2 Remove skin from chicken breasts; cut breasts in half lengthwise. Remove bones. Cut chicken breasts into ½-inch-wide strips. Season with salt and pepper.

3 In reserved drippings in the skillet cook chicken strips and chopped onion over medium-high heat for 4 to 5 minutes or just till chicken is done.

4 Stir in brussels sprouts, lemon juice, ½ teaspoon salt, basil, and ⅛ teaspoon pepper. Reduce temperature to medium-low. Cover and cook for 6 minutes. Stir in tomatoes and crumbled bacon. Cook, covered, 1 to 2 minutes more. Serves 4.

Chicken and Vegetable Skillet

CHICKEN BREASTS CELESTE

Save the bones you remove from the chicken breasts to make broth for later use—

Assembling time: 20 minutes
Cooking time: 20 minutes

3 **whole medium chicken breasts**
¼ **cup all-purpose flour**
½ **teaspoon salt**
¼ **teaspoon paprika**
⅛ **teaspoon pepper**
1 **small onion, finely chopped**
 (¼ cup)
2 **tablespoons cooking oil**
½ **cup dairy sour cream**
¼ **cup mayonnaise** or **salad dressing**
2 **tablespoons dry sherry**
2 **tablespoons water**
 Snipped parsley

1 Remove skin from chicken breasts; cut breasts in half lengthwise and remove bones. Place chicken breast halves between two pieces of clear plastic wrap; pound out from the center with a meat mallet to flatten slightly. Remove wrap. Coat chicken pieces with a mixture of flour, salt, paprika, and pepper.

2 In a large skillet cook chicken and onion in hot cooking oil over medium heat about 15 minutes or just till chicken is done, turning chicken pieces once. Remove chicken to a warm serving platter; keep warm. Drain fat from skillet.

3 Combine sour cream, mayonnaise or salad dressing, sherry, and water; stir till smooth. Add to the skillet and heat through over low heat; *do not boil.* Pour over chicken; sprinkle with parsley. Serves 6.

CHICKEN TARRAGON

Assembling time: 15 minutes
Cooking time: 8 minutes

2 **whole medium chicken breasts**
1 **tablespoon all-purpose flour**
½ **teaspoon dried tarragon, crushed**
¼ **teaspoon salt**
2 **tablespoons cooking oil**
⅓ **cup hot water**
1 **teaspoon instant chicken bouillon granules**
1 **teaspoon lemon juice**
 Snipped parsley

1 Remove skin from chicken breasts; cut breasts in half lengthwise and remove bones. Cut the boned chicken breast halves into ½-inch-wide strips.

2 Combine flour, tarragon, and salt; add chicken pieces, tossing to coat well. In a 10-inch skillet cook chicken in hot cooking oil over medium-high heat for 5 minutes, turning chicken pieces often.

3 Combine hot water, chicken bouillon granules, and lemon juice; add to skillet. Stir, scraping up browned particles. Cover and cook 1 to 2 minutes. Sprinkle with parsley before serving. Makes 4 servings.

SKIP BONING CHICKEN BREASTS

You can purchase chicken breasts already skinned, halved, and boned. By letting the butcher at the supermarket do the tedious work, you can cut 10 to 15 minutes from meal preparation time. Boned chicken breasts cost a little more than whole chicken breasts, but you may find the time you save is well worth the extra money.

COCONUT CHICKEN WITH TROPICAL SAUCE

Assembling time: 18 minutes
Cooking time: 10 minutes

2 **whole medium chicken breasts**
1 **cup coconut**
1 **tablespoon curry powder**
1 **beaten egg**
2 **tablespoons water**
3 **tablespoons cooking oil**
1 **6-ounce can (¾ cup) unsweetened pineapple juice**
1 **teaspoon cornstarch**
2 **tablespoons light raisins**
¼ **cup drained mandarin orange sections** or **pineapple chunks**
 Hot cooked rice (optional)

1 Remove skin from chicken breasts; cut breasts in half lengthwise and remove bones. Place chicken breast halves between two pieces of clear plastic wrap. Pound out from the center with a meat mallet to about ¼-inch thickness. Remove wrap. Sprinkle chicken lightly with salt and pepper.

2 Combine coconut and curry powder. In a dish combine egg and water. Dip chicken pieces in egg mixture, then in coconut mixture, patting to coat well.

3 In a large skillet cook chicken in hot oil over medium heat about 10 minutes or till coating is golden brown and chicken is done, turning chicken pieces once.

4 Meanwhile, for sauce, in a small saucepan combine pineapple juice and cornstarch; add raisins. Cook and stir till mixture is thickened and bubbly; cook and stir 2 minutes more. Stir in mandarin orange sections or pineapple chunks. Serve sauce over chicken. Serve with hot cooked rice, if desired. Makes 4 servings.

TURKEY STROGANOFF SKILLET

Purchase ground raw turkey either fresh or frozen. In the freezer case, look for it in a tube much like packaged pork sausage—

Assembling time: 15 minutes
Cooking time: 25 minutes

1 pound ground raw turkey
1 12-ounce can vegetable juice cocktail
1 10¾-ounce can condensed chicken broth
¾ cup water
1 3-ounce can sliced mushrooms
2 teaspoons minced dried onion
1 teaspoon dried parsley flakes
1 teaspoon Worcestershire sauce
½ teaspoon dried thyme, crushed
⅛ teaspoon pepper
5 ounces noodles
1 cup dairy sour cream *or* plain yogurt
2 tablespoons all-purpose flour

1 In a large skillet cook ground turkey till meat is brown. Stir in vegetable juice cocktail, chicken broth, water, *undrained* mushrooms, dried onion, parsley flakes, Worcestershire sauce, thyme, and pepper. Stir in uncooked noodles.

2 Bring mixture to boiling; reduce heat. Cover and cook for 15 to 20 minutes or till noodles are tender. Combine sour cream or yogurt and flour; stir into turkey mixture in skillet. Cook and stir till thickened and bubbly. Makes 6 servings.

RED CABBAGE AND CHICKEN SKILLET

Assembling time: 15 minutes
Cooking time: 25 minutes

8 chicken thighs
2 tablespoons cooking oil
1 16-ounce jar sweet-sour red cabbage
2 medium apples, cored and sliced
1 teaspoon minced dried onion
1 teaspoon caraway seed

1 In a skillet brown chicken thighs in hot cooking oil over medium heat about 10 minutes, turning once. Remove chicken thighs and drain fat from skillet.

2 In the same skillet combine the remaining ingredients. Return chicken to skillet. Cover and cook 20 to 25 minutes or till chicken is tender. Makes 4 servings.

SAUCY CHICKEN LIVERS

Total preparation time: 15 minutes

1½ pounds chicken livers, halved
¼ cup all-purpose flour
2 tablespoons cooking oil
1 10¾-ounce can condensed cream of chicken soup
1 4-ounce can sliced mushrooms
2 tablespoons chopped pimiento
⅛ teaspoon pepper
Hot cooked noodles

1 Place livers in a plastic bag. Add flour; shake to coat. In a 10-inch skillet cook livers in hot oil over medium heat about 5 minutes or just till livers are no longer pink.

2 Stir in the soup, *undrained* mushrooms, pimiento, and pepper. Cover and simmer about 5 minutes or till heated through. Serve over noodles. Makes 6 to 8 servings.

CHICKEN LIVERS WITH ORANGE SAUCE

Total preparation time: 28 minutes

1 medium onion, chopped (½ cup)
2 tablespoons butter *or* margarine
1 pound chicken livers, halved
2 2½-ounce packages thinly sliced fully cooked ham, chopped (1 cup)
1 4-ounce can sliced mushrooms, drained
1 teaspoon salt
¼ teaspoon dried thyme, crushed
1 cup orange juice
4 teaspoons cornstarch
¼ teaspoon bottled hot pepper sauce
Hot cooked noodles

1 In a 10-inch skillet cook onion in butter or margarine till tender but not brown; add chicken livers and ham. Cook over medium heat about 5 minutes or just till chicken livers are no longer pink; remove mixture from skillet and set aside.

2 In the same skillet combine mushrooms, salt, and dried thyme. Stir together orange juice, cornstarch, and bottled hot pepper sauce; stir into the mushroom mixture in skillet.

3 Cook and stir till thickened and bubbly; cook and stir 2 minutes more. Return chicken liver mixture to skillet; cook till heated through. Serve mixture over hot cooked noodles. Makes 6 servings.

OVEN-BAKED FISH WITH WINE SAUCE

Assembling time: 10 minutes
Cooking time: 30 minutes

**4 individually frozen fish fillets
     (1 pound)**
4 green onions, sliced (¼ cup)
1 tablespoon butter *or* margarine
**1 ⅞-ounce envelope chicken
     gravy mix**
1 cup water
½ cup dairy sour cream
1 tablespoon dry white wine
**1 2½-ounce jar sliced mushrooms,
     drained**
Paprika

1 Place frozen fish fillets on a piece of heavy-duty foil. Season with salt and pepper; wrap securely. Bake in a 450° oven about 30 minutes or till fish flakes easily when tested with a fork.

2 Meanwhile, in a small saucepan cook sliced green onions in butter or margarine over medium heat till tender but not brown. Stir in dry chicken gravy mix; add water. Cook and stir till mixture is thickened and bubbly. Cook and stir mixture for 1 to 2 minutes more.

3 Combine sour cream and white wine; add to gravy mixture. Stir in drained mushrooms. Cook till heated through; *do not boil*. Unwrap fish fillets. With a slotted spatula remove fillets from foil to a platter or individual serving plates; sprinkle with paprika. Spoon sour cream mixture over fish. Makes 4 servings.

FISH VERACRUZ

Assembling time: 25 minutes
Cooking time: 15 minutes

**1 16-ounce package frozen fish
     fillets**
¾ cup water
**¼ teaspoon salt
     Dash pepper**
1 small tomato, peeled and chopped
1 small onion, chopped (¼ cup)
¼ cup chopped green pepper
2 tablespoons chili sauce
1 tablespoon lemon juice
1 tablespoon butter *or* margarine
1 teaspoon dried parsley flakes
¼ teaspoon dried thyme, crushed
**1 4½-ounce can tiny shrimp, rinsed
     and drained**
**1 2½-ounce jar sliced mushrooms,
     drained**
¼ cup dry white wine

1 Allow frozen fish to stand at room temperature for 20 minutes. Slicing on the bias, cut the partially thawed fish into ¾-inch-thick slices.

2 Grease a 10-inch skillet. Add fish, water, salt, and pepper. Bring to boiling; reduce heat. Cover and simmer about 10 minutes or till fish flakes easily when tested with a fork; drain well.

3 Meanwhile, in a medium saucepan combine tomato, onion, green pepper, chili sauce, lemon juice, butter or margarine, parsley flakes, and thyme. Bring to boiling; reduce heat to medium-low. Cook, covered, about 5 minutes or till vegetables are tender.

4 Stir in shrimp, sliced mushrooms, and white wine. Return to boiling. Boil gently, uncovered, about 3 minutes or till of the desired consistency. Arrange fish on a serving platter; spoon tomato mixture over fish. Makes 4 to 6 servings.

CUCUMBER-SAUCED FISH

Try a different coating for fried fish—instant mashed potato flakes. Top with a cool and creamy cucumber sauce and you have a novel way to dress up ordinary fish fillets—

Assembling time: 20 minutes
Cooking time: 20 minutes

**1 16-ounce package frozen fish
     fillets**
1 medium cucumber, chopped
½ cup dairy sour cream
¼ teaspoon celery salt
1 beaten egg
2 tablespoons water
2 teaspoons prepared mustard
¼ teaspoon dried oregano, crushed
⅓ cup instant mashed potato flakes
3 tablespoons cooking oil

1 Allow frozen fish to stand at room temperature for 15 minutes. Meanwhile, for cucumber sauce, stir together cucumber, sour cream, and celery salt; set aside.

2 In a shallow bowl combine egg, water, prepared mustard, and oregano. With a heavy knife cut the partially thawed fish crosswise into 4 portions. Dip fish portions into egg mixture; roll in potato flakes.

3 In a 10-inch skillet cook fish fillets in hot cooking oil 8 to 10 minutes per side or till fish is golden brown and flakes easily when tested with a fork. Transfer fish to a serving platter; top with cucumber sauce. Makes 4 servings.

BROILED FISH AMANDINE

No need to toast the almonds separately in this recipe—they toast atop the fish during the last few minutes of broiling—

Assembling time: 20 minutes
Cooking time: 25 minutes

1 16-ounce package frozen fish
  fillets
¼ cup butter *or* margarine
¼ teaspoon finely shredded
  lemon peel
¼ cup lemon juice
  Few dashes bottled hot pepper
  sauce
¼ cup sliced almonds
1 tablespoon snipped parsley

1 Allow frozen fish to stand at room temperature for 15 minutes. Meanwhile, in a small saucepan melt butter or margarine. Stir in shredded lemon peel, lemon juice, and hot pepper sauce.

2 With a heavy knife cut the partially thawed fish crosswise into 4 portions. Place fish portions on an unheated rack in a broiler pan. Brush fish with some of the lemon-butter mixture; sprinkle with a little salt and pepper.

3 Broil 4 inches from heat for 12 minutes. Brush with lemon-butter mixture; turn and brush again. Broil 10 to 12 minutes more or till fish flakes easily when tested with a fork, topping with sliced almonds the last 2 minutes of broiling.

4 Transfer fish portions to a serving platter. Combine the remaining lemon-butter mixture and snipped parsley; drizzle over fish portions. Makes 4 servings.

HADDOCK KABOBS

Assembling time: 20 minutes
Cooking time: 20 minutes

1 pound fresh *or* frozen haddock
  fillets
2 medium green peppers, cut into
  1-inch squares
½ cup creamy Italian salad dressing
4 cherry tomatoes

1 If frozen, allow haddock to stand at room temperature 15 minutes. Cut into 1-inch cubes. Thread fish cubes and green pepper squares alternately on 4 skewers.

2 Place on a well-greased, unheated rack in a broiler pan. Broil about 3 inches from heat for 10 minutes. Brush occasionally with some of the Italian salad dressing. Turn; broil about 10 minutes more or till done.

3 Meanwhile, heat the remaining salad dressing. Serve kabobs with a cherry tomato threaded on the end of each skewer. Pass salad dressing. Makes 4 servings.

CUTTING PARTIALLY THAWED FISH FILLETS

To cut a partially thawed block of frozen fish fillets into portions, use a large knife and press firmly through the block. The fish still will be icy but it will have thawed just enough for the knife to penetrate.

HALIBUT MANDARIN

Use one 16-ounce package of frozen fish fillets if halibut steaks are not available. Thaw the fillets before cooking to separate, and reduce the cooking time to 6 minutes—

Total preparation time: 15 minutes

4 frozen halibut steaks, cut ¾ inch
  thick (1 to 1½ pounds)
2 teaspoons cornstarch
1 teaspoon freeze-dried chives
½ teaspoon instant chicken bouillon
  granules
½ cup orange juice
2 tablespoons dry white wine
1 teaspoon butter *or* margarine
1 11-ounce can mandarin orange
  sections, drained

1 Place frozen halibut steaks in a greased skillet. Add water to cover. Bring to boiling; reduce heat. Cover and simmer 8 to 10 minutes or till fish flakes easily when tested with a fork; drain well.

2 Meanwhile, for sauce, in a saucepan combine cornstarch, chives, and chicken bouillon granules. Stir in orange juice and wine. Add butter or margarine. Cook and stir till mixture is thickened and bubbly; cook and stir 2 minutes more.

3 Carefully stir mandarin orange sections into sauce; cook till heated through. To serve, arrange halibut steaks on a serving platter: spoon orange sauce over halibut. Makes 4 servings.

CRUNCH-TOPPED FISH STEAKS

Assembling time: 10 minutes
Cooking time: 30 minutes

6 frozen fish steaks, cut 1 inch thick (about 1½ pounds)
⅓ cup creamy French salad dressing
2 tablespoons lemon juice
1 3-ounce can French-fried onions
¼ cup grated Parmesan cheese

1 Arrange fish in an 11×7×1½-inch baking pan. Mix dressing and lemon juice; pour over fish. Crush onions slightly; mix with cheese. Sprinkle over fish.

2 Bake, uncovered, in a 450° oven for 25 to 30 minutes or till fish flakes easily when tested with a fork. Makes 6 servings.

BAKED FISH AND VEGETABLES

Assembling time: 22 minutes
Cooking time: 20 minutes

1 16-ounce package frozen fish fillets
1 4-ounce can whole mushrooms
1 medium green pepper, cut into thin strips
2 tablespoons lemon juice
1 tablespoon snipped parsley
½ teaspoon dried savory, crushed
2 tablespoons butter or margarine

1 Let frozen fish stand at room temperature for 15 minutes. Cut crosswise into 8 portions. Arrange fish in a greased 12×7½×2-inch baking dish.

2 Drain mushrooms; place atop fish. Mix green pepper, lemon juice, parsley, savory, ½ teaspoon *salt*, and ⅛ teaspoon *pepper*; spoon over fish. Dot with butter.

3 Bake, loosely covered, in a 450° oven for 15 to 20 minutes or till fish flakes easily when tested with a fork. Serves 4.

SALMON SAUTÉ

Total preparation time: 20 minutes

2 medium onions, thinly sliced
2 tablespoons olive oil or cooking oil
4 fresh salmon steaks (about 1 pound)
¼ cup wine vinegar

1 In a skillet cook onions in oil till tender but not brown. Remove from skillet; set aside. Drain skillet; add salmon steaks.

2 Cook salmon, uncovered, over medium heat for 3 minutes per side. Add onions and vinegar. Cover; simmer 2 minutes or till heated through. Makes 4 servings.

CREAMED OYSTERS

Total preparation time: 20 minutes

1 medium onion, chopped (½ cup)
1 stalk celery, chopped (½ cup)
¼ cup butter or margarine
1 pint shucked oysters
2 tablespoons all-purpose flour
1 teaspoon prepared mustard
1 teaspoon anchovy paste
½ teaspoon salt
⅛ teaspoon pepper
Dash ground red pepper
1 cup light cream
2 tablespoons dry sherry
4 English muffins, split and toasted

1 Cook onion and celery in butter or margarine till tender. Add *undrained* oysters; cook till edges curl. Stir in flour, mustard, anchovy paste, salt, pepper, and red pepper.

2 Add cream; cook and stir till thickened and bubbly. Stir in sherry; heat through. Serve creamed oysters atop English muffin halves. Makes 4 servings.

ITALIAN-STYLE FISH

A pretty meal-in-one dish that combines family favorites—crispy breaded fish portions, spaghetti, plump Italian green beans, and mozzarella cheese—

Total preparation time: 25 minutes

1 8-ounce package frozen breaded fish portions
4 ounces spaghetti
1 9-ounce package frozen Italian green beans
1 15½-ounce jar meatless spaghetti sauce
½ of a 4-ounce package (½ cup) shredded mozzarella or cheddar cheese

1 Bake frozen breaded fish portions according to package directions. Meanwhile, cook spaghetti according to package directions; drain. Cook frozen Italian green beans according to package directions; drain. In a small saucepan warm spaghetti sauce till heated through.

2 To serve, spread hot cooked spaghetti in the center of a warm platter. Spoon some of the spaghetti sauce over top. Arrange fish portions atop. Pour remaining spaghetti sauce over all. Sprinkle with shredded cheese. Arrange green beans around edge of platter. Serve immediately. Makes 4 servings.

Italian-Style Fish
Mid-East Tuna Salad
(see recipe, page 173)

LEMON-SHRIMP STIR-FRY

Assembling time: 5 minutes
Cooking time: 15 minutes

2 tablespoons cornstarch
2 teaspoons sugar
1 teaspoon instant chicken bouillon granules
1/8 teaspoon pepper
1 cup cold water
1/3 cup lemon juice
2 tablespoons cooking oil
2 12-ounce packages (about 2 cups) frozen shelled shrimp
1 medium green *or* sweet red pepper, cut into 3/4-inch squares
4 green onions, cut into 1-inch pieces
1 6-ounce package frozen pea pods
1 3-ounce can sliced mushrooms, drained
Hot cooked rice

1 In a small bowl combine cornstarch, sugar, chicken bouillon granules, and pepper. Stir in cold water and lemon juice till combined; set aside.

2 Preheat a large skillet or wok over high heat. Add cooking oil. Add frozen shrimp, green or red pepper, and green onions. Stir-fry for 5 to 6 minutes.

3 Stir lemon mixture and then add to shrimp mixture. Cook and stir till thickened and bubbly. Cook and stir 2 minutes more. Stir in pea pods and sliced mushrooms; cover and cook till heated through. Serve over hot cooked rice. Serves 4.

RANGE-TOP TUNA CASSEROLE

Total preparation time: 25 minutes

4 ounces noodles
3/4 cup milk
1 1 1/2-ounce envelope cheese sauce mix
1 1/2 cups cream-style cottage cheese
1 cup frozen peas
1 6 1/2-ounce can tuna, drained and flaked
6 rich round crackers

1 Cook noodles according to package directions; drain. Stir milk into sauce mix; stir in cheese and peas. Cook and stir till thickened; cook 2 minutes more.

2 Stir in cooked noodles and tuna; heat through. Turn into a serving dish; crush crackers and sprinkle atop. Serves 4.

SHRIMP BAKE

Assembling time: 12 minutes
Cooking time: 30 minutes

1 10 3/4-ounce can condensed cream of mushroom soup
1/2 teaspoon Worcestershire sauce
1/4 teaspoon ground ginger
1 cup quick-cooking rice
1 16-ounce can fancy mixed Chinese vegetables, drained
2 4 1/2-ounce cans shrimp, rinsed and drained
1 4-ounce can mushroom stems and pieces, drained
3/4 cup chow mein noodles

1 Combine soup, Worcestershire, ginger, and 1 1/4 cups *water*. Stir in *uncooked* rice. Bring to boiling. Stir in Chinese vegetables, shrimp, and mushrooms.

2 Turn into a 1 1/2-quart casserole. Top with noodles. Bake, uncovered, in a 350° oven for 25 to 30 minutes. Serves 4.

TUNA-VEGETABLE SAUCE WITH PASTA

Total preparation time: 25 minutes

8 ounces spaghetti, linguine, *or* fettuccine
4 green onions, sliced (1/4 cup)
2 tablespoons butter *or* margarine
4 teaspoons cornstarch
1 cup milk
1 tablespoon instant chicken bouillon granules
1/4 teaspoon dried thyme, crushed
1/8 teaspoon pepper
1 16-ounce can mixed vegetables, drained
1 9 1/4-ounce can tuna, drained and broken into chunks
2 teaspoons lemon juice

1 Cook pasta according to package directions; drain. Meanwhile, in a medium saucepan cook green onions in butter or margarine till tender but not brown.

2 Stir cornstarch into onion in saucepan; add milk, chicken bouillon granules, thyme, and pepper. Cook and stir till mixture is thickened and bubbly; cook and stir 2 minutes more.

3 Stir in drained mixed vegetables, tuna, and lemon juice; cook till heated through. To serve, place hot cooked pasta on a warm serving platter; spoon tuna-vegetable mixture over pasta. Makes 4 servings.

SALMON ROLL-UPS

Spread the cheesy salmon filling only to within 1/2 inch of the edges of the crescent rolls before rolling up. This will prevent the filling from squeezing out the ends of the roll-ups and will allow the edges to seal—

Assembling time: 20 minutes
Cooking time: 15 minutes

- 2 packages (16 total) refrigerated crescent rolls
- 1 7¾-ounce can salmon, drained, flaked, and skin and bones removed, *or* one 6½-ounce can tuna, drained and flaked
- 1 4-ounce package (1 cup) shredded cheddar cheese
- ¼ cup finely chopped celery
- 1 green onion, chopped (1 tablespoon)
- 1 tablespoon sweet pickle relish
- 1 tablespoon lemon juice
  Dash pepper
- 1 7½-ounce can semi-condensed savory cream of mushroom soup
- ¼ cup dairy sour cream
  Paprika *or* snipped parsley

1 Unroll crescent rolls. Seal perforations to form 8 rectangles total. Combine salmon or tuna, cheese, celery, green onion, pickle relish, lemon juice, and pepper.

2 Spread some of the salmon mixture evenly over each rectangle. Roll up from short end; place, seam side down, on an ungreased baking sheet. Bake in a 375° oven for 12 to 15 minutes or till golden.

3 Meanwhile, in a small saucepan combine soup and sour cream; heat through. Serve mixture over roll-ups; garnish with paprika or snipped parsley. Makes 4 servings.

SALMON SANDWICH BAKE

Assembling time: 20 minutes
Cooking time: 20 minutes

- 1 15½-ounce can salmon, drained, flaked, and skin and bones removed
- 1 10¾-ounce can condensed cream of celery soup
- ½ cup shredded Muenster cheese
- 1 teaspoon minced dried onion
- 2 cups packaged biscuit mix
- ½ cup milk
- 1 teaspoon sesame seed
- 3 tablespoons milk
- 1 teaspoon dried parsley flakes

1 Mix salmon, ¼ *cup* of the soup, the cheese, and onion; set aside. Combine biscuit mix and ½ cup milk. Pat *half* of the dough into a greased 8×8×2-inch baking pan. Spread salmon mixture atop.

2 On waxed paper, evenly pat remaining dough into an 8-inch square. Invert dough atop salmon mixture; remove waxed paper. Sprinkle with sesame seed.

3 Bake in a 450° oven for 18 to 20 minutes. Meanwhile, heat together remaining soup, 3 tablespoons milk, and the parsley. Serve over sandwich squares. Makes 6 servings.

BUYING SALMON

When you choose canned salmon, keep the use in mind. Sockeye and chinook are perfect for salads because they are deep red and break into large chunks. Coho, pink, and chum are lighter in color, flake easily, and usually cost less. They're great for sandwiches and dishes where color and texture make little difference.

FISH PATTIES WITH CRANBERRY SAUCE

Leftover cooked fish is a delicious and thrifty substitute for the tuna or salmon in this recipe. Use 1½ cups flaked, cooked fish in place of the canned fish—

Assembling time: 20 minutes
Cooking time: 6 minutes

- 1 beaten egg
- ¼ cup milk
- 1 teaspoon minced dried onion
- ¼ teaspoon salt
- 1½ cups soft bread crumbs (2 slices)
- 1 9¼-ounce can tuna, drained and flaked, *or* one 7¾-ounce can salmon, drained, flaked, and skin and bones removed
- ¼ cup milk
- ½ cup finely crushed cheese crackers *or* saltine crackers
- 2 tablespoons cooking oil
- 1 8-ounce can whole *or* jellied cranberry sauce

1 In a bowl combine egg, ¼ cup milk, minced dried onion, and salt. Let stand 1 minute. Add bread crumbs and tuna or salmon; mix well. Form mixture into four ¾-inch-thick patties.

2 Dip patties into ¼ cup milk, then crushed crackers. In a skillet cook patties in hot oil over medium-low heat about 3 minutes per side or till golden brown. To serve, spoon cranberry sauce over each patty. Makes 4 servings.

TUNA-PINEAPPLE BUFFET

Use the 2 teaspoons of curry powder for a mild curry flavor. Real curry lovers may want to add more—

Total preparation time: 20 minutes

- 1 15¼-ounce can pineapple chunks (juice pack)
- 2 tablespoons butter *or* margarine
- 2 stalks celery, sliced (1 cup)
- 2 tablespoons chopped onion
- 2 to 3 teaspoons curry powder
- 1 10¾-ounce can condensed cream of mushroom soup
- ¼ cup raisins
- 2 teaspoons lemon juice
- ¼ teaspoon ground ginger
- 1 12½-ounce can tuna, drained and broken into chunks
  Chow mein noodles

1 Drain pineapple chunks, reserving ⅓ cup juice; set aside. In a 2-quart saucepan melt butter or margarine. Stir in celery, onion, and curry powder. Cover and cook over medium-low heat about 5 minutes or till vegetables are crisp-tender.

2 Stir in reserved pineapple juice, pineapple chunks, cream of mushroom soup, raisins, lemon juice, and ground ginger. Cook and stir till mixture is bubbly.

3 Carefully fold drained tuna into soup mixture. Cook till heated through. Serve over chow mein noodles. Makes 6 servings.

SHRIMP-SLAW TACOS

Assembling time: 15 minutes
Chilling time: 15 minutes

- 1 cup shredded cabbage
- 1 4½-ounce can shrimp, drained
- ½ cup cream-style cottage cheese, drained
- ¼ cup coarsely shredded carrot
- 2 tablespoons mayonnaise *or* salad dressing
- 4 teaspoons chutney
- ½ teaspoon curry powder
- ⅛ teaspoon salt
- 6 taco shells

1 In a bowl combine cabbage, shrimp, cottage cheese, and carrot. Mix mayonnaise or salad dressing, chutney, curry powder, and salt. Stir into shrimp mixture.

2 Cover and chill in the freezer 10 to 15 minutes or in the refrigerator till serving time. Spoon some of the shrimp mixture into each taco shell. Makes 3 servings.

TUNA-VEGETABLE BISQUE

Total preparation time: 12 minutes

- 1 10¾-ounce can condensed cream of shrimp soup
- 1 10½-ounce can condensed vegetarian vegetable soup
- 1 8-ounce bottle clam juice
- ¾ cup milk
- 1 tablespoon minced dried onion
- 1 teaspoon dried parsley flakes
- 1 9¼-ounce can tuna, drained and flaked

1 In a saucepan combine soups, clam juice, milk, onion, and parsley. Cook over medium heat, stirring occasionally, till mixture is bubbly. Stir in tuna; cover and simmer 5 minutes more. Makes 4 servings.

EASY SEAFOOD GUMBO

Purchased cooked bacon pieces and quick-cooking rice streamline this recipe for speed and ease of preparation—

Assembling time: 5 minutes
Cooking time: 20 minutes

- 1 16-ounce can stewed tomatoes
- 1 10¾-ounce can condensed chicken gumbo soup
- 1 10-ounce package frozen cut okra
- 1 cup water
- 1 8-ounce can whole oysters
- 1 6½-ounce can minced clams
- 1 teaspoon instant chicken bouillon granules
- 1 teaspoon dried thyme, crushed
- ¼ teaspoon bottled hot pepper sauce
- 1 bay leaf
- 1¼ cups quick-cooking rice
- ¼ cup cooked bacon pieces
- 1 teaspoon filé powder

1 In a large saucepan combine *undrained* tomatoes, chicken gumbo soup, frozen okra, water, *undrained* oysters, *undrained* clams, chicken bouillon granules, thyme, hot pepper sauce, and bay leaf. Bring to boiling; reduce heat. Cover and simmer 15 minutes.

2 Meanwhile, cook rice according to package directions. Remove bay leaf from seafood mixture; stir in cooked bacon pieces and filé powder. Ladle mixture into bowls over rice. Makes 5 servings.

MID-EAST TUNA SALAD

Pictured on page 169—

Total preparation time: 40 minutes

 2 cups water
 ¾ cup bulgur wheat
 ½ of a 10-ounce package (1 cup) frozen peas
 3 tablespoons red wine vinegar and oil salad dressing
 1 tablespoon lemon juice
 1 teaspoon dried basil, crushed
 1 9¼-ounce can tuna
    Lettuce
    Tomato wedges
    Lemon wedges

1 In a bowl stir water into bulgur. Let stand 30 minutes. Meanwhile, combine frozen peas, vinegar and oil dressing, lemon juice, and basil. Cover and chill. Chill tuna.
2 Drain bulgur; press out water. Drain and flake tuna. Stir bulgur and tuna into pea mixture. Serve in lettuce-lined bowl with tomato and lemon wedges. Serves 4.

TUNA-VEGETABLE SANDWICHES

Assembling time: 15 minutes

 1 9¼-ounce can tuna
 1 8½-ounce can peas and carrots
 ½ cup chopped water chestnuts
 ½ cup dairy sour cream
 ½ teaspoon dried dillweed
 ¼ teaspoon onion salt
 6 rusks *or* 6 slices bread
 1 cup shredded Monterey Jack cheese

1 Drain tuna and vegetables; flake tuna. Mix tuna, vegetables, water chestnuts, sour cream, dillweed, and onion salt. Serve over rusks with cheese. Serves 6.

SEAFOOD OPEN-FACERS

While the seafood mixture chills, enjoy creating decorative garnishes with your favorite assortment of fresh vegetables—

Assembling time: 15 minutes
Chilling time: 30 minutes

 1 7-ounce can crab meat *or* one 6½-ounce can lobster *or* one 6½-ounce can tuna
 ½ cup finely chopped cucumber
 ⅓ cup sour cream dip with chives
 ½ teaspoon dried dillweed
 4 slices pumpernickel, whole wheat, *or* white bread
    Butter *or* margarine, softened
    Sliced radishes, sliced tomato, carrot sticks, celery sticks, sliced fresh mushrooms, snipped parsley, green pepper rings, sliced pickles, *or* sliced olives (optional)

1 Drain and flake the crab meat, lobster, or tuna, removing any cartilage. In a mixing bowl combine the desired seafood, the chopped cucumber, sour cream dip with chives, and dried dillweed. Cover and chill in the freezer for 30 minutes.
2 Spread one side of each bread slice with softened butter or margarine; spread each with about ⅓ cup of the seafood mixture. If desired, garnish each open-face sandwich with any of the fresh vegetables listed above, creating a different garnish for each sandwich. Serves 2.

TUNA-FRUIT SALAD

Total preparation time: 25 minutes

 1 11-ounce can mandarin orange sections
 1 9¼-ounce can tuna
 2 apples
 4 cups torn lettuce
 ⅓ cup broken walnuts
 ½ cup mayonnaise *or* salad dressing
 2 teaspoons soy sauce
 1 teaspoon lemon juice

1 Chill mandarin oranges and tuna in the freezer for 20 minutes. Meanwhile, core and chop apples. In a large salad bowl combine apples, lettuce, and walnuts. Drain oranges and tuna; break up large chunks of tuna. Add to mixture in salad bowl.
2 In a small bowl combine mayonnaise, soy sauce, and lemon juice; mix well. Pour over salad mixture; toss. Serves 4.

OYSTER-BROCCOLI SOUP

Total preparation time: 20 minutes

 1 10-ounce package frozen cut broccoli with cheese sauce
 ½ cup water
 1 10¾-ounce can condensed cream of celery *or* cream of potato soup
 1 8-ounce can whole oysters
 1 cup milk

1 Remove broccoli and cheese sauce from pouch. In saucepan combine broccoli with cheese sauce and water. Cook till thawed, breaking up broccoli with a fork.
2 Pour into blender container; add soup. Cover; blend till broccoli is chopped. Return mixture to saucepan. Stir in *undrained* oysters and milk. Heat through. Serves 3.

SOUFFLÉ OMELET

Assembling time: 15 minutes
Cooking time: 15 minutes

- ¼ **cup butter** *or* **margarine**
- ¼ **cup all-purpose flour**
- ½ **teaspoon salt**
- 1½ **cups milk**
- 4 **beaten egg yolks**
- 4 **egg whites**
- ¾ **cup shredded process Swiss cheese (3 ounces)**
- 2 **tablespoons dry white wine** *or* **milk**
- 1 **tablespoon snipped fresh chives** *or* **freeze-dried chives**

1 For sauce, in a saucepan melt butter or margarine; stir in flour and salt. Add 1½ cups milk all at once. Cook and stir till mixture is thickened and bubbly; cook and stir 1 minute more.

2 Reserve ½ cup of the sauce. Gradually stir the remaining sauce into the egg yolks; set aside. Beat egg whites till stiff peaks form. Fold yolk mixture into whites.

3 Turn egg mixture into an ungreased 8 × 1½-inch round baking dish. Bake in a 400° oven about 15 minutes or till omelet is puffed and golden brown.

4 Meanwhile, in the same saucepan combine the reserved ½ cup sauce, shredded Swiss cheese, 2 tablespoons wine or milk, and chives; cook and stir over medium heat till sauce is bubbly and cheese is melted. Serve sauce over omelet. Makes 4 servings.

CHEESE STRATAS

Assembling time: 10 minutes
Cooking time: 30 minutes

- 4 **slices firm-textured bread**
- 1 **5-ounce jar cheese spread with bacon**
- ½ **cup frozen peas**
- 2 **beaten eggs**
- 1 **cup milk**
- ½ **teaspoon sesame seed**

1 Spread 2 bread slices with *half* of the cheese spread; top with remaining slices. Cut each sandwich into 4 squares.

2 In each of 2 greased 20-ounce casseroles place *half* of the peas and bread squares. Mix eggs and milk; pour over bread mixture.

3 Bake, uncovered, in a 375° oven for 25 minutes. Dollop remaining cheese spread atop; sprinkle with sesame seed. Bake 5 minutes more. Makes 2 servings.

AMAZING QUICHE

Assembling time: 20 minutes
Cooking time: 25 minutes

- 2¼ **cups milk**
- 5 **eggs**
- ½ **cup all-purpose flour**
- 2 **teaspoons minced dried onion**
- ¼ **teaspoon dried marjoram, crushed**
- 1 **cup shredded brick** *or* **Monterey Jack cheese (4 ounces)**
- ½ **cup grated Parmesan cheese**

1 Grease a 10-inch pie plate or quiche pan. In a blender container combine milk, eggs, flour, onion, marjoram, and ¼ teaspoon *salt.* Cover; blend 15 seconds. Pour into pie plate. Top with cheeses. Bake in a 400° oven for 20 to 25 minutes or till a knife inserted near-center comes out clean. Let stand 5 minutes. Serves 6.

CHEESE AND EGG WEDGES

Cheese lovers will appreciate the three types of cheese in this main-dish pie. Cut the wedges smaller and serve as an appetizer or a snack—

Assembling time: 10 minutes
Cooking time: 35 minutes

- 3 **eggs**
- ½ **cup milk**
- ¼ **cup all-purpose flour**
- ½ **teaspoon baking powder**
- ½ **teaspoon seasoned salt**
- 2 **cups shredded Monterey Jack** *or* **mozzarella cheese (8 ounces)**
- ¾ **cup cream-style cottage cheese with chives**
- ½ **of a 3-ounce package cream cheese, cut up**
  Tomato wedges
  Watercress *or* **parsley sprigs**
  Meatless spaghetti sauce, heated (optional)

1 In a small mixer bowl combine eggs, milk, flour, baking powder, and seasoned salt. Beat at low speed of electric mixer till blended. Add Monterey Jack or mozzarella cheese, cottage cheese with chives, and cream cheese. Beat till mixture is combined.

2 Pour into an ungreased 9-inch pie plate. Bake, uncovered, in a 350° oven about 35 minutes or till knife inserted near center comes out clean.

3 Arrange tomato wedges and watercress or parsley sprigs atop. To serve, cut into wedges. Pass heated spaghetti sauce, if desired. Makes 6 servings.

Cheese and Egg Wedges

EGGS

MIXED VEGETABLE QUICHE

Assembling time: 10 minutes
Cooking time: 35 minutes

- 1 **tablespoon butter** *or* **margarine**
- ¼ **cup toasted wheat germ**
- 6 **eggs**
- 1¼ **cups milk**
- 1 **tablespoon minced dried onion**
- ½ **teaspoon dried oregano, crushed**
- 1 **8½-ounce can mixed vegetables, drained,** *or* **1 cup cooked vegetables**
- 1 **4-ounce package (1 cup) shredded cheddar cheese**

1 Grease a 9-inch pie plate or quiche pan with the butter or margarine. Sprinkle wheat germ over bottom and up sides of pie plate. Beat eggs, milk, onion, and oregano till blended. Stir in vegetables and cheese.

2 Pour egg mixture into the pie plate. Bake in a 375° oven 30 to 35 minutes or till a knife inserted near center comes out clean. Let stand 5 minutes. Serves 5 or 6.

TEXAS BAKED EGGS

Assembling time: 10 minutes
Cooking time: 20 minutes

- 1 **15-ounce can chili with beans**
- ½ **medium green pepper, chopped**
- 1 **8-ounce package (2 cups) shredded cheddar cheese**
- 4 **eggs**

1 In a saucepan combine chili with beans and green pepper. Heat through. Stir in *half* of the cheese. Spoon into four 10-ounce casseroles or custard cups. Break 1 egg into each casserole. Sprinkle with remaining cheddar cheese. Bake in a 350° oven about 20 minutes or till eggs are done. Makes 4 servings.

SALAMI-MUSHROOM FRITTATA

Assembling time: 10 minutes
Cooking time: 10 minutes

- 1 **small green pepper, chopped (½ cup)**
- ⅓ **cup chopped salami**
- 1 **clove garlic, minced**
- 2 **tablespoons butter** *or* **margarine**
- 6 **eggs**
- ⅓ **cup milk**
- ½ **teaspoon dried basil, crushed**
- ¼ **teaspoon salt**
  Dash pepper
- 1 **2½-ounce jar sliced mushrooms, drained**
- 2 **tablespoons grated Parmesan cheese**

1 In a 10-inch oven-going skillet cook green pepper, salami, and garlic in butter or margarine till green pepper is tender. In a bowl beat eggs, milk, basil, salt, and pepper till combined; stir in salami mixture and mushrooms. Pour into the skillet.

2 Cook over medium-low heat. As egg mixture begins to set, run a spatula around the edge of the skillet, lifting the egg mixture to allow uncooked portion to flow underneath. Continue cooking and lifting edges till eggs are almost set but still moist.

3 Place skillet under broiler about 5 inches from heat. Broil for 1 to 2 minutes or just till surface is set. Sprinkle with grated Parmesan cheese. To serve, cut frittata into wedges. Makes 4 servings.

FARMER'S POTATO OMELET

Assembling time: 12 minutes
Cooking time: 23 minutes

- 1 **cup hot water**
- ½ **cup milk**
- 1¼ **cups instant mashed potato flakes**
- ½ **cup shredded cheddar** *or* **American cheese (2 ounces)**
- ½ **teaspoon salt**
- 6 **beaten eggs**
- ½ **cup diced fully cooked ham (3 ounces)**
- 2 **tablespoons cooking oil**

1 In a mixing bowl combine hot water and milk. Stir in *1 cup* of the potato flakes, the cheese, and salt. Let stand about 2 minutes or till the liquid is absorbed.

2 Add beaten eggs and diced ham to potato mixture in bowl; stir lightly to combine. In a 10-inch oven-going skillet heat oil. Sprinkle remaining potato flakes over bottom of skillet. Pour egg mixture into the skillet. Cook, covered, over low heat for 15 to 20 minutes or till top is nearly set.

3 Place skillet under broiler 4 to 5 inches from heat. Broil about 3 minutes or till golden. Cut into wedges; serve from skillet. Makes 4 or 5 servings.

OVEN-GOING SKILLETS

The handle of your skillet determines its suitability for use in a hot oven. One-piece cast-iron skillets or skillets with removable handles are safe for oven use. For skillets with other types of handles, check the manufacturer's directions for safe oven temperatures.

PASTA FRITTATA

Assembling time: 18 minutes
Cooking time: 12 minutes

4 **ounces spaghetti**
¼ **cup shredded Gruyère** *or* **grated Parmesan cheese**
2 **tablespoons butter** *or* **margarine**
6 **beaten eggs**
2 **tablespoons snipped chives** *or* **sliced green onion**
⅛ **teaspoon pepper**
Dash salt
1 **8-ounce can (1 cup) tomato sauce**
2 **tablespoons olive** *or* **cooking oil**
¼ **cup shredded Gruyère** *or* **grated Parmesan cheese**

1 Cook spaghetti according to package directions just till tender; drain. In a mixing bowl toss spaghetti with ¼ cup cheese and butter or margarine. Add eggs, chives, pepper, and salt; toss till coated.

2 In a small saucepan heat tomato sauce; keep warm. In a 10-inch oven-going skillet heat oil. Add spaghetti mixture, spreading it evenly in the skillet. Cook over medium-low heat.

3 As egg mixture begins to set, run a spatula around the edge of the skillet, carefully lifting the egg mixture to allow uncooked portion to flow underneath. Continue cooking and lifting edges till eggs are almost set but still moist on top.

4 Place skillet under broiler about 5 inches from heat. Broil for 1 to 2 minutes or just till surface is set. Loosen sides and bottom of frittata; slide out onto a serving platter. Cut into wedges. Spoon heated tomato sauce over wedges. Sprinkle with ¼ cup cheese. Makes 4 servings.

TOASTY HAM AND EGG BAKE

Assembling time: 20 minutes
Cooking time: 25 minutes

3 **slices whole wheat bread**
1 **4½-ounce can deviled ham**
2 **tablespoons hot-style catsup**
8 **eggs**
½ **cup wheat flakes** *or* **40% bran flakes, slightly crushed**
2 **teaspoons butter** *or* **margarine, melted**

1 Toast bread slices. Combine ham and catsup; spread over toast. Cut toast into cubes. Divide cubes among 4 greased 10-ounce casseroles or custard cups.

2 Break eggs one at a time into a sauce dish; slide 2 eggs into each casserole. Combine crushed cereal and melted butter; sprinkle over eggs.

3 Bake in a 325° oven for 20 to 25 minutes or till eggs are done. Serve with additional hot-style catsup, if desired. Makes 4 servings.

EGGS AND TOMATOES

Assembling time: 10 minutes
Cooking time: 12 minutes

1 **medium onion, chopped (½ cup)**
1 **tablespoon olive** *or* **cooking oil**
1 **16-ounce can tomatoes, cut up**
½ **teaspoon dried basil, crushed**
4 **eggs**

1 In a 10-inch skillet cook onion in hot oil till tender. Stir in *undrained* tomatoes, basil, ¼ teaspoon *salt*, and dash *pepper*. Simmer, uncovered, 5 minutes.

2 Break eggs one at a time into a sauce dish; slide eggs into tomato mixture. Season to taste. Cover; simmer 3 to 5 minutes or till eggs are set. Makes 2 servings.

EGG FOO YONG PATTIES

Build a menu around these Oriental egg and vegetable patties. Accompany them with canned fried rice and a spinach salad garnished with mandarin oranges and kiwi fruit. For dessert, serve lemon sherbet topped with slivered almonds—

Assembling time: 10 minutes
Cooking time: 8 minutes

Bottled sweet-sour sauce
6 **eggs**
1 **16-ounce can fancy mixed Chinese vegetables, drained**
3 **tablespoons chopped green pepper**
1½ **teaspoons minced dried onion**
¼ **teaspoon salt**
Dash pepper
Cooking oil

1 Place the bottle of sweet-sour sauce in a bowl of hot tap water to warm. In a mixing bowl beat eggs well. Stir in vegetables, green pepper, onion, salt, and pepper.

2 In a skillet heat about 2 tablespoons oil. Using a scant ⅓ cup of the egg mixture for each patty, fry patties in hot oil over medium-high heat for 1 to 2 minutes per side or till golden. (Spread vegetable mixture to cover egg.)

3 Keep patties warm. Repeat till all of the egg mixture is used. Add more cooking oil as needed. Serve patties with warm sweet-sour sauce. Makes 3 servings.

TOSTADA EGGS RANCHEROS

Total preparation time: 20 minutes

1 small onion, chopped (¼ cup)
1 tablespoon cooking oil
1 8-ounce can stewed tomatoes, cut up
½ to 1 teaspoon chili powder
   Dash garlic powder
1 tablespoon butter *or* margarine
4 eggs
4 tostada shells *or* 4 cups corn chips
1 cup shredded lettuce
   Shredded cheddar *or* Monterey Jack cheese (optional)

1 In a small saucepan cook onion in cooking oil for 2 minutes. Stir in *undrained* tomatoes, chili powder, and garlic powder. Simmer, uncovered, about 8 minutes or till mixture is slightly thickened.

2 Meanwhile, in a medium skillet melt butter or margarine. Add eggs; cook over medium-low heat. When whites of the eggs are set, add about 2 teaspoons *water*. Cover and cook till eggs are done.

3 Coarsely crush corn chips, if desired. On each of 2 plates place 2 tostada shells or *half* of the chips; top with some of the shredded lettuce. Place fried eggs atop shells or chips. Spoon tomato mixture over all. Sprinkle with shredded cheese, if desired. Makes 2 servings.

Tostada Eggs Ranchero

EGG AND SAUSAGE SCRAMBLE

Total preparation time: 20 minutes

4 skinless pork *or* mild Italian sausage links, sliced
1 medium green pepper, chopped
2 tablespoons chopped onion
6 eggs
¼ cup milk
¼ to ½ teaspoon dried oregano, crushed

1 In a 10-inch skillet cook sliced sausage, green pepper, and onion over medium-low heat till sausage is brown. Drain off all but about 2 tablespoons fat.

2 Beat eggs, milk, oregano, and ¼ teaspoon *salt* till combined; add to the skillet. Cook, without stirring, over medium heat till nearly set, lifting and folding partially cooked eggs so uncooked portion flows underneath. Continue cooking about 4 minutes more or till eggs are set. Serves 4.

SCRAMBLED EGG SANDWICHES

Total preparation time: 15 minutes

6 eggs
¼ cup milk
2 tablespoons butter *or* margarine
1 cup shredded smoky cheddar cheese
2 English muffins, split, toasted, and buttered
½ cup fresh alfalfa sprouts

1 Beat eggs, milk, and ¼ teaspoon *salt* till combined. Melt butter; pour in egg mixture. Cook, without stirring, till nearly set, lifting and folding partially cooked eggs so uncooked portion flows underneath.

2 Sprinkle cheese atop; continue cooking just till eggs are set. Top muffin halves with egg mixture and sprouts. Serves 4.

POACHED EGGS WITH CHEESE SAUCE

Total preparation time: 15 minutes

Cooking oil *or* shortening
4 eggs
½ of an 11-ounce can (⅔ cup) condensed cheddar cheese soup
⅓ cup dairy sour cream
½ teaspoon Worcestershire sauce
4 rusks
1 medium tomato, sliced (4 slices)

1 Lightly grease a 10-inch skillet. Add about 1½ inches of water to skillet; bring to boiling. Reduce heat to simmer. Break eggs one at a time into a sauce dish. Carefully slide eggs into water, holding lip of dish as close to water as possible. Allow an equal amount of space between eggs.

2 Simmer, uncovered, over low heat for 3 to 5 minutes. Do not let water boil. For more attractive poached eggs, smooth edges of eggs during cooking by using a spoon to gently pull away any strings of egg white. When eggs are cooked to the desired doneness, lift each out with a slotted spoon.

3 Meanwhile, for cheese sauce, in a saucepan combine cheddar cheese soup, sour cream, and Worcestershire sauce. Heat through; *do not boil*. To serve, on each of 2 plates place 2 rusks. Arrange a tomato slice, then a poached egg atop each rusk; spoon cheese sauce over eggs. Makes 2 servings.

EGG AND BACON HASH BROWNS

Assembling time: 25 minutes
Cooking time: 15 minutes

- **1 cup milk**
- **¾ cup water**
- **1 6-ounce package dry hash brown potatoes with onion**
- **8 slices bacon**
- **8 eggs**
- **2 teaspoons dried parsley flakes**
- **1 teaspoon onion salt**
- **⅛ teaspoon pepper**
- **1 cup shredded Swiss *or* cheddar cheese (4 ounces)**

1 In a medium saucepan bring milk and water to boiling; remove from heat. Stir in dry potatoes; cover and let stand about 20 minutes or till liquid is absorbed.

2 Meanwhile, in a 12-inch oven-going skillet cook bacon till crisp; drain, reserving 3 tablespoons drippings in skillet. Crumble bacon and set aside.

3 Beat eggs, parsley flakes, onion salt, and pepper till combined; stir in hash brown potatoes and crumbled bacon. Add to the reserved drippings in skillet. Cook, uncovered, over medium-low heat for 8 to 10 minutes or till eggs are almost set.

4 Place skillet under broiler about 3 inches from heat. Broil about 2 minutes or just till surface is set. Sprinkle with shredded Swiss or cheddar cheese. Broil 1 to 2 minutes more to melt cheese. To serve, cut into wedges. Makes 6 servings.

SCRAMBLED EGGS BENEDICT

If you don't have a 4-egg poacher, pour the egg mixture into 4 greased 6-ounce custard cups. Place in a 10-inch skillet containing 1 inch of boiling water. Cover and cook about 12 minutes or till the eggs are set—

Total preparation time: 15 minutes

- **1 2½-ounce package thinly sliced ham**
- **6 eggs**
- **¼ cup milk**
- **⅛ teaspoon dry mustard**
- **1 1-ounce envelope hollandaise sauce mix (makes ¾ cup)**
- **4 rusks**

1 In a small skillet place ham and about 1 tablespoon *water*. Cover and heat over low heat till warm. Beat eggs, milk, dry mustard, ¼ teaspoon *salt*, and dash *pepper* till well combined.

2 Pour egg mixture into 4 greased egg-poacher cups. Place cups in poacher over boiling water. Cover and cook about 5 minutes or till eggs are set.

3 Meanwhile, prepare hollandaise sauce mix according to package directions. Top each rusk with some of the ham, then 1 of the cooked egg portions. Spoon hollandaise sauce over eggs. Makes 4 servings.

QUICK OMELET FILLINGS

Heat ½ cup leftover cooked vegetables or meat with one 10¾-ounce can condensed cream of chicken soup and ½ cup milk to fill omelets. (Or, fill omelets with leftovers and top with the heated soup-milk mixture.) Saucy boil-in-a-bag entrées make fast fillings, too.

OMELET WITH RATATOUILLE SAUCE

Total preparation time: 30 minutes

- **1 cup chopped unpeeled eggplant**
- **1 cup chopped zucchini**
- **1 7½-ounce can tomatoes, cut up**
- **1 teaspoon minced dried onion**
- **½ teaspoon dried basil, crushed**
- **¼ teaspoon salt**
- **¼ teaspoon dried oregano, crushed**
- **4 eggs**
- **¼ cup milk**
- **¼ teaspoon salt**
- **2 tablespoons butter *or* margarine Grated Parmesan cheese**

1 In a saucepan combine eggplant, zucchini, *undrained* tomatoes, onion, basil, ¼ teaspoon salt, and oregano. Bring to boiling; reduce heat and simmer, covered, for 8 minutes. Uncover and cook about 3 minutes more or to desired consistency.

2 Meanwhile, beat eggs, milk, and ¼ teaspoon salt just till combined. In an 8-inch skillet with flared sides melt *1 tablespoon* of the butter or margarine till it sizzles. Lift and tilt the skillet to coat sides.

3 Pour *half* of the egg mixture into the skillet. Cook over medium heat. As the egg mixture begins to set, run a spatula around the edge of the skillet, carefully lifting the egg mixture to allow uncooked portion to flow underneath. When eggs are set but still shiny, remove from heat.

4 Spoon ¼ of the vegetable mixture across the center of the omelet. Fold ⅓ of the omelet over filling. Overlap remaining ⅓ atop filling. Slide the omelet out onto a serving plate; keep warm.

5 Repeat cooking and filling for the second omelet. Spoon the remaining vegetable mixture atop both omelets. Sprinkle each with grated Parmesan cheese. Makes 2 servings.

CREAMY EGGS ORIENTAL

Total preparation time: 30 minutes

9 eggs
1 10½-ounce can chicken a la king
½ of a 4-ounce package (½ cup) shredded cheddar cheese
⅓ cup milk
2 tablespoons soy sauce
1 teaspoon minced dried onion
1 8-ounce can sliced water chestnuts, drained
½ small green pepper, thinly sliced
1 cup fresh bean sprouts *or* ½ of a 16-ounce can bean sprouts, drained
Hot cooked rice *or* one 3-ounce can chow mein noodles

1 To hard-cook eggs, place eggs in a large saucepan; cover with cold water. Bring to boiling; reduce heat to just below simmering. Cover and cook for 15 minutes. Run cold water over eggs till cool. Remove shells from eggs; quarter or slice eggs.

2 In a medium saucepan combine chicken a la king, cheese, milk, soy sauce, and onion. Add water chestnuts and green pepper. Cook, stirring constantly, till mixture is bubbly and cheese is melted.

3 Stir in bean sprouts and quartered or sliced hard-cooked eggs; heat through. Serve over hot cooked rice or chow mein noodles. Makes 4 to 6 servings.

HARD-COOKED EGG TIP

A greenish ring around the yolk of a hard-cooked egg is a common, harmless occurrence caused by the formation of iron sulfide. To lessen the possibility of such rings forming, carefully watch the cooking time and immediately cool the eggs in cold water. For faster cooling, add a few ice cubes.

QUICK EGG CURRY

Total preparation time: 30 minutes

6 eggs
1 10¾-ounce can condensed cream of chicken soup
½ cup cream-style cottage cheese
2 to 3 teaspoons curry powder
Hot cooked rice
½ cup canned French-fried onions

1 To hard-cook eggs, place eggs in a saucepan; cover with cold water. Bring to boiling; reduce heat to just below simmering. Cover and cook for 15 minutes. Run cold water over eggs till cool. Remove shells; quarter eggs.

2 Meanwhile, in a blender container or food processor bowl combine chicken soup, cottage cheese, and curry powder. Cover; blend or process till smooth.

3 Pour curry mixture into a medium saucepan. Carefully stir in quartered hard-cooked eggs; cook over medium heat till mixture is heated through, stirring occasionally. Serve over hot cooked rice. Sprinkle French-fried onions atop. Serves 4.

EGGS A LA TETRAZZINI

Add color contrast to the creamy egg sauce by using green noodles—

Total preparation time: 30 minutes

6 eggs
1 stalk celery, sliced (½ cup)
1 tablespoon butter *or* margarine
2 single-serving envelopes instant cream of chicken soup mix
1 teaspoon minced dried onion
1 teaspoon dried parsley flakes
1 cup water
1 cup milk
2 tablespoons chopped pimiento
Hot cooked spaghetti *or* linguine
½ cup grated Parmesan cheese

1 To hard-cook eggs, place eggs in a saucepan; cover with cold water. Bring to boiling; reduce heat to just below simmering. Cover and cook for 15 minutes. Run cold water over eggs till cool. Remove shells from eggs; slice or chop eggs.

2 Meanwhile, in a medium saucepan cook celery in butter or margarine about 5 minutes or just till tender. Add dry soup mix, onion, and parsley; stir in water and milk. Cook and stir till mixture is thickened and bubbly.

3 Fold in cooked eggs and chopped pimiento; heat through. Serve egg mixture over hot cooked pasta. Sprinkle each serving with 2 tablespoons Parmesan cheese. Makes 4 servings.

HAWAIIAN NUT TOSS

Assembling time: 15 minutes

- 1 6-ounce can frozen pineapple juice concentrate
- 1 5⅓-ounce can (⅔ cup) evaporated milk
- 2 tablespoons salad oil
- 3 cups torn iceberg *or* leaf lettuce
- 1 8¼-ounce can pineapple chunks, drained
- 1 fresh papaya, peeled, seeded, and sliced into bite-size pieces
- ⅓ cup cashews
- ½ cup alfalfa *or* bean sprouts

1 For dressing, in a small mixer bowl combine concentrate and evaporated milk; beat well. With mixer still running, slowly add salad oil; beat till smooth and creamy.

2 In a salad bowl combine lettuce, pineapple, papaya and cashews. Pour some dressing over salad; toss lightly. Sprinkle with sprouts. Cover and chill remaining dressing. Makes 6 servings.

CREAMY LETTUCE SALAD

Assembling time: 15 minutes

- ⅓ cup dairy sour cream
- ¼ cup creamy French salad dressing
- 1 tablespoon milk
  Dash pepper
- 6 cups torn lettuce
- 1 11-ounce can mandarin orange sections, drained
- ½ medium cucumber, sliced
- 1 cup shredded cheddar cheese

1 Stir together sour cream, French dressing, milk, and pepper. In a salad bowl combine lettuce, orange sections, cucumber, and cheese. Spoon sour cream mixture atop. Toss lightly. Makes 6 servings.

WALDORF COLESLAW

Assembling time: 15 minutes

- ½ of a small head cabbage, cored and cut into small wedges
- 1 small apple, cored and cut into eighths
- ¼ cup raisins
- ¼ cup chopped walnuts
- ⅓ cup pineapple *or* apple yogurt
- ⅓ cup mayonnaise *or* salad dressing

1 In a blender container place *half* of the cabbage and half of the apple; add cold water to cover. Cover; blend till coarsely chopped. Drain well. Repeat.

2 In a mixing bowl combine cabbage mixture, raisins, and walnuts. Stir together yogurt and mayonnaise or salad dressing. Toss with cabbage mixture. Season with salt. Serve at once. Serves 8.

SESAME TOSSED SALAD

Total preparation time: 20 minutes

- ¼ cup salad oil
- ½ teaspoon finely shredded lime peel
- 2 tablespoons lime juice
- 2 teaspoons sesame seed
- 1 teaspoon sugar
  Dash salt
- 5 cups torn spinach
- 2 small tomatoes, cut into wedges
- 1 small zucchini, sliced

1 For dressing, in a screw-top jar combine oil, lime peel, lime juice, sesame seed, sugar, and salt. Cover; shake well. Chill in the freezer for 10 to 15 minutes.

2 Meanwhile, in a salad bowl combine spinach, tomato wedges, and zucchini. Shake dressing; toss with salad. Serves 6.

CURRIED FRUIT AND NUT SALAD

Halving and seeding grapes is easier if you use kitchen shears to cut the grapes—

Assembling time: 18 minutes

- 1 head red leaf lettuce *or* romaine, torn
- 1 11-ounce can mandarin orange sections, drained
- 1 cup torn spinach
- 1 cup grapes, seeded and halved
- ½ cup slivered almonds
- ½ cup salad oil
- ⅓ cup white wine vinegar
- 1 clove garlic, minced
- 2 tablespoons brown sugar
- 2 tablespoons frozen minced chives *or* snipped chives
- 1 tablespoon curry powder
- 1 teaspoon soy sauce
- 1 avocado, seeded, peeled, and sliced (optional)

1 In a salad bowl combine lettuce or romaine, orange sections, spinach, grapes, and almonds. For salad dressing, in a screw-top jar combine salad oil, vinegar, garlic, brown sugar, chives, curry powder, and soy sauce. Cover and shake well.

2 Just before serving, shake dressing and toss some of the dressing with the salad. Garnish with avocado, if desired. Pass remaining dressing. Makes 8 servings.

Curried Fruit and Nut Salad

HOT SPINACH SALAD

Assembling time: 22 minutes
Cooking time: 5 minutes

8   cups torn spinach
4   slices bacon, chopped
2   beaten eggs
¼   cup light cream
3   tablespoons vinegar
2   teaspoons sugar
¼   teaspoon salt
¼   teaspoon paprika

1 Place torn spinach in a salad bowl. In a 10-inch skillet cook bacon pieces over medium heat till crisp; spoon bacon and the drippings over spinach. Toss gently.

2 In a mixing bowl combine eggs, light cream, vinegar, sugar, salt, paprika, and dash *pepper*. Pour cream mixture into the skillet; cook and stir over medium heat till slightly thickened. Pour over spinach; toss till leaves are well coated. Garnish with sliced tomatoes, if desired. Serve immediately. Makes 4 servings.

MEXICANA CORN SALAD

Assembling time: 7 minutes
Chilling time: 15 minutes

½   cup dairy sour cream
2   tablespoons chili sauce
½   teaspoon chili powder
1   12-ounce can whole kernel corn with sweet peppers, drained
1   tablespoon sliced pitted ripe olives
4   cups torn lettuce

1 In a mixing bowl combine sour cream, chili sauce, and chili powder. Stir in corn and sliced olives. Chill in freezer for 15 minutes. Spoon sour cream mixture atop torn lettuce. Toss lightly. Makes 4 servings.

INDIAN SPINACH SALAD

Assembling time: 25 minutes

8   cups torn spinach
2   small apples, cored and chopped
½   cup light raisins
½   cup peanuts
2   green onions, sliced
¼   cup white wine vinegar
¼   cup salad oil
2   tablespoons chutney, chopped
2   teaspoons sugar
1½ teaspoons curry powder
1   teaspoon dry mustard
½   teaspoon salt

1 Place torn spinach in a large salad bowl; top with apple, raisins, peanuts, and green onion. In a screw-top jar combine vinegar, oil, chutney, sugar, curry powder, mustard, and salt. Cover and shake well. Pour over salad and toss lightly. Serves 8.

BUYING AND USING FRESH SPINACH

When buying fresh spinach, look for large deep-green leaves. Avoid any spinach with yellow or brown spots. Loosely cover the unwashed spinach and store it in the vegetable crisper of your refrigerator. Spinach should be used within a few days for the best flavor.

Before using the spinach, rinse it well to remove any sand or dirt. Pat the leaves dry, and remove and discard the stems and any damaged leaves.

EASY GARDEN ROW SALAD

Assembling time: 10 minutes

½   of a 16-ounce package frozen loose-pack mixed broccoli, carrots, and cauliflower
1   stalk celery, sliced (½ cup)
2   green onions, sliced
¼   cup Italian salad dressing
    Lettuce leaves
2   tablespoons sunflower nuts
1   tomato, cut into wedges (optional)

1 Pour boiling water over vegetables in a bowl; let stand 2 minutes. Drain well. Combine vegetables, celery, and green onion. Add salad dressing; toss lightly. Place in a lettuce-lined bowl. Sprinkle with sunflower nuts. Top with tomato, if desired. Serves 4.

CHEESE AND POTATO SALAD

Total preparation time: 30 minutes

2   eggs
¾   cup mayonnaise *or* salad dressing
2   tablespoons vinegar
1   teaspoon minced dried onion
1   teaspoon prepared mustard
2   stalks celery, chopped (1 cup)
1   cup cream-style cottage cheese
1   16-ounce can sliced potatoes, drained
6   lettuce cups

1 Place eggs in saucepan; cover with cold water. Bring to boiling; reduce heat to just below simmering. Cover; cook for 15 minutes. Run cold water over eggs till cool. Remove shells; chop eggs.

2 Meanwhile, in bowl combine mayonnaise or salad dressing, vinegar, onion, and mustard. Add celery and cottage cheese; mix well. Gently fold in potatoes and eggs. Serve in lettuce cups. Serves 6.

BEAN AND KRAUT SALAD

Assembling time: 15 minutes
Chilling time: 15 minutes

- 1 16-ounce can sauerkraut, drained and snipped
- 1 15¾-ounce can barbecue beans
- ¼ cup sliced pitted ripe olives
- 2 teaspoons minced dried onion
- ¼ cup mayonnaise *or* salad dressing
- ½ teaspoon chili powder
- 6 or 7 lettuce cups
  Corn chips (optional)

1 Mix together the sauerkraut, *undrained* beans, ripe olives, and dried onion. In a mixing bowl combine the mayonnaise or salad dressing and chili powder.

2 Add mayonnaise mixture to bean mixture and toss lightly. Chill in the freezer for 15 minutes. Serve in lettuce cups. Top with corn chips, if desired. Serves 6 or 7.

PEA POD AND WATER CHESTNUT SALAD

Assembling time: 8 minutes

- 1 6-ounce package frozen pea pods
- 1 8-ounce can sliced water chestnuts, drained
- 1 2-ounce jar sliced pimento, drained
- ¼ cup sliced pitted ripe olives
- 2 tablespoons Italian salad dressing
- 2 teaspoons soy sauce

1 Run hot water over frozen pea pods in a colander for 1 minute; drain. In a bowl combine pea pods, water chestnuts, pimento, and olives. Stir together salad dressing and soy sauce. Pour over vegetables; toss. Spoon mixture into salad bowls. Serves 4.

CHEESY FRUIT AND LETTUCE

Assembling time: 15 minutes

- 1 8¾-ounce can tropical fruit salad
- ½ cup seedless green grapes, halved
- 1 stalk celery, finely chopped
- ¼ cup blue cheese salad dressing
- ¼ of a 4-ounce container frozen whipped dessert topping, thawed
- 4 lettuce wedges

1 Drain fruit salad, reserving 2 tablespoons syrup. In a bowl combine the drained fruit salad, green grapes, and celery. Set aside. Stir the reserved syrup into blue cheese dressing; fold in whipped topping. Fold into fruit mixture. Serve over lettuce wedges. Serves 4.

GERMAN POTATO SALAD

Total preparation time: 18 minutes

- 6 slices bacon
- 2 16-ounce cans sliced potatoes
- 3 tablespoons all-purpose flour
- 2 tablespoons sugar
- 1 teaspoon celery seed
- 4 green onions, sliced (¼ cup)
- ¼ cup vinegar

1 In a skillet cook bacon till crisp; drain. Reserve 2 tablespoons drippings in skillet. Crumble bacon; set aside. Drain potatoes, reserving 1 cup of the liquid.

2 Stir flour, sugar, and celery seed into drippings. Stir in onion. Add the 1 cup reserved potato liquid and the vinegar. Cook and stir till thickened and bubbly. Cook and stir 1 minute more. Stir in potatoes and bacon. Heat through. Serves 6 to 8.

HOT BACON-TOPPED SALAD

Total preparation time: 15 minutes

- 4 slices bacon, chopped
- 2 tablespoons chopped onion
- 2 tablespoons vinegar
- 1 to 2 tablespoons sugar
- 3 cups coarsely shredded cabbage *or* other torn greens

1 In a small skillet cook bacon till crisp; drain. Add onion, vinegar, and sugar to bacon; mix well. Heat through. Pour over cabbage; toss and serve. Makes 2 servings.

QUICK SALAD IDEAS

When you want to perk up a meal with a flavorful salad, try one of these quick-to-fix ideas:

Fill pear or apple halves with sour cream dip, shredded cheddar cheese, or whipped cream cheese spread.

Add zip to bottled salad dressings by mixing them with sour cream or mayonnaise. Then serve over torn greens.

Mound cottage cheese with chives atop tomato halves.

Top pineapple slices with whole cranberry sauce and sprinkle with nuts.

Combine chopped apple; chopped dates; drained, crushed pineapple; and shredded carrot. Stir in mayonnaise or salad dressing.

CREAMY BLUE CHEESE SALAD

Assembling time: 12 minutes

 1 3-ounce package cream cheese,
    cut up
 ½ cup crumbled blue cheese
    (2 ounces)
 ¾ to 1 cup oil and vinegar salad
    dressing with seasonings
    Torn greens

1 In a small mixing bowl stir cream cheese and blue cheese together till well combined. Gradually stir in the oil and vinegar dressing to make of desired consistency. Serve atop torn greens. Cover and refrigerate any remaining salad dressing. Makes about 1¼ cups salad dressing.

HERB-DRESSING-TOPPED SALAD

Assembling time: 8 minutes

 ⅔ cup salad oil
 ⅓ cup wine vinegar
 1 teaspoon sugar
 1 teaspoon dried basil, thyme, or
    oregano, crushed
    Dash garlic powder
    Torn greens

1 In a screw-top jar combine oil; vinegar; sugar; basil, thyme, or oregano; and garlic powder. Cover and shake vigorously. Serve atop torn greens. Cover and refrigerate any remaining dressing. Makes 1 cup salad dressing.

GARBANZO BEAN CUPS

Assembling time: 12 minutes

 1 15-ounce can garbanzo beans,
    drained
 ½ cup chopped zucchini or
    cucumber
 1 small tomato, chopped
 ⅓ cup creamy cucumber salad
    dressing
 1 tablespoon vinegar or red wine
    vinegar
 1 teaspoon dried parsley flakes
 ¼ teaspoon minced dried onion
 4 lettuce cups

1 In a mixing bowl combine garbanzo beans, zucchini or cucumber, and tomato. In another bowl stir together salad dressing, vinegar, parsley, and dried onion. Pour over bean mixture. Toss lightly to coat vegetables. Serve in lettuce cups. Serves 4.

PREPARING SALAD GREENS

To prepare salad greens, start by removing the core from head lettuce or separating the leaves of leafy lettuce. Thoroughly rinse the greens with cold water and drain. Remove and discard any wilted outer leaves. Place greens in clean kitchen towel or paper toweling and pat or toss gently to remove clinging water. Tear greens into bite-size pieces to expose the interior and let the greens absorb the dressing.

PEANUT WALDORF SALAD

Assembling time: 15 minutes
Chilling time: 15 minutes

 2 medium apples, cored and
    chopped
 ½ cup tiny marshmallows
 ½ cup dry roasted peanuts
 ¼ cup raisins
 ½ cup mayonnaise or salad dressing
 2 tablespoons dry white wine or
    milk

1 In a bowl combine chopped apples, marshmallows, peanuts, and raisins. Stir together mayonnaise or salad dressing and white wine or milk; spoon atop apple mixture. Mix well. Cover and chill in the refrigerator for 15 minutes. Makes 4 servings.

CREAMY FRUIT DRESSING

Assembling time: 10 minutes

 1 cup dairy sour cream
 2 tablespoons orange juice
 1 tablespoon brown sugar or honey
 1 teaspoon lemon juice
 ⅛ teaspoon ground nutmeg
    Fresh fruit or canned fruit,
    drained

1 In a small bowl combine sour cream, orange juice, brown sugar or honey, lemon juice, and nutmeg. Stir to dissolve brown sugar. Serve atop fruit. Cover and refrigerate any remaining dressing. Makes about 1 cup dressing.

PEANUT BUTTER DRESSING

Assembling time: 10 minutes

½ cup mayonnaise *or* salad dressing
2 tablespoons peanut butter
1 tablespoon orange juice
  Fresh fruit *or* canned fruit, drained
  Lettuce leaves

1 In a small bowl gradually blend mayonnaise or salad dressing into peanut butter. Stir in orange juice. Spoon peanut butter mixture atop fruit on lettuce-lined salad plates. Cover and refrigerate any remaining dressing. Makes about ⅔ cup dressing.

FRUIT AND NUT TROPICAL SLAW

Assembling time: 15 minutes

1 8¼-ounce can pineapple chunks
1 tablespoon lemon juice
1 medium banana, sliced (1 cup)
3 cups finely shredded cabbage
2 stalks celery, thinly sliced (1 cup)
1 11-ounce can mandarin orange
    sections, drained
½ cup chopped walnuts
¼ cup raisins
1 8-ounce carton orange yogurt
½ teaspoon salt

1 Drain pineapple, reserving 2 tablespoons syrup. Stir together the reserved syrup and lemon juice. Coat banana slices with *1 tablespoon* of the syrup mixture; set remaining syrup mixture aside.

2 In a large bowl combine pineapple, banana, cabbage, celery, oranges, nuts, and raisins. Stir together the reserved syrup mixture, yogurt, and salt. Add to cabbage mixture; toss lightly. Makes 8 to 10 servings.

CRANBERRY-CITRUS SALAD

Assembling time: 10 minutes

1 8-ounce can jellied cranberry
    sauce
1 8-ounce can grapefruit sections,
    drained
  Lettuce leaves
⅓ cup mayonnaise *or* salad dressing
1 tablespoon honey
2 teaspoons vinegar
¼ teaspoon celery seed

1 Slice cranberry sauce crosswise into 4 portions. Arrange cranberry slices and grapefruit sections on 4 lettuce-lined salad plates. In a small bowl stir together mayonnaise or salad dressing, honey, vinegar, and celery seed; spoon atop cranberry slices and grapefruit sections. Makes 4 servings.

CHILLING SALAD INGREDIENTS

You may want to store canned salad ingredients in the refrigerator so you can put together a salad that's already chilled. Even if you're short on refrigerator space, it will help to place the canned ingredients in the refrigerator when you start preparing the meal. Make the salad at the last minute to allow for maximum chilling time.

ORIENTAL SPROUT SALAD

Pictured on page 137—

Assembling time: 12 minutes

2 cups fresh bean sprouts
½ cup sliced radishes
2 tablespoons green onions, sliced
¼ cup vinegar
¼ cup salad oil
1 tablespoon sugar
1 tablespoon soy sauce
2 cups torn greens

1 In a mixing bowl combine sprouts, radishes, and green onions. In a screw-top jar combine vinegar, oil, sugar, and soy sauce; cover and shake well. Pour over sprout mixture; toss lightly. Serve atop torn greens. Toss gently before serving. Serves 4.

AVOCADO-ORANGE SALAD

Assembling time: 15 minutes

¼ cup mayonnaise *or* salad dressing
¼ cup chutney, chopped
¼ teaspoon curry powder
  Lettuce leaves
2 avocados, seeded, peeled, and
    sliced
1 orange, peeled and sliced

1 In a small mixing bowl stir together the mayonnaise or salad dressing, chutney, and curry powder. On 4 lettuce-lined salad plates arrange avocado and orange slices. Spoon chutney mixture over fruit. Makes 4 servings.

SUNFLOWER WALDORF SALAD

Assembling time: 12 minutes

2 small apples, cored and chopped
   (1½ cups)
⅓ cup sunflower nuts
¼ cup seedless green grapes, halved
¼ cup chopped celery
1 large banana, sliced
¼ cup plain yogurt
   Lettuce leaves
   Banana slices (optional)

1 In a mixing bowl toss together apples, sunflower nuts, grapes, and celery. Fold in the sliced, large banana and yogurt. Serve on individual lettuce-lined salad plates. Garnish with additional banana slices, if desired. Makes 3 or 4 servings.

PEAR-PECAN SALAD

Assembling time: 10 minutes

1 4-ounce container whipped cream
   cheese
⅓ cup mayonnaise *or* salad dressing
1 tablespoon milk
1 teaspoon sugar
1 29-ounce can pear halves, drained
   Lettuce leaves
⅓ cup chopped pecans

1 In a mixing bowl combine whipped cream cheese, mayonnaise or salad dressing, milk, and sugar; beat smooth with a rotary beater. For each serving, arrange 2 pear halves on a lettuce-lined salad plate; drizzle with cream cheese mixture. Sprinkle with pecans. Makes 4 servings.

Watercress-Endive-Orange Salad

WATERCRESS-ENDIVE-ORANGE SALAD

This elegant salad is quick to put together for special occasions—

Assembling time: 25 minutes

½ cup salad oil
2 tablespoons cider vinegar
1 tablespoon Dijon-style mustard
1 teaspoon honey
3 heads French *or* Belgian endive,
   cut lengthwise into thin strips
1 large bunch watercress *or* Bibb
   lettuce, torn (3 cups leaves)
2 medium oranges, peeled and
   thinly sliced

1 To make dressing, in a blender container combine salad oil, cider vinegar, mustard, and honey. Cover; blend till smooth. On platter arrange endive, watercress or Bibb lettuce, and orange slices. If desired, garnish with an orange rose. Pour dressing over salad. Makes 6 servings.

POPPY SEED FRUIT DRESSING

Assembling time: 10 minutes

½ of a 4-ounce container whipped
   cream cheese
½ cup cherry, vanilla, *or* orange
   yogurt
1 teaspoon poppy seed
   Fresh fruit *or* canned fruit, drained
   Lettuce leaves

1 In a mixer bowl beat together cream cheese, yogurt, and poppy seed. Arrange fruit on lettuce-lined salad plates. Dollop cream cheese mixture atop fruit. Cover and refrigerate any remaining dressing. Makes ¾ cup dressing.

COTTAGE CHEESE AND STRAWBERRY COMBO

Assembling time: 15 minutes

1 cup cream-style cottage cheese,
   drained
2 tablespoons chopped walnuts
2 tablespoons mayonnaise *or* salad
   dressing
⅛ teaspoon ground nutmeg
4 canned peach *or* pear halves
1 cup sliced strawberries
   Lettuce leaves

1 In a mixing bowl stir together cottage cheese, nuts, mayonnaise or salad dressing, and nutmeg. Arrange peach or pear halves and sliced strawberries on 4 lettuce-lined salad plates. Spoon cottage cheese mixture over fruit. Makes 4 servings.

FRUIT MEDLEY SALAD

Assembling time: 15 minutes

1 17-ounce can chunky mixed fruits,
   drained
1 medium apple, cored and chopped
½ cup lemon yogurt
2 tablespoons apricot preserves
2 cups shredded lettuce
1 tablespoon pumpkin seed *or*
   sunflower nuts

1 In a mixing bowl combine drained mixed fruits and apple. Stir together yogurt and apricot preserves. Add to fruit mixture; toss lightly. Spoon atop shredded lettuce in a salad bowl; sprinkle with pumpkin seed or sunflower nuts. Toss before serving. Makes 6 servings.

FAST COOKING
VEGETABLES

SAVORY GREEN BEANS AND TOMATOES

Assembling time: 5 minutes
Cooking time: 8 minutes

1 9-ounce package frozen cut green beans
1 8-ounce can stewed tomatoes, cut up
1 small onion, cut into thin wedges
2 tablespoons cooked bacon pieces

1 In a saucepan combine frozen beans, *undrained* tomatoes, and onion. Bring to boiling. Reduce heat and simmer, covered, for 5 to 7 minutes or till beans are tender, stirring occasionally. Serve in sauce dishes. Sprinkle with bacon pieces. Makes 4 to 6 servings.

TANGY GREEN BEANS WITH BACON

Total preparation time: 8 minutes

1 16-ounce can cut green beans
1 teaspoon minced dried onion
1/4 teaspoon dried thyme, crushed
1 tablespoon butter *or* margarine
1 tablespoon vinegar
2 tablespoons cooked bacon pieces

1 In a medium saucepan heat *undrained* green beans, onion, and thyme; drain. Add butter or margarine and vinegar; toss lightly till butter is melted. Add bacon pieces; toss again. Turn into a serving bowl. Makes 4 servings.

GREEN BEANS AND PEPPERS

Total preparation time: 12 minutes

1 9-ounce package frozen cut green beans
2 medium green peppers, cut into 3/4-inch squares
1 teaspoon minced dried onion
1 tablespoon sesame seed
1 tablespoon butter *or* margarine
2 tablespoons grated Parmesan cheese

1 In a medium saucepan cook beans, green peppers, and onion in a small amount of boiling salted water according to bean package directions; drain.
2 Meanwhile, cook sesame seed in hot butter over medium heat till seed is light brown, stirring frequently. Spoon sesame seed over beans and peppers; toss to mix. Turn into a serving bowl. Sprinkle with Parmesan cheese. Serves 5 or 6.

CURRIED GREEN BEANS

Assembling time: 5 minutes
Cooking time: 10 minutes

2 tablespoons cooking oil
2 teaspoons mustard seed
1/2 teaspoon salt
1/2 teaspoon curry powder
1 medium onion, chopped (1/2 cup)
1 9-ounce package frozen French-style green beans
2 tablespoons coconut

1 In a skillet heat oil; add mustard seed. Cover and cook till seed stops popping. Stir in salt and curry powder. Stir in onion. Add frozen beans, breaking up with a fork.
2 Cover and cook for 8 to 10 minutes or till done, stirring frequently. Stir in coconut. Makes 5 or 6 servings.

MASHED POTATOES DELUXE

Total preparation time: 10 minutes

Packaged instant mashed potatoes (enough for 4 servings)
1/2 teaspoon dried parsley flakes
1/3 cup sour cream dip with French onion
Butter *or* margarine (optional)
2 tablespoons cooked bacon pieces

1 Prepare instant mashed potatoes according to package directions, *except* reduce the water called for by 1/4 cup and add the dried parsley flakes to the water.
2 Add sour cream dip to prepared mashed potatoes; stir till combined. Turn into a serving bowl. Dot with butter or margarine, if desired. Sprinkle with cooked bacon pieces. Makes 4 servings.

CHEESY POTATOES

Assembling time: 5 minutes
Cooking time: 25 minutes

1 7 1/2-ounce can semi-condensed cream of mushroom soup
2/3 cup milk
1 1 1/2-ounce envelope cheese sauce mix
4 cups frozen hash brown potatoes with onion and peppers

1 In a saucepan stir together soup, milk, and dry cheese sauce mix. Add hash brown potatoes; toss to coat potatoes well. Cover and cook over medium heat about 25 minutes or till potatoes are tender, stirring frequently. Makes 6 servings.

CREAMY BAKED CORN

Assembling time: 5 minutes
Cooking time: 25 minutes

¼ cup plain yogurt *or* dairy sour
   cream
2 tablespoons green goddess salad
   dressing
1 tablespoon all-purpose flour
1 teaspoon brown sugar
1 12-ounce can whole kernel corn
   with sweet peppers, drained
1 green onion, sliced
1 tablespoon toasted wheat germ

1 In a bowl combine yogurt or sour
cream, salad dressing, flour, brown
sugar, and dash *pepper*. Stir in drained corn
and green onion. Turn into a 20-ounce casserole; sprinkle with wheat germ.
2 Bake, uncovered, in a 375° oven for 20
to 25 minutes or till mixture is heated
through. Makes 4 servings.

FASTEST CORN CHOWDER

Total preparation time: 8 minutes

1 17-ounce can cream-style corn
1 13-ounce can (1⅔ cups)
   evaporated milk
1 12-ounce can whole kernel corn
   with sweet peppers
1 teaspoon minced dried onion
   Dash pepper
1 tablespoon butter *or* margarine
   Cooked bacon pieces (optional)

1 In a saucepan combine cream-style
corn, evaporated milk, *undrained*
whole kernel corn with sweet peppers, onion, and pepper. Bring to boiling, stirring
constantly. Stir in butter or margarine. Top
each serving with cooked bacon pieces, if
desired. Makes 4 to 6 servings.

BUTTERY SWEET CARROTS

Assembling time: 5 minutes
Cooking time: 20 minutes

6 medium carrots, sliced (1 pound)
   or 3 cups frozen crinkle-cut
   carrots
1 medium apple, cored and sliced
2 tablespoons brown sugar
2 tablespoons butter *or* margarine
1 tablespoon lemon juice

1 In a medium saucepan cook the fresh
carrots, covered, in boiling salted water
about 15 minutes or till tender. (Or cook the
frozen carrots according to package directions.) Drain thoroughly.
2 Add the sliced apple, brown sugar, butter or margarine, and lemon juice to
carrots in saucepan; mix well. Cover and
cook about 5 minutes or till apple is tender.
Makes 6 servings.

SWEET AND SOUR CARROTS

Assembling time: 5 minutes
Cooking time: 10 minutes

4 green onions, cut into 1-inch
   pieces
¼ cup apple juice, orange juice, *or*
   water
2 tablespoons butter *or* margarine
2 tablespoons honey
1 tablespoon lemon juice
2 cups frozen crinkle-cut carrots *or*
   frozen loose-pack vegetables

1 In a saucepan combine onions, juice or
water, butter or margarine, honey, and
lemon juice. Bring to boiling. Add frozen carrots or vegetables; toss to mix. Cover and
cook over medium heat about 10 minutes or
till tender. Season with salt, if desired.
Makes 4 servings.

GLAZED CARROTS AND BRUSSELS SPROUTS

The glaze on this attractive vegetable combination gets its subtle sweetness from the
apple juice. Prepare the glaze while the vegetables cook—

Total preparation time: 15 minutes

2 cups frozen crinkle-cut carrots
1 10-ounce package frozen brussels
   sprouts
½ cup apple juice
1½ teaspoons cornstarch
½ teaspoon instant chicken bouillon
   granules
   Dash ground cloves
1 tablespoon butter *or* margarine
1 teaspoon lemon juice

1 In a covered saucepan cook frozen carrots and brussels sprouts in a small
amount of boiling salted water about 10 minutes or till tender. Drain.
2 Meanwhile, in a medium saucepan
combine apple juice, cornstarch, chick-
en bouillon granules, and ground cloves.
Cook and stir till mixture is thickened and
bubbly. Cook and stir 2 minutes more.
3 Stir in butter or margarine and lemon
juice. Add cooked carrots and brussels
sprouts; stir till vegetables are well coated.
Makes 6 servings.

BLACK TIE PEAS

Make every minute count. Slice the onion while waiting for the water to boil—

Assembling time: 5 minutes
Cooking time: 10 minutes

- 1 10-ounce package frozen peas
- 1 small onion, cut into thin wedges
- ¼ cup sliced pitted ripe olives
- 1 tablespoon butter *or* margarine

1 Cook frozen peas and onion wedges according to pea package directions, *except* omit salt from the cooking water. Drain. Stir in ripe olives and butter or margarine; heat through. Makes 4 servings.

BREADED TOMATO SLICES

Assembling time: 8 minutes
Cooking time: 5 minutes

- 2 beaten eggs
- 1 tablespoon milk
- 4 firm medium tomatoes
- 1 cup fine dry seasoned bread crumbs
- 2 to 3 tablespoons cooking oil
- ½ cup shredded American cheese (2 ounces)

1 In a shallow bowl combine eggs and milk. Cut tomatoes into ¾-inch-thick slices. Dip tomato slices in bread crumbs, then in egg mixture. Dip again in crumbs.
2 In a skillet cook tomatoes in hot oil over medium heat turning to brown on both sides. Sprinkle cheese over tomatoes. Cover and cook over low heat till cheese is almost melted. Makes 4 to 6 servings.

CHEESY ZUCCHINI AND CORN

Assembling time: 6 minutes
Cooking time: 8 minutes

- 1 pound zucchini, cubed (3½ cups)
- 1 small onion, chopped (¼ cup)
- 1 8¾-ounce can whole kernel corn, drained
- ½ cup shredded American cheese
- 1 *or* 2 canned green chili peppers, rinsed, seeded, and chopped
- 1 tablespoon butter *or* margarine

1 In a saucepan combine zucchini, onion, ½ cup *water*, and ¼ teaspoon *salt*; bring to boiling. Reduce heat; simmer, covered, about 5 minutes or till zucchini is crisp-tender. Drain well.
2 Stir in corn, cheese, chili peppers, and butter or margarine; cook and stir over low heat till cheese is melted. Serve in sauce dishes. Makes 6 servings.

ZUCCHINI AND SPINACH STIR-FRY

Assembling time: 8 minutes
Cooking time: 12 minutes

- 1 small onion, cut into thin wedges
- 2 tablespoons cooking oil
- 2 medium zucchini, thinly sliced
- 8 cups coarsely torn fresh spinach
- 1 teaspoon lemon juice
- ½ teaspoon seasoned salt
- ½ teaspoon dried basil, crushed

1 In a large skillet or wok cook onion in hot oil for 3 minutes. Add zucchini; cook, stirring often, for 3 to 5 minutes more. Add spinach *half* at a time, cooking and stirring just till wilted. Stir in lemon juice, seasoned salt, basil, and a dash *pepper*. Makes 8 servings.

ZUCCHINI IN DILL CREAM SAUCE

Assembling time: 10 minutes
Cooking time: 12 minutes

- 2¼ pounds zucchini, cut into 2×½×½-inch strips (7 cups)
- 1 small onion, finely chopped (¼ cup)
- ½ cup water
- 1 teaspoon salt
- 1 teaspoon instant chicken bouillon granules
- ½ teaspoon dried dillweed
- 2 tablespoons butter *or* margarine
- 2 teaspoons sugar
- 1 teaspoon lemon juice
- ½ cup dairy sour cream
- 2 tablespoons all-purpose flour

1 In a saucepan combine zucchini strips, chopped onion, water, salt, bouillon granules, and dillweed. Bring to boiling. Reduce heat; simmer, covered, about 5 minutes or till zucchini is crisp-tender. Drain, reserving cooking liquid. Set zucchini aside; return cooking liquid to saucepan. Stir in butter or margarine, sugar, and lemon juice.
2 Combine sour cream and flour. Stir into reserved cooking liquid. Cook and stir till thickened and bubbly. Cook and stir 1 minute more. Stir in zucchini. Serves 6 to 8.

CAULIFLOWER WITH MUSTARD SAUCE

Assembling time: 3 minutes
Cooking time: 20 minutes

1 medium head cauliflower
1 10¾-ounce can condensed cream of celery soup
1 tablespoon prepared mustard
1 tablespoon butter *or* margarine
½ teaspoon dried parsley flakes
1 tablespoon shelled sunflower nuts

1 Leave cauliflower whole or cut into flowerets. Cook whole cauliflower in 1 inch of boiling salted water for 15 to 20 minutes. (Or cook flowerets for 10 to 15 minutes.) Drain. Place in a serving bowl.
2 Meanwhile, in a small saucepan combine remaining ingredients except nuts; bring to boiling. Pour over cauliflower. Sprinkle with sunflower nuts. Serves 6 to 8.

SWISS CREAM OF VEGETABLE SOUP

Total preparation time: 30 minutes

1 16-ounce package frozen loose-pack French-style green beans, carrots, cauliflower, and onions
1 14½-ounce can chicken broth
1 medium onion, chopped (½ cup)
1 cup cubed process Swiss cheese
1 cup milk

1 In saucepan mix frozen vegetables, broth, and onion. Bring to boil. Reduce heat; simmer, covered, about 10 minutes.
2 Transfer about *half* of the mixture to a blender container; cover and blend till smooth. Return to the saucepan. Repeat with remaining mixture. Stir cheese and milk into vegetable mixture. Cook and stir till cheese is melted. Makes 6 servings.

ASPARAGUS WITH FLUFFY HOLLANDAISE

Total preparation time: 12 minutes

1 10-ounce package frozen asparagus spears
1 egg
1 tablespoon lemon juice
1 4-ounce container whipped cream cheese

1 Cook frozen asparagus spears according to package directions; drain. Meanwhile, in a small saucepan beat together the egg and lemon juice. Stir in cream cheese. Cook and stir over low heat for 2 to 3 minutes or till smooth and thickened. *Do not boil.* Spoon cream cheese mixture over asparagus spears. Makes 3 or 4 servings.

ASPARAGUS WITH FRESH TOMATO SAUCE

Total preparation time: 10 minutes

1 10-ounce package frozen asparagus spears
⅓ cup mayonnaise *or* salad dressing
1 small tomato, chopped
1 teaspoon lemon juice
Dash pepper

1 Cook asparagus according to package directions; drain. Meanwhile, for sauce, stir together mayonnaise or salad dressing, chopped tomato, lemon juice, and pepper.
2 Arrange asparagus in a heat-proof dish; spoon sauce atop. Broil 3 inches from heat about 1 minute or till sauce is heated through. Makes 4 servings.

CARAWAY CABBAGE

Assembling time: 5 minutes
Cooking time: 17 minutes

½ medium head cabbage
½ teaspoon salt
1 3-ounce package cream cheese, cut up
2 tablespoons chopped pimiento
½ teaspoon caraway seed

1 Coarsely chop cabbage. Place in a saucepan; add salt and enough water to cover. Cook, covered, for 10 to 12 minutes or till tender. Drain. Add cream cheese, pimiento, and caraway seed; cook and stir till cream cheese is melted. Serves 6.

COPENHAGEN BRUSSELS SPROUTS

Total preparation time: 12 minutes

1 16-ounce package frozen brussels sprouts
6 slices bacon
⅓ cup Italian salad dressing
1 3-ounce can sliced mushrooms, drained
4 green onions, sliced (¼ cup)
2 tablespoons chopped pimiento
1 ounce blue cheese, crumbled (¼ cup)

1 Cook frozen brussels sprouts according to package directions; drain. Meanwhile, in a small skillet cook bacon till crisp; drain. Crumble bacon; set aside.
2 Combine cooked brussels sprouts, Italian salad dressing, mushrooms, green onions, and pimiento. Cook over low heat, stirring frequently, till heated through. Remove from heat; stir in blue cheese and crumbled bacon. Makes 6 to 8 servings.

SNOWCAPPED BROCCOLI SPEARS

Impressive yet quickly assembled, this broccoli platter is appropriate for special-occasion dinners. A worthy complement to roasts, steaks, and chops—

Assembling time: 15 minutes
Cooking time: 15 minutes

2 10-ounce packages frozen
    broccoli spears
2 egg whites
¼ teaspoon salt
⅓ cup mayonnaise *or* salad dressing
1 tablespoon butter *or* margarine,
    melted
    Grated Parmesan cheese

1 Cook frozen broccoli spears according to package directions; drain well. Meanwhile, in a small bowl beat egg whites and salt with a rotary beater till stiff peaks form. Gently fold in mayonnaise or salad dressing; set aside.

2 Arrange cooked broccoli spears with stem ends toward the center on an oven-proof platter or in a 9-inch pie plate. Drizzle the melted butter or margarine over broccoli spears.

3 Spoon the mayonnaise mixture onto the center of the platter over broccoli stems; sprinkle with grated Parmesan cheese. Bake in a 350° oven for 12 to 15 minutes or till topping is golden. Serves 6.

Snowcapped Broccoli Spears

SAUCY BROCCOLI

Total preparation time: 20 minutes

1 10-ounce package frozen cut
    broccoli
1 1½-ounce envelope sour cream
    sauce mix
⅓ cup mayonnaise *or* salad dressing
2 ounces American cheese, cubed
    (½ cup)

1 Cook broccoli according to package directions; drain. Meanwhile, prepare the sour cream sauce mix according to package directions; stir in the mayonnaise or salad dressing.

2 Stir mayonnaise mixture and cubed American cheese into drained broccoli in the saucepan. Cook and stir broccoli mixture over low heat till cheese is melted. Serve at once. Makes 4 servings.

ORIENTAL-STYLE BROCCOLI

Assembling time: 7 minutes
Cooking time: 10 minutes

½ pound fresh broccoli
1 8-ounce can sliced water
    chestnuts, drained
1 medium onion, sliced
3 tablespoons butter *or* margarine

1 Cut broccoli stalks lengthwise into uniform spears, following the branching lines. In a covered skillet cook broccoli, water chestnuts, and onion in hot butter or margarine over medium heat about 10 minutes or just till tender, turning broccoli occasionally and being careful not to break broccoli spears. Makes 4 servings.

SPINACH AND BROCCOLI WITH CHEESE SAUCE

For flavor variety, try different cheese spreads in this recipe. American or Swiss flavor cheese spread or cheese spread with bacon are tasty alternatives to the blue cheese spread—

Total preparation time: 25 minutes

1 10-ounce package frozen chopped
    spinach
1 10-ounce package frozen chopped
    broccoli
¼ cup water
1 teaspoon instant chicken bouillon
    granules
1 5-ounce jar blue cheese spread
½ cup milk
1 tablespoon cornstarch
½ of a 3-ounce can French-fried
    onions (optional)

1 In a large saucepan combine frozen spinach, frozen broccoli, water, and bouillon granules. Bring to boiling; reduce heat. Cover and cook for 12 minutes, breaking up vegetables with a fork. *Do not drain.*

2 Stir blue cheese spread into vegetable mixture. Combine milk and cornstarch; add to vegetable mixture. Cook and stir till mixture is thickened and bubbly. Cook and stir 2 minutes more. Turn into a serving bowl; garnish with French-fried onions, if desired. Makes 6 to 8 servings.

CREAM-STYLE LIMAS AND MUSHROOMS

Assembling time: 5 minutes
Cooking time: 18 minutes

- 1 3-ounce can sliced mushrooms
- 1 10-ounce package frozen lima beans
- 1 small onion, chopped (¼ cup)
- ½ teaspoon sugar
- ½ teaspoon salt
- Dash pepper
- ½ cup light cream *or* milk
- 2 teaspoons cornstarch

1 Drain mushrooms, reserving the liquid. Set mushrooms aside. Add enough water to mushroom liquid to measure ½ cup. In a saucepan combine the reserved mushroom liquid, lima beans, chopped onion, sugar, salt, and pepper. Bring to boiling; reduce heat. Simmer, covered, about 10 minutes or till beans are tender.

2 Stir together light cream or milk and cornstarch. Stir into bean mixture. Cook and stir till thickened and bubbly; cook and stir 2 minutes more. Stir in mushrooms; heat through. Makes 4 or 5 servings.

MEXICAN BEANS

Assembling time: 3 minutes
Cooking time: 5 minutes

- 1 15-ounce can garbanzo beans
- 1 15-ounce can red kidney beans
- 1 10-ounce can tomatoes and green chili peppers
- ½ teaspoon chili powder

1 Drain beans. Combine beans, *undrained* tomatoes and green chili peppers, and chili powder. Heat through. Makes 6 servings.

MOCK BAKED BEANS

Assembling time: 5 minutes
Cooking time: 12 minutes

- 1 16-ounce can lima beans, drained
- 1 15-ounce can butter beans with molasses sauce and bacon
- 1 8-ounce can tomato sauce
- ¼ cup chopped green pepper
- 2 tablespoons brown sugar
- 1 tablespoon minced dried onion
- ½ teaspoon dry mustard
- ⅛ teaspoon ground ginger

1 In a medium saucepan combine lima beans, *undrained* butter beans, tomato sauce, green pepper, brown sugar, onion, mustard, and ginger. Bring to boiling; reduce heat. Simmer, covered, about 10 minutes or till flavors are blended. Makes 6 servings.

PARSNIPS AND BACON

Assembling time: 10 minutes
Cooking time: 10 minutes

- 2 slices bacon
- 1 pound parsnips
- 2 tablespoons chopped onion
- ½ teaspoon salt
- ⅛ teaspoon pepper
- 1 teaspoon dried parsley flakes

1 In a skillet cook bacon till crisp; drain bacon, reserving drippings in skillet. Crumble bacon; set aside. Meanwhile, peel parsnips and cut into julienne strips.

2 Add parsnips and chopped onion to reserved drippings; toss to coat. Sprinkle with salt and pepper. Cook, covered, over low heat about 10 minutes or till parsnips are tender, stirring often. Stir in bacon and parsley. Makes 4 servings.

ORANGE BEETS

Assembling time: 2 minutes
Cooking time: 5 minutes

- 3 tablespoons orange marmalade
- 4 teaspoons cornstarch
- 1 16-ounce can sliced *or* diced beets

1 In a saucepan combine marmalade and cornstarch. Stir in *undrained* beets. Cook, stirring constantly, till mixture is thickened and bubbly. Cook and stir 2 minutes more. Makes 4 servings.

VERY EASY BORSCHT

A quick, simmered soup with a homemade flavor—

Total preparation time: 20 minutes

- 1 envelope *regular* onion soup mix
- 2 16-ounce cans julienne beets
- 1 16-ounce jar sweet-sour red cabbage
- 1 10½-ounce can condensed beef broth
- Dairy sour cream

1 In a 4-quart Dutch oven prepare onion soup mix according to package directions. Stir in *undrained* beets, *undrained* red cabbage, and beef broth; heat through. Serve in bowls; dollop with sour cream. Makes 8 to 10 servings.

CRANBERRY-GLAZED SWEET POTATOES

Assembling time: 5 minutes
Cooking time: 10 minutes

- 1 8-ounce can whole cranberry sauce
- ¼ cup orange juice *or* apple juice
- 2 tablespoons butter *or* margarine
- 1 17-ounce can sweet potatoes, drained

1 In a skillet stir together cranberry sauce, orange or apple juice, and butter. Cook and stir till combined.

2 Add sweet potatoes; spoon cranberry mixture over potatoes. Cook over medium heat about 10 minutes or till potatoes are glazed, basting often. Serves 4 or 5.

SWEET POTATOES FLORIDA

Assembling time: 8 minutes
Cooking time: 20 minutes

- 1 16-ounce can grapefruit *or* orange and grapefruit sections
- 1 17-ounce can sweet potatoes, drained
- ¼ cup packed brown sugar
- 2 tablespoons butter *or* margarine
- ⅛ teaspoon ground nutmeg

1 Drain grapefruit sections, reserving ¼ cup of the liquid. Arrange grapefruit sections and sweet potatoes in an 8 × 1½-inch round baking dish.

2 In a small saucepan stir together brown sugar, butter or margarine, ground nutmeg, and the reserved ¼ cup grapefruit liquid. Cook and stir till combined.

3 Pour sugar mixture evenly over grapefruit and potatoes. Bake in a 350° oven about 20 minutes. Serves 6.

AU GRATIN TOPPING

Assembling time: 5 minutes

- ½ cup fine dry bread crumbs
- 2 tablespoons grated Parmesan cheese
- ¼ teaspoon paprika
- 1 tablespoon Italian salad dressing
  Hot cooked vegetables

1 Combine crumbs, cheese, and paprika. Stir in dressing; mix well. Sprinkle atop desired *buttered*, hot cooked vegetables. Makes about ¾ cup.

CREAM CHEESE TOPPER

Assembling time: 5 minutes

- 1 4-ounce container whipped cream cheese with chives
- ¼ cup butter *or* margarine, softened
  Hot cooked vegetables

1 In a small bowl combine whipped cream cheese with chives and softened butter or margarine. Serve over desired hot cooked vegetables. Makes about ¾ cup.

VEGETABLE FIX-UPS

Perk up plain cooked vegetables by adding a quick topping. Try the topping recipes on this page when you prepare canned, frozen, or fresh vegetables. Store the topping in a covered container in the refrigerator until you need it.

ZIPPY HORSERADISH BUTTER

Give corn-on-the-cob, sliced carrots, green beans, peas, or new potatoes a flavor boost with this easy butter—

Assembling time: 5 minutes

- ½ cup butter *or* margarine
- 1 tablespoon prepared mustard
- 2 teaspoons prepared horseradish
- ½ teaspoon salt
- ⅛ teaspoon pepper
  Hot cooked vegetables

1 Beat together butter or margarine, mustard, horseradish, salt, and pepper with an electric mixer. Serve over desired hot cooked vegetables. Makes about ⅔ cup.

HERBED NUT TOPPER

Add a new flavor and texture to spinach, cabbage, or broccoli with this easy topper—

Total preparation time: 7 minutes

- ¼ cup shelled sunflower nuts, sliced almonds, *or* coarsely chopped cashews
- ½ teaspoon dried basil *or* oregano, crushed
- 2 tablespoons butter *or* margarine
  Hot cooked vegetables

1 In a small saucepan cook desired nuts and herb in hot butter or margarine. Stir frequently, till nuts are golden. Serve over desired hot cooked vegetables. Makes about ¼ cup.

ORANGE RICE

Assembling time: 10 minutes
Cooking time: 8 minutes

1 stalk celery, chopped (½ cup)
2 green onions, sliced
   (2 tablespoons)
2 tablespoons butter *or* margarine
1 cup quick-cooking rice
1 cup water
1 tablespoon frozen orange juice
   concentrate
½ teaspoon salt

1 In a saucepan cook celery and green onion in hot butter or margarine for 5 minutes. Stir in rice, water, orange juice concentrate, and salt. Bring mixture to boiling; reduce heat and simmer, covered for 5 minutes. Fluff with a fork. Makes 4 servings.

CREAMY MUSHROOM RICE

Assembling time: 5 minutes
Cooking time: 22 minutes

1¼ cups water
½ cup long grain rice
1 4-ounce can mushroom stems and
   pieces
1 tablespoon dried parsley flakes
1 teaspoon instant chicken bouillon
   granules
1 4-ounce container whipped cream
   cheese with chives

1 In a saucepan combine water, rice, *undrained* mushrooms, parsley flakes, and chicken bouillon granules. Bring to boiling. Reduce heat and simmer, covered, about 20 minutes or till rice is tender. Stir in cream cheese with chives; heat through. Makes 4 or 5 servings.

JAPANESE RICE MEDLEY

This colorful combination of rice and vegetables is a good flavor companion for a pork or poultry entrée—

Assembling time: 5 minutes
Cooking time: 8 minutes

1 3-ounce can sliced mushrooms
1 ¾-ounce envelope mushroom
   gravy mix
1½ cups quick-cooking rice
1 10-ounce package frozen loose-
   pack green beans, broccoli,
   onions, and mushrooms
2 green onions, sliced
   (2 tablespoons)
2 tablespoons butter *or* margarine
2 tablespoons soy sauce
¼ cup slivered almonds *or* ½ cup
   chow mein noodles

1 Drain mushrooms, reserving liquid. Add enough water to reserved liquid to measure 1¾ cups. In a medium saucepan stir the reserved mushroom liquid into gravy mix. Stir in mushrooms, rice, frozen vegetables, green onion, butter or margarine, and soy sauce.

2 Bring mixture to boiling, stirring to break up vegetables. Reduce heat and simmer, covered, about 5 minutes or till rice and vegetables are tender. Turn into a serving bowl. Sprinkle with slivered almonds or chow mein noodles. Makes 6 servings.

ITALIAN-STYLE RICE

Total preparation time: 30 minutes

2 cups water
1 cup long grain rice
½ teaspoon salt
   Butter *or* margarine
   Grated Parmesan *or* Romano
   cheese

1 In a medium saucepan combine water, rice, and salt. Bring to boiling; reduce heat. Cover and simmer for 15 minutes. Remove from heat. Let stand, covered, for 10 minutes. Serve immediately with butter or margarine; sprinkle with Parmesan or Romano cheese. Makes 6 servings.

   Rice with Mushrooms: Prepare Italian-Style Rice as above, *except* omit butter and Parmesan or Romano cheese. Meanwhile, cook 2 sliced *green onions* in 2 tablespoons hot *butter or margarine* about 3 minutes or till tender. Stir in one 4-ounce can *sliced mushrooms*, drained; heat through. Serve mixture over hot cooked rice.

RICE WITH SPINACH

Assembling time: 5 minutes
Cooking time: 23 minutes

1 10-ounce package frozen chopped
   spinach
⅔ cup long grain rice
1 medium onion, chopped (½ cup)
2 tablespoons butter *or* margarine
¼ teaspoon ground nutmeg

1 In a medium saucepan combine spinach, rice, onion, butter or margarine, nutmeg, 1¼ cups *water*, ½ teaspoon *salt*, and ⅛ teaspoon *pepper*. Bring to a boiling, stirring to break up spinach. Reduce heat and simmer covered, about 20 minutes or till rice is tender. Makes 6 servings.

TOMATO-MUSHROOM RICE

Assembling time: 5 minutes
Cooking time: 22 minutes

1¼ cups water
 1 8-ounce can stewed tomatoes,
   cut up
⅔ cup long grain rice
 1 4-ounce can sliced mushrooms,
   drained
 4 green onions, sliced (¼ cup)
 1 tablespoon butter *or* margarine
 2 teaspoons instant beef bouillon
   granules
½ teaspoon dried oregano *or* basil,
   crushed

1 In a saucepan stir together water, *undrained* tomatoes, rice, mushrooms, green onion, butter or margarine, bouillon granules, and oregano or basil. Bring to boiling; reduce heat and simmer, covered, about 20 minutes or till rice is tender and liquid is absorbed. Makes 6 servings.

QUICK-COOKING RICE

Ever wonder why quick-cooking white rice cooks in one-fourth the time of long grain white rice and quick-cooking brown rice in one-third the time of regular brown rice? The time savings are due to the fact that the quick-cooking rices are precooked and then dehydrated. The cooking you do rehydrates the rice to finish the cooking process.

BROWN RICE-VEGETABLE RING

For a main dish fill the center with creamed salmon, tuna, turkey, or chicken—

Assembling time: 8 minutes
Cooking time: 16 minutes

 1 10 ¾-ounce can condensed
   chicken broth
1½ cups quick-cooking brown rice
 1 8¾-ounce can whole kernel corn,
   drained
 2 tablespoons chopped pimiento
 1 tablespoon butter *or* margarine
 1 teaspoon dried parsley flakes
½ teaspoon dried basil, crushed

1 In a medium saucepan combine broth, rice, corn, pimiento, butter or margarine, parsley, basil, and 1 cup *water*; bring to boiling. Reduce heat and simmer, covered, about 15 minutes or till rice is tender.

2 Press hot mixture into a well-greased 4-cup ring mold. Unmold immediately onto a serving plate. Makes 6 servings.

FRUITED RICE

Assembling time: 5 minutes
Cooking time: 5 minutes

 1 cup quick-cooking rice
 1 cup water
½ cup cranberry-orange relish
 1 medium apple, peeled and
   coarsely chopped
 1 tablespoon butter *or* margarine
⅛ teaspoon salt
   Dash ground cinnamon

1 In a small saucepan combine rice and water. Bring to boiling. Stir in relish, apple, butter or margarine, salt, and cinnamon. Reduce heat and simmer, covered, about 5 minutes or till rice is tender. Stir before serving. Makes 4 servings.

LEMON RICE

Assembling time: 10 minutes
Cooking time: 8 minutes

¼ cup butter *or* margarine
½ teaspoon salt
½ teaspoon mustard seed
½ teaspoon ground turmeric
1½ cups quick-cooking rice
1½ cups water
 1 tablespoon lemon juice

1 In a medium saucepan melt butter or margarine over low heat. Stir in salt, mustard seed, and turmeric. Cook for 5 minutes, stirring occasionally.

2 Stir in quick-cooking rice, water, and lemon juice. Bring to boiling; reduce heat and simmer, covered, about 5 minutes or till rice is tender. Makes 4 or 5 servings.

RED RICE WITH GREEN BEANS

Assembling time: 3 minutes
Cooking time: 8 minutes

 1 9-ounce package frozen French-
   style green beans
 1 8-ounce can stewed tomatoes,
   cut up
¾ cup quick-cooking rice
⅓ cup water
¾ teaspoon prepared mustard
½ teaspoon instant beef bouillon
   granules
¼ teaspoon chili powder

1 In a medium saucepan combine green beans, *undrained* tomatoes, rice, water, mustard, bouillon granules, and chili powder. Bring to boiling, stirring to break up beans. Reduce heat and simmer, covered, about 5 minutes or till rice is tender and beans are done. Makes 4 or 5 servings.

FETTUCCINE
à la CARBONARA

There's no elaborate sauce preparation involved in this rich, cheesy pasta dish. The heat from the pasta cooks the egg, which thickens the mixture into a creamy sauce—

Total preparation time: 30 minutes

- 4 **eggs**
- 12 **ounces fettuccine, linguine,** *or* **other pasta**
- ½ **pound bacon, sliced**
- ¼ **cup whipping cream**
- ⅛ **teaspoon pepper**
- ¼ **cup butter** *or* **margarine, cut up**
- 1 **cup grated Parmesan** *or* **Romano cheese (4 ounces)**
- ¼ **cup snipped fresh parsley** *or* **1 tablespoon dried parsley flakes**

1 Place *unbroken* eggs in a bowl of warm water; set aside. Meanwhile, cook pasta according to package directions; drain. In skillet cook bacon till crisp. Remove; drain on paper toweling. Crumble and set aside.

2 Beat together eggs, whipping cream, and pepper just till combined. Toss hot, cooked pasta with butter or margarine. Pour egg mixture over and toss till pasta is well coated. Add bacon, grated Parmesan or Romano cheese, and parsley; toss to mix. Serve immediately. Makes 8 servings.

Fettuccine à la Carbonara

PASTA WITH PARSLEY-GARLIC SAUCE

Total preparation time: 20 minutes

8 ounces fettucine, linguine, *or* spaghetti
1 large clove garlic, minced
2 tablespoons butter *or* margarine
2 tablespoons olive oil *or* cooking oil
½ cup snipped parsley
¼ teaspoon salt
⅛ teaspoon pepper

1 Cook pasta according to package directions; drain. Meanwhile, in a small saucepan cook garlic in hot butter and oil just till golden brown. Stir in parsley, salt, and pepper; heat through.

2 Place hot cooked pasta on a serving platter. Pour parsley mixture atop; toss till well coated. Makes 6 to 8 servings.

FETTUCCINE IN ALMOND SAUCE

Total preparation time: 20 minutes

6 ounces fettuccine
½ cup sliced almonds
2 tablespoons butter *or* margarine
1 slightly beaten egg
3 tablespoons cooked bacon pieces
1 tablespoon dried parsley flakes
1 tablespoon lemon juice
Grated Parmesan cheese

1 Cook fettuccine according to package directions; drain. Meanwhile, in a 10-inch skillet cook and stir nuts in hot butter or margarine over medium heat till golden.

2 In a small bowl combine the egg, bacon pieces, parsley, lemon juice, and dash *pepper*. Add nuts. Toss with the hot pasta. Pass Parmesan. Makes 4 to 6 servings.

CHEESE- AND-OLIVE-SAUCED SPAGHETTI

Total preparation time: 22 minutes

8 ounces spaghetti
1 cup shredded Swiss cheese
1 cup sliced pimiento-stuffed olives *or* sliced pitted ripe olives
1 cup whipping cream
½ cup milk

1 In a large saucepan cook spaghetti according to package directions; drain. Add shredded cheese, sliced olives, cream, and milk; toss to combine. Cook and stir over medium heat for 3 to 4 minutes or till cheese is melted and sauce is thickened. Season with salt and pepper to taste. Turn into a serving dish. Makes 8 servings.

SAUCY BROCCOLI AND NOODLES

Total preparation time: 22 minutes

1 5½-ounce package noodles with sour cream sauce mix
1 10-ounce package frozen chopped broccoli
½ cup cream-style cottage cheese
¼ cup milk
¼ cup crushed wheat wafers
1 tablespoon butter *or* margarine, melted

1 Cook noodles from mix according to package directions; drain. Meanwhile, cook broccoli according to package directions; drain. Combine hot cooked noodles, the packet of sauce mix, cottage cheese, and milk. Fold in broccoli.

2 Turn noodle mixture into a serving bowl. Toss crushed crackers with melted butter or margarine; sprinkle atop noodle mixture. Makes 6 servings.

SOUTHERN CHEESE GRITS

A longtime favorite in the South, grits are now a welcome addition to a hearty breakfast or brunch menu anywhere—

Assembling time: 10 minutes
Cooking time: 20 minutes

4 cups water
1 cup quick-cooking grits
½ teaspoon salt
1½ cups shredded American cheese (6 ounces)
2 tablespoons butter *or* margarine
2 drops bottled hot pepper sauce
1 slightly beaten egg
Paprika

1 In a medium saucepan bring the water to boiling. Gradually stir in quick-cooking grits and salt. Return to boiling. Reduce heat and cook, uncovered, for 3 to 5 minutes or till the grits absorb all of the water and the mixture is thick. Remove the saucepan from heat.

2 Add shredded American cheese, butter or margarine, and bottled hot pepper sauce; stir till the cheese is melted. Stir in the slightly beaten egg. Turn the mixture into a greased 8×8×2-inch baking dish. Sprinkle with paprika.

3 Bake, uncovered, in a 325° oven about 15 minutes or till set. Let stand 5 minutes before serving. Makes 8 servings.

PARMESAN SLICES

Pictured on page 137—

Assembling time: 5 minutes
Cooking time: 2 minutes

⅓ **cup mayonnaise** *or* **salad dressing**
⅓ **cup grated Parmesan cheese**
8 **1-inch slices French bread**

1 In a small bowl combine mayonnaise or salad dressing and Parmesan cheese; spread on one side of each bread slice. Place slices, cheese side up, on a baking sheet; broil about 5 inches from heat for 1 to 2 minutes or till golden. Makes 8 slices.

SWISS-SOURDOUGH LOAF

Assembling time: 10 minutes
Cooking time: 20 minutes

½ **cup butter** *or* **margarine, softened**
½ **teaspoon dried tarragon, crushed**
1 **16-ounce loaf unsliced sourdough bread**
6 or 7 **slices Swiss cheese**

1 Combine softened butter or margarine and tarragon. Slice bread into 12 to 14 slices, cutting to but not through bottom crust. Spread one cut surface of each slice with some of the butter mixture.
2 Cut cheese slices into triangles; place a cheese triangle between each bread slice. Wrap bread in foil. Bake in a 375° oven about 20 minutes or till heated through. Makes 1 loaf.

ITALIAN BREADSTICKS

A clever use of leftover frankfurter buns—

Assembling time: 5 minutes
Cooking time: 10 minutes

4 **frankfurter buns, split**
3 **tablespoons butter** *or* **margarine, melted**
¼ **cup grated Parmesan cheese**
¾ **teaspoon Italian seasoning**

1 Cut split frankfurter buns lengthwise into three strips; place in a shallow baking pan. Brush bun strips with melted butter or margarine. Stir together Parmesan cheese and Italian seasoning. Sprinkle atop strips. Bake in a 350° oven for 8 to 10 minutes or till toasted and crisp. Makes 24.

OLIVE-TOPPED BAGELS

Assembling time: 5 minutes
Cooking time: 2 minutes

1 **4-ounce container whipped cream cheese with chives**
2 **tablespoons sliced pitted ripe olives**
4 **bagels, split**

1 Stir together whipped cream cheese and olives. Spread cream cheese mixture on each bagel half. Place on a baking sheet; broil about 5 inches from heat about 2 minutes or till light brown. Makes 8 servings.

ONION-BUTTERED RYE ROLLS

Assembling time: 10 minutes
Cooking time: 10 minutes

¼ **cup butter** *or* **margarine, softened**
2 **tablespoons finely chopped onion**
2 **teaspoons Dijon-style mustard**
6 **small rye dinner rolls, split**

1 In a small bowl stir together softened butter or margarine, chopped onion, and mustard. Spread cut surfaces of *each* roll with about 1½ *teaspoons* of the butter mixture. Reassemble rolls. Wrap in foil. Heat rolls in a 350° oven for 8 to 10 minutes or till warm. Makes 6 rolls.

SESAME BREADSTICKS

For a crisper texture, let these breadsticks cool completely before serving—

Assembling time: 10 minutes
Cooking time: 18 minutes

1 **package (10) refrigerated biscuits**
¼ **cup sesame seed**
Milk

1 With hands, roll each biscuit into an 8-inch rope. Moisten hands, if necessary. (Ropes will shrink back to 6 inches.) Sprinkle sesame seed on waxed paper. Brush each rope with milk and roll in sesame seed. Place on a greased baking sheet. Bake in a 375° oven for 15 to 18 minutes or till golden brown. Makes 10 breadsticks.

PAN-FRIED CORN FRITTERS

Assembling time: 8 minutes
Cooking time: 10 minutes

1 cup packaged biscuit mix
1 8¾-ounce can kernel corn, drained
1 beaten egg

1 In a mixing bowl place biscuit mix. Add corn, egg, and ¼ cup *water*. Stir till combined. Using about ¼ cup of the mixture for each fritter, cook fritters in lightly greased skillet over medium heat about 10 minutes or till brown; turn once. Serve with butter or margarine, warmed applesauce, dairy sour cream, or maple-flavored syrup, if desired. Makes 6 to 8 fritters.

BLUEBERRY PANCAKE WEDGES

Total preparation time: 25 minutes

1 16-ounce can blueberries
1 cup packaged pancake mix
1 teaspoon finely shredded lemon peel
2 tablespoons butter *or* margarine
⅓ cup sugar
1 tablespoon cornstarch

1 Drain blueberries, reserving syrup. Prepare pancake mix according to package directions; stir in lemon peel. Set aside. In a 10-inch oven-going skillet melt butter or margarine; remove from heat.

2 Pour pancake batter into skillet. Drop blueberries into batter. Bake in a 400° oven for 15 to 18 minutes.

3 Meanwhile, in a saucepan combine sugar and cornstarch; stir in reserved blueberry syrup. Cook and stir till thickened and bubbly; cook and stir 2 minutes more.

4 Loosen edges of pancake. Invert onto a serving plate; cut into wedges. Pass syrup mixture. Makes 4 to 6 servings.

WHOLE WHEAT OVEN PANCAKES

Assembling time: 8 minutes
Cooking time: 12 minutes

1 cup whole wheat flour
1 cup whole bran cereal
⅓ cup toasted wheat germ
1½ teaspoons baking powder
½ teaspoon baking soda
1 egg
1 cup buttermilk
¼ cup hot water
¼ cup cooking oil
¼ cup honey

1 Stir together flour, cereal, wheat germ, baking powder, and soda. Add remaining ingredients. Beat till combined.

2 Spread batter evenly in a greased 15×10×1-inch baking pan. Bake in a 425° oven for 12 minutes. Cut into rectangles. Serve warm. Makes 8 to 10.

HONEY-PEANUT ROLLS

Assembling time: 8 minutes
Cooking time: 15 minutes

2 tablespoons butter *or* margarine
¼ cup peanuts, coarsely chopped
¼ cup honey
¼ teaspoon ground cinnamon
1 package (8) refrigerated crescent rolls

1 In a saucepan melt butter or margarine; stir in peanuts, honey, and cinnamon. Pour into an 8×1½-inch round baking pan. Slice roll dough (do not unroll) into 8 slices; place atop honey mixture, cut side down. Bake in a 375° oven for 12 to 15 minutes. Invert onto a plate. Serve warm. Makes 8.

LEMON-CHEESE-FILLED ROLLS

Assembling time: 10 minutes
Cooking time: 12 minutes

1 3-ounce package cream cheese, cut up
1 tablespoon lemon juice
1 teaspoon sugar
1 package (6) refrigerated flaky dinner rolls

1 In a small bowl stir together cream cheese, lemon juice, and sugar till smooth. Split each dinner roll in half horizontally. Flatten *each* half to a 2½-inch circle.

2 Spoon cheese mixture on *half* of the circles. Top with remaining circles; seal edges. Place in greased muffin cups.

3 Bake in a 400° oven about 12 minutes or till golden. Cool slightly. Sprinkle with powdered sugar, if desired. Makes 6 rolls.

CINNAMON-HONEY SCONES

Assembling time: 12 minutes
Cooking time: 12 minutes

1 cup all-purpose flour
1 cup quick-cooking rolled oats
2 teaspoons baking powder
⅛ teaspoon ground cinnamon
⅓ cup butter *or* margarine
1 beaten egg
2 tablespoons milk
2 tablespoons honey

1 Stir together flour, oats, baking powder, cinnamon, and ¼ teaspoon *salt*. Cut in butter till mixture resembles coarse crumbs. Stir in egg, milk, and honey till mixture is moistened. (Dough will be sticky.)

2 On an ungreased baking sheet pat dough with lightly floured fingers to a 6-inch circle; cut into 12 wedges. Bake in a 400° oven for 10 to 12 minutes. Makes 12.

SPICED MUFFINS

You may want to double this recipe. These muffins disappear quickly—

Assembling time: 8 minutes
Cooking time: 15 minutes

 1 **cup packaged pancake mix**
 2 **tablespoons sugar**
 ½ **teaspoon pumpkin pie spice**
 1 **small banana, mashed (⅓ cup)**
 ¼ **to ⅓ cup milk**

1 In a small bowl stir together pancake mix, sugar, and pumpkin pie spice. Add banana and enough of the milk to make a thick batter; stir till all is moistened. Grease muffin cups or line with paper bake cups; fill ⅔ full. Bake in a 375° oven about 15 minutes. Serve warm. Makes 6 muffins.

LEMON YOGURT BISCUITS

Assembling time: 12 minutes
Cooking time: 12 minutes

 2 **cups all-purpose flour**
 4 **teaspoons baking powder**
 1 **tablespoon sugar**
 ½ **teaspoon cream of tartar**
 ½ **teaspoon salt**
 ¼ **teaspoon baking soda**
 ½ **cup shortening**
 1 **8-ounce carton lemon yogurt**
 2 **tablespoons milk**

1 Stir together flour, baking powder, sugar, cream of tartar, salt, and baking soda. Cut in shortening till mixture resembles coarse crumbs. Make a well in center.
2 Combine yogurt and milk; add to dry ingredients all at once. Stir just till dough clings together. Drop from a tablespoon onto a greased baking sheet. Bake in a 450° oven for 10 to 12 minutes. Makes 12.

CHEESE 'N' BACON DROP BISCUITS

Assembling time: 12 minutes
Cooking time: 12 minutes

 2 **cups packaged biscuit mix**
 ¾ **cup shredded cheddar cheese**
 ⅔ **cup milk**
 ¼ **cup cooked bacon pieces**

1 In a mixing bowl combine biscuit mix, cheese, milk, and bacon; stir just till moistened. Drop from a tablespoon onto a greased baking sheet. Bake in a 450° oven about 10 to 12 minutes or till golden brown. Makes 12 biscuits.

SAVORY BISCUIT BREAD

Assembling time: 10 minutes
Cooking time: 20 minutes

 2 **cups packaged biscuit mix**
 ⅔ **cup milk**
 2 **tablespoons grated Parmesan cheese**
 1 **teaspoon dried parsley flakes**
 ½ **cup shredded cheddar cheese**
 2 **tablespoons butter or margarine, melted**
 2 **green onions, sliced**
 1 **teaspoon Worcestershire sauce**
 ½ **teaspoon dried oregano, crushed Few dashes bottled hot pepper sauce**

1 In a bowl combine biscuit mix, milk, Parmesan cheese, and parsley flakes; stir just till moistened. Spread mixture evenly in a well-greased 8×8×2-inch baking dish.
2 Stir together cheddar cheese, butter or margarine, onions, Worcestershire sauce, oregano, and bottled hot pepper sauce. Sprinkle atop biscuit mix mixture. Bake in a 350° oven about 20 minutes or till done. Serve warm. Makes 8 servings.

ORANGE-CORNMEAL MUFFINS

Assembling time: 10 minutes
Cooking time: 15 minutes

 1 **8½-ounce package corn muffin mix**
 ⅓ **cup orange juice**

1 Prepare corn muffin mix according to package directions, *except* replace the liquid called for with orange juice. Grease muffin cups or line with paper bake cups; fill ⅔ full. Bake according to package directions. Makes about 10 muffins.

ONION BISCUITS

Assembling time: 10 minutes
Cooking time: 12 minutes

 ½ **cup milk**
 1 **teaspoon minced dried onion**
 1 **11-ounce package piecrust mix**
 1 **tablespoon baking powder**
 1 **teaspoon dried parsley flakes or**
 ½ **teaspoon sesame seed**

1 In a small bowl combine milk and onion; let stand 5 minutes. Meanwhile, in a mixing bowl stir together piecrust mix, baking powder, and parsley or sesame seed. Make a well in the center of the dry ingredient mixture. Add milk and onion all at once. Stir just till dough clings together.
2 Turn out onto a well-floured surface; knead for 10 to 12 strokes. Roll or pat dough to a ½-inch thickness. Cut with a 2½-inch biscuit cutter, dipping cutter in flour between cuts. Place on an ungreased baking sheet. Bake in a 450° oven for 10 to 12 minutes or till golden brown. Makes 10.

Onion Biscuits

CHERRIES WITH HONEY MERINGUE

Total cooking time: 25 minutes

2 16-ounce cans pitted tart red
   cherries (water pack)
1 cup sugar
3 tablespoons cornstarch
¼ teaspoon salt
1 cup cranberry juice cocktail
1 tablespoon butter *or* margarine
2 egg whites
¼ cup honey
3 tablespoons finely chopped
   walnuts

1 Drain cherries, reserving ⅔ cup liquid. In a 10-inch skillet stir together sugar, cornstarch, and salt. Stir in reserved cherry liquid, cranberry juice cocktail, and butter or margarine.

2 Cook and stir till mixture is bubbly. Cook; stir 2 minutes more. Add cherries; heat through. Keep warm.

3 In a small mixer bowl beat egg whites at high speed of electric mixer till soft peaks form (tips curl over). Gradually add honey in a thin stream, beating till stiff peaks form (tips stand straight). Fold in *2 tablespoons* of the chopped nuts.

4 Drop egg white mixture from a tablespoon onto hot cherry mixture, forming 6 mounds. Sprinkle remaining nuts atop mounds. Simmer, uncovered, for 5 minutes. Serve in dessert dishes. Serves 6.

FRESH FRUIT WITH COCONUT CREAM TOPPING

Assembling time: 20 minutes

2 tablespoons coconut
1 3-ounce package cream cheese,
   cut up
¼ cup coconut syrup *or* cream of
   coconut
½ cup whipping cream
4 cups sliced strawberries, sliced
   bananas, sliced apricots, sliced
   peaches, sliced nectarines,
   peeled and sectioned oranges,
   peeled and sectioned grapefruit
   or any combination of the above

1 Toast coconut, if desired. In a small mixer bowl beat together cream cheese and coconut syrup till smooth. Gradually add whipping cream, beating on medium speed of electric mixer for 1½ to 2 minutes or till mixture is thickened and fluffy. Fold in coconut. Serve atop fresh fruit. Serves 8.

RUM-SAUCED PEACHES

Total preparation time: 10 minutes

1 16-ounce can peach halves
3 tablespoons brown sugar
2 teaspoons lemon juice
2 tablespoons rum

1 Drain peach halves, reserving syrup. In a saucepan combine reserved syrup, brown sugar, and lemon juice. Cook and stir over low heat till sugar is dissolved and sauce is heated through.

2 Stir in rum and peach halves; heat through. Place peach halves and syrup in 4 dessert dishes. Makes 4 servings.

FRUIT 'N' GINGER PEARS

An out-of-the-ordinary fruit concoction that's colorful as well as flavorful—

Assembling time: 10 minutes
Cooking time: 20 minutes

6 small pears
1 8¾-ounce can fruit cocktail
⅓ cup orange juice
2 teaspoons snipped candied ginger
2 tablespoons cold water
1 tablespoon sugar
1 tablespoon cornstarch
3 tablespoons dry sherry

1 Core and peel pears. Drain fruit cocktail, reserving syrup. Add enough water to the reserved syrup to measure ⅔ cup liquid. In a large skillet combine reserved syrup mixture, orange juice, and candied ginger. Place whole pears in liquid and bring to boiling. Reduce heat; cover and simmer about 15 minutes or till pears are just tender. With a slotted spoon transfer pears to 6 dessert dishes.

2 Combine the 2 tablespoons cold water, sugar, and cornstarch. Stir into hot syrup mixture in the skillet. Cook and stir till thickened and bubbly; cook and stir 2 minutes more.

3 Remove from heat; stir in sherry and fruit cocktail. Spoon fruit cocktail mixture over pears. Serve warm. Serves 6.

PEACH MILK SHAKE DESSERT

Assembling time: 7 minutes

- 1 pint vanilla ice cream
- 1 10-ounce package frozen peach slices
- ½ cup milk
- 2 tablespoons Amaretto
  Ground nutmeg

1 In a blender container combine ice cream, peaches, milk, and Amaretto. Cover and blend till smooth. Pour into sherbet or parfait glasses. Sprinkle with nutmeg. Serves 6.

GINGER-PAPAYA PARFAITS

If papaya is not available, try fresh peaches or pears—

Assembling time: 20 minutes

- ¼ cup frozen orange juice concentrate
- 1 medium papaya
- 1 20-ounce can pineapple chunks, drained
- ¼ cup coconut
- 1 medium banana
- 1 8-ounce carton plain yogurt
- 1 teaspoon freshly grated gingerroot

1 Let frozen orange juice concentrate stand at room temperature about 10 minutes or till thawed. Meanwhile, peel, seed, and cube papaya; combine with pineapple. Toast coconut, if desired.

2 In a small bowl mash the banana; stir in yogurt, gingerroot, and thawed orange juice concentrate. In 6 parfait glasses alternately layer papaya mixture and yogurt mixture. Top each serving with coconut. Serve or chill till serving time. Makes 6 servings.

BERRIES 'N' CREAM PARFAITS

Assembling time: 12 minutes
Chilling time: 20 minutes

- 1½ cups milk
- 1 cup dairy sour cream
- 1 package 4-serving-size *instant* vanilla pudding mix
- ¼ teaspoon ground nutmeg
- 1 21-ounce can strawberry *or* red raspberry pie filling
- 1 tablespoon lemon juice

1 In a small mixer bowl combine milk and sour cream. Beat with a rotary beater till smooth. Stir in pudding mix and nutmeg; beat till mixture is smooth and slightly thickened. Combine pie filling and lemon juice.

2 In 6 parfait glasses, starting with pudding mixture, alternately layer pudding mixture and pie filling. Chill in freezer for 15 to 20 minutes or till set. Makes 6 servings.

COCONUT-PEACH PARFAITS

Assembling time: 20 minutes

- ½ of a 6-ounce can (⅓ cup) frozen orange juice concentrate
- 1 16-ounce can peach slices, drained and chopped
- 1 medium banana, sliced
- 1 cup whipping cream
- ½ cup coconut
- ¼ cup sugar

1 Let orange juice concentrate stand at room temperature about 10 minutes or till thawed. Meanwhile, combine peaches and banana. Whip cream to soft peaks.

2 Stir coconut and sugar into concentrate; fold in whipped cream. In 8 parfait glasses alternately layer whipped cream mixture and fruit mixture. Serve immediately or chill till serving time. Makes 8 servings.

LEMON TRIFLES

Assembling time: 28 minutes

- 3 cake dessert cups
- ¼ cup cream sherry
- 1 envelope unflavored gelatin
- 2 tablespoons cold water
- ¼ cup boiling water
- 2 eggs
- ½ cup sugar
- ½ cup lemon yogurt
- 2 tablespoons lemon juice
  Dash salt
- ¾ cup ice cubes (5)
- ¼ cup strawberry preserves
  Slivered almonds

1 Stack cake cups one on top of another; cut into small wedges. Arrange cake wedges in 6 parfait glasses or dessert dishes. Drizzle about *2 teaspoons* of the sherry over cake in each dish. Set aside.

2 In a blender container sprinkle gelatin over 2 tablespoons cold water; let stand 1 minute. Add the ¼ cup boiling water; cover and blend till gelatin is dissolved.

3 Add eggs, sugar, yogurt, lemon juice, and salt. Cover and blend on low speed. With blender at high speed, add ice cubes one at a time, blending till ice is melted. Immediately pour yogurt mixture over cake wedges. Chill in freezer for 10 minutes.

4 Meanwhile, in a small saucepan heat strawberry preserves. Drizzle over each serving; garnish with almonds. Serve or chill till serving time. Makes 6 servings.

TROPICAL PINEAPPLE COMPOTE

Assembling time: 8 minutes

¼ cup lime juice
¼ cup honey
½ cup pitted whole dates
1 20-ounce can pineapple chunks, drained
1 11-ounce can mandarin orange sections, drained
Coconut

1 Stir together lime juice and honey; set aside. Slice dates in half lengthwise and then crosswise. Add dates, pineapple chunks, and mandarin orange sections to honey mixture. Stir lightly to coat. Spoon into 6 sherbet dishes; sprinkle coconut over each serving. Makes 6 servings.

BROILED GRAPEFRUIT

Assembling time: 10 minutes
Cooking time: 3 minutes

2 grapefruit, halved
⅓ cup packed brown sugar
¼ cup flaked coconut
2 tablespoons butter *or* margarine
1 tablespoon water

1 Loosen sections from grapefruit halves. Cut white membrane from center of each half. Combine brown sugar, coconut, butter or margarine, and water. Spoon atop grapefruit halves.
2 Place grapefruit halves in a shallow baking pan. Broil 5 inches from heat for 2 or 3 minutes or till sugar mixture is melted. Makes 4 servings.

PEACH MELBA SUNDAES

Assembling time: 10 minutes
Cooking time: 10 minutes

2 tablespoons butter *or* margarine
2 tablespoons sugar
¼ cup packed brown sugar
2 tablespoons orange juice
2 tablespoons lemon juice
3 medium peaches *or* nectarines, peeled, pitted, and sliced, *or* one 16-ounce can peach slices, drained
1 cup fresh *or* frozen loose-pack raspberries, thawed and drained
¼ cup peach brandy
Vanilla ice cream

1 In a heavy 10-inch skillet melt butter or margarine; stir in sugar, brown sugar, orange juice, and lemon juice. Cook and stir over medium heat till sugar is dissolved and mixture is bubbly.
2 Stir in sliced peaches or nectarines. Simmer, uncovered, about 4 minutes or just till fruit is tender, stirring occasionally. Stir in raspberries and brandy; heat through. To serve, scoop vanilla ice cream into dessert dishes. Spoon hot fruit mixture atop. Makes 4 to 6 servings.

THAWING WHIPPED TOPPING

To thaw frozen whipped topping, allow it to stand at room temperature for 20 to 30 minutes. Or, place it in the refrigerator for several hours.

PEANUT BUTTER BANANAS

Assembling time: 5 minutes
Cooking time: 5 minutes

½ of a 6-ounce package (½ cup) butterscotch pieces
⅓ cup chunk-style peanut butter
4 medium bananas
¼ cup chopped peanuts

1 In a small saucepan combine butterscotch pieces and peanut butter; cook and stir over low heat till melted. Halve bananas crosswise, then lengthwise. Place in dessert dishes; spoon peanut butter mixture over. Sprinkle with peanuts. Serves 4.

LEMON CUSTARD SAUCE ON FRUIT

Assembling time: 12 minutes

2 10-ounce packages frozen mixed fruit (in quick-thaw pouch)
2 egg yolks
2 teaspoons finely shredded lemon peel
2 tablespoons lemon juice
¼ cup sugar
2 tablespoons butter *or* margarine, melted
½ of a 4-ounce container frozen whipped dessert topping, thawed

1 Thaw mixed fruit according to package directions; drain well. Meanwhile, in a small mixer bowl combine egg yolks, shredded lemon peel, and lemon juice. Beat at high speed of electric mixer for 3 minutes.
2 Gradually beat in sugar; beat in melted butter. Fold in thawed dessert topping. Spoon fruit into six dessert dishes; top with lemon mixture. Makes 6 servings.

MAPLE-PECAN WAFFLES

Total preparation time: 12 minutes

1 5-ounce package (6) frozen
   waffles
½ cup maple-flavored syrup
1 tablespoon lemon juice
½ cup chopped pecans
   Vanilla ice cream

1 Bake or toast waffles according to package directions. In a small saucepan mix maple-flavored syrup and lemon juice. Bring to boiling. Cook and stir about 3 minutes or till slightly thickened.

2 Stir pecans into syrup mixture. Place a scoop of ice cream atop each waffle; spoon pecan mixture atop. Serves 6.

VANILLA-MOCHA DESSERTS

Pictured on the cover—

Total preparation time: 18 minutes

½ of a 5⅓-ounce can (⅓ cup)
   evaporated milk
¼ cup semisweet chocolate pieces
1 teaspoon instant coffee crystals
1 17½-ounce can vanilla pudding
⅓ cup almond brickle chips

1 In a saucepan combine milk, chocolate, and coffee. Cook and stir over medium heat till chocolate is melted and mixture is bubbly. Place saucepan in a bowl of ice water, stirring mixture till cooled.

2 Stir together pudding and almond brickle chips. Spoon *half* of the pudding mixture into 4 sherbert or parfait glasses; top with *half* of the chocolate mixture. Repeat layers. Sprinkle with a few additional brickle chips. Makes 4 servings.

SOUR CREAM CITRUS PUDDING

Assembling time: 8 minutes

1⅔ cups milk
1 package 4-serving-size *instant*
   lemon pudding mix
¾ cup dairy sour cream
1 11-ounce can mandarin orange
   sections, drained

1 In a medium bowl combine milk and pudding mix. Beat slowly with a rotary beater or at low speed of electric mixer about 2 minutes. Fold in sour cream.

2 Set *4* of the orange sections aside; fold remaining sections into pudding mixture. Serve in dessert dishes. Garnish each serving with a reserved orange section. Makes 4 servings.

ICE CREAM-FILLED CHOCOLATE CUPS

Assembling time: 15 minutes
Chilling time: 10 minutes

½ cup semisweet chocolate pieces
¼ cup chunk-style peanut butter
1¼ cups crisp rice cereal
   Vanilla *or* peppermint ice cream

1 Cook and stir chocolate pieces and peanut butter over low heat till melted. Remove from heat; stir in rice cereal.

2 Press ¼ of the cereal mixture onto bottom and about halfway up sides of 4 buttered 6-ounce custard cups. Place cups in freezer about 10 minutes or till firm.

3 Dip bottoms of custard cups in hot water for 5 to 10 seconds; carefully remove each chocolate shell. Fill each shell with a scoop of ice cream. Serves 4.

CHOCO-PEANUT SUNDAES

Assembling time: 10 minutes

1 pint vanilla ice cream
½ cup chocolate-covered peanuts *or*
   chocolate-covered raisins *or*
   candy-coated milk chocolate
   pieces with peanuts
½ cup semisweet chocolate pieces
3 tablespoons butter *or* margarine

1 Scoop ½ cup of the ice cream into each of 4 dessert dishes; sprinkle each with *2 tablespoons* of the peanuts, raisins, or candy. Place in freezer. Meanwhile, in a small saucepan combine semisweet chocolate pieces and butter. Cook and stir over medium heat till melted.

2 Remove dishes from freezer. Immediately pour chocolate mixture over each scoop of ice cream. Serves 4.

PINEAPPLE-STRAWBERRY YOGURT SLUSH

Assembling time: 8 minutes

2 8-ounce containers strawberry
   frozen yogurt
1 8-ounce can crushed pineapple
   (juice pack)
1 ripe large banana, sliced
¾ cup ice cubes (5)
2 tablespoons sugar
2 tablespoons coconut
   Mint sprigs

1 In a blender container combine frozen yogurt, *undrained* pineapple, banana, ice cubes, sugar, and coconut. Cover and blend till smooth. Pour into 4 dessert glasses. Garnish with mint sprigs. Serves 4.

EASY CHERRY TORTE

Assembling time: 30 minutes

1 frozen loaf pound cake
1 12-ounce jar cherry preserves
2 tablespoons cherry liqueur
1 cup whipping cream
3 tablespoons Amaretto, cherry
 liqueur, *or* brandy
2 tablespoons sugar
 Slivered almonds (optional)

1 Let frozen pound cake stand at room temperature for 10 minutes to thaw slightly. Meanwhile, in a small mixing bowl stir together cherry preserves and the 2 tablespoons cherry liqueur.

2 To assemble torte, slice pound cake horizontally into 3 layers. Spread bottom layer with about ¼ *cup* of the preserves mixture. Place second layer atop and spread with about ¼ *cup* of the preserves mixture. Place third layer atop and spread with the remaining preserves mixture.

3 In a small mixer bowl beat whipping cream, the 3 tablespoons desired liqueur, and the sugar at high speed of electric mixer just till stiff peaks form. *Do not overbeat.* Frost sides of torte generously with *some* of the whipped cream mixture.

4 Garnish top of torte with slivered almonds, if desired. Serve at once or chill up to 1 hour. To serve, slice torte. Pass remaining whipped cream mixture. Makes 6 to 8 servings.

Easy Cherry Torte

PEANUT BUTTER SHORTCAKE

Total preparation time: 30 minutes

2⅓ cups packaged biscuit mix
¼ cup sugar
¼ teaspoon ground nutmeg
½ cup light cream
3 tablespoons cooking oil
¼ cup chunk-style peanut butter
2 tablespoons honey
½ cup dairy sour cream
⅓ cup chunk-style peanut butter
1 5-ounce can vanilla pudding

1 In a bowl stir together biscuit mix, sugar, and nutmeg. Stir together light cream and cooking oil. Add all at once to biscuit mix mixture. Stir just till moistened.

2 Pat *half* of the dough into a greased 8×1½-inch round baking pan. Stir together the ¼ cup peanut butter and the honey; dollop atop the dough in the pan. Top with the remaining dough. Bake in a 450° oven about 15 minutes or till light brown.

3 Meanwhile for sauce, in a mixing bowl beat together sour cream and the ⅓ cup peanut butter. Fold in vanilla pudding. Serve atop warm shortcake. Serves 6.

LIQUEUR-FLAVORED COFFEE

Total preparation time: 15 minutes

4½ cups hot strong coffee
½ cup coffee liqueur, Amaretto,
 crème de cacao, crème de
 almond, chocolate mint liqueur,
 orange liqueur, crème de cassis,
 or chocolate-almond liqueur
 Pressurized dessert topping

1 Stir together hot coffee and liqueur. Pour into coffee cups. Top with pressurized dessert topping. Makes 6 servings.

FRENCH SILK DESSERTS

Enhance the flavor of this rich chocolate dessert by choosing from a variety of liqueur options—

Assembling time: 25 minutes

1 frozen loaf pound cake
¾ cup butter (not margarine)
1 cup sugar
3 envelopes (3 ounces) pre-melted
 unsweetened chocolate product
1½ teaspoons vanilla
3 eggs
¼ cup brandy, crème de cacao, *or*
 coffee liqueur
 Unsweetened whipped cream
 (optional)

1 Let the frozen pound cake stand at room temperature to thaw while preparing the topping. For topping, in a small mixer bowl beat the butter at medium speed of electric mixer for 30 seconds. Add the sugar and beat about 4 minutes more or till mixture is fluffy.

2 Beat in the pre-melted chocolate and vanilla. Add the eggs, one at a time, beating at medium speed for 1 minute after each addition; scrape the sides of the mixer bowl frequently.

3 Slice the pound cake loaf crosswise into 8 slices. Place cake slices on serving plates and drizzle with brandy, crème de cacao, or coffee liqueur. Spoon topping over cake slices. Garnish with unsweetened whipped cream, if desired. Serves 8.

FRENCH-TOASTED POUND CAKE

Pound cake slices are dipped in an egg mixture, fried to a golden brown, then topped with juicy strawberries. A new twist for strawberry shortcake—

Assembling time: 15 minutes
Cooking time: 5 minutes

1 frozen loaf pound cake
1 10-ounce package frozen halved strawberries (in quick-thaw pouch)
1 egg
½ cup milk
⅛ teaspoon ground nutmeg *or* cinnamon
2 tablespoons butter *or* margarine
   Pressurized dessert topping (optional)

1 Let frozen pound cake stand at room temperature about 10 minutes to thaw slightly. Meanwhile, thaw frozen strawberries according to package directions. Beat together the egg, milk, and nutmeg or cinnamon. Set aside the egg mixture and the strawberries.

2 Slice the pound cake into ½-inch-thick slices. Dip each slice in the egg mixture, coating both sides. In a large skillet fry pound cake slices in hot butter or margarine over medium heat for 4 or 5 minutes or till golden brown, turning once.

3 To serve, spoon thawed strawberries over fried cake slices. Top with dessert topping, if desired. Makes 6 servings.

ORANGE-CHOCOLATE PIE

Assembling time: 15 minutes
Chilling time: 15 minutes

1 4-ounce container frozen whipped dessert topping
1 package 4-serving-size *instant* chocolate fudge pudding mix
1½ cups milk
1 4-ounce container whipped cream cheese
1 graham cracker pie shell
1 11-ounce can mandarin orange sections, drained

1 Let dessert topping stand at room temperature about 5 minutes or till partially thawed. Meanwhile, in mixer bowl combine pudding mix, milk, and cream cheese; beat about 2 minutes or till combined.

2 Spoon *half* of the dessert topping into the pie shell; carefully spoon pudding mixture atop. Arrange orange sections atop. Dollop with remaining dessert topping. Chill in freezer for 15 minutes. Serves 8.

BLACK-BOTTOM TARTS

Total preparation time: 10 minutes

1 5-ounce can chocolate fudge pudding
1 tablespoon crème de cacao
6 graham cracker tart shells
2 5-ounce cans vanilla pudding
⅓ cup dairy sour cream
2 tablespoons fudge topping

1 Stir together chocolate fudge pudding and liqueur. Spoon into the tart shells. Stir together vanilla pudding and sour cream. Spoon atop mixture in each shell.

2 Drizzle about *1 teaspoon* of the fudge topping atop each tart. Serve or chill up to 1 hour before serving. Makes 6 servings.

CREAMY COFFEE LIQUEUR PIE

Just combine the ingredients for the creamy pie filling, then pour it into the chocolate-flavored crumb crust. This delectable fast dessert is perfect for entertaining—

Assembling time: 10 minutes
Chilling time: 20 minutes

1½ cups cold milk
1 package 4-serving-size *instant* vanilla pudding mix
1 1½-ounce envelope dessert topping mix
¼ cup coffee liqueur
1 chocolate-flavored crumb pie shell
1 1¼-ounce bar milk chocolate

1 In a small mixer bowl combine cold milk, *instant* vanilla pudding mix, dessert topping mix, and coffee liqueur. Beat at low speed of electric mixer till combined. Beat at high speed of electric mixer about 5 minutes or till soft peaks form.

2 Turn pudding mixture into the chocolate-flavored crumb pie shell. Chill in freezer for 15 to 20 minutes or till filling is set. Meanwhile, chill milk chocolate bar in freezer; crush and sprinkle chocolate bits atop pie before serving. (*Or,* melt milk chocolate bar in a small saucepan with 1½ teaspoons shortening over low heat; drizzle chocolate over pie before serving.) Makes 8 servings.

PEAR TURNOVERS

Assembling time: 15 minutes
Cooking time: 15 minutes

1 package (8) refrigerated
   crescent rolls
2 tablespoons sugar
2 tablespoons brown sugar
¼ teaspoon ground nutmeg *or*
   cinnamon
1 8½-ounce can pear halves,
   drained and chopped

1 Unroll crescent rolls and separate into 4 rectangles. Pinch together diagonal seam in *each* rectangle. Combine sugar, brown sugar, and nutmeg or cinnamon.

2 Place ¼ of the chopped pears in the center of each rectangle. Sprinkle *each* with *1½ to 2 teaspoons* of the sugar mixture. Moisten edges of *each* rectangle; fold over dough to form a triangle and seal.

3 Place on ungreased baking sheet. Top with remaining sugar mixture. Bake in 400° oven 15 minutes. Cool. Serves 4.

CRANBERRY-NUT COBBLER

Assembling time: 12 minutes
Cooking time: 17 minutes

1 12-ounce package (3 cups)
   cranberries
¾ cup packed brown sugar
1 package (8) refrigerated
   cinnamon rolls
⅓ cup chopped nuts

1 In a medium saucepan combine cranberries, brown sugar, and 1 cup *water*. Bring to boiling. Cook and stir over medium heat about 5 minutes or till cranberries pop.

2 Turn into an 8×1½-inch round baking dish. Top with rolls; sprinkle with nuts. Bake in a 400° oven for 13 to 17 minutes. Drizzle with icing in package. Serves 8.

INDIVIDUAL APPLE CRISPS

Assembling time: 10 minutes
Cooking time: 20 minutes

1 21-ounce can apple pie filling
1 tablespoon lemon juice
¼ cup quick-cooking rolled oats
2 tablespoons brown sugar
2 tablespoons all-purpose flour
¼ teaspoon ground cinnamon
   Dash salt
2 tablespoons butter *or* margarine

1 Stir together pie filling and lemon juice. Divide among four 6-ounce custard cups. Combine oats, brown sugar, flour, cinnamon, and salt. Cut in butter or margarine till mixture is crumbly. Sprinkle atop apple mixture. Bake in a 350° oven for 20 minutes or till heated through. Makes 4 servings.

GINGER-CRUNCH PEACHES

Assembling time: 10 minutes
Cooking time: 20 minutes

8 gingersnaps, crushed (½ cup)
2 tablespoons chopped pecans
2 tablespoons butter *or* margarine,
   melted
1 tablespoon brown sugar
1 29-ounce can peach halves *or*
   slices, drained
¼ cup orange juice
   Vanilla ice cream (optional)

1 In a small bowl combine crushed gingersnaps, pecans, melted butter, and brown sugar; mix well. Place peach halves or slices, cut side up, in an 8×8×2-inch baking pan. Drizzle with orange juice. Sprinkle cookie mixture over peaches.

2 Bake in a 350° oven about 20 minutes or till peaches are heated through. Top with ice cream, if desired. Serves 6 to 8.

SPICY FRUIT AND DUMPLINGS

Assembling time: 10 minutes
Cooking time: 20 minutes

⅓ cup butter *or* margarine
1 tablespoon cornstarch
1 16-ounce can peach slices
1 17-ounce can chunky mixed fruit
2 tablespoons brown sugar
⅛ teaspoon ground cloves
1 cup packaged biscuit mix
1 tablespoon brown sugar
¼ teaspoon ground cinnamon
⅓ cup milk

1 In a large skillet melt butter; stir in cornstarch. Add *undrained* peaches, *undrained* mixed fruit, the 2 tablespoons brown sugar, and cloves. Cook and stir over medium heat till thickened and bubbly. Cook and stir 2 minutes more. Keep warm.

2 For dumplings, combine biscuit mix, the 1 tablespoon brown sugar, and ground cinnamon; add milk. Stir till all is moistened.

3 Drop biscuit mixture from a tablespoon onto boiling fruit mixture in skillet to make 6 dumplings. Cook, uncovered, for 10 minutes. Cover and cook 8 to 10 minutes more or till dumplings spring back when lightly touched. To serve, spoon warm fruit mixture over dumplings. Makes 6 servings.

WALNUT-WHEAT GERM BARS

Delicious warm or cool, these chewy nut-filled bars are ideal for a quick dessert, snack, or lunch-box treat—

Total preparation time: 30 minutes

1 cup all-purpose flour
½ cup packed brown sugar
⅓ cup toasted wheat germ
½ cup butter *or* margarine
2 eggs
1 cup packed brown sugar
¼ cup all-purpose flour
½ teaspoon baking powder
¼ teaspoon salt
¾ cup chopped walnuts
½ cup coconut

1 Stir together the 1 cup flour, the ½ cup brown sugar, and the wheat germ. Cut in butter or margarine till mixture resembles coarse crumbs. Press into the bottom of an ungreased 13×9×2-inch baking pan. Bake in a 350° oven for 8 minutes.

2 Meanwhile, beat together eggs and the 1 cup brown sugar. Stir together the ¼ cup flour, baking powder, and salt; stir into egg mixture. Stir in walnuts and coconut. Carefully spoon over warm crust. Bake in a 350° oven about 15 minutes. Cut into bars. Serve warm or cool. Makes 36 bars.

ORANGE-TOPPED SUGAR ROUNDS

Total preparation time: 30 minutes

1 16-ounce package frozen sliced sugar cookies
1 4-ounce container whipped cream cheese
1 tablespoon honey
1 teaspoon lemon juice
1 11-ounce can mandarin orange sections, drained

1 Arrange pieces of cookie dough on two large cookie sheets. Bake cookies according to package directions. Cool on wire racks for at least 5 minutes.

2 Meanwhile, in a bowl stir together the whipped cream cheese, honey, and lemon juice; spread some atop each cookie. Top each cookie with a drained mandarin orange section. Makes 36 cookies.

QUICK CHOCOLATE BRANDY COOKIES

Assembling time: 15 minutes
Cooking time: 10 minutes

¾ cup all-purpose flour
1 tablespoon unsweetened cocoa powder
⅓ cup butter *or* margarine
¼ cup sugar
2 tablespoons brandy
1 tablespoon milk
¼ cup chopped pecans

1 Stir together flour and cocoa powder. In a mixer bowl beat butter or margarine for 30 seconds. Add sugar and beat till fluffy. Add brandy and milk; beat well. Add dry ingredients to mixture and beat till combined. Stir in pecans.

2 Drop from a teaspoon onto ungreased cookie sheet. Bake in a 375° oven for 10 minutes. Makes about 16 cookies.

CHOCOLATE CHIP SANDWICHES

Total preparation time: 30 minutes

1 16-ounce package frozen sliced chocolate chip cookies
1½ 1¼-ounce bars milk chocolate, broken into 18 pieces
½ of a 7-ounce jar marshmallow creme

1 Bake cookies according to package directions. Top the flat sides of half of the warm cookies with some of the chocolate and marshmallow creme. Top with remaining cookies, flat side down. Makes 18.

SPICE AND ALMOND BARS

Assembling time: 12 minutes
Cooking time: 15 minutes

2 cups all-purpose flour
1 cup butter *or* margarine
1 cup packed brown sugar
1 egg yolk
1 teaspoon vanilla
1 slightly beaten egg white
¼ cup sugar
½ teaspoon ground cinnamon
½ cup sliced almonds

1 Stir together flour and ⅛ teaspoon *salt*. In mixer bowl beat butter on medium speed of electric mixer for ½ minute. Add brown sugar and beat till fluffy. Add egg yolk and vanilla; beat well. Add dry ingredients; beat till combined.

2 Pat dough evenly in an ungreased 15×10×1-inch shallow baking pan. Brush top of dough with the egg white. Combine sugar and cinnamon; sprinkle over dough. Sprinkle with sliced almonds.

3 Bake in a 350° oven about 15 minutes or till light brown. Cut into bars while warm. Makes about 48 bars.

EASY CHOCOLATE SAUCE

Total preparation time: 7 minutes

1 6-ounce package (1 cup)
  semisweet chocolate pieces
2/3 cup light corn syrup
1 5 1/3-ounce can (2/3 cup) evaporated
  milk
  Vanilla ice cream
  Milk (optional)

1 In a small saucepan combine chocolate pieces and corn syrup. Cook and stir over low heat till chocolate pieces are melted. Remove from heat. Gradually stir in evaporated milk. Serve warm or chilled over vanilla ice cream. (If sauce becomes too thick when chilled, stir in a little milk.) Store any remaining sauce, covered, in refrigerator. Makes 1 3/4 cups.

SHERRIED RASPBERRY SAUCE

Assembling time: 15 minutes
Cooking time: 5 minutes

1 10-ounce package frozen red
  raspberries (in quick-thaw
  pouch)
2 tablespoons sugar
1 tablespoon cornstarch
1/3 cup cream sherry
  Ice cream *or* cake

1 Thaw raspberries according to package directions; drain, reserving 1/2 cup of the syrup. In a small saucepan combine sugar and cornstarch; stir in reserved raspberry syrup and the sherry.

2 Cook and stir till thickened and bubbly; cook and stir 2 minutes more. Stir in drained raspberries. Serve warm over ice cream or cake. Makes 1 1/3 cups.

TOASTED FRUIT TOPPER

This nutty topping has the flavor and crunch of macaroons—

Assembling time: 10 minutes
Cooking time: 12 minutes

1/4 cup all-purpose flour
1/4 cup coconut
1/4 packed brown sugar
1/4 cup chopped walnuts
1/8 teaspoon ground cinnamon
1/4 cup butter *or* margarine
  Canned fruit *or* ice cream

1 Stir together flour, coconut, brown sugar, walnuts, and cinnamon. Cut in butter or margarine till crumbly. Spread evenly in an 8×8×2-inch baking pan.

2 Bake in a 350° oven for 10 to 12 minutes or till brown. Cool slightly; crumble. Serve over fruit or ice cream. Makes 2 cups.

BUTTER-RUM SUNDAE SAUCE

Be sure to refrigerate any leftover sauce. To reheat, in a small saucepan cook and stir about 7 minutes or till heated through—

Assembling time: 5 minutes
Cooking time: 8 minutes

1/4 cup butter *or* margarine
2 tablespoons light corn syrup
1 package creamy white frosting
  mix (for 2-layer cake)
1/3 cup evaporated milk
1/4 cup rum
  Vanilla ice cream
  Chopped nuts

1 In a saucepan heat butter till brown; remove from heat. Stir in corn syrup and about *half* of the frosting mix; add remaining mix and gradually stir in evaporated milk.

2 Heat through, stirring constantly. Remove from heat; stir in rum. Serve warm over vanilla ice cream. Sprinkle with chopped nuts. Makes 2 cups.

CRUMBLY PEANUT BUTTER TOPPING

Total preparation time: 5 minutes

1/3 cup all-purpose flour
1/3 cup packed brown sugar
1/2 cup chunk-style peanut butter
  Ice cream, cake, *or* pudding

1 In a bowl stir together flour and brown sugar. Cut in peanut butter till mixture resembles coarse crumbs. Sprinkle atop ice cream, cake, or pudding. Makes 1 1/3 cups.

APPETIZERS, SNACKS, AND BEVERAGES

APPETIZER FRITTATA

Assembling time: 14 minutes
Cooking time: 12 minutes

1 small onion, chopped (¼ cup)
¼ cup chopped celery
2 tablespoons butter *or* margarine
8 beaten eggs
½ cup dairy sour cream
½ cup grated Parmesan cheese
1 3½-ounce package sliced pepperoni

1 In 10-inch oven-going skillet cook onion and celery in butter till tender. Mix eggs, sour cream, and cheese. Chop *half* the pepperoni; stir into egg mixture.

2 Pour egg mixture into skillet. Cook over medium heat for 8 to 10 minutes or till almost set, lifting edges occasionally to allow uncooked portion to flow underneath. Arrange remaining pepperoni around edge. Place under broiler 5 inches from heat; broil 1 to 2 minutes. Sprinkle with sliced green onion, if desired. Serves 12.

BACON AND TOMATO DIP

Total preparation time: 15 minutes

6 slices bacon
1 8-ounce package cream cheese, cut up
2 teaspoons prepared mustard
½ teaspoon celery salt
1 medium tomato, seeded and chopped
¼ cup chopped green pepper
Vegetable dippers

1 Cook bacon till crisp; drain and crumble. In a bowl combine cream cheese, mustard, and celery salt. Stir in bacon, tomato, and green pepper. Cover and chill. Serve with vegetables. Makes 2 cups.

ARTICHOKE APPETIZERS

Assembling time: 10 minutes
Cooking time: 18 minutes

1 medium onion, chopped (½ cup)
4 well-beaten eggs
¼ cup fine dry bread crumbs
⅛ teaspoon dried oregano, crushed
2 or 3 drops bottled hot pepper sauce
1 8-ounce package (2 cups) shredded cheddar cheese
2 6-ounce jars pickled artichoke hearts, drained and chopped

1 Cook onion in a small amount of boiling water about 5 minutes or till tender; drain. Combine eggs, bread crumbs, oregano, hot pepper sauce, ½ teaspoon *salt*, and ⅛ teaspoon *pepper*. Stir in onion, cheese, and artichokes. Spread in a greased 11×7×1½-inch baking pan.

2 Bake in a 350° oven 17 to 18 minutes. Cut into bars. Serve warm. Makes 28.

BAHA SHRIMP DIP

Assembling time: 10 minutes
Chilling time: 18 minutes

1 medium avocado, seeded and peeled
½ cup cream-style cottage cheese
⅓ cup green goddess salad dressing
⅛ teaspoon garlic powder
Dash bottled hot pepper sauce
2 4½-ounce cans tiny shrimp, rinsed and drained
Assorted crackers

1 Chop avocado. In a blender container place avocado, cottage cheese, salad dressing, garlic powder, and hot pepper sauce. Cover; blend till smooth. Stir in shrimp; cover and chill in freezer for 15 minutes. Serve with crackers. Makes 2 cups.

CHEESE OLIVE WRAP-UPS

Assembling time: 15 minutes
Cooking time: 15 minutes

1 stick piecrust mix
½ cup shredded cheddar cheese (2 ounces)
½ teaspoon chili powder
24 medium pitted ripe olives *or* pimiento-stuffed olives

1 In a mixing bowl combine the piecrust mix, shredded cheddar cheese, and chili powder. Prepare the piecrust dough according to package directions.

2 Shape about ½ *teaspoon* of the piecrust dough around each olive. Place on an ungreased baking sheet. Bake in a 375° oven for 12 to 15 minutes or till golden brown. Serve warm or cool. Makes 24.

CURRY CANAPÉS

Assembling time: 12 minutes
Cooking time: 3 minutes

1 5¼-ounce can deviled ham
¼ cup chutney, chopped
2 tablespoons chopped pecans
¼ teaspoon curry powder
30 melba toast rounds *or* crackers

1 In a mixing bowl stir together deviled ham, chutney, pecans, and curry powder. Spread about 1 *teaspoon* on each melba toast round or cracker. Place, spread side up, on a baking sheet. Broil 4 inches from heat for 2 to 3 minutes or till ham mixture is hot and slightly bubbly. Makes 30.

**Bacon and Tomato Dip
Appetizer Frittata**

CHEESE-FILLED ARTICHOKES

Assembling time: 10 minutes
Cooking time: 13 minutes

1 7 ¾-ounce can artichoke bottoms
1 4½-ounce package camembert cheese
Snipped chives (optional)

1 Drain artichokes. Quarter and place in a single layer in a shallow baking pan. Bake, covered, in a 325° oven for 8 to 10 minutes. Meanwhile, cut camembert into wedges the same size as artichoke wedges.

2 Uncover the artichokes; place a wedge of camembert cheese onto each artichoke wedge. Sprinkle with chives, if desired. Bake, uncovered, 2 to 3 minutes more or till cheese is melted. Makes 24.

BLUE CHEESE-STUFFED MUSHROOMS

Assembling time: 14 minutes
Cooking time: 12 minutes

24 to 30 large fresh mushrooms
2 3-ounce packages cream cheese, cut up
½ of a .9-ounce envelope blue cheese salad dressing mix
¼ cup finely chopped walnuts
Paprika (optional)

1 Remove stems from mushrooms. Chop enough stems to make ½ cup (use remaining another time). In mixer bowl beat together cheese and salad dressing mix; stir in nuts and chopped stems.

2 Spoon cream cheese mixture into mushroom caps; place in a shallow baking pan. Sprinkle with paprika, if desired. Bake caps, uncovered, in a 375° oven for 10 to 12 minutes. Makes 24 to 30.

CORN-SAUSAGE SQUARES

Assembling time: 10 minutes
Cooking time: 20 minutes

1 8-ounce package corn muffin mix
1 4-ounce package (1 cup) shredded cheddar cheese
1 5-ounce can Vienna sausages, drained and thinly sliced

1 Prepare muffin mix according to package directions, *except,* add ½ cup of the cheese to the batter. Spread evenly in a greased 11×7×1½-inch baking pan.

2 Arrange sausage slices evenly atop batter. Sprinkle remaining cheese atop. Bake in a 375° oven for 15 to 20 minutes. Cut into squares. Serve warm. Makes 24.

SESAME SHRIMP APPETIZER

Assembling time: 15 minutes
Cooking time: 8 minutes

1 4½-ounce can shrimp, rinsed, drained, and chopped
⅓ cup plain yogurt
1 green onion, thinly sliced
8 thin slices bread
3 tablespoons butter *or* margarine, melted
4 teaspoons sesame seed

1 In a bowl stir shrimp, yogurt, and onion till mixture is almost a paste. Spread *4 slices* bread with shrimp mixture; top with remaining bread. Cut off crusts.

2 Brush both sides of sandwiches with butter. Sprinkle each side with sesame seed. Place on baking sheet. Quarter each sandwich. Bake in 425° oven about 8 minutes or till light brown. Makes 16.

BREADED CHICKEN LIVERS

Assembling time: 15 minutes
Cooking time: 12 minutes

¾ cup finely crushed round sesame bread wafers
2 tablespoons butter *or* margarine, melted
¼ teaspoon paprika
8 ounces chicken livers, cut in half
½ cup sour cream dip with French onion
1 tablespoon Dijon-style mustard
Milk

1 Mix together crushed wafers, melted butter, and paprika. Roll chicken livers in crumb mixture, patting to coat well. Place in ungreased 15×10×1-inch baking pan.

2 Bake in a 400° oven for 10 to 12 minutes or till livers are slightly pink in center. Meanwhile, in a bowl stir together sour cream dip and mustard. Stir in enough milk (about 2 teaspoons) to make of dipping consistency. Serve with hot livers. Makes 30.

TUNA-CHEESE SPREAD

Assembling time: 10 minutes

1 8-ounce package cream cheese, cut up
2 tablespoons chili sauce
1 tablespoon dried parsley flakes
1 teaspoon minced dried onion
Dash bottled hot pepper sauce
1 6½-ounce can tuna, drained and flaked
Crackers

1 In bowl beat together cream cheese, chili sauce, parsley, onion, and hot pepper sauce till fluffy. Fold in tuna. Serve immediately or cover and chill till serving time. Serve with crackers. Makes 1¾ cups.

CHINESE VEGETABLE SOUP

Total preparation time: 10 minutes

2 13¾-ounce cans (about 3½ cups) chicken broth
1 16-ounce can fancy mixed Chinese vegetables, rinsed and drained
1 4½-ounce can shrimp, rinsed and drained
2 green onions, thinly sliced (2 tablespoons)
1 teaspoon molasses

1 In a large saucepan combine chicken broth, Chinese vegetables, shrimp, green onion, and molasses. Bring to boiling. Ladle into bowls. Makes 4 to 6 servings.

RUMAKI SPREAD

Assembling time: 8 minutes

4 ounces liverwurst
1 3-ounce package cream cheese, cut up
1 teaspoon prepared mustard
¼ cup finely chopped water chestnuts
2 tablespoons toasted wheat germ
Crackers

1 In a small mixer bowl beat together liverwurst, cream cheese, and mustard till smooth. Stir in water chestnuts. Spoon liverwurst mixture into a serving bowl; sprinkle with wheat germ. Serve immediately or cover and chill till serving time. Serve with crackers. Makes about 1 cup.

CHICKEN LIVERS IN WINE

Total preparation time: 13 minutes

2 tablespoons butter *or* margarine
1 pound chicken livers, cut into bite-size pieces
2 tablespoons snipped parsley
1 tablespoon lemon juice
¼ cup dry sherry
1 teaspoon cornstarch
Melba toast rounds (optional)

1 In a 10-inch skillet or chafing dish melt butter or margarine. Stir in chicken livers. Cook and stir over medium-high heat for 3 to 4 minutes. Stir parsley, lemon juice, ¼ teaspoon *salt*, and ⅛ teaspoon *pepper* into chicken livers. Combine the sherry and cornstarch; stir into the chicken liver mixture.

2 Cook and stir till thickened and bubbly. Cook and stir 2 minutes more. Serve livers on melba toast rounds or in the chafing dish with wooden picks. Serves 8 to 10.

RUSSIAN SANDWICHES

Total preparation time: 30 minutes

1 egg
32 slices party pumpernickel bread
Butter *or* margarine
1 16-ounce can mayonnaise-style potato salad
1 6-ounce can sliced pickled beets, well drained

1 Place egg in small saucepan; cover with cold water. Bring to boiling. Reduce heat to just below simmering. Cover; cook 15 minutes. Run cold water over egg. Remove shell; sieve or finely chop egg.

2 Meanwhile, spread bread with butter or margarine; top each slice with *1 tablespoon* of potato salad. Place a slice of beet atop each. Garnish with egg. Makes 32.

BEEF 'N' CHEESE SANDWICHES

Assembling time: 14 minutes
Cooking time: 16 minutes

1 package (10) refrigerated biscuits
1 4½-ounce can corned beef spread
¼ cup shredded Swiss *or* cheddar cheese (1 ounce)
2 teaspoons prepared mustard

1 Roll or pat each biscuit into a 6×2-inch rectangle. Stir together corned beef spread, cheese, and mustard. Spread about *1 tablespoon* of the beef mixture on each piece of dough.

2 Bring long side of dough up around filling, pinching edges to seal. Twist each roll of dough and coil around in greased muffin pans. Bake in a 375° oven for 14 to 16 minutes or till golden brown. Makes 10.

ORIENTAL EGG SANDWICHES

Total preparation time: 15 minutes

4 beaten eggs
⅓ cup chopped water chestnuts
¼ cup chopped green pepper
2 tablespoons butter *or* margarine
Bottled sweet-sour sauce
3 small pita bread rounds, halved

1 Stir together eggs, water chestnuts, green pepper, and ¼ teaspoon *salt*. In a skillet melt the butter or margarine. Pour in egg mixture. Cook, without stirring, over medium heat till mixture starts to set. Lift and fold cooked eggs so uncooked portion flows underneath.

2 Continue cooking till eggs are set but still moist. Meanwhile, heat sweet-sour sauce. Spoon egg mixture into pita halves; top with sweet-sour sauce. Serves 6.

HAM 'N' CHEESE SNACK SQUARES

Assembling time: 13 minutes
Cooking time: 17 minutes

1½ **cups finely chopped fully cooked ham (8 ounces)**
 1 **8-ounce carton plain yogurt**
 ¼ **cup shredded Swiss cheese (1 ounce)**
 ¼ **cup finely crushed saltine crackers (7 crackers)**
 2 **tablespoons butter *or* margarine, melted**
 1 **to 2 teaspoons caraway seed**
 6 **eggs**

1 In a medium mixing bowl combine ham, yogurt, Swiss cheese, crushed crackers, melted butter or margarine, and caraway seed. In a small mixer bowl beat eggs on medium speed of electric mixer about 6 minutes or till thick and lemon-colored.

2 Fold beaten eggs into yogurt mixture till well combined. Pour mixture evenly into a greased 8×8×2-inch baking pan. Bake in a 375° oven for 15 to 17 minutes or till lightly browned. Cut into squares and serve hot. Makes 12 to 16.

BACON-CHEESY CELERY STICKS

Assembling time: 15 minutes

 1 **4-ounce container whipped cream cheese with onions**
 1 **tablespoon Dijon-style mustard**
 2 **tablespoons cooked bacon pieces**
 4 **or 5 stalks celery**

1 In a mixing bowl stir together cream cheese and mustard; stir in bacon pieces. Fill stalks of celery with cheese mixture; cut filled celery diagonally into 2- to 3-inch pieces. Makes about 24.

EASY CHILI-CHEESE DIP

Total preparation time: 15 minutes

 1 **15-ounce can chili with beans**
 1 **8-ounce package (2 cups) shredded cheddar cheese**
 1 **to 2 teaspoons chili powder**
 ⅛ **teaspoon garlic powder**
   Few dashes bottled hot pepper sauce
   Corn chips, tortilla chips, *or* vegetable dippers

1 Place chili with beans in a blender container; cover and blend till smooth. In a chafing dish or fondue pot combine chili, cheddar cheese, chili powder, garlic powder, and bottled hot pepper sauce.

2 Heat chili mixture over medium-low heat till cheese melts, stirring frequently. Keep warm over low heat. Serve with chips or vegetable dippers. Makes 2 cups.

ZIPPY COCKTAIL NUTS

Total preparation time: 13 minutes

 2 **tablespoons butter *or* margarine**
 1 **teaspoon curry powder and ¼ teaspoon bottled hot pepper sauce *or* ½ teaspoon five-spice powder *or* ½ teaspoon ground allspice**
 ½ **teaspoon seasoned salt**
 2 **cups untoasted shelled nuts (sunflower, pine, cashews, *or* peanuts)**

1 In a large skillet melt the butter or margarine over medium heat. Stir in the desired seasoning and the seasoned salt. Stir in desired nuts, stirring to coat.

2 Cook nut mixture, stirring frequently, about 10 minutes or till nuts are toasted. Turn out onto paper toweling. Makes 2 cups.

FAR EAST NIBBLE MIX

Assembling time: 8 minutes
Cooking time: 20 minutes

 ½ **cup butter *or* margarine**
 1 **tablespoon soy sauce**
 1 **teaspoon garlic salt**
 4 **cups bite-size shredded bran squares**
 1 **3-ounce can chow mein noodles**
 1 **cup peanuts**
 ½ **cup shredded coconut**

1 In a 13×9×2-inch baking pan melt butter or margarine. Stir in soy sauce and garlic salt. Add bran squares, chow mein noodles, peanuts, and coconut. Stir to mix thoroughly. Bake in a 325° oven about 20 minutes, stirring once or twice. Makes about 8 cups.

CHEESE POPCORN

Assembling time: 10 minutes

 ½ **cup unpopped popcorn**
 3 **tablespoons cooking oil**
 ¼ **cup butter *or* margarine, melted**
 1 **1½-ounce envelope cheese sauce mix**

1 Pop corn in hot oil according to package directions. Place popped corn in a large mixing bowl. Pour melted butter or margarine over warm popcorn; toss to coat. Add dry cheese sauce mix; toss again. Makes about 3 quarts.

PINEAPPLE-BERRY FROST

Assembling time: 22 minutes

1 10-ounce package frozen
  strawberries
1 6-ounce can frozen pineapple juice
  concentrate
1 juice can (¾ cup) light rum *or*
  bourbon
2 cups ice cubes
2 cups carbonated water

1 Allow berries to stand at room temperature 15 minutes. Use a sharp knife to
cut block of strawberries into 6 or 8 pieces.

2 In a blender container combine berries,
concentrate, and rum or bourbon. Cover; blend till smooth. Add ice cubes, one at a
time through hole in lid of blender or with lid
ajar; blend till slushy.

3 Pour into a pitcher; slowly pour the carbonated water down the side of the
pitcher, stirring gently. Pour into glasses.
Makes 8 servings.

CHAMPAGNE SIPPER

Assembling time: 10 minutes

1 750-ml bottle dry white wine,
  chilled
½ cup orange liqueur
¼ cup grenadine syrup
2 750-ml bottles dry pink
  champagne, chilled
1 28-ounce bottle carbonated water,
  chilled
  Orange slices (optional)

1 In a punch bowl combine wine, orange
liqueur, and grenadine. Carefully pour
champagne and carbonated water down the
side of the bowl, stirring gently with an up-
and-down motion. Garnish with orange
slices, if desired. Makes 25 servings.

TOMATO-CUCUMBER SOUP

Assembling time: 10 minutes

1 10¾-ounce can condensed tomato
  soup
1 soup can (1¼ cups) cold water
1 medium cucumber, peeled and
  cut up
¼ teaspoon Worcestershire sauce
  Dash onion powder
  Dash pepper
  Plain yogurt

1 In a blender container combine the tomato soup, water, cucumber, Worcestershire sauce, onion powder, and pepper.
Cover and blend till smooth. Serve cold or
heat through. Dollop with yogurt. Serves 4.

ORANGE-YOGURT-COCONUT DIP

Assembling time: 15 minutes

1 8-ounce carton orange yogurt
1 4-ounce container whipped cream
  cheese
¼ cup flaked coconut, toasted
2 tablespoons brown sugar
  Milk
  Orange slices (optional)
  Fresh fruit dippers

1 In a mixing bowl combine orange yogurt, whipped cream cheese, toasted
coconut, and brown sugar. If necessary,
add a little milk to make mixture of dipping
consistency. Serve immediately or cover
and chill till serving time. Trim with orange
slices, if desired. Serve with fresh fruit dippers. Makes 1½ cups.

FRUIT NOG PICK-ME-UP

Assembling time: 10 minutes

1 8-ounce carton flavored yogurt
  (any flavor)
1 cup milk
1 cup fresh *or* frozen unsweetened
  blueberries, raspberries,
  strawberries, orange sections,
  or sliced peaches
1 egg
¼ teaspoon vanilla *or* almond extract
2 teaspoons sugar (optional)
2 *or* 3 ice cubes

1 In a blender container combine yogurt,
milk, desired fruit, egg, and vanilla or
almond extract. Add sugar, if desired. Cover
and blend till mixture is frothy. Add ice
cubes, one at a time, through hole in lid of
blender or with lid ajar, blending till smooth
after each addition. Pour into glasses. Serve
at once. Makes 4 servings.

CRAN-ORANGE SIPPER

Pictured on page 137—

Assembling time: 5 minutes

4 cups cranberry-apple drink
1 cup orange juice
¼ cup lemon juice
1 28-ounce bottle carbonated water
  Ice cubes
  Orange slices (optional)
  Lemon slices (optional)

1 In a large pitcher combine cranberry-
apple drink, orange juice, and lemon
juice. Slowly pour the carbonated water
down the side of the pitcher; stir gently.
Serve over ice cubes in tall glasses. Garnish
with orange slices and lemon slices, if desired. Makes 6 servings.

CHERRY FIZZ

Assembling time: 5 minutes

⅓ **cup cherry preserves**
2 **teaspoons water**
1 **pint (2 cups) cherry-nut *or* vanilla ice cream**
1 **10-ounce bottle (1¼ cups) lemon-lime carbonated beverage**

1 Combine cherry preserves and water. Pour cherry mixture into 2 tall glasses. Add scoops of cherry-nut and/or vanilla ice cream. Slowly pour carbonated beverage down sides of glasses. Makes 2 servings.

TROPICAL SODA

Assembling time: 6 minutes

Orange sherbet
1 **cup unsweetened pineapple juice**
⅓ **cup orange juice**
Few drops aromatic bitters (optional)
1 **10-ounce bottle (1¼ cups) lemon-lime carbonated beverage**
Strawberries (optional)

1 Place a small scoop sherbet in each of 2 glasses. Combine pineapple juice, orange juice, and aromatic bitters, if desired. Pour ¼ *cup* of the juice mixture into each glass; stir to muddle sherbet.
2 Add remaining juice mixture. Add another scoop of sherbet to each glass. Slowly pour carbonated beverage down sides of glasses. Garnish with strawberries, if desired. Makes 2 servings.

Cherry Fizz
Tropical Soda
Frothy Grasshopper

FROTHY GRASSHOPPER

Assembling time: 5 minutes

2 tablespoons green crème de menthe
2 tablespoons white crème de cacao
1 cup vanilla ice cream
1 10-ounce bottle (1¼ cups) carbonated water
2 sugar cubes (optional)
  Few drops lemon extract (optional)

1 In each of 2 tall glasses combine *1 tablespoon* crème de menthe, *1 tablespoon* crème de cacao, and a small amount of ice cream. Add *¼ cup* carbonated water to each glass; stir to muddle ice cream.

2 Add another scoop of ice cream. Slowly pour remaining carbonated water down sides of glasses. If desired, soak sugar cubes in lemon extract. Place atop ice cream in each glass. Set sugar cubes aflame. Makes 2 servings.

SPICED HOT CHOCOLATE MALT

Total preparation time: 8 minutes

4 cups chocolate milk
¼ cup instant malted milk powder
¾ teaspoon ground allspice
  Marshmallows

1 In a saucepan combine milk, malted milk powder, and allspice. Heat and stir till almost boiling, but *do not boil.* Beat with a rotary beater till frothy. Serve in heat-proof mugs; top each serving with a marshmallow. Makes 4 or 5 servings.

CHOCOLATE-BANANA SHAKE

Assembling time: 5 minutes

1 cup cold milk
3 tablespoons instant cocoa mix
1 banana, cut up
1 pint (2 cups) vanilla ice cream

1 In a blender container combine milk and cocoa mix. Cover; blend till cocoa mix is dissolved. Add banana and ice cream by spoonfuls. Cover; blend till smooth. Pour into glasses. Serves 2.

ORANGE CIDER

Total preparation time: 5 minutes

⅔ cup apple cider *or* apple juice
1 tablespoon orange-flavored instant breakfast drink powder
  Dash ground cinnamon
  Dash ground nutmeg

1 In a saucepan heat cider till hot. Meanwhile, in a mug stir together orange drink powder, cinnamon, and nutmeg. Add hot cider. Stir to mix well. If desired, float a lemon slice atop. Makes 1 serving.

TOMATO-APPLE STARTER

Total preparation time: 5 minutes

1½ cups apple cider *or* apple juice
⅛ teaspoon ground cinnamon
1 10¾-ounce can condensed cream of tomato soup

1 In a saucepan stir apple cider or apple juice and cinnamon into tomato soup. Heat to boiling, stirring occasionally. Pour into mugs or soup bowls. Makes 4 servings.

RED WINE PUNCH

Assembling time: 10 minutes

4 cups dry red wine, chilled
1 6-ounce can frozen red Hawaiian fruit punch concentrate
1 28-ounce bottle (3½ cups) lemon-lime carbonated beverage, chilled
  Ice cubes *or* ice ring (optional)
  Halved orange slices

1 In a punch bowl combine wine and frozen punch concentrate. Slowly pour lemon-lime beverage down the side of the punch bowl; stir gently to mix. Add ice, if desired. Float halved orange slices atop punch. Makes 10 to 12 servings.

CHILLY IRISH COFFEE

Assembling time: 5 minutes

½ cup milk
¼ cup Irish whiskey
1 teaspoon instant coffee crystals
1 quart coffee ice cream
  Frozen whipped dessert topping, thawed *or* pressurized dessert topping

1 In a blender container combine milk, Irish whiskey, and coffee crystals. Spoon in coffee ice cream. Cover and blend till smooth. To serve, pour into 4 tall glasses and dollop each with dessert topping. Makes 4 servings.

CHAPTER 5

EASY COOKING

On those days when you want to start dinner and then go on to other things, choose a recipe from this chapter. Here you'll find easy recipes that you can assemble quickly and then allow to cook, chill, or freeze without much tending. This delicious assortment of foods includes everything from appetizers and beverages for parties to main-dish recipes, salads, and soups to side dishes and desserts.

So, go ahead. Make any of these irresistible recipes and still have time to put your feet up and relax: Peachy Skillet Dinner (see recipe, page 254), Texas Spanish Rice (see recipe, page 270), and Chocolate-Swirled Coffee Cake (see recipe, page 272).

BELGIAN-STYLE BEEF

Assembling time: 10 minutes
Cooking time: 1 hour and 10 minutes

- 1 medium onion, sliced (½ cup)
- 3 tablespoons butter *or* margarine
- 1½ pounds boneless beef round steak, cut ½ inch thick
- 1 cup beer
- 2 bay leaves
- 2 teaspoons dried parsley flakes
- 1 teaspoon sugar
- ¾ teaspoon salt
- ½ teaspoon dried thyme, crushed
   Dash pepper
- ¼ cup cold water
- 2 tablespoons all-purpose flour

1 In a 12-inch skillet cook onion in butter or margarine till tender but not brown. Remove onion and set aside. Cut meat into 6 pieces. In the same skillet brown the meat, half at a time; remove from skillet.

2 Stir the beer, bay leaves, parsley flakes, sugar, salt, thyme, and pepper into the skillet drippings. Return the meat and onion to the skillet. Cover and simmer about 1 hour or till the meat is tender.

3 Remove the meat and onion to a serving platter. Spoon off fat from pan juices. Measure the pan juices. Return *1 cup* of the pan juices to the skillet. Stir together cold water and flour. Stir into pan juices in skillet. Cook and stir till thickened and bubbly. Cook and stir 1 minute more. Spoon atop meat. Makes 6 servings.

TOMATO-SAUCED STEAK

Assembling time: 20 minutes
Cooking time: 1½ hours

- 2 tablespoons all-purpose flour
- 1 teaspoon dry mustard
- 2 pounds beef round steak, cut ¾ inch thick
- 2 tablespoons cooking oil
- 1 10¾-ounce can condensed tomato soup
- 1 medium onion, chopped (½ cup)
- 1 tablespoon Worcestershire sauce

1 Mix flour, mustard, ¼ teaspoon *salt*, and dash *pepper*. Pound mixture into meat with a meat mallet. In oven-going skillet brown meat on both sides in hot oil. Drain.

2 Stir together soup, onion, and Worcestershire sauce; pour over meat. Bake, covered, in a 325° oven for 1 hour. Uncover; bake about 30 minutes more. Serves 8.

BEAN-SAUCED CHUCK STEAK

Assembling time: 15 minutes
Cooking time: 1½ hours

- 1 2-pound beef chuck steak, cut 1 inch thick
- 1 tablespoon cooking oil
- 1 8¼-ounce can refried beans
- 1 8-ounce can tomato sauce
- 1 4-ounce can green chili peppers, rinsed, seeded, and chopped
- ½ teaspoon minced dried onion
- 1 cup broken tortilla *or* corn chips

1 In oven-going skillet brown meat on both sides in hot oil. Drain off fat. Mix beans, tomato sauce, chili peppers, and onion; pour over meat. Cover and bake in a 350° oven about 1½ hours or till meat is tender. Transfer meat and sauce to a platter. Sprinkle with broken chips. Serves 6 to 8.

ROLLED FLANK STEAK

Assembling time: 25 minutes
Cooking time: 2 hours

- 1 10-ounce package frozen chopped spinach
- 1 beaten egg
- 1 cup herb-seasoned stuffing mix
- ½ teaspoon minced dried onion
- ¼ teaspoon pepper
- 1 1- to 1½-pound beef flank steak
- 1 8-ounce can tomato sauce with chopped onion
- ¼ cup dry red wine
- ¼ cup water
- 1 tablespoon cold water
- 2 teaspoons cornstarch

1 Run hot water over frozen spinach in a colander about 5 minutes or till thawed. Drain spinach, pressing out excess moisture. In a bowl combine egg and thawed spinach. Stir in seasoned stuffing mix, dried onion, and pepper. Mix well.

2 Pound meat with a meat mallet to about ¼-inch thickness. Spread spinach mixture atop steak. Roll up steak jelly-roll style starting from long side. Secure with string.

3 Place steak roll in a 13×9×2-inch baking pan. Stir together tomato sauce, wine, and the ¼ cup water; pour over meat. Bake, covered, in a 325° oven about 1¾ hours or till the meat is tender.

4 To serve, transfer meat roll to a serving platter; remove string. Skim fat from pan juices. Stir together 1 tablespoon cold water and cornstarch. In a saucepan combine cornstarch mixture and pan juices. Cook and stir till thickened and bubbly. Cook and stir 2 minutes more. Spoon tomato sauce mixture over meat. Makes 6 servings.

Rolled Flank Steak

OVEN SWISS STEAK

Assembling time: 20 minutes
Cooking time: 1 hour and 20 minutes

¼ **cup all-purpose flour**
1 **teaspoon salt**
1½ **pounds beef round steak, cut**
   ¾ inch thick
2 **tablespoons cooking oil** *or*
   shortening
1 **16-ounce can tomatoes, cut up**
1 **stalk celery, finely chopped**
   (½ cup)
1 **medium carrot, finely chopped**
   (½ cup)
½ **teaspoon Worcestershire sauce**

1 In a small mixing bowl stir together the all-purpose flour and the salt. Use a meat mallet to pound *2 tablespoons* of the flour mixture into the beef round steak. Cut the round steak into 6 serving-size portions.

2 In a large skillet brown the meat portions on both sides in hot cooking oil or shortening. Transfer the meat to a 12×7½×2-inch baking dish, reserving the drippings in the skillet.

3 Stir the remaining flour mixture into the reserved meat drippings in the skillet. Stir in the *undrained* cut-up tomatoes, finely chopped celery, finely chopped carrot, and Worcestershire sauce.

4 Cook and stir till the tomato mixture is thickened and bubbly. Cook and stir 1 to 2 minutes more. Pour the tomato mixture over the meat portions in the baking dish. Bake, covered, in a 350° oven about 1 hour and 20 minutes or till the meat is tender. Makes 6 servings.

OVEN-BAKED STEAK AND ONIONS

Assembling time: 15 minutes
Cooking time: 1 hour and 5 minutes

2 **pounds beef round steak, cut**
   1 inch thick
2 **tablespoons cooking oil**
1 **5¾-ounce can steak sauce with**
   mushrooms
¼ **cup dry red wine**
½ **teaspoon ground sage**
3 **carrots, thinly sliced**
2 **medium onions, sliced**
1 **tablespoon all-purpose flour**

1 Cut steak into 8 pieces. In oven-going skillet brown meat on both sides in hot oil. Drain. Mix the steak sauce, wine, sage, and ¼ cup *water*. Pour over steak.

2 Add the carrots and onions. Bake, covered, in a 350° oven about 1 hour or till meat is tender. Transfer meat, carrots, and onions to a platter; keep warm.

3 Skim the fat from pan juices. Stir together the flour and 2 tablespoons *cold water*; stir into pan juices in skillet. Cook and stir till thickened and bubbly. Cook and stir 1 minute more. Spoon over meat. Serves 8.

BEEF BURGUNDY

Assembling time: 18 minutes
Cooking time: 45 minutes

1 **pound beef round steak, cut**
   ¾ inch thick
1 **tablespoon cooking oil**
1 **cup dry red wine**
2 **tablespoons chopped onion**
1 **clove garlic, minced**
1 **tablespoon catsup**
1 **teaspoon instant beef bouillon**
   granules
¼ **teaspoon dried thyme, crushed**
⅛ **teaspoon pepper**
1 **bay leaf**
1 **3-ounce can sliced mushrooms**
¼ **cup cold water**
2 **tablespoons all-purpose flour**
   Hot cooked noodles

1 Cut the meat into ¾-inch cubes. In a medium saucepan brown the meat, *half at a time*, in hot oil. Drain off fat. Stir in dry red wine, chopped onion, minced garlic, catsup, beef bouillon granules, dried thyme, pepper, and bay leaf.

2 Bring to boiling; reduce heat. Cook, covered, over low heat for 35 to 40 minutes or till the meat is tender. Add the *undrained* sliced mushrooms. Stir together cold water and flour; stir into meat mixture. Cook and stir till mixture is thickened and bubbly. Cook and stir 1 minute more. Remove bay leaf. Serve over hot cooked noodles. Makes 4 servings.

SHORT RIBS WITH LIMAS

Beef short ribs can be cut from the plate or chuck or the ribs immediately below the rib steak section. Short ribs from the chuck usually have more lean meat than the others—

Assembling time: 1¼ hours
Cooking time: 2½ hours

8 cups water
2 cups dry lima beans
3 pounds beef short ribs
2 tablespoons cooking oil
¾ teaspoon salt
⅛ teaspoon pepper
1 12-ounce can beer
1 medium onion, chopped (½ cup)
½ cup water
¼ cup vinegar
2 tablespoons brown sugar
2 teaspoons dry mustard
2 bay leaves

1 In a Dutch oven combine the 8 cups water and dry lima beans. Bring beans to boiling. Reduce heat; simmer 2 minutes. Remove from heat. Cover the Dutch oven; soak beans for 1 hour. Drain the beans.

2 Meanwhile, cut the beef ribs into serving-size pieces. Brown the ribs in hot oil. Drain off fat. Sprinkle ribs with the salt and pepper. Place in a 3-quart casserole.

3 Stir together the drained beans, beer, chopped onion, the ½ cup water, vinegar, brown sugar, dry mustard, and bay leaves. Spoon the bean mixture on top of the ribs in the casserole. Cover the casserole and bake in a 350° oven for 2 to 2½ hours or till beans and ribs are tender. Remove bay leaves before serving. Serves 6.

BEEF PAPRIKA

Assembling time: 15 minutes
Cooking time: 1 hour and 35 minutes

1 pound beef stew meat, cut into 1-inch cubes
1 large onion, chopped (1 cup)
3 tablespoons cooking oil
1 16-ounce can tomatoes, cut up
1 cup water
1 tablespoon paprika
1 tablespoon dried parsley flakes
2 teaspoons instant beef bouillon granules
½ teaspoon dried thyme, crushed
¼ teaspoon salt
⅛ teaspoon minced dried garlic
1 bay leaf
2 tablespoons cold water
1 tablespoon all-purpose flour
Hot cooked noodles

1 In a 10-inch oven-going skillet brown the meat and chopped onion in hot cooking oil. Drain off fat. Stir in *undrained* tomatoes, the 1 cup water, paprika, parsley, beef bouillon granules, thyme, salt, dried garlic, and bay leaf. Bring mixture to boiling.

2 Bake, covered, in a 350° oven about 1½ hours or till the meat is tender. Skim off fat. Combine the 2 tablespoons water and flour. Stir into the meat-tomato mixture. Cook and stir till the mixture is thickened and bubbly. Cook and stir 1 minute more. Remove bay leaf. Serve over hot cooked noodles. Makes 4 servings.

GREEK BEEF STEW

Assembling time: 20 minutes
Cooking time: 2 hours

2 cups water
3 tablespoons quick-cooking tapioca
1½ pounds beef stew meat, cut into 1-inch cubes
3 tablespoons cooking oil
    or shortening
2 medium onions, quartered
1 8-ounce can tomato sauce
⅓ cup dry red wine
1 tablespoon brown sugar
1½ teaspoons garlic salt
¼ teaspoon ground cinnamon
1 bay leaf
1 cup crumbled feta cheese (4 ounces)
½ cup walnut halves

1 In a bowl combine the water and tapioca; let stand at least 5 minutes. Meanwhile, in a 4-quart Dutch oven brown the meat cubes in hot cooking oil or shortening. Drain off fat.

2 Stir in the tapioca mixture, quartered onions, tomato sauce, dry red wine, brown sugar, garlic salt, ground cinnamon, and bay leaf. Bring mixture to boiling. Reduce heat; cover the Dutch oven and simmer over low heat for 1½ to 2 hours or till the meat is tender.

3 Remove bay leaf before serving. Ladle the stew into individual serving bowls. Top each serving with some of the crumbled feta cheese and walnut halves. Makes 6 servings.

BOEUF EN DAUBE

Assembling time: 15 minutes
Cooking time: 1 hour and 45 minutes

2 slices bacon, cut up
2 to 2½ pounds beef stew meat, cut
    into 1-inch cubes
2 cups dry red wine
½ cup water
1 medium onion, chopped (½ cup)
2 cloves garlic, minced
1 tablespoon vinegar
½ teaspoon salt
½ teaspoon instant beef bouillon
    granules
½ teaspoon dried rosemary, crushed
½ teaspoon dried thyme, crushed
½ teaspoon finely shredded orange
    peel
¼ teaspoon pepper
6 carrots, bias-sliced into 1-inch
    pieces
3 medium onions, quartered
1 cup pitted ripe olives
2 tablespoons cornstarch
2 tablespoons cold water
    Snipped parsley (optional)

1 In a Dutch oven cook bacon till crisp.
Add the meat cubes; brown the meat in
the bacon drippings. Stir in the red wine, the
½ cup water, the 1 chopped onion, garlic,
vinegar, salt, beef bouillon granules, rosemary, thyme, orange peel, and pepper.
2 Bring to boiling. Reduce heat; cover
and simmer for 1 hour. Stir in the carrots, the 3 quartered onions, and olives.
Simmer, covered, for 30 to 40 minutes or till
vegetables are tender.
3 Combine the cornstarch and the 2 tablespoons cold water; stir into the meat
mixture. Cook and stir till thickened and bubbly. Cook and stir 2 minutes more. Turn into
a serving bowl. Top with snipped parsley, if
desired. Makes 8 servings.

Boeuf En Daube

SWEET PEPPER
BEEF ROUND

Assembling time: 15 minutes
Cooking time: 2 hours and 10 minutes

1 3- to 3½-pound beef bottom round
    roast
2 tablespoons cooking oil
2 medium onions, sliced
2 green peppers, cut into strips
½ cup dry red wine
¼ cup raisins
2 tablespoons catsup
1 clove garlic, minced
1 teaspoon salt
½ teaspoon dried basil, crushed
½ teaspoon dried tarragon, crushed
½ teaspoon dried thyme, crushed
1 bay leaf
⅛ teaspoon pepper
4 teaspoons all-purpose flour
½ cup dairy sour cream
    Hot cooked rice (optional)

1 In a large Dutch oven brown meat in hot
cooking oil. Stir together the sliced onion, green pepper strips, dry red wine, raisins, catsup, garlic, salt, dried basil, dried
tarragon, dried thyme, bay leaf, and pepper.
Pour over meat in the Dutch oven.
2 Bring to boiling. Reduce heat; cover
and simmer about 2 hours. Remove
bay leaf. Transfer meat and vegetables to a
warm serving platter; keep warm.
3 Measure pan juices; reserve 1 cup. In
the Dutch oven stir flour into sour
cream. Stir in the reserved pan juices. Cook
and stir till thickened and bubbly. Cook and
stir 1 minute more. To serve, slice meat.
Serve meat, vegetables, and thickened pan
juices atop hot cooked rice, if desired.
Makes 8 servings.

DUTCH OVEN
DINNER

Assembling time: 15 minutes
Cooking time: 2¼ hours

2 tablespoons all-purpose flour
½ teaspoon salt
1 3-pound beef round rump roast
2 tablespoons cooking oil
1 large onion, chopped (1 cup)
¾ cup water
½ of a 1.4-ounce envelope butter-
    milk salad dressing mix
    (2 tablespoons)
1 20-ounce package frozen loose-
    pack carrots, potatoes, onion,
    and celery
½ cup milk
2 tablespoons cornstarch
¼ teaspoon Kitchen Bouquet
    (optional)

1 In a bowl stir together the flour and salt.
Coat the roast with the flour mixture. In
a Dutch oven brown roast on all sides in hot
cooking oil. Drain off fat. Stir together onion,
water, and salad dressing mix. Pour over
meat in the Dutch oven.
2 Bring to boiling. Reduce heat; cover
and simmer for 1 hour. Add frozen vegetables. Cover and simmer the mixture
about 1 hour more or till the meat and vegetables are tender.
3 Remove meat and vegetables to a
warm serving platter; keep warm. Measure pan juices; add enough water to equal
1½ cups liquid. Return the reserved liquid to
the Dutch oven.
4 Stir together milk and cornstarch. Stir
into liquid in Dutch oven. Cook and stir
till thickened and bubbly. Cook and stir 2
minutes more. Season to taste with salt and
pepper. Stir in Kitchen Bouquet, if desired.
Spoon some sauce over meat and vegetables before serving. Pass the remaining
sauce. Makes 8 servings.

ORANGE 'N' SPICE POT ROAST

Assembling time: 20 minutes
Cooking time: 2¾ hours

- 3 slices bacon
- 1 3½- to 4-pound beef chuck pot roast
- 2 tablespoons lemon juice
- 1 teaspoon salt
- 1 8-ounce can stewed tomatoes, cut up
- 1 cup orange juice
- 1 medium onion, chopped (½ cup)
- ¼ cup snipped parsley
- 1 teaspoon sugar
- ½ teaspoon ground cinnamon
- 1 clove garlic, minced
- 4 whole cloves
- 1 small bay leaf
- ¼ cup cold water
- 2 tablespoons all-purpose flour

1 In a 12-inch oven-going skillet cook bacon till crisp. Drain bacon, reserving the drippings. Crumble bacon and set aside. Trim excess fat from the pot roast. Sprinkle pot roast with lemon juice and salt. Brown the meat in the reserved bacon drippings.

2 Meanwhile, in a medium bowl combine *undrained* stewed tomatoes, orange juice, chopped onion, snipped parsley, sugar, ground cinnamon, garlic, cloves, bay leaf, and crumbled bacon. Pour over meat.

3 Bake, covered, in a 325° oven for 2 to 2½ hours or till the meat is tender. Remove meat and vegetables to a serving platter; keep warm.

4 Remove cloves and bay leaf from pan juices; skim off fat. Combine cold water and flour. Stir into pan juices in skillet. Cook and stir till thickened and bubbly. Cook and stir 1 minute more. Pass thickened pan juices with meat. Makes 8 servings.

BEEF ROAST WITH SOUR CREAM SAUCE

Assembling time: 15 minutes
Cooking time: 2½ hours

- 1 3- to 4-pound beef chuck pot roast
- 2 tablespoons all-purpose flour
- 1 tablespoon cooking oil
- 1 10¾-ounce can condensed cream of potato soup
- ½ teaspoon Worcestershire sauce
- ¼ teaspoon dried marjoram, crushed
- ¼ teaspoon dried thyme, crushed
- ⅛ teaspoon pepper
- 1 10-ounce package frozen brussels sprouts, thawed
- 1 17-ounce can sweet potatoes, drained
- ½ cup dairy sour cream
- 1 tablespoon all-purpose flour

1 Trim any excess fat from the pot roast. Rub meat with the 2 tablespoons flour. In a large Dutch oven brown meat in hot cooking oil. Drain off fat.

2 In bowl mix soup, Worcestershire sauce, marjoram, thyme, pepper, and ¼ cup *water*. Pour over meat in the Dutch oven. Bake, covered, in a 350° oven about 1¾ hours or till meat is almost tender.

3 In a colander run brussels sprouts under warm water till separated. Arrange sweet potatoes and brussels sprouts around the meat in the Dutch oven. Cover and bake about 30 minutes more or till meat and vegetables are tender. Remove meat and vegetables to a serving platter; keep warm.

4 Skim fat from pan juices. Measure pan juices; add enough water to juices to measure 1½ cups liquid. Return liquid to Dutch oven. Combine sour cream and the 1 tablespoon flour. Stir into liquid in Dutch oven. Cook and stir till thickened and bubbly. Cook and stir 1 minute more. To serve, spoon some of the sour cream mixture over meat and vegetables; pass the remainder. Serves 8 to 10.

CHILI BEAN POT ROAST

Assembling time: 15 minutes
Cooking time: 2¼ hours

- 1 medium onion, chopped (½ cup)
- 2 tablespoons cooking oil
- 3 tablespoons all-purpose flour
- 1 teaspoon salt
- ⅛ teaspoon pepper
- 1 2½- to 3-pound beef chuck pot roast
- 1 16-ounce can red kidney beans, drained
- 1 7½-ounce can tomatoes, cut up
- 1 4-ounce can green chili peppers, rinsed, seeded, and chopped
- ⅓ cup dry red wine
- 2 tablespoons all-purpose flour
- 2 tablespoons cold water
  Flour tortillas
  Dairy sour cream
  Shredded cheddar cheese
  Sliced pitted ripe olives

1 In a 4-quart Dutch oven cook chopped onion in hot oil till tender. Meanwhile, in a small bowl combine the 3 tablespoons flour, salt, and pepper; coat roast with flour mixture. Brown meat in the onion-oil mixture.

2 In a bowl stir together beans, *undrained* tomatoes, chili peppers and wine. Pour over meat. Cover; simmer about 2 hours or till the meat is tender. Remove meat to platter; keep warm.

3 Skim fat from pan juices. Mash vegetables slightly. Combine the 2 tablespoons flour and water; stir into pan juices in Dutch oven. Cook and stir till thickened and bubbly. Cook and stir 1 minute more. Pass thickened pan juices with meat. Serve with tortillas, sour cream, shredded cheese, and sliced olives. Makes 6 servings.

BEEF IN RED WINE

Assembling time: 20 minutes
Cooking time: 2¼ hours

- 1 3- to 4-pound beef chuck pot roast
- 2 cloves garlic, slivered
- 1 teaspoon dried basil, crushed
- 1 teaspoon dried oregano, crushed
- ½ teaspoon salt
- ¼ teaspoon pepper
- 2 tablespoons cooking oil
- 1 cup dry red wine
- ¾ cup beef broth
- 2 medium carrots, chopped (1 cup)
- 1 medium onion, sliced
- ¼ cup snipped parsley
- 1 bay leaf

1 Use a sharp knife to cut several small slits in the pot roast; insert a sliver of garlic into each slit. In a bowl combine basil, oregano, salt, and pepper; rub onto surfaces of meat. In a large Dutch oven brown meat on both sides in hot oil. Drain.

2 In a bowl stir together dry red wine, beef broth, chopped carrot, sliced onion, snipped parsley, and bay leaf. Pour over meat. Bring to boiling. Reduce heat; cover and simmer about 2 hours or till meat is tender.

3 Transfer the meat to a warm serving platter. Skim fat from pan juices; remove bay leaf. Spoon pan juices over meat. Makes 8 to 10 servings.

JIFFY WELLINGTON PIE

Assembling time: 18 minutes
Cooking time: 55 minutes

- 1 beaten egg
- ¼ cup water
- 2 tablespoons dry red wine
- 2 cups soft bread crumbs (about 2½ slices bread)
- 1 teaspoon salt
- ¼ teaspoon dried thyme, crushed
- ⅛ teaspoon pepper
- 1 bay leaf, crushed
- 1½ pounds ground beef
- 1 9-inch frozen unbaked pastry shell
- 1 4¾-ounce can liverwurst spread
- 1 4-ounce can sliced mushrooms, drained
- 1 1⅛-ounce envelope hollandaise sauce mix
  Tomato wedges (optional)

1 In a mixing bowl stir together egg, water, and wine. Stir in crumbs, salt, thyme, pepper, and bay leaf. Add ground beef; mix well. Press mixture into a 9-inch pie plate. Bake in 350° oven 40 minutes.

2 Meanwhile, remove pastry shell from freezer; set aside to thaw slightly. Drain fat from meat; invert onto an oven-proof platter. Increase oven temperature to 450°. Spread meat with liverwurst spread; top with the mushroom slices.

3 Carefully invert partially thawed pastry shell over meat. Remove pan from pastry. Press edges of pastry to platter to seal. Cut slits in top of pastry to allow steam to escape. Bake in a 450° oven about 15 minutes or till golden brown.

4 Meanwhile, prepare hollandaise sauce mix according to package directions. Garnish with tomato wedges, if desired. Serve with hollandaise sauce. Makes 6 servings.

TACO SALAD PIE

Total preparation time: 55 minutes

- 1 beaten egg
- ½ cup taco sauce
- 2 cups cheese-flavored croutons, crushed
- 4 green onions, sliced (¼ cup)
- ¼ teaspoon salt
- ¾ pound ground beef
- 1 15½-ounce can chili beans
- ½ cup shredded cheddar cheese (2 ounces)
- 4 green onions, sliced (¼ cup)
- ½ cup shredded cheddar cheese (2 ounces)
  Shredded lettuce
  Chopped tomatoes
  Dairy sour cream
  Pitted ripe olives, sliced (optional)

1 To make crust, in a bowl combine egg and taco sauce. Stir in crushed croutons, 4 green onions, and salt. Add the ground beef; mix well. Press into bottom of a 10×6×2-inch baking dish. Bake in a 350° oven for 20 minutes. Drain off fat.

2 Meanwhile, combine *undrained* chili beans, ½ cup shredded cheese, and 4 green onions; pour over meat mixture. Bake about 20 minutes more or till meat is done and bean mixture is heated through.

3 Sprinkle with ½ cup shredded cheese. Bake 2 to 3 minutes more or till cheese is melted. Cut into 5 servings. Top individual servings with shredded lettuce, chopped tomatoes, sour cream, and sliced olives. Makes 5 servings.

233

CALZONE CASSEROLE

Assembling time: 20 minutes
Cooking time: 45 minutes

1 pound ground beef, pork, veal, lamb, *or* raw turkey
1 8-ounce can pizza sauce *or* 1 cup spaghetti sauce
½ teaspoon dried oregano, crushed
¼ teaspoon dried basil, crushed
⅛ teaspoon garlic powder
  Several dashes bottled hot pepper sauce
6 slices bread, toasted
1½ cups cream-style cottage cheese, drained, *or* 1½ cups shredded mozzarella, Monterey Jack, Swiss, cheddar, *or* American cheese
2 beaten eggs
1 cup milk
1 tablespoon all-purpose flour
¼ teaspoon salt
¼ cup grated Parmesan cheese
1 teaspoon dried parsley flakes

1 In a large skillet brown the ground meat (if using ground turkey, add 1 tablespoon *cooking oil*); remove from heat. Drain off fat. Stir in pizza sauce or spaghetti sauce, dried oregano, dried basil, garlic powder, and hot pepper sauce.

2 Cut each slice of toasted bread into four triangles. Fit *half* the bread triangles into a greased 10×6×2-inch or an 8×8×2-inch baking dish. Top with the meat mixture. Spoon cottage cheese or sprinkle shredded cheese over meat mixture. Arrange the remaining bread triangles atop.

3 In a bowl stir together eggs, milk, flour, and salt; pour over the bread slices (making sure that all is moistened). Sprinkle with Parmesan cheese and dried parsley. Bake in a 325° oven for 40 to 45 minutes or till egg mixture is set. Makes 8 servings.

BEEF-ZUCCHINI CASSEROLE

Assembling time: 35 minutes
Cooking time: 35 minutes

3 medium zucchini, halved lengthwise and sliced ¼ inch thick (1 pound)
1½ cups water
1 tablespoon minced dried onion
½ teaspoon salt
1½ cups quick-cooking rice
1 pound ground beef
1 10¾-ounce can condensed tomato soup
2 slightly beaten eggs
1½ teaspoons dried oregano, crushed
¼ teaspoon garlic salt
  Dash bottled hot pepper sauce
1½ cups cream-style cottage cheese, drained (12 ounces)
1 4-ounce package (1 cup) shredded cheddar cheese

1 In a medium saucepan cook zucchini in a small amount of boiling water about 4 minutes or till almost tender. Drain zucchini. In a large saucepan bring the 1½ cups water, the dried onion, and salt to boiling; stir in rice. Remove from heat; cover and let stand for 5 minutes.

2 Meanwhile, in a skillet cook ground beef till browned; drain off fat. Add tomato soup, beaten eggs, dried oregano, garlic salt, hot pepper sauce, and zucchini; mix well. Stir in rice mixture.

3 In a 12×7½×2-inch baking dish place *half* of the zucchini-rice mixture. Spread with cottage cheese; top with remaining zucchini-rice mixture. Cover with foil. Bake in a 350° oven for 30 minutes. Sprinkle cheddar cheese on top and bake 3 to 5 minutes more or till cheese is melted. Makes 8 servings.

SKIP-A-STEP LASAGNA

You don't have to precook the noodles to make this easy lasagna—

Assembling time: 15 minutes
Cooking time: 1 hour and 5 minutes
Standing time: 10 minutes

1 pound ground beef
1 15½-ounce jar spaghetti sauce with meat
2 slightly beaten eggs
1½ cups cream-style cottage cheese (12 ounces)
⅓ cup grated Parmesan cheese
½ teaspoon dried basil, crushed
½ teaspoon dried oregano, crushed
9 lasagna noodles
1½ cups shredded Swiss cheese (6 ounces)
1 cup boiling water
2 tablespoons grated Parmesan cheese

1 In a large skillet cook ground beef till browned; drain off fat. Stir in spaghetti sauce. In a mixing bowl stir together eggs, cottage cheese, the ⅓ cup Parmesan cheese, dried basil, and dried oregano.

2 In a 12×7½×2-inch baking dish place *three uncooked* lasagna noodles. Spread *one-third* of the meat-spaghetti sauce mixture atop noodles. Top with *half* of the cottage cheese mixture and ½ *cup* of the Swiss cheese.

3 Repeat the layers of noodles, meat-sauce mixture, cottage cheese mixture, and Swiss cheese. Top with remaining three noodles and remaining meat-sauce mixture. Pour boiling water into baking dish around the edge. Cover tightly with foil.

4 Bake in a 350° oven about 1 hour or till the noodles are tender. Uncover; sprinkle with the remaining Swiss cheese and the 2 tablespoons Parmesan cheese. Return to oven; bake 3 to 5 minutes more or till cheese is melted. Let stand 10 minutes before serving. Makes 8 to 10 servings.

BEEF SANDWICH SQUARES

Assembling time: 20 minutes
Cooking time: 30 minutes
Standing time: 10 minutes

  1 **pound ground beef**
  1 **small onion, chopped (¼ cup)**
  ¼ **cup catsup**
  ½ **teaspoon salt**
  ¼ **teaspoon minced dried garlic**
  1 **10-ounce package corn bread mix**
  1 **8½-ounce can cream-style corn**
  ¾ **cup shredded American cheese**
  2 **eggs**
  2 **tablespoons milk**
  ½ **cup shredded American cheese**
  2 **tablespoons cold water**
  2 **teaspoons cornstarch**
  1 **8-ounce can stewed tomatoes,**
    cut up
  2 **tablespoons chopped, canned**
    green chili peppers
  1 **teaspoon Worcestershire sauce**

1 In a large skillet cook the ground beef and chopped onion till the meat is browned; drain off fat. Stir in catsup, salt, and minced dried garlic; set aside.

2 In a bowl combine corn bread mix, corn, the ¾ cup cheese, eggs, and milk. Stir just till combined. Spread *half* the batter in a greased 8×8×2-inch baking pan. Spoon beef mixture atop batter in pan; sprinkle the ½ cup cheese atop meat mixture. Top with remaining batter. Bake in a 350° oven for 30 to 35 minutes. Let stand 5 minutes before serving.

3 Meanwhile, prepare sauce. In a small saucepan combine cold water and cornstarch. Stir in *undrained* tomatoes, chili peppers, and Worcestershire sauce. Cook and stir till thickened and bubbly. Cook and stir 2 minutes more. Cut corn bread into squares. Serve sauce atop. Serves 6.

Beef Sandwich Squares

235

HEARTY PILAF CASSEROLE

Bulgur is wheat that has been cooked and parched before grinding. It differs from cracked wheat in that it is cooked. You can find bulgur in the cereal section of most supermarkets—

Assembling time: 18 minutes
Cooking time: 48 minutes

 1 **pound ground beef**
 ¾ **cup bulgur wheat**
 8 **green onions, sliced (½ cup)**
 ¼ **cup chopped green pepper**
 1 **clove garlic, minced**
 1 **16-ounce can tomatoes, cut up**
 3 **medium zucchini, sliced ¼ inch thick (1 pound)**
 1 **tablespoon Worcestershire sauce**
 1¼ **teaspoons salt**
 1¼ **teaspoons dried oregano, crushed**
 1 **teaspoon sugar**
   Dash bottled hot pepper sauce
 1 **4-ounce package (1 cup) shredded cheddar cheese**

1 In a large skillet cook the ground beef, bulgur wheat, sliced onion, chopped green pepper, and minced garlic till the meat is browned and the onion and pepper are tender. Drain off fat. Stir in *undrained* tomatoes, zucchini slices, Worcestershire sauce, salt, oregano, sugar, and hot pepper sauce.

2 Turn the meat mixture into a 2-quart casserole. Bake, covered, in a 350° oven about 45 minutes or till heated through. Sprinkle shredded cheddar cheese atop. Bake 2 to 3 minutes more or till the cheese melts. Makes 6 servings.

LAYERED BEEF AND NOODLE CASSEROLE

Assembling time: 30 minutes
Cooking time: 45 minutes
Standing time: 5 minutes

 6 **ounces medium noodles (4½ cups)**
 1 **pound ground beef**
 1 **large onion, chopped (1 cup)**
 1 **15½-ounce jar extra thick spaghetti sauce**
 ½ **teaspoon dried basil, crushed**
 ⅛ **teaspoon garlic powder**
 1 **10-ounce package frozen cut broccoli**
 1 **2½-ounce jar sliced mushrooms, drained**
 1 **beaten egg**
 2 **cups cream-style cottage cheese (16 ounces)**
 1 **4-ounce package (1 cup) shredded cheddar cheese**

1 Cook noodles according to package directions; drain well. Meanwhile, in a large skillet cook the ground beef and onion till the meat is browned. Drain off fat.

2 Stir in the spaghetti sauce, basil, and garlic powder. Run hot water over the broccoli in a colander till the broccoli is separated. Drain well. Stir the drained broccoli and mushrooms into the meat mixture.

3 Arrange the cooked noodles in the bottom of a 12×7½×2-inch baking dish. Mix egg and cottage cheese; spread over the noodles. Top with meat mixture. Bake, covered, in a 350° oven for 40 minutes.

4 Top with shredded cheddar cheese. Bake, uncovered, about 5 minutes more or till the cheese is melted. Let stand 5 minutes before serving. Makes 8 servings.

ITALIAN MEAT PIE

For a slightly different flavor, substitute shredded cheddar or Swiss cheese for the mozzarella—

Total preparation time: 50 minutes

 1 **beaten egg**
 ½ **cup milk**
 ¼ **cup fine dry bread crumbs**
 2 **tablespoons grated Parmesan cheese**
 1 **tablespoon minced dried onion**
 1 **teaspoon Italian seasoning**
 1 **pound ground beef**
 1 **2½-ounce jar sliced mushrooms, drained**
 ½ **of a 3-ounce package sliced smoked beef, cut up**
 1 **8-ounce can pizza sauce**
 ½ **cup shredded mozzarella cheese (2 ounces)**

1 In a mixing bowl combine egg and milk. Stir in the bread crumbs, Parmesan cheese, dried onion, and Italian seasoning. Add ground beef; mix well. Press the meat mixture onto the bottom and up the sides of a 9-inch pie plate.

2 Bake meat mixture in a 375° oven for 15 minutes. Drain off fat. Top with the drained mushrooms and sliced smoke beef. Spoon the pizza sauce over all. Bake meat pie 10 minutes more.

3 Sprinkle shredded mozzarella cheese atop. Bake about 5 minutes more or till the cheese is melted. Let stand for 5 minutes before cutting the meat pie into wedges. Makes 6 servings.

HOT SANDWICH LOAF

Assembling time: 12 minutes
Cooking time: 45 minutes

- ¼ **cup butter** *or* **margarine, softened**
- ¼ **cup mayonnaise** *or* **salad dressing**
- 1 **tablespoon snipped fresh chives** *or* **frozen snipped chives**
- 1 **teaspoon prepared mustard**
- ½ **teaspoon onion powder**
- 1 **unsliced loaf French** *or* **pumpernickel bread**
- 8 **slices olive, pepper,** *or* **pickle and pimiento luncheon meat (8 ounces)**
- 8 **slices Monterey Jack, Swiss,** *or* **American cheese (8 ounces)**

1 In a small bowl stir together butter or margarine, mayonnaise or salad dressing, snipped chives, prepared mustard, and onion powder. Place French or pumpernickel bread on a piece of foil large enough to wrap loaf.

2 Slice the bread crosswise into 16 slices, cutting to, but not through, the bottom crust. Spread mayonnaise mixture in every other opening of the cut bread.

3 Fold the meat and cheese slices in half; insert *one* slice of meat and *one* slice of cheese into *each* mayonnaise-spread opening in the bread.

4 Press bread slices together; wrap loaf in foil and place on a baking sheet. Bake in a 375° oven for 40 to 45 minutes or till heated through. To serve, cut through the bottom crust of the unfilled openings in the bread. Makes 8 servings.

SAUSAGE LASAGNA ROLLS

Pictured on cover —

Assembling time: 40 minutes
Cooking time: 35 minutes

- 8 **lasagna noodles**
- 1 **pound bulk Italian sausage**
- 1 **medium onion, chopped (½ cup)**
- 1 **tablespoon all-purpose flour**
- ½ **cup milk**
- ½ **teaspoon garlic salt**
- ⅛ **teaspoon ground nutmeg**
- 1 **3-ounce package cream cheese, cut up**
- 1 **15½-ounce jar extra thick spaghetti sauce**
- 1 **8-ounce can diced carrots, drained**
- ¼ **cup dry red wine** *or* **water**
- 1 **tablespoon dried parsley flakes**
- ½ **teaspoon dried basil, crushed**
- ½ **cup shredded mozzarella cheese (2 ounces)**

1 Cook lasagna noodles according to package directions; drain. Meanwhile, in a large skillet cook the Italian sausage and onion till meat is browned and onion is tender. Drain off fat.

2 Stir in flour. Stir in milk, garlic salt, and nutmeg. Cook and stir till mixture is thickened and bubbly. Cook and stir 1 minute more. Stir in cream cheese till mixture is smooth. Keep warm.

3 For sauce, in a large saucepan combine spaghetti sauce, diced carrots, wine or water, parsley flakes, and basil; heat through. Pat lasagna noodles dry with paper toweling. Spread noodles with sausage mixture; roll up.

4 Pour *half* of the sauce into a 10×6×2-inch baking dish. Place filled lasagna rolls seam side down in baking dish; spoon remaining sauce atop rolls.

5 Cover and bake in a 350° oven for 30 minutes. Sprinkle with shredded mozzarella cheese. Bake, uncovered, about 5 minutes more or till the cheese is melted. Makes 4 servings.

PIZZA STRATA

Any firm-textured bread, such as sourdough or French bread, can be substituted for the Italian bread—

Assembling time: 15 minutes
Cooking time: 1 hour
Standing time: 10 minutes

- ½ **pound bulk pork sausage**
- 1 **medium onion, chopped (½ cup)**
- 3 **cups cubed Italian bread**
- 1 **2-ounce can mushroom stems and pieces, drained**
- 1 **8-ounce can pizza sauce**
- 1 **4-ounce package (1 cup) shredded mozzarella cheese**
- 3 **beaten eggs**
- 1¾ **cups milk**
- 1 **teaspoon dried parsley flakes**
- ½ **teaspoon dried oregano, crushed**
- ¼ **cup grated Parmesan cheese**

1 In a large skillet cook pork sausage and onion till the meat is browned and onion is tender. Drain off fat. Arrange bread cubes in an ungreased 9×9×2-inch baking pan.

2 Top bread cubes with the meat mixture and mushrooms. Spoon pizza sauce atop. Sprinkle shredded mozzarella cheese over the sauce. Stir together the beaten eggs, milk, dried parsley flakes, and oregano. Pour over all.

3 Sprinkle Parmesan cheese atop. Bake, uncovered, in a 325° oven about 1 hour or till set. Let stand 10 minutes before serving. Makes 6 servings.

PORK ROAST AND VEGETABLES

Assembling time: 20 minutes
Cooking time: 1 hour and 50 minutes

1 **3-pound pork shoulder arm roast**
2 **tablespoons cooking oil**
1 **cup apple juice**
1 **cup water**
¼ **cup dry white wine**
2 **teaspoons instant chicken bouillon granules**
2 **teaspoons minced dried onion**
2 **teaspoons lemon juice**
½ **teaspoon salt**
¼ **teaspoon ground cinnamon**
¼ **teaspoon pepper**
4 **medium carrots, cut into 1-inch pieces**
1 **pound parsnips, peeled and sliced**
2 **tablespoons cold water**
4 **teaspoons cornstarch**

1 In a large Dutch oven brown the roast on all sides in hot cooking oil. Drain off fat. Stir together the apple juice, water, wine, bouillon granules, dried onion, lemon juice, salt, ground cinnamon, and pepper. Pour over the meat in the Dutch oven.

2 Bring to boiling. Reduce heat; cover and simmer for 1 hour. Add the carrots and parsnips to the meat mixture. Cover and simmer for 30 to 40 minutes more or till the meat and vegetables are tender.

3 Remove the meat and vegetables to a serving platter; keep warm. Skim fat from pan juices. Measure juices; add water, if necessary, to make 1¼ cups liquid. Return to Dutch oven.

4 Combine cold water and cornstarch. Stir into the reserved 1¼ cups liquid in Dutch oven. Cook and stir till thickened and bubbly. Cook and stir 1 to 2 minutes more. Pass thickened pan juices with the meat. Makes 8 servings.

Roast Royale

ROAST ROYALE

Use an all-beef sausage to stuff rare- or medium-roasted meats; pork sausage must be cooked to the well-done stage (170°)—

Assembling time: 15 minutes
Cooking time: 2½ hours
Standing time: 15 minutes

1 **5-pound boneless pork loin roast, boneless beef rib roast, *or* boneless leg of lamb**
1 **teaspoon seasoned salt**
½ **pound bulk pork sausage *or* beef sausage**
6 **slices bacon**
2 **tablespoons cooking oil**
1 **tablespoon soy sauce**
1 **tablespoon vinegar**
1 **tablespoon molasses**
1 **12-ounce can apricot nectar**
1 **tablespoon cornstarch**

1 If roast is tied, cut and discard string. Unroll roast. Sprinkle meat with seasoned salt; top with sausage. Reroll the roast and tie the meat securely.

2 Lay bacon slices crosswise over the roast; secure ends of bacon with wooden picks. Place roast on a rack in a shallow roasting pan. Insert a meat thermometer.

3 Roast, uncovered, in a 325° oven till done. (Allow 2½ hours for well-done (170°) for pork, 3¼ hours for medium (160°) for beef, or 2½ hours for medium (160°) for lamb.)

4 Mix oil, soy sauce, vinegar, molasses, and ¼ teaspoon *pepper*. During the last half of roasting, baste meat several times with soy mixture. In saucepan mix nectar and cornstarch. Cook and stir till thickened and bubbly. Cook and stir 2 minutes more. During the last 10 minutes of roasting, baste meat with some apricot mixture.

5 Place roast on a platter; let stand 15 minutes. Remove strings and wooden picks. Spoon additional apricot mixture atop meat; serve remainder with meat. Garnish with parsley, if desired. Serves 12 to 15.

PORK STEW WITH CORNMEAL DUMPLINGS

Total preparation time: 2¼ hours

2 **pounds boneless pork**
2 **tablespoons cooking oil**
1 **28-ounce can tomatoes, cut up**
1 **12-ounce can (1½ cups) beer**
1 **medium onion, cut into thin wedges**
1 **tablespoon sugar**
1 **tablespoon Worcestershire sauce**
1 **teaspoon dried thyme, crushed**
1 **clove garlic, minced**
2 **bay leaves**
¼ **teaspoon ground nutmeg**
2 **tablespoons all-purpose flour**
Cornmeal Dumplings

1 Cut the pork into 1-inch cubes. In a 4-quart Dutch oven brown the stew meat, half at a time, in hot cooking oil. Drain off fat. Return all meat to the Dutch oven. Stir in the *undrained* tomatoes, *1 cup* of the beer, onion, sugar, Worcestershire sauce, thyme, garlic, bay leaves, nutmeg, ¾ teaspoon *salt*, and ¼ teaspoon *pepper*.

2 Bring to boiling. Reduce heat; cover. Simmer about 1½ hours or till meat is tender. Skim off fat. Remove bay leaves. Mix flour and remaining beer. Stir into meat mixture. Cook and stir till bubbly. Cook and stir 1 minute more. Remove from heat.

3 Prepare Cornmeal Dumplings. Return stew mixture to boiling; drop batter by rounded tablespoonfuls onto boiling mixture to make 8 dumplings. Sprinkle with paprika, if desired. Cover and simmer, *without lifting cover*, for 12 minutes. Makes 8 servings.

Cornmeal Dumplings: In a mixing bowl stir together ½ cup all-purpose *flour*, ⅓ cup yellow *cornmeal*, 1½ teaspoons *baking powder*, ¼ teaspoon *salt*, and dash *pepper*. Combine 1 beaten *egg*, 2 tablespoons *milk*, and 2 tablespoons *cooking oil*. Add to flour mixture and stir till combined. Stir in one 8¾-ounce can whole kernel *corn*, drained.

BEER-PORK STEW

Assembling time: 20 minutes
Cooking time: 1¼ hours

1 **pound boneless pork**
1 **tablespoon cooking oil**
1 **16-ounce can tomatoes, cut up**
1 **medium onion, cut into thin wedges**
⅓ **cup beer**
1 **bay leaf**
2 **teaspoons Worcestershire sauce**
1 **teaspoon sugar**
½ **teaspoon salt**
½ **teaspoon dried thyme, crushed**
¼ **teaspoon ground nutmeg**
⅛ **teaspoon minced dried garlic**
⅛ **teaspoon pepper**
1 **20-ounce package frozen loose-pack mixed carrots, potatoes, celery, and onions**
⅓ **cup beer**
2 **tablespoons all-purpose flour**

1 Cut the pork into 1-inch cubes. In a 3-quart saucepan brown the meat in hot cooking oil. Drain off fat. Stir in the *undrained* tomatoes, onion, ⅓ cup beer, bay leaf, Worcestershire sauce, sugar, salt, thyme, nutmeg, garlic, and pepper.

2 Bring to boiling; reduce heat. Cover and simmer for 40 minutes. Stir in vegetables; return to boiling. Reduce heat; cover and simmer for 20 minutes more.

3 Skim off fat. Stir together ⅓ cup beer and flour. Stir into the meat-vegetable mixture. Cook and stir till thickened and bubbly. Cook and stir 1 minute more. Serves 6.

SOUTHERN PORK STEW

Assembling time: 20 minutes
Cooking time: 1 hour

1 **pound boneless pork**
1 **tablespoon cooking oil**
1 **10¾-ounce can condensed golden mushroom soup**
¼ **cup peanut butter**
¼ **teaspoon salt**
Dash pepper
1 **cup water**
3 **medium sweet potatoes, peeled and sliced ½ inch thick**
1 **medium onion, cut into wedges**
1 **small green pepper, cut into bite-size pieces**

1 Cut the boneless pork into 1-inch cubes. In a 3-quart saucepan brown pork cubes in hot cooking oil. Drain off fat. Remove the pork cubes from the saucepan. Set aside.

2 In the same 3-quart saucepan stir together the golden mushroom soup, peanut butter, salt, and pepper. Gradually stir in the water, stirring till the peanut butter mixture is smooth. Stir in the sweet potato slices, onion wedges, and the pork cubes.

3 Bring meat-vegetable mixture to boiling. Reduce heat, cover and simmer for 40 minutes. Stir in green pepper pieces. Cover and simmer for 10 to 15 minutes more or till the meat and vegetables are tender. Makes 4 servings.

CORIANDER PORK STEW

Assembling time: 20 minutes
Cooking time: 55 minutes

1 **pound boneless pork**
1 **large onion, chopped (1 cup)**
3 **tablespoons butter *or* margarine**
4 **small potatoes, peeled and quartered**
2 **carrots, cut into 1-inch pieces**
1 **4-ounce can mushroom stems and pieces, drained**
½ **cup dry red wine**
½ **cup beef broth**
1 **tablespoon quick-cooking tapioca**
1 **teaspoon ground coriander**
½ **teaspoon salt**
½ **teaspoon Kitchen Bouquet (optional)**
⅛ **teaspoon pepper**

1 Cut the boneless pork into 1-inch cubes. In a large skillet cook the pork cubes and chopped onion in the butter or margarine till the meat is browned. Drain off fat. Stir in the quartered potatoes, carrot pieces, and drained mushrooms.

2 Stir together the dry red wine; beef broth; quick-cooking tapioca; ground coriander; salt; Kitchen Bouquet, if desired; and pepper. Pour over the meat and vegetables in the skillet.

3 Bring meat and vegetable mixture to boiling. Reduce heat; cover and simmer about 50 minutes or till pork cubes and potato pieces are tender. Transfer meat and vegetables to a serving platter. Makes 4 servings.

TENDERLOIN WITH MUSHROOM SAUCE

Assembling time: 10 minutes
Cooking time: 1 hour

1 1-pound pork tenderloin
1 3-ounce can sliced mushrooms, drained
3 green onions, sliced
3 tablespoons dry sherry
½ cup cold water
1 teaspoon cornstarch
½ teaspoon instant beef bouillon granules
¼ teaspoon dried basil, crushed
   Dash pepper

1 Place tenderloin on a rack in a shallow roasting pan, tucking under thinner ends of tenderloin, if necessary. Insert a meat thermometer. Roast, uncovered, in a 325° oven about 1 hour or till thermometer registers 170°. Transfer to a warm serving platter; keep warm.

2 Meanwhile, to make sauce, in a small saucepan combine mushrooms, green onions, and dry sherry. Bring to boiling. Reduce heat; cover and simmer for 2 minutes.

3 Stir together water, cornstarch, bouillon granules, basil, and pepper. Stir into onion mixture. Cook and stir till mixture is thickened and bubbly. Cook and stir 2 minutes more. To serve, thinly slice the meat; spoon sauce atop. Makes 6 servings.

RIBS WITH APPLE BUTTER

Total preparation time: 1¾ hours

3 pounds meaty pork spareribs
1 cup apple butter
1 tablespoon vinegar
½ teaspoon minced dried onion
⅛ teaspoon minced dried garlic

1 Cut meat into 2 or 3 rib portions. Place ribs, meaty side down, in a shallow roasting pan. Roast in a 450° oven for 30 minutes. Remove meat from oven; drain.

2 Turn ribs meaty side up. Reduce oven temperature to 350°. Roast ribs, covered, 30 minutes more. Mix apple butter, vinegar, onion, garlic, 1 to 2 tablespoons *water*, ½ teaspoon *salt*, and ¼ teaspoon *pepper*. Pour mixture over ribs. Roast, uncovered, about 30 minutes more. Serves 6.

PORK STEAK DINNER

Assembling time: 12 minutes
Cooking time: 50 minutes

2 pork shoulder steaks, cut ½ inch thick
1 tablespoon cooking oil
2 medium potatoes, thinly sliced
1 small onion, thinly sliced
¼ cup white wine
½ of a ¾-ounce envelope mushroom gravy mix

1 Cut each pork steak into 2 serving-size pieces. In a large skillet brown steaks in hot oil on both sides. Remove from skillet; set aside. Drain fat from skillet.

2 Arrange potatoes and onion in skillet; place pork steaks atop. Mix wine, gravy mix, ¼ cup *water*, and ⅛ teaspoon *pepper*. Pour over all. Cover and cook over low heat for 40 to 50 minutes or till potatoes and meat are tender. Serves 4.

PORK PUFF CASSEROLE

Assembling time: 18 minutes
Cooking time: 35 minutes

1 pound ground pork
1 medium onion, chopped (½ cup)
½ teaspoon dried thyme, crushed
1 beaten egg
¼ cup milk
¾ cup soft bread crumbs (1 slice)
1 teaspoon Worcestershire sauce
¼ teaspoon salt
⅛ teaspoon pepper
3 eggs
3 tablespoons milk
2 3-ounce packages cream cheese, cut up
4 ounces cheddar cheese, cut into cubes (1 cup)

1 In a large skillet cook ground pork, chopped onion, and dried thyme till the pork is browned and the onion is tender. Drain off fat. Stir together the 1 egg and ¼ cup milk. Stir bread crumbs, Worcestershire sauce, salt, and pepper into the egg mixture. Add pork mixture; mix well.

2 Press meat mixture onto bottom of an 8 × 1½-inch round baking dish. In a blender container combine the 3 eggs and 3 tablespoons milk. Cover and blend till smooth. With blender running, add cream cheese and cheddar cheese pieces through the opening in lid. Blend till nearly smooth.

3 Pour cheese-egg mixture over the meat mixture. Bake in a 375° oven for 30 to 35 minutes or till the cheese-egg mixture is puffy and set. (Puff will remain creamy in center.) Serve immediately. Serves 6 to 8.

GROUND PORK AND BARLEY OVEN STEW

This easy oven stew uses barley instead of the more traditional potatoes—

Assembling time: 15 minutes
Cooking time: 1 hour and 10 minutes

1 pound ground pork
1 medium onion, chopped (½ cup)
1 16-ounce can tomatoes, cut up
1 cup frozen crinkle-cut sliced carrots
1 cup vegetable juice cocktail
⅔ cup quick-cooking barley
1 4-ounce can mushroom stems and pieces
1 teaspoon instant beef bouillon granules
¾ teaspoon poultry seasoning
⅛ teaspoon minced dried garlic

1 In a large skillet cook ground pork and chopped onion till the ground pork is browned and onion is tender. Drain off fat. In a 2-quart casserole combine the cooked pork-onion mixture, *undrained* tomatoes, carrots, vegetable juice cocktail, *uncooked* barley, *undrained* mushrooms, bouillon granules, poultry seasoning, and dried garlic; mix well.

2 Bake the ground pork mixture, covered, in a 350° oven about 70 minutes or till the barley is tender, stirring once. To serve, ladle into bowls. Makes 6 servings.

PORK- GREEN CHILIES BAKE

Assembling time: 20 minutes
Cooking time: 45 minutes

1½ pounds ground pork
1 medium onion, chopped (½ cup)
¼ cup catsup
2 teaspoons Worcestershire sauce
¼ teaspoon pepper
½ cup shredded Monterey Jack cheese (2 ounces)
2 beaten eggs
¾ cup milk
½ cup shredded Monterey Jack cheese (2 ounces)
1 4-ounce can green chili peppers, rinsed, seeded, and chopped
1 2-ounce can sliced pimiento, drained and chopped
1 tablespoon all-purpose flour

1 In a large skillet cook the ground pork and chopped onion till the ground pork is browned and the onion is tender. Drain off fat. Stir catsup, Worcestershire sauce, and pepper into meat mixture.

2 Spread pork and onion mixture in the bottom of an 8×8×2-inch baking pan. Sprinkle ½ cup shredded Monterey Jack cheese over meat.

3 In a mixing bowl combine the beaten eggs, milk, ½ cup shredded Monterey Jack cheese, rinsed and chopped green chili peppers, chopped pimiento, and all-purpose flour; mix well.

4 Pour egg-cheese mixture over pork and onion mixture. Bake in a 325° oven for 40 to 45 minutes or till egg-cheese mixture is set. To serve, cut into squares. Makes 6 servings.

SWEET-SOUR PORK LOAF

Assembling time: 10 minutes
Cooking time: 45 minutes

2 beaten eggs
1 8-ounce can tomato sauce
¾ cup soft bread crumbs (1 slice)
1 small green pepper, finely chopped (½ cup)
1 1¾-ounce envelope sweet-sour sauce mix
1 tablespoon minced dried onion
¼ teaspoon pepper
1 pound ground pork, ground beef, *or* ground lamb
½ pound ground fully cooked ham
⅓ cup water

1 In a large mixing bowl combine the beaten eggs and ¾ cup of the tomato sauce. Stir in the soft bread crumbs, chopped green pepper, *half* of the sweet-sour sauce mix, minced dried onion, and pepper. Add the ground pork, ground beef, or ground lamb, and ground ham; mix well.

2 Pat meat-green pepper mixture into a 9-inch pie plate. Use hands to smooth the top of the meat-green pepper mixture. Bake, uncovered, in a 350° oven about 45 minutes or till meat loaf is done. Drain off fat.

3 Meanwhile, to make sauce, in a small saucepan combine the remaining sweet-sour sauce mix, the remaining tomato sauce, and the water. Cook and stir till sauce is bubbly. Transfer meat loaf to serving platter. Spoon sauce over meat loaf. Makes 6 servings.

PORK CHOPS IN ONION SAUCE

Onion soup mix gives the recipe a spicy onion flavor without any chopping or slicing of fresh onions—

Assembling time: 15 minutes
Cooking time: 40 minutes

- 4 pork loin chops, cut ½ inch thick
- 2 tablespoons cooking oil
- ½ cup water
- ½ envelope (¼ cup) *regular* onion soup mix
- ½ cup dairy sour cream
- ¼ cup milk
- 1 tablespoon all-purpose flour
  Hot cooked noodles
  Snipped parsley (optional)

1 Cook pork chops on both sides in hot cooking oil about 10 minutes or till chops are browned. Drain off fat. Stir together water and onion soup mix. Pour over chops in skillet.

2 Bring to boiling. Reduce heat; cover and simmer for 30 to 40 minutes or till chops are tender. Remove chops to a warm serving platter. Keep warm.

3 Skim fat from pan juices. Stir together sour cream, milk, and flour. Stir sour cream mixture into the pan juices. Cook and stir till mixture is thickened and bubbly. Cook and stir 1 minute more. Serve chops and thickened pan juices over hot cooked noodles. Sprinkle with snipped parsley, if desired. Makes 4 servings.

PORK CHOP AND CABBAGE DINNER

Assembling time: 18 minutes
Cooking time: 45 minutes

- 4 pork chops, cut ¾ inch thick
- ¼ teaspoon salt
  Few dashes pepper
- 1 tablespoon cooking oil
- ⅓ cup apple juice *or* apple cider
- 1 teaspoon sugar
- 1 teaspoon instant chicken bouillon granules
- ½ teaspoon caraway seed
- ½ small head cabbage, cored and cut into 4 wedges
- 1 large cooking apple, cored and cut into wedges
- 1 small onion, chopped (¼ cup)
- ⅓ cup apple juice *or* apple cider
- 1 tablespoon cornstarch

1 Sprinkle pork chops with salt and pepper. In a 10-inch skillet brown pork chops on both sides in hot cooking oil. Drain off fat. Stir together ⅓ cup apple juice or apple cider, the sugar, chicken bouillon granules, and caraway seed. Pour over the chops in the skillet.

2 Place cabbage and apple wedges atop chops in skillet; sprinkle with chopped onion. Bring mixture to boiling. Reduce heat; cover and simmer about 35 minutes or till chops are tender. Transfer chops, cabbage, and apple to a serving platter; keep warm.

3 Combine ⅓ cup apple juice or apple cider and cornstarch. Stir into pan juices in skillet . Cook and stir till mixture is thickened and bubbly. Cook and stir 2 minutes more. Pass thickened pan juices with the chops, cabbage wedges, and apple wedges. Makes 4 servings.

PORK CHOPS MEDITERRANEAN

Assembling time: 15 minutes
Cooking time: 40 minutes

- 4 pork chops, cut ½ inch thick
- 2 tablespoons cooking oil
- 1 8-ounce can stewed onions, drained
- 1 7¾-ounce can semi-condensed tomato royale soup
- 1 7½-ounce can tomatoes, cut up
- 1 4-ounce can mushroom stems and pieces, drained
- ¼ cup sliced pimiento-stuffed olives
- 1 teaspoon dry mustard
- 1 teaspoon lemon juice
- ½ teaspoon dried thyme, crushed
- ¼ teaspoon garlic powder
  Hot cooked noodles

1 In a 12-inch skillet brown chops on both sides in hot cooking oil. Remove chops and drain off fat. In the same skillet combine drained onions, tomato royale soup, *undrained* tomatoes, drained mushrooms, olives, dry mustard, lemon juice, thyme, and garlic powder.

2 Bring to boiling. Arrange chops atop tomato mixture. Reduce heat; cover and simmer for 30 minutes. Uncover and simmer about 10 minutes more or till chops are tender and sauce is of desired consistency. Season to taste with salt and pepper. Serve chops and sauce with hot cooked noodles. Makes 4 servings.

ONE-STEP HAM CASSEROLE

Total preparation time: 1 hour

1   10¾-ounce can condensed cream of celery soup
1   cup milk
1   4-ounce can sliced mushrooms, drained
1   tablespoon minced dried onion
2   cups chopped fully cooked ham
1   cup elbow macaroni
2   tablespoons chopped pimiento
½   cup shredded American cheese

1 In a 1½-quart casserole combine soup, milk, mushrooms, and dried onion. Add ham, *uncooked* macaroni, pimiento, and dash *pepper*. Mix well. Bake, covered, in a 375° oven about 50 minutes or till macaroni is tender. Uncover; sprinkle cheese atop. Makes 4 servings.

ORANGE-GLAZED HAM

Total preparation time: 1¾ hours

1   3-pound canned ham
2   tablespoons butter *or* margarine
1   tablespoon cornstarch
¼   teaspoon dried fines herbes, crushed
1   cup orange juice

1 Use a knife to score top of ham, if desired. Place ham on a rack in a shallow baking pan. Insert a meat thermometer. Bake ham in a 325° oven for 1 hour.
2 Meanwhile, in saucepan melt butter. Stir in cornstarch and fines herbes. Stir in orange juice. Cook and stir till bubbly. Cook and stir 2 minutes more.
3 Spoon ¼ *cup* of the sauce over ham. Bake about 30 minutes longer or till thermometer registers 140°. Reheat remaining sauce; pass with ham. Serves 12.

CHOUCROUTE GARNI

Total preparation time: 65 minutes

6   slices bacon, cut up
1   medium onion, chopped (½ cup)
1   27-ounce can sauerkraut, drained
2   medium carrots, bias-sliced
2   tablespoons snipped parsley
1   tablespoon sugar
3   juniper berries, crushed (optional)
⅛   teaspoon ground cloves
⅛   teaspoon pepper
1   bay leaf
¾   cup water
½   cup dry white wine
1   teaspoon instant chicken bouillon granules
4   medium potatoes, quartered
4   medium smoked pork chops (about 2 pounds)
4   fully cooked knackwurst, diagonally scored

1 In a 12-inch skillet cook bacon and chopped onion till bacon is crisp and onion is tender. Drain off fat. Stir the sauerkraut, carrots, parsley, sugar, juniper berries, cloves, pepper, and bay leaf into mixture in skillet.
2 Stir in water, wine, and bouillon granules. Bring to boiling. Reduce heat; cover and simmer for 10 minutes. Add potatoes, pushing them into the sauerkraut. Cover and simmer for 20 minutes.
3 Top with the pork chops and knackwurst. Cover and simmer 20 minutes more. To serve, discard bay leaf. Arrange sauerkraut mixture and potatoes on a serving platter. Top with chops and knackwurst. Makes 8 servings.

Choucroute Garni

APRICOT-HAM LOGS

If you can't purchase ham that's already ground, ask your butcher to grind it for you. Or, grind leftover ham using a food processor or a meat grinder—

Assembling time: 10 minutes
Cooking time: 45 minutes

  2 **beaten eggs**
  ⅓ **cup milk**
1½ **cups soft bread crumbs (2 slices)**
  1 **12-ounce can apricot cake and pastry filling**
  1 **teaspoon minced dried onion**
  1 **teaspoon dried parsley flakes**
    Dash pepper
  1 **pound ground fully cooked ham**
  1 **pound ground pork**
  2 **tablespoons brown sugar**
  2 **tablespoons vinegar**
  2 **tablespoons water**

1 In a mixing bowl combine the eggs and milk. Stir in soft bread crumbs, ½ cup of the apricot filling, the onion, dried parsley, and pepper. Add ground ham and ground pork; mix well.

2 Shape the ground meat mixture into 8 individual meat loaves. Place in a 12×7½×2-inch baking dish. Bake loaves, uncovered, in a 350° oven for 35 minutes. Drain off fat.

3 Combine the remaining apricot filling, brown sugar, vinegar, and water; spoon over meat loaves. Bake for 5 to 10 minutes more. Makes 8 servings.

CREAMY SPINACH LASAGNA

Assembling time: 35 minutes
Cooking time: 35 minutes

  6 **lasagna noodles**
  1 **10-ounce package frozen chopped spinach**
  1 **1-ounce envelope white sauce mix**
1¼ **cups milk**
  2 **tablespoons grated Parmesan cheese**
  1 **beaten egg**
1½ **cups cream-style cottage cheese (12 ounces)**
  4 **ounces boiled ham**
  ½ **cup shredded mozzarella cheese (2 ounces)**

1 Cook the noodles according to package directions; drain. Cook the spinach according to package directions. Drain well, pressing out excess liquid.

2 Prepare the white sauce mix according to package directions, *except* use the 1¼ cups milk. Stir the drained spinach and grated Parmesan cheese into the white sauce. Stir together the beaten egg and cream-style cottage cheese. Cut ham into thin strips.

3 In a 10×6×2-inch baking dish layer *two* of the noodles, trimming as necessary to fit. Spread *half* of the spinach mixture atop. Sprinkle with *half* of the boiled ham strips and spread with *half* of the egg-cottage cheese mixture.

4 Repeat the layers of noodles, spinach mixture, ham, and egg-cottage cheese mixture. Arrange the remaining two noodles atop. Cover and bake in a 350° oven for 30 minutes. Uncover; sprinkle with mozzarella cheese. Bake, uncovered, about 5 minutes more or till the cheese is melted. For easier serving, let stand 10 minutes before cutting. Makes 4 servings.

CHEESY HAM AND POTATO CASSEROLE

Assembling time: 20 minutes
Cooking time: 43 minutes

  1 **pound fully cooked ham**
  1 **cup cream-style cottage-cheese**
  2 **3-ounce packages cream cheese, cut up**
  ½ **teaspoon dried basil, crushed**
  ½ **teaspoon paprika**
1½ **cups frozen loose-pack hash brown potatoes, thawed**
  ½ **cup shredded mozzarella cheese (2 ounces)**
1½ **cups frozen loose-pack hash brown potatoes**
  ½ **cup shredded mozzarella cheese (2 ounces)**

1 Cut the ham into bite-size strips. Set aside. In a mixing bowl stir together cottage cheese, cream cheese, basil, and paprika till well combined.

2 In an ungreased 10×6×2-inch baking dish place 1½ cups hash brown potatoes. Spread cream cheese mixture atop; sprinkle ham evenly over cheese layer.

3 Sprinkle with ½ cup mozzarella cheese. Top with 1½ cups hash brown potatoes. Bake, uncovered, in a 400° oven for 35 to 40 minutes or till heated through. Top with ½ cup mozzarella cheese; return to oven for 2 to 3 minutes or till the cheese is melted. Makes 6 to 8 servings.

LAMB SHANKS A L'ORANGE

Assembling time: 25 minutes
Cooking time: 1½ hours

- 4 lamb shanks (about 4 pounds total)
- 2 tablespoons cooking oil
- 1 cup water
- 2 medium carrots, finely chopped (1 cup)
- 1 medium onion, chopped (½ cup)
- 1½ teaspoons finely shredded orange peel
- 1 teaspoon dried parsley flakes
- 1 teaspoon instant chicken bouillon granules
- ¼ teaspoon salt
- ⅛ teaspoon pepper
- ½ cup dairy sour cream
- 2 tablespoons all-purpose flour
- 2 tablespoons orange juice

1 Sprinkle lamb shanks with a little salt and pepper. In a Dutch oven brown the lamb shanks on all sides in hot cooking oil. Drain off excess fat.

2 Stir together water, carrots, onion, orange peel, dried parsley, bouillon granules, salt, and pepper. Pour over meat in the Dutch oven. Bring to boiling. Reduce heat; cover and simmer about 1½ hours or till the meat is tender.

3 Transfer meat to a warm serving platter; keep warm. Skim fat from pan juices; measure pan juices-vegetable mixture. Return 1½ cups of the mixture to pan.

4 Combine sour cream and flour; stir in orange juice. Stir into the 1½ cups juices-vegetable mixture. Cook and stir till thickened and bubbly. Cook and stir 1 minute more. Pour thickened juices-vegetable mixture over meat. Makes 4 servings.

LAMB WITH TARRAGON SAUCE

Assembling time: 25 minutes
Cooking time: 45 minutes

- 4 lamb shoulder chops, cut ¾ inch thick
- 2 tablespoons cooking oil
- ½ cup water
- ⅓ cup dry white wine
- ½ teaspoon dried tarragon, crushed
- ½ teaspoon instant chicken bouillon granules
- 1 tablespoon cold water
- 2 teaspoons cornstarch
- 1 2½-ounce jar sliced mushrooms, drained
- ¼ cup dairy sour cream

1 In a large skillet brown the lamb chops on both sides in hot cooking oil. Drain off fat. Sprinkle chops with salt and pepper. Stir together the ½ cup water, dry white wine, dried tarragon, and chicken bouillon granules. Pour over lamb chops in skillet.

2 Bring to boiling. Reduce heat; cover and simmer for 40 to 45 minutes or till the lamb chops are tender. Remove chops; keep warm. Skim fat from drippings.

3 Combine the 1 tablespoon cold water and cornstarch. Stir mixture into the hot drippings; stir in drained mushrooms. Cook and stir till mixture is thickened and bubbly. Cook and stir 2 minutes more.

4 Stir about *half* of the hot mixture into the sour cream. Return all to skillet. Heat through; *do not boil*. Pass sour cream mixture with chops. Makes 4 servings.

LAMB-YAM STEW

Assembling time: 15 minutes
Cooking time: 1 hour and 50 minutes

- 1 pound boneless lamb
- 2 tablespoons cooking oil
- 1 medium onion, chopped (½ cup)
- 1 clove garlic, minced
- 1 teaspoon dried oregano, crushed
- 1 teaspoon ground coriander
- ½ teaspoon salt
- ¼ teaspoon ground cumin
- ¼ teaspoon ground ginger
- ¼ teaspoon ground cloves
- ¾ cup water
- 2 tablespoons soy sauce
- 3 medium carrots, thinly sliced (1½ cups)
- 2 medium yams *or* sweet potatoes, peeled and halved
- 1 16-ounce can tomatoes, cut up
- ¼ cup all-purpose flour
- 3 firm medium bananas *or* 2 medium plantains, peeled and cubed

1 Cut the lamb into 1-inch cubes. Brown meat in hot cooking oil. Place the meat in a 2½-quart casserole. Stir in chopped onion, minced garlic, oregano, coriander, salt, cumin, ginger, and cloves. Stir in water and soy sauce.

2 Bake, covered, in a 350° oven for 1 hour. Stir in carrots and yams. Drain tomatoes, reserving juice; stir tomatoes into meat-vegetable mixture. Combine the reserved tomato juice and flour; stir into meat-potato mixture. Bake, covered, for 45 minutes. Stir in plantains; bake about 5 minutes more. Makes 6 servings.

ROAST CHICKEN WITH FILBERT STUFFING

Assembling time: 25 minutes
Cooking time: 2 hours

⅓ cup chopped filberts
1½ cups herb-seasoned stuffing mix
½ cup water
3 tablespoons butter *or* margarine, melted
1 2½- to 3-pound broiler-fryer chicken
Cooking oil
¼ cup honey
2 tablespoons dry sherry
1 tablespoon soy sauce
½ teaspoon ground ginger

1 Place filberts in a pie plate and toast in a 375° oven about 10 minutes, stirring once. Meanwhile, combine stuffing mix, water, and melted butter or margarine, tossing to moisten evenly. Add filberts; toss.

2 Spoon some of the stuffing mixture into neck cavity of chicken. Skewer neck skin to back. Spoon remaining stuffing mixture into body cavity. Tie legs to tail; twist wing tips under back of chicken.

3 Place chicken, breast side up, on a rack in a shallow roasting pan. Brush skin lightly with cooking oil. Insert a meat thermometer in center of inside thigh muscle but not touching bone. Roast, uncovered, in a 375° oven for 1½ hours.

4 Meanwhile, in a bowl combine honey, sherry, soy sauce, and ginger. Baste chicken with some of the honey mixture. Continue roasting 15 to 30 minutes more or till meat thermometer registers 185° and drumstick moves easily in socket, brushing occasionally with remaining honey mixture. Makes 6 servings.

TARRAGON ROAST CHICKEN

Assembling time: 20 minutes
Cooking time: 1½ hours

2 tablespoons butter *or* margarine, melted
1 tablespoon dry white wine
1 teaspoon dried tarragon, crushed, *or* 1 tablespoon snipped fresh tarragon
½ teaspoon salt
⅛ teaspoon pepper
1 2½- to 3-pound broiler-fryer chicken
2 egg yolks
1 tablespoon vinegar
⅓ cup tomato sauce
¼ cup butter *or* margarine
1 tablespoon snipped parsley

1 Combine the 2 tablespoons melted butter or margarine, dry white wine, tarragon, salt, and pepper. Thoroughly brush chicken inside and out with butter mixture.

2 Skewer neck skin to back. Tie legs to tail; twist wing tips under back. Place chicken, breast side up, on a rack in a shallow roasting pan. Insert a meat thermometer in center of inside thigh muscle but not touching bone.

3 Roast, uncovered, in a 375° oven for 1¼ to 1½ hours or till meat thermometer registers 185° and drumstick moves easily in socket. Baste with pan drippings.

4 Shortly before serving, prepare sauce. In a blender container place egg yolks and vinegar. Cover and quickly turn blender on and off. In a small saucepan bring tomato sauce and the ¼ cup butter or margarine to boiling. With blender lid ajar and blender running on high speed, *slowly* pour in butter mixture, blending about 30 seconds or till thick and fluffy.

5 Return sauce mixture to saucepan; stir in parsley, if desired. Heat through over low heat, stirring constantly. *Do not boil.* Place chicken on a serving platter; serve with sauce. Makes 6 servings.

CURRY ROAST CHICKEN

Assembling time: 18 minutes
Cooking time: 2½ hours

1 medium onion, chopped (½ cup)
1 stalk celery, chopped (½ cup)
1 teaspoon curry powder
¼ cup butter *or* margarine
5 cups plain croutons
⅓ cup chopped cashews
⅓ cup raisins
½ teaspoon salt
¼ teaspoon pepper
1 cup chicken broth
1 4- to 5-pound whole roasting chicken
Salt
Cooking oil

1 In a skillet cook onion, celery, and curry powder in butter or margarine till onion and celery are tender but not brown. In a large mixing bowl combine croutons, cashews, raisins, the ½ teaspoon salt, pepper, and onion mixture. Drizzle with chicken broth; toss crouton mixture lightly.

2 Sprinkle neck and body cavities of chicken with salt; stuff loosely with crouton mixture. Skewer neck skin to back. Tie legs to tail; twist wing tips under back.

3 Place chicken, breast side up, on a rack in a shallow roasting pan. Brush chicken skin with cooking oil. Insert a meat thermometer in center of inside thigh muscle but not touching bone.

4 Roast chicken in a 375° oven for 2 to 2½ hours or till meat thermometer registers 185° and drumstick moves easily in socket. Baste occasionally with pan drippings. Makes 6 servings.

QUICK CHICKEN FRICASSEE

Assembling time: 20 minutes
Cooking time: 35 minutes

¼ cup all-purpose flour
¾ teaspoon dried thyme,
  crushed
½ teaspoon salt
⅛ teaspoon pepper
1 2½- to 3-pound broiler-fryer
  chicken, cut up
2 tablespoons cooking oil
½ cup hot water
½ teaspoon instant chicken bouillon
  granules
1 8-ounce package frozen peas and
  potatoes with cream sauce
⅔ cup milk

1 In a paper or plastic bag combine flour, thyme, salt, and pepper. Add 2 or 3 chicken pieces at a time; shake to coat. In a large skillet brown chicken in hot oil over medium heat about 15 minutes, turning as necessary to brown evenly.

2 Stir together hot water and instant chicken bouillon granules; pour bouillon mixture over chicken. Cover and cook over low heat about 30 minutes or till chicken is tender. Transfer chicken to a serving platter; keep warm.

3 Add peas and potatoes with cream sauce and milk to the bouillon mixture in the skillet. Cook and stir till vegetables are thawed and bouillon mixture comes to boiling. Cover and cook for 1 minute more. Spoon vegetable mixture over warm chicken on serving platter. Makes 6 servings.

EASY OVEN-FRIED CHICKEN

Assembling time: 10 minutes
Cooking time: 1 hour

1 2½- to 3-pound broiler-fryer
  chicken, cut up, *or* 3 whole
  medium chicken breasts,
  halved lengthwise
  Cheesy Biscuit Coating *or*
  Herbed Potato Coating

1 Rinse chicken; roll pieces in choice of coating. Place, skin side up, in an ungreased 15×10×1-inch baking pan. Bake in 375° oven 50 to 60 minutes. Serves 6.

Cheesy Biscuit Coating: Combine 1 cup *packaged biscuit mix*, ¼ cup grated *Parmesan cheese*, 2 teaspoons *paprika*, and 1 teaspoon *onion salt*.

Herbed Potato Coating: Combine 1 cup dry *packaged instant mashed potatoes*; 1 teaspoon *paprika*; ½ teaspoon *salt*; ½ teaspoon dried *tarragon*, crushed; and ⅛ teaspoon *pepper*.

CORN BREAD-COATED CHICKEN

Assembling time: 10 minutes
Cooking time: 1 hour

1 8-ounce package corn bread
  stuffing mix
¼ cup butter *or* margarine, melted
1 10¾-ounce can condensed
  cream of chicken soup
⅓ cup milk
1 2½- to 3-pound broiler-fryer
  chicken, cut up

1 In a large bowl combine stuffing mix and melted butter. Mix soup and milk. Dip chicken into soup mixture, then into stuffing, pressing to coat. Place in an ungreased 15×10×1-inch baking pan. Bake in a 375° oven about 1 hour. Serves 6.

CHICKEN WITH WINE-VEGETABLE SAUCE

Use any blend of frozen mixed vegetables in this flavorful sauce over chicken—

Assembling time: 5 minutes
Cooking time: 1 hour

1 2½- to 3-pound broiler-fryer
  chicken, cut up
½ of a 20-ounce package (2 cups)
  frozen loose-pack cauliflower,
  broccoli, and carrots
1 10¾-ounce can condensed
  cream of chicken soup
⅓ cup dry white wine
1 tablespoon minced dried onion
1 tablespoon all-purpose flour
¼ teaspoon dried tarragon, crushed
  Hot cooked noodles

1 Arrange chicken in a 13×9×2-inch baking pan. Bake in a 350° oven for 30 minutes; drain. In a colander run hot water over frozen vegetables to partially thaw. Combine soup, wine, dried onion, flour, and tarragon. Stir in partially thawed vegetables. Pour over chicken.

2 Bake, uncovered, in a 350° oven about 30 minutes or till chicken is done. Arrange chicken on a serving platter. Spoon vegetable mixture over chicken. Serve with hot cooked noodles. Makes 6 servings.

ITALIAN CHICKEN DINNER

The flavor combination in this one-skillet meal is sensational—

Assembling time: 20 minutes
Cooking time: 45 minutes

1 2½- to 3-pound broiler-fryer chicken, cut up
2 tablespoons cooking oil
½ medium head cabbage, cut into 6 wedges
1 3-ounce can sliced mushrooms, drained
1 8-ounce can tomato sauce
1 small green pepper, chopped (½ cup)
1 small onion, chopped (¼ cup)
1 teaspoon dried oregano, crushed
¾ teaspoon garlic salt
1 4-ounce package (1 cup) shredded mozzarella cheese

1 In a 12-inch skillet brown chicken in hot cooking oil over medium heat about 15 minutes, turning as necessary to brown evenly. Drain off fat.

2 Place cabbage wedges and drained mushrooms around chicken. Combine tomato sauce, chopped green pepper, chopped onion, dried oregano, and garlic salt; pour around chicken.

3 Bring mixture to boiling; reduce heat. Cover and simmer for 35 to 40 minutes or till chicken is tender. Spoon off fat. Sprinkle cheese over all. Cover and cook about 2 minutes more or till cheese is melted. Makes 6 servings.

Italian Chicken Dinner

BAKED CHICKEN AND LENTILS

Assembling time: 15 minutes
Cooking time: 2¼ hours

1 large onion, chopped (1 cup)
1 cup dry lentils (8 ounces)
1 tablespoon instant chicken bouillon granules
2 bay leaves
½ teaspoon poultry seasoning
⅛ teaspoon pepper
2 cups boiling water
½ of an 8-ounce package brown-and-serve sausage links, sliced
½ of a 20-ounce package (2 cups) frozen crinkle-cut carrots
1 2½- to 3-pound broiler-fryer chicken, cut up
Salt
Pepper
Paprika

1 In a 3-quart casserole combine the onion, lentils, chicken bouillon granules, bay leaves, poultry seasoning, and pepper. Add boiling water; stir to mix. Cover and bake in a 350° oven for 45 minutes.

2 Stir in sliced sausage links and frozen carrots. Arrange chicken pieces atop lentil mixture. Sprinkle chicken with a little salt, pepper, and paprika. Bake, covered, in a 350° oven about 1½ hours or till chicken is tender. Remove bay leaves before serving. Makes 6 servings.

CHICKEN STEW WITH DOUBLE CORN DUMPLINGS

You don't have to brown the chicken for this hearty home-style stew—

Assembling time: 20 minutes
Cooking time: 55 minutes

3 cups water
1 envelope *regular* onion-mushroom soup mix
1 2½- to 3-pound broiler-fryer chicken, cut up
2 medium carrots, thinly sliced
2 tablespoons snipped parsley
½ teaspoon dried sage, crushed
1 beaten egg
1 8-ounce can whole kernel corn, drained
¼ cup milk
1 8½-ounce package corn muffin mix

1 In a large saucepan or Dutch oven stir together the water and dry soup mix. Add chicken pieces. Bring mixture to boiling; reduce heat. Cover and simmer mixture for 25 minutes. Stir in sliced carrots, snipped parsley, and dried sage. Cover and simmer mixture about 20 minutes more or till chicken is almost tender.

2 In a mixing bowl combine egg, drained whole kernel corn, and milk. Add corn muffin mix; stir just till combined. Drop dough into 6 mounds atop simmering mixture. Cover and simmer about 10 minutes more or till chicken and dumplings are done. Makes 6 servings.

SKILLET CHICKEN AND RICE

Assembling time: 25 minutes
Cooking time: 40 minutes

1 2½- to 3-pound broiler-fryer
 chicken, cut up
2 tablespoons cooking oil
¾ cup long grain rice
1 medium onion, chopped (½ cup)
4 medium carrots, bias-sliced into
 ½-inch-thick pieces (2 cups)
1¼ cups water
1 6-ounce can sliced mushrooms
1 tablespoon dried parsley flakes
2 teaspoons salt
1 teaspoon Italian seasoning,
 crushed
 Salt
 Pepper
 Italian seasoning, crushed

1 In a 12-inch skillet brown chicken in hot oil over medium heat about 15 minutes, turning as necessary to brown evenly. Remove chicken pieces. Drain all but 2 tablespoons fat from skillet.

2 Add rice and chopped onion to skillet. Cook and stir over medium heat till rice is light brown. Stir in sliced carrots, water, *undrained* mushrooms, parsley flakes, the 2 teaspoons salt, and the 1 teaspoon Italian seasoning.

3 Place chicken pieces atop rice mixture. Season chicken with additional salt and pepper. Sprinkle lightly with additional crushed Italian seasoning. Cover and simmer about 40 minutes or till chicken and rice are done. Skim off fat, if necessary. Makes 6 servings.

LAZY PAELLA

Assembling time: 20 minutes
Cooking time: 1 hour and 10 minutes

1 2½- to 3-pound broiler-fryer
 chicken, cut up
2 tablespoons cooking oil
1 6-ounce package saffron rice mix
1 cup water
1 8-ounce can stewed tomatoes
¾ cup frozen peas
1 3-ounce can sliced mushrooms
1 small onion, cut into wedges
1 8-ounce package frozen peeled
 and deveined shrimp
 Paprika

1 In a large skillet brown chicken pieces in hot oil over medium heat about 15 minutes, turning as necessary to brown evenly. Season to taste with salt and pepper, if desired. In a 13×9×2-inch baking dish combine rice mix, water, *undrained* stewed tomatoes, frozen peas, *undrained* mushrooms, and onion. Rinse shrimp; stir into rice mixture.

2 Arrange chicken pieces atop; sprinkle with paprika. Cover tightly with foil. Bake in a 350° oven for 60 to 70 minutes or till done. Makes 6 servings.

COOK WITH FROZEN CHICKEN

If you wrap chicken pieces individually before freezing, you won't need to thaw them before cooking. Just run the pieces under cold water several minutes, then remove wrap. For skillet dishes, brown chicken 5 minutes longer, then finish cooking. For oven dishes, bake an extra 15 to 20 minutes.

SAUCY CHICKEN AND VEGETABLES

Assembling time: 12 minutes
Cooking time: 1 hour and 5 minutes

1 2½- to 3-pound broiler-fryer
 chicken, cut up
1 6-ounce can (¾ cup) hot-style
 tomato juice
1 tablespoon wine vinegar
¾ teaspoon dried oregano, crushed
½ teaspoon garlic salt
¼ teaspoon salt
⅛ teaspoon pepper
6 stalks celery, sliced (3 cups)
2 cups sliced fresh mushrooms
 (5 ounces)
1 tablespoon cold water
1 tablespoon cornstarch

1 In a 12-inch skillet arrange chicken pieces. Combine tomato juice, wine vinegar, oregano, garlic salt, salt, and pepper; pour over chicken. Add celery and mushrooms.

2 Bring to boiling; reduce heat. Cover and simmer for 50 to 60 minutes or till chicken is tender. Remove chicken and vegetables to a serving platter; keep warm.

3 Skim fat from pan juices. Measure 1 cup pan juices; return to the skillet. Combine water and cornstarch; stir into pan juices in the skillet. Cook and stir till thickened and bubbly; cook and stir 2 minutes more. Spoon over chicken and vegetables. Makes 6 servings.

TANGY CURRIED CHICKEN

Assembling time: 10 minutes
Cooking time: 65 minutes

1 8-ounce can tomato sauce
1 tablespoon curry powder
1 tablespoon dried parsley
   flakes
1 teaspoon sugar
½ teaspoon salt
½ teaspoon onion powder
½ teaspoon ground ginger
¼ teaspoon pepper
1 2½- to 3-pound broiler-fryer
   chicken, cut up
   Hot cooked noodles *or* rice
1 8-ounce carton plain yogurt
2 tablespoons all-purpose flour
½ cup chopped peanuts

1 In a 10-inch skillet combine tomato sauce, curry powder, dried parsley flakes, sugar, salt, onion powder, ground ginger, and pepper.

2 Add chicken pieces to skillet, turning once to coat. Bring to boiling; reduce heat. Cover and simmer for 50 to 60 minutes or till chicken is tender.

3 Place hot cooked noodles or rice on a warm platter; top with chicken pieces. Keep warm. Remove tomato mixture from skillet. Skim fat. Add water, if necessary, to make 1 cup; return to skillet.

4 Stir together yogurt and flour; stir yogurt mixture into tomato mixture in skillet. Cook and stir till mixture is thickened and bubbly. Cook and stir 1 minute more. Spoon some of the yogurt mixture atop chicken pieces; sprinkle with chopped peanuts. Pass remaining yogurt mixture. Makes 6 servings.

SAFFRON CHICKEN

Toast the almonds while the chicken cooks. Spread them in a shallow pan, sprinkle with cooking oil, and bake at 300° for 15 to 20 minutes, stirring frequently. Or, toast in a skillet over low heat—

Assembling time: 12 minutes
Cooking time: 1 hour and 5 minutes

2 tablespoons olive oil *or* cooking
   oil
2 large onions, very thinly sliced
   (2 cups)
¾ teaspoon salt
¼ teaspoon pepper
¼ teaspoon thread saffron,
   crushed
⅛ teaspoon ground red pepper
1 2½- to 3-pound broiler-fryer
   chicken, cut up
½ cup raisins
½ cup blanched whole almonds,
   toasted
1 tablespoon lemon juice

1 In a heavy 4-quart saucepan or Dutch oven heat cooking oil. Stir in thinly sliced onions, salt, pepper, crushed saffron, and ground red pepper.

2 Add chicken, turning to coat with onion mixture. Cover and simmer for 50 to 60 minutes or till tender, turning chicken occasionally.

3 Remove chicken to a warm serving platter; keep warm. Skim fat from pan juices; boil pan juices rapidly about 2 minutes or till reduced to a moderately thick sauce. Stir in raisins, toasted almonds, and lemon juice; heat through. Spoon over chicken. Makes 6 servings.

WAIKIKI CHICKEN

Assembling time: 20 minutes
Cooking time: 40 minutes

¼ cup all-purpose flour
½ teaspoon salt
1 2½- to 3-pound broiler-fryer
   chicken, cut up
2 tablespoons cooking oil
1 8-ounce can crushed pineapple
½ cup bottled barbecue sauce
1 tablespoon cornstarch
1 tablespoon brown sugar
½ teaspoon dry mustard
1 medium green pepper, seeded
   and cut into rings
   Hot cooked rice (optional)

1 In a paper or plastic bag combine flour and salt. Add 2 or 3 chicken pieces at a time; shake to coat. In a large skillet cook chicken pieces in hot cooking oil over medium heat about 15 minutes, turning as necessary to brown evenly.

2 Meanwhile, combine *undrained* pineapple, barbecue sauce, cornstarch, brown sugar, and dry mustard. Pour mixture over chicken pieces in skillet.

3 Cover and cook over low heat for 35 to 40 minutes or till tender, turning once. Arrange on a serving platter; garnish with green pepper rings. Serve with hot cooked rice, if desired. Makes 6 servings.

PEACHY SKILLET DINNER

Assembling time: 20 minutes
Cooking time: 45 minutes

- 1 2½- to 3-pound broiler-fryer chicken, cut up
- 2 tablespoons cooking oil
- 1 teaspoon finely shredded orange peel
- 1 cup orange juice
- 1 small onion, chopped (¼ cup)
- 1 teaspoon salt
- ½ teaspoon dry mustard
- ¼ teaspoon pepper
- ¼ teaspoon paprika
- 1 9-ounce package frozen cut green beans
- 1 17-ounce can sweet potatoes, drained
- 1 16-ounce can peach slices, drained
  Orange juice *or* water
- 1 tablespoon cold water
- 2 teaspoons cornstarch

1 In a 12-inch skillet or Dutch oven brown chicken in hot oil over medium heat about 15 minutes, turning as necessary to brown evenly. Combine orange peel, 1 cup orange juice, onion, salt, dry mustard, pepper, and paprika; pour over chicken. Cover and simmer for 20 minutes.

2 Push chicken to one side of the skillet. Add frozen green beans. Bring to boiling; reduce heat. Cover and cook for 10 minutes. Arrange sweet potatoes and peaches around chicken. Cover and cook 10 minutes more.

3 Remove chicken, peaches, and vegetables to a serving platter; keep warm. Pour pan juices into measuring cup; skim off fat. Add additional orange juice or water to make 1 cup liquid. Return to the skillet.

4 Combine the 1 tablespoon cold water and the cornstarch; stir into liquid in the skillet. Cook and stir till mixture is thickened and bubbly; cook and stir 2 minutes more. Serve over all on platter. Serves 6.

NO-PEEK CHICKEN

Assembling time: 12 minutes
Cooking time: 55 minutes

- ⅓ cup long grain rice
- 1 small onion, chopped (¼ cup)
- 2 tablespoons chopped pimiento
- 4 chicken drumsticks *or* thighs, *or* 2 of each (1 to 1¼ pounds)
- 1 7½-ounce can semi-condensed cream of mushroom soup
- ¼ cup dairy sour cream
- ¼ cup dry white wine *or* water
- ¼ cup water
- 1 teaspoon instant chicken bouillon granules
- ¼ teaspoon poultry seasoning
- ¼ cup fine dry bread crumbs
- 1 tablespoon butter *or* margarine, melted
- ¼ teaspoon paprika

1 In an 8 × 1½-inch round baking dish combine rice, onion, and chopped pimiento. Place chicken pieces atop. Stir together soup and sour cream; stir in wine, water, chicken bouillon granules, and poultry seasoning. Pour soup mixture over chicken; cover tightly. Bake in a 375° oven for 45 minutes.

2 Combine bread crumbs, melted butter or margarine, and paprika; sprinkle over chicken and rice. Bake, uncovered, about 10 minutes more. Makes 2 servings.

CHICKEN-CLAM POT PIE

An attractive dinner dish that gives you the flavors of a clambake without the work—

Assembling time: 20 minutes
Cooking time: 42 minutes

- 6 chicken thighs (2 pounds)
- 3 tablespoons cooking oil
- 1 10-ounce can whole baby clams Milk
- 1 10-ounce package frozen peas and carrots
- ¼ cup all-purpose flour
- ½ teaspoon salt
- ½ teaspoon poultry seasoning
- 1 8-ounce can stewed onions, drained
- 1 package (6) refrigerated biscuits Sesame seed

1 Skin chicken thighs, if desired. In a 10-inch oven-going skillet brown chicken thighs in hot oil over medium heat about 15 minutes, turning as necessary to brown evenly. Remove and set aside. Drain all but about 3 tablespoons fat from skillet.

2 Meanwhile, drain clams, reserving juice; add enough milk to reserved juice to make 2 cups liquid. Break up frozen peas and carrots to separate.

3 Stir flour, salt, and poultry seasoning into pan drippings in skillet. Add milk mixture all at once. Cook and stir till thickened and bubbly.

4 Stir in clams, peas and carrots, and drained onions; add chicken thighs. Return to boiling. Cover and cook for 10 minutes. Leave mixture in skillet or transfer to a 10 × 6 × 2-inch baking dish.

5 Place biscuits atop hot mixture; sprinkle generously with sesame seed. Bake in a 400° oven for 18 to 20 minutes or till biscuits are brown. Makes 6 servings.

ROMAN-STYLE CHICKEN

Peel and chop the tomatoes and onion while browning the chicken—

Assembling time: 25 minutes
Cooking time: 50 minutes

¼ cup all-purpose flour
½ teaspoon salt
  Dash pepper
2 whole medium chicken breasts
  (1½ pounds)
2 tablespoons butter *or* margarine
1 medium onion, chopped (½ cup)
1 clove garlic, minced
⅓ cup dry white wine
1 tablespoon cornstarch
2 medium tomatoes, peeled and
  chopped (1½ cups)
1 2½-ounce package very thinly
  sliced ham, cut into julienne
  strips (½ cup)
¼ teaspoon dried rosemary, crushed

1 In a plastic or paper bag combine flour, salt, and pepper. Remove skin from chicken breasts; cut breasts in half lengthwise. Add 2 chicken breast halves at a time to flour mixture in the bag; shake to coat.

2 In a large skillet cook chicken in butter or margarine over medium heat about 10 minutes or till brown on both sides. Remove chicken to a 12×7½×2-inch baking dish. Add onion and garlic to skillet; cook till onion is tender but not brown.

3 Combine wine and cornstarch; stir into onion mixture. Stir in tomatoes, ham, and rosemary. Pour over chicken. Bake, covered, in a 350° oven for 30 minutes. Uncover and bake about 20 minutes more. Makes 4 servings.

ORANGE-CURRY CHICKEN

Assembling time: 10 minutes
Cooking time: 1 hour and 5 minutes

1 16-ounce can sliced potatoes
¼ cup raisins
4 chicken thighs *or* legs
  (1 to 1¼ pounds)
2 tablespoons frozen orange juice
  concentrate
1 to 1½ teaspoons curry powder
1 teaspoon minced dried onion
½ teaspoon salt
  Paprika

1 Drain potatoes, reserving ⅓ cup of the liquid. Place drained potato slices and raisins in a 10×6×2-inch baking dish. Arrange chicken atop the potato mixture.

2 Combine the ⅓ cup reserved potato liquid, orange juice concentrate, curry powder, onion, and salt; pour over all. Cover and bake in a 350° oven for 50 minutes. Uncover and bake for 10 to 15 minutes more or till chicken is tender. Sprinkle with paprika. Makes 2 servings.

CHICKEN TO SUIT YOUR TASTE

If your family prefers white meat over dark meat (or vice versa), don't let that stop you from making a recipe that calls for a whole chicken, cut up, or the wrong type of chicken pieces. Simply substitute an equal weight of the chicken pieces you prefer for the ones specified in the recipe. Don't, however, substitute pieces in recipes that call for stuffed or rolled chicken breasts.

CREAMY CHICKEN AND BROWN RICE SOUP

Assembling time: 12 minutes
Cooking time: 45 minutes

2 cups water
¼ cup regular brown rice
1½ teaspoons instant chicken bouillon
  granules
¾ teaspoon dried marjoram, crushed
1 whole large chicken breast
  (¾ pound)
1 stalk celery, sliced (½ cup)
1 small onion, chopped (¼ cup)
1 cup frozen peas
1 cup milk
1 3-ounce package cream cheese,
  cut up
2 tablespoons chopped pimiento

1 In a medium saucepan combine water, rice, chicken bouillon granules, and marjoram. Add chicken breast. Bring to boiling; reduce heat. Cover and simmer about 25 minutes or till chicken is tender. Remove chicken; allow chicken to cool slightly.

2 Skim fat from bouillon mixture. Add sliced celery and chopped onion. Cover and cook about 10 minutes or till celery and onion are tender.

3 Meanwhile, remove and discard chicken skin and bones; cut meat into short strips. Add chicken strips, peas, milk, cream cheese, and chopped pimiento to vegetable mixture. Cook and stir for 5 to 10 minutes or till cream cheese melts and mixture is heated through. Makes 4 servings.

CORNISH HENS WITH FRUITED RICE

If you want to stuff the hens with the rice mixture, use 4 whole hens and omit the water from the rice mixture. Brush hens with oil. Cover and bake 30 minutes; uncover and bake 1 hour more—

Assembling time: 15 minutes
Cooking time: 1 hour

1 11-ounce can fried rice
1 8¾-ounce can unpeeled apricot
   halves, drained and cut up
1 8¼-ounce can crushed pineapple,
   drained
⅓ cup chopped water chestnuts
¼ cup water
¼ teaspoon ground ginger
3 1- to 1½-pound Cornish game
   hens
   Salt
   Paprika

1 In a mixing bowl combine fried rice, cut-up apricots, crushed pineapple, water chestnuts, water, and ground ginger. Turn into a 1-quart casserole.

2 Cut Cornish game hens in half lengthwise. Place hen halves, cut side down, on a rack in a shallow roasting pan. Sprinkle with salt and paprika.

3 Bake birds, uncovered, and casserole, covered, in a 375° oven for 50 to 60 minutes or till hens are tender and rice mixture is heated through. Makes 6 servings.

POULET AUX FINES HERBES

"Fines herbes" is an herb blend usually consisting of parsley, chervil, chives, and tarragon—

Assembling time: 30 minutes
Cooking time: 45 minutes

4 whole large chicken breasts
¼ cup butter or margarine, softened
1 teaspoon dried parsley flakes
¼ teaspoon dried oregano, crushed
¼ teaspoon dried fines herbes,
   crushed
¼ teaspoon dried marjoram, crushed
2 ounces Monterey Jack cheese, cut
   into 8 strips
½ cup fine dry bread crumbs
¼ cup dry white wine
   Hot cooked noodles

1 Remove skin from chicken breasts; cut breasts in half lengthwise and remove bones. Place each half between 2 pieces of clear plastic wrap; pound with a meat mallet to flatten; remove wrap.

2 In a small bowl combine butter or margarine, parsley flakes, oregano, fines herbes, and marjoram. Using *half* of the herb-butter mixture, dot some on each piece of chicken. Place a strip of cheese on each and roll up tightly, tucking in ends.

3 Melt the remaining herb-butter mixture. Brush over chicken rolls; roll chicken in bread crumbs to coat. Place rolls, seam side down, in a 12×7½×2-inch baking dish. Bake, uncovered, in 350° oven 20 minutes.

4 Pour the wine into the baking dish around chicken. Drizzle any remaining melted herb-butter mixture over chicken. Bake, uncovered, for 20 to 25 minutes more or till chicken is tender and golden brown.

5 Drain chicken, reserving juices. Serve chicken over hot cooked noodles. Pass reserved juices with chicken. Serves 8.

BARBECUE TURKEY DINNER

This dish is easy and mess-free, because the turkey cooks in a sweet, mild barbecue sauce inside an oven roasting bag—

Assembling time: 10 minutes
Cooking time: 1¾ hours

1 teaspoon all-purpose flour
1 1-pound frozen turkey thigh or leg
2 medium potatoes, peeled and
   quartered
2 medium onions, peeled and cut
   into thin wedges
½ cup hot-style catsup
2 tablespoons water
½ teaspoon celery seed
¼ teaspoon garlic salt

1 Place 1 teaspoon flour in an oven roasting bag; shake to coat inside. Place bag in a 13×9×2-inch baking pan. Arrange frozen turkey thigh or leg, quartered potatoes, and onion wedges in bag.

2 Stir together catsup, water, celery seed, and garlic salt; pour over turkey and vegetables. Close bag; fasten with a twist tie. Cut three or four 1-inch slits in top of roasting bag.

3 Bake in a 375° oven 1½ to 1¾ hours or till turkey is tender. Remove turkey thigh and vegetables to a serving platter. Spoon catsup mixture over turkey and vegetables. Makes 2 servings.

Poulet Aux Fines Herbes

CHEESY CHICKEN CASSEROLE

Serve this easy-to-make casserole with green beans, crusty breadsticks, and a quick fruit salad—

Assembling time: 20 minutes
Cooking time: 32 minutes

- 4 ounces curly noodles
- 1 10¾-ounce can condensed cream of chicken soup
- ½ cup milk
- 1 cup cream-style cottage cheese
- 1 5-ounce can chunk-style chicken *or* ¾ cup chopped cooked chicken
- ½ cup shredded American cheese (2 ounces)
- ½ teaspoon dried tarragon, basil, *or* thyme, crushed

1 Cook noodles in boiling salted water according to package directions; drain. Meanwhile, in a large bowl combine cream of chicken soup and milk. Stir in cottage cheese, *undrained* chunk-style chicken or chopped chicken, *half* of the American cheese, desired herb, and cooked noodles.

2 Turn chicken-noodle mixture into an ungreased 1½-quart casserole. Cover and bake in a 350° oven for 25 to 30 minutes or till heated through. Uncover and sprinkle with remaining American cheese. Bake for 1 or 2 minutes more or till cheese is melted. Makes 4 servings.

CHICKEN, HAM, AND BROCCOLI LASAGNA

Assembling time: 40 minutes
Cooking time: 35 minutes

- 4 ounces lasagna noodles
- 1 10-ounce package frozen cut broccoli
- 3 tablespoons butter *or* margarine
- 3 tablespoons all-purpose flour
- 2 teaspoons minced dried onion
  Dash garlic powder
  Dash pepper
- 1½ cups milk
- 1 3-ounce can chopped mushrooms, drained
- 2 tablespoons grated Parmesan cheese
- 1 2½-ounce package very thinly sliced chicken, cut into strips
- 3 ounces sliced *or* shredded mozzarella cheese
- 1 2½-ounce package very thinly sliced ham, cut into strips
- 2 tablespoons grated Parmesan cheese

1 Cook noodles according to package directions; drain. In a colander run hot water over broccoli to separate. For sauce, in a saucepan melt butter or margarine; stir in flour, onion, garlic powder, and pepper. Add milk all at once; cook and stir till thickened and bubbly. Stir in mushrooms and 2 tablespoons Parmesan cheese.

2 In a greased 9×9×2-inch baking pan layer *half* of the cooked noodles (cut to fit, if necessary), *all* of the broccoli, the chicken strips, and mozzarella cheese, and *about ⅔* of the sauce. Top with ham strips, remaining cooked noodles, and the remaining sauce. Sprinkle with the 2 tablespoons Parmesan cheese.

3 Bake, uncovered, in a 350° oven about 35 minutes or till heated through. Let stand 10 minutes before cutting and serving. Makes 6 servings.

CHICKEN QUICHE

Assembling time: 28 minutes
Cooking time: 50 minutes

- 1 9-inch frozen unbaked deep-dish pastry shell
- 3 eggs
- 1½ cups milk
- 1 tablespoon all-purpose flour
- 1 tablespoon minced dried onion
- 1 teaspoon dried parsley flakes
- ¾ teaspoon dried basil, crushed
- ½ teaspoon salt
- ¼ teaspoon dry mustard
  Dash pepper
- 1 cup shredded Swiss cheese (4 ounces)
- 1 5-ounce can chunk-style chicken, drained and chopped, *or* ¾ cup chopped cooked chicken

1 Place unpricked pastry shell on a preheated baking sheet in a 450° oven. Bake at 450° for 6 minutes. Remove from oven; reduce oven to 325°.

2 Meanwhile, in a bowl beat together eggs, milk, flour, minced dried onion, parsley flakes, basil, salt, dry mustard, and pepper. Sprinkle cheese and chicken evenly over the partially baked pastry shell; pour egg mixture over all.

3 Bake in a 325° oven about 50 minutes or till knife inserted near center comes out clean. Let stand 10 minutes before serving. Makes 6 servings.

CHICKEN ENCHILADA BAKE

Assembling time: 15 minutes
Cooking time: 35 minutes

1 12-ounce jar chicken gravy
1 8-ounce carton dairy sour cream
1 4-ounce can chopped green chili
   peppers, drained
2 green onions, sliced
   (2 tablespoons)
   Few dashes bottled hot pepper
   sauce
2 5-ounce cans chunk-style chicken,
   drained and finely chopped, *or*
   1½ cups finely chopped cooked
   chicken
12 6-inch corn tortillas
1 tablespoon all-purpose flour
1 4-ounce package (1 cup) shredded
   cheddar cheese

1 In a bowl combine chicken gravy, sour cream, chili peppers, onions, and hot pepper sauce. In a second bowl combine chopped chicken and *½ cup* of the gravy mixture; spoon about 2 tablespoons onto each tortilla and roll up. Place, seam side down, in an ungreased 13×9×2-inch baking dish.

2 Stir flour into remaining gravy mixture; pour atop rolled tortillas. Cover with foil. Bake in a 350° oven about 30 minutes or till heated through.

3 Remove foil; sprinkle shredded cheddar cheese atop tortillas and sauce. Bake, uncovered, for 3 to 5 minutes more or till cheese is melted. Makes 6 servings.

TURKEY-STUFFING WEDGES

Another time, try these wedges with chunk-style chicken—

Assembling time: 25 minutes
Cooking time: 40 minutes

1 medium onion, chopped (½ cup)
¼ cup butter *or* margarine
½ of a 10-ounce package (1 cup)
   frozen peas and carrots
3 eggs
1⅓ cups milk
1 6¾-ounce can chunk-style turkey,
   cut up, *or* 1 cup chopped
   cooked turkey
½ of a 4-ounce package (½ cup)
   shredded cheddar cheese
1 8-ounce package (2 cups) herb-
   seasoned stuffing mix

1 In a small skillet cook the chopped onion in the butter or margarine till onion is tender but not brown. In a colander run hot water over the frozen peas and carrots to separate; set aside.

2 Meanwhile, in a large bowl beat together the eggs and milk; add peas and carrots, chunk-style or chopped turkey, and shredded cheddar cheese. Stir in the herb-seasoned stuffing mix and cooked onion just till stuffing mix is moistened.

3 Turn turkey-stuffing mixture into an 8×1½-inch round baking dish. Bake in a 350° oven for 35 to 40 minutes. Let mixture stand 5 minutes before cutting into wedges. Makes 6 servings.

SQUASH-CHICKEN CASSEROLE

Squash, peanuts, and seasoned croutons make this recipe a nice change from everyday chicken casseroles—

Assembling time: 20 minutes
Cooking time: 30 minutes

1 12-ounce package frozen mashed
   cooked winter squash
1 stalk celery, sliced (½ cup)
1 medium onion, chopped (½ cup)
1 tablespoon butter *or* margarine
1 teaspoon instant chicken bouillon
   granules
⅛ teaspoon pepper
2 5-ounce cans chunk-style chicken
1 3-ounce can sliced mushrooms,
   drained
¼ cup chopped peanuts *or* cashews
1 cup herb-seasoned croutons

1 In a large saucepan cook squash, celery, and onion in butter or margarine, covered, till squash is thawed and vegetables are tender, stirring frequently. Stir in bouillon granules and pepper.

2 Meanwhile, combine *undrained* chicken, drained mushrooms, and peanuts. Turn into a 10×6×2-inch baking dish. Spread squash mixture over chicken mixture. Top with croutons. Bake, uncovered, in a 350° oven for 25 to 30 minutes or till heated through. Makes 4 servings.

SPANISH BAKED STUFFED FISH

Assembling time: 20 minutes
Cooking time: 60 minutes

1 3-pound fresh *or* frozen dressed
    fish
1½ cups quick-cooking rice
1 8-ounce can stewed tomatoes,
    cut up
1 cup water
1 4-ounce can chopped green chili
    peppers, drained
1 teaspoon instant chicken bouillon
    granules
1 teaspoon chili powder
    Salt
    Pepper
1 tablespoon cooking oil

1 Thaw fish, if frozen. In a saucepan combine rice, *undrained* tomatoes, water, green chili peppers, bouillon granules, and chili powder. Bring to boiling; reduce heat. Cover and simmer for 5 minutes.

2 Rinse the fish and pat dry with paper toweling. Place in a greased large shallow baking pan. Sprinkle the cavity of fish with salt and pepper. Stuff fish loosely with rice mixture. (Spoon the extra rice mixture into a greased small casserole. Cover and bake during the last 20 minutes of fish baking time.)

3 Brush fish with cooking oil. Bake in a 350° oven for 45 to 60 minutes or till fish flakes easily when tested with a fork. Carefully transfer fish to a serving platter. Serve with the extra rice mixture. Serves 6.

FISH FLORENTINE

Assembling time: 20 minutes
Cooking time: 50 minutes

1 16-ounce package frozen fish
    fillets
1 10-ounce package frozen spinach
    soufflé
8 rich round crackers, crushed
    (⅓ cup)
2 tablespoons toasted wheat germ
2 tablespoons grated Parmesan
    cheese

1 Allow frozen fish and spinach soufflé to stand at room temperature for 15 minutes to partially thaw. Cut block of fish crosswise into 8 portions; arrange in an 8×8×2-inch baking dish, allowing 1 inch between pieces of fish.

2 Cut spinach soufflé into 8 portions; place one portion of soufflé atop each piece of fish. Bake, uncovered, in a 400° oven for 15 minutes.

3 Combine crushed crackers, wheat germ, and Parmesan cheese; sprinkle atop spinach and fish. Bake for 30 to 35 minutes more or till fish flakes easily when tested with a fork. Makes 4 servings.

SHORTCUT FOR THAWING FROZEN FISH FILLETS

If you forget to thaw the block of frozen fish fillets for dinner, don't panic. Let it stand at room temperature for 15 minutes, then cut into 1-inch-thick slices or cubes. Let stand 20 minutes if bias-slicing. Cook the fish a few minutes longer than usual, till it flakes easily when tested with a fork.

NUT-CRUSTED FLOUNDER

Try this appealing fish recipe with any kind of white fish fillets that are frozen in block form such as cod, perch, haddock, or sole—

Assembling time: 22 minutes
Cooking time: 30 minutes

1 16-ounce package frozen flounder
    fillets
¼ cup finely chopped cashews *or*
    walnuts
2 tablespoons toasted wheat germ
⅛ teaspoon paprika
3 tablespoons mayonnaise *or* salad
    dressing
1 teaspoon lemon juice
½ teaspoon soy sauce
    Parsley sprigs (optional)

1 Let frozen fish stand at room temperature for 15 minutes. Meanwhile, on waxed paper or in a shallow dish combine chopped cashews or walnuts, wheat germ, and paprika. In a small bowl stir together mayonnaise or salad dressing, lemon juice, and soy sauce.

2 Cut block of fish crosswise into 1-inch slices. Dip slices of fish into mayonnaise mixture; roll in nut mixture to coat. Arrange fish in a greased shallow baking pan. Bake in a 400° oven for 25 to 30 minutes or till fish flakes easily when tested with a fork. Transfer to serving platter; garnish with parsley, if desired. Makes 4 servings.

FISH-POTATO SALAD

Pictured on page 262—

Assembling time: 40 minutes
Chilling time: 30 minutes

1 **pound fresh** *or* **frozen fish fillets**
2 **eggs**
2 **16-ounce cans sliced potatoes,**
   drained, *or* **4 medium potatoes,**
   cooked, peeled, and sliced
1 **cup mayonnaise** *or* **salad dressing**
4 **sprigs parsley**
3 **tablespoons snipped chives** *or*
   sliced green onion tops
6 **pitted green olives**
1 **tablespoon anchovy paste**
1 **tablespoon milk**
½ **teaspoon dry mustard**
   Leaf lettuce

1 If using frozen fish fillets, let stand at room temperature for 20 minutes. Bias-slice the fish into 1-inch-thick slices.

2 Meanwhile, place eggs in a saucepan; cover with cold water. Bring to boiling; reduce heat to just below simmering. Cover and cook for 15 minutes. Run cold water over eggs. Remove shells; chop eggs.

3 In a 10-inch skillet place whole fresh or sliced thawed fish; add boiling water to cover. Cover and simmer for 5 to 8 minutes or till fish flakes easily. With a slotted spatula remove fish from skillet; pat dry with paper toweling. Coarsely break up fish.

4 In a bowl combine eggs and potatoes; set aside. In a blender container or food processor bowl place mayonnaise or salad dressing, parsley, chives or onions, olives, anchovy paste, milk, and mustard. Cover and blend or process till smooth.

5 Gently fold mayonnaise mixture into potato mixture. Add fish; stir gently to coat. Chill for 30 minutes in freezer. Serve on individual lettuce-lined plates. Garnish with tomato slices and snipped chives, if desired. Makes 6 servings.

CURRIED FISH AND CHIP BAKE

Assembling time: 5 minutes
Cooking time: 45 minutes

1 **14-ounce package frozen breaded**
   fish portions
1 **16-ounce package frozen French-**
   fried crinkle-cut potatoes
1 **10¾-ounce can condensed cream**
   of celery soup
¾ **cup milk**
⅓ **cup mayonnaise** *or* **salad dressing**
1 **teaspoon curry powder**

1 Arrange fish in a greased 12×7½×2-inch baking dish; top with potatoes. Combine soup, milk, mayonnaise, and curry; pour over potatoes. Bake, uncovered, in 350° oven about 45 minutes. Serves 4.

MACARONI SEAFOOD SALAD

Assembling time: 25 minutes
Chilling time: 45 minutes

1 **7¼-ounce package macaroni and**
   cheese dinner mix
⅓ **cup mayonnaise** *or* **salad dressing**
⅓ **cup creamy cucumber salad**
   dressing
½ **teaspoon minced dried onion**
1 **6½-ounce can tuna, drained and**
   broken into chunks *or* **two 4½-**
   ounce cans shrimp, drained
1 **medium tomato, chopped**
1 **medium avocado**

1 Prepare dinner mix according to package directions, *except* omit butter. Stir in mayonnaise, cucumber dressing, and onion. Fold in tuna or shrimp and tomato.

2 Cover; chill in freezer for 30 to 45 minutes. Peel, seed, and chop avocado; fold into macaroni mixture. Serve in lettuce-lined bowl, if desired. Serves 3 or 4.

SEAFOOD IN A SPAGHETTI SHELL

If you like, make the crust with fettuccine, linguine, or fusilli in place of the spaghetti—

Assembling time: 35 minutes
Cooking time: 40 minutes

6 **ounces spaghetti**
1 **beaten egg**
⅔ **cup grated Parmesan cheese**
¼ **teaspoon garlic powder**
3 **beaten eggs**
1 **cup evaporated milk**
1 **5½-ounce can crab meat, drained,**
   flaked, and cartilage removed
1 **4½-ounce can tiny shrimp, drained**
2 **green onions, thinly sliced**
   (2 tablespoons)
½ **teaspoon dried dillweed**
   Paprika

1 Cook spaghetti in boiling salted water according to package directions; drain. Meanwhile, in a medium bowl combine the 1 beaten egg, *half* of the Parmesan cheese, and the garlic powder.

2 Add cooked spaghetti to the egg mixture; toss to coat well. Press mixture on bottom and sides of a greased 9-inch pie plate, forming a shell; set aside.

3 In a bowl combine the 3 beaten eggs, evaporated milk, crab meat, shrimp, green onions, dillweed, and remaining Parmesan cheese. Pour mixture into spaghetti shell. Sprinkle lightly with paprika. Cover edges of pie with foil.

4 Bake in a 350° oven for 35 to 40 minutes or till knife inserted just off-center comes out clean (center may seem moist). Remove foil. Let stand 5 minutes before serving. Makes 6 servings.

CHEESY MACARONI AND SALMON PIE

Assembling time: 30 minutes
Cooking time: 35 minutes

1 cup elbow macaroni
1 15½-ounce can salmon
2 eggs
2¼ cups soft bread crumbs (3 slices)
2 green onions, thinly sliced
1 tablespoon lemon juice
¼ teaspoon salt
⅛ teaspoon pepper
¾ cup shredded American cheese
   (3 ounces)
½ cup milk
2 beaten eggs
⅛ teaspoon dried dillweed
1 tablespoon butter *or* margarine,
   melted

1 Cook macaroni in a large amount of boiling salted water for 8 to 10 minutes or just till tender; drain. Meanwhile, drain salmon, reserving 3 tablespoons liquid. Flake salmon, discarding skin and bones.

2 In a mixing bowl beat 2 eggs; stir in *1½ cups* of the soft bread crumbs, the onions, lemon juice, salt, pepper, and the reserved salmon liquid. Add salmon; mix well. Press onto the bottom and sides of a 9-inch pie plate, forming a shell. Set aside.

3 Combine cooked macaroni, cheese, milk, 2 beaten eggs, and dillweed. Turn mixture into the salmon shell. Toss remaining ¾ cup bread crumbs with melted butter; sprinkle over macaroni mixture.

4 Bake, uncovered, in a 350° oven for 30 to 35 minutes or till set. Let stand 5 minutes before serving. Garnish with fresh dill, if desired. To serve, cut into wedges. Makes 6 servings.

Cheesy Macaroni and Salmon Pie
Fish-Potato Salad (see recipe, page 261)

SALMON-VEGETABLE BAKE

Try this family-style casserole with peas or spinach instead of the broccoli—

Assembling time: 12 minutes
Cooking time: 1 hour and 10 minutes

1 10-ounce package frozen chopped
   broccoli
1 10¾-ounce can condensed cream
   of chicken, shrimp, *or* mushroom
   soup
1 8-ounce carton plain yogurt
¼ cup milk
½ teaspoon dried dillweed
1 16-ounce package frozen fried
   potato nuggets
1 15½-ounce can salmon, drained,
   flaked, and skin and bones
   removed

1 In a colander run hot water over frozen broccoli till thawed; drain well. In a medium bowl combine soup, yogurt, milk, and dillweed. Fold in *half* of the frozen potato nuggets and all of the broccoli. Gently fold in flaked salmon.

2 Turn salmon mixture into a 2-quart casserole. Top with remaining frozen potato nuggets. Bake, uncovered, in a 350° oven for 60 to 70 minutes or till heated through. Makes 6 servings.

FLUFFY TUNA-POTATO CASSEROLE

You can use 2 cups leftover mashed potatoes instead of the packaged instant mashed potatoes—

Assembling time: 20 minutes
Cooking time: 50 minutes

Packaged instant mashed
   potatoes (enough for
   4 servings)
1 10-ounce package frozen peas
   and carrots
2 slightly beaten eggs
½ teaspoon dry mustard
   Dash bottled hot pepper
   sauce
1 9¼-ounce can tuna, drained and
   broken into chunks
1 4-ounce package (1 cup) shredded
   cheddar cheese
½ cup corn flakes, crushed

1 Prepare potatoes according to package directions, *except* omit salt. In a colander run hot water over frozen vegetables till separated; drain well.

2 In a bowl combine mashed potatoes, eggs, mustard, and hot pepper sauce; mix well. Spread *half* of the mixture in a 1½-quart casserole. In a second bowl combine tuna, cheese, and the peas and carrots; spoon over potatoes.

3 Spoon remaining potatoes over tuna mixture. Sprinkle crushed corn flakes over top. Bake in a 375° oven for 45 to 50 minutes. Makes 6 servings.

ASPARAGUS SUPREME

Four cups of fresh cut-up asparagus may be substituted for the frozen asparagus—just cook the fresh asparagus in boiling salted water for 5 to 6 minutes or till crisp-tender, drain, and use instead of the cooked frozen asparagus—

Assembling time: 20 minutes
Cooking time: 35 minutes

2 8-ounce packages frozen cut asparagus
1 10¾-ounce can condensed cream of shrimp soup
½ cup dairy sour cream
2 tablespoons coarsely shredded carrot
1 teaspoon minced dried onion
⅛ teaspoon pepper
½ cup herb-seasoned stuffing mix
⅛ teaspoon butter *or* margarine, melted

1 Cook the frozen asparagus according to the package directions. Drain well. In a mixing bowl stir together the cream of shrimp soup, dairy sour cream, shredded carrot, minced dried onion, and pepper. Fold in cooked asparagus.

2 Turn asparagus mixture into an ungreased 1-quart casserole. Toss together stuffing mix and melted butter or margarine; sprinkle around edge of asparagus mixture. Bake casserole, uncovered, in a 350° oven for 30 to 35 minutes. Makes 4 to 6 servings.

SAUCEPAN "BAKED" BEANS

Assembling time: 16 minutes
Cooking time: 20 minutes

4 slices bacon
1 large onion, chopped (1 cup)
2 16-ounce cans pork and beans in tomato sauce
3 tablespoons molasses
1 teaspoon prepared mustard

1 In a 2-quart saucepan cook bacon till crisp; remove bacon. Drain off fat, reserving 2 tablespoons drippings in pan. Cook onion in reserved drippings till onion is tender but not brown.

2 Meanwhile, crumble bacon. Stir bacon, pork and beans, molasses, and mustard into the onion in the saucepan. Bring to boiling. Reduce heat and simmer, uncovered, about 20 minutes or till of desired consistency. Makes 6 servings.

EASY BEAN BAKE

Assembling time: 10 minutes
Cooking time: 1¾ hours

2 16-ounce cans pork and beans in tomato sauce
1 medium apple, cored and chopped (½ cup)
1 medium onion, chopped (½ cup)
⅓ cup catsup
3 tablespoons brown sugar
1 tablespoon Worcestershire sauce
2 teaspoons prepared horseradish

1 Stir together pork and beans, chopped apple, chopped onion, catsup, brown sugar, Worcestershire sauce, and prepared horseradish; mix well. Turn into a 1½-quart casserole. Bake, uncovered, a 325° oven 1½ to 1¾ hours. Makes 6 servings.

PEACHY BAKED BEANS

Total preparation time: 1½ hours

2 16-ounce cans baked beans
¼ cup dark corn syrup
1 small onion, finely chopped (¼ cup)
¼ teaspoon ground allspice
1 16-ounce can peach halves, drained
3 tablespoons orange marmalade

1 In a mixing bowl stir together the beans, corn syrup, onion, and allspice. Turn into a 1½-quart casserole. Bake, uncovered, in a 350° oven for 1 hour.

2 Arrange peach halves, cut side up, atop beans. Spoon about *1 teaspoon* of the orange marmalade into *each* peach cavity. Return to oven and bake, uncovered, about 15 minutes more. Makes 6 servings.

CHEESY GREEN BEAN CASSEROLE

Total preparation time: 32 minutes

2 slightly beaten eggs
1 cup cream-style cottage cheese with chives
¼ cup shredded cheddar cheese
½ teaspoon Worcestershire sauce
⅛ teaspoon pepper
1 16-ounce can French-style green beans, drained
¼ cup fine dry bread crumbs
1 tablespoon butter, melted

1 Stir together eggs, cheeses, Worcestershire sauce, and pepper. Arrange green beans in a shallow 1-quart baking dish; spoon cheese mixture atop.

2 Toss together bread crumbs and butter; sprinkle atop cheese mixture. Bake, uncovered, in a 350° oven for 20 to 25 minutes or till cheese mixture is set. Serves 4 to 6.

MEXICAN CORN CASSEROLE

Total preparation time: 35 minutes

- ½ to 1 teaspoon chili powder
- ½ teaspoon onion salt
- 1 8-ounce can tomato sauce
- ¼ cup taco sauce
- 2 17-ounce cans whole kernel corn, drained
- ½ cup sliced pitted ripe olives
- 1 cup nacho cheese tortilla chips, coarsely crushed
- ½ cup shredded cheddar cheese

1 In a mixing bowl combine chili powder and onion salt. Stir in tomato sauce and taco sauce. Add corn, olives, and ¼ cup of the crushed tortilla chips; mix well. Turn mixture into an 8 × 1½-inch round baking dish.

2 Bake, uncovered, in a 350° oven for 20 minutes; stir. Sprinkle with remaining ¾ cup crushed tortilla chips and cheddar cheese; bake about 5 minutes more or till cheese is melted. Makes 8 servings.

BAKED EGGPLANT SLICES

Total preparation time: 43 minutes

- 1 cup mayonnaise or salad dressing
- ¼ cup milk
- 1 tablespoon lemon juice
- 1 medium eggplant, cut into ½-inch slices (about 1 pound)
- 3 cups finely crushed cheese-flavored crackers

1 Combine mayonnaise, milk, lemon juice, and ¼ teaspoon *salt*. Season eggplant with additional salt; dip into mayonnaise mixture; coat with crushed crackers.

2 Place eggplant slices in an ungreased 15 × 10 × 1-inch baking pan. Bake in a 350° oven 25 to 30 minutes or till slices are crisp and hot. Makes 6 servings.

CRUMB-TOPPED BROCCOLI CASSEROLE

Assembling time: 10 minutes
Cooking time: 25 minutes

- 2 10-ounce packages frozen cut broccoli
- 1 11-ounce can condensed cheddar cheese soup
- ¼ cup mayonnaise or salad dressing
- ⅓ cup crushed rich round crackers

1 Cook frozen broccoli according to the package directions; drain. Stir together the soup and mayonnaise; gently fold in broccoli. Turn into a 1½-quart casserole; sprinkle with cracker crumbs. Bake in a 350° oven about 25 minutes. Serves 6.

CARROTS WITH WATER CHESTNUTS

Total preparation time: 40 minutes

- 1 pound carrots, peeled and bias-sliced ½ inch thick
- 2 tablespoons butter or margarine
- 1 8-ounce can sliced water chestnuts, drained
- ¾ teaspoon dried thyme, crushed
- ¼ teaspoon ground ginger
- 3 tablespoons dry white wine
- 1 tablespoon snipped parsley

1 Cook carrots, covered, in a small amount of boiling salted water for 15 to 20 minutes. Drain; set carrots aside.

2 In the same saucepan melt butter; add water chestnuts, thyme, and ginger. Cook and stir for 2 minutes. Add wine, parsley, and carrots; cook and stir about 6 minutes or till heated through. Serves 6 to 8.

HONEY BAKED ONIONS

Total preparation time: 55 minutes

- 6 medium onions, halved crosswise
- 2 tablespoons honey
- 2 tablespoons dry white wine
- 1 tablespoon butter or margarine
- ¼ teaspoon salt
- ¼ teaspoon paprika

1 Place onion halves, cut side up, in an 11 × 7 × 1½-inch baking dish. In a small saucepan combine remaining ingredients; heat till butter is melted. Spoon over onions. Cover and bake in a 350° oven for 40 to 45 minutes or till tender. Serves 6.

SOUR CREAM POTATO SALAD

Total preparation time: 50 minutes

- 6 medium potatoes (2 pounds)
- ½ cup finely chopped fully cooked ham
- ⅓ cup chopped onion
- ⅓ cup chopped green pepper
- ¼ cup chopped celery
- 1 tablespoon butter or margarine
- ¾ cup dairy sour cream
- 3 tablespoons vinegar
  Pitted ripe or pimiento-stuffed olives, halved

1 In a saucepan cook potatoes, covered, in enough boiling salted water to cover for 25 to 30 minutes or till tender; drain. Peel and slice potatoes to make about 6 cups.

2 Meanwhile, cook ham, onion, green pepper, and celery in butter till tender; drain off fat. Stir in sour cream, vinegar, 1 teaspoon *salt*, and ¼ teaspoon *pepper*. Heat through, but *do not boil*. Combine sour cream mixture and potatoes. Garnish with olives. Serve warm. Makes 10 servings.

EASY CHEESY POTATOES

Assembling time: 5 minutes
Cooking time: 46 minutes

1 16-ounce package frozen hash brown potatoes with onion and peppers
3 tablespoons creamy Italian salad dressing
1 cup shredded American cheese (4 ounces)

1 Place potatoes in a 10×6×2-inch baking dish. Pour Italian salad dressing over potatoes; toss to coat. Cover with foil and bake in a 400° oven about 45 minutes or till potatoes are hot. Top with shredded American cheese. Bake 1 minute more or till cheese melts. Makes 6 servings.

BAKED POTATO SLICES

Assembling time: 8 minutes
Cooking time: 1 hour and 10 minutes

4 large baking potatoes
1/3 cup butter or margarine
1 tablespoon minced dried onion
1/2 teaspoon dried dillweed, basil, or thyme, crushed
2 tablespoons grated Parmesan cheese

1 Scrub potatoes, but do not peel. Cut potatoes crosswise into 1/2-inch slices. Arrange slices in a 10×6×2-inch baking dish or a 9-inch pie plate.
2 Melt butter or margarine; stir in onion and dillweed, basil, or thyme. Drizzle over potatoes. Sprinkle with Parmesan cheese. Sprinkle with salt and pepper, if desired. Cover tightly with foil. Bake in a 375° oven for 60 to 70 minutes or till potatoes are tender. Makes 4 to 6 servings.

PUFFY POTATO BAKE

Assembling time: 12 minutes
Cooking time: 30 minutes

Packaged instant mashed potatoes (enough for 4 servings)
1 4-ounce container whipped cream cheese with chives
1 well-beaten egg
2 tablespoons grated Parmesan cheese

1 Prepare mashed potatoes according to package directions, *except* decrease the water by 1/3 cup. Stir the cream cheese into potatoes till combined. Stir in the egg.
2 Turn into a lightly greased 1-quart casserole. Sprinkle with Parmesan cheese. Bake, uncovered, in a 350° oven about 30 minutes or till puffed. Makes 4 servings.

FRUIT-POTATO PUFF

Assembling time: 70 minutes
Cooking time: 45 minutes

6 medium sweet potatoes (2 pounds)
3/4 cup mashed banana or applesauce
1/4 cup butter or margarine, softened
1/2 teaspoon shredded lemon peel
2 egg yolks
2 egg whites

1 In saucepan cook sweet potatoes, covered, in enough boiling salted water to cover for 30 to 40 minutes or till tender; drain. Peel potatoes; mash on low speed of electric mixer (do not add butter or milk).
2 Add banana or applesauce, butter, peel, and 1/2 teaspoon *salt*. Beat till fluffy. Add yolks; beat well. Beat whites till stiff peaks form; fold into potato mixture. Turn into a buttered 1 1/2-quart casserole. Cover; bake in a 350° oven 20 minutes. Uncover; bake 25 minutes. Serves 10.

SPAGHETTI SQUASH WITH VEGETABLE-TOMATO SAUCE

Total preparation time: 35 minutes

1 2-pound spaghetti squash
1/2 of a 20-ounce package frozen loose-pack broccoli, cauliflower, and carrots
2 teaspoons cornstarch
3/4 teaspoon dried oregano, crushed
1/8 teaspoon salt
1 16-ounce can stewed tomatoes, cut up
1/4 cup pitted sliced green olives
2 tablespoons butter or margarine, melted
Salt
Pepper

1 Use a large knife to cut the squash into quarters; remove seeds. Place squash in a large saucepan or Dutch oven; add about 2 inches water. Bring to boiling. Reduce heat; cover and simmer about 20 minutes or till tender.
2 Just before serving, cook the frozen vegetables according to package directions; drain. In a saucepan combine cornstarch, oregano, and salt. Stir in *undrained* stewed tomatoes and olives. Cook and stir till mixture is thickened and bubbly. Cook and stir 2 minutes more. Stir in cooked vegetables; keep warm.
3 Use two forks to shred and separate the squash pulp into strands. Pile squash onto a serving platter. Toss with melted butter or margarine; season with salt and pepper. Spoon vegetable mixture over squash. Makes 6 servings.

Spaghetti Squash with Vegetable-Tomato Sauce

267

DILL-SAUCED ACORN SQUASH

Total preparation time: 45 minutes

2 small acorn squash
1 8-ounce carton sour cream dip
  with chives
¼ cup sliced radishes
1 green onion, sliced
1 tablespoon milk
¼ teaspoon dried dillweed

1 Cut squash crosswise into 1-inch slices; discard seeds. Arrange in a single layer in a shallow baking pan. Cover; bake in 350° oven about 35 minutes.

2 In a saucepan combine sour cream dip, radishes, green onion, milk, dillweed, ¼ teaspoon *salt*, and a dash *pepper*. Cook and stir over low heat till heated through (*do not boil*). Serve over squash. Serves 4 to 6.

RAISIN-FILLED SQUASH WEDGES

Total preparation time: 40 minutes

2 medium acorn, dumpling, *or*
  golden nugget squash
¼ cup sugar
2 teaspoons cornstarch
⅔ cup raisins
½ cup orange juice

1 Cut squash lengthwise into quarters; discard seeds. Arrange in a 3- to 4-quart saucepan, skin side down; add 1 cup *water*. Season with salt and pepper. Bring to boiling. Reduce heat; cover and steam for 15 to 20 minutes or till tender. Drain.

2 Meanwhile, in a saucepan combine sugar and cornstarch. Stir in raisins, orange juice, and ¼ cup *water*. Cook and stir till thickened and bubbly. Cook and stir 2 minutes more. Place squash, cut side up, on a serving platter; spoon raisin mixture atop. Makes 4 to 6 servings.

SQUASH WITH ALMOND SAUCE

Total preparation time: 1 hour and 10 minutes

2 medium acorn, dumpling, *or*
  golden nugget squash, halved
¼ cup butter *or* margarine
⅓ cup slivered almonds
⅓ cup sliced water chestnuts
1 teaspoon lemon juice

1 Remove seeds from squash halves. Place, cut side down, in a shallow baking pan. Cover; bake in a 350° oven for 30 minutes. Invert squash halves. Season with salt and pepper. Cover; bake 20 to 30 minutes more.

2 Meanwhile, in a saucepan melt butter; add almonds and cook till light brown. Stir in water chestnuts and lemon juice; heat through. Spoon almond mixture atop squash halves. Serves 4.

SUMMER TOMATO SCALLOP

Total preparation time: 52 minutes

6 tomatoes, peeled and sliced
¼ cup butter *or* margarine, melted
1 clove garlic, minced
½ teaspoon dried basil, crushed
½ teaspoon dried tarragon, crushed
4 slices firm-textured bread,
  cut into cubes
⅓ cup grated Parmesan cheese

1 Arrange tomatoes in a 10×6×2-inch baking dish. In a bowl combine butter or margarine, garlic, basil, tarragon, and ¼ teaspoon *salt*. Add bread cubes; toss to mix. Top tomatoes with bread mixture. Sprinkle with Parmesan cheese. Bake in a 350° oven about 40 minutes or till hot. Serves 6.

CHEESE-SPINACH BAKE

Assembling time: 12 minutes
Cooking time: 30 minutes

1 10-ounce package frozen
  chopped spinach
2 beaten eggs
½ cup milk
½ cup shredded American cheese
1 teaspoon minced dried onion

1 Cook spinach according to package directions. Drain well, pressing out excess liquid. Combine eggs, milk, cheese, and onion. Stir into drained spinach.

2 Turn spinach mixture into an ungreased 20-ounce casserole. Bake, uncovered, in a 350° oven for 25 to 30 minutes or till a knife inserted near center comes out clean. Makes 4 servings.

SPINACH-RAREBIT BAKE

Total preparation time: 35 minutes

1 10-ounce package frozen
  Welsh rarebit
2 10-ounce packages frozen
  chopped spinach
2 tablespoons cooked bacon pieces
½ of a 3-ounce can French-fried
  onions

1 Place unopened pouch of rarebit in a skillet; pour in water to a depth of ½ inch. Cover. Place over low heat about 15 minutes or till rarebit is thawed. Meanwhile, cook spinach according to package directions, *except* omit the salt; drain well.

2 In a 10×6×2-inch baking dish combine spinach and *one-third* of the rarebit. Sprinkle bacon atop. Carefully spoon remaining rarebit over all; spread evenly. Top with onions. Bake in a 350° oven for 10 to 15 minutes or till hot. Serves 6.

CORN 'N' SQUASH PUDDING

You can substitute 1½ cups cooked and mashed acorn, buttercup, butternut, hubbard, or banana squash for the frozen winter squash in this recipe—

Assembling time: 17 minutes
Cooking time: 30 minutes

  1 12-ounce package frozen mashed
      cooked winter squash
  1 medium onion, chopped (½ cup)
  ¼ cup butter *or* margarine
  2 slightly beaten eggs
  ¼ cup evaporated milk *or* milk
  1 tablespoon sugar
  ¼ teaspoon salt
  ⅛ teaspoon pepper
  1 cup herb-seasoned stuffing mix
  1 12-ounce can whole kernel corn
      with sweet peppers, drained

1 Cook squash according to package directions. Set aside. In a small skillet cook chopped onion in butter or margarine till onion is tender but not brown. Remove from heat.

2 In a mixing bowl combine eggs, milk, sugar, salt, and pepper; stir in onion mixture. Add herb-seasoned stuffing mix, drained corn, and mashed cooked squash, stirring till well combined. Turn mixture into a 10×6×2-inch baking dish.

3 Bake, uncovered, in a 350° oven about 30 minutes or till a knife inserted just off-center comes out clean. Let stand 5 minutes before serving. Makes 6 servings.

ORIENTAL BAKED VEGETABLES

Total preparation time: 1¼ hours

  1 20-ounce package frozen loose-
      pack French-cut green beans,
      carrots, cauliflower, and onions
  1 16-ounce can tomato wedges
  1 8-ounce can sliced water
      chestnuts, drained
  ¼ cup butter *or* margarine, melted
  1 tablespoon quick-cooking tapioca
  2 tablespoons soy sauce
  1 tablespoon sugar

1 Combine mixed vegetables, tomatoes, and water chestnuts. Mix remaining ingredients. Pour over vegetables; toss. Turn into 2-quart casserole. Cover; bake in a 350° oven 1 hour; stir once. Serves 8.

EASY CHEESY VEGETABLES

Total preparation time: 45 minutes

  ½ of a 20-ounce package frozen
      loose-pack French-cut green
      beans, carrots, cauliflower, and
      onions
  1 1½-ounce envelope cheese
      sauce mix
  1 1⅜-ounce envelope cream
      sauce mix
1½ cups milk
  3 cups frozen loose-pack hash
      brown potatoes
  ½ of a 3-ounce can French-fried
      onions

1 Make vegetables according to package directions; do not drain. Add sauce mixes, then milk. Bring to boiling. Stir in potatoes. Turn into 12×7½×2-inch baking dish. Bake, uncovered, in 350° oven 30 minutes. Top with onions; bake 5 minutes. Serves 8.

BROCCOLI-CAULIFLOWER CASSEROLE

Assembling time: 15 minutes
Cooking time: 25 minutes

  1 10-ounce package frozen cut
      broccoli
  1 10-ounce package frozen
      cauliflower
  1 10¾-ounce can condensed cream
      of chicken soup
  ½ of an 8-ounce jar cheese spread
  1 3-ounce can French-fried onions

1 Cook frozen broccoli and cauliflower together in boiling water just till tender; drain. Stir condensed chicken soup, cheese spread, and *half* of the onions into the drained vegetables.

2 Turn vegetable mixture into a 1-quart casserole. Bake in a 350° oven about 20 minutes. Sprinkle remaining onions atop; bake 5 minutes more. Makes 6 servings.

BAKED POTATO TOPPERS

The next time you make baked potatoes, try one of these easy toppers.
• Stir crumbled bacon, sliced green onion, snipped chives, or shredded cheese into sour cream or cottage cheese.
• Beat together an 8-ounce package softened cream cheese or neûfchâtel cheese and ⅓ cup milk or light cream; beat till fluffy. Add 1 tablespoon snipped chives, 1½ teaspoons lemon juice, and ½ teaspoon garlic salt; beat till well combined.

RICE AND PASTA

SOPHISTICATED RICE

Assembling time: 18 minutes
Cooking time: 20 minutes

- 1 cup long grain rice
- 1 medium onion, cut into thin wedges
- 2 tablespoons butter *or* margarine
- 2½ cups water
- 1 tablespoon dry sherry
- 2 teaspoons instant chicken bouillon granules
- 1 teaspoon dried parsley flakes
- ½ teaspoon garlic salt
- ¼ cup grated Parmesan cheese

1 In a 2-quart saucepan cook rice and onion in butter for 10 minutes, stirring occasionally. Add water, dry sherry, bouillon granules, parsley flakes, and garlic salt.
2 Bring to boiling; reduce heat. Cover and simmer for 15 to 20 minutes or till liquid is absorbed and rice is tender. Stir in Parmesan cheese. Makes 6 servings.

BROWN RICE LYONNAISE

Assembling time: 12 minutes
Cooking time: 50 minutes

- 1 10¾-ounce can condensed chicken broth
- ½ cup regular brown rice
- 1 medium onion, chopped (½ cup)
- 1 medium carrot, shredded *or* finely chopped (½ cup)
- ¼ cup water
- 1 tablespoon butter *or* margarine
- ¼ teaspoon caraway seed

1 In a medium saucepan combine chicken broth, rice, onion, carrot, water, butter, and caraway seed. Bring to boiling; reduce heat. Cover and simmer for 45 to 50 minutes or till rice is tender. Serves 4.

CURRIED RICE CASSEROLE

Assembling time: 8 minutes
Cooking time: 50 minutes

- 2¼ cups boiling water
- 1 cup long grain rice
- 2 tablespoons butter *or* margarine
- 1 tablespoon instant chicken bouillon granules
- 1 teaspoon curry powder
- 1 cup frozen peas

1 In a greased 1½-quart casserole combine water, rice, butter, bouillon granules, and curry powder. Cover and bake in a 350° oven for 35 to 40 minutes or till rice is tender. Uncover; stir in peas. Bake, uncovered, 10 minutes more. Serves 6.

RICE MEXICANA

Assembling time: 8 minutes
Cooking time: 40 minutes

- 1½ cups water
- 1 10-ounce can tomatoes and green chili peppers, cut up
- 1 8¾-ounce can whole kernel corn, drained
- 1 cup long grain rice
- 1 teaspoon instant chicken bouillon granules
- ½ teaspoon minced dried onion
- ½ cup dairy sour cream

1 In a medium saucepan bring water to boiling. Stir in tomatoes and green chilies, corn, rice, chicken bouillon granules, and minced dried onion.
2 Turn into a 10×6×2-inch baking dish. Cover and bake in a 350° oven for 35 to 40 minutes or till rice is tender. Spoon sour cream down center of rice. Serves 8.

CARROT-RICE CASSEROLE

Assembling time: 10 minutes
Cooking time: 40 minutes

- ½ cup long grain rice
- 1 tablespoon butter *or* margarine
- 1 10¾-ounce can condensed chicken broth
- 1 medium carrot, shredded (½ cup)
- ¼ cup water
- 1 teaspoon dried parsley flakes
- 1 teaspoon minced dried onion

1 In a saucepan cook rice in butter or margarine over medium heat till golden, stirring constantly. Add chicken broth, shredded carrot, water, parsley flakes, and dried onion; bring to boiling.
2 Pour rice mixture into a 1-quart casserole. Cover and bake in a 350° oven for 35 to 40 minutes or till rice is tender. Makes 4 servings.

TEXAS SPANISH RICE

Assembling time: 10 minutes
Cooking time: 20 minutes

- ½ cup long grain rice
- 1 tablespoon cooking oil
- 1 7½-ounce can tomatoes, cut up
- 1 cup water
- 2 green onions, sliced
- ½ teaspoon salt
- ½ teaspoon ground cumin
- ⅛ teaspoon garlic powder
- ⅛ teaspoon pepper

1 In an 8-inch skillet cook rice in oil over medium heat till golden, stirring constantly. Remove from heat. Stir in *undrained* tomatoes, water, green onions, salt, cumin, garlic powder, and pepper. Bring to boiling; reduce heat. Cover and simmer for 15 to 20 minutes or till rice is tender. Serves 4.

RATATOUILLE SAUCED SPAGHETTI

Pasta and colorful vegetables in one easy side dish—

Assembling time: 10 minutes
Cooking time: 30 minutes

- 1 medium eggplant, peeled and cubed (1 pound)
- 1 16-ounce can tomatoes, cut up
- 1 medium green pepper, cut into strips
- 1 4¼-ounce can chopped ripe olives, drained
- 1 tablespoon cooking oil
- 1 teaspoon minced dried onion
- 1 teaspoon garlic salt
- 1 teaspoon dried basil, crushed
- ⅛ teaspoon pepper
- 6 ounces spaghetti *or* vermicelli
  Grated Parmesan cheese (optional)

1 In a 3-quart saucepan combine peeled and cubed eggplant, *undrained* tomatoes, green pepper strips, drained chopped ripe olives, cooking oil, minced dried onion, garlic salt, basil, and pepper. Bring eggplant mixture to boiling; reduce heat. Cover and simmer for 30 minutes.

2 Meanwhile, cook spaghetti or vermicelli according to package directions; drain. To serve, spoon the eggplant-tomato mixture over individual servings of cooked pasta. Sprinkle each serving with a little grated Parmesan cheese, if desired. Makes 6 to 8 servings.

WILD RICE PILAF

An extra-special accompaniment for poultry, fish, beef, or pork—

Assembling time: 15 minutes
Cooking time: 50 minutes

- ½ cup wild rice (3 ounces)
- 1¼ cups water
- 1 stalk celery, thinly sliced (½ cup)
- 1 3-ounce can sliced mushrooms, drained
- 2 green onions, sliced (2 tablespoons)
- 2 tablespoons chopped pimiento
- 1 tablespoon instant chicken bouillon granules
- 1 teaspoon lemon juice
- ¼ teaspoon dried thyme, crushed
- ⅛ teaspoon pepper

1 In a strainer run cold tap water over wild rice about 1 minute, lifting rice to rinse well. In a 1½-quart saucepan combine wild rice, 1¼ cups water, sliced celery, mushrooms, green onions, chopped pimiento, chicken bouillon granules, lemon juice, dried thyme, and pepper.

2 Bring rice mixture to boiling; reduce heat. Cover and simmer for 40 to 50 minutes or till rice is tender and most of the excess liquid is absorbed. Serves 4.

ZIPPY NOODLES

Assembling time: 20 minutes
Cooking time: 30 minutes

- 4 ounces noodles
- 1 stalk celery, chopped (½ cup)
- 1 tablespoon butter *or* margarine
- 1 10¾-ounce can condensed cream of chicken soup
- ¼ cup plain yogurt
- 1 tablespoon milk
- ½ teaspoon Worcestershire sauce
- 1 tablespoon toasted wheat germ

1 Cook noodles according to package directions; drain. Meanwhile, in a saucepan cook celery in butter or margarine for 5 minutes. Stir in soup, yogurt, milk, and Worcestershire sauce. Fold in noodles.

2 Turn mixture into a 1-quart casserole. Sprinkle wheat germ atop. Bake in a 350° oven about 30 minutes or till heated through. Makes 6 servings.

BARLEY PILAF

Assembling time: 10 minutes
Cooking time: 25 minutes

- 2½ cups water
- 1 cup quick-cooking barley
- 1 tablespoon instant beef bouillon granules
- 1 teaspoon minced dried onion
- ¼ teaspoon dried thyme, crushed
- ¼ teaspoon garlic salt
- 1 4-ounce can mushroom stems and pieces, drained
- 1 tablespoon butter *or* margarine

1 In a 2-quart saucepan bring water to boiling. Stir in barley, bouillon granules, dried onion, thyme, and garlic salt. Return to boiling; reduce heat. Cover and simmer for 20 to 25 minutes or till barley is tender, stirring occasionally. Stir in mushrooms and butter or margarine. Makes 6 servings.

PIZZA ROLL-UP

This zesty bread can be served as a side dish with a soup or a casserole. Or, it will make a great hot snack—

Assembling time: 1 hour and 10 minutes
Cooking time: 30 minutes

1 13¾-ounce package hot roll mix
⅓ cup tomato paste
1 teaspoon dried oregano, crushed
½ teaspoon sugar
¼ teaspoon garlic powder
4 ounces pepperoni, chopped (1 cup)
1 4-ounce package shredded mozzarella cheese
Milk

1 Prepare hot roll mix according to package directions; cover and let rest 10 minutes. Roll dough out on a lightly floured surface to a 14×10-inch rectangle.

2 Stir together tomato paste, dried oregano, sugar, and garlic powder. Spread tomato mixture over dough. Sprinkle with chopped pepperoni and mozzarella cheese.

3 Starting from narrow end, roll up dough jelly roll style. Pinch edge and ends to seal. Place, seam side down, in a greased 15×10×1-inch baking pan.

4 Use a sharp knife to cut 5 shallow slashes diagonally in the top. Cover with a damp cloth. Place pan in oven. Turn oven on to 200° for *1 minute*; turn oven off. Let dough rise in warm oven till nearly double (about 30 minutes).

5 Remove dough from oven. Preheat oven to 375°. Brush dough with a little milk. Bake in 375° oven for 25 to 30 minutes or till golden. Serve warm. Makes 1 loaf.

CHOCOLATE-SWIRLED COFFEE CAKE

Pictured on page 225—

Assembling time: 1¼ hours
Cooking time: 45 minutes

1 6-ounce package (1 cup) semisweet chocolate pieces
⅓ cup evaporated milk
3 tablespoons sugar
1 13¾-ounce package hot roll mix
¼ cup sugar
¼ cup all-purpose flour
¼ cup sugar
¼ cup butter *or* margarine
¼ cup chopped walnuts

1 In a small saucepan combine ¾ *cup* of the chocolate pieces, the milk, and 3 tablespoons sugar. Cook and stir over low heat till chocolate melts and mixture thickens slightly; remove from heat.

2 Prepare hot roll mix according to package directions, *except* add ¼ cup sugar to the mix. (Not necessary to let rise.) Knead gently on a lightly floured surface for 10 to 12 strokes or till smooth.

3 Roll dough out to a 16×10-inch rectangle. Spread with chocolate mixture. Starting with long side, roll up jelly roll style. Moisten edge and ends; pinch to seal.

4 Carefully place the roll, seam side down, in a greased 9- or 10-inch tube pan. Cover with a damp cloth. Place pan in oven. Turn oven on to 200° for *1 minute*; turn oven off. Let dough rise in warm oven till nearly double (about 30 minutes). Remove from oven. Preheat oven to 350°.

5 Meanwhile, in a small bowl combine flour and ¼ cup sugar; cut in butter. Stir in walnuts and remaining chocolate pieces. Sprinkle mixture atop risen dough.

6 Bake in 350° oven for 40 to 45 minutes or till golden brown. Cool 15 minutes before removing from pan. Serve warm. Makes one 9- or 10-inch coffee cake.

HONEY-DRIZZLED BUBBLE RING

Assembling time: 1½ hours
Cooking time: 25 minutes

1 13¾-ounce package hot roll mix
3 tablespoons sugar
⅓ cup honey
3 tablespoons butter *or* margarine, melted
1½ teaspoons lemon juice
⅓ cup slivered almonds
⅓ cup sugar
½ teaspoon ground cinnamon
½ teaspoon ground nutmeg

1 Prepare hot roll mix according to package directions, *except* stir the 3 tablespoons sugar into the yeast-egg mixture. Cover the dough with a damp cloth. Place bowl in oven. Turn oven on to 200° for *1 minute*; turn oven off. Let dough rise in warm oven till double (about 30 minutes).

2 Meanwhile, combine honey, melted butter or margarine, and lemon juice; turn into an ungreased 6½-cup oven-proof ring mold. Sprinkle almonds atop honey mixture; set aside. Combine ⅓ cup sugar, cinnamon, and nutmeg; set aside.

3 Stir dough down. Drop spoonfuls of dough into sugar-spice mixture, turning to coat. Arrange balls of dough in prepared ring mold. Cover with a damp cloth. Place pan in oven. Turn oven on to 200° for *1 minute*; turn oven off. Let dough rise in warm oven till nearly double (about 25 minutes).

4 Remove from oven; preheat oven to 375°. Bake in 375° oven for 20 to 25 minutes or till done. Cool 1 minute. Loosen sides; invert onto a serving plate. Drizzle with any remaining topping. Makes 1 ring.

Peanut Ring (see recipe, page 274)
Pizza Roll-Up

PEANUT RING

Pictured on page 273—

Total preparation time: 45 minutes

2 packages (10 each) refrigerated
  biscuits
½ cup chopped peanuts
⅓ cup packed brown sugar
1 package 4-serving size *regular*
  butterscotch pudding mix
1 teaspoon ground cinnamon
⅓ cup butter *or* margarine, melted

1 Halve biscuits. Mix nuts, sugar, pudding mix, and cinnamon. Dip biscuit halves in butter, then in sugar mixture. Layer in greased 6½-cup oven-proof ring mold.
2 Drizzle with any remaining butter and sprinkle with any remaining sugar mixture. Bake in a 375° oven about 15 minutes. Invert onto a serving plate. Makes 1.

ITALIAN LOAF

Total preparation time: 2 hours

1 16-ounce loaf frozen bread dough,
  thawed
3 tablespoons butter, softened
2 tablespoons spaghetti sauce mix
2 tablespoons snipped parsley

1 Roll dough out on floured surface to a 12×9-inch rectangle. Combine butter, dry sauce mix, and parsley; spread over dough. From long side, roll up jelly roll style. Seal edge and ends. If desired, sprinkle a greased baking sheet with cornmeal.
2 Place dough, seam down, on baking sheet. Brush with water; sprinkle with salt. Slash top at 2-inch intervals. Cover. Place in oven. Turn oven on to 200° for *1 minute*; turn off. Let dough rise till nearly double (about 30 minutes). Remove. Bake in a 350° oven about 45 minutes, covering with foil last 15 minutes. Makes 1.

SWISS ONION SPIRAL BREAD

You can reheat this bread by wrapping the loaf in foil and warming it in a 400° oven for 15 to 20 minutes—

Assembling time: 1 hour and 20 minutes
Cooking time: 30 minutes

2 slices bacon
1 medium onion, chopped (½ cup)
1 16-ounce loaf frozen bread dough,
  thawed
1 cup shredded Swiss cheese
  (4 ounces)
1 beaten egg
  Poppy seed *or* dillseed

1 In a small skillet cook bacon till crisp. Drain bacon, reserving drippings in skillet. Crumble bacon and set aside. Cook onion in the reserved drippings till tender. Remove from heat.
2 On a lightly floured surface roll bread dough out to a 17×7-inch rectangle; spread cooked onion evenly over dough. Sprinkle cheese and crumbled bacon atop.
3 Starting from long side, roll up jelly roll style. Pinch edge and ends to seal. Place roll, seam side down, in a greased 15×10×1-inch baking pan. Make shallow slashes across the top at 2-inch intervals.
4 Cover with a damp cloth. Place pan in oven. Turn oven on to 200° for *1 minute*; turn oven off. Let dough rise in warm oven till nearly double (about 30 minutes). Remove dough from oven; preheat oven to 350°. Brush top of bread with egg; sprinkle with poppy seed or dillseed. Bake in 350° oven for 25 to 30 minutes or till golden brown. Serve warm. Makes 1 loaf.

SEED-NUT BREAD

Total preparation time: 1¼ hours

¼ cup shelled sunflower nuts
¼ cup sesame seed
3 cups packaged biscuit mix
¼ cup sugar
¼ cup toasted wheat germ
2 eggs
1½ cups milk
¼ cup chopped walnuts

1 Place sunflower nuts and sesame seeds in a 15×10×1-inch baking pan. Bake in a 350° oven 15 minutes or till toasted, stirring occasionally. Mix biscuit mix, sugar, and wheat germ. Add eggs and milk.
2 Beat at low speed of electric mixer for ½ minute. Beat for 3 minutes at high speed. Set aside *1 tablespoon* seeds. Stir remaining seeds and walnuts into batter.
3 Turn into greased 9×5×3-inch loaf pan. Top with reserved seeds. Bake in 350° oven about 50 minutes. Cool 10 minutes. Remove from pan; cool. Makes 1.

APPLE-CHEESE QUICK BREAD

Total preparation time: 1¼ hours

2 beaten eggs
1 cup applesauce
⅓ cup sugar
¼ cup cooking oil
¼ teaspoon ground nutmeg
2 cups self-rising flour
½ cup shredded cheddar cheese
¼ cup chopped walnuts

1 In a mixing bowl combine eggs, applesauce, sugar, oil, and nutmeg; stir in flour just till moistened. Gently fold in cheese and nuts. Turn batter into a greased 8×4×2-inch loaf pan. Bake in a 350° oven for 45 to 50 minutes. Cool in pan 10 minutes; remove from pan. Serve warm. Makes 1.

SPINACH SPOON BREAD

Spoon bread is a traditional corn bread that has a custard-like consistency—

Assembling time: 25 minutes
Cooking time: 37 minutes

- 1 10-ounce package frozen onions in cream sauce
- 1 10-ounce package frozen chopped spinach
- 2 slightly beaten eggs
- 1 cup dairy sour cream
- ½ cup butter *or* margarine, melted
- ¼ teaspoon salt
- 1 8½-ounce package corn muffin mix
- ½ cup shredded American cheese (2 ounces)

1 Prepare onions in cream sauce according to the package directions; set aside. Cook spinach according to the package directions; drain the spinach well.

2 In a large mixing bowl combine beaten eggs, sour cream, melted butter or margarine, salt, onions in cream sauce, and drained spinach. Stir in corn muffin mix.

3 Turn mixture into a greased 1½-quart casserole. Bake in a 350° oven for 30 to 35 minutes or till a wooden pick inserted in center comes out clean. Sprinkle top of spoon bread with shredded American cheese; bake about 2 minutes more or till the cheese is melted. Serve spoon bread warm. Makes 8 servings.

MAPLE-CORNMEAL MUFFINS

Total preparation time: 40 minutes

- 1½ cups self-rising flour
- ½ cup yellow cornmeal
- 1 beaten egg
- 1 cup milk
- ¼ cup cooking oil
- ¼ cup maple-flavored syrup

1 Stir together flour and cornmeal. Make a well in center. Combine egg, milk, oil, and syrup; add all at once to dry ingredients. Stir just till moistened (batter should be lumpy). Grease muffin cups; fill ⅔ full. Bake in a 400° oven for 20 to 25 minutes. Serve warm. Makes 16 muffins.

PEANUT BUTTER ROLLS

Total preparation time: 1 hour

- 2 cups self-rising flour
- 3 tablespoons sugar
- ½ cup shortening
- ⅔ cup milk
- ½ cup chunk-style peanut butter
- ¼ cup honey
- 1 tablespoon sugar
- ¼ teaspoon ground cinnamon

1 Mix flour and the 3 tablespoons sugar. Cut in shortening till mixture resembles coarse crumbs. Stir in milk till moistened. Knead on floured surface 8 to 10 strokes.

2 Roll out dough to a 16×8-inch rectangle. Combine peanut butter and honey; spread over dough. Starting with long side, roll up jelly roll style. Pinch seam to seal.

3 Cut into 1-inch slices. Place, cut side down, in a greased 9×9×2-inch baking pan. Sprinkle with 1 tablespoon sugar and the cinnamon. Bake in a 375° oven for 30 to 35 minutes. Invert onto a plate. Serve warm. Makes 16 rolls.

GOLDEN PEACH NUT BREAD

Total preparation time: 1½ hours

- 2 beaten eggs
- 2 4½-ounce jars strained peaches (baby food)
- ½ cup sugar
- ¼ cup cooking oil
- 2 tablespoons orange juice
  Dash ground nutmeg
- 2 cups self-rising flour
- ½ cup chopped walnuts

1 In a mixing bowl combine eggs, strained peaches, sugar, oil, orange juice, and nutmeg. Stir in flour just till moistened; fold in nuts. Turn batter into a greased 8×4×2-inch loaf pan.

2 Bake in a 350° oven for 60 to 65 minutes or till done. Cool in pan 10 minutes. Remove from pan and cool on a wire rack. Makes 1 loaf.

SPICY MUFFINS

Total preparation time: 35 minutes

- 1¾ cups self-rising flour
- ¼ teaspoon ground cinnamon
- 1 beaten egg
- ½ cup milk
- ½ cup honey
- ⅓ cup cooking oil
- ¼ cup raisins

1 In a mixing bowl stir together flour and cinnamon. Make a well in center. Combine egg, milk, honey, and oil; add all at once to dry ingredients. Stir till moistened.

2 Carefully stir in raisins (batter should be lumpy). Line muffin pan with paper bake cups; fill ⅔ full. Bake in a 400° oven for 16 to 18 minutes. Serve warm. Makes 14.

DILLY CHEESE BREAD

Assembling time: 1¾ hours
Cooking time: 40 minutes

      3 cups all-purpose flour
      1 package active dry yeast
  1½ cups milk
   ⅓ cup shortening
   ¼ cup sugar
   ½ teaspoon salt
      1 egg
   ¾ cup shredded Swiss cheese
   ½ cup Grape Nuts cereal
   ¼ cup grated Parmesan cheese
      1 teaspoon dillseed

1 In a large mixer bowl combine *1½ cups* of the flour and the yeast. In a saucepan combine milk, shortening, sugar, and salt. Heat just till warm (115° to 120°) and shortening is almost melted, stirring constantly. Add the milk mixture to flour mixture; add egg and Swiss cheese.

2 Beat at low speed of electric mixer for ½ minute, scraping sides of bowl constantly. Beat 3 minutes at high speed. Stir in Grape Nuts cereal, Parmesan cheese, dillseed, and the remaining flour.

3 Cover with a damp cloth; place bowl in oven. Turn oven on to 200° for *1 minute*; turn oven off. Let dough rise in the warm oven till double (about 45 minutes). Stir down with a wooden spoon. Let rest for 5 minutes. Spoon batter into two greased 8×4×2-inch loaf pans.

4 Cover with a damp cloth; place pans in oven. Turn oven on to 200° for *1 minute*. Turn oven off. Let dough rise in warm oven till nearly double (about 25 minutes).

5 Remove from oven; preheat oven to 350°. Bake in 350° oven for 35 to 40 minutes or till loaves test done. Cover with foil the last 10 minutes of baking time. Remove from pans. Cool on racks. Makes 2.

Dilly Cheese Bread

LEMON COFFEE BREAD

Assembling time: 1¾ hours
Cooking time: 25 minutes

  2¾ to 3¼ cups all-purpose flour
      2 packages active dry yeast
   ¾ cup milk
   ¼ cup sugar
   ¼ cup butter *or* margarine
      1 egg
      2 teaspoons finely shredded
        lemon peel
      1 cup sifted powdered sugar
      1 to 2 tablespoons lemon juice

1 In a large mixer bowl combine *1 cup* of the flour and yeast. Combine milk, sugar, butter, and ¼ teaspoon *salt*. Heat just till warm (115° to 120°); stir constantly. Add to flour mixture; add egg and lemon peel.

2 Beat at low speed of electric mixer for ½ minute, scraping bowl. Beat 3 minutes at high speed. Stir in as much of the remaining flour as you can with a spoon.

3 Turn out onto floured surface. Knead in enough remaining flour to make a moderately soft dough that is smooth and elastic (3 to 5 minutes). Shape into a ball.

4 Place in a greased bowl; turn once to grease surface. Cover; place bowl in oven. Turn oven on to 200° for *1 minute*; turn oven off. Let dough rise in warm oven till double (about 20 minutes).

5 Punch down. Turn out onto lightly floured surface. Divide in half. Shape into 2 round loaves; place on greased baking sheet. Flatten slightly. Cover; place in oven. Turn oven on to 200° for *1 minute*; turn oven off.

6 Let dough rise in the warm oven till nearly double (about 20 minutes). Remove dough from oven. Preheat oven to 350°. Bake loaves in 350° oven about 25 minutes or till bread tests done. Remove from pan; cool on racks for 30 minutes.

7 Combine powdered sugar and enough lemon juice to make of drizzling consistency; drizzle over loaves. Makes 2 loaves.

ORANGE COFFEE CAKE

Assembling time: 1 hour and 10 minutes
Cooking time: 40 minutes

      2 cups all-purpose flour
      1 package active dry yeast
   ¼ teaspoon ground nutmeg
   ½ cup orange juice
   ⅓ cup sugar
   ¼ cup shortening
   ¼ teaspoon salt
      2 eggs
   ½ of a 10-ounce jar (½ cup) orange
        marmalade
   ¼ cup all-purpose flour
      2 tablespoons sugar
   ¼ teaspoon ground nutmeg
      2 tablespoons butter *or* margarine

1 In a small mixer bowl combine *1 cup* of the flour, the yeast, and ¼ teaspoon nutmeg. In a saucepan combine orange juice, ⅓ cup sugar, shortening, and salt. Heat just till warm (115° to 120°) and shortening is almost melted, stirring constantly.

2 Add orange juice mixture to flour mixture; add eggs. Beat at low speed of electric mixer for ½ minute, scraping bowl constantly. Beat 3 minutes at high speed.

3 Stir in the remaining flour (batter will be stiff). Fold in marmalade. Spread batter in a greased 11×7×1½-inch baking pan. Cover; place pan in oven. Turn oven on to 200° for *1 minute*; turn oven off. Let dough rise in the warm oven till nearly double (about 30 minutes). Remove dough from oven. Preheat oven to 350°.

4 Meanwhile, combine the ¼ cup flour, 2 tablespoons sugar, and ¼ teaspoon nutmeg. Cut in butter or margarine till crumbly. Sprinkle atop coffee cake. Bake in a 350° oven for 35 to 40 minutes or till done. Cool 15 minutes; serve warm. Makes 1.

277

TARRAGON CASSEROLE BREAD

Assembling time: 1 hour and 10 minutes
Cooking time: 40 minutes

    3 cups all-purpose flour
    2 packages active dry yeast
    1 tablespoon dried parsley flakes
 1½ teaspoons dried tarragon, crushed
    1 teaspoon salt
   ½ teaspoon celery seed
    1 cup dairy sour cream
   ⅓ cup water
    3 tablespoons sugar
    2 tablespoons butter *or* margarine
    2 eggs

1 In a large mixer bowl combine *1½ cups* of the flour, the yeast, parsley flakes, tarragon, salt, and celery seed. In a saucepan combine sour cream, water, sugar, and butter or margarine. Heat just till warm (115° to 120°) and butter or margarine is almost melted, stirring constantly. (Mixture may appear curdled.)

2 Add sour cream mixture to flour mixture; add eggs. Beat at low speed of electric mixer for ½ minute, scraping sides of bowl constantly. Beat 3 minutes at high speed. Stir in the remaining flour.

3 Turn into a greased 2-quart casserole. Cover; place casserole in oven. Turn oven on to 200° for *1 minute*; turn oven off. Let dough rise in the warm oven till nearly double (about 45 minutes). Remove dough from oven. Preheat oven to 350°. Bake bread in a 350° oven for 35 to 40 minutes. Remove from casserole. Cool on a wire rack. Makes 1 loaf.

SPEEDY PARMESAN ROLLS

Assembling time: 55 minutes
Cooking time: 25 minutes

    1 package active dry yeast
   ⅔ cup warm water (110° to 115°)
 2½ cups packaged biscuit mix
   ¼ cup grated Parmesan cheese
    2 tablespoons butter *or* margarine, melted
    2 tablespoons grated Parmesan cheese

1 Dissolve yeast in warm water. Stir in packaged biscuit mix and the ¼ cup grated Parmesan cheese; beat well. Drop dough by spoonfuls into a greased 9 × 1½-inch round baking pan.

2 Drizzle with melted butter or margarine; sprinkle with 2 tablespoons cheese. Place pan in oven. Turn oven on to 200° for *1 minute*; turn oven off.

3 Let dough rise in the warm oven till nearly double (about 30 minutes). Remove from oven. Preheat oven to 400°. Bake rolls in a 400° oven for 22 to 25 minutes or till golden brown. Serve warm. Makes 12 rolls.

QUICK-RISE METHOD

The rising times given in the recipes are guidelines for allowing the doughs to rise following the quick-rise method (in a warm oven). You can also allow any of these doughs to rise following the conventional method (just cover the dough and put it in a warm place). You should expect the conventional method to take longer.

RAISIN-NUT BATTER BREAD

Assembling time: 1¼ hours
Cooking time: 35 minutes

    2 cups all-purpose flour
    1 cup whole wheat flour
    2 packages active dry yeast
    1 teaspoon ground cinnamon
 1¼ cups milk
   ¼ cup sugar
   ¼ cup butter *or* margarine
    1 teaspoon salt
    2 eggs
    1 cup chopped walnuts
    1 cup raisins

1 In a large mixer bowl combine *1 cup* of the all-purpose flour, the whole wheat flour, yeast, and cinnamon. In a saucepan combine milk, sugar, butter or margarine, and salt. Heat just till warm (115° to 120°) and butter is almost melted, stirring constantly. Add to flour mixture; add eggs.

2 Beat at low speed of electric mixer for ½ minute, scraping sides of bowl constantly. Beat 3 minutes at high speed. Stir in the chopped walnuts, raisins, and the remaining all-purpose flour.

3 Spread batter in 2 greased 8 × 4 × 2-inch loaf pans. Cover; place pans in oven. Turn oven on to 200° for *1 minute*; turn oven off. Let dough rise in the warm oven till nearly double (about 45 minutes).

4 Remove dough from oven. Preheat oven to 350°. Bake bread in a 350° oven for 30 to 35 minutes or till bread tests done. Cool in pans 10 minutes. Remove from pans; cool on wire racks. Makes 2.

WHOLE WHEAT QUICK-RISE BREAD

Assembling time: 1½ hours
Cooking time: 35 minutes

2¾ to 3¼ **cups all-purpose flour**
  2 **packages active dry yeast**
1⅔ **cups milk**
  ⅓ **cup honey**
  2 **tablespoons butter *or* margarine**
  1 **egg**
2½ **cups whole wheat flour**
  1 **slightly beaten egg white**

1 In a large mixer bowl combine *2 cups* of the all-purpose flour and the yeast. In a saucepan combine milk, honey, butter or margarine, and 2 teaspoons *salt*. Heat just till warm (115° to 120°); stir constantly. Add to flour mixture; add egg.

2 Beat at low speed of electric mixer for ½ minute, scraping sides of bowl constantly. Beat 3 minutes at high speed. Stir in whole wheat flour and as much of the remaining all-purpose flour as you can mix in with a spoon.

3 Turn out onto a lightly floured surface. Knead in enough of the remaining all-purpose flour to make a moderately stiff dough that is smooth and elastic (6 to 8 minutes total). Shape into a ball.

4 Place in a lightly greased bowl; turn once to grease surface. Cover; place bowl in oven. Turn oven on to 200° for *1 minute*; turn oven off. Let dough rise in the warm oven till double (about 30 minutes).

5 Punch down; turn out onto lightly floured surface. Divide in half. Shape into 2 round loaves. Place on greased baking sheet. Cover; place in oven. Turn oven on to 200° for *1 minute*; turn oven off.

6 Let dough rise in the warm oven till nearly double (about 30 minutes). Remove from oven. Preheat oven to 350°. Brush dough with egg white. Bake in 350° oven for 30 to 35 minutes. If necessary, cover with foil the last 10 minutes to prevent overbrowning. Remove from pan; cool on wire racks. Makes 2 loaves.

SOUR CREAM-ONION BREAD

Assembling time: 1 hour and 25 minutes
Cooking time: 40 minutes

  2 **cups all-purpose flour**
  1 **package active dry yeast**
  8 **green onions, sliced (½ cup)**
  2 **tablespoons butter *or* margarine**
  ½ **cup dairy sour cream**
  ⅓ **cup milk**
  2 **tablespoons sugar**
  1 **teaspoon salt**
  1 **egg**

1 In a large mixer bowl combine *1 cup* of the flour and the yeast. In a saucepan cook green onion in butter or margarine till onion is tender. Stir in sour cream, milk, sugar, and salt; heat over low heat just till warm (115° to 120°). Add sour cream mixture to flour mixture; add egg.

2 Beat at low speed of electric mixer for ½ minute, scraping sides of bowl constantly. Beat 3 minutes at high speed. Stir in the remaining flour. Turn batter into a greased 1-quart casserole.

3 Cover; place casserole in oven. Turn oven on to 200° for *1 minute*; turn oven off. Let dough rise in the warm oven till nearly double (about 45 minutes). Remove dough from oven. Preheat oven to 375°.

4 Bake bread in a 375° oven for 35 to 40 minutes or till bread tests done. Cover with foil the last 15 minutes of baking time to prevent overbrowning. Cool 10 minutes in casserole. Remove from casserole; cool on a wire rack. Makes 1 loaf.

EASY PARKER HOUSE ROLLS

Pictured on page 281—

Total preparation time: 2½ hours

3½ to 4 **cups all-purpose flour**
  1 **3-ounce package no-bake custard mix**
  1 **package active dry yeast**
1¼ **cups milk**
  ½ **cup butter *or* margarine**
  2 **tablespoons butter, melted**

1 Combine *1 cup* of the flour, the dry custard mix, and yeast. Heat milk, ½ cup butter, and ½ teaspoon *salt* just till warm (115° to 120°) and butter melts, stirring constantly. Add to flour mixture. Beat at low speed of electric mixer for ½ minute, scraping bowl. Beat 3 minutes at high speed.

2 Stir in as much remaining flour as you can mix in with a spoon. Turn out onto a lightly floured surface. Knead in enough remaining flour to make a moderately soft dough that is smooth and elastic (3 to 5 minutes total). Shape into a ball. Place in lightly greased bowl; turn to grease surface.

3 Cover. Place bowl in oven. Turn oven on to 200° for *1 minute*; turn oven off. Let dough rise in warm oven for 30 minutes. Again, turn oven on to 200° for *1 minute*; turn oven off. Continue to let rise till double (about 30 minutes more). Punch down. Divide in half. Cover; let rest 10 minutes.

4 On lightly floured surface roll each half to ¼-inch thickness. Cut with a floured 2½-inch round cutter. Brush with melted butter. Make an off-center crease in each round. Fold so large side overlaps small side slightly. Place rolls with large sides up in a greased 13×9×2-inch baking pan.

5 Cover; place in oven. Turn oven on to 200° for *1 minute*; turn oven off. Let rise in oven till nearly double (about 30 minutes). Remove; preheat oven to 400°. Bake in 400° oven 10 to 12 minutes. Makes 12.

BOSTON CREAM PIE

Total preparation time: 1¼ hours

2 eggs
1 cup sugar
1 cup all-purpose flour
1 teaspoon baking powder
½ cup milk
2 tablespoons butter *or* margarine
  Vanilla Cream Filling
  Chocolate Glaze
  Vanilla Icing

1 Grease and flour a 9 × 1½-inch round baking pan. Beat eggs for 4 minutes or till light and lemon-colored. Gradually add sugar, beating till dissolved.

2 In a bowl stir together flour, baking powder, and ¼ teaspoon *salt*. Add to egg mixture, beating till blended. Heat milk and butter till butter is melted; add to batter, beating till mixed.

3 Turn batter into prepared pan. Bake in a 350° oven for 25 to 30 minutes. Cool 10 minutes. Remove from pan; cool.

4 Split cake horizontally. Fill with Vanilla Cream Filling. Spread Chocolate Glaze on top layer, drizzling down sides. Immediately drizzle Vanilla Icing in a spiral over cake; draw a knife through icing at intervals to produce a webbed effect. Serves 8.

Vanilla Cream Filling: Prepare one package 4-serving-size *instant French vanilla pudding mix* according to package directions, *except* use 1⅔ cups *milk*.

Chocolate Glaze: In a saucepan melt one square (1 ounce) *unsweetened chocolate* with 1 tablespoon *butter or margarine* over low heat, stirring often. Remove from heat. Stir in ¾ cup sifted *powdered sugar* and ½ teaspoon *vanilla* till crumbly. Beat in 2 teaspoons *very hot water*. Beat in 3 to 4 teaspoons additional *hot water*, 1 teaspoon at a time, to make of pouring consistency.

Vanilla Icing: In a small bowl combine ½ cup sifted *powdered sugar* and ¼ teaspoon *vanilla*. Add enough *milk* (1 to 2 teaspoons) to make of drizzling consistency.

CHEESECAKE PIE

Total preparation time: 2 hours

2 8-ounce packages cream cheese, cut up
⅔ cup sugar
3 eggs
¼ teaspoon almond extract
1 cup dairy sour cream
3 tablespoons sugar
1 teaspoon vanilla

1 Beat together cream cheese, the ⅔ cup sugar, eggs, and almond extract. Pour into an ungreased 9-inch pie plate. Bake in a 350° oven about 35 minutes.

2 In a small bowl stir together sour cream, the 3 tablespoons sugar, and vanilla; spread atop cheese mixture. Cool. Cover and chill at least 1 hour. Serves 8.

RAISIN PIE

Assembling time: 15 minutes
Cooking time: 45 minutes

1½ cups raisins
3 slightly beaten eggs
1 cup dairy sour cream
½ cup milk
¾ cup packed brown sugar
1 tablespoon lemon juice
½ teaspoon ground cinnamon
¼ teaspoon ground cloves
1 9-inch frozen unbaked deep dish pastry shell

1 In bowl cover raisins with *boiling water*; let stand 5 minutes. Drain. Combine eggs, the 1 cup sour cream, and milk. Stir in brown sugar, lemon juice, cinnamon, cloves, and ¼ teaspoon *salt*. Stir in raisins.

2 Pour into frozen pastry shell. Place on preheated baking sheet in a 350° oven. Bake for 40 to 45 minutes or just till filling is set. Cool on wire rack; dollop with additional sour cream, if desired. Makes 8 servings.

FUNNY CAKE

Assembling time: 25 minutes
Cooking time: 40 minutes

1 9-inch frozen unbaked deep-dish pastry shell
1 10-ounce package frozen strawberries *or* red raspberries
¼ cup sugar
2 tablespoons butter *or* margarine
2 tablespoons light corn syrup
⅓ cup sugar
¼ cup shortening
½ teaspoon vanilla
1 egg
½ cup all-purpose flour
¾ teaspoon baking powder
¼ teaspoon salt
¼ cup milk

1 Line pastry shell with a double thickness of heavy-duty foil or line it with foil and fill with dry beans or pie weights. Place shell on preheated baking sheet in a 450° oven. Bake for 6 minutes. Remove from oven; remove foil or foil and beans. Cool.

2 Meanwhile, in a saucepan combine frozen berries, the ¼ cup sugar, butter or margarine, and corn syrup. Cover and cook over low heat till berries thaw, breaking up berries with a fork. Uncover saucepan; bring mixture to boiling. Boil 2 minutes.

3 Sieve berry mixture into a small bowl; discard seeds. Set aside. In mixer bowl beat together the ⅓ cup sugar, shortening, and vanilla for 1 minute. Beat in egg.

4 Stir together flour, baking powder, and salt. Add to creamed mixture alternately with milk. Pour sieved berry mixture into partially baked pastry shell. Spoon batter atop. Bake in a 375° oven about 40 minutes or till done. Serve warm. Makes 8 servings.

**Funny Cake
Boston Cream Pie
Easy Parker House Rolls (see recipe, page 279)**

TOASTED PECAN PUDDING CAKE

Assembling time: 30 minutes
Cooking time: 40 minutes

½ cup chopped pecans
3 tablespoons butter *or* margarine
1 cup all-purpose flour
½ cup sugar
¾ teaspoon baking powder
½ teaspoon salt
½ cup milk
1 teaspoon vanilla
¾ cup packed brown sugar
¾ cup water
¾ cup milk
1 teaspoon instant coffee crystals
Vanilla ice cream (optional)

1 Place pecans in an 8×8×2-inch baking pan. Dot with butter or margarine. Bake in a 350° oven about 15 minutes or till toasted, stirring often.

2 Meanwhile, in a mixing bowl stir together the flour, sugar, baking powder, and salt. Stir in the pecan-butter mixture, the ½ cup milk, and vanilla. Turn batter into the same greased 8×8×2-inch baking pan.

3 Sprinkle the brown sugar evenly over the top. In a small saucepan combine water, the ¾ cup milk, and coffee crystals. Cook and stir just till boiling; slowly pour water-milk mixture atop cake batter in pan.

4 Bake in a 350° oven for 35 to 40 minutes. To serve, spoon each warm serving into a sherbet dish; spoon any additional pudding mixture atop. If desired, serve with vanilla ice cream. Makes 8 servings.

ONE-BOWL CHOCOLATE CAKE

Total preparation time: 1 hour

2 cups all-purpose flour
2 cups sugar
½ cup unsweetened cocoa powder
¾ teaspoon baking powder
¾ teaspoon baking soda
1½ cups milk
½ cup butter *or* margarine, softened
2 eggs
1 teaspoon vanilla

1 In mixer bowl combine flour, sugar, cocoa, baking powder, and baking soda. Add *half* the milk, the butter, eggs, and vanilla. Mix at low speed till blended. Beat 2 minutes at medium speed.

2 Add remaining milk. Beat 2 minutes more. Turn into a greased and floured 13×9×2-inch baking pan. Bake in a 350° oven for 40 to 45 minutes. Serves 12.

DATE CAKE

Assembling time: 10 minutes
Cooking time: 45 minutes

1 cup all-purpose flour
1 teaspoon baking soda
2 eggs
1 8-ounce package pitted whole dates
¾ cup sugar
1 tablespoon butter *or* margarine
½ cup walnuts

1 Combine flour and soda; set aside. In a blender container combine eggs, dates, sugar, butter, and 1 cup warm *water*. Cover and blend till smooth. Add nuts; cover. Blend till nuts are coarsely chopped.

2 Stir date mixture into flour mixture. Pour into a greased 9×9×2-inch baking pan. Bake in a 325° oven for 40 to 45 minutes. Serves 9.

CHERRY QUICK CAKE

The icing makes this cake extra moist—

Assembling time: 18 minutes
Cooking time: 1 hour

1 21-ounce can cherry pie filling
2 cups all-purpose flour
1 cup sugar
1½ teaspoons baking soda
½ teaspoon salt
2 beaten eggs
½ cup cooking oil
1 teaspoon vanilla
½ cup chopped walnuts
1 cup sifted powdered sugar
½ cup dairy sour cream

1 Spread pie filling in a 13×9×2-inch baking pan. In a mixing bowl stir together flour, sugar, baking soda, and salt. Sprinkle evenly over pie filling.

2 In a mixing bowl combine eggs, cooking oil, and vanilla. Add chopped walnuts; mix well. Pour over dry ingredients in pan. Stir just till mixed. Bake in a 350° oven 40 to 45 minutes or till cake tests done.

3 Cool on a wire rack for 15 minutes. Prick cake with tines of a fork. In a saucepan combine powdered sugar and sour cream. Cook and stir just till mixture boils. Pour sour cream-sugar mixture evenly over cake. Serve cake warm or cool. Makes 12 servings.

SHOOFLY CAKE

Assembling time: 10 minutes
Cooking time: 30 minutes

2½ **cups all-purpose flour**
¾ **cup sugar**
1 **teaspoon baking soda**
½ **cup butter** *or* **margarine**
1 **cup hot water**
½ **cup light molasses**

1 In a mixing bowl stir together flour, sugar, soda, and ½ teaspoon *salt*. Cut in butter till mixture resembles fine crumbs. Remove ⅓ *cup* of the crumb mixture; set aside.

2 Stir together hot water and molasses; stir into crumb mixture. Turn into a greased 9×1½-inch round baking pan. Sprinkle reserved crumbs atop.

3 Bake in a 350° oven 25 to 30 minutes. Serve warm with whipped cream or vanilla ice cream, if desired. Makes 8 servings.

OATMEAL COOKIE DESSERT

Assembling time: 15 minutes
Cooking time: 30 minutes

2 **20-ounce cans sliced apples**
½ **cup chopped pecans**
¼ **cup sugar**
½ **teaspoon ground cinnamon**
1 **package 3-dozen-size oatmeal cookie mix**
Vanilla ice cream

1 Drain *one* can of apples. Turn *all* apple slices and liquid of second can into a 13×9×2-inch baking dish. Combine pecans, sugar, and cinnamon; sprinkle atop.

2 Prepare cookie mix according to package directions; drop batter by teaspoonfuls atop mixture in baking dish. Bake in a 375° oven for 25 to 30 minutes or till cookie topping is golden brown. Serve warm with ice cream. Makes 12 servings.

QUICK FUDGE BROWNIES

Assembling time: 15 minutes
Cooking time: 35 minutes

1½ **cups semisweet chocolate pieces**
1½ **cups graham cracker crumbs**
1 **14-ounce can (1¼ cups) Eagle Brand sweetened condensed milk**
1 **slightly beaten egg**
1 **teaspoon vanilla**
½ **cup chopped walnuts**

1 Melt *1 cup* of the chocolate pieces; stir in graham cracker crumbs, sweetened condensed milk, egg, and vanilla. Mix well. Stir in remaining chocolate pieces and nuts.

2 Spread mixture in a well-greased and floured 9×9×2-inch baking pan. Bake in a 350° oven about 35 minutes. Cool on a wire rack; cut into squares. Makes 36.

MINCEMEAT SQUARES

Assembling time: 15 minutes
Cooking time: 30 minutes

2 **cups all-purpose flour**
1 **cup sugar**
½ **cup chopped walnuts**
½ **teaspoon baking soda**
½ **teaspoon salt**
½ **teaspoon ground cinnamon**
½ **cup cooking oil**
¼ **cup orange juice**
1 **28-ounce jar prepared mincemeat**

1 Combine flour, sugar, nuts, soda, salt, and cinnamon. Stir in oil and juice. Reserve *1½ cups* flour mixture; press remainder into a 13×9×2-inch baking pan.

2 Spread mincemeat over mixture in pan; sprinkle with reserved flour mixture. Bake in a 400° oven about 30 minutes or till golden brown. Makes 12 servings.

CHOCOLATE-PEANUT BARS

Total preparation time: 45 minutes

1 **cup peanut butter**
¾ **cup sugar**
1 **egg**
1 **5¾-ounce package milk chocolate pieces**

1 In mixer bowl combine peanut butter, sugar, and egg. Beat on low speed till thoroughly combined. Press into an 11×7×1½-inch baking pan. Bake in a 325° oven for 18 to 20 minutes.

2 Remove from oven and immediately sprinkle with chocolate pieces. Cover pan with foil; let stand 3 minutes and remove foil. Spread chocolate over surface.

3 Sprinkle with chopped peanuts, if desired. Chill in freezer for 10 to 15 minutes or till chocolate is firm. Cut into squares; store in refrigerator. Makes 24 to 30.

SPICY OAT BARS

Assembling time: 20 minutes
Cooking time: 25 minutes

1 **package 2-layer-size spice cake mix**
½ **cup quick-cooking rolled oats**
2 **beaten eggs**
¼ **cup light molasses**
¼ **cup orange juice**
¼ **cup cooking oil**
½ **cup chopped pitted dates**
½ **cup chopped nuts**
Powdered sugar

1 Combine cake mix and oats. Combine eggs, molasses, juice, and oil; mix well. Stir into dry mixture. Stir in dates and nuts.

2 Spread in a greased 15×10×1-inch baking pan. Bake in a 350° oven for 25 minutes. Cool for 10 minutes. Sift powdered sugar atop. Cut into bars. Makes 60.

CHOCOLATE-CARAMEL PECAN BARS

Assembling time: 15 minutes
Cooking time: 15 minutes
Cooling time: 15 minutes

- 1 8-ounce package cream cheese, cut up
- ¾ cup butter *or* margarine
- ¾ cup sugar
- 1 teaspoon vanilla
- 2 cups all-purpose flour
- ½ teaspoon baking powder
- ½ cup caramel topping
- 1 5¾-ounce package milk chocolate pieces
- 1 cup chopped pecans

1 For crust, in a small mixer bowl beat cream cheese and butter or margarine on medium speed of electric mixer about 1 minute or till softened. Add sugar and vanilla; beat till well combined.

2 Stir together flour and baking powder; gradually beat into cream cheese mixture, mixing well. Spread cream cheese mixture in an ungreased 13×9×2-inch baking pan. Bake in a 375° oven about 15 minutes or till a wooden pick inserted in center comes out clean.

3 Immediately drizzle caramel topping over warm crust and sprinkle with chocolate pieces. Allow chocolate to melt slightly. Use a knife to swirl chocolate; sprinkle with pecans. Cool in refrigerator for 10 to 15 minutes. Cut into bars. Makes 32.

FUDGE CHEESECAKE BARS

Assembling time: 18 minutes
Cooking time: 30 minutes

- 2 cups all-purpose flour
- 1½ cups butter *or* margarine, cut up
- ⅔ cup packed brown sugar
- 1 package creamy chocolate fudge frosting mix (for 2-layer cake)
- 1 8-ounce package cream cheese, cut up
- 2 eggs
- ¾ cup slivered almonds

1 In a large mixer bowl combine flour, butter or margarine, and brown sugar. Beat on low speed of an electric mixer till the butter is cut into the dry ingredients (or, cut in by hand with a pastry blender).

2 Pat the flour mixture into an ungreased 13×9×2-inch baking pan. Bake in a 350° oven for 10 to 12 minutes. Meanwhile, in the same mixer bowl combine dry frosting mix and cream cheese; beat on low speed of electric mixer till combined. Add eggs; beat till smooth.

3 Carefully spread chocolate mixture over hot crust. Sprinkle with slivered almonds. Bake in a 350° oven about 30 minutes or till chocolate mixture is set. Cool; cut into bars. Store in refrigerator. Makes 32.

APPLE STRUDEL CUPS

Total preparation time: 35 minutes

- 1 10-ounce package (6) frozen patty shells
- 1 20-ounce can apple pie filling
- ½ teaspoon ground cinnamon
  Frozen whipped dessert topping, thawed

1 Bake patty shells according to package directions. Cool. In a saucepan mix pie filling and cinnamon. Cook over medium heat till warm. Spoon into patty shells. Dollop each with dessert topping. Serves 6.

PEACH MELBA CRISP

Assembling time: 20 minutes
Cooking time: 20 minutes

- 1 10-ounce package frozen red raspberries (in quick-thaw pouch)
- ¼ cup sugar
- 2 tablespoons cornstarch
- 1 16-ounce can peach slices
- ¼ cup butter *or* margarine
- 1½ cups granola
- 1 cup chopped walnuts
  Light cream

1 Thaw raspberries according to package directions. In a medium saucepan combine sugar, cornstarch, and dash *salt*. Stir in *undrained* peaches and *undrained* raspberries. Cook and stir till thickened and bubbly. Cook and stir 2 minutes more. Turn into an 8×1½-inch round baking dish.

2 Meanwhile, in another saucepan melt butter or margarine; stir in granola and walnuts. Sprinkle atop peach mixture. Bake in a 375° oven about 20 minutes. Serve warm with cream. Makes 6 servings.

QUICK FRUIT STRUDEL

Assembling time: 20 minutes
Cooking time: 50 minutes

½ **cup sugar**
1 **teaspoon ground cinnamon**
1 **20-ounce can sliced apples** *or* **one 16-ounce can pitted tart red cherries (water pack)** *or* **one 16-ounce can pear slices, drained**
½ **cup raisins (optional)**
¼ **cup chopped nuts**
5 **tablespoons butter** *or* **margarine, melted**
10 **sheets (16x12 inches) frozen phyllo dough, thawed**

1 In a mixing bowl combine sugar and cinnamon; reserve 1 tablespoon sugar mixture; set aside. Stir drained fruit, raisins, if desired, and nuts into remaining sugar mixture in mixing bowl. Stir till fruit is coated.

2 Brush a 12×7½×2-inch baking dish lightly with some of the melted butter or margarine. Fold a sheet of phyllo dough in half crosswise, forming a 12×8-inch rectangle; place in dish, tucking in edges of phyllo dough as necessary.

3 Brush top of phyllo dough with a little more melted butter. Repeat folding, layering and brushing, using *4 more sheets* of phyllo dough. Spoon fruit mixture atop phyllo dough in baking dish.

4 Repeat folding, layering, and brushing using the remaining *5 sheets* of phyllo and remaining butter. Score in a diamond pattern, using sharp knife and cutting to but not through bottom layer.

5 Sprinkle top with the reserved sugar mixture. Bake in a 350° oven for 45 to 50 minutes or till top is golden brown. Cool; cut along score lines to serve. Makes about 20 pieces.

PEANUT BUTTER-APPLE COBBLER

Total preparation time: 40 minutes

¼ **cup packed brown sugar**
¼ **cup chunk-style peanut butter**
¼ **cup butter** *or* **margarine**
1 **20-ounce can sliced apples**
¼ **cup orange juice**
½ **of a 17-ounce roll refrigerated sugar cookie dough**

1 In a saucepan combine brown sugar, peanut butter, and butter. Heat and stir mixture till sugar dissolves. Stir in *undrained* apple slices and orange juice; bring to boiling. Turn into a 10×6×2-inch baking dish.

2 Slice cookie dough into six equal portions; place atop hot apple mixture. Bake, uncovered, in a 400° oven for 20 to 25 minutes. Serve warm. Serves 6.

CRANBERRY CRISP

Assembling time: 15 minutes
Cooking time: 35 minutes

1 **package creamy coconut-pecan frosting mix (for 2-layer cake)**
2 **cups quick-cooking rolled oats**
½ **cup butter** *or* **margarine, cut up**
½ **teaspoon ground cinnamon**
½ **teaspoon ground nutmeg**
1 **16-ounce can whole cranberry sauce**
1 **16-ounce can pear halves, drained and chopped**

1 In a mixer bowl combine frosting mix, oats, butter or margarine, cinnamon, and nutmeg. Beat on medium speed about 3 minutes or till crumbly. Pat *2 cups* of the oat mixture into a 9×9×2-inch baking pan.

2 Stir cranberry sauce; spoon cranberry sauce and pears over oat mixture. Sprinkle remaining oat mixture atop. Bake in a 375° oven 30 to 35 minutes. Serves 8.

CRANBERRY-APPLE COBBLER

Total preparation time: 32 minutes

1 **20-ounce can sliced apples**
1 **16-ounce can whole cranberry sauce**
¼ **teaspoon ground cinnamon**
1 **cup packaged biscuit mix**
2 **tablespoons sugar**
¼ **cup milk**

1 Drain apples, reserving ¼ cup liquid. In a 10-inch skillet mix reserved liquid, apples, cranberry sauce, and the ¼ teaspoon cinnamon. Bring to boiling.

2 Meanwhile, in a bowl combine biscuit mix and sugar; stir in milk. Drop batter in 6 portions atop boiling mixture. Sprinkle with additional cinnamon, if desired.

3 Reduce heat. Simmer, uncovered, for 10 minutes. Cover and simmer 10 to 12 minutes more or till done. Serves 6.

BLACK-BOTTOM CUSTARDS

Total preparation time: 50 minutes

1 **3-ounce package no-bake custard mix**
1 **tablespoon sugar**
1½ **cups milk**
1 **3-ounce package cream cheese, cut up**
¼ **cup semisweet chocolate pieces**

1 In a saucepan combine custard mix and sugar. Stir in milk. Mix in cream cheese. Quickly bring to boiling, stirring constantly. Remove from heat; beat smooth with a rotary beater.

2 Stir together *half* of the custard mixture and the chocolate pieces; stir till melted. Pour chocolate mixture into five 6-ounce custard cups. Carefully spoon plain custard atop. Chill at least 30 minutes. Serves 5.

286

ANY-SEASON FRUIT COBBLER

Assembling time: 25 minutes
Cooking time: 15 minutes

 1 16-ounce can peach slices
 1 8-ounce can pineapple chunks (juice pack)
 1 16-ounce jar pitted stewed dried prunes, drained and halved
 ¼ cup honey
 ⅛ teaspoon ground cinnamon
 ⅛ teaspoon ground nutmeg
 ¼ teaspoon almond extract
 1 cup whole wheat flour
 ¼ cup toasted wheat germ
 2 teaspoons baking powder
 ⅛ teaspoon salt
 ¼ teaspoon finely shredded orange peel
 ½ cup orange juice
 2 tablespoons butter *or* margarine, melted
 2 teaspoons honey

1 Drain peaches and pineapple, reserving liquid. Add enough water to liquid to make 1½ cups. In saucepan mix reserved liquid, peaches, pineapple, prunes, the ¼ cup honey, cinnamon, and nutmeg. Bring to boiling. Reduce heat; simmer, uncovered, for 10 minutes. Remove from heat; stir in almond extract.

2 For dumplings, in a mixing bowl stir together whole wheat flour, wheat germ, baking powder, and salt. Combine orange peel, orange juice, butter, and the 2 teaspoons honey; add to dry ingredients, stirring till moistened.

3 Turn *hot* fruit mixture into 8×8×2-inch baking dish. *Immediately* drop dumplings by spoonfuls atop hot fruit. Bake in a 400° oven about 15 minutes. Serve warm. Makes 9 servings.

Cherry Crisp Parfaits

CHERRY CRISP PARFAITS

Total preparation time: 35 minutes

 ¼ cup butter *or* margarine
 1 cup quick-cooking rolled oats
 ½ cup packed brown sugar
 1 21-ounce can cherry pie filling
 ½ teaspoon ground allspice
 1 pint vanilla ice cream

1 In saucepan melt butter. Stir in oats and brown sugar. Turn into an 8×8×2-inch baking pan. Bake in a 350° oven for 10 minutes (mixture will be soft). Cool in refrigerator for 10 minutes; crumble.

2 Meanwhile, in a saucepan combine cherry pie filling and allspice; heat through. Divide *half* of the cherry mixture among 8 heat-proof parfait glasses.

3 Divide *half* the oat mixture among the parfaits. Divide the ice cream among the 8 parfaits; top with remaining cherry mixture and oat mixture. Makes 8 servings.

MAPLE BAKED CUSTARD

Total preparation time: 45 minutes

 4 beaten eggs
 2 cups milk
 ½ cup maple-flavored syrup
 ¼ teaspoon salt
    Whipped cream
    Ground nutmeg

1 In a 4-cup measure combine eggs, milk, syrup, and salt. Place six 6-ounce custard cups in a 13×9×2-inch baking pan on an oven rack. Pour egg mixture into the custard cups. Pour boiling water into pan around custard cups to a depth of 1 inch.

2 Bake in 325° oven 30 to 35 minutes or till knife inserted near center comes out clean. Serve warm or chilled with whipped cream and nutmeg. Serves 6.

YOGURT-ORANGE PARFAITS

You can double the amount of coconut crumb mixture when preparing this recipe. Then tightly cover the extra crumbs and store them in the refrigerator till the next time you want to make these parfaits—

Total preparation time: 35 minutes

 ¼ cup all-purpose flour
 ¼ cup coconut
 2 tablespoons sliced almonds
 1 tablespoon brown sugar
 2 tablespoons butter *or* margarine
 1 package 4-serving-size *instant* vanilla pudding mix
 1½ cups milk
 1 8-ounce carton orange yogurt
 1 11-ounce can mandarin orange sections, drained

1 In a mixing bowl stir together flour, coconut, almonds, and brown sugar; cut in butter or margarine till mixture resembles coarse crumbs. Evenly pat coconut mixture to ¼-inch thickness on a baking sheet. Bake in a 375° oven for 10 to 12 minutes or till golden brown. Slide onto a wire rack to cool at least 10 minutes.

2 Meanwhile, in a mixing bowl combine dry pudding mix, milk, and orange yogurt. Beat with a rotary beater according to package directions. Fold in orange sections.

3 Crumble baked coconut mixture into coarse crumbs. Spoon *half* of the pudding mixture into 6 sherbet dishes; top with *half* of the crumbs. Repeat layers with remaining pudding mixture and crumbs. Chill at least 5 minutes. Makes 6 servings.

GINGERY PEAR COMPOTE

Total preparation time: 35 minutes

½ cup unsweetened pineapple juice
¼ cup sugar
1 tablespoon lemon juice
¼ teaspoon ground ginger
6 medium pears, peeled, cored, and halved
Whipped cream
Shaved chocolate (optional)

1 In a 10-inch skillet combine pineapple juice, sugar, lemon juice, and ginger; heat and stir till sugar dissolves. Add pears, turning to coat.

2 Bring mixture to boiling. Reduce heat. Cover and simmer 20 to 25 minutes or just till pears are tender. Serve warm or chilled; top with whipped cream and shaved chocolate, if desired. Makes 6 servings.

COCONUT CRUNCH TORTE

Assembling time: 18 minutes
Cooking time: 35 minutes

1 cup coconut
½ cup graham cracker crumbs
⅓ cup chopped cashews
4 egg whites
1 teaspoon vanilla
1 cup sugar
Vanilla ice cream

1 In a bowl combine coconut, cracker crumbs, and cashews. Set aside. In large mixer bowl beat egg whites, vanilla, and ½ teaspoon *salt* till soft peaks form. Add sugar, a tablespoon at a time, beating till stiff peaks form.

2 Fold in coconut mixture. Spread in a well-greased 9-inch pie plate. Bake in a 350° oven for 30 to 35 minutes. Cool on rack. Serve with ice cream. Serves 8.

FRUIT PIZZA

Total preparation time: 35 minutes

1 package (8) refrigerated crescent rolls
1 10-ounce package frozen halved strawberries (in quick-thaw pouch)
1 4-ounce container whipped cream cheese
1 11-ounce can pineapple tidbits and mandarin orange sections, drained
¾ cup coconut
¾ cup broken pecans
¾ cup orange marmalade
1 tablespoon lemon juice

1 Unroll crescent rolls and separate into triangles. On a lightly greased 12-inch pizza pan place triangles with points toward center. Press crescent rolls together to cover bottom of pan and ½ inch up sides of pan. Bake in a 375° oven for 13 to 15 minutes or till golden brown.

2 Meanwhile, thaw strawberries according to package directions; drain. Dollop whipped cream cheese atop hot crescent roll crust; let stand 1 to 2 minutes or till cream cheese is softened. Evenly spread cream cheese over crust.

3 Arrange drained pineapple tidbits and mandarin orange sections atop cream cheese layer. Sprinkle with coconut and broken pecans. Arrange drained strawberries atop. Stir together orange marmalade and lemon juice; drizzle over fruit. Cut into wedges to serve. Makes 8 to 10 servings.

CHOCOLATE-LAYERED CHEESECAKE

Total preparation time: 1 hour and 20 minutes

1 10½-ounce *or* 11-ounce package cheesecake mix
1½ cups milk
1 3-ounce package cream cheese, cut up
¼ cup unsweetened cocoa powder
Shaved chocolate *or* chocolate curls (optional)

1 Prepare the crumb crust from cheesecake mix according to package directions; reserve *2 tablespoons* of crumbs for garnish. Press remaining crumbs onto the bottom and about 1 inch up the sides of an 8-inch springform pan or a 9-inch pie plate; cover and chill in the refrigerator while preparing filling.

2 For filling, in a mixer bowl combine cheesecake filling mix, milk, and cut-up cream cheese; beat at low speed of electric mixer till blended. Beat at medium speed for 3 minutes more or till mixture is very thick and smooth.

3 Pour *half* of the filling mixture into a small mixer bowl. Sift the unsweetened cocoa powder atop the filling mixture in the small bowl. Beat on medium speed of electric mixer till well combined.

4 Spread the chocolate filling mixture over the chilled crust. Top with the remaining filling mixture. Cover and chill in the refrigerator at least 1 hour before serving. Garnish with the reserved crumbs; add shaved chocolate or chocolate curls, if desired. Makes 8 servings.

PEAR CLAFOUTI

Clafouti is a traditional French pudding made with a fruit and a rich batter. It resembles a pie, but it usually has no crust—

Assembling time: 30 minutes
Cooking time: 1 hour

3 **medium pears, peeled and cored, or one 29-ounce can pear halves**
3 **eggs**
1¼ **cups milk**
½ **cup all-purpose flour**
⅓ **cup sugar**
2 **teaspoons vanilla**
¼ **teaspoon rum flavoring**
⅛ **teaspoon salt**
⅛ **teaspoon ground nutmeg**
Whipped cream

1 If using canned pears, place pear halves on paper toweling to drain thoroughly. Chop fresh or canned pears. In a small mixer bowl beat eggs on high speed of electric mixer till foamy.

2 Add milk, flour, sugar, vanilla, rum flavoring, salt, and ground nutmeg; beat at low speed of electric mixer till mixture is smooth. Spread chopped pears in a greased 10-inch quiche dish or pie plate.

3 Pour batter over pears. Bake in a 350° oven 50 to 60 minutes or till a knife inserted near center comes out clean. Let stand 15 minutes. Garnish with whipped cream. Makes 8 servings.

FUDGE BROWNIE PUFF

This rich dessert puffs like a soufflé, but is fudgy and nutty like a brownie—

Assembling time: 12 minutes
Cooking time: 40 minutes

1 **6-ounce package (1 cup) semisweet chocolate pieces**
½ **cup milk**
4 **egg yolks**
½ **cup walnuts**
¼ **cup sugar**
1 **teaspoon vanilla**
4 **egg whites**
¼ **teaspoon cream of tartar**
Frozen whipped dessert topping, thawed

1 If desired, fit a 1½-quart soufflé dish with a foil collar. Fold foil into thirds, lengthwise. Lightly rub butter and sprinkle sugar on one side. With buttered side in, attach collar to dish. In a blender container place chocolate pieces. In a small saucepan heat milk till almost boiling; pour over chocolate pieces. Cover and blend till mixture is smooth.

2 Add egg yolks, walnuts, sugar, and vanilla to chocolate mixture in blender container. Cover and blend till mixture is well blended and walnuts are coarsely chopped.

3 In a large mixer bowl beat egg whites and cream of tartar till soft peaks form (tips curl over); fold in chocolate mixture. Pour into the ungreased soufflé dish.

4 Bake in a 350° oven for 35 to 40 minutes or till a knife inserted near center comes out clean. Serve immediately with whipped dessert topping. Makes 6 servings.

PEAR OR APPLE DUMPLINGS

Preparing fruit dumplings is easier when you start with a piecrust mix—

Assembling time: 25 minutes
Cooking time: 50 minutes

1 **package piecrust mix (for 2-crust pie)**
1 **tablespoon sugar**
4 **medium cooking apples *or* firm pears, peeled and cored**
⅓ **cup raisins**
¼ **cup orange marmalade**
Light cream (optional)

1 In a mixing bowl prepare the piecrust mix according to package directions, *except* add 1 tablespoon sugar to the piecrust mix before adding water. Roll the pastry dough on lightly floured surface to ⅛-inch thickness and cut into 4 circles about 7½ inches in diameter; reroll leftover dough as necessary.

2 Place apples or pears in an ungreased 9×9×2-inch baking pan. Fill centers with raisins; spoon marmalade atop raisins. Place pastry circles over fruit. Pull pastry down to completely cover the fruit. Pinch pastry together to seal edges at the base of the fruit. Use the tines of a fork to prick top of pastry to allow steam to escape.

3 Bake in a 350° oven 45 to 50 minutes or till the fruit is easily pierced with a fork. Serve warm with light cream, if desired. Makes 4 servings.

PEACH-GINGERBREAD PUDDING

Assembling time: 23 minutes
Cooking time: 1 hour

- 1 **17-ounce can spiced whole peaches**
- 1 **14½-ounce package gingerbread mix**
- ⅓ **cup chopped walnuts**
  Spicy Sauce

1 Drain peaches, reserving syrup. Pit and finely chop peaches; set aside. Prepare the gingerbread mix according to package directions, *except* decrease the water by ¼ cup. Fold in chopped peaches and walnuts.

2 Pour gingerbread mixture into a well-greased 9-cup fluted tube pan. Cover tightly with foil. Bake in a 375° oven 55 to 60 minutes or till gingerbread tests done. Cool in pan for 10 minutes. Loosen edges and unmold onto a serving plate. Meanwhile, prepare Spicy Sauce. Serve gingerbread warm with Spicy Sauce. Serves 10 to 12.

Spicy Sauce: In a saucepan stir together ¼ cup *sugar*, 2 tablespoons *cornstarch*, and ⅛ teaspoon ground *nutmeg*. Add enough water to the reserved peach syrup to make 1½ cups liquid. Stir peach liquid into the sugar mixture in the saucepan. Cook and stir till the mixture is thickened and bubbly. Cook and stir 2 minutes more. Remove from heat. Stir in 2 tablespoons *butter* or *margarine* and 1 tablespoon *lemon juice.*

CHOCOLATE CHIP-PEANUT BUTTER BREAD PUDDING

Assembling time: 20 minutes
Cooking time: 1 hour

Butter *or* margarine
- 4 **slices white bread**
- ½ **cup coconut**
- ½ **cup semisweet chocolate pieces**
- ⅔ **cup sugar**
- ½ **cup peanut butter**
- 2 **eggs**
- 1 **teaspoon vanilla**
  Dash salt
- 2½ **cups milk**

1 Lightly spread butter on one side of each slice of bread. Cut the buttered bread into ½-inch cubes. Place in an 8×8×2-inch baking dish. Sprinkle coconut and chocolate pieces atop bread cubes.

2 In a small mixer bowl beat together sugar and peanut butter on medium speed of electric mixer for 1 minute. Beat in eggs, vanilla, and salt.

3 Add milk; beat on low speed till blended. Pour atop bread cubes in baking dish. Place baking dish in a 13×9×2-inch baking pan on an oven rack; pour boiling water into the outer pan to a depth of 1 inch.

4 Bake in a 350° oven about 1 hour or till a knife inserted near center comes out clean. Spoon into dessert dishes. Serve warm. Makes 8 servings.

CARAMEL-TOPPED RICE PUDDING

Assembling time: 20 minutes
Cooking time: 30 minutes

- 2 **cups milk**
- 1 **cup water**
- ½ **cup sugar**
- ½ **teaspoon salt**
- 1⅓ **cups quick-cooking rice**
- 3 **beaten eggs**
- 1½ **teaspoons vanilla**
- ¼ **cup caramel topping**
  Frozen whipped dessert topping, thawed

1 In a medium saucepan combine the milk, water, sugar, and salt. Bring the milk mixture to boiling; stir in the quick-cooking rice. Remove saucepan from heat. Cover and let stand for 10 minutes. (Rice will not absorb all of the liquid.)

2 Combine eggs and vanilla. Gradually stir about *half* of the hot rice mixture into eggs. Return all to the remaining rice mixture in the saucepan, stirring to thoroughly combine ingredients.

3 Pour caramel topping into a 5½-cup oven-going ring mold, lifting and tilting mold to spread topping over bottom and about halfway up the sides of mold. Pour rice mixture into prepared mold.

4 Place mold on baking sheet or pizza pan to catch any liquid that may bubble over. Bake in a 350° oven for 25 to 30 minutes or till a knife inserted near center comes out clean.

5 Slip the point of a knife or spatula down the sides of the mold to let air in and loosen the sides of the pudding. Immediately place serving plate atop mold; invert mold. Carefully lift off mold. Serve pudding warm with whipped dessert topping. Makes 6 to 8 servings.

PEACH PUFF PUDDING

Assembling time: 27 minutes
Cooking time: 25 minutes

1 29-ounce can peach slices
1 tablespoon brandy
⅓ cup all-purpose flour
¼ teaspoon baking powder
 Dash salt
2 egg yolks
¼ cup sugar
1 tablespoon brandy
½ teaspoon vanilla
2 egg whites
 Powdered sugar

1 Drain peaches, reserving 1 tablespoon of the peach liquid. Combine peach liquid with 1 tablespoon brandy. Arrange peach slices in the bottom of an 8×8×2-inch baking pan. Drizzle brandy mixture over fruit. Heat in a 375° oven for 10 minutes while preparing topping.

2 For topping, stir together flour, baking powder, and salt; set aside. In a mixing bowl beat egg yolks; gradually beat in ¼ cup sugar, 1 tablespoon brandy, and vanilla. Stir in flour mixture. Beat egg whites till stiff peaks form; gently fold beaten whites into yolk mixture.

3 Pour batter over hot fruit, covering surface as much as possible. Bake in a 375° oven about 25 minutes. Cool 10 to 15 minutes. Sprinkle with powdered sugar. Serve warm. Makes 6 to 8 servings.

CHOCOLATE-BARLEY PUDDING

Assembling time: 30 minutes
Chilling time: 1 hour

¾ cup water
¼ cup quick-cooking barley
1 square (1 ounce) semisweet
 chocolate
1 tablespoon butter *or* margarine
1 tablespoon sugar
1½ teaspoons cornstarch
1 beaten egg yolk
3 tablespoons milk
½ teaspoon vanilla
1 egg white
2 tablespoons sugar
½ cup whipping cream
 Broken walnuts (optional)

1 In a saucepan bring water to boiling. Add barley; reduce heat. Cover and simmer 10 to 12 minutes or till tender. Drain off any excess liquid; cool. Set aside.

2 Meanwhile, in another saucepan melt chocolate and butter or margarine over low heat. Stir together the 1 tablespoon sugar and the cornstarch. Stir into chocolate mixture; add egg yolk and milk. Cook and stir till mixture is thickened and bubbly. Cook and stir 2 minutes more. Stir in vanilla and cooked barley.

3 In a small mixer bowl beat egg white on high speed of electric mixer till soft peaks form (tips curl over). Gradually add the 2 tablespoons sugar, beating till stiff peaks form (tips stand straight). Fold beaten egg white into barley mixture. Cover and chill at least 1 hour.

4 To serve, whip the ½ cup cream; reserve *one-fourth* of the whipped cream. Layer barley mixture and remaining whipped cream in parfait glasses, ending with barley mixture. Top with the reserved whipped cream and walnuts, if desired. Makes 4 servings.

PUMPKIN-RUM BREAD PUDDING

If you don't have dry whole wheat bread, arrange slices of whole wheat bread in a single layer on the rack of an oven preheated to 300°. Bake for 5 minutes and then cut into cubes—

Assembling time: 12 minutes
Cooking time: 1 hour

6 cups dry whole wheat bread
 cubes
½ cup finely chopped walnuts
3 slightly beaten eggs
1 14-ounce can Eagle Brand
 sweetened condensed milk
1 cup canned pumpkin
¾ cup packed brown sugar
2 teaspoons ground cinnamon
½ teaspoon ground nutmeg
2 cups milk
¼ cup rum
¼ cup butter *or* margarine, melted
2 teaspoons vanilla
 Whipped cream (optional)

1 Combine bread cubes and walnuts in the bottom of a 12×7½×2-inch baking dish. In a bowl stir together eggs, condensed milk, pumpkin, brown sugar, cinnamon, and nutmeg. Gradually stir in milk, rum, butter or margarine, and vanilla, mixing well.

2 Pour over bread-nut layer in the baking dish. Place baking dish in a 13×9×2-inch baking pan. Pour boiling water into pan to a depth of 1 inch. Bake in a 350° oven 50 to 60 minutes or till a knife inserted near center comes out clean. Serve warm with whipped cream. Makes 10 servings.

FLAKY CHEESE SQUARES

Assembling time: 25 minutes
Cooking time: 18 minutes

1 8-ounce package cream cheese
2 eggs
2 cups shredded Monterey Jack cheese *or* mozzarella cheese (8 ounces)
½ cup cream-style cottage cheese with chives
¼ cup butter *or* margarine, melted
8 sheets (18x16 inches) frozen phyllo dough, thawed
2 tablespoons grated Parmesan cheese

1 In a small mixer bowl beat cream cheese on low speed of an electric mixer about 1 minute or till softened. Add eggs; beat till mixture is smooth. Stir in shredded Monterey Jack or mozzarella cheese and cottage cheese.

2 Brush the bottom of a 15 × 10 × 1-inch baking pan with some of the melted butter or margarine. Layer *4 sheets* of the phyllo dough in pan, allowing sides to overlap edges. Brush each sheet with butter or margarine before adding the next sheet.

3 Spread cheese mixture over the phyllo dough. Layer the remaining sheets of phyllo atop the cheese mixture, brushing each with melted butter or margarine as directed above.

4 Fold edges of phyllo over the top; brush with melted butter or margarine. Sprinkle with Parmesan cheese. With a sharp knife, score top four sheets of phyllo into 1½-inch squares. Bake in a 400° oven 15 to 18 minutes or till golden. Cut into squares along scoring. Serve warm. Makes 60.

STROGANOFF PIZZA ROUNDS

Assembling time: 35 minutes
Cooking time: 10 minutes

1 package active dry yeast
½ cup warm water (110° to 115°)
1 tablespoon cooking oil
2½ cups packaged biscuit mix
1 pound bulk Italian sausage
1 cup dairy sour cream
¼ teaspoon salt
3 tomatoes, sliced
1 teaspoon dried basil, crushed
½ teaspoon dried thyme, crushed
1 4-ounce package (1 cup) shredded mozzarella cheese
¼ cup grated Parmesan cheese

1 In a mixing bowl soften yeast in warm water; stir in cooking oil. Add biscuit mix, stirring just till all is moistened. Cover and let rest 10 minutes. Divide dough into 6 equal portions.

2 On a lightly floured surface roll each piece of dough into a 5-inch circle. Place on greased baking sheets; crimp edges. Bake in a 425° oven for 5 minutes.

3 Meanwhile, in a large skillet cook Italian sausage till browned; drain off fat. Stir in sour cream and salt. Spread meat mixture on each crust. Top with tomato slices; sprinkle with a little additional salt.

4 Sprinkle with basil and thyme. Top each with some mozzarella cheese and Parmesan cheese. Return to a 425° oven; bake 8 to 10 minutes more or till heated through. Makes 6 servings.

GLAZED MEATBALLS AND APPLES

Total preparation time: 35 minutes

1 slightly beaten egg
¼ cup milk
¼ cup fine dry bread crumbs
½ teaspoon salt
1 pound ground beef
½ cup water
¼ cup catsup
2 tablespoons brown sugar
2 apples, cored and cut into chunks
1 tablespoon soy sauce
1 teaspoon cornstarch
½ teaspoon ground allspice
¼ teaspoon dry mustard

1 In a mixing bowl combine egg and milk. Stir in bread crumbs and salt. Add ground beef; mix well. Shape into ¾-inch meatballs (use a rounded teaspoon for each). Place meatballs in a large shallow baking pan. Bake in a 450° oven 10 to 15 minutes or till done.

2 Meanwhile, in a small saucepan combine the water, catsup, and brown sugar; heat mixture to boiling. Add the apple chunks; simmer, covered, about 5 minutes or till the apple chunks are tender.

3 Stir together soy sauce, cornstarch, allspice, and mustard. Stir into apple mixture. Cook and stir 2 minutes more.

4 Using a slotted spoon, transfer baked meatballs to apple mixture; heat through. Keep meatball-apple mixture warm; serve with wooden picks or cocktail picks. Makes about 60.

Stroganoff Pizza Rounds
Glazed Meatballs and Apples

SPINACH STUFFING DROPS

Assembling time: 22 minutes
Cooking time: 10 minutes

1 10-ounce package frozen chopped spinach
3 beaten eggs
1¼ cups corn bread stuffing mix, crushed
⅓ cup grated Parmesan cheese
¼ cup butter *or* margarine, melted
¼ teaspoon onion powder
2 teaspoons brown sugar
1 teaspoon cornstarch
¼ cup prepared mustard
3 tablespoons water

1 In a saucepan cook spinach in a very small amount of water for 5 to 7 minutes or just till thawed. Drain, pressing out excess moisture. In a mixing bowl combine beaten eggs, corn bread stuffing mix, grated Parmesan cheese, melted butter or margarine, and onion powder.

2 Stir in drained spinach. Drop spinach mixture by teaspoons onto a greased baking sheet. Bake in a 400° oven about 10 minutes or till done.

3 Meanwhile, to prepare mustard dip, in a small saucepan combine brown sugar and cornstarch. Stir in prepared mustard and water. Cook and stir till mixture is thickened and bubbly. Cook and stir 2 minutes more. Serve warm spinach drops on wooden picks with mustard dip. Makes about 72.

MEXICAN STACK-UP

Total preparation time: 35 minutes

1 6-ounce container frozen avocado dip
1 16-ounce can refried beans
2 tablespoons finely chopped onion
2 tablespoons water
1 4-ounce package (1 cup) shredded cheddar cheese
2 tomatoes, seeded and finely chopped
⅓ cup chopped pitted ripe olives
Tortilla chips *or* corn tortillas, cut into wedges

1 Place unopened container of frozen dip in a bowl of hot water; let stand about 25 minutes or till nearly thawed. Meanwhile, stir together refried beans, onion, and water.

2 On a round, flat platter, spread refried bean mixture evenly into a 6- to 7-inch circle. Spread avocado dip atop refried bean mixture. Top with layers of cheddar cheese and tomatoes. Sprinkle with olives. Serve with tortilla chips. Makes 4 cups.

CHEESE DOME

Total preparation time: 40 minutes

1 8-ounce package shredded cheddar cheese (at room temperature)
1 4-ounce package Camembert cheese (at room temperature)
⅓ cup dry white wine
⅔ cup sliced almonds
Assorted fresh fruit pieces

1 Combine cheeses and wine. Beat till smooth. Stir in *half* of the almonds; cover and chill in freezer for 25 to 30 minutes. Shape into a dome. Press remaining almonds against outside of cheese. Serve with fresh fruit. Makes 2½ cups.

SALMON-CHEESE SPREAD

Total preparation time: 1 hour

1 8-ounce package cream cheese, cut up
1 7¾-ounce can salmon, drained, flaked, and skin and bones removed
1 4-ounce package (1 cup) shredded cheddar cheese
½ teaspoon dried dillweed
¼ cup onion salad dressing
2 tablespoons snipped parsley
Assorted crackers

1 Mix cream cheese, salmon, cheddar cheese, and dillweed. Beat in onion dressing. Cover; chill in freezer for 15 to 20 minutes. Shape into a ball; chill in freezer for 30 minutes more. Sprinkle with parsley. Serve with crackers. Makes 2½ cups.

BROCCAMOLI DIP

Total preparation time: 1¼ hours

1 10-ounce package frozen chopped broccoli
½ teaspoon minced dried onion
½ cup dairy sour cream
1 tablespoon lemon juice
¼ teaspoon ground coriander
⅛ teaspoon ground red pepper
Tortilla chips *or* vegetable dippers

1 Cook broccoli and onion according to the broccoli package directions *except* add 2 to 3 minutes to the cooking time; drain. Place broccoli mixture, sour cream, lemon juice, coriander, and red pepper in blender container. Cover; blend till smooth.

2 Turn into serving bowl; cover. Chill at least 1 hour; stir. Serve with chips or vegetables. Makes about 1¾ cups.

CARAWAY-CHEESE WEDGES

Total preparation time: 40 minutes

1 9-inch frozen unbaked deep-dish
  pastry shell
4 beaten eggs
¼ cup dairy sour cream
1 cup shredded Swiss cheese
2 tablespoons cooked bacon pieces
1 teaspoon minced dried onion
½ teaspoon caraway seed

1 Place unpricked pastry shell on a preheated baking sheet in a 450° oven.
Bake at 450° for 6 minutes. Remove from
oven; reduce heat to 350°.

2 Combine eggs and sour cream. Stir in
cheese, bacon, onion, caraway, and a
dash of *pepper*. Pour into warm pastry shell.
Bake in a 350° oven about 20 minutes or till
set. Cut into small wedges. Serves 16 to 20.

CARAMEL CORN

Total preparation time: 50 minutes

½ cup butter *or* margarine
1 cup packed brown sugar
¼ cup light corn syrup
¼ teaspoon baking soda
½ teaspoon vanilla
3 quarts popped corn

1 In a heavy saucepan melt butter; stir in
brown sugar, corn syrup, and ½ tea-
spoon *salt*. Bring to boiling, stirring constantly. Boil *without stirring* for 5 minutes.
Remove from heat; stir in soda and vanilla.

2 Gradually pour over popped corn; mix
well. Turn into buttered 17×12×2-inch
baking pan. Bake, uncovered, in a 300°
oven 30 minutes. Stir after 15 minutes.

3 Remove from oven; cool in pan. Loos-
en and break into pieces. Store in a
tightly covered container. Makes 2½ quarts.

FISH 'N' CHIP STICKS

Assembling time: 15 minutes
Cooking time: 30 minutes

1 package (10) refrigerated biscuits
1 9-ounce package frozen fish sticks
¼ cup milk
1 cup finely crushed potato chips
  (about 2 ounces)
½ cup dairy sour cream
2 tablespoons milk
1 tablespoon sweet pickle relish
½ teaspoon prepared horseradish
¼ teaspoon onion salt
  Dash bottled hot pepper sauce

1 Separate biscuits. On a lightly floured
surface roll each biscuit into a 5×4-
inch rectangle. Top each with one frozen fish
stick; wrap biscuit dough around fish stick,
pinching edges of biscuit to seal.

2 Dip each biscuit-wrapped fish stick in
the ¼ cup milk; then roll the sticks in the
finely crushed potato chips to coat.

3 Place coated sticks on a greased baking sheet. Bake in a 350° oven for 25 to
30 minutes or till golden brown.

4 Meanwhile, prepare horseradish dip. In
a small mixing bowl stir together the
dairy sour cream, the 2 tablespoons milk,
sweet pickle relish, prepared horseradish,
onion salt, and bottled hot pepper sauce.
Serve the horseradish dip with the hot fish
sticks. Makes 10.

CIDER-CITRUS PUNCH

Total preparation time: 35 minutes

1 gallon apple cider *or* apple juice
1 6-ounce can frozen lemonade
  concentrate
1 6-ounce can frozen orange juice
  concentrate
½ cup packed brown sugar
1 tablespoon whole cloves
1 tablespoon whole allspice

1 In a large saucepan or Dutch oven
combine the cider, concentrates, and
brown sugar. Heat and stir till concentrates
thaw and sugar dissolves. Tie cloves and
allspice in a cheesecloth bag. Add to the
cider mixture. Heat just to boiling.

2 Reduce heat; cover and simmer 20
minutes, stirring occasionally. Remove
spice bag and discard. Serve hot or cold
over ice. Makes 24 (6-ounce) servings.

HONEY-SPICE PERCOLATOR WINE

Total preparation time: 20 minutes

¾ cup honey
8 whole cloves
6 inches stick cinnamon, broken
1 750-ml bottle dry red wine
¼ cup brandy
2 tablespoons lemon juice

1 In 8- to 10-cup percolator mix honey
and 2½ cups *water*. Place cloves and
cinnamon in percolator basket; perk according to manufacturer's directions.

2 Meanwhile, in saucepan heat wine,
brandy, and lemon juice till warm. Remove basket from percolator; stir in wine
mixture. If desired, serve with cinnamon
stick stirrers. Makes 8 (6-ounce) servings.

CHAPTER 6

MAKE-AHEAD COOKING

Cooking ahead is a trick-of-the-trade that many efficient cooks use often. The recipes in this chapter can save you time by allowing you to switch cooking chores to off hours. Simply prepare the foods and freeze or chill them just until before serving. Glance through the following pages and you'll discover a wide variety of options. Try a main dish based on frozen stew or ground meat mix. Fix up frozen meatballs or poultry starter. Opt for a molded or marinated salad with no last-minute work. Refrigerate bread dough or muffin batter until you need it. Keep ready-made desserts on call. Stash a whole party menu of appetizers in your freezer. By relying on make-ahead foods, you can give show-stopping parties or serve delicious family meals even on the busiest of days.

These mouth-watering dishes are each designed to fix and forget until minutes before you're ready to eat: Marinated Steak Platter (see recipe, page 308), Molded White Wine and Apricot Salad (see recipe, page 331), and Instant Black Forest Pie (see recipe, page 353).

FREEZER BEEF STEW MEAT MIX

Total preparation time: 2 hours and 40 minutes

½ cup all-purpose flour
1 teaspoon salt
⅛ teaspoon pepper
6 pounds beef stew meat, cut into 1-inch cubes
¼ cup cooking oil
1 10½-ounce can condensed beef broth
1¼ cups water (1 soup can)
2 stalks celery with leaves
1 large onion, quartered
2 cloves garlic, minced
2 bay leaves

1 In a plastic bag combine the flour, salt, and pepper. Add stew meat cubes, a few at a time, shaking to coat. In a large kettle or Dutch oven brown meat cubes, ⅓ at a time, in hot cooking oil.

2 Return all meat to the kettle or Dutch oven. Add beef broth, water, celery, onion, garlic, and bay leaves. Bring the mixture to boiling; reduce heat. Cover and simmer for 2 hours or till meat is tender.

3 Skim fat. Drain meat, reserving liquid. Strain liquid; discard vegetables and bay leaves. Cool quickly. Divide meat and broth into 6 moisture-vaporproof containers or freezer bags. Seal, label, and freeze. Makes six (2-cup) portions.

DUMPLING-TOPPED TEXAS STEW

Total preparation time: 1 hour

1 2-cup package Freezer Beef Stew Mix
1 16-ounce can tomatoes, cut up
2 cups tomato juice
1 15½-ounce can red kidney beans, drained
1 medium onion, chopped
2 cloves garlic, minced
1 tablespoon Worcestershire sauce
1 teaspoon sugar
1 teaspoon dried oregano, crushed
½ teaspoon ground cumin
¼ teaspoon salt
¼ teaspoon ground red pepper
Few drops bottled hot pepper sauce
1 4-ounce can green chili peppers, rinsed, seeded, and chopped
2 cups packaged biscuit mix
¾ cup shredded cheddar cheese
⅔ cup milk

1 In a Dutch oven combine Freezer Beef Stew Mix, *undrained* tomatoes, tomato juice, kidney beans, onion, garlic, Worcestershire sauce, sugar, oregano, cumin, salt, ground red pepper, and bottled hot pepper sauce. Reserve *1 tablespoon* of the chopped green chili peppers. Stir remaining chili peppers into the tomato mixture in the Dutch oven. Bring the tomato mixture to boiling; reduce heat. Simmer, uncovered, for 15 minutes. Stir occasionally with a fork to break up the mix.

2 In a mixing bowl combine biscuit mix, cheese, and the reserved chili peppers. Add milk all at once; stir just till mixture is moistened. Drop dough from a tablespoon atop the bubbling stew. Simmer, uncovered, about 10 minutes. Cover and simmer for 10 minutes more. Makes 6 servings.

ORIENTAL-STYLE BEEF AND RICE

Total preparation time: 30 minutes

1 2-cup package Freezer Beef Stew Mix
¼ cup water
2 cups water
1 ¾-ounce envelope mushroom gravy mix
1½ cups quick-cooking rice
1 8-ounce can sliced water chestnuts, drained
1 4-ounce can sliced mushrooms, drained
2 tablespoons chopped green *or* red sweet pepper
1 tablespoon butter *or* margarine
1 tablespoon soy sauce
1 6-ounce package frozen pea pods

1 In a large saucepan combine Freezer Beef Stew Mix and the ¼ cup water. Cover and cook over low heat for 15 to 20 minutes. Stir occasionally with a fork to break up the mix.

2 Meanwhile, combine the 2 cups water and the gravy mix. Stir gravy mixture, uncooked rice, water chestnuts, mushrooms, chopped pepper, butter or margarine, and soy sauce into meat mixture. Bring to boiling; reduce heat. Cover and simmer for 5 minutes.

3 Place pea pods in a colander. Run hot water over pea pods; drain. Add pea pods to meat mixture. Cover and simmer 2 minutes more or till rice and pea pods are tender. Makes 6 servings.

FREEZER GROUND MEAT MIX

Total preparation time: 30 minutes

- 3 beaten eggs
- 2 cups soft bread crumbs
- 1 cup chopped celery
- 1 cup chopped onion
- 1 cup shredded carrot
- 3 pounds ground beef *or* pork

1 In a bowl combine eggs, bread crumbs, celery, onion, carrot, and 1 teaspoon *salt.* Add meat; mix well. In a skillet cook the mixture, half at a time, till meat is lightly browned. Stir with a fork to break up large pieces. Drain fat. Cool quickly.

2 Spoon *2 cups* of the meat mixture into each of 5 moisture-vaporproof containers or freezer bags. Seal, label, and freeze. Makes five 2-cup portions.

CHILI SKILLET

Total preparation time: 30 minutes

- 1 2-cup package Freezer Ground Meat Mix
- 1 15½-ounce can red kidney beans
- 1 8-ounce can tomato sauce
- 1 teaspoon chili powder
- ½ teaspoon sugar
- 1 8-ounce jar cheese spread
- ½ cup dairy sour cream

1 In skillet cook Freezer Ground Meat Mix and ¼ cup *water,* covered, over medium-low heat 15 to 20 minutes. Stir often with a fork to break up large pieces.

2 Drain kidney beans. Stir kidney beans, tomato sauce, chili powder, and sugar into meat mixture. Bring to boiling; reduce heat. Cover and cook for 3 to 5 minutes. Slowly stir in cheese spread till melted.

3 Remove from heat. Dollop sour cream atop mixture. Sprinkle corn chips around the edge, if desired. Serves 6.

CHOP SUEY SANDWICHES

Total preparation time: 35 minutes

- 1 16-ounce can fancy mixed Chinese vegetables, drained
- 1 2-cup package Freezer Ground Meat Mix
- 1 8-ounce can crushed pineapple (juice pack)
- 3 tablespoons soy sauce
- 2 tablespoons cornstarch
- 8 individual French rolls
- ½ of a 3-ounce can chow mein noodles

1 In a saucepan combine the mixed Chinese vegetables, Freezer Ground Meat Mix, and the *undrained* crushed pineapple. Cover and cook over medium-low heat for 15 to 20 minutes. Stir mixture occasionally with fork to break up large pieces.

2 In a bowl combine soy sauce and cornstarch; add to meat mixture. Cook and stir till mixture is thickened and bubbly. Cook and stir 2 minutes more.

3 Meanwhile, cut a thin slice from the top of each French roll. Set aside. Hollow out bottoms of rolls leaving a ¼-inch shell. (Use bread pieces for another purpose.) Spoon meat mixture into the rolls. Crumble the chow mein noodles on top of the hot meat mixture. Cover *each* with top of bun. Makes 8 sandwiches.

SKILLET PIZZA

Total preparation time: 40 minutes

- 1 2-cup package Freezer Ground Meat Mix
- 1 15¾-ounce package cheese pizza mix
- Dash garlic powder
- ½ cup hot water
- 1 4-ounce can sliced mushrooms, drained
- 1 4-ounce package (1 cup) shredded mozzarella cheese

1 In a saucepan combine Freezer Ground Meat Mix, the sauce from the pizza mix, the herbs from pizza mix (if present), and garlic powder. Cover and cook over medium-low heat for 15 to 20 minutes. Stir occasionally with a fork to break up large pieces.

2 Meanwhile, in a bowl combine flour packet and cheese from pizza mix; add hot water. Stir to form a soft dough. With greased hands spread dough into a greased cold, heavy, oven-going 10-inch skillet. Press dough over bottom and ½ inch up sides.

3 Bake, uncovered, in a 425° oven for 5 minutes. Spread the meat mixture over crust. Top with the mushrooms. Sprinkle with shredded mozzarella cheese. Bake 12 to 15 minutes more or till done. Let stand 5 minutes. Loosen sides and bottom of pizza; slide onto large serving plate. Cut into wedges to serve. Makes 6 servings.

STROGANOFF SANDWICH

Total preparation time: 40 minutes

- 1 2-cup package Freezer Ground Meat Mix (see recipe, page 299)
- ¼ cup dry sherry
- ¼ cup water
- 1 teaspoon instant beef bouillon granules
- 1 8-ounce carton dairy sour cream
- 2 tablespoons all-purpose flour
- 1 4-ounce can sliced mushrooms, drained
- 1 loaf French bread, unsliced Butter *or* margarine, softened
- 2 medium tomatoes, sliced
- 1 cup shredded American cheese (4 ounces)

1 In a saucepan combine Freezer Ground Meat Mix, dry sherry, water, and instant beef bouillon granules. Cover and cook over medium-low heat for 15 to 20 minutes. Stir occasionally with a fork to break up large pieces. Cover and cook 5 minutes more.

2 Combine the sour cream and flour. Stir the sour cream mixture and the mushrooms into the meat mixture. Cook and stir till mixture is thickened and bubbly. Cook 1 minute more.

3 Meanwhile, cut bread in half lengthwise. Place halves, cut side up, on a baking sheet. Broil 4 to 5 inches from the heat for 2 to 3 minutes or till toasted. Spread bread lightly with the softened butter or margarine. Spread half of the hot meat mixture on each toasted loaf half.

4 Halve tomato slices and arrange atop the meat mixture. Broil for 5 minutes. Sprinkle with shredded cheese; broil 2 minutes more. Slice to serve. Makes 8 servings.

SOUTH OF THE BORDER-STYLE TACO SALAD

Total preparation time: 25 minutes

- 1 2-cup package Freezer Ground Meat Mix (see recipe, page 299)
- ¼ cup water
- 1 8-ounce can tomato sauce
- 1 tablespoon all-purpose flour
- 1 4-ounce can green chili peppers, rinsed, seeded, and chopped
- 2 teaspoons chili powder
- 12 cups torn greens
- 1 cup cherry tomatoes
- 1 4-ounce package (1 cup) shredded cheddar cheese

1 In a saucepan combine the Freezer Ground Meat Mix and water. Cover and cook over medium-low heat for 15 to 20 minutes. Stir occasionally with a fork to break up large pieces.

2 In a bowl combine the tomato sauce and flour; add to meat mixture along with chopped green chili peppers and chili powder. Cook and stir till thickened and bubbly. Cook and stir 1 minute more.

3 Meanwhile, in a large salad bowl toss together the torn greens and cherry tomatoes. Top with hot meat mixture; sprinkle with shredded cheddar cheese. Toss to serve. Makes 6 servings.

CORN MOUSSAKA

Total preparation time: 1 hour

- 1 2-cup package Freezer Ground Meat Mix (see recipe, page 299)
- ¼ cup water
- 1 17-ounce can whole kernel corn, drained
- 1 8-ounce can tomato sauce
- 2 tablespoons all-purpose flour
- ¼ teaspoon ground cinnamon
- ⅛ teaspoon garlic powder
- 2 beaten eggs
- 1½ cups cream-style cottage cheese
- 1 4-ounce package (1 cup) shredded mozzarella cheese
- ¼ cup grated Parmesan cheese (1 ounce)
  Slivered almonds (optional)

1 In a saucepan combine Freezer Ground Meat Mix and water. Cover and cook over medium-low heat for 15 to 20 minutes. Stir ground meat mixture occasionally with a fork to break up large pieces. Cover and cook 5 minutes more.

2 Meanwhile, spread corn in an ungreased shallow 1½-quart casserole or a 10x6x2-inch baking dish. In a bowl combine tomato sauce, flour, cinnamon, and garlic powder. Add tomato sauce mixture to meat mixture. Cook and stir till mixture is thickened and bubbly. Cook and stir 1 minute more. Spread tomato sauce and meat mixture over corn. Combine eggs and cottage cheese; spread over the meat mixture.

3 Bake in a 350° oven for 15 minutes. Top with mozzarella and Parmesan cheeses. Sprinkle almonds atop, if desired. Return to oven and bake 10 to 15 minutes more. Let stand 5 minutes before serving. Makes 6 servings.

Corn Moussaka

FREEZER MEATBALLS

Total preparation time: 1 hour and 30 minutes

3 beaten eggs
¾ cup milk
3 cups soft bread crumbs
½ cup finely chopped onion
2 teaspoons salt
3 pounds ground beef *or* ground pork

1 In a bowl combine eggs and milk; stir in bread crumbs, onion, and salt. Add ground beef or ground pork; mix well. Shape into 1-inch meatballs.

2 Bake meatballs, half at a time, in large, shallow baking pans in a 375° oven for 25 to 30 minutes. Remove from pan; cool. Arrange cooled meatballs in single layer on a baking sheet so the edges do not touch.

3 Freeze till firm. Using 24 per package, wrap meatballs in moisture-vaporproof containers or freezer bags. Seal, label, and freeze. Makes three 24-meatball portions.

MIXING GROUND MEAT MIXTURES

Making well-blended meat loaf and meatball mixtures is easy. First combine all the wet ingredients with any crumbs and dry seasonings. Then add the ground meat and blend the mixture well with your hands to distribute the ingredients evenly. To prevent the mixture from sticking to your hands, wet them with cold water before you start.

SPAGHETTI AND MEATBALLS

Total preparation time: 30 minutes

1 16-ounce can tomatoes, cut up
1 6-ounce can tomato paste
¾ cup water
½ cup dry red wine
1 4-ounce can sliced mushrooms
2 teaspoons Worcestershire sauce
1 teaspoon dried oregano, crushed
½ teaspoon chili powder
¼ teaspoon salt
¼ teaspoon pepper
2 bay leaves
1 24-meatball package Freezer Meatballs
Hot cooked spaghetti
Grated Parmesan cheese (optional)

1 In a large saucepan or Dutch oven stir together *undrained* tomatoes, tomato paste, water, dry red wine, *undrained* mushrooms, Worcestershire sauce, oregano, chili powder, salt, pepper, and bay leaves.

2 Add the Freezer Meatballs to tomato and mushroom mixture. Bring mixture to boiling; reduce heat. Cover; simmer about 25 minutes or till meatballs are heated through. Stir mixture occasionally with a fork to break apart the meatballs.

3 Remove bay leaves. Serve the mixture over hot cooked spaghetti. Pass grated Parmesan cheese, if desired. Serves 6.

SWEET AND SOUR MEATBALLS

Total cooking time: 30 minutes

1 8-ounce can tomato sauce
3 tablespoons vinegar
2 tablespoons brown sugar
1 teaspoon prepared mustard
1 24-meatball package Freezer Meatballs
Hot cooked noodles

1 Combine tomato sauce, vinegar, brown sugar, prepared mustard, ¼ cup *water*, and dash *pepper*. Add Freezer Meatballs.

2 Bring to boiling; reduce heat. Cover; simmer about 20 minutes or till meatballs are heated through. Stir occasionally with a fork to break apart the meatballs. Serve over hot noodles. Serves 4 to 6.

CRAN-KRAUT MEATBALLS

Total preparation time: 30 minutes

1 8-ounce can sauerkraut, rinsed, drained, and snipped
¾ cup cranberry-orange relish
⅓ cup chili sauce
1 tablespoon brown sugar
1 24-meatball package Freezer Meatballs
4 teaspoons cornstarch
Chow mein noodles

1 In skillet mix sauerkraut, cranberry-orange relish, chili sauce, brown sugar, and 1 cup *water*. Add Freezer Meatballs. Bring to boiling; reduce heat. Cover; simmer about 20 minutes. Stir occasionally with a fork to break apart meatballs.

2 Combine cornstarch and ⅓ cup *water*. Add to skillet mixture. Cook and stir till thickened and bubbly. Cook and stir 2 minutes more. Serve mixture over chow mein noodles. Makes 4 servings.

SPICY MEATBALL HEROES

Total preparation time: 50 minutes

- 1 8-ounce can tomato sauce
- 1 cup water
- 1 6-ounce can tomato paste
- 1 4-ounce can sliced mushrooms, drained
- 1 teaspoon minced dried onion
- 1 teaspoon sugar
- ½ teaspoon dried oregano, crushed
- ½ teaspoon dried parsley flakes
- ½ teaspoon fennel seed
- ¼ teaspoon salt
- ⅛ teaspoon garlic powder
- 2 dashes bottled hot pepper sauce
- 1 24-meatball package Freezer Meatballs
- 8 individual French rolls
- 6 ounces sliced mozzarella cheese

1 In a medium saucepan combine tomato sauce, water, tomato paste, mushrooms, dried onion, sugar, oregano, parsley flakes, fennel, salt, garlic powder, and hot pepper sauce. Add Freezer Meatballs. Bring to boiling; reduce heat. Cover; simmer for 30 minutes. Stir occasionally with a fork to break apart meatballs.

2 Meanwhile, cut a thin slice from the top of each roll. Set aside. Hollow out bottoms, leaving a ¼-inch shell. (Use bread pieces for another purpose.) Place mozzarella cheese in bottom of roll, cutting as necessary to fit. Spoon *3 meatballs* and some of the tomato mixture into each roll. Cover with the top of bun, if desired. Makes 8 servings.

MEATBALL SOUP

Total preparation time: 45 minutes

- 1 16-ounce can stewed tomatoes
- 1 15-ounce can garbanzo beans
- 1 10½-ounce can condensed beef broth
- ½ teaspoon dried thyme, crushed
- ¼ teaspoon dried marjoram, crushed
- 1 24-meatball package Freezer Meatballs
- 2 medium carrots, sliced
- 2½ cups coarsely chopped cabbage

1 In saucepan combine the *undrained* stewed tomatoes, *undrained* garbanzo beans, beef broth, thyme, marjoram, 2 cups *water*, and ⅛ teaspoon *pepper*. Add Freezer Meatballs. Bring to boiling; reduce heat. Cover; simmer 15 minutes. Stir occasionally with a fork to break apart meatballs.

2 Add carrots; cover and simmer 10 minutes more. Add cabbage; cover and simmer for 10 minutes or till vegetables are tender. Makes 6 servings.

SAUCY MEATBALLS

Total preparation time: 30 minutes

- 1 4-ounce can sliced mushrooms
- 1 10¾-ounce can condensed golden mushroom soup
- ½ cup plain yogurt
- ½ cup milk
- ¼ cup dry white wine
- 2 tablespoons all-purpose flour
- 1 24-meatball package Freezer Meatballs
- Hot cooked noodles

1 Drain mushrooms. Mix with soup. Stir in yogurt, milk, wine, and flour. Add Freezer Meatballs. Bring to boiling; reduce heat. Cover; simmer 20 minutes or till meatballs are hot. Stir often to break apart meatballs. Serve with noodles. Serves 6.

BISCUIT-TOPPED OVEN MEATBALL STEW

Total preparation time: 45 minutes

- 1 29-ounce can large-cut mixed vegetables, drained
- 1 10½-ounce can condensed onion soup
- ½ cup water
- 1 tablespoon steak sauce
- ½ teaspoon dried basil, crushed
- 1 24-meatball package Freezer Meatballs
- 1 package (10) refrigerated biscuits
- 2 tablespoons butter *or* margarine, melted
- ¼ cup grated Parmesan cheese

1 In a 2-quart casserole combine mixed vegetables, soup, water, steak sauce, and basil. Add Freezer Meatballs. Cover and bake in a 425° oven for 30 minutes or till meatballs are heated through. Stir once with a fork to break apart meatballs.

2 Arrange the refrigerated biscuits atop the hot meatball mixture. Brush the top of each biscuit with the melted butter or margarine; sprinkle with the grated Parmesan cheese. Bake for 10 to 12 minutes more or till the biscuits are light brown. Ladle stew into soup bowls. Makes 4 to 6 servings.

OVEN-BARBECUED POT ROAST

Advance preparation time: 10 minutes
Final preparation time: 2½ hours

- 1 3-pound beef chuck pot roast
- 1 medium onion, sliced
- ⅓ cup vinegar
- ¼ cup catsup
- 2 tablespoons cooking oil
- 2 tablespoons soy sauce
- 1 tablespoon Worcestershire sauce
- 1 tablespoon prepared mustard
- 1 teaspoon salt
- ¼ teaspoon garlic powder
- ¼ teaspoon pepper
- 1 cup water
- 4 teaspoons cornstarch

1 Place the pot roast and sliced onion in a plastic bag; set in a shallow baking dish. For marinade, in a bowl combine vinegar, catsup, cooking oil, soy sauce, Worcestershire sauce, mustard, salt, garlic powder, and pepper.

2 Pour the marinade over the meat and close bag. Marinate meat in refrigerator for 3 to 24 hours. Turn bag occasionally to coat meat evenly with marinade.

Before serving: Transfer meat, onion, and the marinade from bag to a shallow baking dish or a Dutch oven. Cover; roast in a 350° oven for 1¾ to 2¼ hours, basting occasionally with the marinade.

Place meat and onions on a serving platter; keep warm. Measure 1 cup of the pan juices. Or, add water if necessary to make 1 cup. For the gravy, in a saucepan combine water and cornstarch. Add the 1 cup reserved pan juices. Cook and stir till mixture is thickened and bubbly. Cook and stir 2 minutes more. Slice meat diagonally across the grain; pass gravy. Makes 8 servings.

BEEF TENDERLOIN DIANE

Advance preparation time: 10 minutes
Final preparation time: 1 hour

- 1 2-pound beef tenderloin roast
- ¼ cup dry white wine
- ¼ cup brandy
- 3 tablespoons lemon juice
- 2 tablespoons snipped chives
- 1½ teaspoons salt
- 1 teaspoon Worcestershire sauce
- ¼ teaspoon pepper
- 2 tablespoons water
- 2 tablespoons butter *or* margarine

1 Place beef in a plastic bag; set in a shallow baking dish. For marinade, in a bowl combine wine, brandy, lemon juice, chives, salt, Worcestershire, and pepper.

2 Pour the marinade over meat and close bag. Marinate meat in the refrigerator for 3 to 24 hours, occasionally turning bag to coat meat evenly with marinade.

Before serving: Remove meat, reserving the marinade. Pat meat dry with paper toweling. Place tenderloin on a rack in shallow roasting pan. Insert meat thermometer. Roast in a 425° oven for 45 to 55 minutes or till thermometer registers 140° (the outside will be brown; the inside will be rare), basting the meat occasionally with *half* of the marinade. Remove roasted meat to serving platter; keep warm.

For sauce, in a small saucepan heat the remaining marinade, the water, and butter or margarine till mixture bubbles. Slice meat diagonally across the grain into ¼-inch-thick slices. Spoon sauce over meat. Serves 8.

REUBEN TRIANGLE SANDWICHES

Advance preparation time: 1 hour
Final preparation time: 15 minutes

- 1 16-ounce can sauerkraut, drained and snipped
- 1 12-ounce can corned beef, flaked
- ½ cup shredded Monterey Jack cheese (2 ounces)
- ½ cup taco sauce
- 2 tablespoons sliced green onion
- ½ teaspoon caraway seed
- 2 packages (10 biscuits each) refrigerated biscuits
- Milk

1 In a bowl combine sauerkraut, corned beef, cheese, taco sauce, green onion, and caraway seed. On a lightly floured surface roll and stretch each biscuit into a 4- to 4½-inch circle.

2 Moisten edges of circles with water. Place a generous 3 *tablespoons* of the corned beef mixture in the center of each circle. Fold up 3 sides of dough to form a triangle; pinch edges well to seal dough. Brush with milk.

3 Bake on a lightly greased baking sheet in a 400° oven for 10 to 12 minutes. Remove from oven; cool on a wire rack. Arrange cooled sandwiches on an ungreased baking sheet so the edges do not touch. Freeze till sandwiches are firm. Place frozen sandwiches in a moisture-vaporproof freezer bag or container. Seal and label; return to freezer.

Before serving: Arrange the frozen sandwiches on an ungreased baking sheet. Bake in a 400° oven for 12 to 14 minutes. Makes 20 sandwiches.

WINE-MARINATED BURGERS

The ground meat patties will darken slightly in the marinade—

Advance preparation time: 15 minutes
Final preparation time: 16 minutes

1 cup dry red *or* white wine
2 tablespoons sliced green onion
1 teaspoon instant beef bouillon
   granules
1 teaspoon Worcestershire sauce
1½ pounds ground beef, veal, lamb, *or*
   pork
¼ teaspoon salt
⅛ teaspoon pepper
6 hamburger buns, split, toasted,
   and buttered
6 lettuce leaves

1 For marinade, in a shallow baking dish stir together dry red or white wine, green onion, bouillon granules, and Worcestershire sauce till bouillon granules are dissolved. In a bowl lightly mix together ground meat, salt, and pepper. Shape into six ½-inch-thick patties.

2 Place the patties in wine mixture in dish, turning once to coat. Cover; marinate patties in the refrigerator for 3 to 24 hours, turning several times.

Before serving: Drain patties well, reserving marinade. Place meat patties on the rack of an unheated broiler pan. Broil 3 to 4 inches from the heat, turning once. Brush with marinade once or twice during broiling time. For beef, veal, or lamb, broil to desired doneness. (Allow 8 to 10 minutes total time for medium.) For pork, broil 14 to 16 minutes total time or till well done.

Serve patties on toasted hamburger buns with lettuce. Makes 6 servings.

MEAT AND PICKLE ROLLS

Advance preparation time: 15 minutes
Final preparation time: 45 minutes

1 beaten egg
1 tablespoon fine dry bread crumbs
1 tablespoon cooked bacon pieces
¼ teaspoon salt
⅛ teaspoon pepper
1 pound ground beef
2 whole dill pickles, halved
   lengthwise
⅓ cup bottled barbecue sauce
¼ cup packed brown sugar
¼ cup cooked bacon pieces
3 tablespoons water
2 tablespoons prepared mustard

1 In a mixing bowl combine the beaten egg, bread crumbs, the 1 tablespoon bacon pieces, salt, and pepper. Add ground beef; mix well. Divide ground meat mixture into four equal portions. Shape *each* portion around a dill pickle half. Place meat rolls in a 10x6x2-inch baking dish. Cover and chill in the refrigerator for 3 to 24 hours.

2 For sauce, in a small bowl stir together barbecue sauce, brown sugar, the ¼ cup bacon pieces, water, and mustard. Cover and chill in refrigerator for 3 to 24 hours.

Before serving: Bake meat rolls, uncovered, in a 375° oven for 30 minutes. Drain off fat. Pour sauce over rolls; bake 15 minutes more or till meat is done. Serves 4.

STORING GROUND MEATS

If freshly ground meats are packaged in plastic wrap or are loosely wrapped with paper, you can refrigerate them safely for one to two days. For best results, store them in the coldest part of your refrigerator.

CUBED STEAK AND CHEESY RICE BAKE

Advance preparation time: 25 minutes
Final preparation time: 1¼ hours

1 11-ounce can condensed cheddar
   cheese soup
1 3-ounce package cream cheese,
   cut into cubes
½ cup milk
1 9-ounce package frozen French-
   style green beans
1 cup quick-cooking rice
1 4-ounce can sliced mushrooms,
   drained
½ teaspoon dried marjoram, crushed
4 beef cubed steaks (1 pound total)
2 tablespoons cooking oil
   Paprika (optional)

1 Place cheddar cheese soup, cream cheese, and milk in blender container or food processor bowl. Cover; process cheese soup mixture till smooth. Pour cheese soup mixture into a mixing bowl. Run hot water over frozen green beans in colander about 1 minute or till thawed; drain well. Stir green beans, quick-cooking rice, mushrooms, and marjoram into cheese soup mixture.

2 In a skillet cook beef cubed steaks on both sides in hot oil till brown; drain off fat. Put cheese soup mixture in bottom of a greased 10x6x2-inch baking dish; arrange steaks atop. Sprinkle steaks with paprika, if desired. Cover; chill in the refrigerator for 3 to 24 hours.

Before serving: Bake, covered, in a 375° oven about 1¼ hours or till meat and rice are done. Makes 4 servings.

ROUND STEAK AU POIVRE

Entertain your dinner guests by flaming this steak. Prepare the steak as directed in the recipe. Transfer it to the blazer pan of a chafing dish. Then flame at tableside. You'll find it's a spectacular entrée that's quick and easy to prepare—

Advance preparation time: 5 minutes
Final preparation time: 15 minutes

1 teaspoon whole black
  peppercorns
1 1-pound beef top round steak,
  cut 1 inch thick
2 tablespoons butter *or* margarine
¼ cup brandy

1 Coarsely crack the peppercorns with a mortar and pestle or with a spoon in a metal mixing bowl.
2 Sprinkle one side of steak with *half* of the cracked peppercorns; rub over meat and press in with heel of hand. Turn and repeat on other side. Cover; chill in the refrigerator for 3 to 24 hours.

Before serving: In a 10-inch skillet melt butter or margarine. Cook steaks in skillet over medium-high heat to desired doneness, turning once. (Allow 11 to 12 minutes total time for medium doneness.) Season the steak on both sides with a little salt. Add brandy to skillet. Heat till brandy almost bubbles. Light a long match and hold over the skillet to ignite the brandy. Allow flames in skillet to subside. Remove the steak to a heated serving platter. Pour brandy mixture over the steak. Makes 4 servings.

Steak Carbonnade

STEAK CARBONNADE

Advance preparation time: 25 minutes
Final preparation time: 20 minutes

 1 12-ounce can (1½ cups) beer
⅔ cup catsup
½ cup chopped onion
¼ cup sugar
 3 tablespoons lemon juice
 2 tablespoons Worcestershire sauce
 1 teaspoon salt
 1 teaspoon paprika
½ teaspoon chili powder
 1 1½-pound beef top round steak,
   cut 1 inch thick
12 ounces green noodles
 2 tablespoons butter *or* margarine
½ cup snipped parsley

1 For the marinade, in a 2-quart saucepan combine beer, catsup, onion, sugar, lemon juice, Worcestershire sauce, salt, paprika, chili powder, and ⅛ teaspoon *pepper*. Bring to boiling; reduce heat. Simmer, uncovered, for 15 minutes. Cool.
2 With a sharp knife score steak on both sides in a diamond pattern. Place the steak in a plastic bag; set in a shallow baking dish. Pour marinade over steak and close bag. Marinate meat in refrigerator for 3 to 24 hours, turning bag occasionally to coat meat evenly.

Before serving: Remove steak, reserving the marinade. Place meat on the unheated rack of a broiler pan. Broil 3 inches from heat to desired doneness, turning once. (Allow 6 to 7 minutes total time for medium rare.) Occasionally brush steak with marinade. Reheat the remaining marinade. Meanwhile, cook the noodles in boiling salted water according to package directions. Drain noodles; toss with butter or margarine and snipped parsley.
   To serve, very thinly slice meat diagonally across the grain. Arrange meat slices atop the noodles on a heated serving platter; spoon some of the marinade over. Pass remaining marinade. Makes 6 servings.

ELEGANT STROGANOFF SWISS STEAK

Advance preparation time: 30 minutes
Final preparation time: 45 minutes

1½ pounds beef round steak, cut
    ¾ inch thick
  2 tablespoons all-purpose flour
 ¾ teaspoon salt
 ⅛ teaspoon pepper
  2 tablespoons butter *or* margarine
  2 cups sliced fresh mushrooms
 ½ cup chopped onion
  1 tablespoon cornstarch
 ½ teaspoon instant beef bouillon
    granules
 ⅛ teaspoon pepper
 ½ cup water
 ½ cup milk
  1 3-ounce package cream cheese,
    softened and cut into cubes
    Hot cooked rice *or* noodles

1 Cut meat into 6 serving-size pieces. Combine flour, salt, and ⅛ teaspoon pepper. Pound the flour mixture into the meat using a meat mallet. In a 10-inch skillet brown meat over medium-high heat in hot butter or margarine. Remove meat from skillet; set aside. Cook mushrooms and onion in same skillet till onion is tender but not brown.
2 Stir cornstarch, bouillon granules, and ⅛ teaspoon pepper into onion mixture in skillet. Stir in water and milk. Cook and stir over medium-high heat till thickened and bubbly. Cook and stir 2 minutes more. Add cream cheese cubes to the mixture; stir till cheese is melted. Place meat in a 12x7x2-inch baking dish. Spoon cream cheese mixture over meat. Cover and chill in refrigerator for 3 to 24 hours.

Before serving: Bake, covered, in a 325° oven for 40 to 45 minutes or till heated through. Serve with rice or noodles if desired. Makes 6 servings.

SPINACH AND MUSHROOM-STUFFED STEAKS

Advance preparation time: 25 minutes
Final preparation time: 20 minutes

4 **beef top loin steaks, cut 1 inch thick**
½ **of a 10-ounce package frozen chopped spinach**
1 **cup sliced fresh mushrooms**
¼ **cup chopped onion**
1 **tablespoon butter *or* margarine**
¼ **teaspoon salt**
¼ **teaspoon dried thyme, crushed**
¼ **teaspoon ground sage**
 Dash pepper

1 With a sharp knife make a pocket for the stuffing by cutting a 2-inch-long slit horizontally in the fat side of each steak. Then insert knife into the slits and draw it from side to side to form larger pockets, cutting almost to bone edges. Set aside.

2 For stuffing, in a saucepan cook spinach according to package directions. Drain well; pat spinach dry with paper toweling. In the same saucepan cook mushrooms and onion in hot butter or margarine till onion is tender but not brown. Stir in spinach, salt, thyme, sage, and pepper. Fill each steak pocket with about ¼ *cup* of the spinach stuffing. Cover; chill in the refrigerator for 3 to 24 hours.

Before serving: Place steaks on rack of unheated broiler pan. Broil 4 inches from heat to desired doneness, turning once. (Allow 16 to 18 minutes total time for medium rare.) Makes 4 servings.

TERIYAKI STEAK KABOBS

Advance preparation time: 10 minutes
Final preparation time: 20 minutes

1 **pound beef sirloin steak**
1 **large green pepper**
⅓ **cup soy sauce**
2 **tablespoons water**
2 **tablespoons dry sherry**
1 **tablespoon cooking oil**
2 **cloves garlic, minced**
½ **teaspoon sugar**
½ **teaspoon ground ginger**
 Hot cooked rice (optional)

1 Cut beef sirloin steak into 1-inch pieces and green pepper into 1-inch squares. For kabobs, on 8 short skewers thread steak pieces alternately with green pepper squares.

2 For the marinade, in a shallow baking dish combine the soy sauce, water, dry sherry, cooking oil, minced garlic, sugar, and ground ginger.

3 Place the kabobs in the marinade, turning once to coat. Cover and marinate in the refrigerator for 3 to 24 hours, turning kabobs occasionally.

Before serving: Remove kabobs from the marinade, reserving marinade. Grill the kabobs over *medium-hot* coals to desired doneness. (Allow 15 to 20 minutes for medium.) Turn and brush kabobs occasionally with the reserved marinade. Serve with hot rice, if desired. Makes 4 servings.

MARINATED STEAK PLATTER

Advance preparation time: 35 minutes
Final preparation time: 5 minutes

1 **1½-pound beef sirloin steak, cut 1½ inches thick**
1 **14-ounce can artichoke hearts, drained and halved**
1 **4½-ounce jar sliced mushrooms, drained**
½ **cup dry white wine**
¼ **cup white wine vinegar**
2 **tablespoons cooking oil**
1 **clove garlic, minced**
½ **teaspoon salt**
½ **teaspoon dried basil, crushed**
½ **teaspoon dried marjoram, crushed**
 Dash pepper
2 **small tomatoes, cut into wedges and halved**

1 Place steak on an unheated rack in a broiler pan. Broil 4 inches from heat to desired doneness, turning once. (Allow about 16 minutes total time for medium rare.) Thinly slice meat. In a shallow baking dish combine sliced meat, artichoke hearts, and mushrooms.

2 For the marinade, in a screw-top jar combine white wine, white wine vinegar, oil, garlic, salt, basil, marjoram, and pepper; cover and shake well. Pour over meat mixture. Cover and marinate in the refrigerator for 3 to 24 hours; stir occasionally.

Before serving: Drain meat mixture, reserving marinade. Arrange meat, mushrooms, artichokes, and the tomato wedges on a serving platter. Spoon some of the marinade over. Makes 6 servings.

BARBECUED CHUCK ROAST

Advance preparation time: 10 minutes
Final preparation time: 45 minutes

½ cup catsup
⅓ cup vinegar
2 tablespoons cooking oil
2 tablespoons finely chopped onion
2 teaspoons chili powder
1 teaspoon salt
½ teaspoon dry mustard
⅛ teaspoon pepper
1 3-pound beef chuck pot roast, cut 1½ inches thick

1 For marinade, in a mixing bowl combine catsup, vinegar, cooking oil, onion, chili powder, salt, mustard, and pepper. Without cutting into meat, slash fat edges at 1-inch intervals.

2 Place meat in a shallow dish. Pour marinade over roast, distributing evenly. Cover and marinate roast in the refrigerator for 3 to 24 hours.

Before serving: Remove roast from marinade, reserving marinade; pat excess moisture from roast with paper toweling. Grill roast over *medium-hot* coals about 20 minutes. Turn; cook to desired doneness. (Allow about 20 minutes on second side for rare to medium rare.) Brush occasionally with reserved marinade. To serve, remove roast to a heated platter. Thinly slice meat across the grain. Makes 8 servings.

GARLIC-MARINATED STEAK

Use an oil and vinegar salad dressing for this recipe, not the creamy garlic version—

Advance preparation time: 5 minutes
Final preparation time: 12 minutes

1 1- to 1½-pound beef flank steak
⅓ cup garlic salad dressing

1 With a sharp knife score flank steak on both sides in a diamond pattern. Place steak in a plastic bag; set in a shallow baking dish. For marinade, combine salad dressing and ¼ teaspoon *pepper*. Pour over the steak and close bag. Chill in refrigerator for 3 to 24 hours; turn occasionally.

Before serving: Remove steak from marinade. Place meat on an unheated rack of a broiler pan. Broil 3 inches from heat to desired doneness, turning once. (Allow 8 to 10 minutes total time for medium rare.) To serve, slice meat diagonally across the grain into very thin slices. Makes 4 to 6 servings.

SHARPENING KNIVES

To carve or slice all meat successfully, keep your knife's cutting edge very sharp. For best results, sharpen knives with a hand-held sharpening steel or stone before each use. With the steel or stone in one hand, hold the knife in the other hand almost flat (at a 20-degree angle) against the sharpener. Draw the blade edge over the sharpener, using a motion that goes across and down at the same time. Turn the blade over; reverse directions.

FLANK STEAK SUPREME

Advance preparation time: 10 minutes
Final preparation time: 12 minutes

1 1-pound beef flank steak
¼ cup cooking oil
¼ cup dry white wine
¼ cup lime juice
1 tablespoon sugar
1 clove garlic, minced
½ teaspoon salt
½ teaspoon dried marjoram, crushed
Dash pepper

1 With a sharp knife score flank steak on both sides in a diamond pattern. Place the steak in a plastic bag; set in a shallow baking dish.

2 For the marinade, combine the cooking oil, wine, lime juice, sugar, garlic, salt, marjoram, and pepper. Pour the marinade over the steak and close the bag. Marinate meat in the refrigerator for 3 to 24 hours, turning occasionally.

Before serving: Remove the steak from the marinade. Place meat on an unheated rack of a broiler pan. Broil 3 inches from the heat to desired doneness, turning once. (Allow 8 to 10 minutes total time for medium rare.) Sprinkle with salt and pepper. To serve, thinly slice meat diagonally across the grain. Makes 4 servings.

APPLE-MARINATED PORK ROAST

Advance preparation time: 15 minutes
Final preparation time: 3 hours

- 1 cup dry white wine
- ⅓ cup frozen apple juice concentrate, thawed
- 1 small onion, thinly sliced and separated into rings
- ¼ cup cooking oil
- 1 tablespoon Worcestershire sauce
- 1 teaspoon dried thyme, crushed
- ¼ teaspoon ground cloves
- 1 3-pound pork loin center rib roast

1 For the marinade, in a bowl combine dry white wine, the apple juice concentrate, onion rings, cooking oil, Worcestershire sauce, thyme, and cloves.

2 Place pork roast in a plastic bag; set in a shallow baking dish. Pour the wine-apple marinade over meat and close bag. Marinate meat in the refrigerator for 3 to 24 hours, turning bag occasionally to coat meat evenly with marinade.

Before serving: Remove roast; reserve the marinade. Place roast, rib side down, in a shallow roasting pan. Pour the reserved marinade over roast. Insert a meat thermometer so tip doesn't touch bone. Roast meat, uncovered, in a 325° oven for 2½ to 3 hours or till meat thermometer registers 170°. Baste roast with marinade once or twice during the baking time. To serve, transfer roast to heated serving platter and slice. Makes 6 servings.

ORANGE-PORK CHOP BAKE

Advance preparation time: 15 minutes
Final preparation time: 1 hour

- 4 pork loin chops, cut ¾ inch thick
- 2 tablespoons cooking oil
- ½ teaspoon instant chicken bouillon granules
- ½ cup hot water
- ⅓ cup frozen orange juice concentrate
- 1 11-ounce can fried rice
- ¼ cup raisins
- ¼ cup slivered almonds
- ¼ cup chopped green pepper

1 In a large skillet brown the pork chops on both sides in hot oil. Drain and set chops aside. Meanwhile, dissolve bouillon granules in the hot water; stir in the orange juice concentrate. In a bowl combine the fried rice, raisins, slivered almonds, and chopped green pepper.

2 Spread the rice mixture in bottom of a 12x7½x2-inch baking dish. Place the pork chops atop rice mixture. Pour orange mixture over all. Cover and chill in the refrigerator for 3 to 24 hours.

Before serving: Bake, uncovered, in a 350° oven for 45 minutes. Uncover and bake 15 minutes more or till the pork chops are tender. Makes 4 servings.

ORIENTAL GLAZED RIBLETS

Advance preparation time: 40 minutes
Final preparation time: 45 minutes

- 3 pounds meaty pork spareribs, sawed in half across bones
- 1 15¼-ounce can pineapple chunks (juice pack)
- ¼ cup packed brown sugar
- 2 tablespoons cornstarch
- ¼ teaspoon salt
- 1 cup water
- 2 tablespoons vinegar
- 2 tablespoons soy sauce
- 1 medium orange
  Hot cooked pea pods (optional)

1 Cut meat into 2-rib portions. In a large saucepan or Dutch oven simmer ribs, covered, in enough boiling salted water to cover meat for 30 minutes; drain. Place ribs in a 13x9x2-inch baking dish. Season with salt and pepper.

2 Meanwhile, drain pineapple chunks, reserving juice. In a saucepan combine brown sugar, cornstarch, and the ¼ teaspoon salt. Stir in reserved pineapple juice, the 1 cup water, vinegar, and soy sauce. Cook and stir till mixture is thickened and bubbly. Cook and stir 2 minutes longer.

3 Halve the orange and cut into thin slices. Stir pineapple chunks and orange slices into soy mixture. Spoon over ribs. Cover ribs and chill in the refrigerator for 3 to 24 hours.

Before serving: Bake ribs, covered, in a 350° oven for 20 minutes. Uncover; spoon pineapple mixture from bottom of baking dish over ribs. Bake, uncovered, 20 to 25 minutes more or till done. If desired, place the ribs atop a bed of buttered cooked pea pods. Makes 4 or 5 servings.

Oriental Glazed Riblets

311

LASAGNA

Advance preparation time: 35 minutes
Final preparation time: 45 minutes

- 8 ounces lasagna noodles
- 1 pound bulk Italian sausage
- 1 cup sliced fresh mushrooms
- ½ cup chopped onion
- 1 clove garlic, minced
- 1 15-ounce can tomato sauce
- ¼ cup dry red wine
- 1 bay leaf
- ¾ teaspoon dried oregano, crushed
- ½ teaspoon sugar
- 1 beaten egg
- 1 cup cream-style cottage cheese, well drained
- ¼ cup grated Parmesan cheese
- ¾ teaspoon dried marjoram, crushed
- 1 6-ounce package sliced mozzarella cheese

1 Cook lasagna noodles according to package directions. Drain; rinse noodles. Meanwhile, in a skillet cook Italian sausage, mushrooms, onion, and garlic till meat is browned and onion is tender. Drain off fat.

2 Stir tomato sauce, wine, bay leaf, oregano, and sugar into meat mixture. Bring to boiling; reduce heat. Simmer, uncovered, for 10 minutes. Remove bay leaf; discard. In a bowl combine the beaten egg, cottage cheese, Parmesan cheese, and marjoram.

3 Layer *half* of the lasagna noodles in the bottom of a 12x7½x2-inch baking dish; spread with *half* of the cottage cheese mixture. Add *half* of the meat mixture and *half* of the mozzarella cheese. Repeat the layers of noodles, cottage cheese mixture, and meat mixture. Cover with foil and chill in the refrigerator for 3 to 24 hours.

Before serving: Bake, covered with foil, in a 375° oven for 35 minutes. Uncover, add the remaining mozzarella cheese, and bake 5 minutes more or till heated through. Let stand 5 minutes before serving. Serves 6.

TAMALE PIE

Advance preparation time: 25 minutes
Final preparation time: 50 minutes

- 1 cup water
- ⅓ cup cornmeal
- ¼ teaspoon salt
  Dash pepper
- 1 beaten egg
- ⅔ cup all-purpose flour
- 1 teaspoon baking powder
- 1 4-ounce package (1 cup) shredded cheddar cheese
- ½ pound bulk Italian sausage
- ½ pound ground beef
- 1 small onion, chopped
- 1 clove garlic, minced
- 1 15-ounce can tomato sauce
- 2 to 3 teaspoons chili powder
- 1 teaspoon sugar
- ½ teaspoon salt
  Dash pepper

1 In a small saucepan combine water, cornmeal, the ¼ teaspoon salt, and dash pepper. Bring to boiling; reduce heat and cook, stirring constantly, till bubbly. Cook and stir 1 minute more. Remove from heat; cool slightly. Add 1 beaten egg; beat till well combined.

2 Stir together the all-purpose flour and baking powder; beat into the cornmeal mixture. Stir in *half* of the cheddar cheese. Spread mixture onto the bottom and sides of a greased 1½-quart casserole.

3 In a skillet cook Italian sausage, ground beef, onion, and garlic till meats are browned and onion is tender. Drain off fat. Stir in tomato sauce, chili powder, sugar, the ½ teaspoon salt, and dash pepper. Spread the meat mixture over the cornmeal mixture. Cover; chill in the refrigerator 3 to 24 hours.

Before serving: Bake, covered, in a 375° oven about 45 minutes. Uncover; sprinkle with the remaining shredded cheddar cheese. Return casserole to the oven and bake for 2 to 3 minutes more or till the cheese is melted. Makes 6 servings.

PIZZA PIE FLORENTINE

Advance preparation time: 30 minutes
Final preparation time: 45 minutes

- 1 6½-ounce packet pizza crust mix
- ¼ cup shelled sunflower nuts
- 1 10-ounce package frozen chopped spinach
- 2 8-ounce cans pizza sauce
- 1 2½-ounce jar sliced mushrooms, drained
- 1 tablespoon all-purpose flour
- 1 pound bulk pork sausage
- 1 6-ounce package sliced mozzarella cheese
- ½ cup grated Parmesan cheese

1 Prepare pizza crust according to the package directions, *except* stir in sunflower nuts. Press the dough onto bottom and sides of a greased 12-inch pizza pan. Bake in a 425° oven for 10 to 12 minutes or till light brown.

2 Meanwhile, cook the spinach according to package directions. Drain well. Stir together spinach, pizza sauce, mushrooms, and flour; set aside.

3 In a skillet cook sausage till browned. Drain off fat. Cover all of the pizza crust with slices of mozzarella cheese. Sprinkle sausage atop cheese. Spoon spinach mixture atop sausage. Sprinkle grated Parmesan cheese over all. Wrap in foil. Seal, label, and freeze at least 6 hours.

Before serving: Place unwrapped frozen pizza on oven rack. Bake in a 400° oven for 40 to 45 minutes. Makes 4 to 6 servings.

CHEESY HAM SANDWICHES

Advance preparation time: 15 minutes

¼ cup butter *or* margarine
1 cup diced fully cooked ham *or* leftover cooked meat
1 4-ounce container whipped cream cheese with chives
¼ cup chopped water chestnuts
2 tablespoons sweet pickle relish, well drained
2 tablespoons milk
8 slices rye, whole wheat, *or* white bread
1 teaspoon prepared horseradish

1 Set out butter or margarine to bring to room temperature. For the filling, in a bowl combine ham or cooked meat, cream cheese, water chestnuts, pickle relish, and milk. Spread about *⅓ cup* of the filling on one side of *half* of the bread slices.

2 In a bowl combine butter or margarine and horseradish; spread mixture on one side of the remaining bread slices. Place, buttered side down, atop the meat filling. Wrap sandwiches individually with moisture-vaporproof wrap. Seal, label, and freeze up to two weeks.

Before serving: Thaw sandwiches. Makes 4 sandwiches.

24-HOUR HAM AND PASTA SALAD

Advance preparation time: 35 minutes
Final preparation time: 5 minutes

2 eggs
1 cup frozen peas
1 cup tiny-shell macaroni *or* elbow macaroni
2 cups shredded lettuce
1 cup fully cooked ham cut into julienne strips
½ cup shredded Swiss cheese (2 ounces)
½ cup mayonnaise *or* salad dressing
¼ cup dairy sour cream
1 tablespoon chopped green onion
1 tablespoon prepared mustard
   Dash bottled hot pepper sauce
   Snipped parsley
   Paprika

1 To hard-cook eggs, place eggs in a saucepan; cover with cold water. Bring to boiling; reduce heat to just below simmering. Cover; cook for 15 minutes. Run cold water over eggs till cool. Remove shells; slice eggs.

2 Meanwhile, in a colander run peas under hot water till separated. In saucepan cook macaroni in a large amount of boiling salted water according to package directions. Drain. Rinse in ice water. Drain again. Set aside.

3 Place lettuce in the bottom of a 2-quart casserole or soufflé dish. Sprinkle with a little salt and pepper. Top with the drained macaroni. Sprinkle egg slices with a little salt; arrange atop macaroni, standing some egg slices on edge, if desired. Layer in order atop eggs: ham strips, peas, and cheese.

4 Combine the mayonnaise or salad dressing, sour cream, green onion, mustard, and pepper sauce. Spread atop salad, sealing to edge of casserole. Cover; chill in the refrigerator for 3 to 24 hours.

Before serving: Sprinkle top of salad with snipped parsley and paprika; toss. Makes 4 servings.

HAM AND NOODLE BAKE

Advance preparation time: 20 minutes
Final preparation time: 1½ hours

4 ounces green *or* plain medium noodles
2 cups cream-style cottage cheese with chives
½ cup milk
1 3-ounce package cream cheese, cut up
2 cups cubed fully cooked ham
¾ cup thinly sliced celery
2 teaspoons Worcestershire sauce
1 teaspoon dried marjoram, crushed
   Dash pepper
½ of a 3-ounce can French-fried onions

1 In a large saucepan cook green or plain noodles in a large amount of boiling salted water for 5 minutes or just till tender; drain. Place cottage cheese, milk, and cream cheese in a blender container. Cover and blend till smooth.

2 Combine noodles, cheese mixture, ham, celery, Worcestershire sauce, marjoram, and pepper. Turn into a 10x6x2-inch baking dish. Cover with moisture-vaporproof wrap. Seal, label, and freeze at least 6 hours.

Before serving: Bake frozen mixture, covered, in a 350° oven for 1¼ hours, stirring once. Stir again. Sprinkle with French-fried onions. Return to oven and bake, uncovered, 10 minutes more or till onions are heated through. Makes 4 to 6 servings.

DILLED LAMB CASEROLE

Advance preparation time: 30 minutes
Final preparation time: 1¼ hours

- 3 ounces medium noodles
- 1 pound boneless lamb, cut into ¾-inch cubes
- 1 tablespoon cooking oil
- 1 10¾-ounce can condensed cream of celery soup
- ½ cup dairy sour cream
- ½ cup milk
- 1 tablespoon all-purpose flour
- ½ teaspoon dried dillweed
- 2 medium carrots, shredded
- ½ cup finely crushed rich round crackers (optional)
- 1 tomato, cut into wedges

1 In a large saucepan cook noodles according to package directions; drain. In a skillet brown lamb in hot cooking oil. Drain off fat. In a bowl stir together soup, sour cream, milk, flour, and dillweed.

2 In a bowl combine cooked noodles, lamb cubes, soup mixture, and shredded carrot. Turn into a 12x7½x2-inch baking dish. Cover the casserole with moisture-vaporproof wrap. Seal, label, and freeze at least 6 hours.

Before serving: Bake frozen casserole, covered, in a 375° oven for 45 minutes, stirring twice to break apart pieces. If desired, sprinkle top with cracker crumbs. Bake, uncovered, for 20 to 25 minutes more or till heated through. Garnish with tomato wedges. Makes 5 or 6 servings.

Curried Lamb and Apricots

CURRIED LAMB AND APRICOTS

Advance preparation time: 5 minutes
Final preparation time: 1 hour

- ½ cup dry white wine
- 1 tablespoon cooking oil
- 1 tablespoon curry powder
- ½ teaspoon salt
- ¼ teaspoon crushed red pepper
- 4 lamb leg sirloin chops, cut ½ inch thick (1 to 1½ pounds)
- 1 small onion, cut into wedges
- 1 tablespoon cooking oil
- 1 cup water
- 1 tablespoon brown sugar
- 1 teaspoon instant chicken bouillon granules
- 1 cup dried apricots
- ½ cup dairy sour cream
- 1 tablespoon all-purpose flour
  Condiments (raisins, peanuts, sliced green onions, chopped tomato, *and/or* flaked coconut)

1 For marinade, combine wine, 1 tablespoon cooking oil, curry powder, salt, and red pepper. In a shallow baking dish place the lamb chops. Pour the marinade over chops. Cover; marinate in refrigerator for 3 to 24 hours, turning chops occasionally.

Before serving: Drain meat, reserving marinade. Pat meat dry with paper toweling. In skillet brown chops and onion in 1 tablespoon hot oil about 10 minutes. Add the reserved marinade, water, brown sugar, and bouillon granules. Bring to boiling; reduce heat. Cover; simmer for 20 minutes. Add apricots; cover and simmer for 10 to 15 minutes more or till apricots and meat are tender. Remove chops and apricots to a platter; keep warm.

For sauce, mix sour cream and flour; stir into hot mixture in skillet. Cook and stir till bubbly. Cook and stir 1 minute more. Pour some of the sauce over chops and apricots. Pass the remaining sauce and condiments. If desired, serve with hot cooked rice and garnish with a green onion. Serves 4.

PINEAPPLE-LAMB KABOBS

Advance preparation time: 25 minutes
Final preparation time: 18 minutes

- 1 medium yellow crookneck squash
- 1 medium green pepper
- 1 8-ounce can pineapple chunks (juice pack)
- 1 pound boneless lamb, cut into 1-inch cubes
- ¼ cup soy sauce
- 1 tablespoon cooking oil
- ½ teaspoon ground ginger
- ½ teaspoon dry mustard

1 Cut squash into 1-inch pieces and green pepper into 1-inch squares. Drain pineapple, reserving juice. For kabobs, on 6 skewers alternately thread the lamb cubes, squash pieces, green pepper squares, and pineapple chunks. For marinade, in a 13x9x2-inch baking dish combine reserved pineapple juice, soy sauce, cooking oil, ginger, and mustard.

2 Place the kabobs in the marinade, turning once to coat. Cover and marinate in the refrigerator for 3 to 24 hours, turning kabobs occasionally.

Before serving: Remove kabobs from the marinade, reserving marinade. Grill the kabobs over *medium-hot* coals to desired doneness. (Allow 15 to 18 minutes for medium.) Brush kabobs frequently with the reserved marinade. Makes 6 servings.

WHOLE WHEAT OVEN-FRIED CHICKEN

Use chicken pieces right from your freezer for this no-fuss recipe. Before freezing, wrap chicken pieces individually in clear plastic wrap. Then overwrap all the pieces together in moisture-vaporproof wrap—

Advance preparation time: 18 minutes
Final preparation time: 1¼ hours

- ¾ **cup finely crushed shredded wheat wafers**
- 1 **teaspoon paprika**
- ¾ **teaspoon ground sage**
  Dash pepper
- 1 **2½- to 3-pound broiler-fryer chicken, cut up and frozen (see tip, page 10)**
- 3 **tablespoons all-purpose flour**
- 1 **5⅓-ounce can (⅔ cup) evaporated milk**
- 2 **tablespoons butter *or* margarine, melted**

1 In a bowl or on waxed paper mix cracker crumbs, paprika, sage, and pepper. Dip frozen chicken pieces in flour, then in evaporated milk. Roll chicken in crumb mixture, pressing to coat.

2 Arrange chicken pieces, skin side up, in a 13x9x2-inch baking pan. Sprinkle with any remaining crumb mixture. Drizzle with the melted butter or margarine. Cover and chill in the refrigerator for 3 to 24 hours.

Before serving: Uncover and bake in a 375° oven about 1¼ hours or till chicken is tender. Makes 6 servings.

CRISPY ITALIAN CHICKEN

Advance preparation time: 18 minutes
Final preparation time: 1 hour

- 1½ **cups crisp rice cereal, crushed**
- 1 **.6-ounce envelope Italian salad dressing mix**
- 1 **2½- to 3-pound broiler-fryer chicken, cut up**
- 3 **tablespoons butter, melted**

1 Mix together crushed cereal and salad dressing mix. Brush chicken pieces with melted butter; roll in cereal mixture to coat. Place in a shallow baking pan. Sprinkle chicken with any remaining cereal mixture. Cover and chill the chicken in the refrigerator for 3 to 24 hours.

Before serving: Uncover; bake in a 375° oven about 1 hour or till tender. Serves 6.

FRUITED OVEN CHICKEN

Advance preparation time: 16 minutes
Final preparation time: 1 hour

- 1 **2½- to 3-pound broiler-fryer chicken, cut up**
- 2 **tablespoons cooking oil**
- 1 **8¼-ounce can crushed pineapple, drained**
- 1 **cup bottled barbecue sauce**
- 1 **11-ounce can mandarin orange sections, drained**
  Hot cooked rice

1 In skillet brown chicken in hot oil. Drain; arrange pieces in an 11x7½x2-inch baking dish. Combine pineapple and barbecue sauce; spread over chicken. Cover; chill in refrigerator for 3 to 24 hours.

Before serving: Bake, covered, in a 375° oven for 50 to 60 minutes. Spoon off fat. Trim with oranges; spoon some sauce atop. Serve with rice. Serves 6.

MEXICALI CHICKEN

Advance preparation time: 15 minutes
Final preparation time: 50 minutes

- 1 **2½- to 3-pound broiler-fryer chicken, cut up**
- 3 **tablespoons cooking oil**
- 1 **medium onion, chopped (½ cup)**
- 1 **medium green pepper, chopped (¾ cup)**
- 1 **28-ounce can tomatoes, cut up**
- 1 **16-ounce can yellow hominy, drained**
- 2 **teaspoons chili powder**
- ½ **teaspoon salt**
- ¼ **cup cold water**
- 3 **tablespoons cornstarch**
- ½ **cup shredded cheddar cheese (2 ounces)**

1 In a large Dutch oven brown chicken pieces in hot cooking oil. Remove chicken to a 12x7½x2-inch baking dish; set aside. In same Dutch oven cook onion and green pepper till onion is tender but not brown. Stir in *undrained* tomatoes, drained hominy, chili powder, and salt.

2 Combine the water and cornstarch. Stir into the tomato mixture. Cook and stir till thickened and bubbly. Cook and stir 2 minutes more. Remove from heat. Pour sauce over chicken in baking dish. Cover and chill in refrigerator for 3 to 24 hours.

Before serving: Uncover and bake in a 375° oven about 50 minutes or till chicken pieces are tender. Serve sauce from baking dish over chicken pieces. Pass shredded cheddar cheese. Makes 6 servings.

CRANBERRY CHICKEN

Advance preparation time: 10 minutes
Final preparation time: 1 hour

8 chicken legs
1 8-ounce can jellied cranberry
    sauce
⅓ cup bottled barbecue sauce
1 tablespoon lemon juice

1 Place chicken in a 10x6x2-inch baking dish. Mix remaining ingredients. Cook and stir till cranberry sauce melts; spoon over chicken. Cover; chill 3 to 24 hours.

Before serving: Uncover and bake in a 375° oven about 1 hour. Makes 4 servings.

MUSHROOM-SAUCED CHICKEN

Advance preparation time: 10 minutes
Final preparation time: 1½ hours

4 whole medium chicken breasts
1 10¾-ounce can condensed cream
    of mushroom soup
½ cup dry white wine
1 4-ounce can sliced mushrooms,
    drained
1 teaspoon dried parsley flakes
¼ teaspoon ground sage
1 8-ounce carton dairy sour cream
2 tablespoons all-purpose flour
    Hot cooked noodles

1 Halve breasts; arrange in a 13x9x2-inch baking dish. Mix soup, wine, mushrooms, parsley, and sage. Pour over chicken. Cover; refrigerate 3 to 24 hours.

Before serving: Uncover; bake in a 350° oven 1¼ to 1½ hours. Remove chicken. Pour sauce into saucepan; skim off fat. Combine sour cream and flour; stir in ½ cup sauce. Return to saucepan. Cook and stir till bubbly. Serve over chicken and noodles. Serves 8.

CHICKEN SALTIMBOCCA

Advance preparation time: 25 minutes
Final preparation time: 50 minutes

2 whole large chicken breasts,
    skinned, halved lengthwise, and
    boned
4 thin slices boiled ham
4 slices Swiss cheese
1 medium tomato, peeled and
    chopped
1 beaten egg
2 tablespoons milk
⅓ cup fine dry bread crumbs
2 tablespoons grated Parmesan
    cheese
½ teaspoon dried sage, crushed

1 Place each chicken breast half between 2 pieces of plastic wrap. Pound to ⅛-inch thickness. Remove plastic wrap.

2 Place a ham slice and cheese slice on each chicken breast half. Trim the ham and cheese slices to fit within ¼ inch of the edge of the chicken. Top each with some chopped tomato. Roll up jelly-roll style, tucking in ends; press to seal.

3 Stir together egg and milk. Stir together bread crumbs, Parmesan cheese, and sage. Dip each chicken roll in the egg mixture and then in the crumb mixture. Arrange coated chicken rolls in a 10x6x2-inch baking dish. Cover and chill in refrigerator for 3 to 24 hours.

Before serving: Uncover and bake in a 350° oven for 45 to 50 minutes or till chicken is tender. Makes 4 servings.

CHICKEN KIEV

Serve this elegant chicken dish at your next dinner party, but prepare it ahead and avoid the last-minute hassle—

Advance preparation time: 25 minutes
Final preparation time: 25 minutes

4 whole large chicken breasts,
    skinned, halved lengthwise, and
    boned
2 green onions, sliced
    (2 tablespoons)
1 tablespoon dried parsley flakes
½ teaspoon salt
¼ teaspoon pepper
½ cup butter *or* margarine, well
    chilled
1 beaten egg
2 tablespoons milk
¾ cup fine dry bread crumbs

1 Place each chicken breast half between 2 pieces of plastic wrap. Pound to ⅛-inch thickness. Remove plastic wrap. Stir together the sliced green onion, parsley flakes, salt, and pepper. Sprinkle mixture over chicken breast halves.

2 Cut the well-chilled butter or margarine into 8 sticks, each measuring about 2½ inches long. Place a stick of butter or margarine atop onion mixture on each chicken breast half. Roll up jelly-roll style, tucking in ends; press to seal.

3 Stir together the egg and milk. Dip each chicken roll in the egg mixture and then in the bread crumbs. Arrange coated chicken rolls in a 10x6x2-inch baking dish. Cover and chill in refrigerator for 3 to 24 hours.

Before serving: Uncover and bake in a 400° oven for 20 to 25 minutes or till the chicken is tender. Makes 8 servings.

SOUR CREAM-THYME CHICKEN

Advance preparation time: 20 minutes
Final preparation time: 50 minutes

3 whole medium chicken breasts, skinned, halved lengthwise, and boned
2 tablespoons butter *or* margarine
1 cup sliced fresh mushrooms
1 small onion, chopped (¼ cup)
1 3-ounce package cream cheese, cut up
½ teaspoon dried thyme, crushed
½ teaspoon dried parsley flakes
¼ teaspoon salt
½ cup milk
½ cup dairy sour cream
1 tablespoon all-purpose flour
1 8-ounce package frozen cut asparagus
½ cup soft bread crumbs
1 tablespoon butter *or* margarine, melted

1 In a large skillet cook chicken breasts in the 2 tablespoons butter or margarine about 15 minutes or till chicken is golden and nearly done. Remove from skillet.

2 In same skillet cook mushrooms and onion in remaining drippings till tender but not brown. Remove from heat; stir in cream cheese, thyme, parsley, and salt. Combine milk, sour cream, and flour; stir into mushroom mixture. In a colander run hot water over frozen asparagus till separated; drain. Stir into mushroom mixture.

3 Turn mushroom mixture into a 10x6x2-inch baking dish. Arrange chicken breasts atop. Toss together bread crumbs and the 1 tablespoon melted butter or margarine. Sprinkle atop chicken. Cover and chill in refrigerator for 3 to 24 hours.

Before serving: Uncover and bake in a 325° oven for 45 to 50 minutes or till chicken is done. Makes 6 servings.

LIME-MARINATED CHICKEN BREASTS

Advance preparation time: 13 minutes
Final preparation time: 10 minutes

2 whole medium chicken breasts, skinned, halved lengthwise, and boned
2 tablespoons soy sauce
2 tablespoons lime juice
2 tablespoons water
1 tablespoon cooking oil
½ teaspoon ground ginger
1 small clove garlic, minced
1 teaspoon cornstarch
1 6-ounce package frozen pea pods

1 Place each chicken breast half between 2 pieces of plastic wrap and pound to ¼-inch thickness. Remove plastic wrap. Arrange chicken breasts in a shallow baking dish. For marinade, in a bowl combine soy sauce, lime juice, water, cooking oil, ground ginger, and garlic. Pour marinade over chicken breasts. Cover and chill in refrigerator for 3 to 24 hours.

Before serving: Remove chicken breasts from marinade, reserving marinade. Place chicken on rack of unheated broiler pan. Broil 4 to 5 inches from the heat for 6 to 8 minutes, turning once.

Meanwhile, add additional water to reserved marinade to make ⅓ cup liquid. In a saucepan stir marinade mixture into cornstarch. Cook and stir till thickened and bubbly. Cook and stir 2 minutes more. Stir in frozen pea pods. Cover and cook 3 minutes more, stirring once. Serve over broiled chicken breasts. Makes 4 servings.

POLYNESIAN CHICKEN BREASTS

Advance preparation time: 13 minutes
Final preparation time: 10 minutes

2 whole large chicken breasts, skinned, halved lengthwise, and boned
1 8-ounce can pineapple chunks
½ of a medium green pepper, cut into thin strips
½ cup water
¼ cup frozen orange juice concentrate
2 tablespoons soy sauce
2 tablespoons cooking oil
¼ teaspoon ground ginger
2 teaspoons cornstarch
Hot cooked rice

1 Place each chicken breast half between 2 pieces of plastic wrap. With a meat mallet pound to ¼-inch thickness. Remove plastic wrap. Arrange chicken breasts in a shallow baking dish.

2 For marinade, in a bowl combine the *undrained* pineapple chunks, green pepper strips, the water, frozen orange juice concentrate, soy sauce, cooking oil, and ground ginger. Pour marinade over chicken breasts. Cover and chill in refrigerator for 3 to 24 hours.

Before serving: Remove chicken breasts from marinade, reserving marinade. Place chicken on rack of unheated broiler pan. Broil 4 to 5 inches from the heat for 6 to 8 minutes, turning once.

Meanwhile, in a saucepan stir cornstarch into marinade. Cook and stir till thickened and bubbly. Cook and stir 2 minutes more. Serve over broiled chicken breasts and hot cooked rice. Makes 4 servings.

FREEZER CHICKEN STARTER

Prepare and freeze this chicken mixture ahead to use in making the recipes on pages 319 and 320—

Total preparation time: 2 hours

  2 2½- to 3-pound broiler-fryer chickens, cut up, *or* 1 6-pound stewing hen, cut up
1¼ pounds chicken wings *or* backs
  4 stalks celery with leaves
  1 carrot, quartered
  1 small onion, quartered
1½ teaspoons salt
 ¼ teaspoon pepper

1 Place chicken pieces, celery, carrot, and onion in a large Dutch oven or kettle. Sprinkle with the salt and pepper. Add enough water to cover the chicken. Bring to boiling. Reduce heat; cover and cook over low heat till chicken is tender. (Allow 1 hour cooking time for broiler-fryers or 1½ to 2 hours for the stewing hen.) Remove meat to shallow baking pan; cool. Refrigerate broth.

2 When the chicken is cool enough to handle, remove the meat from the bones, discarding skin and bones. Cut meat into cubes; cover loosely and refrigerate. Skim fat from broth. Strain broth.

3 In three 1-quart freezer containers, pack *2 cups* of chicken meat and *2 cups* of the chilled broth. Pour remaining broth into 2-pint containers. Cover, seal, label, and freeze. Makes 3 quarts chicken mixture and 1 or 2 pints broth.

CHICKEN AND RICE ENCHILADAS

Final preparation time: 1¼ hours

  1 1-quart container **Freezer Chicken Starter**
  1 cup long grain rice
  1 medium onion, chopped (½ cup)
  1 clove garlic, minced
  1 15-ounce can tomato sauce
  1 4-ounce can green chili peppers, rinsed, seeded, and chopped
 ½ teaspoon sugar
 ½ teaspoon ground cumin
 ¼ teaspoon salt
    Cooking oil
12 tortillas
 ½ cup water
 ¾ cup shredded cheddar cheese (3 ounces)

1 In a saucepan cook Frozen Chicken Starter, covered, over medium-low heat about 25 minutes or till thawed, breaking up mixture with a fork once or twice. Stir in uncooked rice, onion, and garlic. Bring to boiling. Reduce heat; cover and simmer about 15 minutes or till rice is nearly done.

2 Meanwhile, stir together the tomato sauce, chili peppers, sugar, cumin, and salt. Stir *¾ cup* of the tomato sauce mixture into the rice mixture. Heat a small amount of cooking oil in a skillet. Dip tortillas, one at a time, in hot oil just till softened. Drain on paper toweling.

3 Spoon a generous *⅓ cup* of the chicken-rice mixture down the center of each tortilla. Roll up. Place in a 13x9x2-inch baking dish. Add the ½ cup water to remaining sauce mixture; pour over tortillas. Cover and bake in a 350° oven for 25 minutes. Sprinkle with cheese. Uncover and bake about 5 minutes more or till cheese is melted. Makes 6 servings.

CLUB CHICKEN CASSEROLE

Final preparation time: 1¼ hours

  1 1-quart container **Freezer Chicken Starter**
 ½ cup water
 ⅔ cup long grain rice
  1 10-ounce package frozen cut broccoli
  3 tablespoons butter *or* margarine
  3 tablespoons all-purpose flour
  1 teaspoon salt
  1 13-ounce can (1⅔ cups) evaporated milk
  1 4-ounce can sliced mushrooms, drained
 ¼ cup slivered almonds
    Snipped parsley (optional)

1 Place Freezer Chicken Starter and water in a saucepan. Cover and cook over medium heat about 20 minutes or till thawed. Remove chicken meat from broth and set aside. Cook rice in chicken broth according to package directions. In a colander run hot water over frozen broccoli till separated.

2 In another saucepan melt butter or margarine. Stir in flour and salt. Add evaporated milk. Cook and stir till thickened and bubbly. Cook and stir 1 minute more. Stir in chicken, rice, broccoli, and mushrooms.

3 Turn into a 12x7½x2-inch baking dish. Sprinkle with almonds. Bake, uncovered, in a 350° oven for 30 to 35 minutes or till heated through. Garnish with snipped parsley, if desired. Makes 5 servings.

CHEESY CHICKEN POT PIES

Final preparation time: 1 hour and 20 minutes

1½ packages piecrust mix
     (for 2-crust pie)
  1 1-quart container Freezer Chicken
     Starter (see recipe, page 319)
 ⅓ cup sliced celery
  1 small onion, chopped (¼ cup)
  1 teaspoon dried marjoram, crushed
 ¼ teaspoon salt
     Dash pepper
 ¼ cup cornstarch
 ¼ cup milk
  1 cup frozen mixed vegetables
1½ cups shredded Swiss cheese
     (6 ounces)

1 Prepare piecrust mix according to package directions; divide pastry in half. Roll out *half* of the pastry; cut into six 6-inch circles, rerolling if necessary. Line six 4¼x1-inch pie pans with pastry circles. Trim even with edges of pie pans.

2 Meanwhile, in a saucepan heat frozen chicken starter, covered, over medium-low heat about 25 minutes or till thawed, breaking up mixture with a fork once or twice. Stir in sliced celery, onion, marjoram, salt, and pepper. Combine cornstarch and milk; add to the chicken mixture in the saucepan. Cook and stir till thickened and bubbly. Cook and stir for 2 minutes more. Stir in frozen vegetables and Swiss cheese.

3 Spoon hot chicken mixture into pastry-lined pie pans. Roll out remaining pastry. Cut pastry into six 6-inch circles, rerolling if necessary. Cut slits in pastry circles for escape of steam; place atop filling. Seal and flute edges. Bake pies in a 375° oven for 35 to 40 minutes or till crust is light brown. Makes 6 servings.

DOUBLE-DECKER CHICKEN SALAD

Advance preparation time: 1 hour
Final preparation time: 5 minutes

  1 1-quart container Freezer Chicken
     Starter (see recipe, page 319)
  3 envelopes unflavored gelatin
  1 cup cold water
  2 tablespoons lemon juice
 ¼ teaspoon salt
  1 cup cream-style cottage cheese
 ½ cup dairy sour cream
 ½ cup mayonnaise *or* salad dressing
  1 8-ounce package cream cheese,
     cut up
  1 10¾-ounce can condensed tomato
     soup
 ¼ cup shredded carrot
 ¼ cup finely chopped celery
 ¼ cup finely chopped green pepper
     Lettuce leaves

1 In a saucepan heat frozen Freezer Chicken Starter, covered, over medium-low heat about 25 minutes or till thawed, breaking up mixture with a fork once or twice. Strain mixture, reserving broth and chicken. Cube chicken; set aside.

2 In saucepan soften the gelatin in cold water. Stir over low heat till dissolved. Stir in the reserved chicken broth, lemon juice, and salt. Stir together ¾ cup of the gelatin mixture, the cottage cheese, sour cream, and mayonnaise. Pour into a 9x5x3-inch loaf pan. Chill in freezer till almost firm.

3 Meanwhile, in a large mixer bowl beat cream cheese for 30 seconds. Add tomato soup; beat till smooth. Gradually stir in the remaining gelatin mixture. Chill in freezer till partially set (the consistency of unbeaten egg whites). Stir in chicken, carrot, celery, and green pepper. Pour over layer in loaf pan. Chill in refrigerator for 8 to 24 hours or till salad is firm.

Before serving: Unmold onto lettuce-lined plate. Garnish with carrot curls, onion fans, and cherry tomatoes, if desired. Serves 8.

SAUCY CHICKEN WITH POTATO DUMPLINGS

Final preparation time: 55 minutes

  1 1-quart container Freezer Chicken
     Starter (see recipe, page 319)
 ½ cup milk
  1 medium onion, chopped (½ cup)
 ¼ cup butter *or* margarine
 ⅓ cup all-purpose flour
 ¾ teaspoon salt
  1 8-ounce carton dairy sour cream
  1 10-ounce package frozen peas
     and carrots
 ¼ cup chopped pimiento
     Packaged instant mashed
     potatoes (enough for 4 servings)
 ¼ cup toasted wheat germ
     Paprika

1 In a saucepan combine the Freezer Chicken Starter and the ½ cup milk. Cover and cook over medium heat about 20 minutes or till thawed. In another saucepan cook onion in butter or margarine till tender but not brown. Stir in flour and salt. Add the thawed chicken mixture. Cook and stir till mixture is thickened and bubbly. Cook and stir for 1 minute more. Remove from heat.

2 Gradually stir about *1 cup* of the hot mixture into sour cream; return to saucepan. Stir in peas and carrots and pimiento. Turn into a shallow 2-quart casserole or a 12x7½x2-inch baking dish. Bake in a 425° oven about 15 minutes or till bubbly.

3 Prepare mashed potatoes according to package directions. Stir in wheat germ. Drop by large spoonfuls onto *hot* chicken mixture. Sprinkle with paprika. Continue baking 5 to 8 minutes more. Serves 6.

**Double-Decker Chicken Salad
Saucy Chicken with Potato Dumplings**

CHICKEN- AND CHEESE-STUFFED PEPPERS

Advance preparation time: 30 minutes
Final preparation time: 40 minutes

½ cup elbow macaroni
6 large green peppers
1 stalk celery, chopped (½ cup)
3 tablespoons butter *or* margarine
¼ teaspoon salt
¼ teaspoon dried basil, crushed
1¾ cups milk
3 tablespoons cornstarch
½ teaspoon Worcestershire sauce
½ cup shredded Swiss cheese
¼ cup dry white wine
2 5-ounce cans boned chicken, drained and chopped
¼ cup fine dry bread crumbs
1 tablespoon butter, melted

1 Cook macaroni in boiling salted water about 8 minutes or just till tender; drain. Cut off tops of green peppers; remove seeds and membrane. Precook in boiling salted water for 5 minutes; invert on paper toweling to drain. (For crisp peppers, omit precooking.)

2 Chop pepper tops. Cook celery and chopped pepper in the 3 tablespoons butter or margarine till tender. Stir in salt and basil. Stir together milk, cornstarch, and Worcestershire sauce. Add to the celery mixture. Cook and stir till thickened and bubbly. Cook and stir 2 minutes more. Add the cheese and wine; stir till cheese melts. Stir in chicken and cooked macaroni.

3 Fill each pepper with some of the chicken mixture; stand upright in a 12x7½x2-inch baking dish. Toss together the bread crumbs and the 1 tablespoon melted butter. Sprinkle some crumb mixture atop each pepper. Cover; chill in the refrigerator for 3 to 24 hours.

Before serving: Uncover and bake peppers in a 350° oven about 40 minutes or till heated through. Makes 6 servings.

HERBED CHICKEN STRATA

Advance preparation time: 20 minutes
Final preparation time: 1 hour

4 cups toasted whole wheat bread cubes
2 cups shredded brick cheese *or* Swiss cheese (8 ounces)
2 5-ounce cans boned chicken, drained and chopped
3 green onions, thinly sliced
4 beaten eggs
1½ teaspoons prepared mustard
¼ teaspoon dried thyme, crushed
Dash ground red pepper
2 cups milk

1 Place *2 cups* of the toasted whole wheat bread cubes in the bottom of an 8x8x2-inch baking dish or pan. Sprinkle the cheese atop. Arrange the chicken and green onions evenly over the cheese. Top the chicken mixture with the remaining 2 cups toasted bread cubes.

2 Beat together the eggs, mustard, thyme, and ground red pepper with a rotary beater. Stir in milk. Pour evenly over the ingredients in the baking dish. Cover and chill in the refrigerator for 3 to 24 hours.

Before serving: Uncover strata and bake in a 325° oven for 50 to 55 minutes or till a knife inserted just off-center comes out clean. Let stand 5 minutes before serving. Serves 8.

CHICKEN BUNDLES

Advance preparation time: 20 minutes
Final preparation time: 25 minutes

1 package (8) refrigerated crescent rolls
2 5-ounce cans boned chicken, drained and chopped
½ cup shredded cheddar cheese
¼ cup bottled barbecue sauce

1 Unroll rolls into 4 portions; pinch perforations to seal. Stir together the chicken, cheese, and barbecue sauce. Spoon *one-fourth* of chicken mixture atop each rectangle. Moisten corners of each rectangle. Bring to center atop filling; seal. Place on baking sheet. Cover with moisture-vapor-proof material. Seal, label, and freeze.

Before serving: Uncover bundles; bake in 350° oven 20 to 25 minutes. Makes 4.

PINEAPPLE AND CHICKEN SANDWICHES

Advance preparation time: 15 minutes

1 8¼-ounce can crushed pineapple, drained
1 5-ounce can boned chicken, drained and chopped
1 4-ounce container whipped cream cheese
⅓ cup chopped pecans
½ teaspoon dried tarragon, crushed
6 slices white *or* whole wheat bread
Lettuce leaves

1 Combine first five ingredients and dash *salt.* Spread on *3* bread slices. Top with remaining slices. Halve diagonally. Wrap in foil. Seal, label, and freeze.

Before serving: Thaw at room temperature. Place lettuce in sandwiches. Serves 3.

DILLED CHICKEN SANDWICHES

Advance preparation time: 12 minutes

1 4-ounce container whipped cream cheese with chives
1 tablespoon lemon juice
1 teaspoon Worcestershire sauce
½ teaspoon dried dillweed
1 5-ounce can boned chicken, drained and chopped
4 slices whole wheat bread
Alfalfa sprouts

1 Stir together whipped cream cheese, lemon juice, Worcestershire sauce, and dillweed. Stir in chicken. Spread chicken mixture on *2 slices* of the bread. Top with remaining 2 slices. Cut in half diagonally. Wrap in foil. Seal, label, and freeze sandwiches at least 6 hours.

Before serving: Thaw sandwiches at room temperature. Place alfalfa sprouts in each sandwich. Makes 4 servings.

THAWING FROZEN SANDWICHES

Frozen sandwiches thaw at room temperature in 3½ to 4 hours. Take a frozen sandwich from the freezer in the morning to carry to work or school. It will be ready to eat by lunch. Pack lettuce leaves, tomato slices, sprouts, or pickles and add them to the sandwich just before eating.

GARDEN CHICKEN-MACARONI SALAD

Tomatoes, cucumber, green onion, and dillweed give this chicken salad its fresh garden flavor—

Advance preparation time: 20 minutes
Final preparation time: 5 minutes

½ cup elbow macaroni
½ cup cherry tomatoes, halved
¼ cup chopped cucumber
2 green onions, sliced (2 tablespoons)
⅓ cup mayonnaise *or* salad dressing
½ teaspoon dried dillweed
¼ teaspoon salt
⅛ teaspoon pepper
1 5-ounce can boned chicken, drained and chopped
Lettuce leaves

1 Cook macaroni in boiling salted water about 8 minutes or just till tender; drain well. Rinse with cold water. In a bowl combine cooked macaroni, tomatoes, cucumber, and green onions.

2 Stir mayonnaise or salad dressing, dillweed, salt, and pepper into macaroni-vegetable mixture; mix well. Fold in chicken. Season to taste with salt and pepper. Cover and chill in the refrigerator for 3 to 24 hours.

Before serving: Spoon macaroni-vegetable mixture onto individual lettuce-lined salad plates. Makes 2 servings.

CHICKEN AND CHEESE FRUIT MOLD

Advance preparation time: 35 minutes
Final preparation time: 5 minutes

2 envelopes unflavored gelatin
1 tablespoon sugar
1 14½-ounce can chicken broth
2 tablespoons lemon juice
1 8-ounce carton plain yogurt
½ cup mayonnaise *or* salad dressing
2 5-ounce cans boned chicken, drained and chopped
1 4-ounce package (1 cup) shredded cheddar cheese
1 8-ounce can crushed pineapple
1 stalk celery, chopped (½ cup)
Lettuce leaves

1 In saucepan combine unflavored gelatin and sugar; stir in chicken broth. Stir mixture over low heat till gelatin and sugar are dissolved. Remove from heat; cool. Stir in the lemon juice.

2 In a large bowl combine the yogurt and mayonnaise or salad dressing; gradually stir in cooled gelatin mixture till smooth. Chill till partially set (the consistency of unbeaten egg whites).

3 Fold the chopped boned chicken, shredded cheddar cheese, *undrained* crushed pineapple, and chopped celery into gelatin mixture. Pour into a 6- or 6½-cup mold. Cover and chill salad in the refrigerator for 6 to 24 hours.

Before serving: Unmold the salad onto a lettuce-lined serving platter or plate. Makes 6 servings.

24-HOUR CHICKEN SALAD

There's no final preparation when serving this chilled salad. Simply serve it right from the refrigerator—

Advance preparation time: 20 minutes

- 1 3-ounce package cream cheese, cut up
- 4 cups torn fresh spinach
- 1 cup shredded Swiss cheese (4 ounces)
- 1 cup frozen peas
- ½ cup shelled pumpkin seed
- 2 5-ounce cans boned chicken, drained and chopped
- ½ cup shredded carrot
- 1 cup cauliflower flowerets
- 4 cups torn iceberg lettuce
- 1 cup mayonnaise or salad dressing
- 1 tablespoon lemon juice
- ½ teaspoon dried dillweed
- ¼ teaspoon salt
- ½ cup shredded Swiss cheese (2 ounces)

1 Let cream cheese stand at room temperature to soften slightly. Meanwhile, place spinach in the bottom of a large glass bowl. Layer in order, the 1 cup shredded Swiss cheese, the frozen peas, pumpkin seed, and chicken. Then, top with shredded carrot, cauliflower, and lettuce.

2 In a bowl stir together the cream cheese, mayonnaise or salad dressing, lemon juice, dillweed, and salt. Spread mayonnaise mixture over top of salad, sealing to edge of bowl. Sprinkle the ½ cup shredded cheese atop. Cover and chill in the refrigerator for 3 to 24 hours. Makes 6 servings.

LEMONY ROASTED TURKEY BREAST

Have your butcher cut the turkey breast into four pieces while it's still frozen—

Advance preparation time: 25 minutes
Final preparation time: 1 hour and 10 minutes

- ¼ cup cooking oil
- ¼ cup lemon juice
- ¼ cup water
- 2 teaspoons curry powder
- 1 clove garlic, minced
- ½ teaspoon salt
- ½ teaspoon instant chicken bouillon granules
- ½ teaspoon ground coriander
- ¼ teaspoon pepper
- 1 3- to 4-pound frozen breast of turkey, cut into quarters

1 For marinade, combine cooking oil, lemon juice, water, curry powder, garlic, salt, chicken bouillon granules, coriander, and pepper. Place frozen turkey breast pieces in a plastic bag set in a bowl. Pour marinade over turkey pieces. Close bag. Chill in refrigerator for 24 hours, turning bag occasionally to distribute marinade.

Before serving: Arrange turkey quarters in a 12x7½x2-inch baking dish. Pour marinade over turkey quarters. Bake, uncovered, in a 350° oven for 60 to 70 minutes or till turkey is tender, basting occasionally with marinade. Makes 4 servings.

TURKEY AND SWISS CHEESE STRATA

Advance preparation time: 20 minutes
Final preparation time: 1 hour

- 5 cups dry rye bread cubes
- 1½ cups shredded Swiss cheese (6 ounces)
- 2 5-ounce cans boned turkey, drained and chopped
- ¼ cup chopped green pepper
- ¼ teaspoon salt
- 4 beaten eggs
- 2½ cups milk
- ½ cup mayonnaise or salad dressing
- 1 tablespoon butter or margarine, melted

1 Sprinkle 2 cups of the rye bread cubes evenly into the bottom of an 8x8x2-inch baking dish. Combine shredded Swiss cheese, turkey, green pepper, and salt; sprinkle over bread in dish. Top with 2 cups more bread cubes.

2 Stir together the eggs, milk, and mayonnaise or salad dressing. Pour mixture evenly over the ingredients in the baking dish. Cover and chill in the refrigerator for 3 to 24 hours.

Before serving: Toss the remaining 1 cup bread cubes with the melted butter or margarine. Sprinkle buttered bread cubes atop ingredients in baking dish.

Bake, uncovered, in a 325° oven for 50 to 55 minutes or till a knife inserted just off-center comes out clean. Let strata stand 5 minutes before serving. Cut into rectangles. Makes 8 servings.

CREAMY MUSHROOM-TURKEY PATTIES

Advance preparation time: 25 minutes
Final preparation time: 55 minutes

- 1 **beaten egg**
- ½ **cup dairy sour cream**
- ½ **cup fine dry bread crumbs**
- 2 **green onions, sliced**
  (2 tablespoons)
- 1 **teaspoon Worcestershire sauce**
- 1½ **pounds ground raw turkey**
- ¼ **cup hot water**
- 1 **teaspoon instant beef bouillon**
  granules
- 1 **10¾-ounce can condensed cream**
  of mushroom soup
- 1 **4-ounce can sliced mushrooms**
  Hot cooked noodles

1 In a bowl stir together beaten egg, sour cream, bread crumbs, green onions, and Worcestershire sauce. Add ground raw turkey; mix well. Shape mixture into six ½-inch-thick patties.

2 Place patties in the bottom of a 12x7½x2-inch baking dish. Combine hot water and bouillon granules. Stir in mushroom soup and *undrained* mushrooms. Spoon over turkey patties. Cover and chill in the refrigerator for 3 to 24 hours.

Before serving: Uncover and bake in a 375° oven about 50 minutes or till turkey patties are done. Remove turkey patties. Stir sauce in baking dish. Serve sauce over turkey patties and hot cooked noodles. Makes 6 servings.

TURKEY AND NOODLE CASSEROLES

If you like, bake one of these casseroles immediately and freeze the other for a later meal. Bake the unfrozen casserole, uncovered, in a 350° oven about 35 minutes or till heated through—

Advance preparation time: 30 minutes
Final preparation time: 1 hour

- 8 **ounces medium noodles**
- 2 **pounds ground raw turkey**
- 1 **medium green pepper, chopped**
  (¾ cup)
- 1 **8-ounce can sliced water**
  chestnuts, drained
- 2 **10¾-ounce cans condensed**
  cream of chicken soup
- 2 **cups milk**
- 1 **6-ounce can sliced mushrooms,**
  drained
- 1 **2-ounce can sliced pimiento,**
  drained
- 2 **tablespoons minced dried onion**
- 1 **teaspoon salt**
- 1 **teaspoon ground sage**

1 Cook noodles according to package directions; drain. Meanwhile, in a large skillet cook ground raw turkey and green pepper till meat is brown; drain off fat. Add sliced water chestnuts to the meat mixture.

2 In a large bowl stir together the soup and milk; add mushrooms, pimiento, dried onion, salt, sage, and cooked noodles. Stir in meat mixture. Divide meat and noodle mixture between two 2-quart casseroles. Cover each with moisture-vaporproof material. Seal, label, and freeze at least 6 hours.

Before serving: Bake frozen casseroles, covered, in a 400° oven for 30 minutes. Uncover; stir and bake about 30 minutes more or till heated through. Makes two 4- or 5-serving casseroles.

TURKEY LOAF

Advance preparation time: 12 minutes
Final preparation time: 1 hour

- 2 **beaten eggs**
- 1 **10¾-ounce can condensed cream**
  of mushroom soup
- 1 **tablespoon milk**
- 1 **stalk celery, chopped (½ cup)**
- ½ **cup fine dry bread crumbs**
- 2 **tablespoons chopped pimiento**
- 1 **teaspoon dried rosemary, crushed**
- ¾ **teaspoon salt**
- ⅛ **teaspoon pepper**
- 2 **pounds ground raw turkey**
- ¼ **cup dairy sour cream**
- 2 **tablespoons milk**
- 1 **tablespoon sherry**
- ½ **teaspoon paprika**

1 In a mixing bowl combine eggs, *half* of the mushroom soup, and the 1 tablespoon milk. (Cover and refrigerate remaining soup for use in making the sauce.) Stir celery, fine dry bread crumbs, pimiento, rosemary, salt, and pepper into soup mixture. Add ground turkey; mix well.

2 Pat the meat mixture into an ungreased 9x9x2-inch baking pan. Cover and chill in the refrigerator for 3 to 24 hours.

Before serving: Uncover and bake in a 350° oven about 1 hour or till done. Meanwhile, for sauce, combine remaining mushroom soup, the dairy sour cream, the 2 tablespoons milk, dry sherry, and paprika. Cook and stir till mixture is heated through; *do not boil.* Serve sauce over turkey loaf. Makes 8 to 10 servings.

326

CHILLED SALMON WITH CUCUMBER RELISH

Advance preparation time: 12 minutes
Final preparation time: 8 minutes

  4 fresh *or* frozen salmon steaks, cut
     ³/₄ inch thick
     Boiling water
  1 small onion, quartered
  ½ teaspoon salt
  ½ cup white wine vinegar
  ¼ cup water
  2 tablespoons sugar
  ½ teaspoon salt
  ½ teaspoon dried marjoram, crushed
  1 small tomato, chopped
  1 small cucumber, coarsely
     shredded
  ¼ cup sliced green onion
  1 tablespoon snipped parsley
     Shredded lettuce

1 Place fresh or frozen steaks in a greased 10-inch skillet. Add boiling water to cover. Add quartered onion and ½ teaspoon salt. Cover and simmer for 5 to 10 minutes or till fish flakes easily when tested with a fork.

2 Remove fish to a baking dish. Combine vinegar, the ¼ cup water, sugar, ½ teaspoon salt, and marjoram. Stir in chopped tomato, shredded cucumber, green onion, and parsley. Pour atop fish. Cover and refrigerate for 3 to 24 hours.

Before serving: Line plates with shredded lettuce. With slotted spoon remove salmon and vegetables from liquid and place atop lettuce. Drizzle with some of the liquid. Makes 4 servings.

Chilled Salmon with Cucumber Relish

YOGURT-SAUCED TURNOVERS

Advance preparation time: 30 minutes
Final preparation time: 40 minutes

  ½ of a 17¼-ounce package (1 sheet)
     frozen puff pastry
  1 medium onion, finely chopped
     (½ cup)
  1 medium carrot, finely chopped
     (½ cup)
  3 tablespoons butter *or* margarine
  1 4-ounce can sliced mushrooms,
     drained
  1 stalk celery, sliced (½ cup)
  1 beaten egg
  1 15½-ounce can salmon, drained,
     flaked, and skin and bones
     removed
  ¼ cup plain yogurt
  ½ teaspoon dried dillweed
  ¼ teaspoon salt
  ⅛ teaspoon pepper
     Milk
  ½ cup plain yogurt
  ½ teaspoon dried dillweed

1 Allow puff pastry to stand at room temperature for 20 minutes before unrolling. Roll puff pastry into a 12x12-inch square. Cut into four 6x6-inch squares.

2 In a saucepan cook the onion and carrot in the butter or margarine till tender but not brown. Stir in mushroom and celery. Stir together the egg, salmon, the ¼ cup yogurt, ½ teaspoon dillweed, salt, and pepper; stir into onion mixture.

3 Spoon *some* of the salmon mixture atop each pastry square. Moisten edges with water. Bring corners to center; seal. Cover; refrigerate for 2 to 4 hours.

Before serving: Place turnovers in an ungreased shallow baking pan. Brush with milk. Bake, uncovered, in a 400° oven for 30 minutes or till pastry is golden brown. In a bowl stir together the ½ cup yogurt and the ½ teaspoon dillweed. Dollop some atop each turnover. Makes 4 servings.

CHEESY SALMON SHELLS

Advance preparation time: 45 minutes
Final preparation time: 1 hour

  4 ounces large shell macaroni
     (12 to 14 shells)
  2 tablespoons chopped onion
  2 tablespoons butter *or* margarine
  1 tablespoon cornstarch
  ¼ teaspoon salt
     Dash pepper
  1 cup milk
  1 3-ounce package cream cheese,
     cut up
  ½ cup shredded Swiss cheese
     (2 ounces)
  1 8-ounce can sliced water
     chestnuts, drained and chopped
  1 7¾-ounce can salmon, drained,
     flaked, and skin and bones
     removed
  ¼ cup milk
  2 tablespoons chopped pimiento

1 Cook large macaroni shells according to package directions. Drain well. Meanwhile, in a saucepan cook chopped onion in butter or margarine till tender but not brown.

2 Stir cornstarch, salt, and pepper into onion. Add the 1 cup milk all at once. Cook and stir till mixture is thickened and bubbly. Cook and stir 2 minutes more. Add the cream cheese and Swiss cheese; stir till cheese is melted. Stir in the water chestnuts.

3 Divide mixture in half. Fold the salmon into *half* of the mixture. Add the ¼ cup milk and chopped pimiento to the remaining half. Fill the cooked macaroni shells with the salmon-cheese mixture. Place in a greased 10x6x2-inch baking dish. Pour pimiento-cheese mixture over all. Cover and freeze at least 6 hours.

Before serving: Bake frozen shells, covered, in a 375° oven for 40 minutes. Uncover and continue baking 15 to 20 minutes more or till heated through. Makes 4 servings.

FISH AND
SEAFOOD

MARINATED SCALLOP KABOBS

Advance preparation time: 8 minutes
Final preparation time: 15 minutes

1 pound fresh *or* frozen scallops
¼ cup cooking oil
¼ cup dry white wine
2 tablespoons lemon juice
½ teaspoon onion powder
¼ teaspoon dried basil, crushed
⅛ teaspoon salt
  Few drops bottled hot pepper sauce
1 large green pepper, cut into 1-inch squares
4 slices bacon, cut into 2-inch lengths

1 Thaw scallops, if frozen. Halve any large scallops. Place scallops in plastic bag set in deep bowl. For marinade, in a bowl combine cooking oil, wine, lemon juice, onion powder, basil, salt, and hot pepper sauce. Pour over scallops in bag. Close bag and chill in the refrigerator for 3 to 24 hours, turning once.

Before serving: Alternately thread scallops, green pepper, and bacon on skewers. Place kabobs on rack of unheated broiler pan and broil 4 inches from heat about 10 minutes or till scallops are tender, turning once and basting with marinade frequently. (Or, grill over *medium* coals 8 to 10 minutes.) Makes 4 servings.

TUNA-STUFFED PEPPERS

Advance preparation time: 30 minutes
Final preparation time: 55 minutes

6 large green peppers
1 stalk celery, chopped (½ cup)
2 tablespoons butter *or* margarine
2 tablespoons cornstarch
½ teaspoon salt
⅛ teaspoon pepper
1¼ cups milk
1½ cups shredded cheddar cheese (6 ounces)
1 4-ounce can green chili peppers, rinsed, seeded, and chopped
1 teaspoon Worcestershire sauce
1 9¼-ounce can tuna, drained and flaked
¾ cup quick-cooking rice
1 7-ounce can whole kernel corn, drained
⅓ cup coarsely crushed tortilla chips

1 Cut tops from green peppers; remove seeds and membranes. In a saucepan precook peppers in boiling salted water for 5 minutes; invert on paper toweling to drain. (For crisp peppers, omit precooking.)

2 In a large saucepan, cook celery in butter or margarine till tender but not brown. Stir in the cornstarch, salt, and pepper. Add milk all at once. Cook and stir till mixture is thickened and bubbly. Cook and stir 2 minutes more.

3 Add the cheddar cheese, chili peppers, and Worcestershire sauce; stir till cheese is melted. Fold in tuna, uncooked rice, and corn. Fill *each* pepper with *some* of the tuna mixture; stand upright in a 12x7½x2-inch baking dish. Cover and refrigerate for 2 to 24 hours.

Before serving: Sprinkle *each* pepper with *some* of the crushed tortilla chips. Bake, uncovered, in a 350° oven about 50 minutes or till peppers are heated through. Makes 6 servings.

CRAB STRATA

Advance preparation time: 20 minutes
Final preparation time: 1 hour

1 10-ounce package frozen cut asparagus
¼ cup sliced green onion
6 slices day-old bread
1 6-ounce can crab meat, drained, flaked, and cartilage removed
2 cups shredded Muenster cheese *or* mozzarella cheese (8 ounces)
4 beaten eggs
2½ cups milk
2 tablespoons Dijon-style mustard
  Dash ground red pepper

1 In a saucepan cook asparagus and green onion according to directions on asparagus package; drain. Cut *3 slices* of the bread into cubes; cut remaining slices in half diagonally and set aside. Place bread cubes in the bottom of a 12x7½x2-inch baking dish. Top with crab, asparagus mixture, and Muenster or mozzarella cheese.

2 Arrange bread halves atop cheese. In a mixing bowl combine eggs, milk, Dijon-style mustard, and red pepper. Pour over ingredients in baking dish. Cover and refrigerate for 3 to 24 hours.

Before serving: Bake strata in a 325° oven for 50 to 60 minutes or till a knife inserted near center comes out clean. Cut into squares to serve. Makes 8 servings.

SHRIMP SAKE

If you don't have sake, try making this recipe with dry sherry—

Advance preparation time: 10 minutes
Final preparation time: 15 minutes

¾ **pound fresh** *or* **frozen shelled and deveined shrimp**
¼ **cup sake**
¼ **cup water**
3 **tablespoons soy sauce**
2 **tablespoons sugar**
1 **tablespoon cooking oil**
2 **teaspoons dried parsley flakes**
¼ **teaspoon grated gingerroot**
   Few drops bottled hot pepper sauce
   Hot cooked rice

1 Place fresh or frozen shelled and deveined shrimp in a mixing bowl. For marinade, stir together the sake, water, soy sauce, sugar, cooking oil, dried parsley flakes, grated gingerroot, and bottled hot pepper sauce. Pour marinade over shrimp. Cover and refrigerate shrimp for 3 to 24 hours.

Before serving: Drain shrimp, reserving the marinade. Place shrimp on the rack of an unheated broiler pan. Broil 5 to 6 inches from heat for 6 to 8 minutes, turning shrimp once and brushing with marinade several times during broiling. Meanwhile, heat the remaining marinade in a small saucepan. Serve shrimp and warm marinade over hot cooked rice on individual plates. Makes 4 servings.

BROCCOLI-SHRIMP CASSEROLE

Advance preparation time: 30 minutes
Final preparation time: 1 hour

4 **ounces spaghetti, broken up**
1 **tablespoon butter** *or* **margarine**
1 **10-ounce package frozen cut broccoli**
1 **pound fresh** *or* **frozen shelled and deveined shrimp**
2 **tablespoons cornstarch**
½ **teaspoon paprika**
1⅔ **cups milk**
¼ **cup dry white wine**
1 **cup shredded Swiss cheese**
1 **4-ounce can sliced mushrooms, drained**
¼ **teaspoon dried basil, crushed**
¼ **teaspoon dried oregano, crushed**
¼ **cup fine dry bread crumbs**
1 **tablespoon butter** *or* **margarine**

1 Cook spaghetti according to package directions. Drain and toss with 1 tablespoon butter or margarine. Meanwhile, cook broccoli according to package directions; drain. Set spaghetti and broccoli aside.

2 In a saucepan add shrimp to 3 cups boiling salted *water*. Return to boiling; reduce heat and simmer for 1 to 3 minutes or till shrimp turn pink. Drain and set aside.

3 For cheese sauce, in a saucepan combine cornstarch, paprika, ½ teaspoon *salt*, and dash *pepper*. Add milk all at once. Cook and stir till thickened and bubbly. Cook and stir 2 minutes more. Stir in wine and cheese; stir till cheese is melted.

4 In a 2-quart casserole combine spaghetti, broccoli, shrimp, mushrooms, basil, and oregano. Pour cheese sauce over all; toss. Cover and refrigerate for 3 to 24 hours. Combine fine dry bread crumbs and 1 tablespoon melted butter or margarine; cover and chill.

Before serving: Sprinkle the crumb mixture atop casserole. Bake, uncovered, in a 350° oven for 50 to 60 minutes or till heated through. Makes 6 servings.

CITRUS FILLETS WITH PINE NUTS

Advance preparation time: 15 minutes
Final preparation time: 15 minutes

1 **pound fresh** *or* **frozen fish fillets**
½ **cup water**
2 **tablespoons frozen grapefruit juice concentrate**
2 **tablespoons pine nuts** *or* **slivered almonds, toasted**
1 **tablespoon cooking oil**
1 **teaspoon dried parsley flakes**
¼ **teaspoon salt**

1 Allow frozen fish to stand at room temperature for 15 minutes. Separate fillets or cut into 4 serving-size portions; place in a shallow pan. Meanwhile, for marinade, in a mixing bowl combine the water, grapefruit juice concentrate, pine nuts or almonds, cooking oil, parsley flakes, and salt. Pour marinade over fish portions. Cover and refrigerate for 3 to 24 hours.

Before serving: Remove fish from pan, reserving marinade. Place fish on greased rack of unheated broiler pan. Broil fish 4 inches from heat till fish flakes easily when tested with a fork. (Allow 5 minutes for each ½ inch of thickness; if fish pieces are more than 1 inch thick, turn halfway through.) Baste often with reserved marinade. To serve, brush fish again with marinade. Makes 4 servings.

CHEESE AND PINEAPPLE MOLD

Advance preparation time: 20 minutes
Final preparation time: 5 minutes

1 15½-ounce can crushed pineapple
1 3-ounce package lemon-flavored gelatin
1 3-ounce package lime-flavored gelatin
1 cup ice cubes
1 3-ounce package cream cheese, cut up
1 8-ounce carton dairy sour cream
1 tablespoon lemon juice
2 cups shredded cheddar cheese (8 ounces)
Endive (optional)

1 Drain pineapple, reserving syrup. Set pineapple aside. Add water to syrup to make 2 cups liquid. In saucepan heat syrup mixture to boiling; remove from heat.

2 Add lemon and lime gelatin; stir till gelatin is dissolved. Add ice cubes to gelatin mixture, stirring till ice is melted.

3 In small mixer bowl beat cream cheese to soften. Stir in sour cream and lemon juice. Gradually add gelatin mixture to cream cheese mixture, beating till smooth. Stir in the cheddar cheese and the drained pineapple. Turn mixture into a 6½- to 7-cup ring mold. Cover and chill in refrigerator for 6 to 24 hours.

Before serving: Unmold salad onto serving platter; fill center with endive, if desired. Makes 12 servings.

CRANBERRY MOLDED SALAD

Advance preparation time: 15 minutes
Final preparation time: 5 minutes

1 3-ounce package cherry-flavored gelatin
1 cup boiling water
1 16-ounce can whole cranberry sauce
½ cup dairy sour cream
1 11-ounce can mandarin orange sections, drained
¼ cup chopped walnuts
Lettuce leaves

1 In a bowl dissolve gelatin in boiling water. Beat the cranberry sauce and sour cream into the gelatin mixture. Fold in the orange sections and chopped walnuts. Spoon mixture into a 5-cup ring mold. Cover and chill in refrigerator for 6 to 24 hours.

Before serving: Unmold salad onto a lettuce-lined plate. Makes 8 servings.

TANGY CRAN-MALLOW SALAD

Advance preparation time: 15 minutes
Final preparation time: 25 minutes

1 medium apple
1 cup cranberry-orange relish
1 cup tiny marshmallows
1 4-ounce container frozen whipped dessert topping

1 Core and chop apple. In a bowl stir together the cranberry-orange relish, tiny marshmallows, and apple. Cover and chill in refrigerator for 3 to 24 hours.

Before serving: Thaw topping. Fold thawed dessert topping into relish mixture. Turn into serving bowl or spoon into lettuce cups on individual serving plates, if desired. Makes 6 servings.

NUTMEG FRUIT SALAD

Rum and ground nutmeg make this fruit salad special—

Advance preparation time: 20 minutes
Final preparation time: 5 minutes

1 1½-ounce envelope dessert topping mix
1 tablespoon rum
¼ teaspoon ground nutmeg
1 medium apple
¼ cup maraschino cherries, drained
1 16-ounce can peach slices, drained
1 15½-ounce can pineapple chunks, drained
⅓ cup chopped walnuts
Lettuce leaves

1 Prepare topping mix according to package directions, *except* omit the vanilla and add the rum and ground nutmeg. Core and coarsely chop the apple. Halve the drained maraschino cherries.

2 In a large mixing bowl stir together the peach slices, pineapple chunks, chopped walnuts, chopped apple, and halved cherries. Fold the whipped topping mixture into the fruit. Cover and chill in refrigerator for 3 to 24 hours.

Before serving: Stir the fruit salad gently. Spoon the salad into a lettuce-lined bowl or onto individual lettuce-lined plates. Makes 8 to 10 servings.

MOLDED BERRY SALAD

Advance preparation time: 25 minutes
Final preparation time: 5 minutes

1 10-ounce package frozen
   strawberries *or* red raspberries
1 6-ounce package raspberry- *or*
   strawberry-flavored gelatin
2 cups boiling water
1 pint vanilla ice cream
1 6-ounce can frozen lemonade
   concentrate
⅓ cup chopped pecans

1 Place package of fruit in hot water to
thaw for 10 minutes. Drain berries, reserving syrup. In a bowl dissolve gelatin in the boiling water. Add ice cream by spoonfuls, stirring till melted. Add lemonade concentrate; stir till melted. Add the reserved syrup. Chill till partially set. Fold in the drained berries and pecans. Turn into a 6-cup ring mold. Cover; chill in refrigerator for 6 to 24 hours.

Before serving: Unmold onto a serving plate. Makes 8 to 10 servings.

DOUBLE-APPLE SALAD MOLD

Advance preparation time: 15 minutes
Final preparation time: 5 minutes

1 large apple
1 3-ounce package lime-flavored
   gelatin
1 8½-ounce can applesauce
   Mayonnaise *or* salad dressing

1 Core and coarsely chop apple. Dissolve lime-flavored gelatin in 1¼ cups *boiling water*. Stir in applesauce. Stir in the apple. Pour into a 3-cup mold. Cover; chill in refrigerator 6 to 24 hours.

Before serving: Unmold and serve with mayonnaise. Serves 6.

PARTY FRUIT FREEZE

Advance preparation time: 15 minutes
Final preparation time: 5 minutes

2 4-ounce containers whipped
   cream cheese
¼ cup mayonnaise *or* salad dressing
1 pint lemon *or* orange sherbet
1 banana
1 16-ounce can diced peaches *or*
   fruit cocktail, drained
¼ cup flaked coconut
¼ cup chopped walnuts

1 Combine cream cheese and mayonnaise; stir in sherbet till smooth. Chop banana. Stir banana, fruit, coconut, and nuts into sherbet. Turn into an 8x4x2-inch loaf pan. Cover and freeze at least 6 hours.

Before serving: Remove from pan; slice into ½-inch-thick slices. Serve on lettuce-lined plates, if desired. Serves 6 to 8.

STRAWBERRY-BANANA SALAD

Advance preparation time: 20 minutes
Final preparation time: 15 minutes

3 medium bananas
¼ cup slivered almonds
1 pint vanilla ice cream
1 21-ounce can strawberry pie
   filling
1 tablespoon lemon juice
   Lettuce leaves

1 Place a large bowl in freezer to chill. Chop bananas and almonds. Stir ice cream in chilled bowl to soften. Stir in pie filling and lemon juice. Fold in bananas and nuts. Turn into 10 individual molds or one 5½- or 6-cup mold. Freeze at least 6 hours.

Before serving: Let stand at room temperature 10 minutes. Unmold onto lettuce-lined plates or platter. Serves 10.

MOLDED WHITE WINE AND APRICOT SALAD

Pictured on page 297—

Advance preparation time: 15 minutes
Final preparation time: 5 minutes

2 envelopes unflavored gelatin
½ cup sugar
¼ teaspoon salt
2 cups apricot nectar
1 cup dry white wine
¾ cup cold water
1 8-ounce carton dairy sour cream
   Lettuce leaves
   Fresh fruit (optional)

1 In a medium saucepan stir together the unflavored gelatin, sugar, and salt. Stir in the apricot nectar. Cook and stir mixture over low heat till the gelatin dissolves.

2 Remove gelatin mixture from heat. Stir in the dry white wine and cold water; add the dairy sour cream. Beat mixture with a rotary beater till smooth. Turn into a 5½- or 6-cup ring mold. Cover and chill in refrigerator for 6 to 24 hours.

Before serving: Unmold gelatin salad onto lettuce-lined plate. If desired, arrange fresh fruit in the center of the ring mold. Makes 8 to 10 servings.

SPICED GRAPE SALAD

Advance preparation time: 30 minutes
Final preparation time: 5 minutes

1 3-ounce package lime-flavored
   gelatin
1 3-ounce package cream cheese,
   cut up
1 16-ounce can light seedless
   spiced grapes

1 Dissolve gelatin in 1 cup *boiling water*;
gradually beat into cream cheese.
Drain grapes, reserving syrup. Add water to
syrup, if necessary, to make ¾ cup. Stir syrup
into gelatin mixture. Chill till partially set.
Fold in grapes. Turn into a 3½- or 4-cup
mold. Cover; refrigerate 6 to 24 hours.
Before serving: Unmold. Serves 6.

LEMON FRUIT MOLD

Advance preparation time: 35 minutes
Final preparation time: 5 minutes

1 16-ounce can grapefruit sections
1 3-ounce package lemon-flavored
   gelatin
1 3-ounce package peach-flavored
   gelatin
2 tablespoons sugar
1 12-ounce can grapefruit
   carbonated beverage
2 tablespoons lemon juice
1 cup seedless green grapes, halved

1 Drain grapefruit, reserving syrup. Add
water to syrup to make 2 cups. Combine lemon and peach gelatin and sugar; stir
in syrup mixture. Cook and stir till gelatin
dissolves. Remove from heat. Stir in carbonated beverage and lemon juice. Chill till partially set. Fold in fruit. Turn into a 6-cup mold.
Cover and chill in refrigerator 6 to 24 hours.
Before serving: Unmold. Serves 8.

BEAN SPROUT-KRAUT RELISH

Advance preparation time: 20 minutes

1 16-ounce can sauerkraut, drained
1 2-ounce jar sliced pimiento,
   drained
2 cups fresh bean sprouts *or* one
   16-ounce can bean sprouts,
   rinsed and drained
1 stalk celery, sliced (½ cup)
1 small onion, chopped (¼ cup)
2 tablespoons finely chopped green
   pepper
½ cup sugar
½ cup vinegar
¼ cup salad oil

1 Snip the sauerkraut and chop the sliced
pimiento. In a bowl combine the sauerkraut, pimiento, bean sprouts, celery, onion,
and green pepper.

2 In a screw-top jar combine sugar, vinegar, and salad oil; cover and shake to
dissolve sugar. Pour over vegetables, tossing to coat. Cover; chill in refrigerator for 3 to
24 hours. Makes 6 to 8 servings.

SCANDINAVIAN CUCUMBERS

Advance preparation time: 15 minutes

½ cup dairy sour cream
2 tablespoons snipped parsley
2 tablespoons tarragon vinegar
1 tablespoon sugar
1 tablespoon finely chopped onion
¼ teaspoon dried dillweed
2 medium *or* 3 small cucumbers

1 In a bowl combine sour cream, parsley,
tarragon vinegar, sugar, onion, and dillweed. Thinly slice the cucumbers. Fold cucumbers into sour cream mixture. Cover
and chill in refrigerator 3 to 24 hours. Makes
6 servings.

BROCCOLI RING

Advance preparation time: 35 minutes
Final preparation time: 5 minutes

3 eggs
1 10-ounce package frozen chopped
   broccoli
1 envelope unflavored gelatin
½ cup water
1 10¾-ounce can condensed
   chicken broth
⅔ cup mayonnaise *or* salad dressing
⅓ cup dairy sour cream
1 tablespoon lemon juice
   Dash onion powder
   Leaf lettuce

1 To hard-cook eggs, place eggs in a
saucepan; cover with cold water. Bring
to boiling; reduce heat to just below simmering. Cover and cook for 15 minutes. Run
cold water over eggs till cool. Remove
shells; chop eggs.

2 Cook broccoli according to package directions; drain well. Meanwhile, in medium saucepan soften the unflavored gelatin
in the water; add the condensed chicken
broth. Heat and stir till gelatin dissolves.

3 Add mayonnaise or salad dressing,
sour cream, lemon juice, and onion
powder; beat with rotary beater till smooth.
Chill till partially set (the consistency of unbeaten egg whites). Fold eggs and cooked
broccoli into gelatin mixture. Turn mixture
into a 4-cup mold. Cover and chill in refrigerator for 6 to 24 hours.
Before serving: Unmold onto lettuce-
lined serving plate. Garnish center of salad
with additional lettuce. Makes 8 servings.

Lemon Fruit Mold
Scandinavian Cucumbers
Bean Sprout-Kraut Relish
Broccoli Ring

MOLDED POTATO SALAD

Advance preparation time: 35 minutes
Final preparation time: 5 minutes

1 16-ounce can sliced potatoes,
   drained
1 stalk celery, chopped (½ cup)
¼ cup sweet pickle relish
2 tablespoons vinegar
1½ cups cold water
1 envelope unflavored gelatin
1 teaspoon instant chicken bouillon
   granules
1 teaspoon dried parsley flakes
½ cup minced dried onion
½ cup mayonnaise or salad dressing
2 teaspoons prepared mustard
   Lettuce leaves
   Paprika

1 Coarsely chop potatoes. In a medium mixing bowl combine potatoes, chopped celery, and pickle relish. Add vinegar; toss lightly. Set aside.

2 In saucepan combine water, unflavored gelatin, and chicken bouillon granules; let mixture stand 5 minutes. Heat and stir till gelatin dissolves. Stir in the parsley flakes and dried onion.

3 Chill mixture till partially set (the consistency of unbeaten egg whites). Add mayonnaise or salad dressing and mustard to gelatin mixture; beat with rotary beater till fluffy. Fold into potato mixture. Turn into a 10x6x2-inch dish. Cover and chill in refrigerator 6 to 24 hours.

Before serving: Cut into squares and serve on individual lettuce-lined plates. Sprinkle with paprika. Makes 8 servings.

MACARONI AND CORN RELISH SALAD

Advance preparation time: 25 minutes

1 7-ounce package elbow macaroni
1 4-ounce jar pimiento, drained
1 13-ounce jar corn relish
1 medium green pepper, chopped
1 cup mayonnaise or salad dressing
½ cup plain yogurt
3 tablespoons milk

1 Cook macaroni in a large amount of boiling salted water about 8 minutes. Drain. Chop pimiento. Combine macaroni, pimiento, corn relish, and green pepper. Mix mayonnaise, yogurt, milk and ½ teaspoon *salt*; add to macaroni mixture, stirring gently to combine. (Mixture will be thin.) Cover and chill in refrigerator 3 to 24 hours. Serves 6.

DIETER'S VEGETABLE MOLD

Advance preparation time: 25 minutes
Final preparation time: 5 minutes

2 envelopes unflavored gelatin
1½ cups plain yogurt
½ cup low-calorie Italian salad
   dressing
1 cup chopped fresh mushrooms
1 medium green pepper, chopped
1 medium tomato, chopped
2 green onions, sliced

1 In a medium saucepan soften gelatin in 1 cup *cold water*. Heat and stir till gelatin dissolves. Stir in 1 cup additional *water*. Stir in yogurt and Italian dressing. Chill till partially set. Fold in vegetables. Turn into a 6-cup mold. Cover and chill in refrigerator 6 to 24 hours.

Before serving: Unmold onto serving plate. Makes 8 to 10 servings.

SPAGHETTI-VEGETABLE TOSS

Advance preparation time: 25 minutes
Final preparation time: 5 minutes

6 ounces spaghetti
1 12-ounce can whole kernel corn
   with sweet peppers, drained
1 cup sliced zucchini, halved
1 tablespoon finely chopped onion
¼ cup salad oil
2 tablespoons white wine vinegar
2 tablespoons lemon juice
1 tablespoon sugar
1 teaspoon seasoned salt
1 teaspoon dried basil, crushed
12 cherry tomatoes, halved
   Lettuce cups

1 Break the spaghetti into 2-inch lengths. Cook spaghetti in boiling salted water according to package directions. Drain, rinse, and drain again. In bowl combine cooked spaghetti, corn with sweet peppers, zucchini, and chopped onion.

2 In a screw-top jar combine the salad oil, wine vinegar, lemon juice, sugar, seasoned salt, and basil. Cover and shake to mix. Pour over pasta and vegetables; toss to coat well. Cover and chill in refrigerator for 3 to 24 hours.

Before serving: Add cherry tomato halves and toss again. Serve salad in lettuce cups on individual serving plates. Makes 6 servings.

MACARONI SALAD WITH DILL

Advance preparation time: 25 minutes
Final preparation time: 5 minutes

**8 ounces corkscrew *or* elbow
  macaroni**
**1 teaspoon instant beef bouillon
  granules**
1 tablespoon hot water
¾ cup mayonnaise *or* salad dressing
¼ cup dairy sour cream
¼ cup milk
¼ cup sweet pickle relish
1 teaspoon dried dillweed
½ teaspoon salt
⅛ teaspoon pepper
1 large tomato, seeded and chopped
**1 small green pepper, chopped
  (½ cup)**
**1 small onion, finely chopped
  (¼ cup)**
Lettuce leaves

1 Cook the corkscrew or elbow macaroni
in boiling salted water for 6 to 8 minutes
or till tender; drain. Dissolve the beef bouillon granules in the hot water.

2 In a small mixing bowl stir together the
mayonnaise or salad dressing, sour
cream, milk, sweet pickle relish, dried dillweed, salt, pepper, and beef bouillon mixture till well blended.

3 Place cooked and drained macaroni in
a large bowl. Stir mayonnaise mixture
into the cooked macaroni. Fold chopped tomato, green pepper, and onion into the macaroni mixture. Cover and chill in refrigerator
for 3 to 24 hours.

Before serving: Spoon macaroni salad onto individual lettuce-lined plates.
Makes 8 servings.

SEVEN-LAYER SALAD

To show off this salad, layer the vegetables
in a clear glass salad bowl—

Advance preparation time: 20 minutes
Final preparation time: 5 minutes

**1 8-ounce package frozen cut
  asparagus**
1 6-ounce jar artichoke hearts
⅓ cup desired herb-flavored vinegar
1 teaspoon sugar
1 pint cherry tomatoes (2 cups)
4 green onions
6 cups torn salad greens
**¼ cup grated Parmesan cheese
  (1 ounce)**

1 Cook frozen cut asparagus according
to package directions; drain well. Drain
artichoke hearts, reserving liquid.

2 In a screw-top jar combine reserved artichoke liquid, herb-flavored vinegar,
and sugar. Cover and chill in refrigerator till
needed.

3 Halve artichokes and tomatoes; slice
onions. In a large bowl layer in order, 3
cups of the torn greens, the artichokes, tomatoes, onions, asparagus, and remaining
3 cups greens. Sprinkle with cheese. Cover
and chill in refrigerator for 3 to 24 hours.

Before serving: Shake the vinegar
mixture; pour evenly over salad. Toss to
coat. Makes 8 to 10 servings.

TOSSED SALAD WITH LEMON-MUSTARD DRESSING

Advance preparation time: 10 minutes
Final preparation time: 15 minutes

1 egg yolk
4 teaspoons tarragon vinegar
4 teaspoons lemon juice
1 tablespoon Dijon-style mustard
¼ teaspoon salt
⅛ teaspoon white pepper
½ cup salad oil
¼ cup olive oil
4 cups torn Bibb *or* leaf lettuce
**1 medium cucumber, sliced
  (1¾ cups)**
1 cup sliced fresh mushrooms
1 cup cherry tomatoes, halved
½ cup broken walnuts

1 In a small mixer bowl combine the egg
yolk, tarragon vinegar, lemon juice, Dijon-style mustard, salt, and white pepper.
Stir till well blended.

2 Combine salad oil and olive oil. Add oils
to mustard mixture in a thin stream,
beating with electric mixer till blended. Continue beating till mixture is slightly thickened.
Cover and chill dressing in refrigerator for 3
to 24 hours.

Before serving: In a large salad bowl
combine the torn lettuce, sliced cucumber,
sliced mushrooms, halved cherry tomatoes,
and broken walnuts. Toss some of the
dressing with the salad. Pass remaining
dressing. (Refrigerate any leftover dressing.) Makes 8 servings.

NAPA-STYLE MARINATED VEGETABLES

Advanced preparation time: 30 minutes

- 1 10-ounce package frozen brussels sprouts
- 1 10-ounce package frozen cauliflower
- 1½ cups dry white wine
- ⅔ cup salad oil
- ½ cup lemon juice
- ¼ cup sugar
- 2 teaspoons salt
- 1 teaspoon mustard seed
- ½ teaspoon whole black peppercorns
- 2 cloves garlic, minced
- 1½ cups yellow crookneck squash, cut into sticks
- 1½ cups sliced cucumber
- 1½ cups cherry tomatoes
- 1 small onion, thinly sliced and separated into rings

1 Cook frozen brussels sprouts and cauliflower according to package directions; drain. Meanwhile, in a screw-top jar combine the dry white wine, salad oil, lemon juice, sugar, salt, mustard seed, peppercorns, and garlic; cover and shake well.

2 In a deep glass bowl arrange cooked brussels sprouts; pour some of the wine mixture over. Repeat with cauliflower, yellow squash, cucumber, and cherry tomatoes, drizzling each layer with some of the wine mixture. Pour any leftover wine mixture over top layer. Place onion slices atop. Cover and chill in refrigerator for 3 to 24 hours. Serve vegetables with a slotted spoon. Makes 12 servings.

**Napa-Style Marinated Vegetables
Chilled Vegetable Potage (see recipe, page 341)**

ANTIPASTO SALAD

Look for pepperoncini (Italian-style pickled peppers) in the pickle section at your grocery or at an Italian specialty shop. If you don't find pepperoncini, use pickled chili peppers—

Advance preparation time: 15 minutes
Final preparation time: 5 minutes

- 1 2-ounce jar sliced pimiento, drained
- 1 8-ounce can cut Italian green beans *or* cut green beans, drained
- ½ of a 15-ounce can garbanzo beans, drained
- ½ cup sliced pitted ripe olives
- ½ cup sliced pepperoncini
- ⅓ cup olive oil *or* salad oil
- 2 tablespoons lemon juice
- 1 teaspoon dried oregano, crushed
- ¼ teaspoon salt
- ⅛ teaspoon garlic powder
- ⅛ teaspoon pepper
  Bibb lettuce

1 Chop pimiento. In a medium bowl stir together the green beans, garbanzo beans, ripe olives, pepperoncini, and chopped pimiento.

2 In a screw-top jar combine olive oil or salad oil, lemon juice, oregano, salt, garlic powder, and pepper. Cover and shake well. Pour over the vegetable mixture; toss gently to coat. Cover and chill in refrigerator 3 to 24 hours, stirring occasionally.

Before serving: Drain vegetables. Serve on lettuce-lined plates. Serves 6.

RED CABBAGE SLAW

Advance preparation time: 25 minutes

- 1 1-pound head red cabbage
- 1 16-ounce can julienne beets
- 1 medium onion
- ½ cup vinegar
- ⅓ cup sugar

1 Cut cabbage into small wedges, removing core. Fill blender container with *half* of the cabbage; add cold water to cover. Blend till coarsely chopped. Drain. Repeat with remaining cabbage. Drain beets, reserving ½ cup liquid. Thinly slice onion.

2 Combine vegetables. In saucepan combine vinegar, sugar, and reserved beet liquid; bring to boiling. Pour over vegetables; toss. Cover and chill in refrigerator 3 to 24 hours, tossing occasionally. Makes 10 to 12 servings.

RUSSIAN-STYLE POTATO SALAD

Advance preparation time: 10 minutes
Final preparation time: 5 minutes

- ¼ cup salad oil
- ¼ cup white wine vinegar
- 1 tablespoon Dijon-style mustard
- ⅛ teaspoon garlic powder
- 2 16-ounce cans sliced potatoes
- 1 4-ounce can sliced mushrooms
- 1 16-ounce can crinkle-cut beets *or* shoestring beets, drained

1 In a screw-top jar combine salad oil, vinegar, mustard, garlic powder, ¾ teaspoon *salt*, and ¼ teaspoon *pepper*. Cover; shake well. Drain potatoes and mushrooms; place in bowl. Pour oil mixture atop. Toss. Cover; chill in refrigerator 3 to 24 hours.

Before serving: Stir drained beets into potato mixture. Serve in a lettuce-lined bowl, if desired. Makes 6 to 8 servings.

MUSHROOM-VEGETABLE MARINADE

Advance preparation time: 20 minutes
Final preparation time: 5 minutes

- ⅔ cup vinegar
- ⅔ cup olive oil *or* salad oil
- 1 small onion, chopped (¼ cup)
- 2 cloves garlic, minced
- 1 teaspoon salt
- 1 teaspoon sugar
- 1 teaspoon dried basil, crushed
- 1 teaspoon dried oregano, crushed
- ¼ teaspoon pepper
- 8 ounces fresh mushrooms
- 1 14-ounce can artichoke hearts, drained
- 1 cup pitted ripe olives
- 2 stalks celery
- 1 2-ounce jar sliced pimiento, drained
- 1 16-ounce jar whole small carrots, drained
  Lettuce leaves (optional)

1 In a saucepan combine the vinegar, olive oil or salad oil, onion, garlic, salt, sugar, basil, oregano, and pepper. Bring to boiling. Reduce heat; simmer, uncovered, for 10 minutes.

2 Halve mushrooms, artichoke hearts, and olives. Slice celery and chop pimiento. In a large bowl combine the mushrooms, artichoke hearts, olives, celery, pimiento, and carrots. Pour hot vinegar mixture over vegetables; stir to coat well. Cover and chill in refrigerator for 3 to 24 hours, stirring occasionally.

Before serving: Drain vegetables; serve in a lettuce-lined bowl, if desired. Makes 12 servings.

CALICO RICE SALAD

Try this easy vegetable and rice fix-up when you need a make-ahead salad. The dressing mixture will seem thin, but it will thicken when chilled—

Advance preparation time: 30 minutes
Final preparation time: 5 minutes

1 cup water
½ teaspoon salt
½ cup long grain rice
1 10-ounce package frozen mixed vegetables
½ cup mayonnaise *or* salad dressing
½ cup milk
2 tablespoons catsup
1 tablespoon buttermilk salad dressing mix
Lettuce leaves

1 In a saucepan bring the water and salt to boiling; stir in the uncooked rice and frozen vegetables. Return to boiling; reduce heat. Cover and simmer for 15 to 20 minutes or till water is absorbed and vegetables are tender. Set aside.

2 In a bowl stir together the mayonnaise or salad dressing, milk, catsup, and dry salad dressing mix. (Mixture will be thin.) Stir dressing mixture into the vegetable-rice mixture. Cover and chill in refrigerator for 3 to 24 hours.

Before serving: Spoon into a lettuce-lined bowl. Makes 6 to 8 servings.

MAKE-AHEAD POTATO SALAD

Advance preparation time: 10 minutes

1 stalk celery, sliced
1 large carrot, shredded
¼ cup French salad dressing
⅛ teaspoon ground red pepper
1 16-ounce can German-style potato salad
1 8½-ounce can lima beans, drained
1 4-ounce can mushroom stems and pieces, drained
¼ cup mayonnaise *or* salad dressing

1 Mix first 4 ingredients and ¼ teaspoon *salt.* Stir in potato salad, beans, and mushrooms. Fold in mayonnaise. Cover; chill 3 to 24 hours. Serves 8.

VEGETABLE-CHEESE SALAD

Advance preparation time: 15 minutes
Final preparation time: 10 minutes

1 10-ounce package frozen mixed vegetables
½ cup milk
1 1½-ounce envelope cheese sauce mix
¼ cup mayonnaise *or* salad dressing
1 tablespoon lemon juice
1 small head lettuce, shredded
1 stalk celery, chopped (½ cup)

1 Cook mixed vegetables according to package directions; drain. Stir milk into sauce mix; bring to boiling, stirring constantly. Remove from heat; stir in mayonnaise and lemon juice. Stir in cooked vegetables. Cover; chill in refrigerator 3 to 24 hours.

Before serving: Fold in lettuce and celery. Makes 8 servings.

SHRIMP-COTTAGE CHEESE MOLD

Reserve a few cooked shrimp to garnish the molded salad—

Advance preparation time: 30 minutes
Final preparation time: 5 minutes

2 envelopes unflavored gelatin
1½ cups cold water
1½ cups cream-style cottage cheese
1 8-ounce carton dairy sour cream
¾ cup chili sauce
2 tablespoons lemon juice
1 8-ounce package frozen peeled and deveined shrimp, cooked
½ cup finely chopped celery
2 tablespoons snipped parsley

1 In a large saucepan soften the unfla-vored gelatin in the cold water; heat and stir over low heat till gelatin is dissolved. Stir in the cottage cheese, sour cream, chili sauce, and lemon juice. Chill till partially set (the consistency of unbeaten egg whites).

2 Meanwhile, split *four* shrimp lengthwise and arrange in the bottom of a 6-cup ring mold. Chop remaining shrimp. Fold chopped shrimp, celery, and parsley into the chilled gelatin mixture. Turn mixture into mold. Cover and chill in refrigerator for 6 to 24 hours.

Before serving: Unmold onto serving plate. Fill center of mold with lettuce and additional cooked shrimp, if desired. Makes 8 servings.

EASY REFRIGERATOR PICKLES

Advance preparation time: 30 minutes

6 cups thinly sliced cucumbers
2 cups thinly sliced onions
1½ cups sugar
1½ cups vinegar
½ teaspoon salt
½ teaspoon mustard seed
½ teaspoon celery seed
½ teaspoon ground turmeric

1 In a glass or crockery bowl place cucumbers and onions. In a saucepan combine sugar, vinegar, salt, mustard seed, celery seed, and turmeric. Bring to boiling, stirring just till sugar dissolves.

2 Pour vinegar mixture atop cucumber-onion mixture; stir lightly. Cool. Cover pickles and chill in refrigerator 24 hours to 1 month. Makes 7 cups.

SPEEDY PICKLED PEACHES

Advance preparation time: 15 minutes
Final preparation time: 5 minutes

1 29-ounce can peach halves
   Whole cloves
½ cup vinegar
½ cup sugar
3 inches stick cinnamon, broken

1 Drain peaches, reserving 1 cup syrup. Stud each peach half with 3 or 4 cloves. In saucepan combine reserved syrup, vinegar, sugar, and cinnamon. Add peaches. Bring to boiling; simmer, uncovered, 3 to 4 minutes. Cool. Cover; chill in refrigerator 3 hours to 2 weeks.

Before serving: Drain peaches and remove cinnamon. Serve with meat, fish, or poultry. Makes about 3 cups.

BLENDER TOFU DRESSING

Advance preparation time: 10 minutes

1 8-ounce package tofu
   (fresh bean curd), cubed
¾ cup milk
1 0.6-ounce envelope Italian salad dressing mix, one 0.7-ounce envelope blue cheese salad dressing mix, *or* one 0.4-ounce envelope buttermilk salad dressing mix
1 tablespoon mayonnaise *or* salad dressing

1 Place tofu, milk, dry salad dressing mix, and mayonnaise or salad dressing in blender container or food processor bowl; cover and blend till smooth. Cover and chill in refrigerator at least 3 hours. Makes about 1¾ cups dressing.

CREAMY GARLIC DRESSING

Advance preparation time: 10 minutes

1 cup mayonnaise *or* salad dressing
3 tablespoons light cream *or* milk
2 tablespoons vinegar
1 teaspoon sugar
½ teaspoon salt
¼ teaspoon garlic powder
   Dash pepper

1 In a mixing bowl combine the mayonnaise or salad dressing, light cream or milk, vinegar, sugar, salt, garlic powder, and pepper. Stir till thoroughly blended. Cover and chill in refrigerator at least 3 hours. Makes about 1¼ cups dressing.

CARROT-CELERY RELISH

Advance preparation time: 20 minutes

4 medium carrots
2 stalks celery
½ cup tarragon vinegar
¼ cup dry white wine
2 tablespoons sugar
2 tablespoons salad oil
1 tablespoon minced dried onion
1 tablespoon diced dried bell pepper
1 teaspoon mustard seed
¼ teaspoon garlic salt
   Dash pepper

1 Cut carrots into julienne strips and bias-slice celery. In saucepan combine vinegar, wine, sugar, salad oil, dried onion, dried bell pepper, mustard seed, garlic salt, and pepper. Bring to boiling.

2 Add carrots and celery to boiling liquid; cover and simmer 10 minutes or just till crisp-tender. Transfer to a bowl and cool. Cover and chill in refrigerator 3 hours to 2 weeks. Stir occasionally. Makes 3 cups.

BEET RELISH

Advance preparation time: 10 minutes

1 16-ounce can diced beets, drained
1 medium apple, peeled, cored, and chopped (1 cup)
1 small onion, chopped (¼ cup)
¼ cup white vinegar
2 tablespoons sugar
1 to 2 teaspoons prepared horseradish

1 Combine beets, apple, onion, vinegar, sugar, and horseradish. Mix well. Cover and chill in refrigerator 3 hours to 2 weeks. Serve with meat. Makes 2⅔ cups.

TOMATOES AND ARTICHOKES AU GRATIN

Advance preparation time: 25 minutes
Final preparation time: 40 minutes

- ⅔ **cup quick-cooking rice**
- ¼ **teaspoon dried basil, crushed**
- 1 **9-ounce package frozen artichoke hearts**
- 4 **green onions, sliced**
- 2 **tablespoons butter *or* margarine**
- 2 **tablespoons all-purpose flour**
- ½ **teaspoon salt**
- ½ **teaspoon paprika**
- 1¼ **cups milk**
- 1 **cup shredded Swiss cheese (4 ounces)**
- 2 **medium tomatoes, peeled and cut up**
- ¼ **cup fine dry bread crumbs**
- 1 **tablespoon butter *or* margarine, melted**

1 Prepare rice according to package directions, *except* add the basil; cool. Meanwhile, cook artichokes according to package directions; drain. Halve any large artichokes.

2 In saucepan cook green onion in the 2 tablespoons butter or margarine till tender. Stir in flour, salt, and paprika. Add milk all at once. Cook and stir till thickened and bubbly. Cook and stir 1 minute more. Add cheese; stir till melted. Fold in artichokes and tomatoes.

3 Press rice mixture into 4 au gratin dishes, forming a crust. Spoon artichoke mixture into rice crusts. Cover and refrigerate for 3 to 24 hours. In a small bowl toss bread crumbs with the 1 tablespoon melted butter or margarine; cover and chill.

Before serving: Sprinkle au gratin dishes with crumb mixture. Bake in a 350° oven about 40 minutes or till heated through. Makes 4 servings.

CAULIFLOWER-TOMATO SCALLOP

Advance preparation time: 23 minutes
Final preparation time: 35 minutes

- 2 **cups cauliflower flowerets**
- 1 **small onion, chopped (¼ cup)**
- ¼ **cup chopped green pepper**
- 2 **tablespoons butter *or* margarine**
- 2 **tablespoons cornstarch**
- ½ **teaspoon salt**
- ½ **teaspoon dried thyme, crushed**
- 1¼ **cups milk**
- ¾ **cup shredded cheddar cheese (3 ounces)**
- 1 **medium tomato, chopped**
- ¼ **cup fine dry bread crumbs**
- 2 **tablespoons sunflower nuts**
- 1 **tablespoon butter *or* margarine, melted**

1 In medium saucepan cook cauliflower, covered, in small amount of boiling salted water for 10 to 13 minutes or just till tender. Drain; set aside.

2 In same saucepan cook onion and green pepper in the 2 tablespoons butter or margarine till tender but not brown. Stir in cornstarch, salt, and thyme. Add milk all at once. Cook and stir till thickened and bubbly. Cook and stir 2 minutes more. Add shredded cheese; stir till melted. Stir in cauliflower and tomato.

3 Turn vegetable mixture into a 1-quart casserole. Cover and refrigerate for 3 to 24 hours. In a small bowl toss together the bread crumbs, sunflower nuts, and the 1 tablespoon butter. Cover and chill.

Before serving: Sprinkle the crumb mixture atop the vegetable mixture. Bake, uncovered, in a 400° oven for 30 to 35 minutes or till heated through. Serves 6.

CORN-CHEESE BAKE

Advance preparation time: 10 minutes
Final preparation time: 50 minutes

- 2 **12-ounce cans whole kernel corn with sweet peppers, drained**
- 1 **stalk celery, thinly sliced**
- 1 **3-ounce package cream cheese, cut up**
- ½ **cup shredded Swiss cheese**
- 1 **teaspoon minced dried onion**
- 1 **teaspoon dried marjoram, crushed**

1 In saucepan stir together drained corn, celery, cream cheese, Swiss cheese, onion and marjoram. Cook and stir till cheese is melted. Turn into 1-quart casserole. Cover and refrigerate for 3 to 24 hours.

Before serving: Bake casserole, covered, in a 400° oven about 50 minutes or till heated through. Makes 8 servings.

FRENCH ONION SOUP

Advance preparation time: 20 minutes
Final preparation time: 15 minutes

- 1 **pound onions, thinly sliced**
- 3 **tablespoons butter *or* margarine**
- 2 **10½-ounce cans condensed beef broth**
- ¼ **cup dry sherry**
- ⅛ **teaspoon ground sage**
- 6 **slices French bread**
- ¾ **cup shredded Swiss cheese**

1 In a 2-quart saucepan cook sliced onion in butter or margarine till tender. Stir in beef broth, sherry, sage, and dash *pepper*. Cover; refrigerate for 3 to 24 hours.

Before serving: Toast French bread. In a saucepan bring soup to boiling; spoon into broiler-proof soup bowls. Float toast slices atop. Top with Swiss cheese. Broil till cheese is melted. Makes 6 servings.

ZUCCHINI-MAC CASSEROLE

Advance preparation time: 20 minutes
Final preparation time: 1¼ hours

½ **cup elbow macaroni**
3 **cups chopped zucchini**
1 **10½-ounce can tomato puree**
1 **teaspoon instant beef bouillon granules**
½ **teaspoon dried oregano** *or* **basil, crushed**
¼ **cup grated Parmesan cheese**

1 Cook macaroni according to package directions; drain. Meanwhile, combine zucchini, tomato puree, bouillon granules, and oregano or basil. Stir in macaroni. Turn into an 8x1½-inch round baking dish. Sprinkle with Parmesan cheese. Cover with moisture-vaporproof wrap. Seal, label, and freeze at least 6 hours.

Before serving: Bake frozen casserole, covered, in a 400° oven about 70 minutes or till heated through. Serves 6.

GLAZED PARSNIPS

Advance preparation time: 10 minutes
Final preparation time: 1 hour

1½ **pounds medium parsnips**
2 **tablespoons brown sugar**
2 **tablespoons orange juice**
1 **tablespoon butter** *or* **margarine, melted**
Dash salt

1 Peel parsnips and slice diagonally into 2-inch lengths. Place in an 8x8x2-inch baking dish. In a bowl combine brown sugar, orange juice, butter or margarine, and salt. Pour over parsnips, coating all the pieces. Cover; refrigerate 3 to 24 hours.

Before serving: Bake chilled parsnips, covered, in a 325° oven for 50 to 60 minutes or till tender. Makes 4 servings.

SPINACH AND NOODLES PARMESAN

Advance preparation time: 25 minutes
Final preparation time: 35 minutes

4 **ounces medium noodles**
1 **10-ounce package frozen chopped spinach**
1 **cup milk**
1 **tablespoon butter** *or* **margarine**
½ **teaspoon dried basil, crushed**
¼ **teaspoon salt**
1 **3-ounce package cream cheese, cut up**
¼ **cup grated Parmesan cheese**
Grated Parmesan cheese

1 In a saucepan cook noodles according to package directions; drain. Meanwhile, in another saucepan cook spinach according to package directions; drain. Set noodles and spinach aside.

2 In saucepan combine milk, butter or margarine, basil, and salt. Stir in the cream cheese and the ¼ cup Parmesan cheese. Cook and stir cheese mixture over low heat till cream cheese is melted. Toss together noodles, spinach, and cheese mixture. Turn into a 10x6x2-inch baking dish. Sprinkle with additional Parmesan cheese. Cover and refrigerate for 3 to 24 hours.

Before serving: Bake chilled noodle mixture, covered, in a 350° oven for 35 minutes or till heated through. Serves 4.

CHILLED VEGETABLE POTAGE

See photo, page 336—

Advance preparation time: 30 minutes
Final preparation time: 5 minutes

1 **small onion, chopped (¼ cup)**
¼ **cup butter** *or* **margarine**
3 **tablespoons all-purpose flour**
½ **teaspoon dried fines herbes, crushed**
2 **cups light cream** *or* **milk**
2 **cups chicken broth**
2 **beaten egg yolks**
1 **8-ounce carton plain yogurt**
8 **cups desired vegetables***

1 In a 3-quart saucepan cook onion in butter till tender. Stir in *1 tablespoon* of the flour and the fines herbes. Stir in cream and broth. Cook and stir till slightly thickened and bubbly. Simmer, uncovered, 5 minutes.

2 In a bowl stir together egg yolks, yogurt, and remaining flour. Stir *1 cup* of the hot cream mixture into the yogurt mixture; return all to saucepan. Cook and stir till thickened and bubbly. Cook and stir 2 minutes more. Stir in vegetables; remove from heat.

3 Place *one-third* of the mixture into a blender container or food processor bowl. Cover; process till smooth. Repeat twice. Season with salt and pepper. Place in a bowl. Cover; refrigerate 3 to 24 hours.

Before serving: If desired, stir a little milk into soup to make of desired consistency. Garnish each serving with radish slices and parsley, if desired. Makes 6 servings.
Note: Choose 1 or 2 of the following—packed-when-measured greens such as lettuce, parsley, spinach, Swiss chard, or watercress; halved and drained canned artichoke hearts; sliced, peeled cucumber; sliced mushrooms; or precooked asparagus or broccoli cuts, cauliflower flowerets, sliced, peeled beets, sliced carrots, sliced parsnips, or sliced rutabagas.

BROCCOLI AND MUSHROOM BAKE

Advance preparation time: 10 minutes
Final preparation time: 1 hour

2 cups frozen loose-pack cut
  broccoli
1 4-ounce can sliced mushrooms,
  drained
2 tablespoons chopped onion
½ cup milk
1 3-ounce package cream cheese,
  cut up
1 cup shredded Swiss cheese
  (4 ounces)
½ teaspoon dried marjoram, crushed
¼ teaspoon salt
⅛ teaspoon pepper

1 Spread the frozen cut broccoli in the
bottom of a 7-inch pie plate. Spoon the
sliced mushrooms and chopped onion atop.
Set vegetables aside.

2 In a mixer bowl beat the milk, cream
cheese, ½ cup of the shredded Swiss
cheese, marjoram, salt, and pepper on low
speed of electric mixer till fluffy. Spoon the
cheese mixture atop vegetables in pie plate.
Cover with moisture-vaporproof wrap. Seal,
label, and freeze at least 6 hours.

Before serving: Bake the frozen casserole in a 350° oven for 50 to 55 minutes or
till vegetables are heated through. Top with
the remaining Swiss cheese. Bake about 5
minutes more or till cheese is melted. Makes
6 servings.

GREEN BEAN-EGG CASSEROLE

Advance preparation time: 35 minutes
Final preparation time: 50 minutes

3 eggs
2 stalks celery, thinly sliced (1 cup)
¼ cup butter *or* margarine
¼ cup all-purpose flour
1 teaspoon instant chicken bouillon
  granules
¼ teaspoon salt
⅛ teaspoon ground nutmeg
  Dash pepper
1¾ cups milk
2 teaspoons lemon juice
2 9-ounce packages frozen Italian
  green beans
2 tablespoons cooked bacon pieces

1 To hard-cook eggs, place eggs in a
small saucepan; cover with cold water.
Bring to boiling; reduce heat to just below
simmering. Cover and cook for 15 minutes.
Run cold water over eggs till cool. Remove
shells from eggs.

2 Meanwhile, for sauce, in covered
saucepan cook celery in butter or margarine till tender. Stir in flour, bouillon granules, salt, nutmeg, and pepper. Add milk all
at once. Cook and stir till thickened and bubbly. Cook and stir 1 minute more. Stir in
lemon juice. Set aside.

3 Cook Italian beans according to package directions; drain well. Slice hard-
cooked eggs. Reserve *½ cup* beans and *1
egg* for garnish; cover and chill. Arrange remaining beans and egg slices in a 10x6x2-
inch baking dish. Pour sauce over all. Cover
and refrigerate for 3 to 24 hours.

Before serving: Bake casserole, covered, in a 375° oven for 40 minutes or till
heated through. Arrange reserved beans
and sliced egg down center of casserole.
Top with bacon pieces; bake 10 minutes
more. Makes 6 servings.

TWICE-BAKED CHEDDAR-BACON POTATOES

Advance preparation time: 1¼ hours
Final preparation time: 45 minutes

4 medium baking potatoes
½ cup shredded cheddar cheese
  (2 ounces)
¼ cup cooked bacon pieces
1 tablespoon butter *or* margarine
1 tablespoon sliced green onion
¼ to ⅓ cup milk
2 tablespoons shredded cheddar
  cheese

1 Scrub baking potatoes with a brush.
Prick in several places with a fork. Bake
in a 425° oven for 40 to 60 minutes or till
potatoes are tender. Cool slightly; cut a
lengthwise slice from the top of each potato.
Scoop out the inside of each potato to form
a shell; place potato in a bowl. Set the potato
shells aside.

2 Mash potato. Stir in the ½ cup shredded cheddar cheese, cooked bacon
pieces, butter or margarine, and sliced
green onion. Beat potatoes till fluffy, gradually adding as much milk as needed. Spoon
potato mixture into reserved shells. Wrap
each in moisture-vaporproof wrap. Seal, label, and freeze at least 6 hours.

Before serving: Place frozen potatoes
on a baking sheet. Bake, uncovered, in a
375° oven for 40 minutes. Sprinkle potatoes
with the 2 tablespoons cheddar cheese.
Bake 5 minutes more or till cheese is melted
and potatoes are heated through. Makes 4
servings.

Green Bean-Egg Casserole

343

FREEZER BREADSTICKS

Advance preparation time: 45 minutes
Final preparation time: 55 minutes

1½ to 2 cups all-purpose flour
2 packages active dry yeast
½ teaspoon onion powder
¾ cup milk
2 tablespoons shortening
1 tablespoon sugar
1 egg white
1 tablespoon water
Sesame seed

1 In small mixer bowl combine *¾ cup* of the flour, the yeast, and onion powder. In saucepan heat milk, shortening, sugar, and 1 teaspoon *salt* just till warm (115° to 120°); stir constantly. Add to flour mixture. Beat at low speed of electric mixer for ½ minute, scraping bowl. Beat 3 minutes more at high speed. Stir in as much of the remaining flour as you can mix in with a spoon. Turn out onto lightly floured surface.

2 Knead in enough of the remaining flour to make a stiff dough that is smooth and elastic (8 to 10 minutes total). Cover; let rest 10 minutes.

3 Divide dough into 4 portions. Divide each portion into 6 pieces. Roll each piece to a rope 8 inches long. Place on greased baking sheet. Cover with clear plastic wrap; freeze till firm.

4 Remove breadsticks from baking sheet; wrap in moisture-vaporproof material. Seal, label, and freeze up to 4 weeks.

Before serving: Remove desired number of breadsticks from freezer. Thaw, covered, 8 to 24 hours in refrigerator. Remove from refrigerator and place on a greased baking sheet. Cover; let rise in warm place for 15 to 20 minutes. Brush with mixture of egg white and water*; sprinkle with sesame seed. Bake in a 375° oven for 10 minutes. Reduce oven temperature to 300°. Bake 15 to 20 minutes or till golden. Makes 24.
Note: Egg white mixture may be stored in refrigerator 3 to 4 days.

ONION ROLLS

Advance preparation time: 45 minutes
Final preparation time: 35 minutes

3 to 3½ cups all-purpose flour
3 tablespoons *regular* onion soup mix
1 package active dry yeast
1¼ cups milk
¼ cup sugar
¼ cup shortening
1 egg
Melted butter *or* margarine

1 In large mixer bowl combine *1½ cups* of the flour, the onion soup mix, and yeast. In saucepan heat milk, sugar, and shortening just till warm (115° to 120°); stir constantly. Add to flour mixture; add egg. Beat at low speed of electric mixer for ½ minute, scraping bowl. Beat 3 minutes more at high speed. Stir in as much of the remaining flour as you can mix in with a spoon.

2 Turn out onto a lightly floured surface. Knead in enough of the remaining flour to make a moderately soft dough that is smooth and elastic (3 to 5 minutes total). Cover and let rest 20 minutes.

3 Punch dough down. Shape into 20 balls. Place each ball in a greased muffin cup. Using floured kitchen scissors, cut each ball into quarters from top *almost* through to bottom. Cover pans with greased waxed paper or clear plastic wrap. Refrigerate 2 to 24 hours.

Before serving: Remove rolls from refrigerator. Uncover and let stand 20 minutes. Brush with the melted butter or margarine. Bake in a 400° oven for 12 to 14 minutes. Remove from muffin pans and cool on wire rack. Makes 20 rolls.

RYE ROLLS

Pictured on the front cover and on pages 346 and 347—

Advance preparation time: 2¼ hours
Final preparation time: 30 minutes

3 to 3½ cups all-purpose flour
2 packages active dry yeast
2 tablespoons caraway seed
2 teaspoons dried dillweed
2 cups water
⅓ cup packed brown sugar
¼ cup cooking oil
3½ cups rye flour
½ cup water
1 tablespoon cornstarch
Caraway seed

1 In a large mixer bowl combine *2½ cups* of the all-purpose flour, the yeast, 2 tablespoons caraway seed, and the dillweed. Heat the 2 cups water, brown sugar, oil, and 1 tablespoon *salt* just till warm (115° to 120°); add to flour mixture. Beat on low speed of electric mixer for ½ minute, scraping bowl. Beat 3 minutes more at high speed.

2 Stir in the rye flour and as much of the all-purpose flour as you can mix in with a spoon. Knead in enough remaining all-purpose flour to make a moderately stiff dough that is smooth (6 to 8 minutes). Shape into a ball; place in a lightly greased bowl. Cover; let rise till double (1 hour).

3 Punch down; divide into 10 portions. Shape each into an oval roll; place 3 inches apart on greased baking sheets. Cover; let rise till nearly double (30 minutes). Gently cut a few slashes atop each roll. Bake in a 325° oven for 20 minutes (rolls will not be brown). Cool. Wrap in clear plastic wrap or foil. Refrigerate up to 2 weeks.

Before serving: Unwrap rolls; place on baking sheet. Bake in a 375° oven for 15 minutes. Combine the ½ cup water and cornstarch. Cook and stir till thickened and bubbly; cook 1 minute more. Glaze rolls. Sprinkle with caraway seed. Bake 5 to 10 minutes more. Makes 10 rolls.

REFRIG-A-RISE WHITE BREAD

Advance preparation time: 45 minutes
Final preparation time: 55 minutes

5¾ to 6¼ cups all-purpose flour
 1 package active dry yeast
2¼ cups milk
 2 tablespoons sugar
 1 tablespoon shortening
 2 teaspoons salt
   Melted butter *or* margarine

1 In large mixer bowl combine *2½ cups* of the flour and the yeast. In saucepan heat milk, sugar, shortening, and salt just till warm (115° to 120°) and shortening is almost melted; stir constantly.

2 Add to flour mixture. Beat at low speed of electric mixer for ½ minute, scraping sides of bowl. Beat 3 minutes more at high speed. Stir in as much of the remaining flour as you can mix in with a spoon.

3 Turn out onto a lightly floured surface. Knead in enough remaining flour to make a moderately stiff dough that is smooth and elastic (6 to 8 minutes total).

4 Cover; let rest 10 minutes. Divide dough in half. Shape into two loaves. Place each loaf in a greased 8x4x2-inch loaf pan. Brush with melted butter or margarine. Cover loosely with clear plastic wrap. Refrigerate 2 to 24 hours.

Before serving: Let loaves stand uncovered at room temperature for 10 minutes. Puncture any air bubbles with a pin or wooden pick. Bake in a 375° oven for 30 minutes. Brush with melted butter or margarine. Bake about 15 minutes more or till done. Remove from pans; cool on wire rack. Makes 2 loaves.

BEEF BRAID

Pictured on pages 346 and 347—

Advance preparation time: 30 minutes
Final preparation time: 2 hours

2¾ to 3 cups all-purpose flour
 2 packages active dry yeast
 2 tablespoons butter
 1 tablespoon sugar
 1 egg
 2 tablespoons butter, melted
 ½ teaspoon dried fines herbes, crushed
 ½ cup shredded Swiss cheese
 ½ cup snipped thinly sliced smoked beef
 2 teaspoons butter, melted

1 In mixer bowl combine *1 cup* of the flour and the yeast. Heat 2 tablespoons butter, sugar, ¾ cup *water*, and ½ teaspoon *salt* just till warm (115° to 120°); stir constantly. Add to flour mixture; add egg. Beat ½ minute at low speed of electric mixer, scraping bowl. Beat 3 minutes more at high speed. Stir in as much flour as you can mix in with a spoon. Knead in remaining flour to make a moderately stiff dough (6 to 8 minutes).

2 Cover; let rest 5 minutes. Roll into a 12x9-inch rectangle; cut into three 12x3-inch strips. Brush with the 2 tablespoons butter. Sprinkle with *half* of the fines herbes. Sprinkle *one-third* of the cheese and beef lengthwise down center of each strip. Bring long edges together over filling; pinch all edges to seal. Place strips, seam side down, on a greased baking sheet. Braid; secure ends.

3 Cover with plastic wrap; freeze. When firm, wrap in moisture-vaporproof material. Seal, label, and freeze up to 4 weeks.

Before serving: Unwrap; place on baking sheet and thaw. Let rise in warm place till double (1½ hours). Bake in a 375° oven for 25 to 30 minutes. Top with the 2 teaspoons butter and remaining fines herbes; cool. Makes 1.
Note: Refrigerator rising time excluded.

BRIOCHE-STYLE ROLLS

Pictured on pages 346 and 347—

Advance preparation time: 2¼ hours
Final preparation time: 1 hour

4¼ cups all-purpose flour
 1 package active dry yeast
 1 cup milk
 ½ cup butter
 ⅓ cup packed brown sugar
 3 eggs
1½ cups sifted powdered sugar
 2 tablespoons butter, melted
   Milk

1 In mixer bowl combine *1 cup* flour and yeast. Heat 1 cup milk, ½ cup butter, brown sugar, and ½ teaspoon *salt* just till warm (115° to 120°); stir constantly. Add to flour mixture; add eggs. Beat at low speed of electric mixer for ½ minute. Beat 3 minutes at high speed. Stir in remaining flour.

2 Place in greased bowl; turn once. Cover; let rise in warm place till double (2 hours). Punch down. Cover with plastic wrap. Chill 2 to 24 hours.

Before serving: Punch down. Turn out onto lightly floured surface. Set aside *one-fourth* of the dough. Cut remaining dough into 6 portions; cut each portion into quarters. With floured hands, shape into 24 balls. Place balls in greased muffin pans or individual brioche pans. Cut the reserved dough into 6 portions; cut each portion into quarters. Shape each piece into a small ball. With your thumb or wooden spoon handle, make a deep indentation in the top of each large ball in muffin pans. Brush with water; press one small ball into each indentation. Cover; let rise in warm place for 15 minutes. Bake in a 375° oven for 16 to 18 minutes or till rolls sound hollow when tapped. Remove from pans; cool. For glaze, combine powdered sugar, melted butter, and enough milk to make of drizzling consistency (2 tablespoons). Drizzle over rolls. Sprinkle with sliced almonds, if desired. Makes 24.

SWISS CHEESE BATTER BREAD

Advance preparation time: 15 minutes
Final preparation time: 1 hour and 10 minutes

2 cups all-purpose flour
1 package active dry yeast
¾ cup milk
1 tablespoon sugar
¾ teaspoon salt
½ cup shredded Swiss cheese (2 ounces)
1 egg
1 tablespoon butter *or* margarine, melted
1 tablespoon shelled sunflower nuts

1 In small mixer bowl combine *1 cup* of the flour and the yeast. In saucepan heat the milk, sugar, and salt just till warm (115° to 120°), stirring constantly. Add to flour mixture; add cheese and egg. Beat at low speed of electric mixer for ½ minute, scraping bowl constantly. Beat 3 minutes more at high speed. Stir in remaining flour to make a soft dough.

2 Spoon dough evenly into a well-greased 1-quart casserole. Cover with greased waxed paper or clear plastic wrap. Refrigerate 2 to 24 hours.

Before serving: Remove cover and let bread stand at room temperature for 20 minutes. Puncture any air bubbles using a greased wooden pick. Brush surface of dough with melted butter or margarine. Sprinkle with sunflower nuts. Bake in a 350° oven about 45 minutes. If necessary, cover with foil the last 15 minutes of baking to prevent overbrowning. Remove from casserole; cool completely on wire rack. Makes 1.

Swiss Cheese Batter Bread
Fruit-Filled Coffee Cake
Brioche-Style Rolls (see recipe, page 345)
Beef Braid (see recipe, page 345)
Rye Rolls (see recipe, page 344)

FRUIT-FILLED COFFEE CAKE

Advance preparation time: 15 minutes
Final preparation time: 1 hour and 10 minutes*

6 cups all-purpose flour
3 packages active dry yeast
1⅓ cups milk
1 cup butter *or* margarine
¼ cup sugar
2 eggs
2 teaspoons vanilla
2 tablespoons butter *or* margarine
¾ cup canned apricot, prune, cherry, *or* almond cake and pastry filling
Butter Glaze

1 In a large mixer bowl combine *2½ cups* of the flour and the yeast. Heat the milk, butter, sugar, and 2 teaspoons *salt* just till warm (115° to 120°); stir constantly. Add to flour mixture; add eggs and vanilla. Beat at low speed of electric mixer for ½ minute, scraping bowl. Beat 3 minutes at high speed. Stir in the remaining flour.

2 Divide into four portions; wrap each loosely in moisture-vaporproof material. Seal, label, and freeze up to four weeks.

Before serving: For *each* coffee cake, use *one dough portion*. Unwrap; place in greased bowl. Cover; let rise in a warm place till double (about 3 to 3½ hours). (Or, let rise overnight in refrigerator.) Melt the 2 tablespoons butter. Divide in half. On a lightly floured surface roll *one* half into an 8-inch square. Place square in a greased 8x8x2-inch baking pan. Brush with some of the melted butter; spoon desired filling over dough. Roll remaining dough into an 8-inch square; place atop filling. Brush with remaining butter. Cover; let rise till double (45 minutes). Bake in a 375° oven 15 to 20 minutes. Cool; drizzle with Butter Glaze. Makes 4.

Butter Glaze: Combine ½ cup sifted *powdered sugar*, 1 tablespoon *butter*, ⅛ teaspoon *vanilla*, and enough *milk* to make drizzling consistency (2 teaspoons).

*Note: Refrigerator rising time excluded.

BROWN 'N' SERVE COFFEE CAKE

Advance preparation time: 1 hour and 40 minutes
Final preparation time: 30 minutes

- 1 13¾-ounce package hot roll mix
- ½ cup warm water (110° to 115°)
- 2 eggs
- ⅓ cup milk
- ¼ cup sugar
- ¼ teaspoon salt
- ¼ teaspoon almond extract
- 2 tablespoons butter *or* margarine, melted
- ½ cup chopped almonds
- ¼ cup sugar
- ¼ teaspoon ground nutmeg

1 In large bowl soften the yeast from the hot roll mix in the warm water; stir to dissolve. Stir in eggs, milk, ¼ cup sugar, salt, and almond extract. Add flour from hot roll mix; mix well. Spread dough into two greased 8x1½-inch round baking pans.

2 Cover and let rise in warm place till double (about 1 hour). Bake in a 300° oven for 18 to 20 minutes. (Coffee cakes should not be brown.) Cool. Remove from pans. Wrap with clear plastic wrap. Store in refrigerator up to 1 week.

Before serving: Place coffee cakes on a baking sheet; brush each with *half* of the melted butter. For topping, combine the almonds, ¼ cup sugar, and nutmeg; sprinkle half over each cake. (If desired, bake one coffee cake at a time and use *half* of the butter, almonds, ¼ cup sugar, and nutmeg.) Bake in a 375° oven about 20 minutes or till done. Cool slightly on wire racks. Serve warm. Makes 2 coffee cakes.

REFRIGERATOR KRINGLE

Advance preparation time: 50 minutes
Final preparation time: 45 minutes

- 5½ to 6 cups all-purpose flour
- 1 package active dry yeast
- 2 cups milk
- ⅓ cup sugar
- ¼ cup shortening
- 1 egg
- 1 egg yolk
- ½ cup chopped red candied cherries
- ¼ cup diced candied citron
- ¼ cup chopped nuts
- 1 egg white
- 1½ cups sifted powdered sugar
- ¼ teaspoon vanilla
  Milk

1 In large mixer bowl combine *2 cups* flour and the yeast. In saucepan heat the milk, sugar, shortening, and 1 teaspoon *salt* just till warm (115° to 120°); stir constantly. Add to flour mixture; add egg and egg yolk. Beat at low speed of electric mixer for ½ minute, scraping bowl. Beat 3 minutes at high speed. Stir in as much remaining flour as you can with a spoon. Knead in enough remaining flour to make a moderately soft dough that is smooth and elastic (3 to 5 minutes). Cover; let rest 20 minutes. For filling, combine cherries, citron, and nuts.

2 Divide dough in half. Roll each half into a 10x6-inch rectangle. Brush egg white over each. Sprinkle filling lengthwise over half of each rectangle. Without stretching, fold the long side over to within one inch of the opposite side; seal. Place each on a greased baking sheet. Cover loosely with clear plastic wrap. Refrigerate 2 to 24 hours.

Before serving: Uncover dough; let stand at room temperature 10 minutes. Break any surface bubbles using a greased wooden pick. Bake in a 375° oven for 25 to 30 minutes. Cool on racks. Mix powdered sugar, vanilla, and enough milk to make of drizzling consistency (1 to 2 tablespoons). Drizzle over breads. Makes 2.

MOCK CROISSANTS

Advance preparation time: 45 minutes
Final preparation time: 1 hour

- 5½ to 5¾ cups all-purpose flour
- 1 package active dry yeast
- ¾ cup milk
- ½ cup water
- ½ cup butter *or* margarine
- ¼ cup sugar
- 1 teaspoon salt
- 1 egg
- 1 cup butter *or* margarine, chilled
- 1 egg yolk
- 1 tablespoon milk

1 In large mixer bowl combine *2 cups* of the flour and the yeast. In a saucepan heat the ¾ cup milk, water, the ½ cup butter, sugar, and salt till warm (115° to 120°); stir constantly. Add to flour mixture; add egg. Beat at low speed of electric mixer for ½ minute, scraping bowl. Beat 3 minutes at high speed; set aside.

2 In a large bowl cut the 1 cup chilled butter into *3 cups* of the flour. Add yeast mixture. Stir in as much remaining flour as you can mix in with a spoon. Turn out onto lightly floured surface. Knead in enough remaining flour to make a moderately soft dough (3 to 5 minutes total).

3 Cover; let rest 20 minutes. Punch down. Place in lightly greased bowl; turn once. Cover with clear plastic wrap. Refrigerate 2 to 24 hours.

Before serving: Turn dough out of bowl. Puncture any surface bubbles using a greased wooden pick. Divide dough into 4 portions. Roll each fourth into a 12-inch circle. Cut each circle into 8 wedges. Roll up each wedge loosely, starting from wide end. Place, point down, on ungreased baking sheets; curve ends. Let stand in warm place 20 minutes. Beat egg yolk with the 1 tablespoon milk; brush over rolls. Bake in a 375° oven for 12 to 15 minutes. Remove from baking sheets. Serve warm. Makes 32.

WHOLE WHEAT-OATMEAL BREAD MIX

Advance preparation time: 15 minutes

8 cups whole wheat flour
2 cups nonfat dry milk powder
3 tablespoons baking powder
1 tablespoon salt
3 cups regular rolled oats

1 In a large bowl stir together flour, milk powder, baking powder, and salt. Add oats and mix thoroughly. Transfer to a covered storage container. Cover; store in a cool, dry place. Store up to 6 weeks. Makes 12 cups of mix.

WHOLE WHEAT-BANANA BREAD

Final preparation time: 1 hour and 20 minutes

1 8-ounce package cream cheese, cut up
¾ cup sugar
1 cup mashed ripe banana
2 eggs
2 tablespoons cooking oil
2 cups Whole Wheat-Oatmeal Bread Mix
½ cup chopped pecans

Before serving: In a mixer bowl beat cream cheese about 30 seconds till softened; add sugar and beat till light. Add banana, eggs, and cooking oil; beat well. Stir in Bread Mix and chopped pecans just till moistened. Turn into a greased 9x5x3-inch loaf pan.

Bake in a 350° oven for 55 to 60 minutes. Cover with foil last 10 to 15 minutes, if necessary, to prevent overbrowning. Cool in pan 10 minutes; remove from pan. Cool thoroughly on wire rack. Makes 1 loaf.

WHOLE WHEAT-OATMEAL BISCUITS

Final preparation time: 15 minutes

1½ cups Whole Wheat-Oatmeal Bread Mix
⅔ cup water
¼ cup cooking oil

Before serving: In a mixing bowl make a well in the Bread Mix. Combine water and oil; add all at once. Stir quickly with a fork just till moistened. Drop from a tablespoon onto a greased baking sheet. Bake in a 450° oven about 10 minutes. Serve with butter and honey, if desired. Makes 12.

WHOLE WHEAT-OATMEAL PANCAKES

Final preparation time: 15 minutes

1½ cups Whole Wheat-Oatmeal Bread Mix
1 beaten egg
1¼ cups milk
1 tablespoon cooking oil
1 tablespoon honey
Honey *or* maple syrup

Before serving: In medium bowl place Bread Mix. Combine egg, milk, cooking oil, and honey. Stir into Bread Mix till mixture is just moistened (batter will be slightly lumpy). For each pancake, pour about ¼ cup batter onto hot, lightly greased griddle or heavy skillet; spread into a 4-inch circle. Cook till golden brown, turning to cook other side when pancakes have a bubbly surface and slightly dry edges. Serve with honey or maple syrup. Makes 8 pancakes.

SWEET MUFFINS

Advance preparation time: 15 minutes
Final preparation time: 30 minutes

8¾ cups all-purpose flour
3 cups sugar
1 tablespoon baking powder
1 tablespoon baking soda
4 beaten eggs
3 cups milk
1⅓ cups cooking oil

1 Combine flour, sugar, baking powder, soda, and 2 teaspoons *salt*. Mix eggs, milk, and oil. Add egg mixture to flour mixture; stir till moistened. Store in covered container in refrigerator up to two weeks.

Before serving: Stir batter. Grease muffin pans or line with paper bake cups; fill ⅔ full. Bake in a 375° oven for 20 to 25 minutes. Makes 48.

BRAN MUFFINS

Advance preparation time: 15 minutes
Final preparation time: 25 minutes

1¾ cups all-purpose flour
½ cup whole bran cereal
½ cup packed brown sugar
1 teaspoon baking soda
¾ teaspoon ground cinnamon
⅛ teaspoon ground cloves
2 beaten eggs
⅔ cup buttermilk *or* sour milk
¼ cup cooking oil
½ cup raisins

1 Stir together flour, cereal, brown sugar, soda, cinnamon, cloves, and ½ teaspoon *salt*. Combine eggs, buttermilk, and oil. Add egg mixture to flour mixture; stir till moistened. Fold in raisins. Store in covered container in refrigerator up to 10 days.

Before serving: Grease muffin pans or line with paper bake cups; fill ⅔ full. Bake in a 400° oven for 15 to 20 minutes. Makes 16.

PUMPKIN TASSIES

Advance preparation time: 1 hour and 40 minutes
Final preparation time: 30 minutes

- ½ **cup butter** *or* **margarine, cut up**
- 1 **3-ounce package cream cheese, cut up**
- 1 **cup all-purpose flour**
- ¼ **cup packed brown sugar**
- ⅛ **teaspoon salt**
- ⅛ **teaspoon ground cinnamon**
- ⅛ **teaspoon ground nutmeg**
- ⅛ **teaspoon ground allspice**
- 2 **beaten eggs**
- ¾ **cup canned pumpkin**
- ¼ **teaspoon rum flavoring**
- ½ **frozen whipped dessert topping, thawed**

1 In mixer bowl beat butter or margarine and cream cheese till fluffy; stir in flour. Cover and chill in the freezer for 15 to 20 minutes. On lightly floured surface roll dough to ¹⁄₁₆-inch thickness. Cut into 2½- to 2¾-inch rounds with cookie cutter. Press rounds into 1¾-inch muffin pans. Bake in a 400° oven about 10 minutes or till golden brown. Cool in pans on wire rack.

2 Meanwhile, in saucepan combine brown sugar, salt, cinnamon, nutmeg, and allspice. Stir in eggs, pumpkin, and rum flavoring. Cook and stir over low heat about 10 minutes or till thickened. Remove from heat; cover. Chill in freezer 20 minutes.

3 Fold whipped dessert topping into pumpkin mixture. Pipe or spoon *2 to 3 teaspoons* of the pumpkin mixture into *each* tart shell. Garnish with coarsely chopped pecans, if desired.

4 Arrange on baking sheet. Freeze, uncovered, about 3 hours. To protect shape, place tarts in single layer in pan or box. Cover with moisture-vaporproof wrap. Seal, label, and freeze up to 2 months.

Before serving: Thaw tarts about 30 minutes at room temperature. Store leftover thawed tarts, covered, in refrigerator. Makes 32 to 36 tarts.

CHERRY-BRANDY PIE

Advance preparation time: 25 minutes

- 1½ **cups finely crushed chocolate wafers (30 wafers)**
- 6 **tablespoons butter, melted**
- 1 **7-ounce jar marshmallow creme**
- ⅓ **cup cherry brandy**
- 2 **tablespoons chopped maraschino cherries**
- 2½ **cups whipping cream**
- 1 **tablespoon maraschino cherry juice**

1 Combine crushed wafers and butter. Press mixture firmly onto bottom and up sides of a 9-inch pie plate. Combine marshmallow creme and brandy; beat till smooth with rotary beater. Fold in chopped cherries. Whip *2 cups* of the cream till soft peaks form; fold into marshmallow mixture. Turn into crust. Whip remaining cream and cherry juice; dollop or pipe atop pie. If desired, garnish with whole maraschino cherries. Freeze at least 6 hours. Serves 8.

MACAROON TARTS

Advance preparation time: 15 minutes

- 1 **1½-ounce envelope dessert topping mix**
- 7 **crumbled soft macaroons (1½ cups)**
- ¼ **cup chopped walnuts**
- 1 **pint raspberry sherbet**

1 Prepare topping mix according to package directions. Fold in macaroons and nuts. Using about ⅓ *cup* mixture for *each*, spread in bottom and up sides of 8 paper bake cups in 1¾-inch muffin pans. Spoon a *small scoop* of raspberry sherbet into *each*. Cover loosely with foil. Freeze at least 6 hours. Makes 8 servings.

PEAR CHIFFON PIE

Advance preparation time: 45 minutes

- 1 **16-ounce can pear halves**
- 2 **tablespoons sugar**
- 1 **envelope unflavored gelatin**
- 3 **slightly beaten egg yolks**
- ¼ **teaspoon finely shredded lemon peel**
- 1 **tablespoon lemon juice**
- 3 **egg whites**
- ¼ **cup sugar**
- ½ **of a 4½-ounce container frozen whipped dessert topping, thawed**
- 1 **graham cracker pie shell**

1 Drain pear halves, reserving ¼ cup syrup. With fork, mash pears. Set aside. In saucepan combine the 2 tablespoons sugar and the gelatin. Stir in reserved pear syrup, egg yolks, lemon peel, and lemon juice.

2 Cook and stir over medium heat till gelatin dissolves and mixture thickens slightly. Remove from heat. Stir in mashed pears. Chill pear mixture till consistency of unbeaten egg whites (partially set).

3 Beat egg whites till soft peaks form (tips curl over). Gradually add the ¼ cup sugar, beating till stiff peaks form (tips stand straight).

4 Gently fold the gelatin mixture into stiff-beaten egg whites. Fold in thawed dessert topping. Chill till mixture mounds when spooned. Turn into graham cracker pie shell. Cover and refrigerate for 6 to 24 hours. Makes 8 servings.

Cherry-Brandy Pie

COOKING AHEAD
DESSERTS

LEMON PIE HAWAIIAN

Advance preparation time: 1 hour and 50 minutes
Final preparation time: 5 minutes

- 1 **9-inch frozen unbaked deep-dish pastry shell**
- 1 **8¼-ounce can crushed pineapple, drained**
- ¼ **cup packed brown sugar**
- ¼ **cup coconut**
- 2 **tablespoons butter *or* margarine, softened**
- 1 **package 4-serving-size *regular* lemon pudding mix**
- ½ **cup sugar**
- 1¾ **cups water**
- 2 **slightly beaten egg yolks**
- 2 **tablespoons lemon juice**
- 1 **tablespoon butter *or* margarine**
- 2 **egg whites**
- ¼ **cup sugar**
  Toasted coconut (optional)

1 Thaw frozen pastry shell for 10 minutes at room temperature. Combine drained pineapple, brown sugar, the ¼ cup coconut, and the 2 tablespoons butter or margarine; spread over bottom of pastry shell. Cover edge of pastry with foil. Bake in a 425° oven for 15 minutes, removing foil after first 5 minutes of baking. Cool.

2 Meanwhile, in saucepan combine pudding mix and the ½ cup sugar. Stir in the water and yolks; cook and stir till thickened and bubbly. Cook and stir 2 minutes more. Remove from heat. Stir in lemon juice and the 1 tablespoon butter or margarine. Cover with clear plastic wrap; cool, stirring occasionally.

3 Beat egg whites on high speed of electric mixer till soft peaks form (tips curl over); gradually add the ¼ cup sugar, beating till stiff peaks form (tips stand straight). Fold whites into cooled filling; spoon into pastry shell. Cover; refrigerate 6 to 24 hours.
  Before serving: If desired, garnish with toasted coconut. Makes 8 servings.

FRUIT-TOPPED PIE

Advance preparation time: 30 minutes

- 1 **9-inch frozen unbaked deep-dish pastry shell**
- ⅓ **cup sliced almonds**
- 1¼ **cups milk**
- 1 **cup dairy sour cream**
- 1 **package 4-serving-size *instant* vanilla pudding mix**
- ½ **of a 21-ounce can (about 1 cup) cherry, strawberry, *or* peach pie filling**

1 Thaw frozen pastry shell for 10 minutes at room temperature. Prick sides and bottom of shell with fork. Press sliced almonds into bottom of pie shell. Bake according to package directions. Cool slightly.

2 Meanwhile, in mixer bowl combine milk, sour cream, and pudding mix. Beat on low speed of electric mixer for 1 minute. Turn pudding mixture into pie shell. Spoon pie filling atop. Cover and refrigerate for 6 to 24 hours. Makes 8 servings.

FREEZING HOMEMADE PIE SHELLS

Save time by freezing pastry and graham cracker pie shells ahead. Simply prepare the shells using your favorite recipe. Then bake, if desired. Cool and wrap in moisture-vaporproof material. Seal, label, and freeze. Frozen pie shells can be stored as long as two months. To thaw a baked pie shell, heat it in a 325° oven for 8 to 10 minutes. To use unbaked frozen shells, bake as you would unfrozen shells.

NO-CRUST GERMAN CHOCOLATE PIE

Advance preparation time: 1 hour and 20 minutes
Final preparation time: 5 minutes

- ½ **cup butter *or* margarine**
- ½ **of a 4-ounce package German cooking chocolate**
- 1 **teaspoon vanilla**
- 3 **beaten eggs**
- 1 **cup sugar**
- 3 **tablespoons all-purpose flour**
- ¼ **teaspoon salt**
- 1 **cup chopped walnuts**
  Pressurized dessert topping
  Chopped walnuts

1 In a small saucepan melt butter or margarine and chocolate over low heat; remove from heat. Stir in vanilla; cool.

2 In a small mixer bowl combine beaten eggs, sugar, flour, and salt. Beat on high speed of electric mixer just till mixed. *Do not overbeat.* Fold in cooled chocolate mixture; fold in the 1 cup chopped walnuts. Pour into a lightly greased and floured 9-inch pie plate.

3 Bake in a 325° oven for 1 hour or till knife inserted near center comes out clean. Cool slightly. Cover and refrigerate for 6 to 24 hours.
  Before serving: Dollop pie with dessert topping and garnish with additional chopped walnuts. Makes 8 servings.

INSTANT BLACK FOREST PIE

Advance preparation time: 55 minutes
Final preparation time: 10 minutes

1 9-inch frozen unbaked deep-dish
   pastry shell
2 8-ounce cartons cherry yogurt
1 package 4-serving-size *instant*
   chocolate pudding mix
2 tablespoons crème de cacao
1 teaspoon vanilla
1 4½-ounce container frozen
   whipped dessert topping
½ cup cherry preserves
1 tablespoon brandy

1 Thaw frozen pastry shell for 10 minutes at room temperature. Bake according to package directions; cool slightly. Combine yogurt, pudding mix, crème de cacao, and vanilla; beat well with rotary beater. Spread in bottom of pie shell. Cover and refrigerate for 6 to 24 hours.

Before serving: Spread whipped topping over filling. Combine preserves and brandy; spoon over topping. Serves 8.

YOGURT PIE

Advance preparation time: 15 minutes
Final preparation time: 15 minutes

½ cup boiling water
1 package fluffy white frosting mix
   (for 2-layer cake)
2 8-ounce cartons fruit yogurt
   Graham cracker pie shell

1 In mixer bowl pour the boiling water over frosting mix; beat on high speed of electric mixer 5 minutes or till stiff peaks form. Fold in yogurt; spoon into pie shell. Cover; freeze at least 6 hours.

Before serving: Let stand at room temperature for 10 to 15 minutes. Makes 8 servings.

BANANA-CHEESECAKE PIE

Advance preparation time: 1 hour and 20 minutes
Final preparation time: 5 minutes

1 9-inch frozen unbaked deep-dish
   pastry shell
2 eggs
2 cups cream-style cottage cheese
¾ cup milk
¾ cup sugar
1 3-ounce package no-bake custard
   mix
2 tablespoons lemon juice
¼ cup apricot preserves
1 tablespoon orange juice
2 large bananas

1 Thaw frozen pastry shell for 10 minutes at room temperature. Prick bottom and sides of pastry shell. Bake in a 450° oven for 5 minutes; cool slightly. Reduce oven temperature to 350°.

2 In blender container or food processor bowl combine eggs, *undrained* cottage cheese, milk, sugar, and dry custard mix. Cover; blend or process till smooth. Stir in lemon juice. Pour into crust.

3 Bake in a 350° oven for 40 to 50 minutes or till knife inserted near center comes out clean. Cool slightly. Cover and refrigerate for 6 to 24 hours.

Before serving: For glaze, in a small bowl stir together apricot preserves and orange juice. Slice bananas; arrange atop pie. Spoon glaze over fruit. Makes 8 servings.

TOFFEE PIE

Advance preparation time: 15 minutes

1½ cups finely crushed chocolate
    wafers
6 tablespoons butter, melted
1 cup whipping cream
⅔ cup Eagle Brand sweetened
   condensed milk
¼ cup cold strong coffee
½ teaspoon vanilla
2 1⅛-ounce bars chocolate-coated
   English toffee

1 Mix wafers and butter. Press mixture into 9-inch pie plate; chill. Beat cream, milk, coffee, and vanilla on low speed of electric mixer. Beat on high speed 4 minutes. Crush toffee; reserve *2 tablespoons*. Stir remaining into cream mixture. Spoon into crust. Sprinkle with reserved toffee. Cover; freeze at least 6 hours. Serves 8.

FROZEN PUMPKIN CREAM PIE

Advance preparation time: 40 minutes
Final preparation time: 10 minutes

1 9-inch frozen unbaked pastry shell
1 cup canned pumpkin
1 cup chopped nuts
½ cup sugar
½ teaspoon ground ginger
¼ teaspoon ground nutmeg
   Dash salt
1 4½-ounce container frozen
   whipped dessert topping,
   thawed

1 Thaw pastry at room temperature for 10 minutes; bake according to package directions. Cool slightly. Mix next 6 ingredients. Fold topping into mixture. Spoon into shell. Cover; freeze at least 4 hours.

Before serving: Let stand 10 minutes at room temperature. Makes 8 servings.

354

FROZEN CHOCOLATE CHIP CHEESECAKE

Advance preparation time: 30 minutes
Final preparation time: 45 minutes

1¼ **cups graham cracker crumbs**
¼ **cup sugar**
6 **tablespoons butter** *or* **margarine, melted**
1 **8-ounce package cream cheese, cut up**
1 **3-ounce package cream cheese, cut up**
1 **quart chocolate ice cream**
½ **cup chopped semisweet chocolate pieces**
Pressurized dessert topping
Semisweet chocolate pieces

1 To prepare crust, in a bowl combine cracker crumbs and sugar. Stir in melted butter or margarine. Press onto bottom and 1½ inches up the sides of a 9-inch springform pan. Chill.

2 Meanwhile, in a large mixer bowl beat cream cheese on high speed of electric mixer till fluffy; set aside. In a chilled mixing bowl stir ice cream just to soften. Gradually add ice cream to cream cheese, beating till smooth. Fold in chopped chocolate. Spoon into crust. Cover and freeze at least 8 hours.

Before serving: Let stand at room temperature for 30 to 40 minutes. Loosen sides and remove rim from pan. If desired, garnish with dessert topping and semisweet chocolate pieces. Makes 8 to 10 servings.

Lemon Mousse (see recipe, page 356)
Praline Cheesecake

PRALINE CHEESECAKE

Advance preparation time: 1¾ hours
Final preparation time: 10 minutes

1¼ **cups graham cracker crumbs**
¼ **cup sugar**
¼ **cup chopped pecans**
¼ **cup butter** *or* **margarine, melted**
3 **8-ounce packages cream cheese, cut up**
1 **cup packed brown sugar**
1 **5⅓-ounce can (⅔ cup) evaporated milk**
2 **tablespoons all-purpose flour**
1½ **teaspoons vanilla**
3 **eggs**
1 **cup pecan halves**
1 **cup dark corn syrup**
¼ **cup cornstarch**
2 **tablespoons brown sugar**
1 **teaspoon vanilla**

1 For crust, in small mixing bowl combine cracker crumbs, the sugar, and the chopped pecans. Stir in the melted butter or margarine. Press crumb mixture onto bottom and 1½ inches up the sides of a 9-inch springform pan. Bake in a 350° oven for 10 minutes.

2 Meanwhile, beat cream cheese till fluffy; add the 1 cup brown sugar, the evaporated milk, flour, and the 1½ teaspoons vanilla; beat till smooth. Add eggs; beat just till blended. Pour into baked crust.

3 Bake cheesecake in a 350° oven 50 to 55 minutes or till set. Cool in pan 30 minutes; loosen sides and remove rim from pan. Cool. Cover; chill 6 to 24 hours.

Before serving: Arrange nut halves atop cheesecake. For sauce, in small saucepan combine corn syrup, cornstarch, and the 2 tablespoons brown sugar. Cook and stir till thickened and bubbly. Cook and stir 2 minutes more. Remove from heat; stir in the 1 teaspoon vanilla. Cool slightly. Spoon some of the warm sauce over the nuts on the cheesecake. Pass remaining sauce. Makes 12 to 16 servings.

APPLE-CHEDDAR CHEESECAKE

Advance preparation time: 2 hours

½ **cup all-purpose flour**
2 **tablespoons sugar**
½ **teaspoon finely shredded lemon peel**
¼ **cup butter** *or* **margarine**
1 **slightly beaten egg yolk**
¼ **teaspoon vanilla**
2 **8-ounce packages cream cheese, cut up**
1 **cup shredded cheddar cheese (4 ounces)**
¾ **cup sugar**
2 **tablespoons all-purpose flour**
2 **eggs**
¼ **cup milk**
1 **21-ounce can apple pie filling**
¼ **teaspoon ground cinnamon**

1 For crust, combine the ½ cup flour, the 2 tablespoons sugar, and lemon peel. Cut in butter or margarine till mixture resembles coarse crumbs. Stir in egg yolk and vanilla till well combined. Pat *one-third* of the dough onto bottom of a 9-inch springform pan (sides removed). Bake in a 400° oven for 5 to 6 minutes; cool. Grease sides of pan; attach to bottom. Pat remaining dough up sides of pan to height of 1 inch. Set aside.

2 In large mixer bowl beat cream cheese and cheddar cheese till fluffy. Add the ¾ cup sugar and 2 tablespoons flour; beat till smooth. Add eggs; beat just till blended. Gently stir in milk. Turn into crust-lined pan.

3 Bake in a 375° oven for 30 to 35 minutes or till center is set. Cool in pan for 30 minutes; loosen sides of cheesecake pan with narrow metal spatula. Remove rim from pan. Cool completely. Stir together apple pie filling and cinnamon. Spoon apple mixture over cheesecake. Cover and refrigerate for 6 to 24 hours. Makes 12 servings.

PEANUT BUTTER AND JELLY CHEESECAKE

Advance preparation time: 2 hours

- 1 cup graham cracker crumbs
- 3 tablespoons sugar
- 3 tablespoons butter *or* margarine, melted
- 2 8-ounce packages cream cheese, cut up
- 1 cup sugar
- ½ cup peanut butter
- 3 tablespoons all-purpose flour
- 4 beaten eggs
- ½ cup milk
- ½ cup grape jelly

1 In a small bowl combine graham cracker crumbs and the 3 tablespoons sugar. Stir in the melted butter or margarine. Press mixture evenly onto bottom and 1½ inches up sides of a 9-inch springform pan. Bake in 350° oven 10 minutes. Set aside.

2 In large mixer bowl beat cream cheese till fluffy; add the 1 cup sugar, the peanut butter, and flour; beat till smooth. Add eggs; beat just till blended. Stir in milk.

3 Pour mixture into baked crust. Bake in a 350° oven for 45 to 50 minutes or till set. Cool in pan for 30 minutes. Loosen sides and remove rim from pan. Cool completely. In small saucepan heat grape jelly till melted; spoon over cheesecake. Cover and chill for 6 to 24 hours. Serves 12 to 16.

FRUIT-TOPPED RICE DESSERT

Advance preparation time: 1 hour and 50 minutes
Final preparation time: 10 minutes

- 3 cups milk
- ⅔ cup long grain rice
- ⅓ cup sugar
- 1 envelope unflavored gelatin
- 1 cup milk
- ¼ cup chopped almonds, toasted
- 1 teaspoon vanilla
- ½ cup whipping cream
- 1 10-ounce package frozen red raspberries *or* frozen sliced strawberries (in quick-thaw pouch)

1 In a heavy 2-quart saucepan stir together the 3 cups milk, the uncooked rice, and the sugar. Bring mixture to boiling. Reduce heat. Cook, covered, about 45 minutes or till the rice is tender, stirring occasionally.

2 Meanwhile, soften the unflavored gelatin in the 1 cup milk. Stir gelatin into *hot* rice mixture till gelatin dissolves. Stir in the chopped toasted almonds and vanilla. Chill till consistency of unbeaten egg whites (partially set).

3 Meanwhile, whip the cream till soft peaks form. Fold the whipped cream into the rice mixture. Turn into an 8x8x2-inch baking pan. Cover and refrigerate the dessert for 6 to 24 hours.

Before serving: Place frozen raspberries or strawberries in a bowl of hot water to thaw, about 10 minutes. Cut rice dessert into squares. Top with thawed raspberries or strawberries. Makes 9 servings.

LEMON MOUSSE

Pictured on page 354—

Advance preparation time: 30 minutes

- 1 envelope unflavored gelatin
- 1 6-ounce can frozen lemonade concentrate
- ¼ cup water
- 4 slightly beaten egg yolks
- 1½ cups whipping cream
- 4 egg whites
- 2 tablespoons orange liqueur
  Lemon slices, halved (optional)

1 In a small saucepan soften gelatin in frozen lemonade concentrate and water. Cook and stir till gelatin dissolves and mixture thickens slightly.

2 In a bowl gradually stir about *half* of the hot mixture into egg yolks. Return all to saucepan. Cook and stir till thickened and bubbly; cook and stir 2 minutes more. Remove from heat; chill in ice water about 10 minutes till consistency of unbeaten egg whites (partially set).

3 Meanwhile, whip cream till soft peaks form. Wash beaters thoroughly. Beat egg whites till stiff peaks form (tips stand straight). Stir orange liqueur into gelatin mixture. Fold beaten egg whites and whipped cream into gelatin mixture. Turn into a 5- or 6-cup serving bowl. Cover and refrigerate for 6 to 24 hours.

Before serving: Garnish with lemon slices if desired. Makes 10 to 12 servings.

DATE CREAM

Advance preparation time: 30 minutes

- 1 **envelope unflavored gelatin**
- 1 **cup milk**
- ½ **cup maple *or* maple-flavored syrup**
- 2 **beaten eggs**
- 1 **cup whipping cream**
- ½ **cup finely snipped pitted dates**
- ½ **cup chopped pecans**

1 Combine gelatin and ¼ teaspoon *salt.* Stir in milk and syrup. Cook and stir till gelatin dissolves and mixture thickens slightly (mixture will appear curdled).

2 Gradually stir about *half* of the mixture into beaten eggs; return all to saucepan. Cook; stir till thickened slightly *(do not boil).* Chill in bowl of ice water 10 minutes or till consistency of unbeaten egg whites.

3 Meanwhile, whip cream till soft peaks form. Fold cream, dates, and nuts into gelatin mixture. Spoon into 8 dessert dishes. Cover; refrigerate 6 to 24 hours. Serves 8.

MOCK TRIFLE

Advance preparation time: 20 minutes

- 2 **10-ounce packages frozen red raspberries, sliced strawberries, *or* peach slices (in quick-thaw pouch)**
- 1 **3-ounce package no-bake custard mix**
- ¼ **cup milk**
- ¼ **cup cream sherry**
- 8 **cake dessert cups**

1 Place fruit in a bowl of hot water to thaw for 10 minutes. Meanwhile, prepare custard mix according to package directions, *except* add an additional ¼ cup milk before cooking. Stir in sherry. In 8 dessert dishes spoon thawed fruit over dessert cups. Spoon custard mixture atop fruit. Cover; refrigerate for 3 to 24 hours. Serves 8.

CHOCOLATE-NUTMEG DESSERT

Advance preparation time: 15 minutes

- ¼ **cup cold water**
- 1 **envelope unflavored gelatin**
- 1 **tablespoon sugar**
- ¼ **teaspoon ground nutmeg**
  Dash salt
- ½ **cup boiling water**
- 1 **6-ounce package (1 cup) semisweet chocolate pieces**
- ½ **teaspoon vanilla**
- 2 **egg yolks**
- 1 **cup whipping cream**
- ¾ **cup ice cubes (about 6)**

1 In a blender container combine the ¼ cup cold water, gelatin, sugar, nutmeg, and salt. Let stand 2 minutes. Add the ½ cup boiling water; cover and blend at high speed about 40 seconds or till gelatin dissolves.

2 Add chocolate pieces and vanilla. Cover; blend at high speed about 10 seconds or till smooth. With blender running on low speed, add egg yolks and cream through hole in lid. Add ice cubes with blender running. Blend 40 seconds more or till mixture begins to thicken and ice cubes melt. Pour into 6 dessert glasses. Cover; refrigerate for 3 to 24 hours. Serves 6.

FREEZING WHIPPED CREAM

To avoid whipping cream at the last minute, whip the cream several days ahead and spoon it in mounds onto a waxed paper-lined baking sheet. Freeze till firm; transfer mounds to a freezer container. To serve, place a mound on each serving of dessert; let stand at room temperature 20 to 30 minutes before serving.

SPICY PUMPKIN SQUARES

This easy chilled dessert is reminiscent of pumpkin pie—

Advance preparation time: 25 minutes

- 32 **marshmallows (about 3½ cups)**
- 1 **cup canned pumpkin**
- ½ **teaspoon ground cinnamon**
- ¼ **teaspoon ground ginger**
- ⅛ **teaspoon ground cloves**
- 1 **cup graham cracker crumbs**
- ¼ **cup butter *or* margarine, melted**
- 1 **1½-ounce envelope dessert topping mix**

1 In a large saucepan combine marshmallows, pumpkin, cinnamon, ginger, and cloves; cook and stir over low heat till marshmallows are melted. Cool about 15 minutes.

2 Meanwhile, combine the graham cracker crumbs and the melted butter or margarine; reserve ¼ *cup* of the crumb mixture for the topping. Pat the remaining crumb mixture firmly into the bottom of an 8x8x2-inch baking dish.

3 Prepare dessert topping mix according to package directions; fold into cooled marshmallow mixture. Spread marshmallow mixture over crust. Sprinkle reserved crumb mixture atop. Cover and refrigerate for 6 to 24 hours. Makes 12 servings.

COCONUT-FILLED CHOCOLATE ROLL

Advance preparation time: 1 hour

3 **eggs**
⅓ **cup water**
2 **tablespoons cooking oil**
½ **package (2 cups) 2-layer-size chocolate cake mix (pudding type)**
   Powdered sugar
2 **3-ounce packages cream cheese, cut up**
¼ **cup butter** *or* **margarine, softened**
2 **tablespoons sugar**
1 **teaspoon vanilla**
1 **cup coconut**
½ **cup chopped nuts**

1 Line a 15x10x1-inch baking pan with foil or waxed paper; grease well. In small mixer bowl beat eggs on high speed of electric mixer about 5 minutes or till thick and lemon colored. Gradually add the water and cooking oil; beat till well combined. Add the dry cake mix; beat for 1 minute on low speed. Spread evenly into prepared pan. Bake in a 350° oven for 12 to 15 minutes or till done.

2 Immediately loosen edges of cake from pan and turn out onto a towel sprinkled with powdered sugar. Peel waxed paper or foil off cake. Starting with narrow end, roll warm cake and towel together; cool, seam side down, on wire rack.

3 For filling, in mixer bowl beat cream cheese, butter or margarine, sugar, and vanilla till fluffy. Stir in coconut and nuts. Unroll cake; spread evenly with filling to within 1 inch of edges. Roll up cake. Cover and refrigerate for 6 to 24 hours. Makes 10 servings.

CREAM HEARTS

Advance preparation time: 30 minutes
Final preparation time: 10 minutes

1 **10-ounce package frozen red raspberries (in quick-thaw pouch)**
6 **6-inch squares cheesecloth**
1 **8-ounce package cream cheese, cut up**
½ **teaspoon vanilla**
½ **cup sifted powdered sugar**
1 **cup whipping cream**
¼ **cup currant jelly**
2 **tablespoons dry red wine**

1 Place raspberries in a bowl of hot water to thaw. Moisten cheesecloth squares. Line six 3-inch heart-shaped coeur à la crème molds or ½-cup molds with cheesecloth squares, allowing cheesecloth to overhang. In small mixer bowl beat cream cheese and vanilla. Gradually add powdered sugar, beating on high speed of electric mixer till fluffy.

2 In another bowl whip the cream just till soft peaks form; fold into cheese mixture. Spoon the mixture into molds. Cover and refrigerate for 3 to 24 hours.

3 Meanwhile, for raspberry sauce, in small saucepan heat currant jelly till melted. Drain raspberries well (reserve juice for another use). Stir the raspberries and the dry red wine into jelly. Cover and refrigerate for 3 to 24 hours.

Before serving: Invert each mold on an individual serving plate. Holding onto cheesecloth ends, lift off mold; peel off cheesecloth. Spoon raspberry sauce atop each serving. Makes 6 servings.

EGGNOG FREEZE

Advance preparation time: 15 minutes
Final preparation time: 15 minutes

2 **cups finely crushed sugar cookies**
¼ **cup butter** *or* **margarine, melted**
¼ **cup chopped pecans**
1 **package 4-serving-size** *instant* **vanilla pudding mix**
1½ **cups dairy eggnog**
1 **cup whipping cream**

1 Combine cookie crumbs, butter, and nuts; press *1½ cups* into bottom of a 9x9x2-inch baking pan. Prepare pudding mix according to package directions, *except* use the 1½ cups eggnog for the liquid. Whip cream till soft peaks form; fold into pudding mixture. Turn pudding into pan. Sprinkle remaining crumbs atop. Cover; freeze at least 6 hours.

Before serving: Let stand at room temperature 15 minutes. Cut into squares. Makes 9 servings.

CRANBERRY-ORANGE MOUSSE

Advance preparation time: 1 hour
Final preparation time: 15 minutes

2 **cups cranberries**
¾ **cup sugar**
½ **cup orange marmalade**
1½ **cups whipping cream**

1 Combine cranberries and ½ cup *water*; bring to boiling. Reduce heat. Simmer, covered, for 5 minutes or till berries are soft. Sieve berries; discard skins. Add sugar and marmalade to mixture; mix well. Cool to room temperature.

2 Whip cream till soft peaks form; fold into cranberry mixture. Turn into a 5-cup mold. Cover and freeze at least 6 hours.

Before serving: Let stand 10 minutes at room temperature; unmold. Serves 8.

LEMON CHIFFON ALASKA

Advance preparation time: 40 minutes
Final preparation time: 10 minutes

1 cup finely crushed vanilla
  wafers
3 tablespoons butter *or* margarine,
  melted
3 egg yolks
1 14-ounce can Eagle Brand
  sweetened condensed milk
½ cup lemon juice
1 4½-ounce container frozen
  whipped dessert topping,
  thawed
3 egg whites
⅓ cup sugar

1 Combine finely crushed wafers and melted butter or margarine. Press into bottom of an 8x8x2-inch baking dish; chill.

2 Meanwhile, in a small mixer bowl beat egg yolks about 5 minutes or till thick and lemon colored. Beat in sweetened condensed milk. Stir in lemon juice. Fold thawed dessert topping into the lemon mixture. Pour over crumb crust, spreading the mixture evenly.

3 Wash beaters thoroughly. Beat egg whites till soft peaks form (tips curl over). Gradually add sugar, beating till stiff peaks form (tips stand straight). Spread over filling mixture, sealing to edges. Bake in a 500° oven for 1 to 2 minutes or till golden. Cool to room temperature. Wrap loosely in foil. Freeze at least 6 hours.

Before serving: Let stand 10 minutes. Makes 12 servings.

ROCKY ROAD DESSERT

Though frozen, this delicious dessert is soft and easy to serve—

Advance preparation time: 35 minutes
Final preparation time: 10 minutes

1 envelope unflavored gelatin
¼ cup sugar
¾ cup milk
2 tablespoons cold water
1 square (1 ounce) unsweetened
  chocolate, cut up
¼ cup coffee liqueur
1 cup whipping cream
1 cup tiny marshmallows
½ cup chopped pecans

1 In a small saucepan combine gelatin and sugar. Stir in milk, water, and unsweetened chocolate. Cook and stir till gelatin dissolves and mixture thickens slightly (flecks of chocolate may be visible). Remove from heat; stir in coffee liqueur. Chill the chocolate mixture till consistency of unbeaten egg whites (partially set).

2 Meanwhile, whip cream till soft peaks form. Fold whipped cream, marshmallows, and chopped pecans into gelatin mixture. Pour into an 8x8x2-inch pan or an 8x4x2-inch loaf pan. Cover and freeze at least 6 hours.

Before serving: Let stand 10 minutes; cut into squares or slices. Makes 8 or 9 servings.

FROZEN APRICOT TORTE

A tasty way to dress up an ordinary pound cake—

Advance preparation time: 20 minutes
Final preparation time: 20 minutes

1 frozen loaf pound cake
1 egg white
1 8¾-ounce can unpeeled apricot
  halves, well drained
⅓ cup sugar
1 tablespoon lemon juice
⅛ teaspoon almond extract
½ cup whipping cream
  Powdered sugar

1 Let pound cake stand at room temperature for 15 minutes to thaw slightly. Meanwhile, in large mixer bowl combine egg white, drained apricots, sugar, lemon juice, and almond extract. Beat on low speed of electric mixer about 2 minutes or till mixture begins to thicken. Beat on high speed for 10 to 12 minutes or till stiff peaks form (tips stand straight).

2 Cut the partially thawed pound cake into cubes. Whip the whipping cream just till soft peaks form (tips curl over); fold into the apricot mixture. Stir cubed pound cake into the mixture.

3 Turn mixture into an 8x4x2-inch loaf pan; pack lightly into pan. Cover and freeze at least 6 hours.

Before serving: Let torte stand at room temperature about 15 minutes. Unmold onto serving platter. Sprinkle torte lightly with powdered sugar. Makes 8 to 10 servings.

COFFEE-COCONUT MOUSSE

Advance preparation time: 40 minutes
Final preparation time: 15 minutes

- ⅔ **cup sugar**
- 2 **tablespoons instant coffee crystals**
- 1 **envelope unflavored gelatin Dash salt**
- ¾ **cup milk**
- 2 **cups whipping cream**
- 1 **3½-ounce can (1⅓ cups) flaked coconut, toasted Maraschino cherries (optional)**

1 In a 2-quart saucepan combine sugar, coffee crystals, gelatin, and salt. Stir in milk. Cook and stir till the sugar, coffee granules, and gelatin dissolve and the mixture thickens slightly. Remove the saucepan from heat; chill in bowl of ice water for 10 minutes or till consistency of unbeaten egg whites (partially set).

2 Whip the cream till soft peaks form (tips curl over). Fold the whipped cream and *1 cup* of the toasted coconut into the gelatin mixture.

3 Attach a 2-inch-wide strip of foil around each of eight ½-inch soufflé dishes so the foil collar extends 1 inch above the top of dishes; fasten with tape. Spoon coconut mixture into soufflé dishes. (*Or*, turn mixture into a foil-lined 8x4x2-inch loaf pan.) Cover and freeze for 6 to 24 hours.

Before serving: Let mousse stand for 10 minutes at room temperature. Remove foil collars from soufflé dishes or spoon mousse from loaf pan into sherbet glasses. Sprinkle remaining coconut atop and garnish with a maraschino cherry, if desired. Makes 8 servings.

FROSTY ORANGE ROLL

Advance preparation time: 1 hour and 20 minutes

- ¾ **cup all-purpose flour**
- 1 **teaspoon baking powder**
- ¼ **teaspoon salt**
- 3 **eggs**
- 1 **cup sugar**
- 1 **teaspoon finely shredded orange peel**
- ¼ **cup orange juice Powdered sugar**
- 3 **tablespoons orange liqueur**
- 1 **tablespoon white crème de cacao**
- 1 **quart vanilla ice cream**

1 Grease and lightly flour a 15x10x1-inch jelly roll pan. In a bowl stir together flour, baking powder, and salt. In small mixer bowl beat eggs on high speed of electric mixer about 5 minutes or till thick and lemon colored. Gradually add sugar, beating till sugar dissolves. Stir in orange peel and juice. Fold flour mixture into egg mixture.

2 Spread evenly into prepared pan. Bake in a 375° oven for 12 to 15 minutes or till done. Immediately loosen edges of cake from pan and turn out onto a towel sprinkled with powdered sugar. Starting with narrow end, roll warm cake and towel together; cool, seam side down, on a wire rack.

3 Unroll cake. Combine orange liqueur and crème de cacao; sprinkle evenly over cake. In chilled mixer bowl stir ice cream just till softened. Spread cake with ice cream to within 1 inch of edges. Roll up cake. Cover and freeze at least 6 hours. Makes 10 servings.

CHOCOLATE MALTED FREEZE

Advanced preparation time: 1¼ hours

- 1 **cup all-purpose flour**
- ¼ **cup instant malted milk powder**
- ½ **cup butter *or* margarine, melted**
- 1 **cup whipping cream**
- 1 **quart chocolate ice cream**
- 1 **cup chopped pecans**
- ¼ **cup instant malted milk powder**

1 Combine flour and ¼ cup malted milk powder; stir in butter. Spread in an ungreased 9x9x2-inch baking pan. Bake in a 350° oven for 20 to 25 minutes; stir occasionally. Remove from oven; cool. Remove ⅓ *cup* of crumb mixture; set aside. Press remaining mixture into bottom of pan. Whip cream till soft peaks form. In chilled bowl stir ice cream just till softened. Stir whipped cream, nuts, and ¼ cup malted milk powder into ice cream. Spoon over crumb mixture in pan. Top with reserved crumb mixture. Cover; freeze at least 6 hours.

Before serving: Cut into squares. Makes 12 servings.

SUNDAE CAKE

Advance preparation time: 20 minutes

- 1 **frozen loaf pound cake**
- ¾ **cup raspberry sherbet**
- ¾ **cup lemon sherbet**
- ¾ **cup lime sherbet**
- 2 **tablespoons sliced almonds**

1 Let cake stand at room temperature 15 minutes to thaw slightly. Meanwhile, chill 3 bowls for softening sherbets. Hollow out cake, leaving ½-inch shell (reserve center for another use). Return hollowed cake to foil pan. In chilled bowls stir each sherbet just till softened. Layer sherbets in cake. Sprinkle with almonds. Cover and freeze at least 6 hours. Serves 8 to 10.

DOUBLE-BERRY SHERBET

Advance preparation time: 2 hours and 20 minutes

½ of a 3-ounce package raspberry-flavored gelatin (3 tablespoons)
1½ cups orange juice
2 16-ounce cans jellied cranberry sauce
2 egg whites

1 In saucepan soften gelatin in orange juice. Cook and stir till gelatin dissolves and mixture thickens slightly. Add cranberry sauce; beat till smooth. Turn mixture into a 13x9x2-inch pan. Freeze for 2 hours or till almost firm.

2 Meanwhile, chill a large mixer bowl. Spoon cranberry mixture into chilled bowl; add unbeaten egg whites. Beat on high speed of electric mixer about 6 minutes or till fluffy. Return to pan. Cover and freeze at least 6 hours. Makes 8 cups.

EASY STRAWBERRY SHERBET

Advance preparation time: 2¼ hours

2 cups buttermilk
1 cup strawberry preserves

1 Stir buttermilk into preserves. Pour into refrigerator tray; freeze for 2 hours or till firm. Break up frozen mixture and place in chilled mixer bowl. Beat on high speed of electric mixer till fluffy. Return to tray; cover and freeze at least 6 hours.

Before serving: If desired, garnish with fresh strawberries and mint leaves. Makes about 1 quart.

MARBLED EGGNOG ICE CREAM

Try this at the end of a heavy holiday meal—

Advance preparation time: 2½ hours
Final preparation time: 10 minutes

1 3-ounce package no-bake custard mix
4 cups dairy *or* canned eggnog
1 4½-ounce container frozen whipped dessert topping, thawed
1 16-ounce can jellied cranberry sauce

1 In saucepan combine the dry custard mix and eggnog. Cook and stir over medium heat till mixture is thickened and bubbly. Remove from heat. Cover surface with clear plastic wrap; cool slightly. Pour mixture into a 13x9x2-inch pan. Cover; freeze about 2 hours or till almost firm.

2 Break up eggnog mixture in chilled mixer bowl; beat on high speed of electric mixer till fluffy. Fold in the thawed dessert topping. Break up cranberry sauce with fork; gently fold into eggnog mixture just till slightly marbled. Carefully return mixture to pan, retaining marbled effect. Cover and freeze at least 6 hours.

Before serving: Let stand at room temperature for 10 minutes. Makes 9 cups.

Easy Strawberry Sherbet

COOKING AHEAD
DESSERTS

DIXIE ICE CREAM

Advance preparation time: 15 minutes

- 1 quart vanilla ice cream
- 1 cup marshmallow creme
- 1 8-ounce can sweet potatoes, drained and mashed
- 2 tablespoons frozen orange juice concentrate
- ½ cup chopped pecans

1 In a large chilled mixing bowl stir ice cream just till softened. Stir in marshmallow creme, potatoes, and orange juice concentrate till potatoes and juice are combined and marshmallow creme is marbled throughout. Fold in pecans. Turn into shallow pan. Cover and freeze at least 6 hours. Makes 1½ quarts.

MINCEMEAT ICE CREAM

Advance preparation time: 30 minutes

- 4 egg yolks
- 1 cup milk
- 1 cup light cream
- 1 cup sugar
- ⅛ teaspoon salt
- 1⅓ cups prepared mincemeat
- 2 tablespoons brandy or rum
- 1 teaspoon vanilla
- 2 cups whipping cream

1 In a heavy saucepan beat egg yolks; stir in milk, cream, sugar, and salt. Cook and stir over medium heat till mixture thickens and coats a metal spoon. Place pan in a bowl of ice water; stir till cold. Stir in mincemeat, brandy or rum, and vanilla.

2 Whip cream till soft peaks form. Carefully fold egg mixture into whipped cream. Turn mixture into shallow pan; cover tightly with moisture-vaporproof wrap. Freeze at least 6 hours. Makes 2 quarts.

FRUIT COMPOTE

Advance preparation time: 25 minutes
Final preparation time: 5 minutes

- 1 16-ounce can whole, unpitted purple plums
- 1 16-ounce can pitted dark sweet cherries
- 3 tablespoons sugar
- 1 tablespoon cornstarch
- ⅓ cup orange marmalade
- 4 inches stick cinnamon
- 1 16-ounce can peach slices, drained

1 Drain plums and cherries, reserving 1¾ cups syrup. Halve and pit plums. Mix sugar and cornstarch. Stir in reserved syrup, marmalade, and cinnamon. Cook and stir till bubbly. Stir in fruit. Cover; simmer 5 minutes. Cover; chill 3 to 24 hours.

Before serving: Remove cinnamon. Serve with sour cream, if desired. Serves 8.

BRANDIED FRUIT

Spoon this topper over angel cake slices—

Advance preparation time: 5 minutes

- 1 17-ounce can unpeeled apricot halves, drained
- 1 11-ounce can mandarin orange sections, drained
- 1 8¼-ounce can pineapple chunks, drained
- 1 cup sugar
- ¼ cup brandy
- 1 package active dry yeast

1 In glass bowl combine first 5 ingredients. Stir in yeast. Let stand, loosely covered, at room temperature for 24 hours. Stir. Chill at least 1 week. Makes 3 cups. *Note*: To replenish fruit, for each cup removed, add 1 cup drained, canned *fruit*. Let stand at room temperature 24 hours; chill.

HARD SAUCE

Advance preparation time: 2¼ hours
Final preparation time: 15 minutes

- ½ cup butter *or* margarine
- 2 cups sifted powdered sugar
- 1 teaspoon vanilla

1 In mixer bowl beat butter on medium speed of electric mixer for 30 seconds. Add sugar; beat till fluffy. Add vanilla; beat well. Spread into a foil-lined 7½x3½x2-inch loaf pan. Cover and refrigerate at least 1 hour. Cut into squares; place on baking sheet. Freeze about 1 hour or till firm. Remove to freezer bag. Seal, label, and freeze.

Before serving: Let stand at room temperature 10 to 15 minutes. Serve over warm cake, if desired. Makes 18.

CRANBERRY CAKE

Advance preparation time: 1¾ hours

- 2 beaten eggs
- 1 16-ounce can whole cranberry sauce
- 1 cup buttermilk
- ¼ cup cooking oil
- 2 17-ounce packages date quick bread mix
- 1 cup chopped walnuts
- ½ cup orange juice
- ½ cup sugar

1 Combine eggs and cranberry sauce; stir to break up sauce. Stir in buttermilk and oil. Stir in bread mix. Fold in nuts. Pour into a greased 10-inch fluted tube pan. Bake in a 350° oven 60 to 65 minutes. Cool 20 minutes; turn out onto wire rack over a tray.

2 Meanwhile, for syrup, combine orange juice and sugar; cook and stir till bubbly. Cool 20 minutes. Prick top of warm cake. Spoon syrup over cake; spoon any syrup on tray over cake. Cool. Cover; refrigerate for 6 to 24 hours. Serves 12.

DRIED FRUIT FRUITCAKE

Advance preparation time: 4 hours

2 cups dried apples, finely chopped
1½ cups chopped dried apricots
1 8-ounce package pitted whole
    dates, snipped (1⅓ cups)
1 cup dried currants
1 cup raisins
1 cup chopped walnuts
½ cup apple juice
3 cups all-purpose flour
1 tablespoon ground cinnamon
1 teaspoon baking powder
1 teaspoon ground nutmeg
1 teaspoon ground allspice
1 cup butter *or* margarine
1 cup sugar
6 eggs
1 16-ounce can applesauce
    Brandy (optional)

1 In a large mixing bowl combine apples, apricots, dates, currants, raisins, nuts, and apple juice; let stand 1 hour. Stir together flour, cinnamon, baking powder, nutmeg, and allspice.

2 In large mixer bowl beat butter or margarine on medium speed of electric mixer for 30 seconds. Add sugar and beat till fluffy. Add eggs, one at a time; beat well after each addition. Add flour mixture and applesauce alternately to butter mixture. Stir into fruit mixture.

3 Pour into a greased 10-inch tube pan. Bake in a 300° oven for 2 hours. Cool; remove from pan. Wrap in brandy-soaked cheesecloth and foil, if desired, or just wrap in foil. Store in cool place. Makes 1 cake.

LEMON-SPICE SLICES

A light and crispy cookie with a delicate lemon flavor—

Advance preparation time: 1 hour
Final preparation time: 15 minutes

1¾ cups all-purpose flour
¾ teaspoon ground ginger
½ teaspoon baking soda
½ teaspoon ground cinnamon
½ teaspoon ground nutmeg
¾ cup butter *or* margarine
⅔ cup sugar
1 egg
1 teaspoon finely shredded lemon
    peel

1 In a bowl stir together flour, ginger, baking soda, cinnamon, and nutmeg. In a mixer bowl beat the butter or margarine on medium speed of electric mixer for 30 seconds. Add the sugar and beat till fluffy. Add egg and lemon peel; beat well. Add the flour mixture to the beaten mixture and beat till well combined.

2 Cover; chill about 45 minutes for easier handling. Shape into a 12-inch-long roll. Wrap in waxed paper or clear plastic wrap; chill at least 3 hours.

Before serving: Cut into ¼-inch slices. Place cookie slices on an ungreased cookie sheet. Bake in a 350° oven for 10 to 12 minutes or till done. Makes about 48.

OATMEAL SLICES

Advance preparation time: 20 minutes
Final preparation time: 15 minutes

1½ cups all-purpose flour
1 cup quick-cooking rolled oats
¾ cup packed brown sugar
½ cup coconut
2 tablespoons shelled sunflower
    nuts
½ teaspoon baking soda
½ cup shortening
½ cup butter *or* margarine
1 teaspoon vanilla

1 Combine first 6 ingredients and ½ teaspoon *salt*. Cut in shortening and butter till mixture resembles coarse crumbs. Combine vanilla and 2 tablespoons *water*. Toss with flour mixture till moistened. Shape into a 9x2-inch roll. Wrap; chill 3 to 24 hours.

Before serving: Slice ¼ inch thick. Bake on an ungreased cookie sheet in a 350° oven 10 to 12 minutes. Makes 36.

CHOCOLATE DROPS

Advance preparation time: 35 minutes

1 14-ounce can Eagle Brand
    sweetened condensed milk
1 6-ounce package (1 cup)
    butterscotch pieces
1 6-ounce package (1 cup)
    semisweet chocolate pieces
½ teaspoon vanilla
4 cups coarsely crushed pretzels
1 cup crisp rice cereal

1 Cook and stir milk and butterscotch and chocolate pieces over low heat till chocolate is melted. Remove from heat; stir in vanilla. Combine pretzels and cereal. Stir chocolate mixture into pretzel mixture. Drop by teaspoonfuls onto a waxed-paper-lined cookie sheet. Cover; chill 3 to 24 hours. Store in refrigerator. Makes 84.

ORANGE-CUSTARD FONDUE

Advance preparation time: 3 hours
Final preparation time: 30 minutes

1 3-ounce package no-bake custard mix
1¾ cups milk
1 4-ounce container frozen whipped dessert topping
2 tablespoons orange liqueur
1 teaspoon grated orange peel
Fresh fruit dippers
Chocolate cake and pound cake cubes

1 Prepare custard mix according to package directions, *except* use the 1¾ cups milk and omit the egg yolk. Cover surface with clear plastic wrap. Chill 2½ hours or till thickened. Thaw dessert topping.

2 Beat custard with rotary beater till smooth. Fold in dessert topping and liqueur. Top with orange peel. Cover and chill in the refrigerator for 2 to 24 hours.

Before serving: Prepare choice of fruits and cake cubes. If using banana chunks or apple slices, brush with lemon juice to prevent browning. Makes 3½ cups.

BASIL VEGETABLE DIP

Advance preparation time: 5 minutes
Final preparation time: 10 minutes

½ cup mayonnaise *or* salad dressing
⅓ cup dairy sour cream
2 teaspoons dried basil, crushed
⅛ teaspoon garlic powder
Assorted fresh vegetable dippers

1 Stir together mayonnaise, sour cream, basil, and garlic powder. Cover and chill in the refrigerator for 2 to 24 hours.

Before serving: Cut up vegetables. Serve with dip. Makes ¾ cup dip.

CREAMY BEEF SPREAD

Advance preparation time: 10 minutes

1 8-ounce package cream cheese, cut up
½ cup dairy sour cream
1 3-ounce package sliced smoked beef, finely chopped
2 tablespoons sliced green onion
1 tablespoon milk
Several dashes bottled hot pepper sauce
Assorted crackers

1 With electric mixer beat together cheese, sour cream, beef, onion, milk, and pepper sauce. Cover and chill in the refrigerator for 2 to 24 hours. Serve with crackers. Makes 2 cups spread.

PIMIENTO-HAM SPREAD

Advance preparation time: 45 minutes

2 cups shredded pimiento cheese
½ cup hot-style tomato juice
1 2¼-ounce can deviled ham
1 tablespoon prepared horseradish
⅓ cup finely chopped fresh mushrooms
½ of a 4-ounce can mild green chili peppers, rinsed, seeded, and chopped (about 3 tablespoons)
Assorted crackers

1 Place cheese in mixer bowl; cover and allow to come to room temperature (about ½ hour). Gradually add tomato juice, beating with electric mixer till fluffy. Beat in ham and horseradish; fold in mushrooms and chili peppers. Cover and chill in the refrigerator for 2 to 24 hours.

Before serving: Garnish with a green chili pepper and a sprig of parsley, if desired. Serve with crackers. Makes 2¼ cups.

FLUFFY HALIBUT PÂTÉ

Advance preparation time: 25 minutes
Final preparation time: 5 minutes

12 ounces frozen halibut *or* other fish fillets
1 8-ounce package Neufchâtel cheese, cut up
¼ cup cooked bacon pieces
¼ cup water *or* milk
2 tablespoons toasted wheat germ
1 tablespoon snipped parsley
1 tablespoon lemon juice
1 teaspoon onion salt
1 teaspoon soy sauce
½ teaspoon dried dillweed
Leaf lettuce
Cooked bacon pieces *or* paprika (optional)
Assorted crackers *or* fresh vegetable dippers

1 Place frozen halibut or other fish in a greased skillet and add enough water to cover. Bring to boiling; reduce heat. Cover and simmer 6 to 8 minutes or till fish flakes easily when tested with a fork. Drain and flake fish.

2 In a mixer bowl combine cooked fish, Neufchâtel cheese, the ¼ cup bacon pieces, water or milk, wheat germ, parsley, lemon juice, onion salt, soy sauce, and dillweed. Beat with electric mixer till all ingredients are well combined.

3 Press mixture into an oiled fish-shaped mold or 3-cup bowl or mold. Cover and chill in the refrigerator for 3 to 24 hours.

Before serving: Unmold onto a lettuce-lined plate. Sprinkle with additional bacon pieces or paprika, if desired. Serve with crackers or vegetable dippers. Makes about 3 cups spread.

Orange-Custard Fondue

SMOKED CHEESE AND WINE LOGS

Pictured on page 368—
You can also make these logs a week ahead and store them in the refrigerator—

Advance preparation time: 45 minutes
Final preparation time: 2 hours

- 2 8-ounce packages cream cheese, cut up
- 2 cups shredded smoked cheddar cheese (8 ounces)
- ½ cup butter *or* margarine, cut up
- ¼ cup dry red wine
- 1 tablespoon finely snipped chives
- 2 teaspoons prepared horseradish
- 1 cup finely chopped walnuts
  Assorted crackers

1 In mixer bowl combine cream cheese, cheddar cheese, butter or margarine, wine, snipped chives, and the prepared horseradish. Beat with electric mixer till fluffy. Cover and chill 30 minutes.

2 On waxed paper shape mixture into two logs about 1½ inches in diameter. Roll logs in chopped walnuts. Wrap in moisture-vaporproof material. Seal, label, and freeze up to 6 weeks.

Before serving: Thaw cheese logs for 1½ to 2 hours at room temperature or overnight in refrigerator till soft enough to slice without crumbling. Serve as a cheese spread with crackers. Or, slice with a wire cheese slicer or serrated knife into even rounds. Makes 2 logs.

SUNFLOWER SNACKS

Advance preparation time: 45 minutes

- 1 stick piecrust mix
- ½ cup shredded cheddar cheese (2 ounces)
- ⅓ cup sunflower nuts
- ½ teaspoon chili powder

1 Prepare piecrust mix according to package directions, *except* stir in cheese, sunflower nuts, and chili powder. Roll out pastry on lightly floured surface into a 10x8-inch rectangle.

2 Cut into squares, diamonds, or triangles. Place on greased baking sheet. Bake in a 400° oven for 8 to 10 minutes. Remove to rack to cool. Store in a tightly covered container. Makes about 24.

BARBECUE SNACK MIX

Advance preparation time: 1 hour

- 2 cups bite-size shredded wheat biscuits
- 1 cup peanuts
- 1 3-ounce can chow mein *or* rice noodles
- ¼ cup butter *or* margarine, melted
- 1 tablespoon Worcestershire sauce
- ¾ teaspoon barbecue spice
  Dash garlic powder

1 In a large bowl combine shredded wheat biscuits, peanuts, and chow mein or rice noodles. Stir together butter or margarine, Worcestershire sauce, barbecue spice, and garlic powder. Sprinkle over wheat biscuit mixture, stirring to coat.

2 Spread in a shallow baking pan. Bake in a 300° oven for 30 minutes, stirring occasionally. Cool, stirring occasionally. Store in a tightly covered container. Makes about 4½ cups mix.

HAM PINWHEELS

Advance preparation time: 30 minutes
Final preparation time: 1¼ hours

- 3 3-ounce packages cream cheese with chives, cut up
- 1 4½-ounce can deviled ham
- 1 tablespoon chili sauce
  Dash bottled hot pepper sauce
- 1 loaf unsliced whole wheat bread

1 In mixer bowl beat first 4 ingredients with electric mixer till smooth. Trim crusts from bread; cut horizontally into eight ¼-inch slices. Flatten each slice with a rolling pin. Spread *3 tablespoons* ham mixture over *each*. From narrow end, roll up jelly-roll style. Wrap; freeze up to one month.

Before serving: Thaw 45 minutes. Cut crosswise into ¼-inch slices. Cover; thaw 25 to 30 minutes more. Makes about 78.

CHEESE PUFFS

Advance preparation time: 45 minutes
Final preparation time: 15 minutes

- ½ of a 17¼-ounce package (1 sheet) frozen puff pastry
- 1 4-ounce container whipped cream cheese with chives
- 1 egg yolk
- 1 teaspoon lemon juice
- ½ cup shredded cheddar cheese
- ¼ cup cooked bacon pieces

1 Thaw pastry 20 minutes. Meanwhile, beat cream cheese, egg yolk, and lemon juice till smooth. Stir in cheddar cheese and bacon. On floured surface roll pastry into a 12-inch square. Cut into 2-inch squares. Top each with *1 teaspoon* cheese mixture. Moisten edges. Fold dough over to form a triangle; seal. Place on baking sheet. Cover; chill in refrigerator 3 to 24 hours.

Before serving: Bake in a 400° oven for 12 to 15 minutes. Makes 36.

MUSTARD-GLAZED HAM BALLS

Advance preparation time: 30 minutes
Final preparation time: 10 minutes

- 1 8-ounce can crushed pineapple (juice pack)
- 1 beaten egg
- ¼ cup fine dry bread crumbs
- ⅛ teaspoon pepper
- ½ pound ground fully cooked ham
- ½ pound ground beef
- ¼ cup packed brown sugar
- ¼ cup catsup
- ¼ cup vinegar
- ¼ cup water
- 2 tablespoons prepared mustard

1 Drain pineapple, reserving juice. In a bowl combine *2 tablespoons* of the reserved pineapple juice, egg, bread crumbs, and pepper; mix well. Add ground ham, ground beef, and the drained, crushed pineapple; mix well.

2 Shape into 48 meatballs. Place on rack in shallow baking pan. Bake in a 450° oven for 12 to 15 minutes or till lightly browned. Drain on paper toweling. Cool to room temperature.

3 Meanwhile, stir together brown sugar, catsup, vinegar, water, mustard, and remaining reserved pineapple juice. Cover and chill in the refrigerator for 2 to 24 hours. In separate container, cover and chill ham balls in the refrigerator for 2 to 24 hours.

Before serving: In skillet combine sauce and ham balls. Heat to boiling. Reduce heat and simmer, uncovered, about 5 minutes. Makes 48 meatballs.

SAUCY FRANKS

Advance preparation time: 15 minutes
Final preparation time: 10 minutes

- ½ cup catsup
- ¼ cup maple-flavored syrup
- 3 tablespoons prepared mustard
- ¼ teaspoon ground ginger
- 2 16-ounce packages frankfurters
- 1½ cups frozen small whole onions

1 Mix catsup, syrup, mustard, ginger, and ¼ cup *water.* Bias-slice franks into 1-inch lengths. Stir franks and onions into mixture. Cover; chill 3 to 24 hours.

Before serving: Heat catsup mixture to boiling. Reduce heat; simmer 5 minutes. Serve with wooden picks. Makes 60.

CRAB PIROSHKI

Advance preparation time: 45 minutes
Final preparation time: 20 minutes

- 1 package piecrust mix (for 2-crust pie)
- 1 8-ounce container (1 cup) sour cream dip with French onion
- 1 7-ounce can crab meat, drained, flaked, and cartilage removed
- ¼ teaspoon bottled hot pepper sauce

1 Prepare piecrust mix according to package directions, *except* substitute ½ *cup* of the sour cream dip for the water called for; set aside. Combine remaining dip, crab, and pepper sauce. Divide pastry in half. Roll each half into a 10-inch square. Cut into 2½-inch squares. Top each with *1 teaspoon* crab mixture. Moisten edges; fold over to form a triangle. Seal edges with a fork. Freeze on baking sheet 20 minutes. Wrap; freeze up to 3 months.

Before serving: Place piroshki on ungreased baking sheet. Bake in a 450° oven for 18 to 20 minutes. Serve hot. Makes 32.

RASPBERRY-ORANGE SOUP

Advance preparation time: 55 minutes

- 1 10-ounce package frozen raspberries (in quick-thaw pouch)
- 1 tablespoon cornstarch
- 1 cup cold water
- 1 8-ounce carton orange yogurt
- ½ cup light cream *or* milk
- ⅓ cup dry white wine

1 Place package of raspberries in a bowl of hot water; let stand 10 minutes. Drain raspberries, reserving syrup. In saucepan stir reserved syrup into cornstarch; add water. Cook and stir till thickened and bubbly. Cook and stir 2 minutes more. Cover surface with clear plastic wrap or waxed paper; cool 30 minutes. Blend the syrup mixture into the yogurt. Stir in raspberries, cream or milk, and wine. Cover and chill in the refrigerator 3 to 24 hours. Makes 4 to 6 servings.

CHILLED CREAMY ZUCCHINI SOUP

Advance preparation time: 20 minutes

- 1 10¾-ounce can condensed chicken broth
- 4 small zucchini, sliced (about 1 pound)
- 4 green onions, sliced (¼ cup)
- ¼ teaspoon dried thyme, crushed
- 2 tablespoons dry sherry
- ½ cup whipping cream

1 In saucepan bring undiluted chicken broth to boiling; add zucchini, onions, and thyme. Simmer, covered, about 8 minutes or till zucchini is tender.

2 Pour into blender container. Cover and blend till smooth. Stir in sherry; add cream. Salt to taste. Cover and chill in the refrigerator 3 to 24 hours. Makes 6 servings.

368

SUNSHINE SLUSH

Advance preparation time: 20 minutes
Final preparation time: 35 minutes

3 cups water
1 cup sugar
1 6-ounce can frozen orange juice
   concentrate
1 6-ounce can frozen lemonade
   concentrate
2 ripe medium bananas, cut up
3 cups unsweetened pineapple juice
2 tablespoons lemon juice
1 28-ounce bottle carbonated water,
   chilled

1 In a saucepan combine water and sugar. Bring to boiling; stir till sugar is dissolved. Boil gently, uncovered, 3 minutes. Remove from heat. Stir in orange juice and lemonade concentrates. Meanwhile, in blender container combine bananas and *half* of pineapple juice. Cover; blend smooth. Stir into sugar mixture. Stir in remaining pineapple juice and lemon juice.

2 Turn into a 13x9x2-inch pan or plastic freezer container. Cover with moisture-vaporproof material. Seal, label, and freeze at least 6 hours or up to 2 months.

Before serving: Let stand at room temperature about 30 minutes. Spoon slush into each glass. Slowly pour in carbonated water, using equal amounts of slush and water. Stir gently. Makes 12½ cups.

Rum Sunshine Slush: Prepare Sunshine Slush as above, *except* stir in 1½ cups light *rum* or *vodka* before turning mixture into pan or freezer container. Continue as directed above, *except* let frozen mixture stand at room temperature for 5 to 10 minutes instead of 30 minutes. Makes 14 cups.

Mulled Beverage Mix
Sunshine Slush
Apricot Cordial
Smoked Cheese and Wine Logs
(see recipe, page 366)

MULLED BEVERAGE MIX

Advance preparation time: 20 minutes
Final preparation time: 5 minutes

¾ cup sugar
6 inches stick cinnamon, broken
6 whole cloves
   Peel of ¼ lemon, cut into strips
½ cup lemon juice
   Chilled *or* heated apple juice,
   cranberry juice cocktail, dry red
   or white wine, or rosé wine

1 In saucepan mix sugar, cinnamon, cloves, lemon peel, and 1½ cups *water.* Bring to boiling; stir till sugar is dissolved. Reduce heat; cover. Simmer for 10 minutes. Stir in lemon juice. Strain through cheesecloth. Cover tightly; chill in the refrigerator up to 6 weeks.

Before serving: Mix *2 tablespoons* mix and ¾ *cup* desired beverage in a mug. Serve with ice, if desired. Trim with orange slices and maraschino cherries, if desired. Makes 1½ cups mix.

ZIPPY EGGNOG

Advance preparation time: 10 minutes
Final preparation time: 10 minutes

1 3-quart package nonfat dry milk
   powder
2 3-ounce packages no-bake custard
   mix
1 6-ounce jar powdered non-dairy
   creamer
2 teaspoons ground nutmeg

1 Combine milk powder, dry custard mix, non-dairy creamer, and nutmeg. Store in an airtight container.

Before serving: In blender container place 1 cup *water* and *1 cup* eggnog mix. Cover; blend smooth. Add 1 cup *ice cubes,* one at a time; blend till slushy. Serves 6.

APRICOT CORDIAL

Advance preparation time: 45 minutes

1 8-ounce package dried apricots,
   quartered
¾ cup sugar
2 cups vodka
1 cup brandy
2 inches stick cinnamon, broken
¼ teaspoon cardamom seed

1 In saucepan combine apricots and 2 cups *water;* bring to boiling. Reduce heat; cover. Simmer about 15 minutes or till fruit has absorbed as much water as possible. Cool.

2 Combine fruit mixture and sugar; pour into a ½-gallon screw-top jar. Add vodka, brandy, cinnamon, and cardamom; cover tightly. Shake well. Let stand at room temperature for 2 weeks, inverting jar once each day. Strain through cheesecloth into a decanter. Cover. (Serve apricots over ice cream.) Makes about 3 cups liqueur.

MINTED HOT CHOCOLATE MIX

Advance preparation time: 10 minutes
Final preparation time: 5 minutes

2 cups chocolate-flavored instant
   malted milk powder
½ cup white buttermints
3 cups nonfat dry milk powder
½ cup presweetened cocoa powder

1 In blender container combine *1 cup* malted milk powder and the mints. Cover; blend 1 minute. Turn into bowl; stir in remaining malted milk powder, dry milk powder, and cocoa powder. Store in airtight container.

Before serving: Stir ¼ *cup* of the minted hot chocolate mix into ¾ cup *boiling water* in a mug. If desired, top with a marshmallow. Makes 6 cups mix.

INDEX

INDEX

373

INDEX

INDEX

379

INDEX

S

INDEX

INDEX